Richard H. Lucero
November 1972

Presidential
Election
Mc Govern vs Nixon

DRAGON HARVEST

DRAGON HARVEST

Upton Sinclair

The Viking Press · New York

1945

COPYRIGHT 1945 BY UPTON SINCLAIR

FIRST PUBLISHED BY THE VIKING PRESS IN JUNE 1945
PUBLISHED ON THE SAME DAY IN THE DOMINION OF CANADA
BY THE MACMILLAN COMPANY OF CANADA LIMITED

SECOND PRINTING JUNE 1945
THIRD PRINTING AUGUST 1945
FOURTH PRINTING AUGUST 1945

PRINTED IN THE U. S. A. BY THE AMERICAN BOOK—STRATFORD PRESS, INC.

TO

BEN W. HUEBSCH

Kindest of friends and most patient of publishers

Contents

Book One: Regardless of Their Doom

Book Two: Who Sups with the Devil

Book Three: Let Joy Be Unconfined

Book Four: The Brazen Throat of War

vii

Book Five:
Ancestral Voices Prophesying War

Book Six: Let Slip the Dogs of War

Book Seven: The Winds Blew and
Beat upon That House

Book Eight:
The Flinty and Steel Couch of War

BOOK ONE

Regardless of Their Doom

1

The Little Victims Play

THE telephone rang, and it chanced to be answered by the lame but-ler whom Lanny had hired in Spain. "Someone for you, Monsieur Lanny. He says his name is Branting."

It was a call for which Lanny had been waiting, but with only a faint hope. He thought quickly, knowing that José, the servant, was keenly interested in everything his master did and said, and especially when it had a political flavor. Camouflage was called for, and Lanny spoke: "Hello, Branting; glad to hear your voice. Have you got a price on that painting?" Waiting just long enough for the other to have answered if he had been quick enough: "You say you want to walk? Well, it's a fine day. I'll meet you half way."

He went on to give the necessary instructions. Take the tram from Cannes, get off at the village of Juan-les-Pins, and take the road which runs along the west shore of the Cap d'Antibes. "I'll meet you on the road. Yes, I still want that picture, and very much." Branting wouldn't be too greatly puzzled, since they had agreed to use Lanny's trading in old masters as camouflage for a different form of activity.

"Tell my mother I'll not be back for lunch," said Lanny to the black-clad Spaniard. "I have a deal on."

II

The art expert went to his room and unlocked a desk in which he had a roll of paper money, some twenty thousand francs. It sounded like a lot, but wasn't, the franc being down to three cents. However, it would buy things in France, and Lanny stuffed the roll into the pocket of his gray flannel trousers. He stepped out to investigate the weather; it was late January, and the sun was shining brightly—something it does on the Riviera, but not so often as you would gather from the adver-tising folders of railroads and hotels. He decided that he didn't need an overcoat; and he hardly ever wore a hat here at his mother's home.

It had been Lanny's own home through most of his years, which now were thirty-nine. As a rule he passed for younger, because he had had life easy and permitted himself no vices. A handsome, well-set-up man with wavy brown hair and a little brown mustache showing no signs of gray, he was now and then taken for one of the movie stars who came to the hotel on the point of the Cap; they displayed their athletic figures, diving from springboards into the clear blue water, or toasting themselves brown on apricot-colored mattresses laid out on the rocks.

From the loggia of the villa was a view of the Golfe Juan and the little harbor of Cannes crowded with sailboats and yachts. Across the wide *golfe* were the red Estérel mountains, and to the southwest lay the blue Mediterranean, always with vessels in sight, from tiny fishing boats with red sails to the biggest ocean liners. The loggia was a sort of paved terrace, so smooth that it often served as a ballroom for the family and their friends. Steps led down from it, and a graveled path took you to the gate, where tall agaves, or century plants, grew at each side, so big that their spiked leaves, sharp as porcupine quills, had to be trimmed of their inhospitality.

Strolling along the familiar paved road which led to the village, Lanny came within sight of a solidly built man in his forties, walking erect like a soldier, though he wore a not very new or well-kept business suit. He was one of those squareheaded Prussians who could not conceal their origin if they wanted to. His dark hair had been cropped when Lanny had last seen it, but now he had let it grow and you saw that it was showing gray. He had no superfluous flesh on him, and his face had been lined by many cares.

The two quickened their pace when they saw each other, and when they were near, each held out a hand. "Oh, Monck, I'm so glad to see you!" Lanny exclaimed. "I've been fearing you wouldn't get away!"

"I had a League of Nations Commission, no less, to bring me out," said the other, smiling. "You have read about its efforts?"

"Enough to form the opinion that it isn't very active."

"It worked quite diligently so long as there was any chance of our side's winning," declared Bernhardt Monck, alias Branting, alias El Capitán Herzog. The last had been his title when Lanny had visited him, a little over a year ago, on the Ebro front in the Spanish civil war. Then he had been gaining the victory of Belchite—the last victory, as he had feared and as fate had willed. "*Eine gottverdammnte Farce!*" he exclaimed, speaking German, as he always did when they were alone.

Said Lanny: "There is a leaflet being circulated by the Franco supporters here on the Riviera, claiming that there are forty-seven thousand foreign troops among the Loyalist forces."

"Well, the League Commission has just reported something less than thirteen thousand, including doctors and nurses and such. You know that Franco has ten times that number of Italians—and be sure they haven't been shipped out!"

III

It was characteristic of these two that they began talking international politics the moment they met on a public highway. That was the subject which engaged all their thoughts and was the basis of their friendship. Besides Monck, there was only one person on the Riviera who knew Lanny's true opinions on these matters; so he was like a bottle of carbonated water, sealed under pressure, and when the lever was pressed, he went off with a fizz.

The shore was not far away, and there were rocks with no houses near. A pleasant place to sit on a warm day, and he led his friend there. "The tide is in," he said, "so nobody can walk below, and there's no chance of our being overheard." When they were seated, he remarked gravely: "Things look terrible, my friend." It was the beginning of the year 1939.

"We have to write Spain off," replied the other. "Barcelona was taken the day after I got out. It won't take more than a week or two to clean up the rest of Catalonia; and then there'll be Madrid, with the provinces around it, entirely cut off from the outside world, and able to make hardly any munitions. If they can hold out a couple of months longer, I shall be surprised."

"A ghastly thing to think about, Monck!"

"I spend my time trying not to think about it. Franco is the most efficient little murderer that any devil could have invented; he doesn't know the meaning of mercy, or even of statesmanship, and his one idea is to slaughter every man, woman, and child who has opposed him. The safest way, he figures, is to kill all who did not actively support him. He has a whole hierarchy of priests to tell him that this is God's will, and to absolve him every night for mistakes he may have made during the day. After all, if they were good people, he has sent them to heaven, and they won't complain when they arrive."

Thus spoke a former captain of the Thälmann Battalion. The Communist leader for whom it had been named had been, and presumably was still, in a Nazi concentration camp, and the German "Reds"—which in Spain as in Naziland meant not merely Socialists of every shade, but democrats, liberals, even Freemasons—had most of them been withdrawn from the Generalissimo's clutches just in time. Said the embittered ex-soldier: "If the League Commission had known how near to collapse we were, they would surely not have urged our removal!" There was acid in his tone.

He talked about his experience in getting out of Spain. With the enemy only a few miles to the north, and bombing of Barcelona going on incessantly, he had burned his uniform, which might have cost the life of anyone possessing it. He discovered that a good part of the population of this port and manufacturing center had been seized by the same desire as himself—to get into France. A trip which ordinarily took a motorist three hours had taken Monck two days and nights. He had walked most of the way, in a pitiful stream of peasant carts, burros, and trudging fugitives with their belongings in suitcases or bundles on their backs. It was a sight he had been witnessing for two years and a half, all over this unhappy land; one peasant family told him they had moved a dozen times.

In a crowded village street, narrow and crooked, a traffic jam had occurred, and there they had been bombed, seemingly for the amusement of some "Nationalist" aviators. That was an experience not soon to be forgotten, with motorists vainly honking horns and panic-stricken people breaking down fences and beating at the doors of houses. Monck had got out by a side lane, and had been picked up by a government truck which he suspected was carrying treasure out of the country. In the town of Figueras, near the border, the truck had been stalled in a mass of humanity, and had stayed the night in the plaza with people sleeping under the wheels. Food was unobtainable, and everywhere were babies wailing and older children begging, or stealing, where they could.

That was war, said the ex-Capitán: a bad thing in any case, but worse when you lost. He was one of the fortunate ones who had been provided with a passport, and so had got across the border. Now he was in a free land, and could draw free breaths, at least for a while; but he was pessimistic about the future of France, which stood high up on the dictators' list. The fear of war which the French had displayed had destroyed whatever influence they might have had in the councils of Europe. What nation would aid one which had broken its pledges to Czechoslovakia, and had permitted a sister republic at its side to be starved and beaten into enslavement?

IV

Lanny agreed with all this, but he laid a great share of the blame upon the British Tories, who had put their class before their country and were so blinded by fear of the Soviet Union that they felt less than hate for the Nazis. It was Lanny's business to know the leaders in both Britain and France, and he told his friend about their purposes and attitudes. Monck was one who had a right to know, and would make good use of his information.

"What are you going to do now?" the American inquired.

"My wife and children are in Paris," was the reply. "I feel a bit seedy, and think I've earned a couple of weeks' furlough."

"More than that, I should say."

"Maybe so, but I have a date in Berlin."

"*Du lieber Gott!* You are going there again?"

"There were a couple of boys in my battalion who have cooked up a scheme that promises results. You won't want me to go into details."

"Assuredly not," responded a secret agent who kept his secrets even from Monck. "You will be needing money?"

"That is always the first problem."

"It happens that I am in funds right now. I have sold several pictures since we parted in Paris; and since my wife's death it is not so easy for me to spend money."

Lanny told how he had managed to learn definitely that the Nazis had murdered his wife in Dachau—once the beautiful picnicking place of the people of Munich, and now a name of horror throughout the world. Trudi had been the means of distributing what funds he had been able to contribute to the German underground; and now Monck would have to take her place. They talked out arrangements for the future. Monck would have a new name; he chose Braun, the Nazi color. He would be free to write Lanny, here to Bienvenu, or to Lanny's hotel in Paris, or to the Adlon whenever the art expert was visiting Berlin. The notes would always be brief, and would refer exclusively to paintings. The price asked would mean the amount of money that Monck needed. They appointed places, known to both, where they would meet at any time the Capitán might set. They would do the proper amount of walking and turning of corners to make certain they were not being trailed to the rendezvous. All this was an old story, and they could talk in shorthand, as it were.

Lanny put into his fellow-conspirator's hands the money he had taken from his desk. "This is all right," he said; "I mean, it's in small denominations and you can spend it safely. I'll get a larger sum, but it will mean delay, for I have to change the notes before I give them to you. You understand, I cannot ask my bank for used notes or small denominations, for that would look peculiar, and in these days of so many kinds of intrigue the least hint may be followed up and become a clue. The bank gives me a lot of shiny new thousand-franc or ten-thousand-franc notes, all with consecutive serial numbers, and if I gave them to you and you were caught with them, they could be traced back to me. So I have to go and spend each for some small purchase, and get the change."

"I understand all that," replied the German, who had been a sailor, a dockworker, then a union leader and Social-Democratic official, and for six years—since the coming of the Nazis into power—an underground worker in Germany and aboveground fighter in Spain. "I'll wait, and meet you wherever you say."

V

Lanny felt it necessary to apologize for a lack of hospitality. "You know, I am sure, I'd like nothing better than to spend some time with you. But I have lived here most of my life, and everybody knows me; I am supposed to be the most fashionable of playboys, and do only the right things—play tennis with ex-King Alfonso and the King of Sweden, drink tea with the Duchess of Windsor, and listen to the Aga Khan, Moslem prince and pope, discuss his mistresses. I cannot invite you to my mother's home, even privately, because the servants would notice an unusual sort of person."

"Forget all that," said the ex-roustabout. "Trudi told me a lot about you, and I have been able to guess more."

"I don't want you to think I'm doing no more than just making money. I gather items of information and deliver them where they will count."

"Don't tell me about it, *lieber Genosse*. Money is enough for us, believe me!"

"It is so with many other persons I know, *lieber Bernhardt*. In my youth I learned some verses by an English poet which are supposed to be sung by an infernal spirit: 'How pleasant it is to have money, heigh-ho, how pleasant it is to have money!' "

"Most of the time, yes; but not when the Gestapo catches you and starts asking where you got it."

That thought wiped the smile from the one-time playboy's face. "I am counting upon you, *Genosse*, as I counted upon my dear Trudi in the past. My ability to go on helping the cause depends upon your never speaking my name to any living soul."

"Your trust will be kept." The German gave Lanny his hand, and in their warm clasp was all the faith and honor of which men are capable, and upon which depends their ability to build and maintain a civilization.

Before they parted, Lanny said: "By the way, did you happen in Barcelona to run into a friend of mine, Raoul Palma?"

"I don't recall the name."

"He drove with me to the Ebro, but I didn't introduce him to you. He has been employed in the Foreign Press Bureau. He and his wife are old-time Socialists, and have carefully kept secret the fact that I am still their friend. She is here in Cannes, and has not heard from him in the last week or more."

"There are many persons who have got out of Barcelona but have not got into France. They are being held at the border for lack of passports—but judging from the mob that I saw at the frontier post, it will take machine guns to hold them much longer. I doubt if French troops would obey orders to fire on them, and I doubt if the government would dare to give such an order."

"I tell Julie that Raoul got over the mountains once, escaping from the last counterrevolution, and he may do it again."

"Not many can stand that trip in midwinter," replied the ex-Capitán. "But the wife should not give up hope, for thousands will escape by one means or another, and many will be hidden in barns and cellars and caves and other places in Spain. The masses of the people are against Franco, and not all his murders will be able to change them."

VI

Lanny walked back to his home, dressed himself for the fashionable city of Cannes, and stepped into his car. At his bank he drew the sum of fifty thousand francs, something which occasioned no surprise, for he frequently paid for paintings in cash, because of the moral effect which the sight of large banknotes exercised. Now he set out upon a shopping expedition, buying not paintings but odds and ends of objects which he could use as birthday gifts to servants and friends. Each time he would pay with a shiny new banknote; now and then the clerk would say: "Have you nothing smaller, Monsieur Budd?" and Lanny would reply with what he considered a white lie. Before long his pockets were stuffed with bills of all sizes, and he would have presented a shining mark for bandits, had any chanced to be operating in that fashionable city.

His task completed, he returned to the car, pulled down the curtains, and wrapped up a small fortune in a neat brown paper parcel. After consulting his watch, he drove along the splendid Boulevard de la Croisette which runs along the Golfe Juan, and presently, far ahead, he saw the sturdy erect figure walking. Lanny stopped his car a few feet ahead, and held out the package. The man said: "*Danke schön.*" Lanny said: "*Glückliche Reise,*" and that was all. Monck turned back toward the main part of town, and Lanny sat for a while, watching in the mirror of his car the figure receding into the distance.

Ever since boyhood, Lanny Budd had lived with a troubled conscience because he had things so easy and couldn't see what he was doing to earn his passage through the world. He traveled wherever he pleased, and always de luxe; he ate the best of foods, he had several lovely homes always open to him, and he never had to worry about where his next roll of bills was coming from. Fate had willed that he should collect his money in dollars and spend it in francs, which was the surest of ways to a comfortable life. But, beginning at the age of thirteen, he had met persons whom he considered to be heroes, and this had made an indelible impression upon him, spoiling the taste of his food and the tranquillity of his thoughts.

A hero—now and then a heroine—was a person who enjoyed no income, whether in dollars or francs, and seemed to leave it for the ravens to feed him or her. A hero was a person absorbed in the effort to save the world from falling into a condition of enslavement, which just now appeared to be its certain destiny. In many countries an outlaw, the hero was hunted like a wild beast, or worse—for beasts are merely killed, they are not tortured to make them reveal the hiding places of their kind. In the countries which still considered themselves "free," the hero was left to his own devices, but was looked upon as a dangerous character, and feeding him was left to the ravens, of whom Lanny had often felt impelled to take the role.

Bernhardt Monck, alias Herzog, alias Branting, was a self-educated man, but he had made a good job of it, and might have earned a comfortable living for himself and family in the bourgeois world. Instead he had risked death and torture worse than death, first in Germany, then in Spain—and now he was going back into Germany, in spite of the fact that the Gestapo had his photograph and fingerprints. What drove him was the sense of justice and the love of freedom, the same force which had caused thousands of American boys, British boys, French boys to leave their homes and schools and come to the red hills of Aragon, furnace-hot in summer and swept by icy blasts in winter, there to risk death and mutilation. A large percentage of them were the cream of their countries' intellectuals, who might have become successful writers, politicians, scientists, whatever they had chosen; but they had been infuriated by the sight of greed and lies enthroned, and had chosen to become what the world called fools and would later call martyrs.

VII

For exactly a quarter of a century the grandson of Budd Gunmakers and son of Budd-Erling had been watching events like this, and helping a little here and there when he could. The leaders of his cause had told him that money was important, and he had been generous. "Distributing to the necessity of saints" had been St. Paul's formula, which had a certain comical sound to unsaintly modern ears. But the more unsaintly the world became, the more it had need of new saints, by whatever name they were called—persons who believed in justice and freedom more than they believed in personal comfort and the good opinion of the personally comfortable.

Of late Lanny had been told that there was something even more important than money, and that was information. All over this old continent intrigues were going on which might decide the destiny not merely of Europe but of the rest of the world for centuries to come. These secrets were supposed to be kept locked up in the minds of a very few powerful persons. But there is no person so cautious that he does not tell somebody, his secretary, his wife, his lady love; that person tells some other person, and presently there are rumors and confidential whispers. It takes expert listeners to judge these, for there are all sorts of pretenders, trying to peddle secrets or perhaps inventing rumors, and giving them out as warships in battle pour out clouds of black smoke to confuse the foe.

So, more than ever, it had become necessary for Lanny Budd to travel on luxurious steamships and stop at expensive hotels and cultivate the rich and famous in the great capitals of Europe. There were few better places than his mother's home on the Cap d'Antibes at the height of the winter season of 1939: a lovely villa, not too gaudy, and old enough to have dignity and reputation. Statesmen long since departed had found relaxation here. Oil magnates and munitions kings had discussed deals with cabinet ministers in its drawing-room; great musicians had played here; Isadora Duncan had danced on the loggia and Marcel Detaze had painted his masterpieces in a studio on the estate. Now the hostess of Bienvenu was close to sixty, and contemplated the very word with dismay; but she was still a lovely woman, whose kindness of heart was apparent to all, and whose understanding of human nature and the ways of the *haut monde* would be useful to any man of large affairs.

Beauty Budd had specialized in friendship, and while she had often been disappointed she had never been embittered. She was not what was called rich on the Côte d'Azur; on the contrary, she called herself poor, having only a thousand dollars a month to live on, and an accumulation of bills which had to wait until Lanny sold another of the paintings of Marcel Detaze, his former stepfather. Everybody who was anybody in the neighborhood knew all about Beauty Budd, or thought they did, for she talked freely, or made people think that she did. She had been something of a scandal in her day, but now she had settled down and become the most respectable of *grandes dames*, and had made a new marriage so proper that it seemed slightly comical to her smart friends.

The white-haired and rosy-cheeked Parsifal Dingle, New Thought devotee and religious healer, wandered about this beautiful estate, of which by a strange whim of fortune he had become the master. He took it serenely, for his convictions forbade him to be concerned with worldly affairs. He read his books and pamphlets, and prayed frequently to perfect himself in order that he might be able to help others. He never spoke an angry or impatient word to anyone, and to the servants and the flower-growing peasants of the Cap he was a new and unheard-of kind of saint, disapproving of church machinery and seeking no permission to work miracles.

Beauty Budd considered him the most wonderful man in the world, and she strove to follow his ideals and really thought she was succeeding. The result was an odd mélange of this- and other-worldliness. The mistress of Bienvenu loved everybody, but at the same time she listened to gossip about them, that being the way of smart society. She tried to be humble in spirit, and told herself that she was succeeding, but at the same time she paid large sums for costumes which would give her what she called "distinction." She told her friends that she no longer cared about money, but when she played bridge and gin-rummy she tried her best to win. When she asked her husband if it was right for her to play for money, he answered that some day her inner voice would speak to her on the subject. So far the only voice that Beauty had heard told her that if she didn't gamble she wouldn't have any friends at all.

VIII

Marceline, child of Beauty's marriage to the painter Marcel Detaze, was in Paris, making her career as a dancer. She had left behind her a baby boy, not quite a year old, who bore his grandfather's name and gave a new atmosphere to the estate. Every day at lunchtime, which was Marceline's breakfast time, she would telephone to make sure the darling was all right, and someone would hold the precious bundle close to the receiver so that his mother could hear him coo; if he didn't, his little toes would be tickled so that he would gurgle. The report was always favorable, for Bienvenu was a grand place for children. The villa was built around an open court, where flowers were encouraged and spiders not; the dogs were gentle, and an English·nurse had been found, one who had reared several titled infants and was as dependable as sunrise.

Lanny himself had been reared in that court, and other little ones had followed—one at a time, and at wide intervals, according to custom in the fashionable world. Marceline herself, and then Lanny's little daughter Frances, and Freddi Robin's little Johannes, who had been brought out of Germany and was now living in Connecticut. Lanny had watched them, one after another, and renewed his sense of the infinite mysteries of being. He had played music for them and watched their responses; he had taught them to dance, and in Marceline's case had thus determined her career. He would have liked nothing better than to stay in this peaceful spot and watch the unfoldment of a new mite of life—half Italian, a quarter French and a quarter American. What other strains might have been mixed in, back through the centuries, all the way to Adam and Eve?

Duty called to the son of Budd-Erling, and he couldn't stay for the delights of child study; he couldn't play the beautiful piano scores piled on the shelves in his studio; he couldn't read the wonderful old books which had been willed to him by a great-great-uncle in Connecticut and had been calling to him for a matter of twenty years. There were devilish forces loose in the modern world, and if they could have their way, they would burn all the vital books and make fine music futile. They would make any Franco-American mother wish she had never brought a man-child into the world; they would turn a half-Italian boy into such a monster as history would grow sick at the thought of.

So Lanny had to dress himself up and go out into that world which called itself great and high and noble and select. He had to drink tea or coffee in fashionable drawing-rooms and listen to the chatter of pleasure-loving ladies. He had to dance with them, flirt with them a little, and know how far he could go without offending them when he avoided going further. He had to sit in fashionable bars and learn to sip mild liquor while his companions drank it stronger. He would sail boats, swim, play tennis, watch polo and horse-racing, and now and then gamble, so as not to be offensively good. And all the time, day and night, his mind would be on the alert for the things he wanted to know: the names of key persons, and ways to meet them, and conversational devices to lead them to talk about what was happening in Europe, and what was being planned by those who had the future in charge.

IX

In Lanny's happy childhood Juan-les-Pins had been a tiny fishing village, but now it had become an all-year-round playground of the rich from places as far apart as Hollywood and Buenos Aires, Batavia and Calcutta. There was a new casino, very swanky, a day and night club for everybody who had money and wanted to eat or drink or gamble or dance. In the restaurant of this establishment Lanny sat at lunch with a gentleman of sixty or so, bald, bespectacled, with a hooked nose, a large drooping mouth, and a complexion which made one think of gray rubber. Juan March was his name and he had begun life as a tobacco-smuggler in Spain. By the shrewd combination of finance and politics which characterizes the modern world he had become owner of the tobacco monopoly of his country; owner also of docks, steamship companies, banks, and a potash industry in Catalonia. He was an international pawnbroker and the financier of kings, and it was he who had made the Franco rebellion against the people's government. He had put up five million dollars in New York and later half a million pounds in London for the purchase of war supplies. Don't imagine that he had given it—any more than the twenty million dollars he had invested in an attempted comeback of ex-King Alfonso. He had got gilt-edged securities and the choicest concessions, and now, with the victory of the Fascists, he saw himself on the way to becoming the richest man in the world.

Also, he was one of the most close-mouthed; very little was published about him, and nothing that he could help. He worked behind the scenes, as Zaharoff had done, and Kreuger, and Stinnes—as Schneider was still doing, and Deterding, and all the other really powerful men whom Lanny had ever known. The politicians and generals and kings lived in the limelight and enjoyed the glory, while the men of money stayed in the background and gave the orders, politely when possible, but making sure they would be obeyed. Señor Juan wouldn't admit even in private that he was a man of great power; he was just a plain businessman, interested in getting things done, in producing useful goods; no public benefactor or anything pretentious like that, but making money, since without money you couldn't do anything; using the money to build docks and steamships, and to produce potash—in short, the same line of talk that Lanny had heard from his father since earliest childhood.

To Lanny Budd the Señor talked as one insider to another. Robbie Budd made excellent fighter planes, and March's money paid for some of them, and would doubtless pay for more from time to time. Lanny knew all about these planes, and was doubtless looking out for his father's business; March would respect him for that. Dealing in old masters was all right, too, for a tobacco-smuggler become gentleman wanted to know how gentlemen spent their money, and meant to have a palace as good as the best. Young Budd must be all right politically, for he had been into Franco Spain at the height of the conflict, and in Seville had visited General Aguilar, Fascist Commander. Lanny had lived most of his life in France, and was a sort of left-handed member of the de Bruyne family; he knew Baron Schneider, of Schneider-Creusot, which was about as sound a credential as anybody could present to the tobacco king. Also, he had traveled over Germany, and had been a guest many times at Karinhall and Berchtesgaden; he could tell what had happened when Schuschnigg, Chancellor of Austria, had come to the Führer's mountain retreat to get a dressing-down. Very certainly Juan March had never attained to such honors, nor did he know anybody else who could make such claims—and prove them by authentic details.

X

Lanny referred to the recent effort of an organization known as the Cagoule to bring about in France the same coup d'état as Franco had achieved in Spain. March knew all about it, and doubtless had helped to finance it, though he did not say so. Lanny had an amusing story of how he had got himself implicated in that conspiracy, and had sought refuge in the château of Graf Herzenberg of the German embassy in

Paris; the Graf had been scared to death of him but hadn't quite had the nerve to put him out, and the story of the nobleman's perplexity caused the heavy drooping mouth of the international pawnbroker to spread into a wide grin.

So after that it was possible for Lanny to say, in a casual tone: "By the way, Señor Juan, I wonder if there is any truth in the report which I hear, that the four interested powers have agreed upon spheres of influence in Spain."

"It is a lot of nonsense," replied the Señor. "Who tells such tales?"

"I have heard it from persons who ought to know. They say Germany is to have the north, Italy the south, France Catalonia, and Britain a district around Gibraltar. Manifestly, the British would pay a high price for airplane bases for their Rock, which is now so difficult to defend."

"The people who repeat such rumors do not know the Caudillo. He would sooner part with his own eyes and hands."

"He will be heavily in debt when this war is over, Señor."

"That is true; but it is well known that international debts have been allowed to stand for long periods."

"You don't have to tell that to an American," said the son of Budd-Erling, fetching a smile.

"My country has many resources, and we expect to allow a fair share to our friends—but very little to those who sat by and criticized us while we fought for their safety. Anyone who thinks otherwise will find Franco a stubborn man."

Lanny observed that an ex-smuggler, like all other Spaniards, had pride in his race. He talked freely about the great future in his native land, and especially her role as motherland to the South American countries. Spain had never had any love for the so-called Monroe Doctrine, considering it presumptuous as well as superfluous. "We Falangistas," said he, "are firm in our conviction that we have the right method for dealing with populations which consist in great part of red and yellow and black races. Democracy is out of the question in such parts of the world, and becomes merely a device of demagogues and troublemakers."

"By the way, Señor Juan," ventured the American, "I wonder if anyone has ever called your attention to the fact that the word for a member of your organization, etymologically I mean, should be *Falangita*. The *falangista* is a small tree-climbing animal."

The tobacco king expressed himself as surprised, and promised to look it up in the dictionaries and communicate with General Franco.

He was impressed by the attainments of Robbie Budd's son, and hoped that he might have the pleasure of meeting Robbie on the latter's next visit to the Continent. That was the sort of thing Lanny could do for his father, as a by-product of his other activities.

From this luncheon Lanny would go straight to his studio in Bienvenu, seat himself at his typewriter, and put into the fewest possible words what he had learned about the future of Franco Spain. He would seal this in an envelope and mark it "Zaharoff 103," his code name and number as a "presidential agent." This he would seal up in a second envelope and address to a man named Baker, at an inconspicuous small brick house in Washington, D.C. Baker would carry it at once to a personage commonly referred to as "That Man in the White House" and cordially hated by nearly everyone Lanny knew.

XI

On one of the many rocks, large and small, which jut out into the Mediterranean between Cannes and Juan there stood a terraced white château with a red-tiled roof, the home of a woman whose name had once been famous in New York and London. Maxine Elliott, the stage queen, had been linked in gossip with well-known names, including J. P. Morgan and King Edward VII. Now she was an old woman with high blood pressure, who took the role of royalty and played it with due arrogance. To her home came persons who had made successes in any and every walk of life, and Lanny Budd had made the discovery that this was an excellent place for the plying of his trade. Maxine provided the indispensable private swimming-pool, beside which wealthy and important persons lounged in deck chairs, relaxing from the world which had been too much with them. She was a backgammon addict and played endlessly under a red-and-yellow striped canopy, but there was never a lack of players, so Lanny could listen to conversation, and now and then put in a few words to guide it.

Among the visitors at this retreat was the grandson of Maxine's long-dead royal protector. Until recently this grandson had been King Edward VIII of England, but recently he had been forced from the throne on account of his determination to marry a lady from Baltimore who had two divorces and no royal blood. Now he was Duke of Windsor, and the lady was Duchess to everybody on the Coast of Pleasure except a few stiff-necked Britishers. The couple came to this "Château de l'Horizon" and impressed Lanny as two bewildered and shell-shocked human creatures who could have been benefited by Parsifal

Dingle's lessons in Divine Love. They were the objects of ravenous curiosity among all chic and would-be-chic people, and the first time Lanny met the royal pair, and his mother mentioned it—as of course she did at once—the ladies of her set came swarming to ask questions. "What has she got that we haven't?" they all wanted to know, and Lanny replied with a *mot* that was repeated up and down the coast: "Well, she's got the duke."

She was small and slender—Lanny judged that she couldn't weigh more than a hundred pounds. She was extraordinarily trim, *soignée* with all the skill of French hairdressers and costumers, and neat to the point of primness. She had the brightest of blue eyes, always alert, watchful, with tiny wrinkles all around them—for she was in her forties. Among those she trusted she had a keen sense of humor, and moods of gaiety which recalled the Southern "charmer"; but she trusted very few, and most of the time her expression was rather grim, as of one who had had to fight her way through the world, and hadn't yet made certain of her victory. Her accent showed no trace of her years in England; she spoke with a languid drawl, though her words were never slurred and were carefully chosen, never any clichés or slang. There was a sort of rising inflection, almost a questioning where no question was involved. Her voice was soft, and her manner gentle.

Lanny decided that she was what is called "a man's woman"; she stood by her one and only man and fought for him, keeping him away from drinkers and gamblers, parasites and notoriety seekers. The unhappy man had been torn up by his roots and now had no place in the world. He had taken seriously his royal duties, and one of his major mistakes lay in having been too deeply moved by the poverty and squalor he had seen among the miners of Britain, and having tried to do something about it. Lanny had wondered if he might not be a bit to the Left, and sounded him out by mentioning the subject of Spain. "But what else could have been done to keep Communism out of Western Europe?" asked the little man, earnestly. There the conversation came to a halt because of the passing of an express train on the Mediterranean line. It made such a roaring that you thought it must be going straight through the château; but it missed and went on, past the gates or doors of numerous other homes of the well-to-do on that somewhat narrow shore.

XII

One of the unwritten rules of this unconventional château was that all the guests wore bathing clothes until lunchtime. For the men that meant a pair of trunks and for the women two or three dabs of bright-colored and expensive cloth. This was fine for the young folks, but less so for the Right Honorable Winston Churchill, who kept his hunched and pudgy figure wrapped in a bright red bathrobe, and the top of his head, which had once had a red thatch, protected by a wide-brimmed loose straw hat. Thus accoutered, he sat on the edge of the bright blue and green pool and discoursed on world politics to all who cared to listen or pretend to.

He had been several times a cabinet minister over the years, but now for a long time he was out, and at the age of sixty-five he amiably described himself as a political failure. He wrote histories, and a biography of his ancestor, the Duke of Marlborough; he painted pictures, and at home on his estate he built brick walls of which he was proudest. He had had an American mother, which was perhaps the reason he was informal and easy-going. He had been for years an ardent Liberal, but then had decided that they were becoming socialistic. When Lanny Budd had met him just twenty years ago in Paris he had come to the Peace Conference with the determination to bring about the putting down of the Bolsheviks by the Allied armies.

Now the whirligig of time had taken several turns, and an imperialist statesman's thoughts had changed once more. He saw that there was a greater menace in the world than Communism, and he had been tirelessly calling upon his countrymen to arm and put a stop to the appeasement of Hitler. He was even willing to admit that he had blundered in supporting Franco's conquest of Spain: and this of course came pleasantly to Lanny Budd's ears. But Lanny dared not show such feelings; in this company he kept his pose of ivory-tower art lover, rich man's son, playboy—anything but politician, whether Red, Pink, White, Black, or Brown.

In his compulsory role he wouldn't be of special interest to a former Chancellor of the Exchequer; but he made a good listener, and as such was appreciated in this gadabout company. There were seldom fewer than thirty persons sitting down to lunch, and often twice that many gathered round the pool; when Churchill denounced Nazism the hostess would look up from her backgammon—or maybe six-pack bézique—and exclaim: "Winston, you are a social menace!" The guest would reply, most amiably: "Don't worry, my dear Maxine, there isn't a single person here who knows what I am talking about."

Most interesting to the son of Budd-Erling was the occasion when Lord Beaverbrook became one of the house guests. Here was somebody who knew what Winston was talking about, and would talk back;

all Lanny had to do was to sit and listen, while the insides of Tory politics were spread before him like a map. Startling indeed was the change of mind in the four months since Neville Chamberlain had come back from Munich hoping that it was "peace for our time." Every action of the Nazis since then had made clear that it wasn't going to be peace, and that Hitler's solemn declaration that he had no further territorial demands upon Europe was just another Hitler lie. His "co-ordinated" press was carrying on a fresh campaign against Prague, and the most besotted of "Munichmen" could see that this meant further disturbances.

Even "the Beaver" had come to see it—the busiest little money-making and speech-making Beaver that Canada had ever contributed to English public life. Listening to him, Lanny Budd could tell himself that he was reaping a harvest he had been secretly sowing over a long period of years. He had been bringing out of Germany the facts about Nazi-Fascism and seeing his English friend Rick put them into literary form and get them published in English newspapers and weeklies. Great is truth, and it will prevail!

The Beaver had met Lanny at Wickthorpe Castle, and knew that he had been a guest of the high-up Nazis on many occasions. When Churchill learned this he was greatly interested, even excited. Lanny explained that his visits had had to do only with art; he had sold some of Marshal Göring's paintings abroad, and had purchased paintings for the Führer. He was free to talk about the aims of these great men, since they had authorized him to do so. Both desired friendship and co-operation with Britain more than anything—or so they said; as to the sincerity of their professions, the tactful son of Budd-Erling refrained from expressing or even having any opinion. His father's business as well as his own made that necessary, and a noble lord who was also a businessman, owner of the *Daily Express* and the *Evening Standard*, would understand and respect that attitude.

XIII

The mistral blew, and scattered the crowds at the outdoor swimming-pool. The Right Honorable Winston, who did not care for card games and was important enough to say so, phoned to Lanny, asking him to come for a talk. They sat alone in the library of this very fine château, and the Englishman asked questions about the personalities of Nazi-land: Hitler, Göring, Hess, Ribbentrop, and Goebbels; Himmler, now head of the Gestapo, Heydrich, now in charge of the Sudetenland, Dr.

Wiedemann, who had come as an emissary to England at the height of the Munich crisis. And then, their agents in France: Otto Abetz, and Kurt Meissner, who had been Lanny Budd's chum from boyhood; and the Frenchmen of the Right, including Laval and Bonnet, and the three de Bruynes, who had been in jail for their efforts to overthrow the Third Republic. Churchill must have known these men, but he wanted Lanny's opinion, and was tireless in asking questions.

At one point he remarked: "Franklin Roosevelt seems to be one man who is really informed about these matters." Lanny smiled, thinking what a sensation he might have made by replying: "I have been keeping him informed for the past year and a half."

They talked as long as their imperious hostess would permit; and at the end Churchill remarked: "This information may be very useful some day."

The other added: "If you should find yourself called on to become Prime Minister."

The Englishman's laugh had a touch of bitterness in it. "No, no, Mr. Budd. They have put me on the shelf to stay. They don't want a man who says what he thinks."

Lanny would have liked to ask who "they" were; but Maxine was calling loudly from the grand salon: "I want somebody to take me to the movies!"

2

Cherry Ripe, Ripe, Ripe!

I

A WOMAN of the fashionable world who owns a lovely villa with several acres of choice land, and who at the same time has a kind heart, inevitably acquires in the course of years a number of old servants and other pensioners. She complains about these burdens but cannot find a way to get rid of them, and she tries, mostly in vain, to find something useful for them to do. Among Beauty Budd's pensioners was Leese, the Provençal cook, who was now bedridden, and Miss Addington, who had been Marceline's governess, and then Frances's, and was waiting for Baby Marcel to be old enough. Also there was the elderly Polish woman with the unusual name of Madame Zyszynski, who had been the agent of Lanny Budd's introduction into the mysteries of the sub-conscious world.

Parsifal Dingle, her discoverer, would invite her to his study, and there, with the doors left open for propriety's sake, the old woman would go into one of her strange trances. Parsifal would make notes of her utterances, and would study them and compare them, and when Lanny came he would have a report of new incidents which neither of them could explain. Lanny, too, would try experiments—he had enough notes for several volumes of the British or the American Society for Psychical Research.

The result of these activities, now in their tenth year, had been a transformation in Lanny's way of thinking. Just as the modern physi-cist has changed this solid earth into an infinity of universes, each made up of minute electrical charges whirling about in relatively immense spaces, so Lanny had come to think of his conscious mind as a brilliant and scintillating bubble floating on top of an infinite ocean of some kind of mind-stuff. What was the mind that nourished his blood and renewed his tissues and attended to his breathing while he slept? Was he to say that all this activity was a matter of chance? Accidents may happen; but systematic, continuous, and perfectly co-ordinated acci-dents are contrary to logic and common sense. The mind that shaped the petals of the rose and painted the colors of the hummingbird's wing was a real mind, even though Lanny did not share its secrets.

Madame had a conscious mind, entirely commonplace, slow, and un-enterprising. But when she rested her head back and shut her eyes and went into one of her trances, she revealed a quite different mind, which spoke with different voices and knew things that Madame had no way of finding out. What was that trance mind, and where did it come from? Did it inhere in her brain, or did it exist without a brain, and if so, would it survive after Madame's brain had turned into a spoonful of gray dust? Was it a person? A spirit? A mental creation, like a dream, or like a character in a novel or play? Lanny was willing to believe anything, provided he could prove it. Until that time he would keep his mind open, not fooling himself with the idea that he knew some-thing when he didn't.

Whenever he was in Bienvenu he would have sittings with this old woman, who in her secret heart adored him as a son. He was hoping for communications purporting to come from his dead wife—though he never would be able to make up his mind whether what he got was Trudi or his own subconscious memories of Trudi, as when he dreamed of her. But she came no more in the séances; that page in his life had apparently been turned. Likewise Grandfather Samuel Budd seemed to have given up this bar-sinister grandson as a hopeless case, who refused to heed the Word of God as set down in the Hebrew Testament.

The communications of Madame had become tiresome and disappointing. Tecumseh, the Indian control, was cross with Lanny, and Claribel, old-time English lady, bored him with her feeble poetry. Only one thing new: both these "controls" said to the son of Budd-Erling, in solemn tones: "Your fate is approaching!" But when he tried to find out what that fate was, they either didn't know or wouldn't take the trouble to answer him. In the course of his unusual duties, Lanny had been in danger more than once, and might be again. His conscious mind was well aware of that, and doubtless his subconscious mind was equally so.

II

Parsifal Dingle had discovered another method of tapping this mental underworld. He had got himself a crystal ball and set it up on a table in his darkened study; lighting a candle and setting it just beyond the globe, and then sitting at the table, resting his head on his arms, he stared into the globe in silence and with intense concentration. Such concentration and fixed staring are among the established ways of inducing trances and thus tapping the subconscious forces. Lanny's stepfather was interested, because by this means he was seeing visions of the Buddhist monastery of Dodanduwa in Ceylon, from whose old-time monks he had been getting communications for years. He had written letters and received replies from the now-living monks, and the pictures they had sent him of the monastery buildings corresponded exactly to what he had seen in the crystal ball.

So, of course, Lanny wanted to try this experiment. The visions were not in the ball, but in the mind of the gazer, so presumably Lanny could use Parsifal's ball without being affected by what Parsifal had seen there. But even that you couldn't be certain about; for who could say what effect mind might have on matter, and what traces of mental activity might remain in a piece of glass? There is a faculty called "psychometry," based on the fact that objects appear to carry some trace of the persons who have owned and used them. If Lanny had seen Dodanduwa, would it have been Parsifal's visions of Dodanduwa, or

Lanny's thoughts about what Parsifal had been telling him? In a universe so full of fantastic things, who could say what was too fantastic?

What Lanny saw, from the very first attempt, were crowded streets in the Orient: Chinese shops with Chinese signs, rickshaws running fast, pagodas and walls with towers, and everywhere Chinese faces; all sorts of men and women, old and young, rich and poor, some angry, some laughing, all astonishingly vivid and fascinating. Lanny had never been especially interested in China; he had met a few traveling students and diplomats, and of course he had seen pictures, but never anything with the vividness of detail that he got in this crystal ball. An astonishing thing; and naturally Lanny didn't fail to recall an experience of the previous autumn, when he had consulted a young Rumanian astrologer in Munich, and had been told: "You will die in Hongkong." Lanny hadn't then and hadn't now any interest in Hongkong, but he perceived that he might have to, if the subconscious powers were so determined upon it.

The clear-minded art expert disliked every form of superstition, and especially when it took the ugly aspect of fear. But he could not rule out the possibility of precognition, one of the most ancient beliefs. Modern physics now gave support to Kant's conception of time as a form of human thinking; and why might it not be that among the many forms of mind in the universe there were some to which the future was as clear as the past is to our own? Some day there might be a Society for the Study of Dreams, with thousands of members recording their dreams according to the technique of J. W. Dunne, and watching to see how many came true.

Through this crystal ball came a long train of camels with ragged Chinese drivers. They went through a narrow city gate, and Lanny followed them, just as if he had been on one of those photographic trucks by which motion pictures travel with a moving object. He didn't hear any camel bells or shouts of drivers, but watched the silent train, and saw them passing over barren wastes, past ruins of ancient cities half buried. They might have been the palaces of Ozymandias, king of kings, where, boundless and bare, the lone and level sands stretched far away.

Lanny told Parsifal about these visions, and also his mother; Beauty reminded him that he had read a book about Marco Polo when he was a small boy. Maybe this was it, all coming back. As for his "fate" which was approaching, Beauty hoped it was so; for to her the word meant one thing: a woman, the right woman, so that Lanny would settle down, preferably here in Bienvenu, and supply more babies to play in the court and make old age less intolerable to a one-time professional beauty. Ten years ago she had had her way in the Irma Barnes match, but that failure hadn't discouraged her; she wouldn't give up while there was a single heiress left on the Riviera, in Paris, London, or New York.

III

A few days later Lanny tried the crystal ball again, and here came something new. Blue water, sparkling in sunshine—everything was always bright in that globe, like a technicolor film. Little boats sailed across, and that had been one of the most familiar sights ever since Lanny could remember. Then came a yacht, stately, white, with gleaming brass and everything spick-and-span, gliding by and spreading a wake behind her: another sight that had always been familiar, not merely from the Cap but all over the Mediterranean and the Atlantic. In boyhood Lanny had cruised to the Isles of Greece in the yacht *Bluebird*, owned by the creator of Bluebird Soap; later in the yacht *Bessie Budd*, named for his half-sister. The German-Jewish financier, Johannes Robin, had taken the Budd family all over the Mediterranean, and then over the North Sea, and up to the Lofoden Islands and across to Newcastle, Connecticut, home of Budd Gunmakers and now of Budd-Erling. So there was nothing strange about yachts.

This was a different one; the image was small, so Lanny couldn't read the name, but the picture was so vivid that the curiosity of a psychic researcher was aroused and he got up and walked out of his studio for a look over the Golfe Juan. By heck!—there was a yacht, having just rounded the Cap, and gliding past the shore toward the breakwater of Cannes. It wasn't more than a mile or two away, and on a clear day with calm water, that seems right at your front door. Straightway began an argument in the mental works of a researcher: was this the same yacht he had seen, or was he just fooling himself as to the details? And was it a coincidence?—for of course at the height of the winter season there was never a day that yachts were not coming and going along the Côte d'Azur.

Lanny got the little pair of glasses with which he had been wont to examine vessels. When he lifted the glasses to his eyes, the yacht leaped toward him, as if it were right by the shore. *Oriole* was the name; vaguely familiar, but he didn't connect it at once. By the rail stood a line of people, enjoying the view; one was a tall gentleman in a white suit and yachting cap, and beside him stood a girl: Lanny could see that she was blonde and graceful, and then he saw her lift glasses to her eyes. Quickly he put his down, for it didn't seem polite to be staring at a lady, even so far away. When he raised the glasses again the yacht had moved on, and the girl had lowered her glasses and turned her eyes to the man at her side.

Lanny smiled to himself at the thought: "Your fate is approaching!" Assuredly that was how it would happen if Beauty Budd could have her way; the girl who got Lanny would arrive on a large and elegant private yacht! Of course she must be a good girl, too, and spiritual like Parsifal Dingle and his spouse; but there was no reason why she shouldn't be those things on a yacht belonging to her father or her brother or some other close relative.

Lanny found it amusing to tell his mother at lunchtime: "I observed my fate on its way to the yacht basin. The name sounds familiar—the *Oriole*."

"Why, of course!" exclaimed Beauty, whose mind was an international *Who's Who*. "The *Oriole*, of Baltimore. It belongs to Mr. Holdenhurst; you met him at Emily's, three years ago."

Lanny remembered, but vaguely, for he was interested in yacht owners only if they collected paintings, or if they took part in pro-Fascist activities. "There was a pretty girl standing by his side."

"That would be his daughter. I forget her name. She was wearing pigtails when she was here before."

"Well, I couldn't tell about that," replied the incorrigible. "She didn't turn her back."

"He takes a cruise every winter," remarked his mother, ignoring his foolishness. "His health is delicate. It is a very distinguished Baltimore family, old friends of Emily's. No doubt we'll be meeting them again."

"It is my fate!" grinned Lanny.

IV

Mrs. Parsifal Dingle, née Mabel Blackless, then Beauty Budd and Madame Detaze, was only mildly interested in problems of precognition, and didn't care if she spoiled an experiment by meddling and taking charge of the future. It didn't take her more than a minute to get her wealthy friend Emily Chattersworth on the telephone and let her know that the *Oriole* was arriving. "Oh, yes," said Emily. "I had a postcard from Reverdy at Cairo saying they were coming. No doubt he'll be phoning me, and we'll get up some sort of shindig."

"Lanny saw them through the glasses, and says there's a nice-looking girl on board."

"That is Lizbeth, the daughter. She was a lovely child. She's about eighteen now, and should be ready for her début."

That was all the instrument of fate needed to know at the moment; she waited till lunch was over and Lanny had gone off to keep one of his mysterious engagements. Then she called again, and revealed her dark purpose. "Lanny seems to have noticed that girl, and that doesn't happen very often. It might be a good idea to invite him alone, and leave me out of it. You know what I mean."

Yes, Emily knew; she was more than ten years older than Beauty, and was even less pleased with what she saw in the mirror. She understood that the mother was performing an act of self-abnegation, for nobody in the world got more pleasure out of smart luncheons and dinner parties and the gossip of people just off a yacht. But young people, in the bottom of their hearts, resent the existence of the old; so the wise *châtelaine* of Sept Chênes would invite father and daughter, and Lanny alone to meet them. She would keep "Reverdy" busy, and leave opportunity for Lanny to get interested in Lizbeth if he would. In any case he would be polite and friendly, as always when his mother and near-foster-mother had placed some débutante on the carpet before his fastidious eyes.

It is the custom, wherever in the de luxe world a yacht draws up alongside a pier, for a cable to be run on board, so that owner and guests can communicate with the outside world. So presently Emily reported that father and daughter were coming to dinner—black tie and tux would do—and Beauty had only to get hold of her wayward son and send him up to the villa on the heights. The mother spent the afternoon telephoning off and on to various places where Lanny might be, but he wasn't there. The provoking fellow came strolling in, bland and insouciant, a half hour or so before dinnertime; Beauty grabbed him and shoved him into his room, and laid out his things with her own hands while he washed and shaved.

Meantime she poured out upon him all the details she had been able to gather concerning the people he was to meet. When she had got him exactly right, even to the nice little waves which appeared spontaneously in his brown hair, she saw him out to his car and then went back to her boudoir and locked herself in for a few minutes of prayer after the fashion which her husband had taught her. God was All-good and All-wise and you must never tell Him what to do; you must

say, and mean it: "Thy will be done, not mine." But in the deeps of
Beauty's soul rested the firm conviction that God couldn't help agreeing with her this time, and, as a sort of contrabass to all her other
prayers, was the one: "Dear God, please take a hint!"

V

The gentleman with the somewhat unwieldy name of Reverdy
Johnson Holdenhurst was the scion of one of the old Baltimore families; he had been named after a Supreme Court justice, a states' rights
Democrat who had stood by the Union and therefore occupied an
honored place in Maryland's history. The present Reverdy's father
had been one of those domineering men who have their own way
regardless. In a fast-growing harbor he had seen docks, railroad sid-
ings, and other privileges to be obtained from a pliable city council
and state legislature, and he had been the one to shove his way in
and grab them. The World War had come along and he had become
one of the city's richest men; he had left behind him three sons, neglected by a preoccupied father and spoiled by an indulgent mother.
The family fortune was now represented by securities, among the
most secure in the land, so that all the sons had to do was to clip
coupons off the bonds and deposit dividend checks in the family
bank, and then take life easy.

The other sons were "drinking men," in Emily's polite phrase.
Reverdy was the best of them, and he was almost too good for his
own good: a kindhearted fellow whom everybody had imposed
upon. Some politicians had persuaded him to run for United States
Senator—wanting his money, of course. What he had discovered of
treachery and corruption in his home city and state had given him
a case of shellshock and caused him to retire from the world.

"He enjoys delicate health," said Emily, and that was not a "bull";
she meant that her friend was following the medical formula for
longevity, to get yourself a good disease and take care of it. His
trouble was his throat; it began to give warning at the least exposure
to cold and dampness, and he had convinced himself that it would
mean his end if a single snowflake ever had a chance to light upon
his shoulder. So he had got himself a perfectly appointed yacht,
custom-built, and about the first of every November the *Oriole* of
Baltimore sailed out of Chesapeake Bay and headed south. Anywhere, it didn't make much difference, so long as it was a place free

from atmospheric disturbances. Anybody would be taken along who wanted to go, provided it was somebody free from emotional disturbances.

Reverdy was a tall, slender man of fifty or so, not especially frail-looking, well tanned by tropical suns. His features were sensitive, his chin rather weak, his manner hesitating and absent-minded. But when he started talking you were surprised to find that he was quite free-spoken. Lanny guessed that he had adopted this as a matter of conviction, a way of combating his inferiority complex. He was a conscientious person and had given much thought to what he ought to do; some of his decisions were unusual and took you some time to get adjusted to.

VI

And then Lizbeth; that was her name, not an abbreviation. Just as, in the precession of the equinoxes, there is a moment when the sun is at its highest point, so in the development of a girl there must be some moment when she is at her loveliest, and it seemed to Lanny Budd that this must be the day and hour for Lizbeth Reverdy Holdenhurst. She had fair hair, so light in texture that it was hardly to be confined; she had sweet features, a complexion which made you think of all the flower petals you had ever seen, and lips of the sort which had caused an old-time English poet to cry: "Cherry ripe, ripe, ripe!" Doubtless she had been told that she was to meet an "attractive" man; and doubtless there had been women friends on the yacht, and a well-trained maid who had helped to choose this low-cut dress of filmy pink chiffon with velvet shoes to match. Lanny knew what such things cost, for he had watched ladies being arrayed in them and chattering about prices since the time when he had been knee-high to a grasshopper.

Her father adored her—you could see that in every glance. No doubt he had done his best to spoil her, as his mother had done with him. How much he had succeeded was a question which could hardly be answered on short acquaintance. When people have nothing to do but eat a properly prepared meal and engage in mild conversation concerning the places they have visited and the friends they have met, you get only the most agreeable impression concerning them—and that is the way they have planned it. That constitutes "good" society, and you are not supposed to probe deeply, saying: "Well, lovely belle from Baltimore with the flower-petal cheeks and the cherry-ripe lips, how is it with your soul? What faith do you live by, and what is your conception of your duty to your fellow-man?"

Reverdy's grandmother had been a schoolmate of Emily Chatters-worth's mother. Lanny remembered well the latter old lady, Mrs. Sally Lee Sibley, who had come from the city which she called "Bawlamaw," and had seen the Fifth Massachusetts regiment attacked while marching through the city at the outbreak of the Civil War. He spoke about her now, and heard reminiscences of the two families, and then of the cruise of the *Oriole*, seven-eighths of the way around the world. Lizbeth had a girl friend whose parents were medical mission-aries in the Fiji Islands, and they had taken her home by the Panama Canal. That was the way with all their cruises, the father explained: somebody wanted to go to some unlikely place, and they took him. They had known somebody in Bali, so they had gone on to that island. A cousin was wintering in Cairo, so that had been the next port, and now they had stopped in Cannes on Emily's account. They would stay a week or so if the mistral, the cold north gale, didn't start up; if it did, the *Oriole* would skirt the lee shores of France and Spain, and flee down the coast of Africa.

Presently Lanny found himself sitting alone with Lizbeth in the library. It had been that way many times at Sept Chênes; mothers and fathers would take the *châtelaine's* word for it that Lanny was the proper sort of man for young girls to be left with. Lanny would tell about his travels, and the adventures which had befallen him in the line of his profession of art expert, unique and distinguished. He had made two different trips into "Red" Spain to bring out old masters, and one into "Nationalist" Spain for the same purpose; bullets had come whin-ing past his ears in Barcelona, and several had come down through the top of his car from a plane near Saragossa. He discovered that Lizbeth knew nothing about the politics involved in this war, and he did not attempt to enlighten her, or say anything about new wars expected soon on this unhappy old continent. It would have frightened her, and to what purpose?

VII

Returning to Bienvenu, Lanny faced one of those scenes which had become routine. "Well, what is she like?" and "What did you talk about?" and "What did she have on?" and even "What did you have for dinner?" All questions had to be answered in detail, and no answer was ever enough—he must go back and recall more to satisfy his mother's impatient clamor.

"Listen, old darling," said the son—and this too was routine. "She's a beauty, and apparently a nice girl; she will make some man happy, but it can't be me, so don't waste your time scheming."

"Oh, Lanny!"—and then all the arguments. "What on earth is the matter with her?" and "What is the matter with you?"

That would have been quite a story, and Lanny couldn't tell it. He had his work to do, and it wasn't buying paintings; but he couldn't give his mother the least hint of that fact. He would only have set her to worrying, even more than over the fact that he had no wife. All he could say was: "I could never make a girl like that happy; it would be the Irma story all over again. She would want me to go cruising in the yacht, or to settle down in suburban Baltimore—and what would I do there?"

"You say that without knowing a thing about her! It might be that she'd find Bienvenu the most romantic place in the world. There's The Lodge that you could have—" It was the house which Irma had built, but years had passed, and it had been well disinfected, so to speak, by other friends who had occupied it. "A girl at that age is unformed, and the man who wins her love can make her into what he pleases."

"Yes, old darling—I don't think! That's the spiel you women give us; but the truth is she was formed when she was in the cradle, and all the years afterwards, by her mother and her nurses and servants and every woman who got near her—all helping to teach her the routine of fashion. Now she is what you call 'finished'—and I would be the same if I let the ladies fool me."

Beauty Budd, whom nobody could fool, sat gazing at her son intently. "Lanny, you are still tied up with that German woman!"

He would have liked to reply: "That German woman is dead." But if he said it, what excuse could he give for refusing to tell about her—when, where, how, and what did she look like, and have you got a picture of her, and so on? Better to keep her as a protecting shield behind which to retire when his mother started probing into his love life! "Bless your heart!" he evaded. "I wish I could be what you want and do what you want; but you know that we all have our different ideas and interests, and have to live our own lives."

"Lanny, I have never objected to your living your own life, but I can't see why you have to shut your mother out of it."

"I have always told you my own secrets, but I can't tell you other people's. That is the law of the Medes and Persians, which altereth not." Beauty Budd had been a preacher's daughter, and knew what he was quoting.

VIII

She couldn't give up, of course; but she would work underground. It became Lanny's social obligation to escort his mother and their best friend to the yacht. Once on board, it became his duty to take Lizbeth for a stroll about the deck, and tell her about the sights of the harbor; to point out the Île Ste.-Marguerite where the German residents of the Riviera had been interned during the World War, and the place where he, as a boy, had seen a submarine emerge from the *golfe* at night, and, farther out, the place where he had seen a tanker blown up and burning. He told about goggle-fishing, which is swimming under water and spearing fish; about flower-growing on the Cap, and the perfume factories where women worked half buried in rose petals, and got headaches from it. In all this he tried to be fatherly, but he was aware that a girl ready for her début wasn't mistaking an eligible man for her father. She was going to sail away for the Gold Coast and the bulge of Brazil and he would probably never see her again; he didn't want her to carry away any memories or dreams that would cast a shadow over her happiness.

But Lanny's fate wasn't through with him yet, not with a bevy of ladies of fashion co-operating with it and against him. There was every reason why the Holdenhurst family and guests should be entertained by American society on the Riviera; and it didn't take long for word to spread that Beauty and Emily were playing at matchmaking, a delightful game in which everybody wishes everybody success. For example, good old Sophie, Baroness de la Tourette—she was still that, according to European custom, though she had long ago divorced her French husband and taken one from her native land. Sophie got up a real affair at her villa on the other side of the Cap: an afternoon lawn party, with a colored band in red and gold uniforms, and dancing on a platform which she had built for the purpose—in sections which could be unscrewed and stored away out of the weather. The hardware lady from Cincinnati had what she wanted whenever she wanted it, including fair weather; for it was like the first day of spring, and all the smart folk came, the ladies in the dizziest costumes and hats which had been created since the days of Marie Antoinette.

Sophie had known Lanny Budd since he was a babe in arms, and had on her drawing-room walls half a dozen examples of French paintings which he had brought out of Spain and sold to her at a price she could boast of. She turned this show into an occasion for the glorifying of her protégé. Her grand piano was hauled out onto the loggia, and the guests drew up their lawn chairs and listened while Lanny displayed his finger technique, a mixture of half a dozen styles taught to him in boyhood by half a dozen teachers whom Sophie had helped to select.

"None of your heavy stuff now," she commanded. "They like it short and sweet." So Lanny played the Rachmaninoff *C-Sharp Minor Prelude*, which gives people the shivers, though they don't know what it's about, and perhaps the composer didn't either; and for an encore a piano transcription of Schumann's *Widmung*. "I love thee in time and eternity!"—Lizbeth Holdenhurst wouldn't have heard the words, but she would get the excitement if she cared anything about music. In any case she would have impressed upon her young mind the fact that here was a talented man, known to all the important people in this ultra-fashionable place and cordially applauded by them.

Also, he danced well; and if he didn't make love to her, but was just friendly and respectful, that was perhaps the best thing he could have done; for in her heart the girl was still a child, and was in a tumult of excitement, not unmixed with alarm. This was really her début, and a wonderful experience, almost beyond imagining. All these important grand people, many of them foreigners with titles; the women staring at her through lorgnettes, the men ogling her, even the old ones. She needed someone to tell her that this was the European way and she mustn't mind; someone to tell her who was who, and where they came from—romantic-sounding names out of the history books.

Lizbeth had a teacher on the yacht, a maiden lady who gave her lessons in history and literature every morning. The girl hadn't studied enough to hurt her, but she had picked up odds and ends, and of course had learned geography in the chart room of the yacht, and from seeing it loom up on the horizon. She could chatter in French, and when she stumbled over a word, she blushed so exquisitely that where was the Frenchman who could not forgive her? Surely not in the Midi! They swarmed around her like bees on a dish of sugar water; they poured out their hearts to her on the dancing floor, greatly to her confusion, and in the ten-day stay of the *Oriole* her father received half a dozen formal proposals by mail. "The French are fast workers—where American money is involved." So declared the Baroness of the Little Tower, who had been worked that way herself, and now said: "Never again!"

IX

Beauty Budd made no formal proposals, for that was not the American way. What she did was to invite father and daughter to Bienvenu;

no showy affair, but a quiet dinner *en famille*, with Emily and Sophie and Sophie's husband as the only other guests. The one-time artist's model preferred the evening, when she could see to the lighting in all the rooms. Here at home she could show what she had been, for on the wall hung the painting which Marcel had made of her, standing in the doorway of the studio in the fullness of her glory—and Miss Lizbeth of Baltimore surely had nothing on the former toast of the Paris ateliers. On the opposite wall was the painting called *Sister of Mercy*, which Marcel had made after his face had been burned off in the early days of the war, and after Beauty had nursed him back to life. That was one of the famous paintings of modern France, and had been shown in one-man exhibitions in Paris, London, New York, and Berlin. In Munich it had been shown to Hitler in the Braune Haus; and while that didn't add to the work's value as art, it certainly helped to make drawing-room conversation.

There were other Detazes on the walls of this home: landscapes and seascapes of the Cap, and others of Greece and Africa which Marcel had painted during the cruise of the *Bluebird*. The family from the *Oriole* might learn that other people, also, had seen the world from the deck of a trim white vessel. There is such a thing as owning docks and railroad terminals on Chesapeake Bay, and again there is such a thing as owning treasures of beauty which mankind will enjoy for ages—and who but the most purse-proud would question which is the more honorific possession? Reverdy Holdenhurst was apparently not among the questioners, for he asked to be taken to Lanny's studio and shown more of the paintings, and before he left he made a timid inquiry as to buying a couple of them for the saloon of the *Oriole*. He had to be careful, these days, he said, for the new income tax schedules made it hard to own and operate a yacht; but when he learned that he could have his choice of the land and seascapes for eight thousand dollars each, he elected to come the next day and make a daylight view.

Dinner one day and tea the next was getting really chummy. Lanny opened up the storeroom which formed the back part of his studio, and José, the lame Spaniard, carried out the paintings and set them up on easels for inspection. Lanny delivered one of those carefully studied discourses whereby he impressed and at the same time instructed the well-to-do. Since money was being spent for art, it might as well be for good art, and the improving of public taste was a service, as well as the means to a comfortable livelihood. Lanny was assisting in the making of several collections which would someday be willed to the public, and he took a lofty tone, not merely in order to impress his clients, but because that was the way he felt about his job. Somebody had to study and think and compare, and learn art values, and money values in relation to art; if persons who hadn't had time for all that wanted expert advice, Lanny Budd would furnish it to them on a ten-per-cent commission basis. They would trust his integrity, and if at any moment they showed hesitation in so doing, he would advise them to get some other expert.

X

The picture viewing completed, Lanny took the belle of the *Oriole* for a stroll about the grounds of Bienvenu. They were full of a lifetime's memories, and he told her some. This second studio had been built for Kurt Meissner, during the years he had been preparing to become a great *Komponist*. Lizbeth had never heard of him, so Lanny told about him, of course not mentioning that he had been Beauty's lover, or that he was now a Nazi agent in Paris. When Lanny mentioned the Nazis, it was only to tell amusing and picturesque things, such as Marshal Göring keeping a lion cub in his home, and the retreat which Hitler had built himself on the top of a mountain, the only access being through a tunnel and a shaft in which a bronze elevator went up seven hundred feet through solid rock.

It was as if Lanny were saying: "Would you like to travel to Germany and see all these fascinating sights?" And again: "Would you like to live in these houses, and see these views and meet these friends every day?" He could be pretty sure that Lizbeth was thinking these thoughts; no doubt her father was doing the same, and surely Beauty and Emily and Sophie were helping all they could. A girl thinks such thoughts about every likely man she meets, and picks up hints from the older women, and watches for the signs of what the man is thinking. There is a tumult in her heart, for it is all so new and strange to her; she is taken by surprise and overwhelmed by thumpings inside and warm flushes of the cheeks. She has to make an all-important decision, and sometimes it is now or never.

Lanny perceived that Lizbeth was on tiptoe with excitement; the world was marvelous to her—and this always seemed tragic to Lanny, because he knew it was in so many ways a cruel world, and especially hard on women. Many kinds of trial lie before them, and those who are having things easiest are often the least prepared. This one, he realized, had led a sheltered life—very much like that which his own little daughter, Frances, was now leading in England. Another "poor little rich girl," with servants to wait on her and hand her everything she asked for; never having to make any effort, no struggle or strain, nothing to develop her mental muscles. The result was, she was a woman in body, but in mind and character a child; nobody could say what her capacities were—not even she herself.

He talked to her on her own level. On this little beach below them he had played as a boy with the children of the fishermen. They had hauled little seines—they ragged and barefooted, he in bathing trunks. They had brought in strange creatures; he described them, and Lizbeth was interested. On the beach in front of the village, now littered with the almost nude bodies of pleasure-seekers, there had been thirty years ago only a few bathers, and there had come a strolling fiddler each day; Lanny's mother provided a centime, for which price the man would play for a while, and the children would dance and caper. That, too, pleased Lizbeth, who had always had her pleasures laid out for her and had never known what it was to wander at her own sweet will. There had always been a governess or someone to tell her where to go and what to do.

Lanny sounded her out tactfully, and decided that she had no trace of what he called "social" feeling. She took the great and powerful to be exactly what they claimed; she admired them, and was thrilled to meet them, and imagined fairy tales about them. She was a snob, but not self-made; she had received the opinions of the people about her and had never thought of questioning them. The rich were that because they were superior and had the right to be. The poor existed to be servants, and to produce things and be paid and be grateful. The world was a garden of delights made for the Holdenhurst family and their friends, and now Lizbeth was about to be turned loose in it to take whatever pleased her fancy.

Lanny might have taught her some of his ideas; at any rate he might have made gentle tentatives, to see what interest he could awaken. But his tongue was tied, his job kept him mute. Imagine Lizbeth going to her father and saying: "Mr. Budd thinks we rich people have too much money, and that income taxes are all right." Imagine her saying to the guests on the yacht: "Mr. Budd says there aren't enough jobs to go round, and that is why the working people are getting so discontented." Such a story would go the rounds of the smart set in a few days; and how then could Lanny expect to have confidential talks with Juan March and the Duke of Alba, with Charles Bedaux and Baron Schneider, with Lord Beaverbrook, the Duke of Windsor, and ex-King Alfonso of Spain? In his youth Lanny had been conspicuous as a "Pink," and it had taken years of careful and subtle maneuvers to slide himself into the position of ivory-tower dweller and sympathizer with the status quo. Even his own mother and father had to be kept uncertain, and the persons who shared his secret could be counted on the fingers of his two hands: Bernhardt Monck and the two Palmas, President Roosevelt and one of his aides, and the members of the Pomeroy-Nielson family in England. That was all, and there must be no more.

So if Lanny asked this girl to marry him he would be hiding his real self, and taking a chance of wrecking her happiness and his own. What would she make of his trips into Germany, of the cryptic notes and the meetings on street corners at night? Of visits to Washington, about which no word must be said? And suppose he got caught in Naziland, as had several times come so close to happening in the past? He could hear Lizbeth saying, as he had heard Irma: "What right did you have to lie to me? If you loved me, why couldn't you trust me?" Thinking such thoughts, Lanny would become reserved—and at the same time aware that this aloofness might only be making him more attractive.

XI

Hospitality such as the Holdenhursts had enjoyed had to be returned, and so the father planned an excursion. The first warm and calm day, Lanny would bring his mother and her husband, and Sophie would bring her husband and Emily to the yacht at about eleven in the morning, and they would proceed eastward along the coast, having lunch on board; they would go ashore at Monte Carlo, visit the casino and try their luck at gambling, maybe dance for a while or attend a picture show, dine at Ciro's, most swanky, and then come home in the evening. A delightful expedition, shared by guests who had come seven-eighths of the way around the world in the *Oriole*, and by the French lady teacher and a man secretary.

In the course of the sailing or steaming, or whatever it is that a Diesel-powered yacht may be said to do, Lanny found himself strolling on deck with the host, who had just sent him a check for sixteen thousand dollars, and now surprised him by an invitation to become a guest for the trip to the United States. They would go down the African coast, but not ashore, it being a fever district. They would cross to the bulge of Brazil and pay a visit to Rio; then northward, perhaps to Havana and to the Bahamas and Florida. Reverdy always planned his cruises to arrive in the Chesapeake by the latter part of April, but if business called Lanny Budd he could take a plane from Rio or from some other stop on the way.

A man of the world realized at once what such an invitation meant. He was what his world called "eligible," and Reverdy was an attentive father, who would not have failed to note his daughter's enjoyment of this eligible man's company. Reverdy had listened to Lanny's conversation, as well as his piano playing; he had visited his home and met his mother and the people of her set; most important of all, he had had long talks with his old friend, the *salonnière* of Cannes, who had known both Lanny and Reverdy from their beginnings on earth, and talked to them both as a mother. Reverdy wouldn't hesitate to tell her what was on his mind, and to ask questions about a possible son-in-law. Emily would explain Lanny's divorce on the grounds that Irma Barnes had been a thoroughly selfish woman. Having helped to make that match, Emily had it on her conscience, and she loved Lanny as if he were her son.

Would she have mentioned that Lanny's father had never married Lanny's mother and divorced her, as the world had been led to believe? Probably so; for Emily shared a bitter secret about Reverdy himself, which had broken his married life and precluded his being too severe upon other men's irregularities. A few years after his marriage his rigid and proper wife had found him in the embraces of a maid in the household. The wife had never been able to forgive him, in spite of his efforts at atonement; they had never since been man and wife, though she kept the home and conformed to all the proprieties. She was a beautiful woman, rich in her own right, and devoted herself to building up the musical and other cultural life of her home city, which was growing too fast for what she considered its good. Reverdy still adored her, and perhaps as a means of making his life tolerable, had persuaded himself that a celibate life was advisable for one in his delicate state of health.

Doubtless he was taking a great deal upon himself to plan his daughter's future without waiting to consult her mother. Certainly he was doing that deliberately when he invited the genial and fascinating Lanny Budd to be her traveling companion over a period of ten weeks or so. Moonlight in tropical and subtropical climes, the swish of water from a yacht's prow and its sparkle on the waves, the murmur of the wind through palm branches ashore—these things are surely not conducive to celibacy. What Reverdy Johnson Holdenhurst was saying to Lanny Prescott Budd, only a decade or so younger than himself, was something like this: "I am offering you first chance, over all the swains who will be waiting for her and will begin laying siege to her the moment she arrives under her mother's wing."

And likewise Lanny knew exactly what he was doing when he answered: "You are paying me a compliment, Mr. Holdenhurst, and I wish I could accept; but I have just had a letter from my father, telling me that he is expecting to be in Paris very soon, and needs me to go into Germany with him. I have business there, too, and engagements which I can hardly break."

XII

After that these two men of the world talked about public affairs. Reverdy knew that Lanny had contacts with influential persons in the great capitals, and he asked what the prospects were. Lanny had to tell him that he thought they were as bad as possible; Europe was teetering on the edge of war, and it could hardly be postponed more than a year. Lanny told what he was free to tell about preparations in Germany, France, and Britain; he was in a strategic spot because his father made fighter airplanes—the B-E P11 the latest, though the U.S. Army had given it a different designation. Robbie Budd had staked his future upon the belief that such planes would decide the destiny of nations, and now he was winning out. Those same officials of army and navy who had formerly given him the cold shoulder were coming to him, or calling him on the telephone from far parts of the world. Formerly they had been exacting and dilatory; now they would take whatever they could get, and price appeared to be no object. The plant was getting under full steam, as Robbie had been dreaming it and promising his stockholders for years.

Reverdy was interested. He had found the business game too strenuous for himself, but he liked to hear about other men's efforts. Robbie Budd's had been a success story, typical of America; he had been slighted all his youth and manhood by his stern old Puritan father, and his efforts had been a sort of defiance of that father, even after the father was dead. Ten years ago the family had got caught in the panic, and a Wall Street syndicate had taken over Budd Gunmakers; but here was Robbie on his own, showing his fellow-townsmen that he was the best Budd of them all. If war actually broke out, the company would be caught up in a whirlwind; Lanny had seen it happen to the munitions plant a quarter of a century ago, and it had made an indelible impression upon his boyish mind.

Did all this make an impression upon the mind of a valetudinarian who had retired from money-getting, but who still lived in a world that was run by money? He said: "Your father must be a remarkable man. I should like to meet him."

Lanny, who also lived in a money world, and had never been allowed to forget it, replied, politely: "It would give him great pleasure, I am sure." He didn't add: "If you could run up to Paris—" for that might suggest eagerness on his part.

"I suppose," ventured Reverdy, "that with a business expanding like that, he can always use more capital."

"Yes, indeed; it is a perpetual problem for him."

"I don't have much to invest these days, for, as you know, we have a government which seems determined to exterminate us 'economic royalists.' But I sometimes have a few dollars left over."

This was an old, old song in Lanny's ears, and he knew that he must take it seriously and look sober, as at a funeral. The rich were becoming poor, and everything was going to the demnition bow-wows. Men of great affairs couldn't see how the world could possibly get along without them; and yet Lanny had seen them, one by one, descending into their graves, and becoming futile spirits trying to give advice through Madame Zyszinski—and nobody but Lanny and his stepfather paying the slightest attention to them!

XIII

He couldn't very well help telling his mother about the yachting invitation, and of course it was like poking into a beehive. "Oh, Lanny! How could you refuse?" and "Don't you see what that means? The girl is in love with you! He'd never dream of asking you if she hadn't wanted it." And then a barrage of questions: "What is it that you really have to do in Germany? Robbie knows everybody there by now; and what is the sale of a picture compared with a chance like this?"

The ladies of the beehive got busy. The yacht was supposed to sail the next day, but Emily Chattersworth, most dignified and even austere of schemers, sat down to telephone. She called a villa in a place called Californie on the heights above Nice, temporarily occupied by a certain Edward Albert Christian George Andrew Patrick David, Duke of Cornwall and Earl of Chester, and recently created Duke of Windsor. She spoke with His Grace's bride, who had been born Warfield and christened Bessie Wallis, and had been raised in a little red brick house on Biddle Street in Baltimore. It was an unfashionable neighborhood, and few Baltimoreans had paid any attention to either the birth or the christening; but they had all heard of her now, and recalled that her mother was a Montague, and the Montagues were "F.F.V.'s"—which, if you live in that part of the world, you know means "First Families of Virginia."

What Emily said was that the *Oriole* was about to sail, but it would seem that the Holdenhursts ought to meet Wallis, and be in a position to tell the home folks how their best-known daughter was getting along. "Wally," of course, would never forget Baltimore, or the imposing brownstone mansion on Monument Square which had been the town house of the Holdenhurst family in her childhood. She would have had to be superhuman not to enjoy receiving their tribute of homage. Home-town girl makes good, so to say! "Bring them to tea tomorrow," said the duchess.

So, of course, the sailing of the yacht was postponed, and all the ladies were in a flutter, most of all Lizbeth. She knew that she shouldn't have been, for, after all, any American is as good as any king, to say nothing of an ex-king, or a duchess who had hoped to be a queen and missed it by—who could say how closely? But Lizbeth knew quite well the first questions everybody at home would ask her—whether she had met "Wally," and what was she like and what did she say and what did she wear and what did she have that they didn't have, excepting the duke.

The idea was, of course, that Lanny should drive Emily and Reverdy and Lizbeth to the tea party. Since he had already met the hosts, this would be no intrusion. But the stubborn fellow put his foot down; he had another engagement and he wasn't going to break it—the first time in all his life that he had ever turned down a request from his near-foster-mother. "No, darling," he said, over the telephone, "I am not going one step farther with that girl. I don't love her, and it's not fair to her to let her think that I do, or that I might. Irma was enough for me, and it ought to be for all my friends."

The truth was, he was going to the Château de l'Horizon because he had learned that Charles Bedaux was a guest there, and this Frenchman who had made his millions in America was a gold mine and treasure chest for a "P.A." He was that peculiar type of person who is dazzled by famous names and flies to a celebrity as a moth to a candle flame. He had watched the rise of Mussolini, and then of

Hitler, and now of Franco, and it had become clear to him that these were the men of the future, to whom history would belong. He had attached himself to them, housed them, fed them, financed them; he had a château here in the Midi, and a villa on the Obersalzberg, and a shooting box in Scotland, all of which were always crowded with his Fascist friends. He shared their secret schemes, invested in their enterprises, carried their gains abroad and hid them safely—and all he asked in return was that the big businessmen of these countries should be instructed to install the Bedaux system of timing every movement made by every workingman!

Emily's chauffeur drove her and her friends to the villa in Californie, while Lanny sat by the blue and green swimming-pool and sipped ginger ale and told how he had so nearly been caught by the French police in the Cagoulard conspiracy of the previous year. That set the pace, and for a couple of hours thereafter he listened to Bedaux's account of the new coup d'état that was going to be carried out from Algeria and French Morocco—just as Franco had started from Spanish Morocco, you remember! In Belgium, also, events were preparing; in two or three years, you would see, there wouldn't be a single labor union left in Europe, nor a political demagogue fattening himself on labor discontent, nor an income or inheritance tax squeezing the "free enterprise system." "I am an economic royalist," declared the inventor of the Bedaux system, with grim defiance.

XIV

Common decency of course compelled Lanny to accompany his mother and her friends to the pier to see the *Oriole* cast off and slide out of the harbor. Before that they all went on board and drank a toast. Lizbeth looked fresh and lovely in a simple sailor suit, and Lanny thought she wouldn't have much trouble in finding a Baltimore husband.

Before they parted, the father said: "I shall probably have to run up to New York, and I might come to Newcastle and talk with your father."

"Certainly," replied the son. "Will you come and visit us?"

"I will be on the yacht. I might come directly to Newcastle, before I go into the Chesapeake. I suppose the best way would be to come into Long Island Sound from the east."

"By all means avoid the congestion of New York harbor and the East River. Perhaps I shall have the pleasure of seeing you at Newcastle. I will arrange it if I can."

He couldn't say less, for in the previous conversation he had mentioned that he would be coming to America when he was through with his affairs in Germany. Driving home, he thought it over and found it strange that a man who had been away from home for more than half a year should by-pass his home and make a long detour, just for a business call. How easy it would have been to call Robbie on the telephone and make an appointment to meet him in New York. But that way, Lizbeth wouldn't be along, and Robbie's son wouldn't be there either!

The more Lanny .thought about it the more uneasy he became. Could it be that Lizbeth had fallen completely under the spell of an American who was half a European, who played the piano better than anybody she knew and delivered suave lectures on art—and who, at the same time, knew all the famous people a subdeb from Baltimore had ever heard of, and who seemed to spend most of his time in palaces and châteaux? And one who didn't run after her and her father's money as other men did, but on the contrary turned her down, politely but firmly! What did he want that Lizbeth Reverdy Holdenhurst didn't have?

Could it be that Lizbeth had taken this problem to her father and clamored for his aid? A girl who had always had everything she wanted would hardly submit without a struggle to not getting the thing she wanted most of all. Could it be that the invitation for Lanny to join the cruise of the *Oriole* had been her idea? And that she had then persuaded her father to visit Newcastle, Connecticut, before returning to their home—to see the man she wanted for a husband before seeing even her mother?

Lanny realized that his fate might still be on his trail!

3

Gold Will Be Master

I

A WIRELESS message came from Robbie Budd; he was on a steamer and bound for Paris. So Lanny packed his bags and wrote a few notes. Then, as he was about to leave in his car, the postman brought a note signed "Bruges," saying: "I have a painting for you to look at." The art expert was happy indeed to get that word, for the name was code for his old friend Raoul Palma, concerning whom he had become deeply anxious.

In the old days as a "parlor Pink" Lanny had been pleased to go to the workers' school in Cannes, and had made no secret of his sympathy with its ideas. But now he couldn't afford to go near the place, or to be seen with either Raoul or his wife. While the school director was in Spain, it had been the practice for Lanny to write to Julie Palma, naming an hour, and he would pick her up on an obscure street and drive her out into the country. This would have looked suspicious to the world, but few would have guessed that the purpose was to give her money for the support of Socialist education.

Now Lanny typed a note arranging for a rendezvous; he did not sign it but sealed it tightly in an envelope, and addressed it to Raoul. On the outside he typed: "Pay two francs to bearer," and then set out on his journey, which took him through the city of Cannes. The school was in a working-class district, the so-called "Old Town," near the harbor, and two or three blocks away Lanny parked his car and went for a stroll. Observing a fellow who appeared to be loafing, he offered him four francs to deliver the note, two to be paid by Lanny and two by the person who received the note. The man accepted, and Lanny went back to his car and sat reading the morning paper until his Spanish friend stepped into the back seat of the car.

In a forest of friendly oak trees which would surely not betray any secrets, Raoul told what had happened to him during the past sixteen months. He was still tense with his memories; the bombing had not been incessant, but the expectation of it had been, and even now, when a plane was heard in the sky overhead, Raoul's heart missed every other beat. Barcelona during the past few weeks had been a nightmare of hunger, disease, and death. The official of the Foreign Press Bureau, always too optimistic, had clung to the hope that the invading armies would be beaten back. Then he had hoped that Franco would make some civilized terms with his conquered foes. Only when he had realized that the Fascists were proceeding to grab every official of the Loyalist government, even down to the humblest clerk or porter, and stand them against a wall and shoot them without ceremony, did he decide that his Spanish dignity permitted him to take flight.

The roads were jammed, and being machine-gunned continually from the air; it had been a question of walking cross-country, and Raoul had been weakened by a long period of underfeeding. He and two colleagues had found a fisherman who agreed for a very high price to row them along the shore during the night. That, they figured, would give them a head start, and a chance to rest; but unfortunately it had been a moonlit night, and they had been spotted by an Italian hydroplane whose pilot was amusing himself by bombing and machine-gunning vessels large and small. The fisherman and one of the passengers had been killed and the boat filled full of holes. Raoul and one of his friends had managed to get ashore, and with money redeemed from the dead fisherman's pockets they had bought a burro. By taking turns, one riding and the other walking alongside, they had managed to make their way across country and get themselves smuggled into France.

II

So here was this former school director, many pounds underweight, and suffering from what were doubtless stomach ulcers. His delicately chiseled features had never shown up so clearly; with his melancholy eyes and black hair in need of cutting he looked like one of Goya's saints. But he was still optimistic, confident that Madrid would hold out. He had been there, and knew the spirit of the people; with what they had learned about the atrocities in captured Valencia and Barcelona, every man and woman would understand that it was better to die fighting.

Lanny had to say: "You might as well forget it, Raoul. Count those people dead, and Spain as through. Nobody can fight bombing planes and artillery with rifles and revolvers—at least not for many weeks."

Tears ran down the Socialist's pale cheeks, and he did not try to wipe them away. He had heard others say it, and had denounced them as defeatists; but he knew that the son of Budd-Erling went among the people who decided the destiny of nations. "All those comrades, Lanny! We simply *have* to save them!"

"We simply *can't* save them, Raoul; and what good does it do to fool either them or ourselves? Only a few days ago I talked with the man who has been raising the money, and putting up a large part of it. Whatever it takes, he will furnish, or has already furnished. When money is in the bank, and munitions have been purchased and put on shipboard, it is something we can no more change than the coming of spring or the phases of the moon. Let's get busy at our next job, and try to do it better."

"What *is* that job, Lanny?"

"To try to save France. We have more workers here, and they are better organized, and if we can make them understand what is being plotted against them, they may be able to act in time."

So Raoul dried his tears and took out a pencil and paper and made notes while Lanny told what he knew about the Cagoulards, whose conspiracy to overthrow the Republic had been exposed some fourteen months ago, since Lanny had last seen his friend. Lanny didn't say from whom he had got this information; he was learning to be more and more cautious, putting his duties as a "P.A." above all others. But it could do no harm to tell the inside facts, which Raoul would put into articles for the Socialist press of France. Such is the help which men of social conscience can give to the masses, and when in future years the records are opened and secrets laid bare it will be found that in every country there were men and women who rebelled against the despotism of *la haute finance*, and found ways to tip off its opponents.

The situation of Marianne, as Lanny portrayed it, was perilous indeed. The Cagoulards, or "Hooded Men," had been exposed, but nobody had been seriously punished, and the authors of the conspiracy were so highly placed that they had not even been named. The heads of the "two hundred families" which ruled France had made up their minds that their interests required the overthrow of the Third Republic, and the establishment of some sort of dictatorship which would break the power of the labor unions, as had been so efficiently done in Italy, Germany, Austria, and Spain. The conspirators had retired "underground" for the moment, but they were as strong as ever, and as determined: great industrialists and bankers, cabinet members and other officials, and the heads of army and navy—such men as Admiral Darlan, General Weygand, and Marshal Pétain, the most honored names in France.

Such was the situation, and the triumph of Franco promised to bring matters quickly to a head. *La patrie* was caught in a vise, with enemies on both sides of her, and others within. The middle classes of France had been pretty well corrupted by the Fascist poison, and were fed new doses of it every day through a purchased press. The one hope lay in the workers; it was the task of Raoul and his friends to awaken them to the peril, to hold up before them the hateful image of Fascism, and make them realize that for the masses it was an issue of freedom or slavery, of life or death.

The director had been at home only a few hours, but already had heard the situation in the school explained by his wife. It was a miniature of what existed throughout the whole country. The working-class world was split into factions, which spent the greater part of their energies in fighting one another instead of concentrating upon the common enemy. The Communists, by far the most active group, insisted upon following in the footsteps of Russia; they went to such an extreme as to argue that from the point of view of the workers there was no difference between a bourgeois republic and a Fascist dictatorship. Therefore, why fight for France? All wars were capitalist wars, and the workers could never win one.

"We have been teaching the workers pacifism for a century," explained Raoul, "and it is almost impossible to unteach them, even after what they have seen in Spain. Some of our best lads have gone over to the Communists, because Julie kept insisting that France has to be armed now."

Said the son of Budd-Erling: "It is hard for a man to practice pacifism while his neighbor is planting dynamite under his house."

III

Lanny put a bundle of banknotes into his friend's hand, enough to keep the school going for another two or three months. It wasn't an expensive undertaking, for the building was old and dingy, and Raoul and his wife lived humbly. The wife had invented an aunt in Paris who was supposed to be putting up the funds; thus Lanny, reclining in the lap of luxury, could salve his conscience with the idea that he was doing something concrete for the workers of the Midi, with whom he was forbidden to have direct contact. From childhood on he had been eager to find out about such people—fishermen, peasants, workers in the perfume factories—anybody he ran into in his neighborhood. But now he was sentenced to live among those greedy and coldhearted persons who called themselves the *grand monde*.

Driving over the familiar *route nationale* up the valley of the river Rhone, Lanny brooded over the confusions of this world in which his lot had been cast. Men had invented means of production capable of making plenty for everyone, but their mental development had not kept up with their techniques, and their moral equipment was centuries behind. They were still predatory animals, trying to enrich themselves at the expense of others, and thus filling their hearts with jealousy and hatred. If anyone suggested the development of co-operative techniques, they called him a "crackpot"—or what Maxine Elliott had dubbed Winston Churchill, "a social menace."

"That Man in the White House," another such menace, had said to Lanny: "You are under orders." So the son of Budd-Erling would go on leading a double life, associating exclusively with persons whose ideas and purposes he despised, studying their wishes, saying what they wanted him to say, thinking up devices to cause them to talk out their inmost hearts. Then he would retire to his room, lock himself in, type out a summary of what he had learned, and find a way to get it safely mailed. He would do that even with his own father, and not have to worry about it, because he was making his father happy, in the belief that his son had become dutiful and what the father called "sensible."

IV

So there was Lanny, waiting at Le Bourget airport with his car, ready to transport the president of Budd-Erling to the Hotel Crillon, and listen to the news about the large family of Budds in and about the city of Newcastle, Connecticut. They did not a little quarreling among themselves, but considered that they got along fairly well as families go. They had various kinds of eccentrics among them, but one and all they were proud of themselves, and had learned to adjust themselves to their world; they all made money, or at any rate hung on to what their forefathers had made. They all had to be proud of Robbie Budd, whether they wanted to or not, and the knowledge of this was one of the quiet and solid satisfactions which Robbie took with him wherever he traveled.

They had called him a wild one, and later on in life an adventurer and gambler; he had started a new gamble at the age of sixty or so, when a sensible man would have been settling down to play with a hobby: collecting old china, or building toy boats, or sending missionaries to the Hottentots. All the old Budds—and the woods were full of them—had shaken their heads and said that he would lose his last night-shirt. Airplanes to fight in, of all things on earth, or above it! But he had gone his stubborn way, and now he sat at the gambling table, preparing to rake in the chips, and grinning at those townsmen who had been invited to come in with him and had declined.

Even Robbie was surprised by the recent picking up of his business, and wanted Lanny to tell him what had happened in the world. Only four or five months since the Prime Minister of Britain had come home with tears of joy in his eyes and told his people that it was "peace for our time," and here, all at once, the governments of Europe had been seized by a mad impulse to increase their military aviation!

Lanny said: "They've got onto Hitler at last."

"You think the British mean to fight him?"

"They've got to make a stand somewhere, and they've pretty nearly reached the point. The Cabinet is split, and different members wobble this way and that; but even a near-Fascist like Beaverbrook has decided that they can't go on making concessions forever."

This was the service Lanny could render to his father, as a sort of world scout and prognosticator. Robbie was like a farmer who knows how to plant and tend crops, but needs to be told whether the demand for wheat is going to increase or decrease, and whether it will be better to sell the corn at once or use it to fatten hogs. Robbie's business involved the ordering of a great variety of materials, and the hundreds of gadgets which went into a fighter plane, all of them increasing in complexity. They had to arrive at his fabricating plant precisely on time—otherwise everything else would be held up. Orders had to be placed far in advance and could rarely be canceled; so, truly, he was gambling, staking everything he had achieved so far upon his ability to guess what the ruling groups of a half dozen great countries would be doing six months from now.

It was no job for a grandfather; but this one seemed to be thriving under the burden. He was a hearty, solid man, with only his gray hair to indicate his age. He had just had a checkup by his doctors and was limiting himself to a cocktail before lunch and another before dinner, and one cigar after each of these meals. He was proud of his ability to obey these stern orders; he was a sensible man and put first things first, so he never tired of declaring. What he put first wasn't making large sums of money; he had been touchy on that point all his life, and had been wont to explain it to his idealistic son on the slightest provocation.

What came first was the protection of their homeland, God's own country, the greatest in the world, the freest and best. What Robbie sold to Europe was just a by-product; what really counted was the tools and the know-how, which Robbie was keeping. Someday America would want planes for defense and want them in a hurry, and there Budd-Erling would be, in a safely protected spot, ready for the job.

As a boy Lanny had believed all that; as a young man he had decided that it was "the bunk"; but now he had come back to agreement with his father—at least so far as concerned the importance of getting fighter planes built. Instead of making toplofty remarks and going off to look at paintings or listen to concerts, Lanny was pleased to accompany his father everywhere, act as chauffeur and social secretary, help him to meet the right people, and then sit and listen, now and then putting in a shrewd word to guide the conversation. These were valuable services, and Lanny could have come into the firm and had a generous salary if he had wanted it; but he made plenty of money, so he said—more than the government would let him keep. This last was taken for a slap at the New Deal, and was the kind of conversation pleasing to the rich and powerful.

V

Lanny watched this well-poised eupeptic man, washing up after his long journey and getting ready for his business forays. Lanny remembered a saying of Clemenceau, the "Tiger," that you could always tell the men of the Right—they were not merely stupid, they were the wickedest. Was Robbie stupid? Certainly not by ordinary standards; he was shrewd, well informed within his self-chosen limits, and he had a sense of humor that made him a good companion. But he was like a man who builds a house to suit himself and then goes inside and shuts the door and locks it and will not open for any knock. Robbie Budd refused to be bothered by the greater part of the universe. If anybody, including Lanny, played music above the grade of college songs, he would sit still and think about his business problems. He appreciated art to the extent that a painting looked like the thing it was supposed to represent; but the finer qualities meant little to him, and that little because Lanny had explained them like a schoolteacher. He had no religion, he never looked at the stars, and the mysteries of being born and dying concerned him hardly at all.

Was Robbie wicked? That again depended upon the standard of judgment. Merely to ask the question caused Lanny to wince, and throughout past years had cost him much mental suffering. Lanny loved his father, and in boyhood had adored him; now his attitude was full of contradictions, clashes of ideas and emotions, a secret war that went on internally whenever they met: admiration mixed with disgust, curiosity mixed with boredom, affection mixed with anger.

In his own eyes Robbie Budd was a sound and well-balanced man, a useful citizen and master of affairs who had demonstrated his capacity to direct the labors of thousands of other men. He had earned that right, and his attitude was, by God, let anybody try to take it away from him! He considered that the New Deal was trying to do this, and he was ready in his own phrase to fight it to hell and back. How far he would go in this fight was something he had perhaps not thought out, but when he came to Paris he found no difficulty in doing business with men who had gone so far as to organize and help to finance a secret murder society. If Lanny had mentioned the fact that the Cagoulards had taken the Rosselli brothers, editors of an Italian anti-Fascist newspaper of Paris, out into the woods and beaten them to death, Robbie would have answered coldly: "Well, they asked for it."

Circumstances had made Robbie, with his own hearty co-operation, a "merchant of death." He had begun selling munitions as soon as he had come out of Yale, which had been some four and forty years ago. His grim old Puritan father had provided him with a complete set of intellectual and moral defenses, supported by numerous texts from ancient Jewish Scripture. Robbie had forgotten the texts, but had taken up the selling techniques and improved upon them; now he was a merchandising machine, and no longer admitted to his mind any idea that this was not the highest destiny of man. He called it patriotism, common sense, the nature of life, which he hadn't made and which nobody could change. Criticism of it he would repudiate with quiet contempt, which would turn to annoyance if the argument was pressed hard.

VI

Robbie told the news from home and then listened to what there was from Bienvenu, not very much. (A French philosopher had said: "Happy the people whose annals are tiresome.") Then, without preliminaries, Robbie started telling the purposes of this trip, the principal one being to visit Berlin and have it out with Hermann Wilhelm Göring, Reichsminister and Reichsmarshal. Robbie was far from satisfied with the outcome of a deal he had made with the old-time robber baron; the men whom Göring had sent to Newcastle were getting everything the Budd-Erling plant had, but those whom Robbie had sent to Berlin were ill-satisfied with what they had been allowed to see and learn, and one of them had tipped Robbie off that a delicate approach had been made to find out if it was possible to buy him. All that was exactly what Lanny had expected and had warned his father about; but he didn't mention that now, having in the meantime become the fat Marshal's art expert and friend.

Robbie said he was just about fed up with the Nazis; they didn't play the game according to American rules. He had decided that the relations he had established with Baron Schneider in Paris were likely to prove more profitable in the long run; but the situation was complicated, and Robbie was eager to hear what data his son had picked up. He listened attentively and asked many questions. Schneider was going to make Budd-Erling planes in Czechoslovakia, and that meant, of course, that in case of war Göring would get both planes and plant. Robbie wouldn't worry about that, for he had got cash, and as a businessman he had to take the stand that he had nothing to do with Europe's quarrels and it made no difference who won the next war. But if Germany should succeed in breaking the Maginot Line, then Schneider would be "out" as a customer, and Robbie might wish that he had kept his friendship with *Der Dicke*, no matter how big a rascal he was.

Lanny said, well, if Germany invaded France, Britain would certainly have to come in, and in that event there would be a tight blockade, and Göring might have trouble in getting any Budd-Erling planes, or in paying what he might owe. Robbie didn't like the British, on account of their being too-forceful trade competitors, and their military men very stiff and stand-offish; but he agreed with Lanny's remark that it was the British fleet which would help to keep the Nazis away from Long Island Sound.

Lanny argued that in the event of war in Europe involving Britain, Robbie wouldn't have to worry, because it would mean that the American government would have to start buying planes for its own protection, and the Budd-Erling plant would be kept busy to capacity. Robbie's answer was: "It may be; but I have so little faith in our brass hats, and their ability to foresee anything, that I'll not stake the future of our plant upon them. What I'm told right now is that the French government has been sufficiently scared, and that I may get a cash order from them at once. If so, I'll be in a position to talk turkey to the fat Hermann."

VII

So that was the scheme on which they went to work. Robbie had cabled the Baron of his coming, and now Lanny phoned to the secretary and was invited to come with his father to dine. They got out their evening clothes and had them pressed; since it was raining, they went in a taxi, so that Lanny wouldn't have the problem of parking his car. They entered the mansion, in which on previous occasions they had met a great company; this time there were no other guests, and three men were served in solemn state by a butler and a footman in livery.

Charles Prosper Eugène Schneider was in his early seventies. He was dapper, elegant, extremely French, and might have been taken for a dandy by one who didn't understand this people. He wore a trim little gray mustache, and spoke English with a sort of mincing voice; but Robbie knew him well, and had never made any mistake about him; he was a man of power, one of the greatest in the world. He had been carefully trained for his job by his father and his grandfather before him, and had taken the family's steel and munitions property and expanded it into an empire. He owned not merely the huge Le Creusot works, those at Chantiers, and the Tréfileries du Havre; he controlled the still larger Skoda works in Czechoslovakia; altogether he owned or controlled some four hundred heavy industry plants at home and in various parts of Europe; he was one of the directing brains of the Comité des Forges, the real government of France.

Outside, he was all courtesy, serenity, and charm; but inside, he was worry and strain, which it was hard for him to conceal in a conversation with friends from overseas. He was bitterly contesting in the courts the moves which had been taken by the Blum government for the nationalizing of Le Creusot; he hated it so that he had walled off the privately owned portion of his plant from the portion which had been taken over by the government, so that there might be no communication between the two.

And foreign affairs worried him even more, for his training had not included the managing of either Bolsheviks or Nazis, two monstrous forces which had developed in his world, the former causing the latter, and each warring against the other. For more than two decades the Baron and his associates had been trying to undermine the empire of Lenin and Stalin, without success; for more than a decade they had been watching the rise of Hitler, wondering if this was the proper answer, hoping and fearing alternately, or even simultaneously, trying to make up their minds and disagreeing, even quarreling among themselves. It was a set of problems without parallel in history, so far as Eugène had read it—and he had read a great deal, he said.

France had one age-old trouble, which had been summed up in a sentence by the shrewd old Clemenceau: there were too many Germans. Forty million Frenchmen, facing eighty millions of the hereditary foe, if you included those which Hitler had taken or was clamoring to take under his dominion. France had Britain for an ally, but Britain was a sea power, and could not put on the Continent an army large enough to even the balance. France had been saved last time by her ally on the east, but now that ally had been ruined by the cancer of Bolshevism. The struggle inside France was between the Left, which had made an alliance with the Reds, and the Right, headed by the Comité des Forges, which wanted to break up this alliance, make friends with Germany, and join her in putting the Reds down for good.

Such was the situation. But now the most awful doubt had assailed the soul of Europe's uncrowned munitions king. Suppose he had been making a mistake! Suppose Hitler refused to be a friend of the French steelmasters! Suppose he was worse than the Bolsheviks, and refused to fight them! Here he was, chewing up Czechoslovakia, and apparently planning to chew up Poland; and suppose he came to some sort of understanding with the Bolsheviks—where would Britain and France be then? It was this sort of nightmare which destroyed the sleep of Baron Schneider of Schneider-Creusot, put lines of care into his face, and threatened him with stomach ulcers.

VIII

Something had to be done, the great man declared. The army mobilization of the previous September, preceding the Munich settlement with Hitler, had cost France eight billions of francs; that had to be made up in taxes, and where were they to come from? Labor was in revolt against the increase in the cost of living, and the abolition of the forty-hour work week; there had been desperate strikes in the airplane industry, where France most needed loyalty and efficiency. The Baron and his friends had been clamoring for a "strong" government, which would tolerate no nonsense, and Premier Daladier had got from the Chamber the right to govern "by decree." He had crushed the strikes by the method of mobilizing the strikers, with the result that labor had been driven to fury and was practicing sabotage, a sort of dull, slow civil war going all the time. Internal enemies were eating out the heart of France, at the very time that her external foes were menacing her life.

The Baron would not have betrayed these torments, except to his intimates; but these visitors came from a happier land overseas, one which had managed to preserve a little of the old-time prosperity. Perhaps they could see the problem through fresh eyes, and throw some gleam of light upon it. *Que faire, que faire?* Robbie Budd had to tell him that things were by no means so rosy at home; there was an evil thing called the New Deal, and the country was now facing a crisis and perhaps another panic. America's only advantage lay in the fact that a great ocean lay between her and any possible enemy.

The munitions king of Europe revealed items of news which had not got into the American press, at least not in such form that it had caught Robbie Budd's attention. Mussolini was demanding portions of French North Africa—actually meaning it, apparently, and threatening to seize them. "That graceless wretch!" exclaimed the Baron. "We of the Right gave him money to help him into power and have fought for him and sustained him over a period of seventeen years; we supported his claim to Abyssinia, we let him have his way in Spain—and now he turns upon us! He must have a 'Munich' of his own, and at the expense of *la patrie!*"

Ingratitude, thou marblehearted fiend! Robbie Budd had experienced it, though never upon such a cosmic scale. He expressed sympathy, so warm that the Frenchman replied by entrusting him with another confidence: he was making plans to start work upon a great munitions plant in Canada. A dethroned monarch of guns and tanks might wish to have at least one principality left to him!

"There is, as you doubtless know, Monsieur Budd, a little enclave of France in that vast land. Its people are still loyal to our Catholic faith, and not corrupted by the cynicism and perversities of their unhappy motherland. It is no longer possible to foresee what lies ahead for my country, but I feel certain that no enemy can reach to a plant in Sorel, Quebec. You agree with me, messieurs?"

Robbie said: "You can count upon the fact that we ourselves would have to protect it in case of its being threatened."

IX

Baron Schneider's mind was in a state of uncertainty on many subjects, but there was one to which he came back again and again—

France must have more airplanes. At this moment, he revealed, she had some sixteen hundred first-line planes, while Germany had three times as many; Robbie Budd substantiated this. During the present year of 1939, the Baron continued, France expected to produce about twenty-five hundred combat planes of all types—"and again Germany will beat us three to one—is it not so?"

"My information is that Göring expects to produce from nine hundred to a thousand planes every month this year." Robbie wasn't breaking any confidence when he said this, for he knew that the fat Marshal hoped to get what he wanted by terrifying his enemies.

"*Eh, bien?* We must have more without delay; and that means American planes." Robbie knew that it meant Budd-Erlings, for the munitions king had made investigations and satisfied himself that Robbie had the fastest single-seater pursuit plane in the world, and with a few changes it could meet French requirements.

"Just what can you do for us, Monsieur Budd?" They talked about time schedules, and then the host said: "I have been carrying on a little campaign, and I want you to meet some of my friends." There was to be a dinner in this palace, three days hence, a stag dinner, much like that which Schneider had given for Lanny a year ago. The same men would come, to meet both father and son: François de Wendel, senator of France and head of the great mining trust; Max David-Weill, representing the most-powerful banking group in France; René Duchemin, of the chemical trust; Ernest Mercier, the electrical magnate; and so on.

The radicals were fond of saying that France was governed by two hundred families, but Robbie knew that no country in the world had ever been governed by any such number of persons; there were always a few powerful ones whom the others trusted, and who had the final say. These were the men who signed documents or spoke words and caused French industry to move along this line or that; and Charles Prosper Eugène Schneider, in many ways the most powerful of them all, invited them to meet an American industrialist, solid and substantial like themselves, yet a man of vision, who had foreseen what was coming and prepared for it, and who now in this crisis might be able to turn the tide of history and save imperiled Marianne from a fate worse than death.

X

Robbie knew that this was an important occasion for him; in some ways the most important of his later years. It might mean not merely a big order for planes; it might mean new expansion, fresh capital—for these men had gold, all the gold of the Banque de France, hidden in the most marvelous vaults in the world, underneath the sidewalks of Paris. They didn't own it, of course, but they could cause it to be expended by politicians whose careers had been financed by them and whose future was theirs to determine. If Robbie could really manage to frighten them—and he was an expert frightener, having been working at it four and forty years—there was no telling what might come of it. Budd-Erling plants in Quebec, in North Africa, even in France itself—who could guess?

For the first time since the Wall Street panic of ten years ago, Lanny saw his father nervous. Robbie wanted to talk about that dinner and everybody who was going to be there. He had met several of them, and done business with them in the old days; but the others—what were they like, and what questions would they ask? Robbie sent for a financial reference book and looked up impressive lists of directorships and connections. Would they want to see documents, or would they have a business meeting later? Would they understand English? Robbie had been speaking business French off and on for two-thirds of his life, and had got along, but he knew that his diction wasn't elegant and wished he had been a scholar like his son.

When Robbie wanted to know about their personalities, Lanny said: "Don't bother about that—there are too many complications and you'd find it hopeless. France has longer memories even than New England. For instance, de Wendel looks down upon Schneider, because Schneider's ancestor was an employee and went off and set up a rival business." When Robbie inquired what they would want to know about, the easy-going son smiled and replied: "Don't worry, they'll tell you. They pinned me down and questioned me as if I were in the witness box in a murder case."

"Don't talk too much," the father cautioned, knowing that the youngster—so he still thought of him—had what is called "charm" and enjoyed exercising it.

"Bless your heart!" the youngster replied. "I won't say a word unless they ask me. But don't be surprised if they want to know about Hitler even more than they do about Budd-Erling."

XI

Here they sat, the rulers of modern France, in a dining room lined with tapestries some five centuries old, representing the crusades, at a table made small so that a dozen men could be close for conversation. According to the French custom the host sat at the middle, not at the head; Robbie, as guest of honor, sat at his right and Lanny at his left. So that no feelings might be hurt, the others were ranged according to seniority, which put the youngest in the positions of least esteem, *au bout de la table*. Several were old men, partly bald, with white hair and closely trimmed beards or mustaches; others were the alert executive type of these modern days, wearing pince-nez, and one a monocle. All were formal, precise, quick-spoken in the French fashion; they had had military training in their time, and none lounged in his seat and took things easy as Americans would have done at a dinner party where there were no ladies. Several wore the *rosace* of an *officier* of the Légion d'Honneur, a tiny little red object no bigger than your finger-nail, and which you would hardly have noticed unless you knew what it meant in this land of ancient culture.

They were served an elegant meal upon dishes of solid gold. There were several wine glasses of shining crystal at each place, and velvet-footed servitors in pink plush livery kept these filled with the proper wine in turn. When the meal was over these men withdrew, and the host arose and said briefly that he had invited them to meet an American business associate, a man who had had the foresight to know what was coming in the world and to prepare for it—"*quelque chose que nous Français, hélas, ne pouvons pas dire.*" He spoke French, which was Robbie's cue to do the same.

The guest started to rise, but the host suggested that they all say what they had to say from their seats, and thus make the occasion less formal. This was a relief to Robbie, who was uneasy enough to feel it in his knees. But he soon got going; for, after all, what he had to tell them was what he had said a thousand times in the course of his life. He referred to Budd Gunmakers, which his family had founded and of which he had been the European representative for some thirty-five years. He told how, foreseeing that future wars would be fought and decided in the air, he had set out to build a plant on the Newcastle River, just above the Budd Gunmakers property. It was an exception-ally favorable location, the entrance to Long Island Sound being a part of the defenses of New York City, as strong as American skill could make them. He described the railroad and inland water connections, the Hudson River and many canals. He told about the young genius he had subsidized and trained, and the Typhoon engine which had devel-oped more horsepower per pound of weight than any in the world so far—though of course their rivals were in close pursuit, including the French—very tactful of a speaker from overseas.

Robbie told of the present output of his plant, and of the records which the Budd-Erling P11 had made. He mentioned his efforts to interest the British and French aviation authorities—they had been slow, and he was sorry to say that the Americans had been equally so. Robbie was a businessman, and took the position that it was first come, first served with his product. General Göring—as he had been then—had made an advantageous offer for the sharing of manufacturing secrets; that agreement had run for two years and either party had the right of withdrawal; whether it would be continued depended in part upon what Marshal Göring—as he now was—had to offer, and in part upon whether the French were interested to make a bid for the co-operation of the Budd-Erling organization.

Robbie made all this brief; and by his son's advice—since the French were inclined to be full of *amour propre*—he did not attempt to tell them anything about the European situation or the dangers confronting France. "Let them ask your opinion, if they want it," Lanny had recommended; so the father contented himself with saying that he had had the pleasure of knowing the head of the German Luftwaffe very well, and had been shown all over Kladow and other of their secret bases. What he had seen had convinced him, just as it had convinced Colonel Lindbergh, that Germany was overwhelmingly strong in the air. He was at liberty to talk about it, by Göring's express authorization. Germany had no secrets, so the Reichsmarschall had declared.

Robbie smiled slightly as he said this last, and his hearers smiled even more openly. "Germany wants peace," he added; "at any rate, that is what the Marshal assures me. He wants other nations to respect Germany's strength and concede to her what she considers her just dues."

XII

The speaker stopped; and the host thanked him, and remarked: "We are all anxious to know, just what does Germany consider her just dues?"

"That is a political question," Robbie evaded, "and outside my field as a businessman. Hitler has stated what he wants in numerous speeches."

"Yes," put in Sénateur de Wendel. "But does he mean what he says? He told us: 'I do not want any Czechs'; but now it begins to appear that he wants Prague."

"Well," replied the American, "apparently he means to give his answer in action, and then we'll both know." The men at the table laughed, but it was not a merry sort of laughter. "I have never met Herr Hitler," Robbie added, "but my son knows him well."

So the company turned to this son, who, having been reared in France, had behaved with propriety and let his parent do the talking. "Have you met Herr Hitler since you last talked with us?" asked Mercier, who controlled a good part of the electric power of his country.

Lanny answered that he had been in Munich at the time of the Four-Power Pact of last September, and not long afterwards had had a chat with the Führer in the Braune Haus. He had seemed very cheerful, and pleased with the settlement; he had spoken highly of Chamberlain's eloquent plea for peace. He called himself a man of peace.

"And do you consider that he means to confine his demands to the return to the Reich of those territories whose inhabitants are more than fifty per cent German?"

"I wish I could give you the sort of answer that would please you," replied Lanny; "but I have learned that Herr Hitler is a person of temperament. I would say that he means what he says when he is saying it; but later some new circumstance arises and he means something else." It was the answer of a man who expected to have his words repeated, and who was planning to go into Germany before long.

There began a discussion in which all had their say, and Lanny listened with close attention, turning his eyes from one speaker to the next, and thinking his own secret, unorthodox thoughts. These were the men of money, masters of the life of France. They told the workers where to live and what work to do; they told the editors what to publish, and thus told the French public what to believe; they told the politicians how to vote, which meant telling the police whom to arrest and the soldiers whom to shoot. They had so arranged the country's economic life that you could not buy a pin for your wife's dress or a nail for your horse's shoe without paying tribute to them. Here they sat, enjoying their money as well as their troubles permitted, and considering how to protect it and to increase it—two things which were fundamentally the same, since in order to hold on to money you have to have more than the fellow who threatens to get it away from you.

That was what they were here for: trying to figure out how to get more money than the moneymasters of Germany, who were turning their money into the tools of war with the intention of conquering the moneymasters of France and depriving them of their money. At least, that was what the Frenchmen feared, and the reason they had assembled at the bidding of their money chief. They couldn't be thinking about anything else, really, for they were money men; money made them and money kept them where they were. Money made all things possible and the lack of money made all things impossible. With their money they were all-powerful, and without their money they would be miserable, half-sick old derelicts, humiliated and neglected. Everybody who came near them, everybody they dealt with, was thinking about their money and wanted some of it. How could anybody think about anything but money in such a money world?

Lanny, watching them and listening to their discussions, found himself asking the old questions: "Are they stupid men? Are they wicked men?" And, as ever, the answer depended upon the standards of judgment. They were what the world had made them; they were part of an era, a stage of civilization; of a system which they called business and which Lanny called capitalism. They had the same saying as Americans: *"Les affaires sont les affaires"*—business is business. When you said that, you set moral considerations aside as irrelevant; the brotherhood of man and the fatherhood of God were idle dreams; liberty, equality, and fraternity were bait to catch votes; the only question was, did you have the price? The poet Racine had written: *"Point d'argent, point de Suisse!"*—no money, no Swiss, referring to Swiss guards. Soldiers were for hire, and if you wanted your life protected you had to pay cost plus a profit.

And that was the way matters stood at this dinner party. This elegance, this elaborate hereditary dignity, this long-established, minutely studied courtesy—all this was window-dressing. These men hadn't come here for friendship, nor for a good dinner, nor for Robbie's beautiful eyes; they had come because Robbie owned the most deadly killing machine in the world, the highest flying and fastest. Robbie himself had never killed anybody in his life, and it was probable that these French gentlemen had never done so either; they were members of the "two hundred families," the rulers of France, who killed by writing their names on pieces of paper, and by speaking words over the telephone, and by asking questions and expressing opinions over the cigars and coffee and liqueurs. They did not kill at retail, only wholesale, and preferably by the million; they did not get blood on their hands, nor even guilt on their consciences; they killed with legality, courtesy, and dignity. If anyone had called them stupid, they would have known that the person was ill-bred, and if anyone had called them wicked, they would have known that he was a dangerous Bolshevik.

"It appears certain that we must have planes." So Schneider summed up the discussion. "We cannot be sure whether we shall use them against Germany or against Russia—but in either case, it is advisable to have them." He said it with a smile, but it was a serious matter indeed that the rulers of France couldn't make up their minds which enemy they had chosen.

XIII

Somebody must have spoken a commanding word, for things began to happen immediately after this dinner. The president of Budd-Erling was invited to a conference with Guy la Chambre, the new Minister of Aviation; just one more politician, Robbie reported, without qualifications except the votes he could control in the Chamber of Deputies. That was the way in France; the Cabinet was changed every year or so, a grand shuffle, and everybody was expected to know everything, with the result that few knew anything. In whatever country Robbie Budd was visiting, he could be counted upon to pick a quarrel with the politicians and their ways.

But there were subordinates in the department who knew their business, and presently came army officers who knew more than even Robbie. There came also an invitation for father and son to the American embassy, just across the street from the hotel; the ambassador wanted to see them on an urgent matter. He was an old friend of Lanny's; they had shared ideas and ideals in the days of the Peace Conference, twenty years in the past. William C. Bullitt, wealthy Philadelphian, had recently been ambassador to the Soviets, and had come to hate them most heartily. Now, as ambassador to France, he had been working ardently against the Franco-Russian alliance.

Had he had a sudden change of heart? Lanny had no chance to ask him. All he learned was, "Bill" wanted France to get American airplanes, and was moving heaven and earth to bring it about. He had learned that Budd-Erling had a contract to make planes for the American army, and was now working on that; he wanted Robbie's consent to put the matter up to President Roosevelt and have the army release those planes to the French. He even wanted Robbie to take back some planes from the army and make changes which the French would require. Would Robbie send test-pilots here to France, and bring technical men to discuss these matters?

"O.K. by me," said the president of Budd-Erling, "—if they'll pay the costs." He got busy on the transatlantic telephone and ordered two of his best men to come, together with a secretary who knew French.

They were fortunate in catching a fast steamer, and a plane met them at Cherbourg; a taxi delivered them to the Crillon, and they went to work without even time to wash up.

Officials of various sorts came to the hotel; they kept Robbie busy all day, and social duties called him at night. It was as if somebody had said: "This American is important, and he and his son must be won away from the Germans." Invitations came, more than Robbie could enjoy. When he grumbled, his son grinned and remarked: "*La patrie est en danger*"—the battlecry of the old French Revolution.

XIV

The women did not vote in France, but they intrigued. It was an art they had been practicing for hundreds of years, and in which they had perfected themselves. They knew how to flatter and cajole, to seek favors and to grant them; they knew how to worm out secrets, and to drop subtle hints, or menaces on occasion; they knew how to detect weaknesses and to play upon them, to pick up scandal and repeat it by delicate innuendo, perhaps even to invent it. They understood men, and how to get what they wanted from them. As soon as some fervid young *ami du peuple* had garnered votes and attained political power, there would come an exquisite highborn lady, ready to attach herself to him and guide his career; out of this she got glory, and the thrill of exercising power, of getting the better of rivals who perhaps had snubbed her in the past. Incidentally, it was a service to her class, a way of keeping the French government conservative, of keeping politics stable.

So an American airplane manufacturer and his son were invited to a *soirée* at the establishment of the wealthy Marquise de Crussol, pretty blue-eyed young daughter of a sardine-canning family and wife of a French nobleman. Lanny, who knew his way about, said they must not miss this, as they would probably meet the Premier of France here. So they went and they did. Edouard Daladier was a man of the people, a baker's son who had begun as a humble *lycée* teacher; his political start had been as a Radical Socialist, which meant in France that he was a Liberal and Anti-clerical of the old tradition. Now in his middle fifties he was a stoutish, heavy-set politician, who had learned that there was little honor and good faith in his country's public life; instead of shouting about *égalité*, he was trying to keep his Cabinet together by finding out what policy the big business interests of France would support. He was a well-meaning man, but awed by the rich and aristocratic, and suffering from indecision, a disease epidemic in his country at the moment.

It was like being the captain of a ship in a storm, and being driven toward the rocks. The captain ought to know what to do, but he doesn't, and everybody from the first mate to the cabin boy shouts into his ears, and whose advice shall he take? Daladier had listened to the appeasers, and had gone to Munich and signed on Hitler's dotted line. Coming home, he had found a vast throng at Le Bourget airport, and had expected to be mobbed, but they had carried him under the Arc de Triomphe on their shoulders. He had thought everything was fixed to stay; but, alas, four months later these laurels had withered, and everybody was calling him names, and there was war in the Cabinet between the out-and-out, die-hard appeasers, and those who wanted to ride two horses at once: to keep friends with Hitler and at the same time to keep the Russian alliance going, on the chance that it might be needed later.

Nobody expected much loyalty in a French Cabinet, for all the members knew that it was a jerrybuilt affair, and half a dozen were hoping to take their chief's place. Social life went on just the same; pretended friends swarmed to the home of your *amie* and ate your food and drank your wine, and took the occasion to undermine you and get ready to cut your political throat. So it was that Robbie and his son met Bonnet, the Foreign Minister, long-nosed and pop-eyed, with his pro-German wife; Herriot with a charming young actress from the Comédie Française; and Paul Reynaud, Minister of Finance and tireless little intriguer against Daladier, his chief. Lanny reported that the last stood a chance to succeed to the premiership, so it was necessary to make themselves agreeable to him and to his *amie*, Madame de Portes. Nervous, intense, hollow-eyed, she was a busy political woman with a spoon in every kettle, a reactionary and friend of all the appeasers. Robbie would get along better with her by saying, not that he wished to help *la patrie*, but that he was trying to make money after the fashion proper to businessmen, and that he did not forget to reward those who did him favors.

But there were drawbacks to this role also; for France was poor, and her taxpayers reluctant, so all the politicians reported, and had to report in order to preserve their political necks. It was a dubious matter indeed to be spending large sums abroad, giving to workers in Connecticut jobs which workers in France were able and eager to perform. To buy planes in a hurry was to admit that somebody had been negligent, and who wanted to shoulder that burden? At receptions and dinner parties everybody would be polite to visitors from overseas, but a large percentage would be wishing they would go back where they came from, or to the devil.

This situation called for·understanding and tact, and in it Robbie had the tireless help of his son. Lanny didn't seem to have anything else to do, and was so useful that Robbie insisted on paying his bills and charging it against the company. Lanny knew most of the personalities involved, and when he didn't, he knew how to find out. He listened attentively to everything that was said, and if he asked questions, it was to help Robbie in getting to the bottom of some important matter. Only now and then, when the father was absorbed in technical matters, plans and specifications and prices, Lanny would shut himself up in his own room and say nothing about what he was doing. One more report would be typed and sent off to the Big Boss in Washington.

4

Portents of Impending Doom

I

"GAY PAREE" had never been more so. People who had money seemed to have no end of it, and they spent it freely, as if they feared the time for spending might be short. On the fashionable shopping streets just back of the Crillon the elegant ladies stepped out of their limousines and tripped in to inspect jewels, furs, luxury goods which had been brought from every part of the world to tempt their fancy. Men milliners, men dressmakers inspected them, discussed their "points," and murmured advice as to the enhancing of their charms. In the previous summer the King and Queen of England had paid a visit of state to the city; the Queen had changed her costume three times daily, and everything she wore had been photographed and minutely studied. So now there was an "English trend" to be noticed in costuming; the ladies all asked to be clad *à l'anglaise.* "But of course," murmured the *couturiers,* "the fashions came originally from here; everything is French fundamentally." Never would it do to have one of the "ten best-dressed ladies" betake herself to London for an *ensemble!*

In the evenings the shiny limousines lined up in front of mansions where the two hundred families gave sumptuous entertainments to one another; and in the neighborhood of the theaters, the smart restaurants, and night clubs, champagne flowed freely, and on the stage you might see a hundred young females, their skins painted every color of the rainbow, dancing the *danse du ventre* or whatever might excite the jaded old men who crowded below. The French would tell you that such sights were for the tourists, that Parisians did not care for them; and maybe it was so—newspaper readers might have found it amusing if someone had taken a census.

Surrounding the luxurious city of pleasure were suburbs with factories old and new, and here the workers were crowded into five-story tenements, standard for cities on five continents. Hard times were threatening again; the masses were at the mercy of economic forces which they understood only dimly; they lived in poverty and insecurity, and their discontents were distilled into a hatred of their masters, whose way of life was revealed in shop windows, in newspapers, and on the cinema screen. The great fashion capital of the world was a hell of class antagonisms; to the workers the rich took the form of slavedrivers with whips, while to the rich the workers were wild beasts in cages—the bars being made, not of steel, but of laws and institutions which now seemed on the point of dissolving.

Lanny walked the streets of this ancient city, so magnificent in some places and so depressing in others. It had been one of his homes since childhood. In its buildings and monuments he read the history of a thousand years, while other spots brought to his mind personal adventures since his youth. He knew that Paris had been besieged and taken more than once, that it had been the scene of revolutions and civil wars, yet always it had managed to survive. Doubtless it would survive whatever calamities now lay ahead; but oh, the suffering, the waste of life! The misery of the poor, who had no part in the glory of the conquerors, in the corruption of politicians, the guilt of traitors—but who would pay with their blood and tears for the blunders and the crimes!

This man of fashion, who had been called a playboy in his youth and still dressed and behaved like one, would stop in front of one of the kiosks and survey the reading matter on display. Inside him it would be as if he were shedding tears of blood, grief unutterable for the madness, the folly, the misuse of human effort which was there embodied! He didn't need to pay a single sou in order to appraise it; he didn't even need to read the headlines; the names of the papers told him everything. This pair, the most respectable, were controlled by Baron Schneider and his Comité des Forges; they had been the paymasters of the

Croix de Feu, and later, more secretly, of the Cagoule. Several were in
the pay of the Nazis, and printed whatever the German Minister of
Propaganda and Public Enlightenment supplied to them. This one represented the effete and rather silly Royalists, while the next was the organ of the deadly Camelots du Roi. Here was the paper of Pierre Laval,
traitor friend of the people, as vile a man as had appeared in French
public life. Next to it, the organ of the Communists, following the
Party line, not easy to foresee. Pathetic seemed the paper of Léon
Blum—old friend whom Lanny no longer dared to visit; he was still
Vice-Premier, but with little power, demanding protection for what
was left of the Czechoslovak republic and making public confession of
his blunder in having failed to protect Spain.

II

Through this dark jungle of French public life roamed the Nazi
hunters, armed with the deadliest of all weapons, gold. They seemed to
have unlimited quantities. The aristocratic and elegant agents bought
the publishers of newspapers, the politicians, the fashionable ladies
whose influence counted in drawing-rooms. The less highly placed but
no less highly trained agents, assuming a hundred disguises, made the
acquaintance of clerks in military establishments, workers in munitions
plants, anyone who had access to secrets which might be useful to a
nation preparing an attack upon its neighbors.

The fact that the Nazis were so getting ready, and that their businessmen, traveling salesmen, scientists, students, artists, tourists, were
working for a score of government agencies—these facts were known
to everybody who cared to know; but the accusations were drowned
out in the general clamor of French journalism, French politics, French
intellectual life, in which Fascist and Nazi, Communist and Bolshevik,
had become terms of abuse no longer taken literally. When you called
your opponent a *cochon*, you didn't mean that he grunted and ate out
of a trough, and when you called him a *chien*, you didn't mean that he
ran on four legs and lifted one of them in public. You just meant that
he had got in your way somehow and you hated him.

At an ultra-fashionable *soirée* Lanny and his father ran into Kurt
Meissner. Robbie hadn't seen him for quite a while, and now was
pleased, and showed it. Highbrow music didn't mean a thing to a manufacturer of airplanes, but other people admired it, and Robbie admired
Kurt as a man who had chosen his job and made a success of it; a dignified and self-contained man, no long-haired and greasy genius. The

fact that Kurt had been a secret agent of the German General Staff in Paris at the time of the Peace Conference didn't worry Robbie; he hadn't known it until it was all over, and then he had thought it a good joke. The fact that Kurt was now playing the same role, and had been for several years, was a matter for the French to worry over if they saw fit. Robbie knew that all the nations of Europe were spying on one another, and he had hired many a secret agent himself.

Did Kurt know that Robbie was now making a deal to supply the French with airplanes? Certainly it was his business to know, and he was an efficient worker. He would understand that a Yankee business-man was out to make money; Robbie didn't pretend to be anything else, and wished to be dealt with on that basis. If Reichsmarschall Göring wanted the planes, he would offer a higher price, and if he didn't, it meant that he was making enough planes at home, and better. As for Lanny, he would be trailing along with his father, taking things easy, as always. Kurt would be cordial to father and son, because they were sources of information and had important connections. Both the Reichsmarschall and the Führer professed to like Lanny, and that was unusual; it must mean that they were getting something out of him, probably information about Britain and France.

So Kurt's long and solemn Prussian face lighted up with a smile of welcome. He asked about Bienvenu, and about Beauty Budd, whose lover he had been for many years; he took a dignified attitude to this fact—he was endlessly grateful to a woman who had taught him much, and indeed saved his life. He asked about Marceline, whom he had helped to raise; yes, he had heard about her success as a dancer, but his many duties had left him no leisure to see her. He had been home for Christmas, and told the news from Stubendorf; there were six little ones in his family now; the older ones still remembered Lanny Budd and asked about him, though he hadn't been to see them for a long time. Kurt's oldest brother, the General, was now stationed near Berlin, and the Budds must not fail to see him on their trip.

III

In the course of the evening the hostess requested Kurt to play for them, and he did so. He played, with dignity and repressed passion, his own compositions, which in past years Lanny had admired extrava-gantly. Now Lanny had decided that they were largely "derivative"; they were echoes of the German classics which the two of them had known by heart. But you had to know German music well in order to pass this judgment, and few in this fashionable audience did so. Kurt had made several of his compositions popular, and had played them with more than one of the Paris symphony orchestras, an unusual honor. For his friends he made no charge, and that was in the nature of a polite bribe to hostesses and caused him to be invited constantly.

So he knew all the key people, not merely in the musical and stage worlds, but those who governed France: the elegant rich ladies, the haughty ones who set the social tone and could change the course of events by expressing opinions to their husbands or lovers. A celebrated German *Komponist* would teach these ladies to respect German music; and then he would say, in his grave, pontifical manner: "Our two nations are the wellsprings of European culture, and its guardians; why can we not unite and protect our common heritage? That is the message I have been charged to give to our friends here in France. Our Führer has said to me a hundred times: 'Tell them that I respect French culture as I do our own, and that I desire nothing in the world so much as peace and friendship, complete and permanent, with France.'"

Nothing could be more impressive. If it happened that Lanny Budd was in hearing, Kurt would turn to him and say: "You, too, have heard him say it. Tell us, is it not so?"

Lanny would reply: "It is something he says continually." Lanny hated to say anything that would further the Nazi cause, but it was his role and he had to play it. He had voiced his uneasiness on this subject to the President of the United States, and had been told: "The information you bring is worth the price you have to pay."

IV

Uncle Jesse Blackless, New England born but now a citizen of the French Republic and member of its Chamber of Deputies, did not put his feet under the dinner tables of the rich and was not to be met at their *soirées*. He still lived in a humble tenement on Montmartre, and had no elegant *amie*, but a wife who was a devoted Party worker. In the old days Lanny had eaten their bread and cheese and drunk their *vin ordinaire*, but of late years he had had to be cautious; he couldn't afford to have his reactionary friends know that he associated with one of the most rabid "Reds" in France. Also, it would have worried his father. Robbie wouldn't have gone so far as to forbid a grown man to visit his mother's elder brother, but the idea would have disturbed him, and perhaps have started a swarm of bees to buzzing in his hat; so let sleeping bees lie, or whatever it is they do.

Paris was full of paintings, all sorts, new and old, good and bad; and this fact provided Lanny with a pretext. He would say: "There are some paintings I ought to look at." He would stroll and visit the dealers—the highest priced were near the hotel. After a look he would telephone to his Red uncle, make an appointment, and pick him up on the street. Driving on roads not used by the rich and prominent, they would not be noticed or overheard. Jesse took it for granted that his nephew was getting information for his Spanish friend Raoul and his English friend Rick, both of them Socialists. A Party Communist, Jesse quarreled with the Socialists, but not with Lanny; they kidded each other, and if an argument started, Lanny would turn it aside with a joke. They swapped information, kept each other's confidences, and enjoyed each other's company.

Uncle Jesse had been bald ever since Lanny could remember him. Now he was an old man, lean and wrinkled, but still spry and full of ginger and other spices. He hated the rich and all their ways; he loved the poor, and in his leisure hours painted them, following the Party line in art as in politics. In his own revolutionary way he was a saint, and had been responsible for the first impulses toward the Left which his nephew received. That had been a quarter of a century ago, when the Party line had existed only in the heads of a few fanatics in Russia and in exile outside.

Lanny told the news from home: about Raoul Palma's escape from Spain, and about the new baby, who was Jesse's grandnephew; also, how Beauty was getting along with her husband and her prayers. The brother's comment was that she was a good soul, but had always been a little weak in the head. (This, too, was the Party line: Religion is the opium of the people!) Lanny and his father had been to see Marceline dancing; but her Red uncle said he wouldn't go—it would cost him a lot of votes to be seen in a night club. When Jesse said such things, you had to watch him and catch the twinkle in his eye.

V

What was Robbie doing in Paris, Robbie's almost-brother-in-law wanted to know, and Lanny reported that he had a big deal on with the government. Robbie hated Jesse's very name, but Jesse did not return this feeling; Robbie suited Jesse because he fitted so perfectly into the formulas of economic determinism. Robbie, great capitalist, was making money, regardless of whether he wrecked the world in the process. Jesse could point to his near-brother-in-law and say:

"You see?"—and everybody would see at once. Jesse "class-angled" Robbie, as the Communists liked to phrase it.

The Red deputy had just delivered a red-hot speech in the Chamber, denouncing the collaboration of the Right with the Hitlerites, declaring that smart society in Paris was swarming with Nazi agents, and naming them. The papers of the extreme Right had raved at him; *Gringoire* had called him an ape, also a hyena, two creatures it would seem rather difficult to combine, even in a metaphor. The Communists, who preached dictatorship, used the freedom of France to tear down that freedom: so said the capitalist press, and in order to protect freedom they proposed to destroy freedom and set up an anti-dictatorship dictatorship. Look at Daladier and his "governing by decree"!

Lanny gave his Red uncle a number of "tips" which might be useful to him. He mentioned that Baron Schneider was wavering on the subject of Munich and Prague. Jesse replied: "*Der Adolf* will make him waver till he's seasick." Jesse told a curious anecdote of the struggle over the Soviet alliance, which had been the crux of French political life for the past two or three years. The treaty still stood, on paper, but the French generals—most of them in their seventies, several in their eighties, and all reactionary to their swords' points—wouldn't let the government implement the bargain by an exchange of plans and information. Schneider-Creusot had been under contract to manufacture big guns for Soviet fortifications, but these guns had not been forthcoming; the Soviet embassy in Paris had pleaded and argued, but without results. This had been a couple of years ago, when the Blum government was in process of nationalizing munitions plants, and Schneider had been fighting it tooth and toenail. One day a director in Le Creusot and member of the Baron's family had called upon the Soviet ambassador and tactfully suggested a way by which the delivery of the guns might be speeded up—if the Soviet government would intimate to the French government that it did not wish to have Le Creusot nationalized!

Lanny had heard rumors of this episode, and said: "Do you really know that, Uncle Jesse?"

The other replied: "I was told it by the man to whom the proposal was made."

VI

This Franco-Russian alliance was the most important thing in the world to Jesse Blackless: the criterion by which he judged all ideas, all nations and individuals. Now that Spain was gone, it represented the last contact of Russia with the western world, her last hope of a friendship in Europe. The Soviets wanted protection against Hitlerism, and were willing to promise protection in return; they had been willing to help Czechoslovakia, but the British Tories and the French Rightists had sold that small republic down the river. Now it was going to be a question of Poland; and what could Russia do for Poland when the Poles wouldn't let them? Poland, in the view of the Red deputy, was not much more enlightened than Franco Spain; the country was governed by a clique of great landowners and military men. They wouldn't admit Russian armies to Polish soil even to defend Poland against Germany, and France wouldn't demand that they alter this policy; so what was the Soviet Union to do?

A complicated situation, which it was Lanny's business to probe and investigate; everywhere he went, he questioned people of all classes and groups, and devised subtle ways of leading them to reveal their attitudes. Now he said: "I keep hearing rumors that the Soviet Union may make some sort of deal with Hitler that will leave them safe and out of the war."

"You can put that down as propaganda of the reactionaries," was the Red deputy's prompt reply. "That's the worst they can think of to say about us—that we have no more principles than themselves."

"Have you never thought of the possibility, Uncle Jesse? The Soviets have been betrayed in about every way there is, and it might occur to them to play tit for tat."

"But a deal of that sort would mean giving Hitler the green light to attack the West!"

"Of course; but then, I could name scores of reactionaries right here and in London who are working day and night to give Hitler the green light to attack Russia."

"Jesus Christ, Lanny! Do you suppose the men in the Kremlin can't see any farther than their noses? If Hitler were to smash the Maginot Line and take Paris, what chance would the Russians have after that? Hitler would go all the way to Spain, and set up his submarine bases and airplane bases there—and what chance would the British have to hold Gibraltar? Once Hitler had the Mediterranean he would have all the Balkans; he would drive to the Caucasus and take the oil, and the rest of Russia would wither up like fruit on a girdled tree."

"I hope they see that clearly, Uncle Jesse."

"Of course they see it. Put the idea out of your mind. Ideologically it's monstrous. We are the opposite pole from Hitler in everything; we are internationalists, proletarians, modern men—while the Hitlerites are blood and soil worshipers, human sacrifice mystics out of the dark forests of Germany before the dawn of civilization."

"I can tell you, Uncle Jesse, the Führer has some sort of proposal up his sleeve. He has just made a long speech, and for the first time he failed to denounce the Soviet Union. He may be coming to you with an offer any day."

"We'll give him a kick in the pants," said the Red deputy—only he used less refined and elegant language.

VII

Herr von Ribbentrop, Foreign Minister of the German Reich, had paid an extensive visit in Paris a month or so ago. He had signed a solemn declaration of amity with the French, and had toasted it in innumerable bottles of Pommery-Greno, a brand of champagne about which the wits of Paris made jokes, it being the brand for which the Reichsminister had formerly been head salesman, and which he had married—that is to say, his wife was the daughter of this prosperous wine establishment. To celebrate his advancement in the world he had persuaded an aunt to adopt him and thus give him possession of the coveted "von." The champagne was not of the best, but smart Paris had laid in a supply, by way of compliment to their distinguished and somewhat dangerous guest.

The ex-salesman had left behind him a staff of busy intriguers, supplied with unlimited funds. They whispered doubts concerning the good faith of Britain, the ex-salesman's especial *bête noir;* Britain had always been ready to fight to the last Frenchman, and now she had made a deal with Mussolini, one of the implications of which was that Italy was to expand at the expense of France. Nobody was ever to expand at the expense of Britain! Otto Abetz, handsome and genial intellectual, friend of all the intellectuals of Paris, was tireless in his search for talent, and any writer who could be persuaded to realize the dangers which British intrigue offered to the French people could be certain of selling his writings—and certain of a publisher, too, for Abetz had a string of papers on his list, and paid them even more generously.

Among the Embassy staff was a Prussian nobleman, Graf Herzenberg, whose guest Lanny had been at his country place, the Château de Belcour. The Graf's *amie* was the Austrian actress Lili Moldau, whose friendship Lanny and his mother had gained. Both this couple were tireless intriguers, and at an evening affair Lanny was one of a group who listened while Seine Hochgeboren explained the passionate interest which all Nazis took in the freedom of the Ukrainian people. In the process of splitting up the Czechoslovakian republic the Nazis had taken to calling the province of Ruthenia a new name; it was the Carpatho-Ukraine—and what an advancement toward European welfare it would be if these Ukrainians could be united to the rest of their brethren, now groaning in the chains of Bolshevism!

That would be at the expense of Russia, of course; and the elegant ladies and gentlemen who danced in the ballroom of the Duc de Belleaumont guzzled his elaborate buffet supper, washed it down with Pommery-Greno, and listened with delight to the idea that France should break off with the hated Reds and give her assent to the Nazis' setting up an "independent" Ukraine, under Nazi protection. It would probably not require a war, the Graf suavely explained, for the Bolsheviks knew well the German strength and their own impotence. All it needed was the friendly neutrality of France, and afterwards the two great peoples might divide the hegemony of the Continent, Germany taking the east as its sphere of influence and France the west—of course in a benevolent and constructive way. Britain had so much land overseas—surely Britain did not have to meddle in Europe!

This would mean peace for a hundred years, perhaps for a thousand, declared the Graf. "The desire for an understanding with France has become almost an obsession with the Führer—he talks about it to everyone who comes to Berchtesgaden. Herr Budd, who has been a guest there many times, can tell you that."

So once more Lanny had to say: "Yes, indeed, *lieber Graf*"—avoiding formality. He knew most of these guests, and some had been his guests in this same drawing-room—it being the palace which Irma Barnes had rented a few years ago to launch her career as *salonnière*. Strange things went on in this modern world, where you swapped partners as if marriage were a quadrille; and equally strange things went on in the diplomatic world, where you swapped allies as freely.

VIII

Having a brief chat with *die schöne Lili*, the son of Budd-Erling remarked: "I have never had a chance to return Seine Hochgeboren's hospitality to me in a time of danger. Just now my sister is dancing at the Chanteclair, and she's worth while, I believe. Would you let me take you both there some evening?"

An actress who might have to go back to her profession some day couldn't afford to look down her nose at it, and Lili said that she had heard about Marceline, and would be delighted to see her performance. She would consult with the Graf and they would choose some evening when they had a dull dinner date and could get away between nine and ten o'clock. She would phone Lanny. He said: "Don't delay, because I have to leave for Berlin with my father in a few days; he has promised to see Marshal Göring before the Marshal leaves for Italy."

They talked about *Der Dicke*—not by that disrespectful name, of course. He was much less so, for he had been dieting and had taken off no less than forty-two pounds—so he had told Robbie over the telephone. But it had weakened his heart, and he had been ordered away to Italy for a rest. Robbie had wondered if it was so, or if the chief of the German Air Force could be trying to get him away from the French. Impossible to guess, and of course Lanny didn't try to guess in the presence of this Nazi enchantress. Instead, he remarked that Hermann Göring was worth several thousand airplanes to the Reich, and they must all take care of him. If necessary, the Budds would travel to Italy for their meeting.

Evidently Herzenberg considered the matter important, for Lili phoned the next morning; they had the evening free, and she wanted Lanny to come to dinner at her apartment, and later they would go to the night club. The Graf's oldest son, Oskar, an SS Leutnant, had recently become an attaché of the legation, and they would take him along, if Lanny had no objection. Lanny said, of course, he would be pleased to meet the Graf's son.

To his father he said: "They must be wanting to find out about your business. What shall I tell them?"

Robbie answered: "Tell them the truth. I am a businessman and I am here to sell planes. Presently I'm going to Germany and sell some there if I can. Don't say anything about my dissatisfaction with Göring, of course."

IX

But it wasn't that: it was another effort to enlist Lanny's services in the cause of Franco-German understanding. A cozy dinner for four: the Graf, a shaven-headed Prussian of the top caste, wearing a monocle and surveying the world with a condescending air—though he was careful not to use it with the son of Budd-Erling; his Titian-haired mistress, trained for a decade in the state theater of Vienna, and still playing the ingénue in private life; and the next generation, a yellow-haired and arrogant young aristocrat with a dueling scar on his left cheek, here to learn the technique of approaching a tiptop leisure-class secret agent. While Lili's maidservant ladled out the consommé, Lili ladled out the flattery; she revealed that she knew everything about the Budd family, and about Marcel Detaze and his paintings and his beautiful wife; she knew about Lanny's high repute as an authority on old masters, and the social triumphs he had won in Munich and Berlin. Then while the servant revealed the contents of steaming casseroles—double lamb chops with *petits pois* at one end and *champignons* at the other—the Graf talked confidentially concerning Germany's position at the moment. No real secrets, of course, but things that looked exactly like them.

Just now the situation in Central Europe was most delicate, a balance that might be upset by the weight of a hair. The wretched imbecile Czechs, instead of abiding by their agreement with the Führer, were waging ideological war on him, threatening the excellent government which Father Tiso had set up in Slovakia with the Führer's approval. The irresponsible British press was inciting them, regardless of the consequences to the peace of the world. Even now, with Madrid about to fall, the French demagogues were still denouncing Franco, and holding the menace of the Russian alliance over all Europe. It was the Jewish bankers of Paris—"but I don't need to tell you things like that, Herr Budd, for you have lived here most of your life and understand the situation much better than we do.".

And so on. What the Graf wished tactfully to suggest was that if Herr Budd could make it convenient to remain in Paris for a while, or to return after accompanying his father to Germany, his aid in advising the Embassy staff and promoting friendly feelings between the two peoples would earn the everlasting gratitude not merely of the Graf but of the Führer and all his friends in Germany. "I am hesitant about suggesting any reward to one in your high position, Herr Budd, but this you can be sure of—if there is anything in our possession that you desire, you have only to suggest it."

Very handsome indeed; and Lanny said: "Be sure that I appreciate your kindness, *mein lieber Graf*. What you suggest is much the same as Reichsmarschall Göring has suggested to me on more than one occasion, and as the Führer suggested to me at the Berghof. I explained to them both that if I were to accept employment, however politely disguised, I should be limiting my ability to be of use to them; in the first place, they would expect more of me than I should be able to perform, and in the second, the secret would soon become known, and I should lose the ability, which I now enjoy, to meet influential persons wherever I travel and to share their confidences. My profession of art expert brings me all that I need, and I am happier as a free lance, able to say what I think. Marshal Göring has been kind enough to let me market some of his paintings which he wanted to get rid of, and that gives me an excuse to visit him now and then, and tell him whatever I have learned that may be helpful. I'll be happy to tell them to you, so far as it's in my power. It so happens that in the Château de Belcour are some French historical paintings in which you probably have no special interest, and the Duc de Belcour has given me an intimation that he might consider putting a price upon them. If you, as the tenant, would consent to release them, I might be able to interest some of my clients in the States, or the Reichsmarschall might like to have them for a collection illustrating various periods in the history of Europe."

"Why certainly, Herr Budd, I wouldn't stand in the way. I might even consider purchasing one of the paintings myself and presenting it to the Reichsmarschall's collection."

So it was settled, in the most elegant way imaginable. The Graf considered this suave American as good as hired—and at a very cheap price. They could go on to discuss Germany's problems, her hopes and fears; and afterwards, having earned the right to some recreation, they could go off to a night club with four faces wreathed in smiles.

X

The Chanteclair was a place of bright lights and glamour. When the Graf's limousine drew up before the marquee, its door was opened by a magnifico in purple and gold, and the doors of the establishment were opened by a boy in a sky-blue uniform with four rows of brass buttons. Lanny of course had telephoned to reserve a table and had told Marceline whom he was bringing, so everything would be done in state. A sort of assistant to the master of ceremonies met them in the crowded lobby, a polyglot personage of many bows. "*Bon soir, Ihre Hochgeboren*," and then: "Good evening, Mister Budd."

The painted ladies of the evening, young, undernourished, and infinitely pitiful, swarmed in that lobby, and an unattached gentleman would have difficulty in getting through without forming an attachment; but escorted as the Graf's party was, its members escaped molestation. The M.C. himself met them at their table; he knew the proper way of addressing all four of the party, and when he returned to his podium, the spotlight was turned upon the eminent guests, and as he

introduced them over the loudspeaker, each arose and "took a bow."
Members of an embassy were expected to show themselves in public,
and the applause which greeted their names was an indication of the
attitude the money-spending and pleasure-seeking part of Paris took
toward their country. The sight of three men with only one woman
was an abnormal one, and the painted ladies gazed hungrily as they
passed; ordinarily they would have introduced themselves, but in
this case there must have been some secret sign which warned them
away.

Lanny ordered Pommery-Greno, which was like raising the swastika
above their table. They sat watching the floor show, in which a couple
of comedians cracked jokes at the expense of the politicians of the day:
very slangy and full of esoteric references which Lanny had to explain
to his guests. Then came Marceline's turn; a burst of music and she
came tripping in, clad in rather scanty white veils, and pursued by her
dancing partner, a youth whom she had picked in the casino at Nice
and had been training for nearly a year. Marceline herself was only
twenty-one, exulting in her youth, freedom, success, and the money
it was bringing.

Lanny himself had loved dancing from childhood, and had had many
teachers. He had begun teaching his half-sister when he had had to
hold her up by her tiny hands. Later, as a child, she had joined Isadora
Duncan's troop of dancing children on the Riviera, and had watched
that great artist and listened to all the world singing her praises. For
ten years now she had been dreaming of doing what Isadora had done;
the previous summer, when she had divorced her Italian husband and
launched herself on a career, it had been first Isadora and then Irene
Castle, both Americans, that she had desired to emulate. Lanny had
said: "Nobody ever saw either of them do a sex-dance. They were
youth, gaiety, springtime. Let the men supply the sex with their
imaginations, if they wish—and they will. But you be the nymph whom
they cannot catch, the dream they can never realize."

"But will that go in Paris, Lanny?" Marceline had clamored.

"It will if you do it well enough. All the others know how to be
seductive, they know everything there is to know, and your only
chance is to be different."

She had made a success in Cannes, because all her friends had come
to the Coque d'Or to support her. She was the daughter of one of
France's great painters, a man who had given his life for his country.
It was the sort of story that is easy to write about and talk about: a
soldier in a blimp on fire and having his face burned off; wearing a

white silk mask, and painting on canvas his grief and hatred of the enemy; and finally, when *la patrie* was in the last of her desperate hours, going back into battle and dying at the Marne. Who could forget such a story? Surely not the press agents! There had been times when there was happiness in France, and Marcel had seen it and painted it; and here came his daughter to reincarnate it in her person.

XI

She was beautiful to look at, and graceful in every movement. She fled with quick eager steps, and her partner pursued her timidly, as if afraid to catch her; perhaps she would disappear entirely if pursued too boldly. She cast mocking glances back at him; she made herself the incarnation of that happy irresponsibility which has never existed in nature, but which poets have made out of some of nature's appearances. It was Marceline herself, saying: "I have what I want. I am sufficient to myself. No man is ever going to hold me!" She felt safe enough from the advances of her partner to cast laughing glances at some of the diners who happened to catch her fancy; she would pass near them and give them a flirt of the filmy veils, and then be off like a hummingbird to the next group of blossoms.

Knowing who was coming with Lanny, she had prepared a little drama. She stopped when she came to his table, and the music stopped also. The dancing youth fell back, as if in awe of such important personages; Marceline bowed to each, and then held out her hand to Lanny. She didn't need to speak, for she had done the same thing many times, in different companies; wherever they happened to be, they entertained their friends with dancing. They knew each other's every whim, and a whispered word was enough prelude to a whole dance. Lanny arose and took her hand; the music started the *Vienna Woods* waltz, and they swept away in what in Lanny's youth had been known as "society dancing." Said the M.C.: "Mademoiselle Marceline is dancing with her brother, Mister Lanny Budd, of Newcastle, Connecticut." So much more romantic to hail from three thousand miles away and a strange Indian name, than from the Riviera, where everybody went in for sun-bathing! The audience applauded, and the couple treated them to a whirl which made the white veils fly out like the cream in a separator.

They returned to the table amid a storm of applause. Marceline, breathing hard, bowed in all directions. Lanny looked at his friends, and observed that the younger of the two Germans was gazing at the lovely dancer with a look of open-mouthed and open-eyed admiration. Marceline wouldn't fail to notice it, and to like what she saw. He was a handsome youth, well set up, a soldier and an aristocrat in a showy and elegant uniform; his cheeks were pink with health, and the dueling scar, being symbolic, was not supposed to be a disfiguration. Oskar had bright blue eyes, and just now they were seeing nothing but the daughter of Beauty Budd and her French painter.

She smiled, and held out her hand, and that was enough. The young Prussian leaped to his feet, bowed from the waist, and came quickly and took Lanny's place. Away they went—no "fancy dancing," for Marceline wouldn't know if he was capable of that, and to try and fail would be humiliating. They would dance as all gentlemen learned to dance in that day, gravely and with complete dullness. "Mademoiselle Marceline is dancing with the Herr Leutnant Oskar von Herzenberg, son of Seine Hochgeboren, Graf von Herzenberg of the German embassy in Paris." The announcement pleased everyone, for appeasement was the mood and watchword of the hour. Up with the Nazi-Fascists and down with the Reds!

Lanny watched the young couple, so well matched and so obviously pleased with each other. His mind was full of thoughts which he would not utter. Marceline had been deeply hurt in her love life, and in her fury she had declared: "The next man that wants me will pay!" Would this handsome Junker pay? Would he have anything to pay with? Would his father, who was keeping an actress and making her earn her keep, favor the idea of his son's following in the same course? Lanny could see that the youth was dangerously charming; and would Marceline have to learn about Brownshirts in the same painful way that she had learned about Blackshirts? Political ideas, he knew, meant nothing to her. She had been brought up to be beautiful, to be admired, and to enjoy herself, all as a matter of course.

One turn about the dancing floor was enough. Marceline returned her partner to his seat, and once more the orchestra took up her flight from reality. Her partner chased her from the scene amid polite applause; and the young Prussian, with cheeks flushed and blue eyes shining, exclaimed: "*Herr Budd, Ihre Schwester ist ein Frühlingslied!*" A song of spring—and Lanny knew that it would soon be spring in Paris, and that Leutnant Oskar would not fail to come again to the Chanteclair, and that if he sent in his card to the *danseuse* it would not go where so many others had gone, into the trashbasket.

XII

A week-end at the Château de Bruyne was compulsory for Robbie Budd whenever he came to Paris; otherwise the feelings of that family would have been deeply wounded. Denis *père* had not been invited to the dinner which Baron Schneider had given for Robbie and the French magnates, and all the family knew the reason; Denis and his two sons had been in jail, and while that was an honor, it was also sensational and conspicuous, and the very rich don't like things of that sort; they prefer to hide what they do, and shudder at the thought of seeing their names in newspapers. Not all the two hundred families were in sympathy with the Cagoulards—and especially not when these "Hooded Men" got caught and had their homes raided by the police, and pictures published of the concrete fortifications they had built on their country estates! Schneider had been the one who got Denis into the Cagoule, but now he was beginning to think that maybe he had gone too far, or at any rate too fast, and so he would leave Denis out of a dinner conference to which he would invite de Wendel and Mercier and others who were still playing along with politicians of the Cabinet.

The pillbox had been broken up and carted away, that having been one of the conditions on which the three men had been released. So now the garden told only of peace, as it had some seventeen or eighteen years back, when Marie de Bruyne had first brought Lanny there. The branches of the trees and shrubs were bare and the ground was black and wet, but already it was growing warm against the wall which faced the south, and a few little green things were timidly peeking from the well-worked and well-manured soil. Soon it would be spring, and the apricot trees spread out against the wall like vines would put on a curtain of pink blossoms before they showed a green leaf, and iris and heart's ease and tulips would make a sort of fringe or wainscoting beneath. The gray-haired old gardener would say to Lanny: *"Comme madame les aimait, m'sieu'!"*

Of the five women whom Lanny had loved in the course of his checkered life, Marie de Bruyne had been the one to give him the most happiness. She had been more than ten years dead, but everything on the place was still hers, the flowers, the piano, the books. There were secrets he shared with nobody but her memory. Soon after her death he had received what purported to be spirit communications from her, but these had ceased, and he had only the question he could never answer to his own satisfaction, whether that gentle ministering spirit still existed somewhere, somehow, in this strange incomprehensible universe, and whether there was any chance that he might see her or hear her voice again. Two women who had loved him were now in that spirit world; Marie and Trudi, one French and one German, different in as many ways as the languages they spoke; yet both were women, and both had loved him, and would not quarrel with each other in that realm where there was no marriage or giving in marriage.

Marie, an unhappily married woman, had charged Lanny on her deathbed to do what he could for the welfare of her two sons. Lanny didn't know quite what to call himself, foster-father, stepfather, god-father; but here he was, a sort of left-handed member of the family in a fashion peculiar to France. He came to visit them whenever he could, and had helped to see them properly married and their families in-stalled in the home—again the fashion of the French, whose aristocratic and Catholic families retain the patriarchal attitude. Denis the elder was over eighty and was feeling his age—this had begun, so he said, in prison, though they had treated him with courtesy and permitted him to purchase comforts. Trying to overthrow your government is an an-cient and respectable practice in Europe, and only among the Nazis was it harshly dealt with.

XIII

Three Frenchmen and two Americans sat in front of a log fire in a drawing-room full of old furniture, books and *objets d'art*, and talked out their hearts on the subject of their two countries. Both were in the hands of evil and incompetent men—so the five agreed. The peril of France was the greater, because she lacked the advantage of three thou-sand miles of protecting ocean. France ought to make peace with her hereditary German foe; but the corrupt and incompetent politicians wouldn't let her, and before long it would be too late, and then would come *"l'irréparable"*—the phrase by which men of their way of think-ing referred to war between Germany and France.

Robbie Budd couldn't say much to console these friends. He had been asking questions of army officers and businessmen, and the tech-nical men he had brought over had been doing the same. All agreed that French aviation, as compared with German, was in a backward state. It was not merely that labor was in revolt and that sabotage was common; it was that so many of the manufacturers were incompetent. The factories were small, and fathers passed on the control to sons who were timid and old-fashioned in their ideas, afraid to spend money upon new developments.

One of the greatest dangers was the concentration of airplane manufacture in and about Paris. This would be fatal in wartime, and "decentralization" was endlessly talked about, but nothing was done. In the southwest of France were great numbers of quarries which offered excellent places for the concealment of aircraft manufacture; surveys had been made and plans drawn, but no steps had been taken to run power lines and railroads to these places. Also, and worst of all, was the neglect to promote the manufacture of motors; anybody could make planes in a hurry, but motors required foundries and machine tools, and France was a second-class nation where these were concerned.

To Robbie Budd all these evils were the result of so-called "democracy" run wild: labor unionism meddling in politics and electing demagogues who presumed to tell businessmen how to run their affairs. Worst of all was this Red business of "nationalizing" airplane plants, something which to Robbie was on the same moral plane as highway robbery. In France the program had produced chaos, for no manufacturer knew when his turn would come, and his business life depended upon his knowing which politicians to buy. The plants which had been taken over might as well have gone out of business; materials didn't arrive on time, investigating commissions kept the administrators from their work, standards were a matter of whim and jobs a matter of political pull. All this Robbie knew on the authority of his own experts, men who had looked into conditions in one "nationalized" plant with a view to having it make changes in Budd-Erling planes.

Lanny listened to this tale of woe with secret amusement, for he had talked with these same experts, and had been told their conclusion, that this government plant was in competition with one of the most powerful privately owned plants in France, and the private concern had hired the French Minister of Aviation in his capacity as a private lawyer. The assistant director of the public plant, the man responsible for most of the chaos, had informed Robbie's men that he didn't have to worry about any of the investigations, since he had such political influence that he couldn't be removed. Robbie's experts had told him that fact, but Robbie didn't consider it important enough to be mentioned in his conversation. What the great private concern was doing in France was exactly what Robbie would have been doing if he had found himself faced with government competition at home. Fight the devil with fire!

XIV

Denis de Bruyne *père* was a stockholder in the Budd-Erling enterprise, so he had a double reason for wishing his country to be provided with these planes. The contract wasn't going through as quickly as Robbie had hoped, and Denis had paid a call on General Gamelin, Chief of Staff of the French army, and the man who had most to say about what weapons it should have. Denis had been received in the École Militaire, where the Generalissimo used a study which had once served his great master, Joffre, whose equestrian statue now stood in the square in front of the building. Denis described the Louis XV room, decorated with gold crowns and fleurs-de-lis, and large paintings representing the battles of Fontenoy and Lawfeld—victories which the French army had won nearly two hundred years ago and which it dreamed of repeating.

The general himself was a neat little man with a round head, bright rosy cheeks, and light silky mustaches turned up at the ends like Kaiser Wilhelm's. He had been friendly and courteous to the head of an old French family, and had discussed the problems of *la patrie* quite frankly. It was the same old trouble: there were twice too many Germans, and this had made it necessary for the French to dig great holes in the ground and to line and cover them with concrete. The French holes were called the Maginot Line and the German holes opposite to it were called the Siegfried Line, and each nation was destined to spend a long time in them, according to the French Chief of Staff; whichever side was reckless enough to come out first would surely be lost. This old gentleman had reached the retiring age, but had been kept on because he was the only general the Leftists did not actively hate. He declared earnestly that he believed in airplanes, they would be most useful in getting information and perhaps in an emergency in getting food and ammunition to the men in the concrete holes; but the notion of planes as an active weapon of offense was one in which he could not bring himself to take stock.

So apparently Robbie's order wasn't going to be as big as he had hoped. He was vexed, of course, and pointed out that unfortunately the French had failed to continue their holes along the Belgian border to the sea. They had counted upon their alliance with the King of the Belgians; but that monarch had taken up the idea of remaining neutral, if he could, and that had left the French republicans in a most uncomfortable position. They left Robbie in one, also, for he had to keep his assembly line full, and if he couldn't persuade the French to protect themselves, he would be forced to make the best deal he could with Marshal Göring.

Denis the elder, greatly disturbed, said that he would go on Monday morning to interview Premier Daladier, a man whom he disliked because he was carelessly dressed, and not very clean, and always smelled of absinthe. Annette, the very intelligent young wife of Denis *fils*, volunteered to pay a call at 103 avenue Henri Martin, the home of pretty, blue-eyed Marie-Louise, Duchesse de Crussol d'Uzes, and try to persuade her of the seriousness of the situation. She was the one whose opinion counted most with the Premier; and that was the way you put through business deals in present-day France!

BOOK TWO

Who Sups with the Devil

5

The Pitcher to the Well

I

A SPELL of mild weather, and Lanny persuaded his father that they might as well motor to Berlin; they could leave after business hours and drive up the valley of the Oise by night, spend the night in Belgium, and reach their destination the following night. Lanny had plans of his own for which he would want the car later. So Robbie's experts returned to Connecticut, taking with them a brief case full of documents, including some contracts—not so big as Robbie had hoped, but then it was always that way in dealing with politicians and brass hats. It was Robbie's inescapable fate to be dealing with one or the other or both, and it would have been hard for him to say which pleased him less. For the president of Budd-Erling, life's greatest mystery was the lack of harmony between production and marketing; the former was so easy and the latter so difficult. Efficiency was Robbie's god, and sales resistance was his devil, and in all the religions of the world these two forces may be observed in conflict.

Speeding by night on a fine military road, with a driver who knew it well, the father discussed his problems past and future. He had given the French every chance in the world; and since they were so niggardly —clamoring for long-term credits and hanging on with a kind of frenzy to every ounce of that gold under the Paris streets—all right, their folly would rest on their own heads. Not for the first time Robbie Budd announced that whatever might befall the Third Republic was not going to worry him. The problem now was to get as much business as he could out of Germany—and that was a matter that required tactful handling, for Germany had very little gold, and American banks were taking very few Hitler bonds these days. The German-Americans were still getting together and heiling one another and spitting Nazi gutturals into their beer, but when it came to investments, most of them preferred A.T. and T. So Dr. Schacht had complained to Robbie, and for once he wasn't lying.

All the way from Paris to Berlin, Robbie talked about how he **was** going to deal with *Der Dicke,* no longer so *dick*. He had proved himself a man of bad faith, but then, how many would show themselves otherwise, in a situation such as Germany faced? The fat Marshal was figuring on war—why else would he be building an air force? In case of war, Britain might be blockading Germany, and America's sympathies would be with Britain; whatever Göring gave to America he would be giving to Britain—so naturally he would want to get as much and give as little as possible.

All right, meet the old-style robber baron on his own ground, laugh with him, and take his rascality for granted. Don't quarrel with him—for if he gets angry, you'll get nothing out of him. Remember that he may win the next war, and then you'll be doing business with him again. "The way I figure it," said the cautious businessman, adopting his son's theory for his own, "if America gets into the war, I don't have to worry—there'll be a market for every·plane we can produce. The problems arise in the case of our staying out; I don't want to make an enemy of the winner, and I certainly don't want to have any paper of the losers. Better to worry along on what cash business I can get."

That was the way the world was run, and it wasn't Lanny's job to find fault with it. Lanny would tell his father all he knew about the British, French, and German leaders, and in return would have the right to ask questions about matters of importance to him. He would pretend that he was interested in the value of stocks, or that he was thinking of some man as a possible client, or just that he was curious about some item of gossip. That was part of the pleasure of living in the great world: one heard so many entertaining stories. Thus Lanny told his father about a one-time Senator from Maryland who went sailing around the world in a yacht every winter, and who wanted to come up to Newcastle to discuss putting money into Budd-Erling. Robbie said: "Send him along. I can always use more." Lanny didn't mention the marriageable daughter, not wanting to have his father questioning him on that subject.

II

Lanny Budd's life had settled into more or less of a routine. He stayed a while on the Riviera and then in Paris; he went to Germany, and then to England. In each place he put on the proper clothes and made himself interesting to the wealthy and powerful, told them what they wanted to know, and used his tact to steer the conversation where he wanted it to go. After each effort he would make out a report—unless it was in Germany, where he never put anything on paper. There were some things he wouldn't write anywhere, and when he had enough of these he would take a trip to the land of his fathers, make sure that the Big Boss had duly received the reports, hear his comments and questions, and take on board a fresh load of courage and determination.

Every now and then Lanny would fall to wondering: how long would he be able to keep up this routine? He knew the old saying, the pitcher that goes too often to the well is broken at last. How long could he expect to continue this double life, and what would be the obstacle over which he would trip? Perhaps if he knew about it in advance, he might be able to sidestep it. He had raised that question with the young astrologer in Munich who had told him that he was going to die in Hongkong. Lanny had asked: "What if I refuse to go to Hongkong?" and the answer had been: "If you would refuse to go, it would not be written in the stars that you would die there."

What did Lanny seek to learn in Berlin? First of all, when was Hitler going to strike again, and in what direction? That was the number one question for the whole world just now. Lanny had told F.D. that either Prague or the Polish Corridor would be taken this spring. He wasn't "rooting" for these things to happen, but naturally he couldn't help feeling a certain amount of satisfaction whenever his prophecies were verified. Just as Robbie Budd exulted when he had turned out the deadliest killer-plane in the world, so when several million people lost their liberties, Robbie Budd's son would say: "Well, Governor, you remember what I told you on my last visit?"

Now, driving through northeastern France and Belgium where so large a part of Europe's industries are crowded, this active-minded conspirator was thinking: "What am I going to ask Göring?" and then: "What am I going to say if he has heard about any of my Red friends?" He would think about Schacht and Krupp von Bohlen and Charles de Wendel and others he was likely to meet and what he wanted to learn from them. He would think about Hess, and of some new psychic adventures to tell him, Rudolf being one who lived according to the advice of the spirits and the astrologers. Above all, Lanny thought about that strangest of human creatures, half-genius, half-madman, whose career he had been following for some seventeen years, and the end was surely not yet: the *Gefreiter*, or sub-corporal, whose father's name had been Schicklgruber, and whose sufferings and

humiliations as a child and youth the whole human race was paying for
with blood and tears.

III

The Hotel Adlon stands at the corner of Wilhelmstrasse and Unter
den Linden, which is right in the heart of Berlin, near the statues and
monuments and huge cold gray public buildings. It is not a large hotel,
according to American standards; only six stories, but solid and dignified, and inside very elegant. It was the place where all Americans went
if they could afford leisure-class prices; they spoke of its bar and lounge
as "the Club," and if you stayed there long enough you would meet
"everybody," just as you would at the Crillon in Paris or the Savoy in
dear old London. Diplomats, big businessmen, newspaper correspondents with unlimited expense accounts, and pleasure-seekers in the upper
brackets—all found the comforts of home here. In the rear was a garden, very pleasant in summertime; in the winter American tempera-
tures were maintained indoors, and only the English complained.

The president of Budd-Erling and his son had been long and favor-
ably known here, and when they telegraphed for a suite they got it.
Marshal Göring's six-wheeled baby-blue and chromium limousine had
been seen to stop at the door and take them away; that placed them
among the Olympians, and even the haughty SS officers in the hotel
lobby bowed to them. Likewise the help beamed upon them, knowing
that all services would be generously rewarded. The hotel management
would tip off the newspapers and there would be reporters waiting,
ready to ask about the errands which had brought them to Germany.
This was convenient, letting their friends know that they were in
town. For Lanny it was an especial convenience, because it might bring
him a note from Bernhardt Monck.

Luxury you could purchase in this "palace hotel," but privacy and
security you could not have at any price. This was not the hotel's fault;
such privileges were beyond the reach of anyone in Naziland. Arriving late at night, and tired after a long drive, the tail end of it in a
snowstorm, Lanny turned back the fine linen coverlet and the soft
warm blankets of his bed, and there he saw a scrap of paper; he picked
it up and read: "*Achtung. Abhörapparate im Zimmer!*" Your room is
wired! Without a word he handed it to his father, who read it, and exchanged a significant look but no sound, for both were aware that the
new apparatus which the Gestapo had at its service made the faintest
whisper audible.

The meaning of this message required little guessing. *Der Dicke* knew that they were coming, and where they always stopped; it might be of importance to him to know what they wanted and what their attitude was going to be. The hotel people would have no choice but to co-operate, and inform the authorities when the Americans were to arrive and what rooms were being held for them. The servants, of course, know everything that goes on in one of these de luxe establishments; gossip spreads like wildfire, and everyone would learn that Gestapo agents had come and wired the suite, and perhaps were in the next suite listening. Among the help would be old-timers, Reds and Pinks who had had to take a Brown protective coloration. Anything the Gestapo wanted would be hateful to these persons, and it would be an act of sabotage to tip off two American visitors, who might double their *Trinkgeld* to the whole staff as an expression of their gratitude.

Lanny held the scrap of paper over the toilet and lighted it; when the ashes dropped he sent them down into the well-arranged sewer system of the Reichshauptstadt. Neither he nor his father took the risk of hunting for a tiny vibrating disk, or wires which might have been run up inside the leg of an iron bedstead. They would follow with redoubled care the rule which a munitions salesman had taught his son in boyhood: never to say any but complimentary things concerning the country of which you were a guest. Confine your plain speaking to a time when you were driving in a car—and had taken the precaution to look into the trunk before you set out.

So now Lanny said: "Did you notice on this trip how many of the factory chimneys in France and Belgium were dead; but in Germany we didn't see a single chimney that wasn't smoking?" He allowed himself a grin—since dictaphones have not yet been provided with television attachments.

His father replied in kind. "They are a marvelous people, the Germans. I only wish there was some way we could learn from them."

And Lanny again: "I wonder if Hermann will invite us to Karinhall this time. That lovely little girl must be learning to walk by now!" They knew from previous experience that there was no goo on this subject that *Der Dicke* and his beloved Emmy wouldn't swallow.

IV

The first thing Robbie wanted was a conference with the two men who for a considerable time had been representing Budd-Erling in Germany, on the arrangement of sharing patents and techniques with

Göring. Robbie wouldn't talk with these men in his hotel or in theirs; he wanted Lanny to take them in the car, the only really safe place. The car was heated, provided that the engine was running. Lanny would have to drive—wherever he chose to go.

He was there to oblige, and he said "O.K." Robbie settled himself in the back seat, with one of the men on each side of him. Lanny took them out toward Potsdam and beyond, past snow-covered fields; presently, in one of them, he saw great tanks maneuvering, for all the world like a herd of elephants rushing this way and that, scattering the snow in clouds and making a great roaring. But the three men gave hardly a glance; they were absorbed in the study of diagrams and charts. Each of the three had brought a well-stuffed brief case, and their conversation was full of figures, and of technical terms which puzzled even Lanny, who had listened to the details of airplane construction and operation through many a boresome hour. They were concerned for a while about the coffeepot, and then about the alarmclock, and then about the birdcage—none of which objects would have seemed to an outsider to be essential to flying six or seven miles up in the air; but these men found it so, and did not smile while they said it.

The coffeepot had a more formal designation, of course; it was 32-708-4B, but that was hard to say and still harder to remember. It was a heater for the pilot's cockpit, and was attached to the exhaust. The operator in the sheet metal department who first made it had called it the coffeepot because that was its shape; the name had spread through the plant, and had stuck. The gearbox looked like an alarmclock, and a fitting in the tail assembly looked like a gambling device known as a "birdcage." In the same way the tubes supporting the seats were flutes, and the electrical conduits piled into boxes were spaghetti. Somewhere in the complex structure were horsecollars and slingshots and hayhooks and violin pegs; butterflies, elbows, stars, fingers, half-moons, and even rabbit ears. All this in Connecticut, of course; to the serious-minded Germans such a development would have been lèse-majesté.

The sun, low in the winter sky, came out from behind the steel-gray clouds, and they stopped for a while to stretch their legs. Down the broad highway came marching a great column of men in gray-green woolen uniforms; a whole battalion, a thousand or more young Prussians in the prime of life, sturdy and grim, loaded down with heavy packs; a route march, doubtless a long one—for they could never tell when the Fatherland might need them, and they must be in condition winter or summer. Coming near to the car, they burst into song: "Today Germany belongs to us, tomorrow the whole world." It was a defiance, and they meant it, personally and directly, for the *Ausländer* in a car with French license plates. American boys under such circumstances would have grinned as they passed, but on these faces there was not a smile; most of them looked straight ahead, as if they had been on parade instead of a tedious march. This was the *Hitlerjugend*, which had been in the Führer's keeping now for six years. Lanny wanted to say: "Hurry up and improve your planes, Robbie; and don't give any more secrets to *Der Dicke!*"

V

Returning to the hotel, Lanny stopped in the lobby, and so ran into an adventure. His path crossed that of a lady, a smallish, birdlike lady who moved quickly and glanced here and there as a bird does when it is picking up whatever it lives on; a lady who might have been thirty, and would have been younger if she had taken off her gold pince-nez. She was rather pretty, and wore a brown plaid coat of English tweed with a mink collar, welcome in the month of February on the flat lands which had once been the marshes of Brandenburg, and were still swept by icy gales from the Baltic and the snow-covered mountains to the north.

The lady's alert eyes swept over a youngish-looking gentleman wearing a tweed overcoat and a Homburg hat, both from London. The eyes showed no signs of interest, but the gentleman stopped and exclaimed: "Well, well! Isn't this Miss Creston?"

"It is," replied the lady, and stopped. "But—" she began.

"Don't you remember me?" That was very ill-bred indeed, but Lanny had had a rumpus with her the last time they had met, and he chose to tease her.

"You have me at a disadvantage," replied the lady, with that firmness which was a part of her personality.

"I am the troglodyte," said the creature.

"Oh! I remember. You are Mr.— Mr.——"

Again Lanny waited, just to be mean. Then he said: "Budd, the art expert who lives in an ivory tower, and doesn't care anything about politics or humanity or any of those ethical things."

"I see that I offended you," replied the lady, drawing herself up to what little height she had. "I am sorry."

"Don't spoil it all," responded the other. "You impressed me greatly. Now I find you—of all places in the world—among the people upon whom you have declared war!" He said it with his best grin, and when he saw that she didn't know quite how to take it, he was still more pleased. "You are staying at the Adlon?" he inquired.

"No, Mr. Budd; I am a mere writer, and nothing even approaching a plutocrat."

"But here is the place for local color! Have you an engagement at the moment?" When she admitted that she hadn't, he suggested: "Shall we sit down and improve our acquaintance? We were in the same room for only an hour, and most of the time we listened to other people."

He led her to a couple of the heavy leather chairs which were not too close to others; and when they were seated he ventured: "You wanted to see this new world with your own eyes? I won't ask you whether you are pleased with what you have seen. Some people change their opinions here, while others have them confirmed."

"I am a person with some fixed principles, Mr. Budd."

"I gathered that from our discussion in my friend Sophie's drawing-room; and I was interested in what you said. Since then I have looked for your name in such magazines as I have seen, but I haven't come upon it."

"I happen to have a story in the current *Bluebook*."

"Thank you for telling me. I'll get it without fail."

"I'm not sure if you'll find it here in Berlin; and perhaps I'd better advise you to forget it. The story is called 'The Troglodyte.' "

"Oh, how charming!" exclaimed the socially trained creature. "You mean that I have the honor of being in it?"

"We writers have to use the material which comes to us. But naturally, we change things; one character becomes a composite of many."

"I dare say you have met more than one man who loves beauty and peace, and tries to keep himself aloof from the hatefulness he sees around him. Is the scene of your story the Cap d'Antibes?"

"It is Capri, which I have also visited."

"But the villa you have described bears some resemblance to that of the Baroness de la Tourette?"

"In some details, possibly."

"It may amuse you to hear that when my mother was discussing our little passage at arms, she predicted that the room and everything in it would appear in a story. She saw you making mental notes."

"Explain to your mother, Mr. Budd, that writers have to live."

"Dr. Samuel Johnson once remarked that he failed to see the necessity."

"I know: but he went on living and so did the victim of his wit."

VI

Lanny's encounter with Laurel Creston had been an unusual one, and every detail of it was still vivid in his mind. She had heard someone remark that Lanny knew Hitler personally; she hated Hitler, and had said so without restraint. Lanny hated Hitler, too, but couldn't say so, and had to stay hidden behind his camouflage; he was an art expert, an ivory-tower dweller, haughtily aloof from politics. The outspoken lady had called him a troglodyte, which had greatly shocked the polite company; most of them didn't know what the word meant, but when they learned that it was a cave-dweller, they didn't think any better of the manners of Miss Creston. Driving home afterwards, Beauty had called her a perfectly odious creature, and her wayward son had let it go at that.

All his life Lanny had been accustomed to the society of women, and now he missed them greatly. He met many, of course, but they had to be ladies of the smart set, whose opinions he despised; he had to lie to them, and that wasn't his idea of enjoying feminine company. In the old days, with Rosemary and then with Marie, and for a while with Irma, he had been able to say what he thought, and to share interests and pleasures with a woman. He couldn't see how, as a secret agent, he could ever have that privilege again; but when he came upon a woman who believed what he believed in his secret heart, he was naturally drawn to her, and found pleasure even in a short talk in a hotel lobby. He wouldn't have dared that on the Riviera, where everybody knew him, and where the encounter in Sophie's drawing-room had become the subject of gossip. But here it was different; for presumably Miss Creston hadn't been calling the Führer bad names in the Berlin pension where she was staying!

He was curious about her, and assumed that a writer would be interested in all sorts of people, even troglodytes. He explained that he was here on art business, and didn't mention his father for fear of provoking a discussion on the ethical aspects of the manufacturing and marketing of killing machinery. He asked if she was traveling alone, and she answered that she traveled with one or more short stories for company; she enjoyed these companions because they always did exactly what she wished them to. Lanny remarked that he had heard of fictional characters who took the bit in their teeth and insisted on having their own way; to which Miss Creston replied that that might happen to a great writer, but she wasn't anything like that—just an observer of people, curious about their motives and the ways in which they fooled themselves.

Said the man: "When I read 'The Troglodyte' am I going to find out how I fool myself?"

Said the woman: "If you're really fooling yourself, you won't recognize it."

He laughed. "I have a friend who is a playwright, and has put me into a play several times, so he tells me; but I don't think I should have recognized myself if I hadn't been told in advance."

"Well, you know what Robert Burns says on the subject. I won't bore you by quoting it."

"Perhaps you are the power that will gie me the giftie; and if so, I'll promise to reward you liberally."

"In what coin, Mr. Budd?"

"I've been trying to think what might be acceptable. The most valuable coin I possess is what I know about art. My mother was a painters' model, and I knew painters and their work from as far back as I can remember. Then Marcel Detaze became my stepfather, and I watched him work and listened to his instructions during his greatest period. Now I earn my living as a student of paintings, whose judgment some of our collectors are willing to take. Does any of that interest you?"

"Very much, Mr. Budd."

"Well, it occurs to me that you might be interested to travel through one or two of the great museums here in Berlin, and listen to some of those discourses by which I am accustomed to bewilder and charm our American Maecenases and Lorenzos, and cause them to part with their wealth. On one occasion I persuaded a Long Island heiress to exchange four hundred and eighty thousand cans of spaghetti with tomato sauce for a piece of canvas not much more than a foot square. It so happened that that surface had been painted by Jan van Eyck with a representation of the Queen of Heaven in her golden robes."

"You wish to heap coals of fire upon my head, Mr. Budd?"

"No, I am offering to pour them into your ears. Would you consider an hour or two of my discourse as adequate compensation for that giftie of seeing myself as you see me?"

They made a date for the following afternoon.

VII

At his father's request, Lanny called up the Reichsmarschall's official residence, which was just around a couple of corners from the hotel.

There was the voice of Oberst Furtwaengler, greeting him with his usual cordiality—but of course you never could tell what any Nazi was really thinking. They were invited to call at the Residenz at eleven o'clock the following morning; they were not being asked to lunch, the staff officer explained, because Seine Exzellenz was being carefully dieted, living on milk and mush and other baby foods, so that it was really distressing to be with him at mealtimes. Lanny took this gravely, as it was meant to be taken—for Prussian staff officers do not make jokes about their exalted superiors.

Robbie wanted to make the best use of his limited time, and bethought himself of persons he might meet in the interim. Dr. Schacht enjoyed the company of Americans, having lived in the United States; he knew everything that was going on in Hitlerland, and was a free and easy talker. The table in the dining room might be wired, but that would be the doctor's lookout, not Robbie's. Lanny phoned, and the great man said he was free for dinner and would come with pleasure.

When last the two Americans had a chat with Dr. Hjalmar Horace Greeley Schacht, he had been the Nazi Minister of Economics and President of the Reichsbank. He had been extraordinarily pessimistic in his conversation, but Lanny had guessed that it was all a sham; the Nazis wanted the rest of the world to think they were going bankrupt, so that the rest of the world wouldn't arm. But now more than a year had passed, and calamities had fallen upon the square Prussian head of the world's most feared financial wizard; first he had lost his job in the Cabinet, and a few days ago he had been ousted as head of the Reichsbank—so this time there could be no doubt as to the genuineness of his distress. Apparently he had come here for the pleasure of pouring out his tale of woe upon two visitors from overseas.

A curious-looking Prussian, like a cartoon by someone who did not like the breed. He was tall and big, his head square and knobby, his face bulbous and red; he had watery blue eyes behind large spectacles, and a prominent Adam's apple inside an abnormally tall stiff collar. He was a heavy eater and voluble talker, and these two activities had a tendency to conflict; he would pour out rapid sentences in English, and then suddenly he would remember his oysters in their half-shells; he would make a stab at one, gulp it down, make a stab at another, gulp it down, and so on. Each time, the Adam's apple would rise up, and then sink into the collar again; apparently the financial wizard would have the idea that he had got something out of place, for he would adjust the collar nervously, and then resume the pouring out of lamentations.

Presently Lanny observed that the two procedures were synchronized with the movements of the waiter in this decorous hotel dining room. When the waiter was present, the guest was swallowing something, if only a chunk of bread. When the waiter departed, the conversation started again. Once, when the man lingered too long, the old turkey-cock turned upon him. "What are you standing there for? Go on about your business!" The waiter fled, and the guest remarked: "This hotel is full of spies. All Germany is full of spies. But I don't care. I have told them what I think. I have told the Number One himself; if he trusts the finances of a great nation to a vulgar clown who is drunk half the time—what can anybody hope for?"

What the Herr Doktor desired more than anything else, it appeared, was to express his opinion of another Herr Doktor, whose name was Walther Funk and who had taken both his jobs by vile and filthy intrigue. He was a lazy fat fellow who called himself a "thwarted artist" —he had wanted to be an actor and considered himself a musician. "Imagine, if you can," exclaimed Schacht, "a man who cannot make up his mind whether he wishes to play the piano or to run a Reichsbank!"

"In our family we have divided the roles," replied Robbie, with a chuckle. "My son is the piano player and I am the financier."

"Exactly! *Aber*—when Funk gives an *Abend* and plays the piano for his guests, they all agree that he is a great financier; when he makes a speech to the Party chiefs, telling them how he is going to abolish the gold standard all over the world and compel all nations which wish to trade with Europe to use Reichsmarks instead of Sterling—then everybody declares that he is one of Germany's admirable musicians."

VIII

The two visitors got a fairly complete biography of this new finance administrator before the meal was all consumed. Dr. Walther Funk had risen in the world by the same method as Ribbentrop, a rich marriage. He was a Rhinelander, and in the early days had seen his chance and been the means of bringing Hitler together with Thyssen and the other steel and coal magnates of the Ruhr. They had undertaken to finance him, and Funk had clung to his coattails. Schacht, well schooled in English, quoted the bitter words of Cardinal Wolsey: "Had I but served my God with half the zeal I served my king, he would not in mine age have left me naked to mine enemies." The large frame of the ex-minister was amply covered by black vicuna cloth, but he felt himself naked politically. Power was the thing he craved, and for which he had changed his political coat many times throughout his career.

He had invented "blocked marks" and other devices whereby the Reich could persuade other nations to part with their goods. Just before his recent dismissal he had been in consultation with Montagu Norman, Governor of the Bank of England, working out a plan to help the Jews who wanted to get out of Germany. They were to be allowed to take their money, but it would have to be used to purchase German imports in the country to which they went. The watery blue eyes of the financial wizard seemed to light up as he told about this; he was very proud of a smart device for pushing German credits abroad, and he grinned when Robbie said: "Aren't you afraid that would rather have a tendency to promote pogroms?"

All such subtleties would now cease, and the Reich was going in for crude inflation, under Dr. Funk's careless-happy regime. The printing presses were going to work on a thing called *Steuergutscheine,* or tax certificates, with which all public obligations were to be paid. "They are simply a means of financing huge loans to the Party, which has grown until it is sucking the lifeblood of the nation. It was my crime that I refused to sanction this any longer." The worthy doctor lowered his voice and looked about him nervously; it was a practice so common in this Haupstadt that it had a special name—the *Berliner Blick,* the Berlin glance.

The waiter had gone for another bottle of wine, so the guest added: "These pieces of paper fall due in the course of next year, and it means that the government will have no income then. What are we supposed to do?"

"A great many people fear that you may be forced into war, Dr. Schacht."

"Nobody fears it more than I, Mr. Budd. The head of our state is taking the worst advice these days." The speaker took another nervous glance, and then said: "I am a conservative man, I assure you. Many of my measures have been novel, but all have been practical steps designed to restore German economy to full production. That has been done, and now I feel that my usefulness to my native land is ended."

So it came out why the ex-president of the Reichsbank had come so promptly at the invitation of an American industrialist. Not for a sumptuous luncheon, but to inquire whether this gentleman knew of any group of financiers who might be disposed to make use of his talents for their personal enrichment! Governments were ungrateful, and private industry was free and offered a place of refuge for a man of modest tastes like Dr. Horace Greeley Hjalmar Schacht.

Alas, the president of Budd-Erling had to tell him that America was no longer that sweet land of liberty which he had visited years ago. The same evil tendencies were coming to fruitage overseas; a greedy party and a swarm of bureaucrats had shifted the center of power from Wall Street to Washington. Nine years ago Robbie had been bitter against the Wall Street crowd which had taken Budd Gunmakers away from his family; but now, to hear him talk, you would have thought that the big Wall Street banks were run by sound conservatives like Dr. Schacht himself. Robbie didn't know them very well, but he promised to make inquiries immediately upon his return. He said that American financiers ought to appreciate the abilities of the man who had managed to persuade Germany's conquerors to lend her the billions of dollars with which to pay them reparations. Robbie said this without a trace of irony, and the Herr Doktor accepted it as an elegant and well-deserved compliment; they parted as two men of large affairs who understood each other perfectly.

IX

From the Adlon to the ministerial residence of Hermann Göring is only a couple of minutes' walk, and the weather next morning was pleasant; but would Robbie Budd take that walk? He would not! Would he go in a taxi? Again not! He would have a hotel chauffeur in livery bring Lanny's car and drive them and then wait for them in proper state. Everybody would understand that when you are going to call upon the Nummer Zwei Nazi—Reichsminister, Air Marshal, and Commissioner of the Four-Year Plan, to give only three of a dozen titles—it is a ceremony; the whisper goes all over the place, and even the haughty SS officers in the hotel bar are set to guessing.

Just across the street from the Residenz was the elaborate and highly ornamented Reichstag building, where the fire had been. The Nazis had had six years in which to repair the burned-out dome, but had made no move to do it; they left the wreck as a monument to "Red" malice—for if there were persons in Germany who knew that the Nazis had started that fire, those persons kept it to themselves. Lanny had been told that there was a three-hundred-foot tunnel from Göring's residence into the Reichstag building, and he always thought of that whenever he walked or drove past. The building was guarded but left unused—as was the Reichstag itself; once a year or so it would be summoned to meet in the Kroll Opera House and listen to Hitler make a speech; then it would vote unanimous approval of everything he had done or promised to do, and at once adjourn *sine die*.

The SS guards at the door of the Residenz had no doubt been told that the two Americans were coming. Inside, Oberst Furtwaengler met them with every sign of cordiality and escorted them up the wide staircase to the Marshal's private office. A heavy black table in the center, heavy gold curtains at the windows, a lionskin rug before the fire and a live lion cub lying on it—all these were the appurtenances of power and represented the powerful man's own taste. Göring himself shocked them by his appearance, for when you have accumulated masses of fat all over your body and then suddenly starve it out, your skin is left full of wrinkles and folds, and there appears to be no way to have it taken up except by a surgical operation. Tailoring, of course, can be done more easily, and the Marshal's bright blue uniform with wide white lapels and cuffs was new and perfectly fitted; but the great man himself appeared to be a bad job. The corners of his mouth drooped, and he did not rise to meet his guests, but held out a languid hand, saying mournfully: "You must excuse me; I am not myself."

Lanny's instant thought was: "You old rascal, you are play-acting!" Göring might have injured his heart, as reports said, but he would remain the old robber baron just the same, and he had every reason to expect a disagreeable interview with the president of Budd-Erling.

The two visitors could safely count upon Göring's having read a transcript of their conversation in their hotel room, so they would follow along that line. They were glad to see him, they hoped he would soon be all right, and how were the lovely little Edda and the lovely large Emmy? The former had been named in honor of Mussolini's daughter, the wife of Count Ciano, and in Lanny's opinion father, mother, and grandfather were three of the most objectionable persons in the world. He suspected that Göring had the same opinion; but politics makes strange bedfellows, and in this case it had given a strange name to a Nordic blonde baby. Lanny sang the little one's praises, and left it for his father to do the same for the retired stage queen, *Der Dicke's* statuesque and showy second wife.

X

In due course they got down to business; and in a very short while every trace of Göring's depression disappeared, and he became the greedy bargainer that Lanny had met six years ago in this same room, with the same ebony table and the same gold curtains, but a different lion cub from the Berlin Zoo. Then the Nummer Zwei had been making known his intention to rob a Jewish *Schieber* of every dollar he owned in the world; now he was trying to hold on to what he had got from a Yankee trader, and to get more, if bonhomie and bluff could achieve it.

For Lanny it was like watching two master swordsmen at rapiers' points. Lanny had to hold aloof and keep strict neutrality; even if he should see any way to help his father, he would not dare to put in a word, for he had to keep friends with Göring even though Robbie might quarrel with him. The business of presidential agent was more important than that of any salesman of anything, and Lanny must remain the debonair man of the world, the combination playboy-art lover who knew all the headliners of two continents and chatted gaily about their characters and purposes. When this business duel was over he must be prepared to tell the reduced fat man that he had a customer for another painting; also about the dinner with the French financiers, and what had been the results of the Ribbentrop visit to Paris and the signing of the friendship pact.

The fight was over the meaning of certain words in a carefully drawn contract. Did "all essential appurtenances" of a fighter plane include, for example, its supercharger? This is a device which compresses air and forces it into the carburetor, thus enabling a plane to fly higher and get above its enemies. Robbie had believed that he had the best in the world; but now it had been reported to him that the Messerschmitt was flying higher than the Budd-Erling, and Robbie was insisting that he wasn't getting access to the records. Göring insisted that superchargers weren't included in the bargain, and anyhow its secrets were not his; it was made by a private concern and the government did not own the patents. That, of course, was nonsense, for there were no secrets kept from the government of Nazi Germany. If the gadgets were made in a separate plant, that was because Göring had ordered it so, no doubt to protect himself in this particular tight corner.

But Robbie couldn't afford to say so, unless he wanted to quarrel. He had to say: "All right, Hermann, if that is your interpretation, I'll be guided by it in future." That carried a sinister threat; it meant: "All right, Hermann, I'll have my gadgets made in a separate plant, and your observers in Newcastle will never hear of them." That is the way business duels are fought, at least by the high-up experts; they don't cry "Touché!" but just press harder and with more deadly concentration toward the vital spots.

A couple of hours of this was too much for the Reichsmarschall with a possibly weakened heart; he lay back in his chair and breathed hard, and said: "I'm afraid I'm overdoing it." And so then, of course, Robbie had to quit, and say that he was sorry. The invalid, real or pretended, said that he would be forced to turn these decisions over to his experts; Robbie said, with all consideration, that he would be happy to meet with them. So for a while they talked about cheerful things; Lanny said he had a customer for one of the Canalettos at twenty-two thousand dollars, and Hermann said he was leaving it entirely to Lanny's judgment. The money was to be deposited to Hermann's account in a New York bank—something Hermann had arranged quite a while ago, and hadn't seen fit to explain. Lanny had heard that the Nazi leaders were accumulating funds in Stockholm and Zurich, Buenos Aires and New York; he understood that it was a subject about which they wouldn't care to talk, and he didn't invite them to.

Instead he asked the Reichsmarschall about his proposed trip to Italy, and mentioned the possibility that Lanny himself might be coming there on picture business. He told very good news from Paris; the collapse of the Reds in Spain was having a powerful effect, and the advocates of the Russian alliance were about at the end of their rope. *Der Dicke* had never told Lanny who his own agents in Paris were, but Lanny had met so many Nazis there that he could make a pretty good guess, and he named this one and that and gave good reports—in short, everything that would enable a semi-invalid to retire with his mind at peace. That is the way to make a social success of yourself; and later, if there was some information that a P.A. needed, he could motor through the Brenner Pass and spend several pleasant days in the ancient Mediterranean town of San Remo, where he had attended an international conference in the far-off days before he had ever heard mention of a World War flying ace named Hermann Wilhelm Göring.

XI

Lanny had approached the porter of the Hotel Adlon, a polyglot and international-minded personage who was accustomed to receiving unusual requests. Lanny handed him a five-mark note and asked him to find somewhere in Berlin a copy of the *Bluebook* magazine for February. When he came back from the ministerial residence he found it lying on the escritoire in his suite, and he sat down at once to find out what sort of fiction writer Laurel Creston might be. Previously he had seen himself as a hero in plays by Eric Vivian Pomeroy-Nielson, and he had once been caricatured in a skit by a journalist who had been annoyed by the flighty conversation of a young "parlor Pink." Now the situation had been oddly turned around; Lanny was a near-Fascist, and was called a troglodyte and had his hide taken off by a "Pink" writer. It was an unpromising subject, for editors and publishers in New York as a rule shared the prevailing opinion that the Fascists represented a bulwark against Bolshevism, and it was rarely that any other point of view was suggested in one of the big-circulation magazines.

Laurel Creston had solved the problem by inventing a little comedy-melodrama. Some fashionable Americans had rented a villa on the island of Capri; at least the author had said it was Capri, though it was Sophie's home in all details, including the hardware lady from Cincinnati whose henna hair was now being allowed to come out gray. Sophie had a loud laugh and a sharp tongue, and to her had been assigned the role which Miss Creston herself had played in Sophie's home, that of arguing with a fashionable young fop who called himself an esthete, an ivory-tower dweller; but the fictional Sophie called him a troglodyte, a cave-dweller, because he had no social vision and no concern about the squalor and corruption so obvious all about him.

An amused auditor of the dispute was a local Fascist official who might well have been Vittorio di San Girolamo, Marceline's ex-husband; it was quite possible that Miss Creston had met him, or at any rate had heard the story of how he had stolen three Detaze paintings from the storeroom on the Bienvenu estate. Anyhow, the discussion in the story was interrupted by screams from upstairs—a maid had found a man looting the mistress's jewel box. The burglar got away, the Fascist official rushed out to look for him—and the climax of the tale came when the official met the burglar in a near-by woods and divided the jewels with him. It was a smart plan they had worked out, a method of punishing an American woman who had presumed to speak blasphemously concerning Il Duce and his new Impero Romano. Being guilty of such an offense, she could hardly expect Fascist officials to work hard to recover her property.

What got this story by with the editors, Lanny guessed, was the vigor of the characterizations and the sharp wit of the dialogue. The climax of the story was carefully prepared. The Fascist official had been so bland and tolerant, you didn't know quite what to make of it, having got the idea that Il Duce's followers were inclined to be somewhat arrogant; when you discovered what the official had been up to all the time it came like the snap of a whip, the sort of effect that O. Henry labored to achieve.

Lanny thought, what a lot of activity was going on inside that small feminine head! Here was a writer who knew what she wanted, gathered it diligently, and wove it into a pattern that moved you to ironic laughter. The picture she had drawn of himself of course didn't worry him; it wasn't Lanny, but the mask he was wearing, and he didn't expect any person with social insight to admire it. Quite the contrary, he liked those persons who disliked it—a phenomenon which troubled his mother, who had been so vexed with Miss Creston. "It would be just like you to look her up and fall in love with her!" Beauty had exclaimed. Lanny didn't intend to go to such extremes, but he thought she would be an agreeable person to know, and he tried to imagine on what terms they might be friends. It would have to be more or less clandestine, for she wouldn't like his rich and important acquaintances, and he couldn't explain to them his interest in a writer who so obviously belonged in the enemy camp.

Could he make a confidante of her, even partially? Lanny had considered that problem in connection with other persons he had met. Without exception, those who shared his secret were old and tried friends; he had been bringing them information for years, and they had got used to the idea that he lived a double life. They understood that they must not talk about him, and that if they were questioned, they must shake their heads sadly and declare that he had lost interest in the "cause." But could he expect any new friend to appreciate the importance of this, and to guard such a secret? And especially a writer, who lived by turning her limited personal experiences into copy? In his hands was a story called "The Troglodyte"; and suppose he should some day come upon a story called "The Secret Agent," or perhaps "The Spy," or "The Underground"?

XII

The weather was pleasant, and he didn't drive to the pension in his car and thus attract a lot of attention. It wasn't far to the Kaiser-Friedrich Museum, and Miss Creston appeared to be an active person. He gave his name to the maid, and the boarder came downstairs, wearing the same brown plaid coat with a mink collar and tiny hat to match. During the walk he told her that he had read her story, and discussed its literary qualities in a way that pleased her; he didn't say anything about the personal side of it, and presumably she would consider this very gracious. He appreciated her work, and that is what writers live on. Without it, life is empty; with it, all things become possible. Her cheeks were glowing, and perhaps it was the winter's cold, plus the exercise; or again, perhaps it was the presence of a personable man—even though he dwelt in a cave!

Presently he was telling her about this great *nouveau riche* city, and the significance of these monuments to Kaisers, generals, and glory. Most of the ornate granite buildings had arisen in the past three-quarters of a century; it was Prussian taste, and the rest of Germany didn't like it; the word *preussisch* had half a dozen meanings in half a dozen sections of the country, all unfavorable. You could walk down the Siegesallée and see the most laughable statuary in the world. This line of conversation might have been taken to have a slightly Pinkish tinge, but Lanny confined it strictly to art.

The Kaiser-Friedrich Museum stands at the head of an island in the middle of the small river Spree. It was built to fit snugly, and looks like a great two-story barge forcing its way up the current. At present the river was frozen over, and skaters were gliding under the bridges; but in summer, Lanny said, you could look out of the museum windows and see the dark water sweeping past, and crude barges loaded with bricks or lumber being poled laboriously by men with dark skins and low foreheads—the descendants of the original Wendish inhabitants of the swamps and forests of Brandenburg. This river had been theirs for centuries and they probably still thought it was theirs, knowing little and caring less about the great civilization which had crowded along the river's banks and spread out for miles in every direction.

The name of this museum was Hohenzollern, but the soul of it was Dr. Bode, so Lanny explained; a great *Kunstsachverständiger*, he had lived to be eighty-four, and to be worshiped by art lovers all over Europe. He had made an exemplary collection; and Lanny took his pupil up to the second floor where the paintings were and began those discourses which he had promised. Here were the Defreggers, and he told how he had found a couple of good ones in Vienna, and the *Nummer Eins* had them at his mountain retreat. They were simple *genre* paintings of the peasant life which the painter had known and which the statesman loved to contemplate—from a distance. A harmless sort of taste, but the same could not be said for all this personage's dabbling in art. Lanny lowered his voice and looked about in the Berlin fashion, explaining: "You understand, in this connection it is customary not to name names."

Also, the Lenbachs. Here was a painter after the German's own heart. The son of a workingman, he had trained himself by a long life-time of patient labors. "A combination of boor and courtier," said Lanny; "he admired the great world, and won his way into it. Wearing a long beard and spectacles, he was interested in men, and painted them as they were in Berlin, proud, cold, methodical, busy, intense, full of thought and cares. He had little interest in their uniforms or broadcloth coats, and didn't bother much with their hands and feet; their faces were what told the story, and he studied these minutely, willing even to learn from photographs, which most painters regard as an unfair form of competition. You see the stern-set mouths, the wrinkles, the hard eyes, the knitted brows. Bismarck, Graf von Moltke, Prinz Hohenlohe Schillingsfürst, these are the men who were making modern Germany, forcing her to the front, forcing the other states out of her way; men who believed in science, in exact knowledge, in things which they could touch and possess—I am speaking of the master class, of course: the men who took power and held it; not of the dreamers, the sentimental folk who didn't know what was being done to them or to the world they lived in."

And the Rembrandts, one of the finest collections of this great master. "He was the first modern painter," said Lanny; "I mean in the sense that he painted what he wanted to paint instead of what somebody ordered. He paid for it by a life of sorrow and trial. He painted himself often, and so we have a record of what time and suffering will do to a magnificent human countenance."

Stopping before the portrait of Hendrickje Stoffels: "Here you see the lovely and pathetic young woman who was his servingmaid and became his second wife. That marriage was an offense which his contemporaries would not forgive. We observe the same situation in the life of Beethoven—only it wasn't the composer but his brother who wished to marry beneath his social station, and it was Beethoven who was horrified and made a great scandal out of it. This strikes us as strange, for we think of Beethoven as a democrat, and fail to realize how castebound the peoples of Europe were, and still are."

"I am not failing to observe it," remarked the woman writer. "But what sort of talk is this for an ivory-tower esthete? I don't believe you are nearly so much of a troglodyte as you try to make yourself think, Mr. Budd!"

Achtung, Lanny!

6

Fighting the Devil with Fire

I

THE reduced Marshal departed for Italy with his entourage, and Robbie was left to negotiate with his subordinates. These gentlemen were as polite as possible, and answered all questions except such as were important. They promised to make inquiries, but they never brought the answers, and it became plain that they weren't going to purchase any more Budd-Erlings and had no authority to decide anything; they were just "stalling." Robbie said to his son that two could play at that game; he would go home and adopt the same methods with the technical men whom *Der Dicke* had in Newcastle.

He proposed to stop in London, and make one more try with the brass hats there. They certainly had good reason to be scared by now, and the fact that Robbie was coming from Berlin ought to add to their uneasiness. Would Lanny come with him? Lanny answered that there was nothing he could do to help, and he had learned of some paintings in Danzig that it might be worth his while to inspect; also, he wanted to meet Hitler, if possible, and find out how he was satisfied with the paintings he had bought, and give him a chance to ask for more. Robbie said: "Take care of yourself, driving in this bad weather."

Before leaving, the Yankee manufacturer had one more talk with the Luftwaffe experts, and the outcome made him more cross than ever. "They think they are making a fool of me," he said, and added: "Take me for a drive"—which meant that he had something important to get off his mind. When they were in the Tiergarten, on an unfrequented road, Robbie said: "Stop and have a look in the trunk and under the back seat." The car was kept in the hotel garage, and Robbie had several times wondered whether the Nazis might have some sort of recording apparatus which could be concealed inside or under it.

Lanny made a search, but found nothing; and when they had started again, the father opened up: "I've been wondering if I couldn't find some way to get hold of one of those new superchargers."

"Gosh!" exclaimed the son. "When did you dream up that one?"

"You understand, I wouldn't be thinking of such a thing if I hadn't given Göring full value, and perhaps twice over."

"I know that, of course."

"I want it because I've a right to it; and everything I've heard leads me to believe the thing works on a new principle and may be very important. I'm sure Göring wouldn't risk a break with me unless that were so. I'd be willing to gamble—up to as much as a hundred thousand freimarks for one of his new models."

"That's a lot of money." (It was about forty thousand dollars.) "Have you any idea how to set about it?"

"I thought it possible you might know the address of some of those Reds you used to meet here."

"Nothing doing, Robbie! You know, I dropped all that sort of thing years ago. One of the reasons was because I realized how it worried you."

"Quite so; and I don't want to get you back in. But if there's any way you could find one of those people and give him enough money to come to Newcastle, I could handle the matter and you wouldn't be involved in any way."

Lanny wasn't so greatly surprised by this approach; for he knew that his father had worked all his life on the maxim of fighting the devil with fire. Lanny explained: "All those people look upon me as a renegade. They're bound to have read in the papers about my hobnobbing with Hitler and Göring, and they might even think that I've betrayed them to the Gestapo. A lot of them have been arrested, and some killed, and you can be sure the rest are not advertising their whereabouts."

"I know all that, and maybe I'll have to put Bub Smith on the job and let him find a couple of good old-fashioned American gangsters to come in and do the job for me. But if you put your mind on it you might think of somebody here who hates the Nazis and would be glad to earn some money to fight them."

"A name occurs to me, but I'm not sure if I can find the man, or if he'd take such a risk. You know, from the Nazi point of view, it would be high treason, and they'd cut off his head with an ax."

"No doubt; and I don't want to get you mixed up in it. You don't need to tell the man anything at all; don't even admit that you know what it's all about. Just give him his traveling money and a bonus and let him get a tourist's visa and come to Newcastle."

"I'll figure over it," Lanny promised. "We'd better have a password, so that the man can identify himself."

All about them were the lawns and beautiful trees of Berlin's famous park. Robbie said: "Tell him 'Tiergarten.'"

The son assented, and then added: "If I write you that I haven't had a chance to visit the Tiergarten, you'll understand that I haven't been able to find a man, and if I write that I won't have time to visit it, you'll understand that I have had to give up." Lanny had been used to codes of this sort ever since the days before the World War, when his father had worn a belt which concealed a long list of words he used in communicating with Grandfather Budd of Budd Gunmakers.

II

The name which had leaped into Lanny's mind was, of course, Bernhardt Monck. But he mustn't let his father know that he was keeping in contact with the German underground; and anyhow, he hadn't heard from Monck, and had no assurance that he was going to hear. After delivering Robbie to the Tempelhofer Feld and seeing him safely launched into the air, Lanny drove for a while, racking his brains to think of some method of getting hold of the former Capitán. The Budds' arrival had been mentioned in the papers, but perhaps Monck hadn't happened to see those papers; he might be elsewhere in Germany, or out of Germany; he might be ill; he might be in the hands of the Gestapo, or buried in a bed of quicklime, Nazi fashion.

The underground couldn't work very long without money, and sooner or later, if Monck was still alive, Lanny would get a message from him. The thing to do now was to give Lanny's presence some further advertising. He bethought himself of a Berliner whose card had been presented to him some six years ago: *Doktor phil. Aloysius Winckler zu Sturmschatten, Privatdozent an der Universität Berlin.* This was a Nazi hanger-on who knew how and where to distribute funds, and at the time of the Detaze show in Berlin he had proved himself a competent press agent. Twice since then he had called at the Adlon for the purpose of offering his services, but Lanny had had to tell him that he wasn't doing any picture promoting.

Now, assuming that the Herr Privatdozent was still alive and in need of funds, there was a service he might render. He was not in the telephone book; but the Reichsmarschall's secretary could find anybody in Germany in five minutes, and was glad to do this favor for the

Reichsmarschall's friend. Lanny sent a telegram to the address given, and in a very short time the bespectacled scholar made his appearance at the Adlon. Lanny remembered him as wearing a derby hat, and in midsummer a vest clip on which to hang the hat, thus preserving both his comfort and his respectability. Now, in winter, he needed no clip, but held the hat in his hand in the hotel lobby, and his voice was as oily and at the same time as pompous as ever.

Lanny explained: "Herr Privatdozent, I am not sure that what I have to suggest will appeal to you as important. Let me make it clear at the outset that I am not promoting anything, and am not offering to pay you money; but it occurred to me that, with your excellent journalistic connections, you might be interested to write an interview on the subject of the Führer's taste in art, based on what I have learned about him during the time which has passed since I last had the pleasure of cooperating with you."

The round rosy face of the scholar-journalist lighted up like a full moon coming out from behind the earth's shadow. "*Wunderbar, Herr Budd! Ausgezeichnet!*"

"You may recall that at the time of our show in Munich, the Führer expressed admiration for the Detaze painting, *Sister of Mercy*, which I took to him. Since that time I have visited him several times at Berchtesgaden, and he has purchased half a dozen Detazes and put them in the Bechsteinhaus on the estate. Also he commissioned me to get him a couple of Defreggers in Vienna, and on these and other occasions he has confided to me his opinions concerning painting and architecture. I know that he is anxious to promote the improvement of taste in Germany, and it might be that testimony to this effect from a foreigner would be welcomed by your public."

The Privatdozent would have rubbed his two hands together if it hadn't been for the derby hat and an imitation-leather brief case. He found more adjectives to express his pleasure, and wanted to go right to work, lest this golden opportunity might somehow slip through his fingers. Lanny invited him up to the suite and cleared a table; the journalist spread out a loose-leaf notebook, tested his fountain pen, and then said: "*Darf ich bitten, Herr Budd.*"

So Lanny talked for an hour or more. He had told many people about the Führer's art ideas, and his memory needed no refreshing. He was acquainted with the German public and the Nazi ideology, so he knew exactly what to say and how to say it. He didn't talk about himself, except incidentally, or in answer to questions from the interviewer. Once the latter remarked, in a tone of envious worship: "You must find the business of *Kunstsachverständiger* extremely profitable, Herr Budd!" That gave Lanny the opportunity he wanted; he smiled complacently and replied: "I make more money than I know what to do with." That would go into the interview—and when Monck read it he would take it as a hint!

III

Lanny had another date with Laurel Creston. She had thanked him cordially for his discourses; she had gone so far as to say that she had never learned so much in one morning in her life. This was practically suggesting that he should favor her with more of the same; and, of course, there were other great collections in Berlin, especially the National Gallery. It seemed in a way a duty for Lanny to escort her there, for some day she might be wishing to write a story called "The Art Expert," and however satirical she might be, it would be better if she had her facts right.

The same thing applied to music, of which she was fond, but possessed little technical knowledge, so she admitted. He had taken her to the Berlin symphony, then conducted by Furtwängler, who had made his peace with the Nazis—no relative of Oberst Furtwaengler of *Der Dicke's* staff. Before and after the concert, Lanny treated her to discourses on the three B's of German music, and incidentally revealed the fact that he himself had been pounding the piano since early boyhood, and had several times had the honor of playing for the Führer of all the ogres and troglodytes.

In short, Lanny was permitting himself to enjoy the company of a charming and intelligent lady, and the pleasure of making an impression upon her. The lady, for her part, could not have failed to be aware that this was an unusual man, and with her shrewd mind she had begun to realize that there was something mysterious about him. His *Weltanschauung*, as the Germans call it, appeared to be in a state of *Verwirrung*. He would express that lofty indifference to politics which had so exasperated her at their first meeting; but before long, in the course of a discussion of art or music, he would express opinions which seemed indisputably political. She was a lady who knew what good manners were, even though she didn't always choose to have them, and now she did not challenge his remarks, but listened, and put this and that together, and wondered if it could be business that caused his extreme reticence. He told amusing stories about his rich clients— though never naming them. Were they all so intolerant of any political or economic heresy that an art expert had to alter his entire life pattern to please them?

There was a Detaze in the National Gallery. Lanny remarked: "We sold it to them after we had our one-man show in Berlin, six years ago. We let it go for a nominal price, because we thought it would pay to have him represented here." That was taking a point of view of art which Laurel Creston found new. This genial Mr. Budd didn't appear to be a greedy person; why did he have to talk so much about money—and to make so much?

They stood in front of the painting, a view of the Roman ruins of Antibes, and Lanny told the story of Marcel Detaze, gay yet wise Frenchman who had been a growing boy's guide; of his technique, the ideas he had held and sought to express, and some of the episodes of his life. They had sailed on the yacht *Bluebird*, owned by a soap manufacturer, and Marcel had painted every day, while the other guests tried to win one another's money at bridge. They had visited the Isles of Greece, celebrated by Lord Byron; they had sat among the ruins of Athens and later of Carthage. "Ruins always fascinated him," said the painter's stepson; "you see how he tries to give you the sense of melancholy, the futility of human labors. 'Even my paintings will some day be ruins,' he would say, with a smile. 'All our efforts at permanence are doomed to failure, and the only thing that survives is change.' He would recite Shelley's sonnet about Ozymandias, king of kings. 'Look on my works, ye Mighty, and despair!'"

IV

Later on Lanny told about the tragic changes which had come in the painter's own life; the war, and the peril of his beloved *patrie*, and his service in the army, and having his face burned off, and sitting in his studio at Bienvenu, wearing a white silk mask and painting masterpieces. "His sufferings had a great deal to do with his fame, for it seems that humanity has to have martyrs. But Marcel's technique has won the praise of the most exacting critics. We don't make any effort to push his work, but there is a steady demand for it, and the more we raise the prices, the more people seem to value it. Only a few weeks ago an American yacht turned up at Cannes, and the owner asked to see the works and insisted upon buying two of them."

"What was the name of the yacht?" asked Miss Creston; and when Lanny said, "The *Oriole*," she exclaimed: "How odd! It's owner is my uncle."

So then they had something else but paintings to talk about. Lanny hadn't asked any personal questions about Miss Creston; but now he learned that she was a Baltimorean, a daughter of Reverdy Holden-hurst's sister. She didn't say any more about her parents, or why she had left home in a manner unusual for Southern ladies. She said that she had taken one of the *Oriole* cruises, several years ago, and Lanny mentioned that Reverdy had invited him on the voyage to the States. "You would have found it rather slow, I am afraid," she remarked.

She asked who had been on board, and he named several of the guests, persons whom she knew. He mentioned Lizbeth, but of course said nothing about the conspiracy of his mother and her friends, which would have been boorish of him. "A very lovely child," he remarked; and the woman replied: "She ought to be more than that by now. I'm afraid she's somewhat spoiled."

"She adores her father," Lanny countered, with his usual amiability.

"She must know that he is not a happy man. He would like to do something useful, but his desires exceed his capacities. That is true of all the members of our family, I think."

"I don't know," said Lanny, gallantly. "If I had been asked about you, the first thing I should have said is that you know exactly what you can do, and are doing it."

The woman smiled a brave little smile, and replied: "That means that you have read one of my short stories; but you have never seen the trunkful of manuscripts at home—to say nothing of all the ashes!"

V

The Herr Privatdozent had feared delays in the publication of his interview, because everything which quoted the Führer had to be submitted to a member of his staff who had been especially deputized for that purpose. But evidently that unknown personage was friendly to the American visitor, for the permission was granted at once, and the interview appeared in the *Völkischer Beobachter*. This was the Führer's own paper, published by his close friend, Herr Ammann, who also published *Mein Kampf* and vast quantities of other Party literature from which the Führer derived his income. Thus he could say that he took no salary as Reichskanzler, and thus increase his reputation for saint-hood.

The interview with Herr Lanning Prescott Budd was restrained and dignified, and even the ivory-tower art world couldn't call it fulsome. It was a fact that Adi Schicklgruber loved art, and had done his best to encourage it; his tastes were limited and somewhat commonplace, but there were many good things within the limits of such taste and Lanny had talked about these. Included were the works of Marcel Detaze, and it was money in Lanny's pocket to mention them to the German public. He was perfectly willing to have the art authorities suspect that that was the motive behind his praise of the Führer. What he wanted was to keep himself solid with the inner circle, and be able to continue his visits to the Berghof and to the office in the New Chancellery building on the Wilhelmstrasse.

"Everybody" read the article, and those whom Lanny met praised it. He bought a bundle of copies and mailed them around: one by airmail to Robbie, to let him know what was going on, and one to Göring in San Remo, to let him know what a competent art expert he had; copies also to Kurt and to Lili Moldau and other Germans in Paris; to Forrest Quadratt in New York, and other Nazi agents and sympathizers there—it was a chance to make himself solid with a host of people whom he might want to make use of. He would keep some spare copies, for use whenever and wherever he might seek to establish himself as a friend of the *Neue Ordnung*.

Naturally he sent one to Laurel Creston. Her German was far from perfect, but she would get the gist of it, and anyone in the pension would be glad to help her out. He didn't take it to her, because he was sticking close to the hotel, on the chance that Monck might telephone. Meantime he carried on imaginary arguments, in which the article made her mad, and she called him a nasty Nazi; he amused himself by letting her pour out her irritation, and then revealing the truth to her, witnessing her consternation and accepting her apologies—all this, of course, in his innermost secret heart.

Oddly enough, this sequence of scenes was not entirely new to Lanny; for it was the procedure which had been suggested by Nina Pomeroy-Nielson, one of his old friends, as a way by which he might find himself a wife. He would meet some anti-Nazi woman, and she would be angry with him, and argue with him; he would listen to her respectfully and gradually let her convert him, until he knew her well enough to trust her, and to be sure that he loved her. Then—grand dénouement!—he would tell her the truth about himself, and they would clasp each other in their arms and live happy ever after.

But where? And how? Would the woman forsake her anti-Nazi world and go away and hide somewhere, never letting one of her friends know that she was consorting with a Nazi sympathizer notorious for his intimacy with Hitler, Göring, and Hess? Would she give up writing anti-Nazi stories, or would she take to publishing them under a pen name and concealing her identity, even from her publisher? That was a chain of imaginings hard to make plausible. How, for example, would she get her royalty checks?

Thus Lanny, staying close to the hotel and keeping watch on his mail. Surely now, if Bernhardt Monck was alive and anywhere near Berlin, he would see that published interview, or hear about it from some friend. Surely he would understand that it was an offer of money; and what a novel kind of political agitator he would be if he didn't want some!

Sure enough, here came the letter; Lanny knew it as soon as it was handed to him at the hotel desk; a plain envelope, with no return address, and undistinguished handwriting. Lanny took a seat in the lobby, not showing any haste; he opened the envelope casually and read:

"Sir: I wish to call your attention to the work of a painter of talent. I would be pleased if you would call Wednesday evening at eight. If this is not convenient, I'll expect you on the first evening possible. Yours respectfully, Braun."

Nothing in that to excite the suspicions of any Gestapo agent! No place mentioned, because they had previously agreed upon a place—the same street corner in the Moabit, a working-class district where Trudi Schultz had been accustomed to meet Lanny in the old days before she had become his wife. *Absit omen!*

VI

In the years while the son of Budd-Erling had been helping to finance the underground against the Nazis, he had worked out a technique which had become semi-automatic. First, there would be the business of getting money which could not be traced. Large bills from the bank would be exchanged in stores where luxury goods were sold: a handsome box of candy, some costly flowers, some toys for children. Kurt's frugal and hard-working little blonde wife in Stubendorf would appreciate useful gifts for their six little ones, and would tell Kurt about it, and both would find it touching that this wealthy playboy should remember the old days and the happy visits he had paid. The same thing applied to the family of Heinrich Jung—Lanny had the names of all these little ones in his notebook, so that he could put in cards with the gifts.

The candy would be for the Fürstin Donnerstein, who appeared to need fattening, and the flowers would be for some other hostess who had entertained him, or some owner of a painting which Lanny had recently purchased. Thus one made and kept contacts in *die grosse Welt;* and thus Lanny would have his pockets stuffed with mark notes of various denominations and no consecutive serial numbers. Thus if the Gestapo caught a member of the underground they couldn't start calling on the banks to find out who had recently drawn thousand-mark notes of consecutive numbers.

After that, the conspirator would drive to the place appointed, on some obscure and unfrequented street, always at night. On the way he would turn several corners, watching in the little mirror of the car to make sure he was not being followed. He would approach the place slowly, as if looking for a street number. Seeing his man Lanny would draw up at the curb, somewhat in front of him, and if at the last moment there should be any sign that they were being watched, the man would walk on without paying attention; on the other hand, if all seemed safe, the man would slip into the seat beside the driver and they would speed away, not forgetting to turn several corners and make sure no car was following.

This time Lanny's confederate was, presumably, traveling on a forged passport; the police had his photographs, fingerprints, and record—they had these for everyone in Germany, and for everyone who had ever been in Germany; if for any reason they had occasion to investigate him, it would be his end—his head would be chopped off in a public ceremony by an executioner wearing a dress suit. This meant that Monck, alias Herzog, alias Branting, alias Braun, couldn't stop at any hotel or lodging house, for all such visitors had to be at once registered with the police. He couldn't stay in a home where there were servants without risk of being reported and having a whole family thrown into a concentration camp. He would have to stay in a hiding place by day, and never go into any public place where one of his numerous enemies might recognize him.

How he was managing all this Lanny had no idea. It was the first principle of underground life that you neither asked questions nor answered them. If you asked, it made you an object of suspicion. In the far-off days which now in retrospect seemed so happy, being a Social Democrat had been like being an amoeba in a pond; you circulated freely, and encountered thousands of others. But now what few were left were like those amoeba which grow in chains; you knew the one who was joined to you, but you didn't know the one who was joined to him. If your contact was broken, if your comrade disappeared, you waited in fear and trembling to learn if he had weakened under the dreadful tortures he would have to endure. If a new man approached you, it was hard to make sure whether he was a friend or a would-be betrayer, and you watched him for a long time before you let him know that you were anything but the Führer's most loyal servant. It was "living dangerously," as Nietzsche had advised.

Lanny had trusted Bernhardt Monck because Trudi had told him to; but he hadn't felt really sure of the man until he had seen him marching with the International Brigade to the defense of Madrid. From that time on, this ex-sailor and trade-union leader represented the anti-Nazi cause in Lanny's mind. It was the fashion among smart people to sneer at "parlor Pinks" like Lanny, and to picture them as the dupes of cunning "Reds" like Monck; but to Lanny it appeared that if there were any heroic souls on this earth, they were the men and women who were keeping the sparks of truth and freedom still burning in the inferno of cruelty and torment which Germany had become.

VII

"I saw that interview about Hitler," Monck began. "*Wirklich fein!*"

"It was meant for you," was the reply.

"*Na klar!* I was waiting to get something important; and now I have it." Monck paused for a moment. "Tell me, could you leave Germany at once?"

"I haven't finished what I came for; but I could leave and come back, if it was necessary."

"Here is the situation: I have some information which cries out to be spread widely. It's of such a character that I have not put it into writing; I have memorized it, and you would have to do the same. I am hoping that you can find some way to get it published."

"I'll make a try, if it is as urgent as you say."

"Well, here is the situation. You recall that in the Four-Power Pact, signed in Munich last September, Hitler undertook to guarantee the borders of Czechoslovakia as they were there agreed upon. Since then Ribbentrop has steadily evaded carrying out that promise. The British and French have been pressing him, but not very hard."

"Decidedly not hard," said Lanny. "They are scared to death of provoking Hitler to fresh rage."

"He is making further demands upon the Czechs, and negotiations have been going on for months, but the outside world has no idea what the demands are. A few days ago Hitler served an ultimatum—'take it, or I will take Prague.' I have those terms."

"That is indeed important, Monck—if you are sure you really have them."

"I cannot give you the slightest hint as to how I got them—I have taken an oath. But I assure you they are correct, beyond the shadow of a doubt. They amount to making the country into a puppet state, and it seems to me the rest of the world should know what is going on right now behind the curtain."

"If you care to trust me with this information, I'll take a trip out of Germany and see that it is published."

"You can manage it without too much danger to your own work?"

"You remember that Trudi's documents were published; the same channel is still open."

"All right. Do you have a good memory?"

"Fairly so. You can give me time, I suppose."

"All the time you want. I'll summarize the terms first, and let you get over the shock." So Monck began to recite: "One: Complete neutralization of the Czech frontiers. Two: Adhesion of Czechoslovakia to the Anti-Comintern pact. Three: Withdrawal from the League of Nations. Four: Drastic reduction of military effectives. Five: Surrender of most of the Czech gold reserves. Six: Czechs to furnish raw materials to redeem Czech currency now in the Sudetenland—that currency is now worthless, you understand. Seven: Sudeten industries to have full access to Czech markets. Eight: No new Czech industries to compete with them. Nine: Czech anti-Semitic legislation conforming to the Nuremberg decrees. Ten: Dismissal of all state employees objectionable to Germany. Eleven: Permission for all Germans in Czechoslovakia to wear Nazi badges and carry the Nazi flag. That's all."

"Well, I'll be damned!" said Lanny Budd.

"So will the Czechs, if they yield to this hold-up," replied the man of the underground.

VIII

The P.A. didn't have to hesitate over such a decision. He said: "I'll get that news out," and then drove slowly about the boulevards of Berlin, learning and reciting a lesson. In the days of his youth he had attended his Grandfather Samuel's Bible class in Newcastle, and there had learned to recite the Ten Commandments and at least a few of the articles contained in a pamphlet called *A Brief Digest of the Boston Confession of Faith.* Somewhat later, in course of his duties as a secretary-translator at the Paris Peace Conference, he had learned the Fourteen Points of Woodrow Wilson; and now in the same way he learned the Eleven Points which were designed as the funeral services of the Czechoslovak Republic. He recited them one by one and then two by two, and when he had gone through them three times over from beginning to end without an error, his mentor said that would do.

"I'll leave tomorrow morning and get the news started by night," he said. He didn't offer to tell where or how, and Monck didn't ask. "Have you anything else on your mind?"

"Not at the moment, but I may have later, if you come back."

"I'll be back in about three days, if all goes well. My mail will be waiting here for me. Do you need some money?"

"I'll be needing it later."

"You had better take it now. I have been to some trouble to get it ready for you." Lanny handed over the large wad of notes, and then said: "Now for something of mine that may or may not be important to you. My father has just been here, and he has about come to the parting of the ways with Göring. He isn't getting what he wants. It's a long story, and no use bothering you with the details. The point is, the Luftwaffe has a new type of supercharger for airplanes, and my father is entitled to the use of the drawings, and he hasn't got them. The last thing he said before he left was that if I could find somebody who could get one of those superchargers out of Germany, he would pay a hundred thousand freimarks for it."

"*Herrschaft!*" exclaimed Monck. "He doesn't want much for his money!"

"Maybe it wouldn't be easy; but I remember that Trudi once had a man in Göring's office."

"I don't even know if that man is still alive."

"Well, if it can't be done, that's all there is to it. I must make this plain at the outset—I can't give any help myself. This is my father's affair, and you must judge it on that basis. My father is a businessman, and his purpose is to make money for himself and his stockholders. He wants the Budd-Erling pursuit plane to be the deadliest in the world, and of course Göring wants to cheat him if he can. I warned him that this would happen, but he's pretty sure of himself, and thought he could match *Der Dicke*'s moves. At the present moment it's Robbie's move, and *Der Dicke* is grinning over the situation."

"Did you tell your father about me?"

"Not the faintest hint. I'm supposed to have broken all contact with the Reds, as my father calls them. He hates them, but he wouldn't mind making use of them. He asked if I could find one and I said I'd try. He wants to keep me out of it, and suggested that I send the man to New-castle, pretending that I didn't know what it was for. But of course that would be a waste of time. If you can get the supercharger, all you have to do is to take it to my father. He is a man of his word, and will pay the money on the spot."

"Just what is a supercharger?"

"A device to take rarefied air and condense it and force it into an airplane engine. The purpose is to enable the plane to maintain its speed in high altitudes."

"What would it weigh?"

"That's hard to guess. The effort of every airplane manufacturer is to reduce the weight of everything, and the merit of this new appara-tus will lie in the fact that it will do more work per pound of weight. How much Göring's technicians have achieved is what my father wants to find out. My best guess would be seventy-five or a hundred pounds. You understand, of course, the blueprints or drawings would do as well."

"That would depend on where I could make a connection—with the office, or the shop, or one of the airfields. Do you know where the thing is made?"

"One of our men has become convinced that it is being made by Siemens, here in Berlin."

"Well, of course I'd like to earn that lump of money for the cause. I'll make inquiries, and let you know."

"One thing has to be got clear—nothing is any good but the newest model. If there's any uncertainty, my father will show you what he has already, and what the performances are."

"I catch myself fooling around your father's plant and then going back to Germany!" laughed the ex-sailor. "No, indeed, this is a job to be done on a moonless night. If either the gadget or the drawings were missing, the Gestapo would go to work all over the world, and you can be sure your father's place would be one of the first."

"That's true enough; and you understand that my father must never be named to anyone. That would be practically the same as naming me. You'll have to say that it's the British or the French who want the de-vice; that's perfectly plausible, and no doubt they'd pay a good price for it. I don't suppose your comrades would care very much who was going to get hold of it."

"We would take the position that anything that hurt the Nazis would help us. They are a gang of criminals in our eyes, and there's no ques-tion of patriotism involved."

"All right then. How soon shall I expect to hear as to the prospects?"

"That's hard to guess. I have to consult someone who knows the situation better than I, and he has to start a chain of inquiries. It might be a day or two and it might be a week before I'll have anything worth reporting."

"I'm not sure just how long I can stay in Germany; but you can write me to the Adlon or to Juan. Let's call it a Defregger; you can say that you can get the Defregger, or whatever you have to tell me about the Defregger. If you manage to get it to England, or to Canada, you can cable or telephone to my father from there. The keyword for him is *Tiergarten*. All you have to do is to say that word and he'll send someone with the money."

"Just as simple as that!" said Monck.

IX

Lanny deposited his friend on the street at a place requested, and then drove back to his hotel, his mind buzzing with the new job he had taken. Ordinarily, when he had "P.A." letters to mail he drove into Holland or Switzerland; but this time he had been planning a trip to the Polish Corridor—for a reason having to do with his last talk with Adolf Hitler. Trying to find out the Führer's intentions regarding Poland, Lanny had invented on the spur of the moment a tale to the effect that he was thinking of purchasing a property in the Corridor and making it his home. Real-estate values would of course be affected by any action the Nazis took; if they moved in, many Poles would move out. Hitler had smiled and said that a little later Herr Budd might be able to drive a better bargain.

Now Herr Budd was uneasy in mind, because he knew that the Führer never forgot any detail, even the smallest; he would bring the matter up and ask questions, and you had better be sure you had your story straight. "Where is the property?" and "How big is it?" and "What are they asking for it?" To Lanny it appeared the part of wisdom to go and look at properties, and pick out one that seemed plausible; so he would be able to answer questions, and would have a pretext for bringing up the all-important subject of the Corridor once more. "Adi" would take up the conversation and blaze away at the Poles, and at their British and French and Jewish supporters; he would shout what he was going to do to them, and perhaps even set a date for the doing!

This Polish Corridor ran between Germany on the west and Danzig and East Prussia on the east; it gave Poland access to the Baltic, and represented one of the bright ideas of the Peace Conference of Paris, in which Lanny had played his small part as a youth. Twenty years ago, perhaps to a day, he had taken Lincoln Steffens and Colonel House to the apartment of his Red uncle, where they had met three representatives of the dreaded Bolsheviks, this being a part of President Wilson's effort to bring about a conference between the Russians and the western Allies. How Lanny and his liberal friends had agonized over the blunders being made by those elder statesmen, so hopelessly diverse in their points of view! The young liberals had clamored, foreseeing many calamities—but nothing so bad as the realities which now confronted the world.

Hitler had appeared in Europe; and by fraud and force, cunningly combined, he had got the German people behind him, as blindly fanatical as himself. Whenever he wanted some territory, his Nazis would begin singing, yelling, and beating up their opponents in that place; when the government put the disturbances down, that was an outrage against the *Herrenrasse*, one of a series of atrocities. Dr. Goebbels would spread them across the front pages of the newspapers he controlled—which was all the papers inside Germany, and others in the border countries, and in many of the great cities of the world, including New York and Chicago.

One of the earliest victims of this technique had been the "free city" of Danzig, supposed to be under the supervision of the League of Nations. The Danzig Nazis had seized the government, and the League had given up the struggle. Hitler was now demanding that both Danzig and the Corridor be turned over to him, and negotiations with Poland were going on, as secret as those with Czechoslovakia. Lanny's program was to travel to the Corridor and put the Czech terms into the airmail; then return to Berlin and begin a campaign to find out the terms for Poland.

X

There was a swarm of American journalists in Naziland, and the son of Budd-Erling took a lot of trouble to keep away from them; the last thing he wanted was publicity—except, of course, as an art expert. So as a rule he walked fast through the lobby of the Adlon, and never went into the bar or the lounge which these visiting journalists called their "Club." But that evening he made a slip; he ran into Pietro Corsatti in the lobby, face to face, and couldn't cut him dead. Pete was an old friend, dating back to the days soon after Mussolini had taken power and had had the Socialist Matteotti beaten to death by his gangsters; Lanny, visiting in Rome, had got word about it, had tipped Pete off, and then been bounced from Il Duce's New Roman Empire.

A long time ago, and it had been forgotten, and should have stayed so. Lanny should have made some quick excuse and ducked into the elevator; but it was his weakness that he liked people, and here was somebody he hadn't seen for several years. Pete had helped to get Lanny married to Irma Barnes, and naturally he wanted to ask how Irma was, and how Lanny was getting along, and what he was doing in Berlin. This Brooklyn-born Italian-American, who referred to the natives of his fatherland as "wops," now had a job as roving correspondent, picking up interesting stories wherever he could find them. Lanny had seen his stuff occasionally in New York papers which were to be bought at hotel newsstands in the capitals he visited.

They chatted for a bit, and it was self-indulgence on Lanny's part, because Pete was one of those journalists who had a lack of admiration for the Nazi-Fascists; and of course the spies in the Adlon would make note of everyone he talked to. Presently he remarked: "I'm on my way to the Polish border; there's a story I've got wind of."

Lanny then did something still more injudicious, saying: "I'm leaving for the Corridor, first thing in the morning. Why not let me take you in my car?"

"The place I have to visit is farther to the south, across the border from Schneidemühl."

"I could go that way just as well," said Lanny. "I'll be delighted to have your company."

"All right; it's a date!"

Belatedly the P.A.'s caution asserted itself. "One thing, Pete; you mustn't put me into any story. I have my reasons."

"Oh, sure thing," replied the newsman. "Never forget, I kept the secret of you and Irma—and that wasn't easy, believe me!"

XI

They had an early breakfast and by gray winter daylight were rolling across the flat plains of Prussia, deeply buried in snow. The soil which lay beneath was sandy and poor, and when the snow had melted, Polish workers would be imported to begin planting it with potatoes, the main staple of the German workers' diet. The land was cut by many small streams, but you hardly knew you were passing them, for the road was one of those four-lane *Autobahnen* which the engineer

Dr. Todt had built for his Führer's wars. Fruit trees had been planted on both sides of the road, according to a custom in this frugal country; by the size of the trees you could tell when the road had been built. The snow was kept cleared from it, and you could drive as fast as you thought safe.

On the way, the journalist told about the errand which was bringing him. Somebody had given him a tip as to where he might find the father of Herschel Grynspan. The name sounded familiar, but Lanny couldn't place it until his friend reminded him—the Jewish youth who had shot and killed Edouard vom Rath, of the Nazi embassy in Paris. Oh, yes, Lanny remembered; he didn't say that he had met this Prussian diplomat in Paris, a year or so before his death. The Jewish boy, only seventeen years of age, had emptied a revolver into him, and was now a prisoner of the French, awaiting trial for his life. Pete had got a tip that the boy's family were among the tens of thousands of Polish Jews who had been driven out of Germany only a week or two prior to the killing. Very probably that cruelty to his parents had had something to do with the mad act; anyhow, a man with a nose for news had decided that the world would be interested in learning about that family, and what its members had to say concerning the son, and his crime, and the tragic consequences it had brought upon the helpless Jews still in Naziland.

They talked about these dreadful events, Lanny, of course, being watchful of every word. Gone were the days when he was a young rebel full of dreams of a happier society and ready to take risks in the cause of the underdog. Here, instead, was a placid man of the world, who had learned that the unhappy planet wasn't going to be changed overnight, and that the old continent of Europe was especially set in its wicked ways. Lanny explained that his profession of art expert obliged him to meet all sorts of persons, and his father's activities as a manufacturer of military airplanes made it necessary for him to do business with the Nazis; the son had found that he was antagonizing everybody he knew, and had made up his mind that his only course was to forget the evil subject of politics.

A secret agent had used this camouflage many times; but it always hurt him, and he wasn't comforted by Pete's reply, that he could understand how Lanny felt, for he had a problem of much the same sort. He was a reporter, and wasn't supposed to express opinions, but merely to tell what he had seen and heard; his job depended upon his ability and willingness to "take policy," as newspapermen phrased it. Lanny was left to guess whether his old friend really meant this, or was just trying to comfort the son of Budd-Erling. In the former case it meant that Pete was corrupted, and in the latter it meant that Lanny was now helping to corrupt him by a bad example. In either case it was painful, and made Lanny wish he hadn't come on this trip. He resolved all over again that he mustn't permit himself the luxury of meeting the friends of his Pink days. Also, he dropped the idea which had crossed his mind, that Pete might be the man to make known to the world the Führer's demands upon the government of Czechoslovakia!

XII

The drive to Schneidemühl, capital of the province of Grenzmark, took about three hours. The border was near, and they obtained their visas and soon were in Poland; you knew it at once because the roads were of a poorer class, and likewise the houses. They were looking for a village with a superfluity of consonants in its name, and the track they followed had had only enough snow cleared away for a single vehicle; if you met another, you had to back up to a passing place. Presently they came to the village, and then began a strange experience; they were looking for a Jew named David Grynspan, and who knew where any Jew lived? They were scattered along the border, more than ten thousand of them, and nobody knew their names, or if they had any.

You just had to follow one track and then another, and question every Jew you saw. "*Bitte, wo wohnt David Grynspan?*" They all understood German, but not all would answer; they weren't deaf, but were dumb with fear; anybody in an automobile must be *Autorität*, which meant more trouble for the children of Israel. When Lanny realized this, he took to saying: "*Wir sind Amerikaner.*" That magic word would loosen tongues, but it didn't bring the information. No lists of the exiles had been furnished, there were no means of communication, and nobody knew anybody except the few who were neighbors in misery.

These hordes of Polish Jews had been gathered from all over Germany in the previous autumn. Many had never been in Poland and didn't know a word of the language; but because their parents had come from that land, they were Polish, and were loaded into cattle cars and transported to the border and dumped across with only such possessions as they had been able to carry in their hands or on top of their heads. Poland didn't want them, and wouldn't admit them into the country; they were existing in the most incredible destitution in a sort of No Man's Land along the border—always the Polish side, because armed Nazis marched on the German side of the barbed wire, ready to shoot anyone who ventured across. The exiles had sheltered themselves in tents, or in hastily built sod huts, many of them half underground, and roofed with poles, old boards, and scraps of tarpaper and tin. Where they got food the travelers had no chance to ask.

It took a couple of hours to find the Grynspan family. They were living in an abandoned cowshed with a dirt floor and a roof that would leak as soon as the snow melted. Three other families shared the place, each having its own corner. David Grynspan, a black-bearded man old in his fifties, sat shivering in a corner of this poorly heated place, wrapped in an old bathrobe. He was greatly disturbed by the appearance of two well-dressed strangers, and even the word *Amerikaner* failed to reassure him; he didn't want to be interviewed, he didn't want to say anything about his son, he was horrified at what the boy had done and at the dreadful pogrom which had followed in Germany. That much news had come across the border, it appeared.

In the Grynspan corner of the hut were his bowed and wrinkled wife, also a son and a daughter, both older than the unfortunate Herschel; they were orthodox Jews, and left it to the elder of the household to speak or be silent. They were literate people—the father had been a tailor for twenty-six years in Hanover, and they had thought they were Germans, and that a lifetime of hard work and honest living had guaranteed them security. Lanny, whose German was better than Pete's, stood for quite a while—there was nothing to sit on—explaining that they were friends, and that the only way the Jews could be helped was to let the outside world know about their condition. The Polish government very much needed the friendship of America, and a story published there might be the cause of persuading the Poles to give the exiles work.

"They will let us work in the fields in the spring," said the father; "but in winter there is no work to be done."

Little by little Lanny succeeded in gaining the wretched man's confidence. He had been badly beaten by a Gestapo agent at the time of his deportation, and was not sure if he would be well again. Since the coming of the Nazis none of his family had been allowed to work in Germany, and they had survived by selling their possessions from time to time. That was why David now had no overcoat to face the bitter winter of these Polish fields. At heavy sacrifice the family had sent Herschel to an agricultural school in Frankfurt-am-Main—this preparatory to the family's emigrating to Palestine. But troubles with the

Arabs had nullified that plan, and the boy had gone to Paris, where he had become a sewing-machine operator for an uncle. He had always been a quiet, studious fellow, and had never taken any part in politics— the only organization he had belonged to was the Jewish Misrachi.

When the father tried to talk about the killing, he broke down, and his wife had to put her arms about him and hold him up; he hadn't heard from the boy since the tragic event and didn't know what had happened. The older brother had written to Herschel, telling him about the beating of the father and the deportation of the family, and doubtless that news had driven Herschel out of his mind. None of the family had ever heard of Edouard vom Rath, and could only surmise that the boy had decided to shoot the first high Nazi official he could get near. Lanny didn't say anything about the terrible sights he had witnessed in Munich and Regensburg immediately after the news of the assassination had reached Germany.

XIII

That was the end of the interview. Lanny would have liked to put a couple of hundred-mark notes into the miserable man's hands, but he was afraid of the consequences—for how could a Jew change such notes, or keep from being robbed? The story would be pretty sure to travel, and the attention of the German authorities might be attracted to the visit and the visitors. Lanny took out of his pocket such small change as he had, and the journalist did the same; the poor exile couldn't refuse it, and tried to pour out his gratitude, but broke down again. The two Americans hurried away, for they had been reared in a different world, and the sight of such suffering made them mentally if not physically ill.

They got into the car and drove back to the village with too many consonants in its name. On the way they were both ashamed of themselves: of their way of life, and of the words they had spoken in the course of the day. They drove on by Bydgoszcz, which was the way the Poles preferred to spell Bromberg. The correspondent wished to write and file his story there—since it wasn't the sort that could be sent from Naziland. Lanny Budd, embarrassed, had to say: "Don't say anything about having had company, Pete. It could be very bad for me. I'd rather you didn't talk about me at all, if you don't mind." Pete said he wouldn't; and Lanny thought: "What a skunk he must think me!"

He consoled himself by locking himself in his hotel room, setting up his little portable typewriter, and writing out Adolf Hitler's eleven-point program for the liquidation of the Czechoslovakian Republic.

He made a copy and a carbon, and added on another sheet various items he had gathered from the Herr Doktor Schacht and from the airplane experts. One set of these documents he put into an envelope which he sealed and marked "103" and sealed this in a slightly larger envelope addressed to the man named Baker in a little brick house in Washington, D.C. The other set was addressed to Mrs. Nina Pomeroy-Nielson, in an obscure village on the river Thames. Both would carry airmail postage. Lanny had taken to sending important letters to Nina, because Rick was known as a writer, and a woman's name was less apt to attract attention.

Rick, being a very old hand at anti-Nazi propaganda, would recognize a world sensation when he saw one. He had an understanding with Lanny that he never used such material under his own name, which might direct suspicions of Gestapo agents toward Lanny. Rick knew an M.P. who would read this document in the House of Commons, while keeping secret the source from which he had got it. That was fighting the devil with his own fire—and it was the reason why Adolf Hitler hated democracy with such furious intensity, and could not endure to have a democratic nation anywhere near him, or indeed anywhere on the same earth with him.

7

Heute Gehört Uns Deutschland

I

THE Polish Corridor lies in what is called the Baltic plain: flat land with many lakes, and small streams meandering here and there, and what would be swamps if they were not drained. It is farming country with a mixed population, having been fought over since the dawn of history and conquered by Pomeranians and Brandenburgers, Poles, Danes and French. The survivors had stayed on, and seemed willing enough to live peaceably, if their politicians had let them; but they wouldn't. Just now it was the Nazis, strutting everywhere in their shiny boots, demanding as a matter of principle a freedom which they denied to everyone else.

There were many small estates suited for a country gentleman, and Lanny found one near the small town of Kartuzy. There was a double row of ancient beech trees leading from the road. The house appeared to be in good repair, and there was an orchard, and a stream which would contain trout—or would it be carp? Anyhow, the asking price, thirty-two thousand marks, was about right. "This is my home," the visitor said to himself, with an inward grin; it looked desolate with the trees bare and everything snowbound, but in spring it would be pleasant enough, though lonely, unless he chose to cultivate the local gentry.

The owner was a Pole, a veteran of the last war, now in his fifties, tall, erect, with flashing dark eyes and black mustaches beginning to turn gray. He was excited by the appearance of an American millionaire—so Lanny with his fine car must assuredly be. He insisted on the visitor's coming inside to inspect the house, and then upon serving coffee. He was anxious to find a purchaser, and gave many reasons: he was a widower, his two sons were officers in the army, he had business in Warsaw—every reason except the right one, that he feared the Nazis and the trouble that was coming. Lanny engaged him in conversation, for it was worth while to know how the Poles were thinking. This one had been in the cavalry, and his long lance stretched across one wall of his smoking room, with a sword and brace of pistols underneath.

The fire of combat still smoldered in his eyes. The Poles were a peace-loving people, he declared, but proud, and by no means to be trampled on. They had constructed a magnificent new port at the foot of this Corridor, and meant to keep it. They had seen what happened to the Czechs, and it was surely not going to happen to Poles—not if the present speaker had to take down his lance and ride forth on the great-grandson of the charger he had ridden all the way to Lemberg, which he spelled Lwow and pronounced Lvuff. Lanny had a sudden vision of Polish cavalry with pennons on its lances charging against those monster tanks which he had seen roaring about the practice fields near Berlin and Munich—any one of them able to spit enough fire to wipe out a whole squadron of horses and men. But he didn't say anything; he was here to listen.

The landowner forgot his role as salesman, and talked about the iron determination of his country. The spirit of the army was magnificent, and the Nazis, if they ventured an attack, would get the shock of their lives; but of course the holding of a district so advanced would depend upon prompt support from the West. Did Monsieur Budd—they were speaking French, never the hated German—believe that the French would appreciate the importance of prompt attack? Lanny replied that it was difficult to say; the Maginot Line was not planned for attack, and the attitude of Belgium was problematical.

"You wouldn't take help from the Russians, I suppose," the visitor remarked, and the other replied: "*Jamais, jamais! Les Bolchœviques sont pire que les Nazis—si une telle chose est possible.*"

The ex-lancer talked freely about conditions in Danzig, a half-hour drive away, where the Nazis had seized power, and were trying to wrest control of the city's foreign affairs away from the Poles. Border incidents were frequent, and they all followed one pattern, of aggression followed by brazen lying in the Nazi press; it was hard for a civilized man to believe that such things were happening, and the Polish host seemed to have the idea that if he could convince one American visitor of the facts he would go out and do something to remedy the situation.

Only when the guest was prepared to leave did he seem to realize that he had been giving the wrong line of talk for a real-estate salesman. He hastened to declare that none of these matters should trouble an American; the Germans had great respect for that nation, on account of the licking they had got in the Meuse-Argonne, and which they would not soon forget. Lanny said he understood that; he was looking at properties, but couldn't say as yet what he would do. The host expressed the pleasure it had been to meet him, and the polyglot guest replied: "*Dzieke tobie, panie*"—which he had learned on his last visit to this country, some seventeen years ago.

II

Driving back to Berlin, Lanny turned on the radio of his car, and came upon a station playing a transcription of Beethoven's *Eighth Symphony*. The Nazis played him continually; they played all the classics, having so few creative artists of their own, and these few third-rate. Beethoven in association with Dr. Goebbels' propaganda always started a war in Lanny's mind; he took the liberty of speaking for the great soul-compeller, saying that he wanted nothing to do with this gangster crew, these poisoners of civilization. Just as Beethoven had torn up the dedication page of the *Eroica* when Napoleon had accepted a crown, so now he spurned the praises which Juppchen Goebbels' hirelings showered upon him.

Pessimistic thoughts besieged an art lover on this solitary drive. It seemed to him that Beethoven's Germany had been dying for at least a quarter of a century. The people of courage and vision had all been murdered, or were languishing in concentration camps, being undermined mentally as well as physically. Modern Germany was a garden in which the flowers had been rooted out and the weeds had grown into a mephitic jungle. The same thing was true of the Italy of Garibaldi and Mazzini; it was true of Spain, and now of Austria; it would soon be true of Czechoslovakia, and then of France. Ever since Lanny's boyhood he had watched the France of the revolution decaying by slow stages, and the France of the new revolution being aborted. A year of the dreariest prospects, this 1939!

But the music of Beethoven went on dancing, went on singing, went on calling to Lanny Budd. The great soul-compeller had been burdened with many cares, had suffered pain, had faced the agony of knowing that his deafness was increasing, and that soon he would never again hear his own music or others'; yet he had risen above these troubles, and written this gayest of symphonies, without a note of sorrow. The tripping themes came back again and again, inviting Lanny to laughter, shouting to him; they were Beethoven in his "unbuttoned mood," not to be resisted. He was proclaiming that hope springs eternal in the human breast; that new generations of men would arise, stronger, braver, wiser than those who were now failing so dismally in their tasks. Evil things would pass, and God would not always be mocked.

The music swept on to that climax which is generally accepted as a burlesque of the pompous music of Beethoven's time, the thumping and blaring with which every composer felt it necessary to conclude every composition of any size. Lanny, diverted from the sorrows of Europe, found himself thinking: "What is a joke in music, and how can you be sure it is a joke unless the composer tells you so?" He thought: "How many of the critics today would know it was a joke if they hadn't been taught it in music school? How many of the uninstructed concertgoers know it, and how many think it is a grand and stirring climax, such as every composition of any size ought to have?"

These questions brought Laurel Creston into Lanny's mind. She asked them and he answered in another learned discourse. He liked to talk, and she, apparently, liked to listen. They had got along very well together, and now it seemed the most natural thing in the world that Miss Creston should have been hearing the *Eighth Symphony*, and should wish to know what he thought about it, and what his half-sister Bess and her husband, Hansi Robin, had said about it. A mass of human experience has been stored up in art, and it has been discussed and commented upon in millions of books and billions of conversations; this is called "culture," and Miss Creston had some and wanted more. She had taken to coming frequently into a P.A.'s imagination with her questions.

III

A lonesome sort of job that Lanny Budd had drifted into. Here in a land of seventy million people, just increased to eighty, there wasn't a single one to whom he might speak his real thoughts. Monck was a partial exception, but Lanny wasn't even sure if he would meet Monck again. But here was one woman with whom he could at least have chats concerning music and art and family and friends and home; to whom he could at least make playful remarks concerning the humorous behavior of the Germans *zu Hause*. A great temptation, and Lanny thought about it from many aspects. He had just had an experience of meeting his old friend Pete and not being happy over it; how was it going to be with this new friend?

Awkward, from every point of view that he could think of. So far, he had been meeting Miss Creston semi-clandestinely; but how long could that go on? She was living in a pension, and Lanny knew that these places are hotbeds of gossip; his friend Jerry Pendleton had married one in Cannes, and helped to run it, and told funny stories about it. Everybody knew everything about everybody else and Lanny could be sure that in the Pension Baumgartner of Berlin everybody was wondering about that elegant American Herr Budd with whom *"die Miss"* went out.

Doubtless they had read an article about an American *Kunstsachverständiger* named Budd who enjoyed the friendship of the Führer. Lanny could imagine the clamor: *"Ach, Fräulein, ist das Ihr Herr Budd?"* Is that *your* Mr. Budd? She couldn't very well have said *Nein*; and if she had said *Ja*, they would all have one idea in the world, to meet him, or at least to have a look at him the next time he came. To the servants and guests of the pension the Führer would be God; purely and simply God, with no qualifications; not the Jewish God with a long gray beard, of course, but the modern *echt deutscher Gott* with a little Charlie Chaplin mustache. *Preis und Ehre sei Gott!*

And what would *die amerikanische Miss* say about this God? Would it be anything less than full reverence? If so, there would be a scandal; *die Amerikanerin* was going out with the Führer's intimate friend, but she herself frowned, made faces, sneered, or at any rate displayed something less than adequate appreciation of the greatness of the greatest man in the world. That scandal might grow until it became something to be brought to the attention of the Gestapo.

And could Lanny warn the lady concerning these dangers? Could he say: "I am doing business with these Nazis, and my father is doing the same. Our interests compel us to pretend that we like and admire them. If I am to take you to concerts and art galleries, you will have to pretend that you feel the same way"? He had already said something much milder than that in Sophie's home, and the lady's reply had been to call him a troglodyte. Now he would be saying, in effect: "I am a troglodyte, and intend to remain one." That was his right, of course; but who wants to hear what a troglodyte thinks about Beethoven, or Rembrandt, or any of the great soul-compellers of the ages?

No, it just wouldn't do. He could not go on cultivating a friendship with this woman writer in Berlin. And where else in the world could he cultivate it? Surely not on the Riviera, where she had already made a scandal about him! Or in Paris, or London, or New York? These five places, Lanny's haunts, were, from the point of view of smart society, the most important in the world; and in no one of them could he carry on any sort of clandestine relationship. He had his circle and Miss Creston had hers, but these circles had intersected on the Cap, and would surely intersect anywhere else.

Laurel Creston was going out from Hitlerland to write short stories about it. She had been observing the people of the Pension Baumgartner for that purpose—she had said it in so many words; she had described one person after another, in her bright satiric way. And she wouldn't deal with them from the purely human point of view, *Pickwick Papers* style; no, she would ridicule them as worshipers of the Charlie Chaplin *Gott*. It might very well be that her stories would make a hit, and be incorporated into a book and reviewed widely. Dr. Goebbels might write a smear article about it in *Das Reich;* and what sort of *dossier* would that provide for the Gestapo, that the son of Budd-Erling, the friend of the leading Nazis, was an intimate of this female defamer of the Herrenvolk and their heaven-sent Führer? *Nein, Nein* and again *Nein!* It was playing with dynamite, and a form of treason to the job of presidential agent! There simply could be no more of Laurel Creston in Lanny Budd's life—so he decided, once for all.

IV

Arriving in Berlin, Lanny got his mail. There was nothing from Monck, so he resumed his duties as collector of gossip. He called up the

Fürstin Donnerstein, who had been Irma's friend long ago, and who knew everybody who was anybody in Germany. A peculiar psychological phenomenon, the state of mind of these old-time aristocrats of Prussia toward the Nazi upstarts—a mixture of contempt and grudging respect. They were crude, they were ridiculous—but they had arrived and apparently meant to stay for a while, so make the best of them and get what you could out of them. They were, in effect, a measure of the gullibility of the German masses; they were what it took to hold these masses down; and while it was humiliating to have your country represented by such men, at least your property was safe and there were no more Red agitators to mess up either politics or industry.

So, in the privacy of your own drawing-room, after you had made sure the servants were not within earshot, you could relieve your mind by repeating the latest choice anecdotes—about *Die Nummer Zwei* taking to drugs again and pretending that his breakdown was because he was reducing weight; about *Die Nummer Drei's* latest astrological mentor, and the high price of *Die Nummer Vier's* champagne. The numbers were uncertain beyond that, but the little club-footed propaganda Doktor was still sleeping with a new actress every night, in spite of the Führer's strict orders. Doktor Ley was drunk every night and so was Doktor Funk; there were rumors that Doktor Schacht wanted to move to Wall Street, and that Fritz Thyssen had fled to Switzerland and was going to tell the story of how and why he had given five million marks to the Führer.

Lanny sat in the Fürstin Hilde's cozy sitting-room before a coal-grate fire, and watched this thin and rather hectic lady smoking many cigarettes and getting what pleasure she could out of a sense of superiority to the rest of the world. It seemed to him a thin sort of pleasure, but many enjoyed it, and millions would have given their right arms to be addressed as "princess" and be able to meet all these great and powerful persons. It saved Lanny a lot of time going about to tiresome receptions, and he repaid the *hohe Dame* by telling her the latest news from Paris: how the French had received the Ribbentrop visit and what this and that member of the Cabinet had said about the champagne deale. and his friendship proposals. The Prussian aristocracy do not like having persons break into their sacred fold by the method of adoption; they despised this *Emporkömmling* and found it hard to remain patriotic with him as Foreign Minister.

Lanny said that what had done most to weaken German prestige in France was the pogroms, and to this Hilde assented without reservation. He remarked that the French were postponing the trial of the

Jewish boy, Grynspan, because they were afraid of stirring up mani-
festations on behalf of the Jews. There came a gleam into Hilde's blue
eyes, and she said: "Have you heard what happened at Rath's funeral?"

No, Lanny hadn't; and the Fürstin got up and went to the door of
her sitting-room, opened it, and looked out—a ceremony meaning that
words of dangerous import were about to be spoken.

"They brought the body to Düsseldorf in state; the casket was set
up in church and the old father came to mourn. *Die Nummer Eins*
came in, and started to console him, saying that the son had died for
Germany, and that the whole nation would avenge the murder. But
the father stopped him. 'I do not wish to hear of vengeance,' he said.
'It is you who are to blame for Edouard's death—you with your cruel
persecution which drove the poor Jewish boy to madness.' *Die Nummer
Eins* stood there, pale with fury, then turned on his heel and walked
out, and refused to deliver the funeral address. But he did not dare
to punish the father, or even to dispute with him, for fear of the scandal. Apparently we of the old nobility still enjoy a certain amount of
immunity."

"Don't count upon it too much," warned the American. "Remember
General von Schleicher!"

V

Next on the list was Heinrich Jung. Lanny telephoned to his home
and heard an official of the Hitlerjugend exclaim, what a charming and
informative interview that was in the "*Völkischer.*" Everybody was
talking about it, and Heinrich was proud to be able to say that he had
known Lanny Budd since boyhood, and indeed had been the first to
make him acquainted with National-Socialist principles. "How far we
have traveled in twenty-five years, Lanny! And how surprised we
should have been, had we been able to foresee it! No doubt we'd be
even more surprised if we could foresee the next twenty-five!"

Heinrich wanted to introduce this famous *Kunstsachverständiger* to
his Party associates. Wouldn't he come to dinner and a reception the
following evening? Lanny couldn't think of anything that would bore
him more, but it was a duty and he accepted. He took his presents for
the children, and they were appreciated by both young and old. Heinrich was, apparently, one of the few Party officials who didn't make
money on the side; at any rate, he lived in a style commensurate with
his salary. Also, he and his wife were among the not-too-numerous
Nazis who conformed to the Aryan ideal; they were both blonds, and

pleasant to the eye—if you didn't mind that a middle-aged man had grown large about the waist, and that the mother of a brood had become plump and pudgy.

How proud they were to have this elegant man of the world in their humble home, and how much they made of him, pressing food upon him, laughing over his witticisms, and doing everything in their power to show him off to the *Parteigenossen!* A living proof that the great land across the seas was coming to appreciate the Herrenvolk, its Führer, and the wonderful movement he had made! Indeed, it was as if the son of Budd-Erling were America, all by himself, and a little bit of France and England, too. They who came to this *Empfang* were Germany; they, the chiefs of the Hitlerjugend, were most of them people of humble origin, *Kleinbuerger* like Hitler himself, and now they had charge of the new generations, and taught them what to think, and how to prepare for the defense of the Fatherland and the spreading of its message and its glory over the world.

They were sitting on the top of that world right now. They had seen their wonderful Führer marching from one triumph to the next, and had become certain that there was nothing he could not do. He had militarized the Rhineland, established conscription in Germany, and forced the Allies to abandon their control over German arms manufacture; he had taken Austria, and then the Sudetenland—unimaginable victories! The Munich settlement represented to all Party comrades the collapse of British and French resistance to the Führer's will, and they took it for granted that Prague, Danzig, Memel, Vilna, the Corridor—all would tumble like ninepins. Then would come the colonies, and the Ukraine—the Führer had invited them to contemplate the marvels he would be able to perform if only he had the wheat and coal and oil, the nickel and manganese of that vast territory—and they were doing that contemplating. They did it in the presence of Herr Budd, who was no stranger, but a blood brother. It was well known that the best blood in America was German, and the second-best was English, which had come originally from Germany, as was proved by all the basic words in their language: *Gott und Mann, Vater und Mutter, Blut und Land und See und Himmel und Donnerwetter*.

So it was a family reunion, and as tiresome as such affairs are apt to be. The men were nearly all World War veterans, which meant that they were close to their fifties. They had thick necks and red faces, and when they had filled themselves with sausage sandwiches and beer the necks were thicker and the faces redder. They were all propagandists, having risen by that means, and this meant that they made speeches even when talking to one another. The honor they paid to Lanny Budd was based upon the fact that he had had the good sense to recognize them and their achievements; he shone by reflected light, and was grateful for having it shed upon him. The *Parteigenossen* sputtered and coughed over their mouthfuls of gutturals and *Wurst*, and Lanny wasn't supposed to flinch from any attack, whether salivary or dialectical. This was the *Neue Ordnung*, and you had better hurry up and learn to like it.

VI

Rudolf Hess, Deputy Führer and Reichsminister, had also read the article in the "*Völkischer*" and found it "O.K."—so he said over the phone. He was very busy, for he had all the conduct of the NSDAP on his hands, and as the Reich extended its boundaries, so did the Party, and the Party manager had new groups of subordinates to choose and to direct. But he took time off to take Lanny to lunch at Horcher's, in the Lutherstrasse, a place frequented by the leading Nazis. They had a private dining room and sat for a long time discussing the things that were near to their hearts.

Lanny had taken the trouble to think up psychic matters which would interest his host. For this black-browed, stern fanatic, so greatly dreaded by all the self-seeking and self-indulgent Party chieftains, had a soft side to his nature; he had had supernormal experiences, and he didn't have enough understanding of the subject to distinguish between what might be true and what couldn't be. He was a patron of every sort of eccentric—astrologers and palmists, numerologists and readers of tea-leaves. Lanny had brought Madame Zyszynski to him and might bring her again—which was one reason why he would always have access to the head of the NSDAP, even at the head's busiest times.

Lanny had visited America since their last meeting, and had learned about the work being done at Duke University in what was there called "parapsychology." Lanny preferred dealing with truth wherever truth would serve his purposes, so now he told how in hundreds of thousands of tests it was being proved that one person could really tell the face of cards which another person was turning up in another room. Some persons could even tell what cards were going to be turned up before they were turned. Nothing less easy to believe had ever been claimed by any astrologer or palmist, and the orthodox psychologists were behaving as Galileo's contemporaries had done when he invited them to watch him drop weights from the leaning tower of Pisa. Lanny told

Hess about it, and the Deputy listened eagerly, and doubtless would take it as reason for believing anything that any of his astrologers and palmists would tell him.

For purposes of his own Lanny had caused Hess to believe in the psychic gifts of a certain Professor Pröfenik, an elderly mystagogue who was practicing in Berlin. Now Lanny asked if Hess had seen him of late, and the Deputy replied that he had paid another visit, and had been told a number of significant things, including the fact that the Führer was soon to achieve another great victory. "Will he?" asked the American, smiling; and the reply was: "It looks as if he will have to, whether he wishes it or not." That was a remark which needed no soothsayer to interpret.

Lanny inquired how the Führer was, and the devoted Deputy reported him well in health but annoyed by the complex of problems which had developed out of the Munich settlement. Both Führer and Deputy had talked to Lanny about their fears, and now the latter said that these fears had been justified. The miserable Czechs—the dregs of creation—showed no gratitude for the favor which had been done them in permitting them to retain their "independence." They were devoting themselves to thwarting the arrangements which the Führer had made for the administration of Slovakia—and of course the British and French were egging them on. "They seem determined to find out how much we will stand," remarked the Deputy. "They may make the discovery that it is less than they thought."

Said Lanny: "I have heard reports that the Führer is annoyed with those who persuaded him to accept the Munich settlement."

"Well, Herr Budd, you know how he is; he has a hunch, and has learned to follow it. If he weakens and gives way to others, and troubles result, as they are doing now, he naturally says: 'I should have done what I wanted to do. I am the one who knows!' "

"That means that you and I are both in the doghouse?" They were speaking English, which Hess knew as well as German, having been born and brought up in British-ruled Egypt.

"I wouldn't say it's quite that bad," smiled the Deputy, a genial person when you got under his dour exterior. "At any rate, it won't be so with you."

"Is that the reason why Hermann has decided to have a rest in Italy?"

The Deputy smiled even more broadly. "I didn't have a chance to ask him. But I warned him years ago how much easier it is not to put on weight than to take it off again."

Lanny knew how to interpret that. Hess was a fighting man, an athlete who kept himself in trim; like his adored Führer, he neither drank nor smoked. But Göring was one of those Nazis whose hoggish greed, for money as well as for food and drink, constituted a scandal in the Deputy's eyes. It was, perhaps, too much to expect that Number Three should approve entirely of Number Two; yet Lanny knew that Göring and Hess were fairly close together in their views of policy; they were the conservatives among the group surrounding the Führer, and wanted him to go slow and to conciliate Britain and France, at least for the present. The radicals and activists were Goebbels and Ribbentrop, and the hatred of Göring and Hess for this pair was positively poisonous; they would have been at one another's throats if it had not been for the fact that the Führer needed all four, and managed them like a trainer with a cageful of wild animals.

VII

Lanny sat studying the countenance of this apostle of National Socialism. His heavy black eyebrows met over his eyes, forming a straight line across his face. His mouth made another such line when he was in his dour mood, which was often. His eyes were grayish-green, and when he fixed them upon some Party delinquent he made the wretch tremble. He had been the Führer's secretary in the early days and had helped to write *Mein Kampf* in the fortress of Landsberg. He was fanatical in his loyalty, and Lanny had seen enough of the world to know that this is a quality far from common.

This was a man with whom Lanny might have made a friendship in happier days. They might have played tennis and taken walking tours in the mountains; they might have undertaken researches into the nature and causes of psychic phenomena, and tried to sort out fact from fancy in that universe of the subconscious mind. But they had been born in a period of wars and revolutions, and it was their fate to be on opposite sides. Which one of them was right was something that history would decide. Meantime, the fact stood that Hess was fanatically determined to compel Europe to take his path; and Lanny was here as a false friend, watching him, studying how to worm his secrets out of him, with the intention of ultimately tripping him up and binding him hand and foot.

Whenever Lanny wanted to receive, he first gave generously. He discussed the attitude of the French politicians to the new German friendship agreement; he told about the Schneider banquet and what had been said there. The collapse of the Reds in Spain had pretty nearly broken the back of those elements in Paris, and "appeasement" was now accepted as an inevitability. The same thing was true in London, which Lanny had visited since he had last seen Hess. "You mustn't pay too much heed to their commercial press," declared the American. "The people who really govern Britain are now pretty nearly solid for a settlement with Germany."

"It means a lot to me to hear you say that," replied the other. "I have just about staked my reputation with the Führer on that subject. He doesn't know the English very well, and it is a question whether he will take my word or Ribbentrop's."

"It will require time, but I feel certain that with a little good will on both sides, difficulties can be ironed out."

Lanny mentioned his trip to the Corridor, to have what he called "another look" at his future home. "I am waiting," he remarked with a smile, "because I wouldn't want to live in Poland."

"I think you can be sure that situation will not remain in its present unsatisfactory state."

"Yes—but I'm being mercenary. I don't see any reason for paying a Pole more money than I have to."

"I am not so sure the price will come down," remarked the Deputy Führer. "There are a great many Germans who have the same idea as you, and are planning to move into both the Corridor and the Danzig district the moment it becomes a part of the Reich."

"Maybe so," laughed Lanny, "but this Polish landowner hasn't met any of them. He behaved like the Jew proprietor of a second-hand clothing store, trying to pull a customer in."

"Somebody ought to explain to those people that they can't behave the way the Czechs did a few months ago, and have been doing ever since. The Führer is in no mood to be bluffed a second time, and I doubt if anybody can restrain him much longer. I know for one that I'm not going to try."

"Nor is Hermann?" inquired Lanny, with a grin.

VIII

More than anything else the Führer's closest friend wanted to know about the French attitude to their alliance with the Bolsheviks. Was there any chance of its being implemented by military preparations? Was there any possibility that secret exchanges of plans and information were now going on? Lanny told about the visit of Denis de Bruyne to General Gamelin, embellishing it somewhat. The high-up French officers were old and tired; the World War had been too much for them, and they hadn't learned anything in twenty years. They looked upon Russia with the same abhorrence that Hess did, and their ideas of law and order differed very little from those of the Nazis. Day by day they were coming to realize more clearly that the Russian deal had put them in the wrong camp.

"For God's sake try to wake them up!" exclaimed Hess. "That situation is a perpetual provocation to us, a red rag waved in the Führer's face. Why cannot the French leaders make up their minds, and be either our friends or our enemies?"

"It takes time to overcome an hereditary antagonism like that between the two countries. The Führer must have patience."

"Patience is not the most conspicuous of his qualities, Herr Budd. We see our country surrounded by intrigues and treacheries; and we are people who know our own minds, and say frankly what we mean."

"I know; that is why I am here, as your friend and the Führer's. Tell me this: can there be any truth in the rumors as to a possibility of your making some sort of counter-deal with the Russians?"

"No man that lives can say what might or might not come out of this situation. I can only tell you my own attitude—I would regard it as the greatest calamity in history. All my hopes are staked upon friendship between Germany and the Anglo-Saxon peoples, including your own. It is almost as if I were part English, having been brought up in an English community, and knowing them so well. During the twenty years that I have been the Führer's secretary and closest associate, I have tried to persuade him to that point of view, and I know that I've had some influence—you will see many traces of it in *Mein Kampf*. But I am not all-powerful, and cannot work miracles. We offer friendship and make one concession after another; but the British ruling classes seem hopelessly tied to their balance-of-power tradition. How can we persuade them to trust us?"

"I see many signs that you are making headway, Herr Hess."

"They are our friends so long as they see France rich and strong. The moment France shows signs of weakness, they become our enemies again. They play dirty politics with the Bolshevik bandits—just enough to keep us worried, and to compel us to spend more money on armaments. When the Führer presents me with fresh evidences of this treacherous policy, what can I say? When he quotes to me the ancient phrase, *perfide Albion*, what can I appear to him but a dreamer and dupe?"

"I hope you will not give way, my friend. I know some of Ribbentrop's crowd, and have heard the arguments he presents to the Führer."

"Not a day passes that I do not hear them, Herr Budd. Germany and Russia are natural allies, because we are an industrial country and they are agricultural. They can supply us with unlimited quantities of raw materials, taking our machine products in return. Our enemies in the last war set up barriers to keep us apart, and nothing in the world would cause those enemies so much pain as to see us tear down those barriers, and divide the land between us. Nothing stands in the way but ideological differences; and men who are cynical and have no real beliefs find it easy to contemplate taking off one coat and putting on another."

"It is indeed a painful thing to contemplate, Herr Hess. Some who claim to know tell me that there is a strong pro-German party in Moscow at the present time."

"I don't suppose Stalin has shot them all—and possibly he wishes that he hadn't shot so many."

"I am expecting to leave for London before long, and one of the first questions Lord Wickthorpe is going to ask me is about this possibility of appeasement moves between you and the Soviets. There is nothing that worries the British quite so much."

"That is the most dangerous element in this situation. We use these threats to worry each other, and presently we work ourselves into a situation where we are tempted to make the threats good. So far as I am concerned, I would rather you told the truth, that I contemplate the idea with abhorrence, and am striving with all my heart for a settlement of all the problems outstanding between us and both Britain and France."

"And what shall I say about the Führer's attitude?"

"I think he would prefer to tell you that himself."

"He will have time to see me?"

"I am sure he will take time."

"And not be too cross with me for having helped persuade him into the Munich settlement?"

"He gets cross with me because I am a German, and he thinks I should not let myself be taken into camp by Germany's enemies. But it will seem perfectly natural to him that an American should be pleading for patience and understanding. He saw last time how the British succeeded in dragging America into the quarrel, and he surely doesn't want that to happen again."

"Indeed not, Herr Hess. My father and I find that as painful to contemplate as you find co-operating with the Bolsheviks."

"Tell that to the Führer, and try to persuade him not to take the Jewish-owned press of London too seriously. I am going to see him tomorrow and will try to make an appointment for you. I'll put him in as amiable a mood as possible, though I cannot promise, for just now the miserable Czechs are behaving like a gang of rowdy boys on our back doorstep."

IX

In spite of all resolutions and all preoccupations, Lanny found himself thinking about Laurel Creston. Was she still at the Pension Baumgartner, and if so, what was she doing, and especially, what was she thinking about him? It was extremely rude of him to break off the acquaintance without a single word; but what word could he say? After all, was there any reason, because he had taken a lady to a concert and two art museums, that he should be considered under obligation to take her somewhere else, or to explain why he didn't? She knew that he was here on business, and mightn't she assume that he had become suddenly busy, and just didn't have time to spend on sightseeing?

But Lanny knew that she wouldn't assume that. She would assume that he was tired of her, and had decided that she didn't come up to his expectations, whatever they were. Well, that was his privilege, surely, and no moral wrong. She had taken the right to tell him what she thought of him, and surely he had the right not to hear any more of it if he didn't wish to! He had satisfied his curiosity, and now had taken the privilege of going elsewhere and meeting persons who would say pleasant things to him—or at least wouldn't call him long names of Greek origin: *trogley*, a cave, and *duein*, to enter.

Her feelings would be hurt; and Lanny was a softhearted fellow who didn't like to hurt anybody's feelings, especially not somebody whom he admired and would have been glad to have for a friend. It was out of the question, of course; he had figured over it from every point of view, and given it up as hopeless. He couldn't write her a polite note and give some excuse—because there just wasn't any excuse. To say that he was too busy would be worse than nothing, because his work obviously wasn't of that sort. He could surely have found a couple of minutes to telephone and say that he had been called out of town. Now he was back in town; and if she saw him, or read about him in the paper, or was told about him by somebody in the pension, matters would be no better.

He just had to drop her. He couldn't have any woman friend, except those he had already—most of them old enough to be his mother. His duty required that; but then, Mother Nature has made man so that he often comes into conflict with his duty, a man-made thing the greater part of the time. Neither Nature nor God had made presidential agents, and laid upon them the injunction to pretend to love the things they hated and to hate the things they loved. Now Mother Nature kept bringing Laurel Creston to Lanny Budd's mind, and causing him to worry because he was treating her with heartless discourtesy.

It couldn't do any harm to think about her—so he told himself. What sort of person was she really, and how had she come by ideas so different from those of "good society" in the conservative old city of Baltimore? He might run into her again some day, either through the Holdenhursts or through her friends on the Riviera, and he was impelled to imagine how he would greet her, and what they would talk about. He mustn't be too cordial; no, rather cold, dignified—as much as to say: "Yes, of course I am a what-you-may-call-it, and it doesn't worry me in the least." Lanny, in his double role, had to learn to feel the emotions he expressed, and when he made these speeches he was quietly contemptuous of the impertinent Miss Creston.

But then, another mood, he was curious about her as a writer: a woman of talent, who really ought to be encouraged. In the great Prussian State Library, which was on Unter den Linden close to Lanny's hotel, were the many large volumes of the *Reader's Guide* indexes, in which are listed all the articles which have been published in American magazines of any importance. These volumes go back to the beginning of the century—which was considerably farther than Laurel Creston went. Lanny was tempted to stop in and look up her name, and he found half a dozen short stories listed. Three were in bound volumes in the Bibliothek, so Lanny spent part of an afternoon in the company of the lady whom he had just permanently renounced.

He found these stories like the one he had read previously: full of sharp, not to say acid humor. They all dealt with Americans of the leisure classes, with whom the author had been brought up. The locale didn't matter, for such Americans were always the same, well meaning but futile, and a target for satire in their efforts at self-importance. They all wanted to be "somebody"; they were bored at home, but took home with them wherever they went, and brought back only a few labels on their suitcases and a few tags of foreign words. "Coelum Non

Animum" was the title of one of the stories, in a highbrow magazine; the title was taken from a line of Horace: "They change their sky but not their mind who travel overseas." All three of the stories had what Lanny was pleased to call a "social" point of view, and when he went out from the library he was enjoying the privilege of telling the author his true opinion.

Then he said: "Oh, hell!" and went back to the Adlon to see if there was any message from Monck or Hess.

X

Lanny watched the co-ordinated press of Berlin. Morning, afternoon, evening, it was always the same, and its circulation kept falling because the Germans thought, what was the use of paying money when you knew in advance what you were going to find? In these early days of March it was Prague which held the front page, for Prague was insulting the government of Father Tiso which the Nazis had set up in Slovakia, and Berlin was raving at Prague, and it was obvious that something was being prepared, and was not far off. In his speech just prior to the Munich settlement Hitler had denied that there was any such country as Czechoslovakia, and now he was proving it by splitting the Slovaks off from the Czechs, to make a separate meal of each.

In the middle of this, London broke into the headlines; one of its hateful "democratic" newspapers published what it alleged to be the terms which Hitler had served upon Prague. The co-ordinated press of Berlin didn't say what the alleged terms were, but denounced them as fantastic, wholly without any basis in reality, and then went on to explain the impossibility of doing business with a people whose press was uncontrolled and irresponsible, Jewish-owned and Bolshevik- or banker-subsidized. So Lanny knew that his airmail letter had reached Rick, and that Rick had known what to do with it. He knew also that the head Nazis would know there was a highly placed spy among them, and a serious leak in their carefully constructed diplomatic machine.

Lanny had been planning to attend an *Empfang* at the town house of his old friend Graf Stubendorf that evening. The top Nazis would be there, and Lanny knew that whatever they talked about, the first thing in their thoughts would be this mystery; they would be eyeing one another and asking, inwardly, who was the traitor that had sold out or the fool that had blabbed? Lanny saw them in his mind's eye, for he had been several times to that palace of gray Swedish granite on the Königin Augustastrasse, and met the elegant company in the paneled drawing-rooms. He saw the poisonous little doctor, limping here and there on his clubfoot—he would not be fooled by his own propaganda, but would know that somebody had betrayed the Führer, and he would be turning his keen dark eyes from one face to the next, trying to pierce to the secret thoughts behind them. Very dangerous to be near "Juppchen" Goebbels that evening!

And the champagne salesman, handsome, urbane, looking like a diplomat in the movies; cynical, unscrupulous, and with a fire of hatred burning in his heart against England and Englishmen, who had judged him a clown and by no means the gentleman he aspired to be. He would hate Americans because they spoke English and looked English and were generally on the English side when it came to a showdown. He would look about the room and espy an American; the only one, in all probability—for Stubendorf was a Junker from the *Junkertum*, and only tolerated the grandson of Budd Gunmakers because he had been a visitor to Stubendorf since boyhood and had known the old Graf, and, moreover, had been married to one of the richest women in the world.

Ribbentrop wouldn't know all that. His eyes would light on Lanny, and his thoughts would be: "What, exactly, is this *Ausländer* doing among us, and could it be that he is the source of this dangerous leak?" Others might have the same thought, and any one of them might be moved to pick up the telephone and call Gestapo headquarters and speak to the ex-schoolteacher with the blank face and the demon's soul, whispering: "Has it ever occurred to you to watch that fellow Lanny Budd, who boasts of being the Führer's friend?" Heinrich Himmler never went to receptions—he had no time for such nonsense; he would be in his office, day and night, giving hell to his subordinates because they hadn't plugged that leak. He would be ransacking his files and his memory, trying to get some hint as to the identity of the traitor or fool; and if ever his attention were called to Lanny Budd, the career of a P.A. would be just about finished; even if they didn't get anything definite, they would follow him everywhere he went, open all his mail, cross-question and alarm his friends and in general make it impossible for him to enjoy life in Naziland.

XI

Lanny decided to lead a strictly inconspicuous life for the next few days. He bethought himself of Emil Meissner, Kurt's brother, whom he had promised to look up. The sound of Lanny's voice over the telephone touched one of the deepest heartstrings of a Prussian general; he heard, not a middle-aged art expert, but a little American boy who had come as a guest to his father's home at Christmas time, gazing with open-eyed wonder at a great Schloss with snow on its towers, and loving everybody and everything German. Lanny Budd had won the heart of Emil's mother and father, both now dead; he had been Kurt's loyal admirer and patron over a long period of years; and these things made him a member of the Meissner family so long as he chose to have it so. "Come to dinner, *en famille*," said Emil, and Lanny replied: "Fine!"

The Meissners had never been rich people; the father had had a modest salary as manager of the great Stubendorf estate. But Emil had a fine home and lived in style, far beyond what his pay as a general of the Reichswehr could cover. He had followed the practice of the Prussian officer caste, not to marry until he could find the daughter of a wealthy bourgeois family and induce the bride's parents to settle a handsome dowry upon her. Since you can't have everything, Emil's wife was somewhat lanky and bony; but she had borne him half a dozen children, and the boys were all in military schools, prepared to follow in their father's footsteps. Frau Meissner, daughter of a leather manufacturer, was keenly aware of her exalted position, dressed with elegance even *en famille*, sat as straight as a ramrod, watched her servants' every move, and rarely intruded her opinions upon the conversation.

Lanny could look back upon the time when Leutnant Emil Meissner had been interested to expound the Hegelian philosophy, very abstract and metaphysical, and Fichte's patriotic elaboration of the same; when he had attended art exhibitions with his youngest brother, and had played the flute in family *Weihnachts* gatherings. But those days were far in the past, and General Emil Meissner was now a professional man, absorbed in the technical problems of the most rapid and efficient killing of his fellow-men. Strange as it might seem, he was very little interested in those forces which might be leading up to war. "I leave politics to the politicians," he remarked, implying a dignified and patrician contempt for such activities. An army officer's job was simpler and more elementary: to be ready to go to war at the moment the order was given, and from that moment on to push forward to victory.

Lanny's job was to learn something from each and every person he met. So now he became the son of an airplane manufacturer, familiar with the technical terms of that industry both in English and in German. Emil warmed up, for his specialty was the co-ordinating of air activity with that of infantry and artillery; he and his fellow staff-members amused themselves by setting such problems for one another to solve. This tall, long-faced, solemn, and tightly buttoned officer got out charts and diagrams, and behaved like a child with his first set of tin soldiers.

So Lanny, who had never killed anybody in his life and never expected to, learned to consider the killing of thousands and even tens of thousands as a problem of mathematics, a function of trajectories, fire power, the expansion rates of gases, logistics, and other sciences with long technical names. His old friend withheld no secrets from him, for Lanny was Budd-Erling, and Emil knew a lot about the performance of Budd-Erling planes, and didn't know that Lanny's father was on the verge of a quarrel with the head of the Luftwaffe. Lanny listened attentively and remembered everything he could, for Rick had been a flyer, and so had Rick's son, Alfy, and they were intimate with Royal Air Force men who would be glad to have this information. Also, it might be possible for Denis de Bruyne to use it in an effort to frighten the pink-cheeked old General Gamelin into a semblance of mental activity.

XII

Coming back from this quiet evening, Lanny found in his mail one of those inconspicuous letters which made his heart beat faster. This one informed him, in a single sentence, that there was a possibility of getting a good Defregger if he would meet the writer that evening or the following one. It was too late for that evening, so Lanny had to spend a day rather restlessly, trying to occupy himself with picture business and wishing that he hadn't bunched his dangers so closely. If the most precious secret of the Wilhelmstrasse and that of the Luftwaffe were both stolen in the same week, the Gestapo would just about go crazy!

Promptly on schedule, Bernhardt Monck stepped into Lanny's car; and, as was his custom, he came straight to the point. "I cannot say positively, but I am assured that there is a good chance of our having what we want. I have not been told any of the details, except that if it can be done, it will be on next Saturday night, the idea being that the discovery will not be made until Monday morning, which will give us time to get the stuff out of the country."

"Is it the drawings or the actual thing?"

"The thing. I'm guessing it's a factory job, somebody in the manufacturing plant."

"Did you find out anything about the size or weight?"

"It's about the size of two suitcases put side by side, and it weighs about forty pounds. The problem is, how to get it past the border. My connections with ships have been severed, and I am afraid to try to renew them. Trudi had contacts with locomotive engineers who used to carry parcels for her—but most of those comrades are in concentration camps now. Much literature has been smuggled into Germany under loads of hay in peasant carts; but it takes time to arrange a thing like that, and if the alarm were given in this case, they would go through every vehicle leaving the country. I have thought of the possibility of taking the gadget to pieces and getting the parts out separately—or possibly hiding them here and there in a car or under it. The thing consists mostly of pipes, I am told, and I suppose your father's experts would know how to put it together again."

"You can reasonably assume that."

"I have the idea that a fast motor car would be my best bet; one that would get me to the Dutch border in a few hours."

That sounded like a hint, and Lanny said: "I wish I could help you, Monck, but I have told you my circumstances."

"All I'm looking for is advice—two heads being better than one. The money you have given me would suffice to buy a good car; the only problem is, if I have the purchase made, and then the gadget is not obtainable, I have wasted a lot of money."

"The car could be sold again; and anyhow, don't hesitate to take the chance. When my father wants something, he wants it, and he would wreck a dozen cars to get his way."

"All right; if that's the word, I'll go ahead. I can arrange to have a chauffeur's uniform bought for me, and if the car is registered in the name of some person who lives abroad, I imagine I could get past the border unless a special alarm had been given."

"That sounds like a risky project to me, Monck."

"Of course it would be better if I could have a passenger; someone who would be the owner, and would look as if he was used to being driven by a chauffeur. Can you think of any person of a liberal turn of mind who might enjoy an automobile ride, say to Le Havre?"

Lanny answered: "Even if I knew a liberal-minded person in this country, I would not dare to communicate with him, and he would hardly trust an art expert who has just been wooing Hitler in public."

"That is true," assented Monck. "But if I had the name of a trustworthy person, I might approach him myself, or have someone else do it."

"Wait a moment," said the art expert. He thought: "Pete Corsatti! He spoke cynically, but he's a decent fellow at heart—he showed it when he met those wretched Jews." And then: "Yes, but he's a newspaperman, and even if he didn't write anything about the story, he could hardly be expected not to talk about it to his friends."

Aloud, Lanny said: "I suppose that if I could think of some person who is honest and wouldn't betray you, it might be possible for you to approach him without his having any idea that I was mixed up in it."

"Something like that is what I had in mind."

"The person wouldn't even have to know about the supercharger. It could be just a proposition to help an underground worker escaping from Germany."

"Exactly."

"Even if this plan failed and the police caught you, my guess is it wouldn't be such a serious matter for a foreigner. He bought a car and engaged a chauffeur to drive him; or you came to him, saying that you had a car for hire and offering to drive him wherever he wished to go. You could have letters of reference, I suppose."

"Those are easy to prepare; and people seldom check up on them."

"I am thinking of a friend, a Hungarian, Zoltan Kertezsi; you have perhaps heard me speak of him in Paris. He is an art expert, and taught me most of what I know about the trade. I could telephone him that I have an important painting in view, and he would take a plane and come at once. If he had a painting to take out, and I wasn't in position to drive him, he would be open to a proposition from a man who was going out in a car and offered to take him for a reasonable price."

That sounded all right. But then, after thinking more about it, Lanny began throwing cold water on his own project. "The trouble is, Zoltan is a grasshopper. He was in London the last time he wrote me, and he might be in New York by now. Then, too, telephone calls are a matter of record, and telegrams are open to the Gestapo. It'll have to be someone who is already here, and whom you can deal with direct."

XIII

They were rolling along on a wide boulevard, with the lights of many cars flashing past. Wealthy Berliners were going to their pleasures, or coming from them; in great cities, night was the same as day. So long as Lanny obeyed the traffic regulations, nobody would stop his car; he could drive here and there, all night if he wished; and Monck said he was in no hurry.

At last another idea, a promising one. "There is an American lady visiting in this town: a writer, and a clever one. She is sympathetic, and I am certain that she is honest—I mean, even if she refused to help you, she would keep your secret. I only know her slightly, and she must never have the slightest hint that I am connected with the matter."

"How would I meet her?"

"She is staying at a pension, and I'm afraid you'd have to take the chance of going there and calling on her. The risk of one visit wouldn't be great, for the maid who opens the door would hardly have access to the files of the Gestapo."

"No, but I couldn't talk to anybody in the public reception room of a pension."

"It would be up to you to choose your words carefully, convince her that you are an honest man, and persuade her to take a walk with you—on some street not too lonely and yet not too frequented."

"How could I explain that I heard of her?"

"One of the servants of the pension has observed a look on her face, or noted some words that she spoke. That caused you to go to the State Library, where you consulted the *Reader's Guide* indexes, and found several of her short stories listed; you read them, and drew the conclusion that she was a person to be trusted. You are being hunted by the Gestapo and it is necessary for you to get out of Germany; your supporters have put up the money for a car, and she is to buy it and let you act as chauffeur. Once you are outside of Germany, the car will be hers."

"*Donnerwetter!*"

"That will be a small price to pay, in my father's view. From the lady's point of view, it would be an experience, and might be good for her writing career. So far, her observation has been confined to one small class; and you could teach her more about Germany in one day than she would learn in the Pension Baumgartner in a year."

"That all seems reasonable enough," declared the man of the underground. "Of course you'd have to tell me about her writings; I couldn't go into the State Library."

"Surely not. I'd tell you all I know about her. But I can't take a decision like this without more thought. I should have to go over every detail of the program, from the point of view of the chances of my connection with it being traced. If the woman got into trouble, the police would question everybody at the pension, and it would be known that I have called on her there. I am at a disadvantage, because I don't know how you would conceal the supercharger in the car, and so what the risks would amount to. I can think of a score of emergencies for which you would have to be mentally prepared. Give me until tomorrow night and I'll let you know."

XIV

Lanny went back to his hotel room, undressed and got into bed, but didn't go to sleep. He lay there scolding himself, because once more he was breaking his promises to himself; he was doing those things which he ought not to have done and he was leaving undone those things which he ought to have done and there was no health in him. So runs the Episcopal Church formula, which he had learned at St. Thomas's Academy long, long ago. But Thou, O Lord, have mercy upon us—and let us have our own way this one more time, and we'll promise to be good forever after!

The point was, Lanny's presidential agent job ought to have sufficed; he ought to have put it first, and the rest nowhere; he ought to have left the stealing of superchargers to Bub Smith, ex-cowboy who had been Robbie's confidential agent for thirty years and was now the head of the private police force at the Budd-Erling plant. Instead, he was yielding to the temptation to help earn a hundred thousand marks for the anti-Nazi underground, and incidentally help to bring the airplanes of his own country to a parity with those of *Der·Dicke*. These were definite and tangible things, whereas the reports to F.D.R. seemed like shooting arrows into the dark. Was this overworked man really reading them, and remembering what he read? And would he ever do anything about them—would the course of human events be altered by the millionth part of a degree by all Lanny Budd's wandering over the earth, intriguing and questioning and typing and mailing?

Lanny always told himself that he didn't believe in worrying. But this time, he argued, it wasn't worrying, it was foresight; it was anticipating possible events and making the necessary provisions. He imagined a dozen different ways of packing a double-sized suitcase into an automobile and keeping it from looking like what it was; and then as many different ways of persuading border guards that a supercharger was really a lady's vanity case—or what was it? There were so many things he must tell Monck; he didn't dare to make written notes, but he ticked them off on his fingers and learned them by heart, as he had done with the eleven points of Hitler's demands on Czechoslovakia. He went through the whole routine of Monck's visit to the pension, and his whispered speech which would persuade a properly brought-up society lady of Baltimore to come for a walk with an ex-sailor whom she had never laid eyes on before and who would appear to her as something of a rough customer.

Lanny didn't worry especially about Laurel Creston, because, after all, she didn't have to go for a walk if she didn't want to, nor did she have to be taken for a ride. If she consented—well, Lanny thought of the remark of Franz Liszt concerning a certain woman who had voice but no temperament, that he would like to marry her and break her heart so that she could really sing. If Laurel Creston got a real scare from the Nazis, it would serve to put the shivers into her writing, and if they arrested her and it got into the newspapers it would quadruple the prices she could charge magazine editors.

But then right away Lanny thought: "Gosh! She'd write about this episode! She'd make it into a short story!" So he ticked off on his fingers one more caution which he must pass on to Monck: he must extract from the honorable lady the solemn promise that she would never write anything which could give the Gestapo any hint as to the methods by which the underground got its emissaries into Naziland and out!

It must have been nearly morning when Lanny fell into a troubled sleep. After that, he couldn't remember what happened, but it must have been terrible, because at the end he found himself tied down on some sort of chopping block, and over him stood *Der Dicke,* having regained his full size and muscular power. He was dressed in evening clothes with tails such as the Nazi executioner wore on state occasions, but also his chest was covered with a mass of decorations, including the great gold eight-pointed star. His face was contorted with rage, and he was waving over Lanny's head a huge bloody battleax, and yelling: *"Dummer Narr! Mit solcher Stümperei wollst du mich hinters Licht führen?"*—and Lanny, struggling frantically against his bonds, opened his eyes and discovered that he had forgotten to turn off the steam heat in his room, and he had over the lower half of him one of those extraordinary feather quilts called *plumeau* which they have in Germany, as thick as bolsters but only half long enough, so that one half of you perspires while the other half freezes.

8

Face of Danger

I

LANNY had planned to spend the next morning taking a long walk in the Tiergarten. He hadn't yet decided whether he would say the word Yes or the word No—two short words which have decided the fate of men and of empires. He wanted to go over all those difficulties again, and check off on his fingers the things that Monck had to learn by heart. But no sooner had he bathed and shaved and dressed and eaten a late breakfast than the telephone rang and there was announced the **Herr** SS Oberleutnant Jaeckel of the Führer's personal staff, whom Lanny had met at Berchtesgaden and driven in his car to the last Parteitag at Nuremberg. Lanny went down into the lobby, bowed ceremoniously, and shook the young officer's hand, for secretaries and aides-de-camp of great men are important personalities—they can arrange appointments, drop subtle hints, and now and then make or break careers. They become aware of their own powers, and suspicious of every sort of approach; so it is necessary to deal with them with exactly the correct amount of dignity, yet with a touch of cordiality and awareness of them as human beings.

Lanny was informed that the Führer would receive him in his New Chancellery office at two o'clock that afternoon. It was, of course, a royal command, and for a P.A. the most important thing in the world. Herr Budd said that he was greatly honored and would be on hand promptly. So then Lanny took his walk in the park, through a light and not unpleasant snowstorm; but he didn't think much about Monck and Miss Creston. He had to put his mind on Adi Schicklgruber: just what he hoped to get out of him, and just how to approach each topic.

Such an interview is a battle, and a commander who means to win has to study his enemy, also the maps of the terrain, and foresee every move and plan his countermove. In this case the terrain was the soul of Adi, and Lanny knew it thoroughly, having been a guest in his home and studied him under a variety of circumstances. He was a compulsive personality, pathologically so, and his reflexes were as automatic as those of an electrical machine. If you pressed certain buttons, the machine would run smoothly, and for a long time; if you pressed certain others, the machine would blow out a fuse, or perhaps blow up and blow you clean off the premises. *Achtung*, Lanny!

II

There was an Old Chancellery building, which had been good enough for the Kaisers, but was not good enough for the one-time occupant of the refuge for the shelterless in Vienna. There was a frustrated architect in Hitler—he had wanted to follow that profession, and now wanted to show both Austria and Germany that they had rejected and humiliated one of the great constructors of all time. So now stretching along the Wilhelmstrasse was a three-story granite building which looked exactly like a barracks—and this effect was maintained by SS guards of the Führer's own Leibstandart, armed with submachine guns. Lanny had a card of admission, and was passed into an immense long corridor with red marble floors. Walking down this corridor, he came to double doors with a bronze coat of arms made of the initials AH. Opening one of these doors, precisely on the stroke of two, he encountered a secretary who knew him and escorted him into the inner sanctum.

It would have been lèse majesté to suggest it, but Lanny was quite sure that the Führer had taken his idea of an office from Mussolini—just as he had taken his program, his technique, and a lot of his paraphernalia. The office of a dictator must be immense, so that the visitor will be overwhelmed; the desk must be immense, and the visitor must be compelled to walk a long way to it, all alone and with nothing to sustain his tottering footsteps. Rightly, the dictator himself should have been of superhuman size, like a sculptured Egyptian pharaoh; but unfortunately Il Duce was a stubby fellow, fond of good eating, and Der Führer was barely of medium size, and would have been taken for the proprietor of a *Kolonialwarenladen* in a small German town—that is to say, a grocery.

The room was paneled in dark wood, and had great doors leading out to the Chancellery park, now covered with snow. There was a fireplace with blazing logs, and over it one of the several Lenbach Bismarcks; near by was a statue of Frederick the Great, much larger than that little man's life size. There were heavy draperies, thick rugs, and great chandeliers hanging from a high ceiling. On the desk were a pair of horn-rimmed spectacles, which the Führer put on when he wanted to read, but which he would not have worn on any public occasion for ten million marks.

He wore a plain business suit and an agreeable smile. He arose and said: "*Wilkommen, Herr Budd,*" and led his guest to one of the big chairs in front of the fire. Lanny said: "*Sie erwiesen mir eine grosse Ehre, mein Führer*"—and then he waited, for royalty must be permitted to indicate what has caused it to summon a visitor.

"You have been to America since I last saw you?" inquired the Führer of all the Germans.

"Yes, Exzellenz; also in Britain and France."

"A most delightful profession, Herr Budd. I cannot think of anything I would like better than to travel over the world picking out masterpieces for great art collections."

"You would have been another Dr. Bode if you had taken up that duty." It was a compliment of the sort which one *Kunstsachverständiger* would pay to another.

"You know how to flatter me," replied the Führer. The smile said that he accepted the compliment, but that a little was enough. After a moment the great man added: "Rudi tells me that you have talked with some of our friends in London and Paris."

So there was a lead; the Führer wanted to hear Lanny's views of the international situation. Adi was in the position of a soldier who walks at night through a field which his enemies have sowed with deadly mines; every time he puts his foot down is a new decision; and if only someone had watched the sowing and made a map of the field! The Führer will listen gladly; but when he is through, he won't be quite sure whether his informant really knows what he claims to know, and whether his map is accurately drawn; in the end the great man will decide to follow what he calls his "intuition," putting his foot down and at the same time shutting his eyes.

Talking about ruling-class opinion in London and Paris is a P.A.'s specialty. He has listened to conversations for hours at a time and for weeks and months on end, and with every sentence he stows away in his memory he is thinking: "This will interest Adi!" Then, of the next sentence: "This would tell him more than he ought to know!" A delicate question, which troubles Lanny's conscience continually; in order to keep in favor with these high-up Nazis he has to bring them information which is worth while, and which time will prove to be right; but if he imparts secrets which help them too greatly, he may be defeating his own cause.

What, in particular, was Lanny going to do about the war which he judged now to be inevitable? Was he going to help to bring it on, or to postpone it? At the time of the attack on Spain he had wanted war, because he knew that the dictators were not ready for it and would have had to back down. Now they had had nearly three years more in which to get ready, and they had been straining every resource to that end. The British and French were supposed to be doing the same, but their efforts were limited, partly by an uninformed public opinion, and partly by the fact that the ruling classes didn't really want to fight Fascism, but on the contrary wanted a modified form of it in their own countries—just enough to hold down labor, without being so rough or so nasty as Mussolini and Hitler and Franco had been!

III

These attitudes were the subject of Lanny Budd's discourse. He told about the banquet which Baron Schneider had given in his town house, who had attended and exactly what had been said. Adi was feminine in his interest in personalities—especially those from whom he expected to get something; he studied them with care and remembered everything about them. These leading French financiers were mere names to him and he wanted to know what they looked like, their family positions and business interests, and just how they could be approached. Several had sustained losses in the taking over of Skoda and other enterprises in Czechoslovakia; they were making a fuss about it, and Hitler, who was expecting to take over everything everywhere, was a stickler for the forms of legality, and was willing to pay bribes if they were not too big. "They should ask somebody in this country," he said. "My businessmen don't have any trouble in getting along with me. They are making three times as much money as they ever made in their lives before—and I mean that literally."

This was a matter of real importance; for this Budd playboy was going back among the enemy financiers, and what he told them would count. So Adi went into particulars. "When I took power, more than forty per cent of German enterprises were unable to pay any dividends at all; but today there isn't a single one that isn't paying. Before my coming, the average of all dividends paid was 2.8 per cent, whereas today it is well over six."

"Do you mind if I make note of that?"

"Not at all, Herr Budd," and Hitler repeated the figures while Lanny jotted them down. "You doubtless know Dr. Krupp von Bohlen und

Halbach; he told me just the other day that the gross income of his steel business has increased more than seven times in the past six years, and is now well over half a billion marks. Or ask Kirdorf, honorary chairman of our steel cartel—he will tell you that last year he paid a five-per-cent dividend, and at the same time set aside for expansion of plant and as a reserve to cover depreciation a sum greater than the original capital of his corporation. We put our industry to work, Herr Budd—sometimes even faster than it likes."

"I understand you, Herr Reichskanzler," said Lanny, responding to the great man's smile.

"Our enemies will tell you that it is because we are arming the country; but our answer is that we can turn the same energies to the ends of peace—any day they are willing to grant us our rights and let us enjoy a feeling of security."

"I am glad to have the exact figures, and will make good use of them. The men I have been telling you about are keenly aware of what you have achieved, and are not a little envious of it. That is particularly true of England, where they do not have the same hereditary suspicion of German accomplishments."

"Tell me frankly, Herr Budd—what in your judgment is the principal obstacle in the pathway to British-German understanding? I am sure I need not repeat that this is the goal I most desire to reach."

"At the moment, Exzellenz, it appears to be the question of Prague. Everywhere I tried to argue with people I would hear: 'Yes, but he guaranteed the independence of Czechoslovakia and now he doesn't intend to make good on it.'"

"But when I guarantee the independence of a country, does that mean that I am guaranteeing its right to make ideological war upon me? I want peace on my eastern border; and what I find is that I have perpetual insults and humiliations, a policy of pinpricks with the sharp end of the pin always in my direction. I find the British and French press egging the Czechs on, supporting them in a propaganda war. If I object, I am told that this is what freedom of the press means. If I talk about underground Jewish influences, I am called a fanatic; but I think I know a rat when I see it, and especially when I feel it gnawing at the tips of my toes."

Lanny didn't want to get Adi started on one of his rat hunts, which might last the rest of the afternoon; nor did he want to talk about the fate of Czechoslovakia, for he had counted that unhappy little country as already on its way down the boa-constrictor's gullet, and had so reported to F.D.R. He hastened to say: "I can only report to you what I hear, Exzellenz. The second objection raised has to do with your intentions toward Poland."

"There again you have it, Herr Budd. They confront me with the same situation as existed in the Sudetenland; I am invited to see German citizens abused and deprived of their rights by an inferior and backward people, and if I protest, that constitutes me an aggressor and tyrant. I can only reply that the aggression was committed by the Versailles *Diktat*, and that I do not intend to rest until those lands having a majority of German population are returned to my Reich, where they belong and are determined to be."

"So I am accustomed to report, Herr Reichskanzler. And by the way, it may interest you to know that I have just returned from a visit to the so-called Corridor."

"Have you bought that property you spoke of?"

"I went to have another look at it. At the moment it is not so cheerful, covered with snow, but a couple of months will make a difference, I assume."

"What is the size of the property?"

"About twenty hectares. That isn't much if you want to be a farmer, but it is enough for privacy, and to sustain a family. It belongs to a Polish gentleman who rode with a lance against your troops in the last war. I took occasion to sound him out on the present situation, and learned that he considers the Polish army fully prepared and ready to demonstrate itself the best in Europe."

"They do the Polish people a poor service who encourage them in such vain delusions. I am being patient and polite with the Poles, because I know that they are merely pawns, being used by stronger and more cunning powers. But if the only effect is to bring an increase of insults and humiliations, the blood-guilt will not be found on my hands."

"I am keeping my Polish lancer dancing on a string," said the art expert, with one of his engaging smiles. "I have not told him that I wouldn't consent to live in Poland, but I have hinted that I am concerned as to the immediate future."

"He may sow one more crop in Poland," replied the Führer of the Germans; "but I think you may safely reckon that he will reap it in Germany. He has nothing to fear, for we are not robbers, and shall treat our Polish minority with even-handed justice—provided, of course, that they obey our laws and keep their mouths shut."

So that was that, and it seemed to a presidential agent well worth a motor ride to the Corridor and back.

IV

They talked for a while about the horror that lurked on the other side of Poland—so the Führer termed it. He said that one reason he did not want to quarrel with the poor pathetic Poles—*die armen traurigen Polen*—was that they had at least intelligence enough to hate the Bolsheviks and were, geographically and politically, a barrier against them. As tactfully as possible, Lanny led up to the fact that the statesmen of France and Britain were now disturbed by rumors of secret negotiations going on for some sort of understanding between Germany and Russia. The Führer burst out: "It is their guilty consciences! France herself has committed this crime against western civilization, and Britain has been dallying with the idea for years. Now they are terrified by the fear that I might shoot first."

"They are truly terrified, Herr Reichskanzler. They ask me the question: 'Is this serious or is it a bluff?' What do you wish me to tell them?"

"Tell them that in the world of universal distrust which they have made it is impossible ever to know reality from bluff. What is bluff one day becomes by force of necessity a reality on the next. I am a simple man of the people, Herr Budd, and do not know the ways of these subtle diplomats. I say what I mean; and quite by accident I have made the discovery that this is the most effective form of diplomacy. Everybody is ready to believe that I mean anything in the world except what I say. Is not that an odd development?"

"It has its humorous aspects, Exzellenz."

"*Nun wohl*, let them enjoy the humor if they can. I tell them that I am trying to defend western civilization from the foulest scourge that has appeared in modern history; and I invite them to help me. If they are willing to do it, all right, the world is safe; but if they are trying to sell out western civilization, and it is a question of who is going to collect the price, then let them tremble in their boots at the thought that I may collect ahead of them. As you say in your wild West, I will shoot more quickly than they."

"I am surprised to find you familiar with our American customs," smiled Lanny.

"You forget that I was brought up on the stories of Karl May. Did I fail to show you my Old Shatterhand collection at the Berghof?"

"I heard about it, Herr Reichskanzler."

"I have a whole room filled with first editions and relics of that most delightful of romancers, who made your country live in my youthful imagination. From him I learned what a great part the Germans have played in the making of your culture; and it is one of the reasons why I am so anxious to preserve a friendship which ought never to have been broken by war. Have you read any of those books, Herr Budd?"

"I have to admit that I had never heard of them until I had the honor of making your acquaintance, Exzellenz. Then I read several—because I wanted to understand your mind and the influences which had shaped it." Lanny would have liked to add: "It struck me that the creator of Old Shatterhand had been reading about Cooper's Leatherstocking." But he knew that such a statement would have cast him into outer darkness. Instead, he remarked: "Speaking of the Berghof reminds me of Madame Zyszynski and the strange experiences we had with her. She is back on the Riviera now and quite well again. We tried some more experiments, with interesting results."

V

This was a subject which interested the Führer greatly, but he didn't want the fact to be known, for he had forbidden the occult arts in his Reich and couldn't afford to break his own laws. Lanny assured him that he had kept the promise not to talk about the matter, but added: "I live in the hope that before long the investigation of the subconscious mind and its secrets may become as respectable as, for example, research into the nature of the atom. A few days ago I was telling Herr Hess about the work which is now being done at Duke University, in the state of North Carolina."

So Lanny talked for a while about "extrasensory perception" and "the psychokinetic effect," and other phenomena with names long and impressive enough to be respectable even in a German university. Hitler remarked: "Perhaps I can arrange to have some of our authorities look into these matters; and perhaps in the summer you and I can try some of these experiments. I hope by that time to be free from the swarm of petty annoyances which have been burdening my mind of late. I am going to do my best to that end."

The son of Budd-Erling smiled one of his most winning smiles and remarked: "The rest of us await history, Exzellenz; you create it." And after allowing a moment for this unction to permeate the dictatorial mind: "I wonder if Exzellenz is familiar with Napoleon's profound saying, that 'politics is fate.'"

Hitler sat staring into the blazing log fire. It was a remark exactly to his taste, as Lanny knew well. "One of the greatest of minds," he mused. "It is too bad that he was not a German and could not have had a fair chance to try out his political ideas."

Lanny had known the Führer of the Germans for a matter of nine years, and had made him the subject of close study. He understood that it is the fate of dictators to have to listen to flattery and to grow more susceptible to it. There are few who dare to say No in their presence, and it becomes less and less tolerable to them to hear that presumptuous word. Just as Lanny had observed Adi's cheeks growing a little rounder and his bulbous nose a little fatter, so he had observed the great man's satisfaction with himself growing a little more naïve and obvious at each visit. And how could it be otherwise? When everybody else in his country considered him a worker of miracles, why should he be the one to disbelieve them?

Lanny thought it safe to say: "Napoleon began his career a century and a half ago, Herr Reichskanzler, and mankind has learned a lot in that time. I really believe it is going to be possible for a second 'little corporal' to achieve what the first one dreamed—that is to say, the unifying of Europe."

The second little corporal took it just as Lanny had expected—that is, as a matter of course. "You, Herr Budd, are able to see my career in its large outlines, and possibly you do not realize how much easier that is for you than for me. To a man of great affairs life too often takes the aspect of a series of treacheries of his foes and stupidities of his followers. Such a man's life is like groping in the dark along an unknown path, beset with traps and broken by precipices."

"All life is like that, Exzellenz; and the great man is the one who knows his way and keeps to it. Now and then comes a flash of lightning which makes it plain to all the world: the Rhineland, the Anschluss, Munich—and what next?"

"What next proved to be a series of miserable intrigues, of futilities and insults and humiliations which make me feel that what the world calls my latest victory was in reality my first defeat. I took your advice, you remember; I waited, I played safe, I compromised—and what do I see? My opponents have decided that I am a weakling, that I do not mean what I say, that I can be bluffed and made into a mockery. Czechoslovakia, that nest of many kinds of vermin with which I am supposed to be at peace—to enjoy having them buzzing under my bed and to find them wriggling in my dinner plate! Do you know about these wretched 'patriots' with whom I have to deal, and the Slovakian and Ruthenian and Carpatho-Ukrainian and what-not politicians to whose idiotic gabble I have to listen and whose treacherous plots I have to thwart?"

"Yes, Exzellenz," replied Lanny, meekly, "I read your press and I listen to your radio."

VI

The son of Budd-Erling knew that he was to blame in Adi's eyes, and he took the attitude of a schoolboy confronted by a master with an upraised ruler. He was prepared to have his knuckles well cracked; but he was saved at the critical moment by one of those coincidences which cause people to speculate about the possibility of extrasensory perception. The far-distant entrance door was opened and a decorous, black-clad secretary entered, very timidly, as if he were not sure of his reception and was prepared to take flight at the least hint of hostility. The Führer turned and looked, then waited; thus encouraged the man came quickly, almost on the run across the great room.

In his hand he held a strip of paper which apparently had come off a teletype. Without a word he put it into the Führer's outstretched hand, and the great man took one glance. Then it was as if his chair had been wired with electricity and the current had been suddenly turned on. "*Teufelsdreck!*" he shouted, and bounced once and then a second bounce that brought him to his feet. There followed a stream of language which could not have been printed in any German book. It was interrupted by a single glance at the secretary and the word "'*R-r-r-raus!*" The man fled, even faster than he had entered, and Hitler took half a dozen steps across the room, cursing furiously, then turned and came toward his guest, holding out the scrap of paper: "*Sehen Sie, Herr Budd—die gottverdammten Schurken!*"

Lanny took the paper and read four words: "*Hacha hat Tiso abgesetzt.*" He didn't have to ask any questions—indeed he couldn't, for Hitler was off across the room again, raging and storming in that raucous voice which the whole civilized world had learned to know over the radio. It was one of his peculiarities over which Lanny never ceased to wonder, that he shouted just as loud for one person as for ten thousand, and was willing to take just as much trouble to scold or exhort or educate or inspire one person as a million. "You see, Herr Budd, what I have to endure! This wretched, presumptuous creature was represented to me as a tame Czech, a man who would cultivate friendship with Germany—a weakling, a sick man who could not do anything if he wished—but this man has been intriguing, lying to my agents, putting obstacles in my path for nearly half a year. He presumes to be dissatisfied with the government which Father Tiso has been giving to the province of Slovakia—and on no grounds except that this able priest is favorable to our National-Socialist point of view and will no longer permit his native land to be victimized by Jewish intrigues and his peasants to be robbed by Jewish moneylenders! So I read: 'Hacha has deposed Tiso!' A defiance of my will, of my precise instructions! So, you see how it is—they no longer believe that I mean what I say, they force me to teach them all over again. *Gut, Sie sollen haben was Sie wollen!*"

The Führer rushed to his desk and pressed a button; there was some sort of telephone apparatus apparently sunk into the desk, and it probably didn't require a loud voice, but the Führer's voice was always loud when he was angry. *"Ich wünsche Ribbentrop! Keitel! Rudi! Sie sollen so schnell wie möglich kommen!"* You could know that there had been a revolution in Germany when the head of the government referred to these august persons without their titles. Very certainly the Kaiser would never have done such a thing, no matter who had defied his imperial and imperious will!

VII

Good manners suggested that Lanny Budd should offer to retire at this juncture; but his duties as P.A. prompted him to stay and hear what Adi Schicklgruber was going to do to the swarm of vermin which were buzzing under his bed and wriggling in his vegetable plate with one poached egg on top. And apparently this suited Adi; he had to have somebody to rave to until such a time as his Foreign Minister and his Field Marshal and his Deputy Führer and Party Chief could leap into their cars and be rushed to the New Chancellery building. If he had been alone in such an emergency he might have burst a blood vessel, or even his lungs!

Lanny had seen Hitler in this state of frenzy on several occasions, and it was always the same thing. He paced the floor, almost running; he poured out a flood of words, so fast that it was difficult for a foreigner to distinguish them—especially as he fell into the dialect of the Innthal where he was born. He shook both fists at his imaginary foes and called them the vilest names he knew—*Marxisten, jüdische Schweinehunde, Agenten der plutocratischen Democratie*. If he came close to you it was rather disagreeable, for the explosions were accompanied by a fine spray, and gradually this gathered in the corners of his mouth and made a foam. Lanny had heard many times that when this rage reached a climax, it became a sort of epilepsy, and Adi Schicklgruber would throw himself onto the floor and chew the carpet; but Lanny hadn't seen this happen.

Of course he had to agree with everything the Führer said, otherwise that would have been the end of their acquaintance. Yes, of course, the Slovaks were entitled to the independence which Father Tiso had claimed for them, and the Hlinka Guards he had formed was a body of heroic patriots. Hacha, president of the Czech Republic and a devout Catholic, was undoubtedly a Marxist tool. General Keitel would surely agree that the troops must be mobilized. The Air Force, no doubt, was ready for action—Hitler rushed to the transmission device and yelled for a message to be sent to Göring, ordering him to fly at once from San Remo, health or no health.

There was a peculiar thing which Lanny had observed about these blind rages—that there was part of Adi's mind that was watching and calculating and knowing exactly what it did. In the homes of the rich, especially among Americans, Lanny had seen spoiled children who had learned to get their own way by flying into such tantrums. These, too, knew what they were doing, and when they got what they wanted the tantrums stopped; they even learned that there were certain persons who would not give in to tantrums, and with these persons they used other tactics. Lanny suspected that the son of Alois Schicklgruber's old age, the only child of an adoring young mother, had learned the business of rug chewing when he was a year old or less, and had continued it because he found that it frightened people and made them give way to his demands.

VIII

Rudolf Hess arrived, and a minute or two later Marshal Keitel, recently appointed Chief of the Supreme Command of the Reichswehr. By that time Lanny had learned as much as he needed to know, and it was really time for him to take himself out of the way. He said that he was sure the Führer had matters of state to discuss, and that he should be excused—something which put him in an excellent position with the other men. He went for a walk up the Wilhelmstrasse, and it was only a few minutes before the extra editions of the newspapers made their appearance. "Juppchen" Goebbels, *le diable boiteux*, hadn't needed to wait for instructions from his Führer; they had been co-operating for almost two decades, and knew each other's technique. Lanny read the headlines and thought that the press of Naziland had become a device for spreading the Führer's tantrums to the entire German public. The same state of mind, the same words, the same images, the same menaces—the son of Budd-Erling could imagine that by nightfall every *Spiessburger* in the Fatherland would be lying on the floor chewing his own rug, or perhaps the concrete pavement of the town in which he resided.

There was nothing for a P.A. to do about all this. He had already informed his Chief what was coming; and now the cables and radio were spreading the news that the German army was being mobilized and that an ultimatum to Prague was being prepared. What Lanny had to do was to put international affairs out of his mind for the moment and decide whether or not he wished to give the green light to Bernhardt Monck. Would the coming of Marshal Göring and the readying of the German Air Force interfere with Monck's project? Probably not, if it was to be a "factory job"; but Lanny couldn't be sure, and had to wait until evening to ask his fellow-conspirator. This day was Thursday, and if the job was to be done, it must be on Saturday night; which meant that Monck would have two days and two nights in which to persuade Laurel Creston and for her to purchase a car and obtain the necessary documents to leave Berlin for Holland. No time to be wasted in hesitation!

It would be hard indeed to say No, when matters had gone this far and there was no other plan in sight. Lanny couldn't think of any other; and when he met his friend that evening his first question was: "What have you decided?" Monck answered: "I haven't decided anything. I have been waiting for you to decide. Apart from that I am stumped." So Lanny said: "All right, you can try Miss Creston if you wish. Whatever she does, I am certain she won't give you away."

IX

The two men of the underground took a long drive about the streets of the Hauptstadt of Naziland, keeping on the main boulevards, where a good car was no different from any other good car, carefully obeying traffic signals and traveling neither fast nor slow, the driver watching in his little mirror to make certain that any car which made one turn behind them did not make the next turn also. To one who had been driving a car for a quarter of a century and had been engaging in conspiracies almost as long, these things were second nature and interfered very little with conversation.

Lanny told all he knew about Laurel Creston: her character, her ideas, her manners and upbringing; her uncle, her cousin, their yacht, and the family at home in Baltimore. Then her short stories, and the magazines they had appeared in, and just how one would find these volumes in the Preussische Staats-Bibliothek on the Wilhelmstrasse; the literary style of the episodes, their social significance, and just what there was about them which might have awakened the interest of a Marxist ex-sailor and labor leader, self-educated and fond of reading. Lanny told about the Pension Baumgartner, the people who lived in it and whom Monck was likely to see there and be seen by. After he had made certain that his friend had learned all this thoroughly, he made, in the manner of a well-trained play actor, an eloquent and moving speech which Monck would repeat in the hope of persuading this lady to go out on the street with a strange man—something which no real lady of Baltimore had done in the three hundred years since an English lord had first attempted to found the city.

Monck asked questions about the psychology of such ladies, so foreign to his own. Lanny explained that they are reserved, and do not shake hands with a man when they are introduced. They do not like excitement, or loud voices, or intense emotions of any sort; no matter how satirical they may be in what they write about their own class, they are subconsciously bound by its manners and prejudices, and repelled by anything foreign or eccentric. Monck could not be taken for a man of fashion, but should be dressed inconspicuously, clean and freshly shaven. He should speak English, not necessarily well, but slowly and distinctly; his manner should be quiet and self-controlled, and he should flatter the lady in only one way, by the assumption that her understanding of psychology, the shrewdness of her mind, would enable her to recognize integrity and idealism when she met it. "And of course not the faintest hint of sex," added the old-maidish Lanny Budd.

X

So, at nine o'clock in the morning, after the employed boarders had had time to depart, *"Die Miss"* was summoned to the telephone, and heard a deep-toned voice say in precise English: "Miss Creston, my name is Anton Siebert; you have never heard of me, but I happen to be a great admirer of your literary work, and I am taking the liberty of asking permission to tell you so."

Now the lady from Baltimore had not yet reached the stage where the number of her "fans" had become a burden, and she could not help being pleased as well as startled. "I did not know that I had readers in Germany," she replied.

"I have just finished reading everything of yours that I could find in our great State Library and I am tremendously impressed by the social insight and quiet irony which I find in your writings. I know that I am doing something presumptuous in calling you, but there is a fraternity in the world of letters which transcends the ordinary social conventions."

"May I ask, Mr. Siebert, how you came to know that I am at this place?"

"I know persons in the pension and heard them speak of you. That caused me to wish to read what you have written, and now I am presuming to ask the privilege of paying my respects. It happens that I have traveled to far parts of the world, and I have had experiences which you might possibly find suited to your pen. For that reason I urge you to pardon this unusual approach."

There was a moment when the issue hung in the balance. "Well, really, Mr. Siebert——" began the troubled lady.

"I assure you that you will find me a respectful person, and I promise not to take very much of your time. It won't take me long to give you an idea of my story, and I am offering it quite freely. Perhaps I should make it plain that I am a man who has done well in the world, and the story of how I have done it is decidedly out of the ordinary."

Now a lady who aspires to write for popular magazines cannot but be aware of the limitations of her experience, and unless her name is Jane Austen she cannot get along with a tea-party atmosphere and no more. Laurel Creston replied: "You are most kind, sir. When would you wish to call?"

"I am in your neighborhood, and would be glad to come now if you say so. I will promise to leave whenever you tell me that you have another engagement."

So the woman, feeling delightfully daring and unconventional, replied: "You may come, sir."

XI

She entered the reception room of the pension wearing a prim tailored suit of some brown woolen material. He saw that she was small, rather pretty, with brown eyes and hair; she wore glasses and was rather pale, as if she had stayed indoors too much in the harsh Berlin winter. What she saw was a man of heavy build, with big shoulders, a bull neck, and hands evidently used to rough labor, his dark hair close cut on his round head which he bowed to her with deference. He was very German, she decided, but couldn't guess anything more; she had expected to meet an intellectual and here appeared to be a sea captain or something like that, and how on earth could he have got anything out of her sophisticated tales of idle-rich Americans? She fixed upon him a pair of alert intelligent eyes and prepared to discover something new about this foreign and decidedly frightening people.

He seated himself in a chair a few feet away and did not lean toward her, but folded his hands in front of him and began to speak, in slightly hesitating English and a voice so low that she could just hear him. "Miss Creston, I know from your writings that this must seem to you a surprising approach. But I know also that you are a judge of character. You are fascinated by the problems of personality; you watch people closely, and try to understand what really moves them. Frequently these motives are not of the highest, and in order that you may not be too greatly distressed, you teach yourself to smile at their pretensions. That is true, is it not?"

"I should say it is a reasonable guess about me," replied the prim lady.

"It is my hope that you will apply that psychological equipment to the present situation. A stranger presents himself, coming from a quite different world—a man who has seen a rough and hard life. But there are fundamental human qualities, integrity of spirit and moral conscientiousness, which can be recognized and honored anywhere. It is my hope that you will find these qualities in me."

"Proceed, Mr. Siebert."

"I went to work as a boy, and had very little schooling; but I have read whenever I had a chance—history, philosophy, poetry, all that came my way. What I am about to say is not meant to demonstrate my literary attainments, but for a far more important reason. There have been times and places when scholars and thinkers found it desirable to speak in parables, to use metaphors, historical allusions, references to ancient mythology and religions." This learned discourse was what Lanny Budd had outlined for his friend, and he knew it pretty nearly by heart. "In the history of Rome, Miss Creston, there were two brothers known as the Gracchi; their story was told by Plutarch—do you happen to recall it?"

"I am afraid my classical education has been neglected, Mr. Siebert."

"Well, then, let us come down to the history of Virginia. You have read something about Patrick Henry?"

"Oh, yes."

"He made a speech. I cannot claim to have read it, but there is one sentence—seven words which I am told that every school child learns in your country. Do not speak those words, but just tell me if you know them."

"I know them quite well."

"Think of them for a moment, not as something in a school book, but as a reality of this hour." The strange visitor paused, to permit a lady born only a short distance from Virginia to say over to herself: "Give me liberty, or give me death." Then he resumed: "It is out of such sentiments that great literature is made; not the kind that is popular with the magazines, perhaps, but the kind which engages the deepest feelings of the human soul, and which calls to all that is best and noblest in us. Do you happen to be familiar with Lord Byron's poetry?"

"Fairly so."

"He wrote a sonnet about an old castle which stands on a lake in Switzerland. Do you recall that, by any chance?"

"Yes, I think I do."

"The first words are: 'Eternal spirit.' It would seem that I am putting you through an examination; but there are definite reasons for my speaking as I do." The visitor looked this way and that about the reception room of the pension. Once more the *Berliner Blick!*

"I believe I understand what you mean, Mr. Siebert."

"Recall to yourself the first two lines of the sonnet, if you can." He waited, long enough for her to repeat mentally:

> Eternal Spirit of the chainless Mind,
> Brightest in dungeons, Liberty! thou art: . . .

Then he continued: "Every nation has its poetry dealing with this high theme; and when we read it, something stirs in us and we have a feeling of oneness with the poet. You may recall that the last word of that sonnet is 'God.' I am not a religious man; but there is a sense in which all of us have a feeling of identity with the universe. You know the attitude of Wordsworth, no doubt."

"He is one poet I know well."

"He loved nature, and identified himself with it in a sort of pantheistic way; it was a matter of feeling, of instinct, which he would hardly have been able to justify by his reason. He was happy when he was in the open air, walking amid the sights of nature which he loved; that benefited his health, and at the same time gave him things to write about. He escaped from the haunts of men—you remember, he wrote:

'The world is too much with us.' " Again the speaker paused, and let his eyes roam about the room, with its three doors and many window curtains. There appeared to be no eavesdropper, but who could be sure?

"Sometimes the poet roamed the hills alone; but at other times he was glad to have a friend with him, and they talked about the great events of those days. You remember those events, Miss Creston?"

"In a vague way."

"They made the theme of great poetry, by Wordsworth, Byron, Shelley, and others in other lands. They have made the theme of fiction, also. Many a writer would have been glad to hear first-hand accounts of such events, from those who had actually witnessed them, and experienced the height of human effort and the depth of human suffering and despair. The writer of genius can imagine these things, but even he must have local color and the details of personality. You know how eagerly Shakespeare seized upon the stories of Holinshed's chronicles, and the Italian tales of bloodshed and terror which he heard. Those things mean a lot to a writer. Am I taking too much of your time, Miss Creston?"

"Not at all. I am deeply interested."

"I noticed that it is a fairly pleasant morning; a gray sky, but that is the best we can expect in March. Wordsworth learned to love such skies, and the mist on the little hills of his Lake Country. It occurs to me that you might like to take a stroll and enjoy a little fresh air. It would be good for you, and give me pleasure to escort you and talk to you as we stroll."

The man of mystery had said his say, making careful use of parables, metaphors, historical allusions, and references to mythology, all taught him by the learned Lanny Budd. He waited for the lady to think it over, meantime keeping his eyes upon her, meeting her inquiring and perhaps frightened glances. She had read much about what was going on in Naziland, and knew that the eternal spirit of the chainless mind must be at work here—some brave and devoted souls must be fighting the terror. By his strange indirect words this man had conveyed to her that he was one of these persons, and was desirous of narrating his experiences to an American writer. This might be dangerous, but also interesting, and in her soul there was a war between the lady of good society and the aspiring writer of fiction.

The visitor interrupted to remark: "It goes without saying that when a man of good manners goes walking with a lady, he permits her to choose the route, so that she may feel perfectly safe."

So the writer of fiction won out in the internal contest. "I think I would enjoy a walk, Mr. Siebert," she remarked. "Will you wait while I put on my things?"

XII

The man of the underground stood by the window, looking out, but occasionally turning his head to see if there were any signs that he was being spied upon. The lady from Baltimore appeared, wearing the same plaid coat and small mink hat as on her expeditions with Lanny Budd. They went out, and she chose to proceed in the direction of the Brandenburger Gate. They walked side by side and there was no one immediately in front of or behind them; the man drew a deep breath, and without any preliminaries, began:

"Miss Creston, I appreciate what it means for one in your position to receive a stranger and to trust him as you are doing. I am grateful, and assure you that you will find me a person worthy of your kindness. As I tried to tell you by that roundabout talk, I am one of those Germans who have refused to submit to the present dictatorship and are actively fighting it. May I tell you a little about my life?"

"That is what I came for, Mr. Siebert."

"First, I am in Germany illegally, on forged passports, and the police are actively seeking me."

"But then—how can you be walking on a frequented street?"

"I am taking that chance, for reasons which I will explain."

"Wouldn't it be wiser for us to walk on some quieter street than Unter den Linden?"

"It was my promise to let you choose the route, Miss Creston."

"We will turn off at the first corner. I have no desire to subject you to needless risk."

Still speaking in a low voice, and slowly, so as to make as few errors as possible in a language he only half knew, the man told about his childhood in a factory district near one of the canals; the search for knowledge in a Socialist workers' school; the work of the trade unions and the co-operatives; the life of a sailor who would not give up his convictions and persisted in teaching his comrades in the strictly disciplined German merchant marine. He told about the war, in which he had been drafted onto a blockade-running vessel and taken prisoner by a British destroyer; his return to Germany, and the efforts to build a Socialist state, which had failed because the leaders lacked the courage to put down the militarists and great industrialists of their country; the struggles against the Communists on the one side and the Nazis on the other; the long agony of inflation and depression, and then the coming of Hitler—Monck named no names, but told of his experiences in concentration camps, and his two escapes. They were stories to make a gently nourished lady somewhat dizzy; he offered to spare her, but she said No—if some people could endure tortures, others ought to be able to hear about them.

XIII

A long walk and a long talk. Monck told the story of Trudi Schultz —not naming her, or giving any hint concerning a husband, or funds from America. He told about the millions of pamphlets which had been smuggled into Germany, telling the truth as to the Nazis and their régime; also the documents which had been brought out and published abroad. He told about various devoted comrades who had been caught and had been heard of no more. He told about Spain, and the International Brigade, and the heroism of young men who had come from every part of the earth to fight Fascism on the battlefield which Fascism had chosen. "You see, Miss Creston," said the man of the underground, "this is a struggle which makes demands upon all who have consciences. When I read your stories, I said: 'Here is a woman whose heart is with us, and when she knows the facts she will do her part.'"

"But what *is* my part, Mr. Siebert? What can a stranger do?"

"Right now I am in an especially dangerous position. I am being hunted day and night, and wherever I stay I bring deadly peril to my comrades. I cannot stop at any hotel or lodging house, because the fingerprints on my passports would give me away to the police. I must get out of the country without delay, and it is my hope to be your chauffeur and drive you into Holland."

"But where could you have got that idea, Mr. Siebert? I have no car!"

"You must understand that I have a movement behind me; I have friends who want to save me, and are willing to put up the money it would cost. I am in position to put into your hands enough to purchase a medium-priced car. It would be registered in your name and would be your property. When you reached Holland, or England, if you were willing to travel that far with me, the car would be yours."

"Mr. Siebert, you take my breath away. I don't know how to drive a car, and I could not afford the luxury of owning one."

"Then you could sell it; that would be entirely up to you."

Not once in this long walk had the woman looked at the man by her side, nor he at her. They had walked straight on, absorbed in their conversation—except when someone passed them and they stopped, perhaps in the middle of a sentence. Now the man took a glance and saw that the woman was biting her lips together.

"I know that this seems a mad proposal," he went on; "but let me explain my plight. I have been in and out of the country a dozen times; but just now all my old haunts are being watched, and most of my old associates are dead or in jail."

"Mr. Siebert," she exclaimed, "this is a terrible thing you are asking!"

"I am not going to urge you, Miss Creston; it is a matter for your conscience to decide. I point out that the trouble I am in is not because of anything I have sought for myself. I might have lived freely and safely in Germany if I had been willing to abandon my faith in human decency, as so many others have done. Moreover, as it happens, I have information of vital importance to the outside world, if I can get it out. Germany is a jail, and it so happens that you possess the magic key. You are an American, and you belong to that class which is privileged to move freely about the world and to be treated with respect."

"You are mistaken, Mr. Siebert, if you think that I am a rich woman or anything near it."

"Anyone who looks at you, or who hears you speak, will know that you are what is called a lady—that you do not smuggle goods, do not consort with Reds, and have the right to purchase a car and have a chauffeur to drive you about Europe. The guards at the border will be polite, and will ask what amount of German money you are taking out, and may possibly say that they are required to look into your purse. They will do no more than glance at your servant, and will take up his exit permit without comment."

"And suppose it does not go that way? Suppose someone recognizes you?"

"In that case you will have a perfectly clear story. You had planned to buy a car and hire a driver, and a strange man appeared who represented himself as a chauffeur, and brought you letters of reference; I will furnish you with such letters—they will not be genuine, and it will be easy to believe that you accepted them and employed the man. I take it that you have not been meeting any Reds or anti-Nazis in Germany, and so your record is clear. The Nazis are not making much trouble for Americans; they are anxious that your country should keep out of the next war when it comes. It is my firm belief that your country will not be able to keep out, and so you will some day realize that in helping me to escape from the madman of Europe you were also helping your own people."

XIV

This proved to be a long walk; so long that the woman's strength gave out, and she wanted to sit on a bench in a park they were passing. But the bench was painted yellow and had a large black letter "J" on it, so the man had to explain and lead her farther on to where there was an "Aryan" bench. There they sat for a while and nobody paid any particular attention to them. Laurel Creston asked one question after another—questions she would not have bothered to ask unless she was thinking seriously of granting the man's request. He had managed, with the help of the fine words Lanny Budd had taught him, to convince her completely that he was what he represented himself to be. It never even occurred to her that he might be a master criminal trying to escape from the German police—say a counterfeiter, or a jewel smuggler, to say nothing of the head of a gang that was going to burglarize the Siemens-Halske plant and steal a supercharger for a fighter plane!

Laurel Creston wanted to know how soon he desired to leave, and he told her that Sunday would be the best day for passing the border; there would be many pleasure cars out, and the guards would be kept busy. "We would leave at about nine in the morning, and be at the border by fifteen."

"That doesn't give me much time to make my arrangements, Mr. Siebert."

"I cannot say about that, but you should not have to make many arrangements, since you could come back to Berlin very soon. You could invent some friend in England who was ill and whom you wished to visit and help; this friend could get well quickly and you could then return without exciting any comment."

"But I would have to buy the car and get the necessary papers."

"You could step into a taxicab and be driven to a dealer's, and in ten minutes you would be the owner of a car and the document proving your ownership."

"And the car license and all that?"

"The dealer would be happy to attend to that for an American lady, and to deliver the car wherever you ordered. I would take charge of it, and at nine o'clock on Sunday morning I would appear in front of the pension in a proper chauffeur's uniform, and you would depart in state."

"You have thought of everything, it appears!"

"One has to learn to do just that when one goes to war with the Gestapo. Sometimes there are slips, but I don't think there will be in this case. Your own position is too secure."

"And you mean that you brought me this extraordinary proposal solely on the basis of my stories that you had read?"

"You have no idea how much of yourself you have put into your stories, Miss Creston. I found there both a warm heart and a keen mind, two things which do not always come together. I perceived that the writer knows what parasitism is, and how it weakens and in the end destroys human character. I ventured the guess that such a writer would not be a lover of the Nazi dictatorship, and would certainly not betray the confidence placed in her."

"I admired the skill with which you managed to convey your ideas to me in that pension, without saying a word that anyone there could understand."

"Naturally, I had thought that out carefully, and prepared it with some books before me. Let me ask if you really know that sonnet of Byron's."

"What I know better is a longer poem, called 'The Prisoner of Chillon.' It is about a man who fought for the freedom of Switzerland and was confined in a dungeon."

"Bonnivard was his name."

"Yes. I am not sure that I can recall the sonnet."

"I learned it for this occasion. Let me recite it for you—and point out in advance that there are literally hundreds of thousands of men and women—nobody but the Gestapo knows how many—who are confined in dungeons throughout Germany at this moment, and for no crime except that they have refused to bow to the will of an ignorant and fanatical despot. Let me repeat Byron's lines, which apply to the present situation without the change of a single word."

"Please do," said the woman, and Monck recited:

> Eternal Spirit of the chainless Mind!
>   Brightest in dungeons, Liberty! thou art:
>   For there thy habitation is the heart—
> The heart which love of thee alone can bind;
> And when thy sons to fetters are consigned—
>   To fetters, and the damp vault's dayless gloom,
>   Their country conquers with their martyrdom,
> And Freedom's fame finds wings on every wind.

Chillon! thy prison is a holy place
And thy sad floor an altar—for 'twas trod,
Until his very steps have left a trace
Worn, as if thy cold pavement were a sod,
By Bonnivard!—May none those marks efface!
For they appeal from tyranny to God.

9

Time Gallops Withal

I

LANNY BUDD had learned by long practice not to let himself worry when it wouldn't do any good. He went to see an American movie that Friday evening, and then he went to sleep, and if he had any nightmares he didn't know it. In the morning, his hands did tremble a little as he opened a letter signed Braun. It told him: "The lady is going to help me find a good Defregger." Lanny thought: "All right, she has fallen for it"—just as Lanny had fallen in so many cases, beginning when he was only fourteen, and his Red uncle had taken him to visit the Italian syndicalist, Barbara Pugliese. He had got into a lot of trouble, off and on ever since, trying to help people who were battling for a new kind of freedom, in the field of economics. It wouldn't be so bad in Laurel Creston's case, he told himself, for she wasn't a presidential agent, and surely hadn't anything more important to do than to learn to understand the struggle against the Nazi-Fascist counterrevolution, and to write about it.

Lanny burned the note, according to his practice, and sent the ashes down into the sewer. Then he put his mind on the screaming Nazi press; he saw that Hitler was going to war again—at any rate, he was going to have his way, and let the other nations of Europe make it a fight if they chose. This Saturday, the 11th of March, the scoundrelly Czechs were terrorizing Germans all over their domains —at least, that was what you believed if you were a German and read Hitler's newspapers or listened to Hitler's radio. Lanny decided that he had got about enough material and was ready to take it out; but it wouldn't do for him to go just at the moment when the supercharger was going, so he looked up a concert for the afternoon and listened to a Bruckner symphony.

This was the night when the burglary was supposed to be committed, and Lanny wanted to have an air-tight alibi; so he called Oberst Furtwaengler, of *Der Dicke's* staff, apologized for having neglected him, and invited him and his very dull provincial wife to a performance of *Die Fledermaus;* then he took them to a night club where they watched grotesquely depraved dancing. The SS officer and his lady drank enough champagne so that they didn't want to go home, and Lanny took them to still another "spot"—it was the fashion to go the rounds like that, and at four o'clock in the morning he drove them home, and made jokes about the time, so as to be sure it was firmly fixed in their minds. They lived some distance out in the suburbs, and thought it was an imposition for him to have to drive back to the Adlon so late, so they invited him to occupy their spare room. Beat that for an alibi if you could!

Lanny lay in a strange bed and counted sheep, doing his best not to think about what Monck was supposed to be doing at that hour. He and his fellow-conspirators would have the supercharger and be taking it to pieces with wrenches, or an acetylene torch, or whatever might be required. The frame, or box, or whatever the device was contained in, would be cut into two or more flat sections and welded under the chassis of the car where they would be inconspicuous. The pipes and whatever else was inside, would be cut to proper lengths and wrapped up in bundles to look like tool kits; they would be hidden under the back seat, and on top of them would be Miss Creston and some of her suitcases and hatboxes. The border guards would hardly move all that—at least, not unless an alarm had been sent out and everything in Germany was being turned upside down.

II

On Sunday morning the Oberst and his lady had hangovers, and Lanny pretended to have one, too. He read the morning papers and now and then turned on the radio—for if an alarm was given, it might possibly be a public one; however, Lanny didn't hear anything. His hosts urged him to stay, and it was a safe way to spend Sunday morning. He had known this couple for some five or six years and had always made himself agreeable, so if they had ever had any suspicions of him, these had long ago been dissipated. He was an art expert who possessed the Führer's favor and had made a lot of money for General Göring by selling paintings which Göring had bought for a song from wealthy Jews. The Reichsmarschall had authorized him to sell the rest of these treasures for whatever he could get, and had naturally expected that the expert would make a quick clean-up; but Lanny hadn't behaved that way—he had been extremely conscientious and had insisted upon getting good prices, thus earning his commissions many times over. Both the great man and his aide appreciated this, and it hadn't occurred to either of them that by these tactics Lanny was providing himself with an excuse for coming into Germany several times a year and enjoying the honor of intimacy with the Nazi Number Two.

Right now this reduced fat man had flown back from Italy and was occupied in preparing the German Air Force for action. Not that it needed much preparing; it had practiced over Madrid and Valencia and Barcelona and Guernica and many other cities and towns of Spain. It had practiced getting ready to bomb Vienna, and then Prague, and now it was Prague again; the Oberst was proud because all his chief had to do was to press a few buttons and speak a few words. That was German *Gründlichkeit*, and the Nazis had brought it to its highest point.

Lanny had had conferences with both Hitler and Hess, and both had told him that what they said was not confidential, they wanted it made known to the world. So Lanny pleased and flattered a faithful aide-de-camp by repeating the words of these almighty personages. In return the aide would talk freely about his own chief, what he said and what he planned to do. It was all along the lines of Herr Budd's wishes, for he, too, wanted reconcilement between Germany and Western Europe, and giving the Fatherland a free hand in the east. The Reichsmarschall had pleaded with the Führer for the Munich settlement, but this time he would surely not plead, and a thousand bombers were loaded and ready to fly the moment the word was given.

III

Lanny had decided that it was the part of wisdom for him to see Göring once more before going out of Germany. A difficult decision to make, for Monday would be the most likely day for *Der Dicke* to get the news of the missing supercharger. If he got it, he would be in a fury, and of course one of his first thoughts would be of the Budd father and son; he might even say something about it—and Lanny judged it would be better so, affording him a chance to be horrified and to give the solemn assurance that he knew nothing whatever about the matter; also to point out that Britain, France, and Russia had agents in Germany, all more active and more capable than the Americans. Göring might well believe that.

Paying such a call was, of course, a different matter from going to a public reception where Lanny would have met scores of prominent Nazis, many of whom did not know him except by reputation. Göring was his friend, and in a time of crisis like this it would not have been natural for Lanny to depart without hearing what messages the Reichs-marschall might have to send to Lord Wickthorpe and Gerald Albany and others of Lanny's highly placed friends in England. Also, there were the paintings; Lanny would say: "I think I'm going to get an offer for that Canaletto; and I may be cabling you about a Sargent before long." *Der Dicke* had surprised Lanny by asking him to assemble a collection of representative American paintings, and he didn't want them shipped to Germany, but to be stored in New York. That was something significant—now, while the Nazi war machine was on its toes and ready to leap, the leaders were preparing for emergencies by stowing things away in safe corners of the world!

Now Lanny asked Furtwaengler if Seine Exzellenz would have time to see him in the midst of his many duties, and the Oberst said that Seine Exzellenz had never failed to take the time; he was the kind of executive who had competent subordinates and saw that they did their jobs and left him free to have a little pleasure now and then. Lanny thanked his two hosts and drove back to his hotel early in the after-noon. In his mind was the picture of the Baltimore lady and her chauf-feur approaching the Dutch border, and all the many different things that might be about to happen to them. He turned on the radio set in his room and sat listening to recordings of Beethoven, Mozart, and Schubert, interspersed with Nazi orators raving at the Czechs. It was three o'clock—and now the car should be at the border; at any moment the radio might report that a notorious Red saboteur and criminal had been arrested trying to escape from the country, posing as the chauf-feur of an American woman writer. There were news periods on one radio and then on another, and Lanny's palms were moist as he turned the dial.

No such news was given; and then he would think: "The discov-ery hasn't been made yet. It will come at seven in the morning, or thereabouts." Then he would think: "But it may not come at all! They may not have got the gadget!" It was possible that Monck had had to call up Miss Creston and tell her that some trouble had developed in the car and the trip would have to be postponed. If that had happened, presumably Lanny would get a note in the morning. It could even be that the crime would never be detected. If it was an inside job, there would not necessarily be any marks of breaking in; and if the gadget was being turned out in quantities, there would be a storeroom, and how often would they take an inventory? Somebody might decide that there had been a miscount; or some subordinate might discover the error and keep it quiet for fear of being held to blame. It might even happen that the one who did the counting might be the one who had done the stealing! All sorts of possibilities to occupy the imagination of a man sitting before a radio, listening to Nazi marching songs and war cries and wondering if even now a thousand bombers might be winging their way toward the beautiful and romantic old city on the river Moldau, portrayed in a Smetana tone poem.

IV

On Monday morning Lanny again sat glued to the radio, and in between broadcasts he skimmed through the papers. Apparently all Germany was absorbed in the problem of Prague, and what reply the Führer intended to make to Czech insolence. Father Tiso, Premier of Slovakia, had been interned in a monastery, which seemed a proper abode for a priest; but now the reverend statesman had fled the monastery and was on his way to Hitler to beg for help against his oppressors. German troops were on the way to the border—that new border of Czechoslovakia which the Führer had "guaranteed" less than half a year ago.

There was nothing about any supercharger having been stolen; and for the hundredth time Lanny asked himself: Would they give a public alarm, or would it be a secret action of the Gestapo, a message to all their agents at the border? Would they be willing to tell the world that they had a secret supercharger for fighter planes? Lanny was still imagining it one way and then the other, when the telephone rang; it was Furtwaengler, saying that Seine Exzellenz would be pleased if Herr Budd would come to lunch. Of course Herr Budd was pleased, likewise; and right away he thought: "He can't have got any word yet, or he wouldn't be feeding me!"

This impression was reinforced when Lanny entered the ministerial residence and *Der Dicke* came to welcome him with both hands. The great man's rest in the land of sunshine and flowers had done him good and he had forgotten that he had any heart trouble; also he had forgotten his fear of embonpoint, judging by the way he attacked the luncheon of turbot followed by broiled venison which he had ordered for his guest. He was the same fat Hermann that Lanny had known for the past six years, talking about his food at the same time that he gobbled it, telling jokes, many of them sexual, and in general exhibiting his joy at being the incomparable person that he was.

Very quickly he made evident the cause of this exuberance. He had ordered the Air Force to be ready for action on the morrow, and it was going to be ready and was going to act. The dream of Hermann's life, which he had been cherishing for a quarter century—ever since, as a humble lieutenant in the trenches, he had worked some kind of "pull" and got himself transferred to aviation. For twenty years he had been building the National-Socialist movement and for six years he had been building the Air Force, and now at last he would have a chance to show what it could do! A strictly professional attitude, Lanny perceived; and as grandson of Budd Gunmakers and son of Budd-Erling he shared it with proper geniality. A beautiful and romantic old city would be blown into dust and rubble, some tens of thousands of civilians would be massacred, and the fat Hermann would say to the world: "Knuckle down to your master!"

"The Führer has given me his word," he declared; "and this time he isn't going to back down. We have seen that it does no good." Lanny understood that Göring had decided to swim with the current.

"I have a picture deal which is taking me to England and then to the States," remarked the art expert. "What do you want me to say to people there?"

So the Air Marshal entered upon a long recital of the inconveniences to which his government had been subjected ever since the Munich compromise. Lanny had already heard Hitler tell it, and had read it in the papers and listened to it over the radio *ad nauseam*. A fat man emitting sounds from the same orifice into which he is stuffing food is not a pleasing spectacle, but Lanny had asked for it and he listened politely. At the end he was not surprised when the great man revealed that he was not really so bursting with confidence as he acted. "Do you think that England or France will fight?" he demanded.

"I'm sure it won't be England *or* France," said Lanny, just to tease him. "If anything, it will be England *and* France."

"Will it be that?"

"I haven't had the opportunity to ask, but if you want my guess, they won't. I know they certainly don't want war; and how far they will let themselves be pushed is something—well, I doubt if Chamberlain himself knows at this moment. I doubt if he *wants* to know."

Lanny would have liked to put a counter-question: "What will *you* do if they take a stand?" But he was quite sure that Hermann didn't know the answer to that one. Hermann was doing what Hitler told him, and Hitler himself didn't know, any more than Chamberlain knew. Chamberlain was muddling through, English fashion, and Hitler was following his intuition, Hitler fashion, and that was the way the world was being run. Hitler was bluffing, and when he saw how his opponents reacted to his bluff he would decide how to react to *their* bluff.

V

"I don't suppose you want to talk about paintings in a crisis like this," the visitor remarked; and the host replied: "Why not? If I had decisions to make at this late hour, I would be a poor executive indeed."

It would not do to assume anything like that, so Lanny said: "I have my car with me, and it might be worth while to take out the Canaletto, as I feel pretty sure of getting a good offer."

"*Ausgezeichnet!*" replied *Der Dicke.*

Lanny went on to discuss Winslow Homer, whose paintings of waves and sailors and fishermen in action had unexpectedly attracted a military man's attention; he told about Grant Wood and other Americans whose work was beginning to be recognized. It was better to get the new men before their prices went too high. Lanny understood that when Hermann Göring bought works of art he expected them to pay dividends, exactly like the shares of the Hermann Göring Stahlwerke. If ever the time came that he had to take flight to America by way of Portugal and the Cape Verde Islands, the paintings he had salted away in New York without ever seeing them would be worth enough to buy an estate in the Pocantico hills.

Der Dicke's thoughts were perhaps on that subject now, for after he had O.K.'d Lanny's recommendations—to sell old masters which American collectors greatly overvalued and to purchase American painters who were as yet greatly undervalued—the fat commander suddenly burst out: "Tell me, Lanny—can it possibly be that the French air force is as weak as all my reports tell me?"

The visitor replied: "I'll tell you the story which Denis de Bruyne had from a member of the Cabinet about six months ago. Before Daladier came to Munich to discuss the settlement, he summoned Darlan, Gamelin, and Vuillemin to the ministry and said: 'Now, gentlemen, tell me frankly, just how well is France prepared if war should come?' Darlan replied: 'The navy is completely ready.' Gamelin replied: 'The army can be mobilized in three days.' Then Daladier turned to the head of the air force, who hesitated, until the Premier urged him. Then he said: 'In two weeks after war starts we shall not have a plane left capable of fighting. It will have to be my policy to put in our second-grade pilots, and save the best until I can get some good planes.' "

Lanny told that story because he knew it was all over Paris, and he was sure that men like Herzenberg and Abetz and Kurt Meissner must have heard it. When Göring added the question: "What have they procured in the past six months?" Lanny replied: "You know how much aviation anybody can procure in six months. I don't know what they've ordered from my father, but I know that he was pretty disgusted when he left Paris. You are familiar with the situation: they are split into a dozen factions that hate each other more than they can ever hate an outside enemy."

"God knows we don't want to fight them," declared *Der Dicke*. "All we want is to pull them away from Russia, and have our friends somehow manage to get control."

"It will surely come that way if you give it time," replied the visitor, and added, with a smile: "But I understand you're not saying that to the Führer any more!"

VI

Lanny went back to the Adlon, fully convinced that Hermann Göring hadn't yet missed his supercharger; he just couldn't be that good an actor! Inquiring for his mail, the guest received a postcard—a plain, open card with a color photograph such as you could buy for five pfennigs at newsstands. This one bore a Netherlands stamp and showed the town hall of the Dutch town of Zutphen, famous on account of Sir Philip Sidney, his wounds and his cup of water. On the card was written: "Aunt Sally is feeling better and I am taking her to London."

Now Lanny had no Aunt Sally, nor had he agreed upon any such name as code. But the stamp and postmark were all he needed, and Monck, of course, was playing with that fact. Lanny took the card upstairs and burned it; then he wrote a few notes and sent a few cablegrams, and by that time a messenger had come from the ministerial residence bringing the Canaletto, not a very large painting, carefully wrapped in oilcloth and canvas. There was a document authorizing him to take it out of the country; also his exit permit—the Oberst always obliged him with services of that sort.

The traveler had decided to wait till morning, on chance that there might be developments which needed explaining. He went for an after-dinner call on Hilde von Donnerstein, and heard the latest gossip concerning the insides of the Nazi machine. They listened to the radio for a while: Father Tiso had flown to the Führer to beg for help and it had been promised him. Hacha, the defiant Czech, had been summoned to Berlin, and was coming; they were all going to learn to come at the master's call. Lanny observed the curious fact that this sophisticated lady, who told so many stories poking fun at the Nazis, was nevertheless proud of the fact that it was a German who was giving the commands. Lanny, of course, had to agree with her; the only possible basis of order in Central Europe was for the lesser breeds to do what they were told.

But nothing about any supercharger, or burglary of the Siemens-Halske plant! In the morning, after his usual comfortable routine, Lanny took the precaution to phone Oberst Furtwaengler, to thank him for his many favors and to say good-by. No hint of anything but cordiality; so Lanny had his painting and his bags and his portable radio set carried down and packed in the car, distributed the proper gratuities, and rolled away to the west. He was going to take the ferry at the Hook that night, and his stateroom had been engaged by wire—the hotel porter had seen to it. Other men had oiled and greased the car, and put gas in the tank, water in the radiator, air in the tires. How comfortably everything had been arranged and how smoothly everything went for those who had plenty of money in the spring of the year 1939!

On the way he listened to Berlin, and when he tired of that he could shift to Amsterdam, Brussels, Paris, London—that is, whenever the car was out in the open country. Great events were rushing on with hurricane speed. The President of the Czech Republic—so the Nazi radio and press were careful to call it, since they had recognized the independence of Slovakia—Hacha, had arrived in Berlin, along with his Foreign Minister and his daughter, the latter on account of his failing health. They were received with military honors, with flowers and even a box of candy for the daughter—let nobody ever say that the

Führer was lacking in gallantry! The poor old man was going to surrender his country and so it wasn't going to be bombed—let no one ever say that the Führer was lacking in mercy!

A swarm of newspapermen had rushed to Prague—and now all the world, including Lanny rolling westward at sixty miles an hour, could listen to an American correspondent telling the world how the people of Prague were taking the prospect of submission to Hitler's will. Would they resist or wouldn't they? Would Britain or France help them? Other Americans in Paris and in London discussed the intentions of those governments. But how could newspaper and radio correspondents foretell the behavior of statesmen who were in the condition of a swarm of bees when someone turns the hive upside down?

VII

The son of Budd-Erling would listen for a while, and then his thoughts would wander off to the supercharger, which ought to be in London by now. It wouldn't take Monck long to get the pieces of the gadget loose from the car, and after that it would be a question of getting on board the first steamer. Monck surely wouldn't delay, for what he had was stolen property, and if the Gestapo got on his trail they could appeal to the British authorities and land him in jail.

Laurel Creston was in a different case; she didn't have any stolen property; she had a car which she had bought in Germany, paying spot cash and getting the dealer's receipt. Lanny was amused to speculate on the question of what she would do with it; would she learn to drive it and blossom out in style, or would she sell it and use the money to prolong her European tour? Certainly she had earned it, for she must have been under intense nervous strain, from the moment she gave her consent on Friday morning until she was past the Dutch border on Sunday afternoon. It had been a test of character—for Lanny felt certain that she hadn't done it for the sake of the money; she had done it for the cause which Monck represented, and which he had convinced her was the cause of freedom and decency.

Lanny had no trouble in imagining the scenes, for he knew both the persons and had written the whole scenario. It had been a test of a woman's nerve, as well as of her belief in the cause. Lanny thought: "She's a real person"; he thought: "I ought to know her better." So there started up that old argument in his mind. How could he know her? How could he be seen with her, or she with him? No, it was absurd to think of, and would just be shirking his duties to F.D.R. Why did he always have to be yielding to temptation and thinking about some woman? Right now he ought to be thinking about what message he would get off to Washington, and what information he would give to Ceddy Wickthorpe and the other Foreign Office men in England.

At the Hook of Holland Lanny went on board the long narrow nightboat, very comfortable, very safe. He was in a free land now, and shut himself up in his stateroom and set up his little portable and went to work. He wrote that Hitler had definitely made up his mind to take Danzig and the Corridor, and that the time would be not longer than six months. He wrote that Hitler would probably force the issue and take the whole western half of Poland; the Führer's former statement that he wanted nobody but Germans was now forgotten, as he was showing in the case of the Czechs. The P.A. wrote that Hitler was seriously thinking of some sort of deal with the Russians, possibly giving them the eastern half of Poland and thus beating the others "to the draw." He added that the high-up Nazis were dubious about the outcome of these ventures, and were salting away money and property abroad; but the Führer's will was implacable, and when it came to a showdown not one would refuse to obey him.

VIII

The passage across the foot of the North Sea took all night. It happened to be a stormy night, and when that ferry boat got into the open it rolled in a most disturbing fashion. Lanny began to feel queer inside, and kept on feeling that way for many hours. If he had any of those psychic gifts which he studied so eagerly in others, he might have got some sense of painful events going on back in Berlin, in that New Chancellery building which he had visited only a few days ago. For this was the night, or rather the small hours of the morning, when the death warrant of the Czech Republic was signed.

Poor old President Hacha! After the military honors and the flowers and the box of candy, he and his minister were taken into Hitler's splendid office and had the document set before them. The Führer made a brief speech; this was the agreement, and all the visiting pair had to do was to write their names on it. Bohemia and Moravia were to become a part of the Third Reich, and Prague was to be occupied the next morning. If Hacha and his minister refused to sign, the thousand bombers would fly and the city would be wiped out of existence. That was all; take it or leave it.

After that speech, Hitler wrote his name and then left the room, bequeathing the elderly invalid to the tender mercies of Ribbentrop and Göring. The two Czechs protested against the outrage, and Göring's answer was that the air force already had its orders; it was to fly at six A.M. There was the document; sign. Göring held out the pen, and when the horrified president shrank from it, Göring pursued him around the table. Sign, or the bombs will soon be falling.

Hacha fell into a faint and had to have restoratives. The thoughtful Führer had ordered his physicians to be on hand, and the sick man was revived. He declared that he could not sign without consulting his Cabinet. All right, there was a direct telephone line—the thoughtful Führer had seen to that, also, and the president might do his consulting at once. The president collapsed again, and again was revived. Such was the duel of wills going on all night, while Lanny Budd was being rolled by the great waves which started in the Arctic Ocean and came sweeping down the coast of Norway, and to the foot of the North Sea as if into a funnel. It was half-past four in the morning when the almost-dead man wrote his name on the death warrant of his country, and already German troops were crossing the border in a dozen places. While Lanny was leaving Harwich they were entering Prague, and when he got to London the extra editions of the newspapers were announcing that the Führer himself was on his way to make a triumphal entry into the Czech capital.

IX

In times such as this a man couldn't very well think about anything but politics. As soon as he came ashore at Harwich, Lanny had phoned to Rick, saying that he had a load of news; Rick took the train, and no sooner had Lanny got settled in the Savoy than his friend appeared. And then what a feast of misery they had! There was no chance of this hotel room being wired and they didn't have to go for a drive in order to enjoy privacy. They could say what they thought, in a tight little island that had been free since the days of Magna Charta; but how much longer would it be free—with despotism spreading like black thunder clouds over the European sky?

Eric Vivian Pomeroy-Nielson was a man who took his politics hard; his belief in democratic Socialism was his religion, and the events of this hour were to him no vague and far-off abstractions, but personal tragedies which he witnessed with his mind's eye and felt to the depths of his soul. He had been in a state of rage mingled with despair ever since

"Munich"; and now he saw the worst of his forebodings being realized —a melancholy satisfaction indeed. It so happened that the sudden death of Prague fell at the same time as the last agonies of Spain; in these black hours traitors were tearing that republic to pieces, and starving, disease-ridden Madrid was to collapse in a couple of weeks.

Rick was only a year and a half older than Lanny, but already his hair was showing signs of gray. He didn't have his friend's happy faculty of losing himself in a piece of music or the study of a great painting; he worried about the world which he couldn't save; he saw it rushing toward a precipice, and he shouted warnings which very few heeded. He had been a successful playwright, and could still have been if he had been willing to cater to the "carriage trade"; instead he wrote political articles, and turned the news which Lanny brought him into diatribes signed "Cato." Of late he had been so violent in his anti-Fascism that Lanny was afraid to visit his home, and met him privately in hotel rooms.

Lanny had never mentioned F.D.R. to his friend, and now he didn't mention the supercharger; but he was free to tell about his talks with the Nazi leaders, and about their intentions. Rick, a skilled journalist, would know how to use this information without giving any clue as to its source. For years he and Nina had avoided mentioning Lanny to their friends, and the general assumption was that the son of Budd-Erling had drifted away from interest in the leftwingers and their ideas. That was something to be expected; it was in accord with the materialistic interpretation of history, and when it happened, the rigid Marxists would shrug their shoulders and say: "You see? It's the class struggle."

Rick was in such a state of fuming that he could hardly sit still; he wanted to pace the floor in spite of his lame knee. "Blind imbeciles" was the kindest phrase he would find to characterize the people who guided his country's destinies in this crisis. He told of something which Alfy, his oldest son, had told him: in London on the previous day one of the newspaper placards had proclaimed, in letters half a foot high: "ANOTHER GREAT STAND!" "And what do you think that was?" inquired the father. "A stand of the British Empire against the madman who is tearing Europe to pieces? No—it was a cricket match!"

Rick's favorite thesis was that this blindness of the British rulers was not accidental. "Class is more than country," was his formula to describe the "Cliveden set," as it was called. They didn't want to fight Hitler, because they believed that he had found the answer to the peril of labor unionism, which was steadily encroaching upon the privileged classes in every land where industrialism had made advances. Hitler had taught labor its place, and was going to crown his career by exterminating Bolshevism. If he would do that, the British landlords and press-lords and beer and coal and shipping and money lords would be perfectly willing to allow him a big chunk of Europe as his reward.

Never had this thesis seemed more clearly justified than in these last critical days. "The Government are disturbed, of course," declared the one-time aviator; "they are afraid of any sort of change, and especially when it is sudden. But they don't care a tinker's dam about Czechoslovakia; they don't care about a republic, they don't care about freedom. When they know that a murder is being committed, they just look the other way. To read our great press this morning makes you want to vomit."

"I had enough of that on the Channel last night," smiled Lanny. "I take it I was right in telling Hitler that Britain won't fight for Prague."

"You were right, but I don't think you should have told him."

"Trust me, old man. I had reasons." That was the nearest a P.A. could come to self-justification.

X

Rick went off to discuss with an editor the information which Lanny had brought him; and Lanny sat at the telephone and called the Foreign Office in Whitehall. He guessed that in a time like this the hard-working Ceddy Wickthorpe would be at his desk, and so he was. "I have just come from Berlin," said the American. "I talked with Number Two the day before yesterday, and with Number One just before that. They gave me messages for you."

"Ripping!" exclaimed his lordship. "Can you drop in?"

"No doubt you're busy now. Are you free for dinner?"

"Come to the club, and we'll have a room. I'll bring Gerald."

"O.K.," replied the American.

"By the way," added the fourteenth Earl of Wickthorpe, "the Prime Minister is going to make a statement to the Commons in a couple of hours. You might like to attend."

"By all means—thanks."

A day of thrills for a dabbler in international crises! Lanny got Prague on his radio and heard a correspondent describe the behavior of the people of that city while the German troops were entering. Apparently the invaders hadn't yet got their censorship going, and the reporter described women standing on the sidewalks with tears streaming down their cheeks. And then, a little later, all airlanes were cleared—Hitler was going to tell the Czech people about their future. Lanny listened to that raucous voice which he knew so well, bellowing the message of *Lebensraum* which had been Adi's obsession for the past two decades, ever since, as a police spy in Munich, he had taken charge of a group of seven bewildered Bavarians who were calling themselves the National Socialist German Workingmen's Party. Only six months ago the Führer had shouted to the world: "I want no Czechs!" Now he told these same Czechs: "For a thousand years Bohemian and Moravian lands were part of the *Lebensraum* of the German people. . . . It is by the law of self-preservation that the German Reich is determined to intervene again decisively to erect the foundations of a reasonable European order and proclaim decrees accordingly. Germany has already proved in its thousand-year-old past that, by reason of its size and the character of the German nation, it alone is predestined to solve these problems."

After which Lanny took a stroll to Westminster and entered that mass of brownstone Gothic buildings in which was housed the "Mother of Parliaments." Wickthorpe had got him a ticket to the visitors' gallery, and he climbed into one of the topmost seats, looking down into a narrow chamber, only seventy feet long, in which the destinies of the British Empire were debated. The speaker sat at the head of a long table in the center, with a wig on his head and the mace of office in front of him. The members sat on uncomfortable benches ranged on both sides of the oblong table. Until recently they had all worn top hats; then the labor members had heralded the social revolution by appearing in caps. Now an excited debate was under way, and the visitor from overseas was cheered to make the discovery that there were a few members of this august body who cared about freedom and democracy and had voices to shout it to the world.

In came the tall and lanky, black-clad and solemn manufacturer who had once been Lord Mayor of Birmingham and now was head of the Conservative Party and of the British government. He had left his rolled black umbrella in the cloak room, but had brought his cadaverous face and prominent Adam's apple behind an old-fashioned wing collar. In a dry dull voice he told his party, his people, and such others as might care to read about it, that he had "so often heard charges of a breach of faith bandied about," which did not seem to him "to be founded upon sufficient premises." He went on to declare: "It is natural that I should bitterly regret what has occurred. But finally do not let us on that account be deflected from our course. Let us remember that the desire of all the peoples of the world still remains concentrated on the hopes of peace and of a return to the atmosphere of understanding and good will which has so often been disturbed."

So that was that; and the Führer of the Germans could be sure that any time he wanted to murder another republic, the British Prime Minister would bitterly regret it. Lanny went back to his hotel to dress for dinner; and there he turned on the radio and heard that Hungarian troops had crossed the borders of the Carpatho-Ukraine and were driving disorganized Czech troops before them. A new Hungarian government was expected to take power, one that was pro-Nazi and anti-Semitic, and the report was that Hitler had agreed to let this government have that portion of Czechoslovakia which was immediately adjacent to Hungary.

XI

The fourteenth Earl of Wickthorpe was a serious-minded and conscientious English gentleman. He possessed a magnificent estate and his rich American wife made it unnecessary for him ever to worry about the high taxes which were ruining so many of his fellow peers. He might have taken things easy and enjoyed his life, but he had chosen a job as a career man in the Foreign Office, something which meant hard work, and was unusual for one in his station. His title wasn't exactly a handicap, but it made him conspicuous, and made it harder for him to withdraw his hand from the plow, once he had put it there. Especially was this true now, when the British Empire, which was his life, found itself suddenly in such dire peril. The realization of this was slowly penetrating the minds of high-ranking Englishmen, and it kept Ceddy Wickthorpe chained to his desk in dreary smokestained London when he would far rather have put on an old raincoat and boots and gone wandering over his lawns and meadows, looking at horses and cows and deer, rabbits and dogs, swans and geese.

His relationship to Lanny Budd was peculiar, since he was married to the woman who had cast Lanny off. Marriages can be broken under the laws of the State of Nevada, but under the laws of nature this one continued on in the form of an eager little girl who was going to finish her ninth year this spring. Frances Barnes Budd revealed in her name that she was part Irma and part Lanny, and so long as she lived her parents could not be entirely separated. Because she was the heiress of a great fortune, her mother wanted her kept safely on the Wickthorpe estate, and that meant that Lanny had to be free to come there and be welcomed as an honored guest.

This wasn't so hard for Ceddy as it might have been for some other men, for he was the impersonal type of Englishman. When he met you he didn't ask about the state of your soul, whether you were happy or unhappy, in love or out, prosperous or on the verge of bankruptcy. The nearest he came to intimacy was an inquiry about your cold, or your recent flu. "Beastly weather," he would say—a remark quite common in London—and then would ask what you thought was likely to be the outcome of Reynaud's efforts to replace Daladier—or it might be Mussolini's intentions as to Albania. His mind was an encyclopedia of details regarding the affairs of the Empire on which the sun never sets and the experienced group of people who managed it. Really you would have thought that he knew *Burke's Peerage* by heart; he could tell you right off that Baron Boskage was the fifth cousin of Viscount Tarpington, and just how that had come about. He could tell you without looking it up the name of the chargé d'affaires at Buenos Aires, whose son he was and what school he had attended.

Now of course he was ready to hear every word the son of Budd-Erling had to tell him about the masters of Germany: what they had said, what they were going to do, and when, and how. They sat in a small private dining room in the Carlton Club, Ceddy and Lanny and Gerald Albany, who was Ceddy's colleague and Lanny's friend of some years. They paid no attention to the waiter, a well-trained elderly man who was assumed to have no ears except when you gave him an order. What did Hitler really mean, and was he gone quite berserk? He had solemnly declared that he had no further territorial claims on Europe; he had said: "I want no Czechs." Was he going on breaking his word like that? And what would be next—Danzig, the Corridor, Memel? It was like living in a kaleidoscope!

XII

The position which Lanny took with these two friends was that of an art expert, aloof and somewhat precious; also a citizen of a neutral country, in that half of the world which had not yet gone mad. The Nazis One and Two gave him commissions, and Number Three was interested in psychic research. They had presumed upon his kindness enough to give him messages, things they wanted influential Britons to understand. All three of the Nazi masters wanted to be friends with Britain, wanted it cordially and genuinely, but only on the terms that

Germany must be free to take what she wanted in parts of the world that did not concern Britain. Danzig, the Corridor, Memel, and after that colonies—but not colonies of Britain; no—only those of small nations like Belgium, Holland, Portugal, which had more than they could use and certainly more than they could defend.

That was the problem; and while consuming first mutton broth with barley and then honest roast beef which is the Englishman's food, Lanny listened to a discussion of whether or not the British government could disinterest themselves in these matters and what would be the effect upon the safety of the Empire if they did. Ceddy and Gerald were not supposed to have any voice in the deciding of policy, but in practice the Cabinet leaned heavily upon the permanent officials, for it was the tradition that British foreign policy was always continuous, and these were the men who were always on hand, who had all the records and the answers to all the questions.

Lanny knew that both these men had been firm in their determination for "appeasement"; but now they had got a violent jolt, and were in the painful state of having to change their minds. That afternoon, in the House of Commons, Lanny had heard Lady Astor expressing her horror at what Hitler had done, and had heard a Labour member jeering at her: "What, Cliveden? Why don't you have another lunch?"—referring, of course, to that famous occasion when Lindbergh had come back from his tour of Europe and told her ladyship's guests that the Russian air force was worthless, and the German was superior to anything which Britain, France, Russia, and Czechoslovakia combined could put up against it. If the mistress of Cliveden had changed her mind, the pillars of the British Empire must be crumbling!

Lanny couldn't say: "I was shocked at the position which the Prime Minister took this afternoon. It is practically turning Hitler loose." Instead he remarked, tactfully: "I wonder if anyone has called the Prime Minister's attention to the significance of Hungary's move today?"

"How do you mean, Lanny?" inquired the dignified and austere Gerald Albany, a clergyman's son and Wordsworth scholar.

"Hungary is certainly not invading any part of Czechoslovakia without Hitler's permission, and if the reports are true that Count Teleki is taking over the government, that settles the matter, for he is to all practical purposes a Nazi. I noticed in the last few days that some of the Berlin papers suddenly stopped referring to the district as the Carpatho-Ukraine and took to calling it by its right name, Carpathian Ruthenia. That is enormously significant—in fact it seems to me the most important development of years, from your point of view."

Lanny stopped. Was he speaking in shorthand to two top experts, or was he being a little bit malicious and forcing those experts to ask for the answer to a problem which they should long ago have worked out for themselves?

"You mean," said Gerald, "that Hitler is giving up his scheme for an independent Ukraine at the expense of Russia?"

"Much more than that. If you look at the map you see that eastern Czechoslovakia is a long finger pointing straight into Russia and only a few miles short of that goal. Carpathian Ruthenia is the tip of that finger, and it affords Hitler a means of getting into Russia without crossing Poland. If he gives it up to Hungary, it means that he isn't going into Russia, and wants to assure Russia of the fact. Stalin is afraid to death of Hitler, but he's not in the least bit afraid of Teleki, and what the deal means is that Hitler is working behind the scenes for some arrangement with Stalin, just as he intimated to me he might do. Get the drop on Britain and France, was his idea."

"My God!" said the blond and pink-cheeked Ceddy, looking at his Foreign Office colleague with consternation in his bright blue eyes.

XIII

Ordinarily these two important men might have tried to cover up their confusion and give the impression that all this had been considered in their last office conference; but times were too serious right now, and neither felt like acting a part. What they wanted was for this American to repeat to them every word that Adi Schicklgruber had spoken on the subject of Bolshevism, the Soviet Union, the Russo-French alliance, and the attitude of Britain to both countries. Could it possibly be that the cynical wretch would be capable of turning his back on the principles he had been proclaiming over a period of—well, as far back as any Englishman had ever heard his name? The rotter, the cad—he was capable of anything! Lanny Budd, who had known Ceddy since boyhood, thought he had never seen him in such a state of mental upset. The whole policy of Britain had been based on the program that Hitler was to do his expanding to the eastward; and now he was letting the Hungarians close a gate across the highway.

"The Prime Minister must have his attention called to this," declared his lordship, and the clergyman's son assented quickly. That was as far as they would go in the presence of an outsider, even an old friend. They thanked Lanny, of course, but they wouldn't tell him any more.

However, there was nothing to keep Lanny from observing that the

Prime Minister traveled to his native city of Birmingham and delivered a scheduled address on Friday, there completely reversing the stand he had taken before Parliament on Wednesday. Then he had said, in substance, that what had happened was none of Britain's concern; but now, addressing the Birmingham Conservative Association, and with all Britain listening over the radio, he recited once more the story of his negotiations with Hitler, and how the Führer had signed a solemn agreement that future problems between the two nations should be settled by consultation. "Instead of that," said Chamberlain, "he has taken the law into his own hands." Referring to the policy of appeasement he declared: "I am convinced that after Munich the great majority of the British people shared my hope and ardently desired that that policy should be carried further, but today I share their disappointment, their indignation, that those hopes have been so wantonly shattered."

Yes, and more than that! The Prime Minister went on to ask: "Is this the end of an old adventure, or the beginning of a new? Is this the last attack upon a small state or is it to be followed by others? Is this, in fact, a step in the direction of an attempt to dominate the world by force?" He went on to serve a solemn warning to the dictator: "I feel bound to repeat that while I am not prepared to engage this country by new and unspecified commitments operating under conditions which cannot now be foreseen, yet no greater mistake could be made than to suppose that because it believes war to be a senseless and cruel thing, this nation has so lost its fiber that it will not take part to the utmost of its power in resisting such a challenge if it ever were made."

Lanny Budd had been watching statesmen most of his life, and it seemed to him that in all those years he had never known one to reverse himself so completely and in so short a time!

XIV

Lanny talked over these problems with Rick and then sent off a report to Washington, in which he ventured the prophecy that, as soon as the storm of popular protest had blown over, Chamberlain would go back to his policy of wobbling. He would never be able to take a firm stand against Hitler, because of his deeply rooted fear that Nazi-Fascism, if defeated, might turn into Bolshevism. "That is the key to the understanding of all political events in Europe," wrote the P.A. "In the long run, every statesman's acts today are dominated by the dread of social revolution in his own country and those of his neighbors."

Lanny's job was done for the nonce, and he was entitled to a holiday. He phoned to Irma, to ask if his coming would be agreeable, and she answered in her smooth, placid voice that it would be entirely so. This was a formality never omitted; they were scrupulously cordial to each other—both being satisfied with the new lives they had made since their parting four years ago, and anxious to make it possible for both to love their child and guard the child's peace of mind.

In a larger cottage on the estate lived Lanny's former mother-in-law, whom he still called "Mother," and her brother, called "Uncle Horace." They were all cream and honey to him; Fanny Barnes forbore urging him to play bridge because she knew it bored him, and she would quickly interrupt when her brother got started on one of his long-winded stories of the good old days when he had made fortunes in Wall Street and how he could do it again if only he had the money. All this watchfulness because of the horrid idea that if Lanny were not made comfortable and happy he might propose to take the little one on some sort of tour, say to Juan-les-Pins or to Newcastle.

Lanny had a three-hundred-year-old cottage which had been remodeled and supplied with all modern conveniences. He had to stoop slightly to come through the doorway, but once inside he had everything he wanted; a man-servant to wait upon him and prepare meals when he didn't care to come to the castle; the free use of a telephone, and it didn't matter if he chose to call Berlin or Juan or New York; a small piano and a radio set; his mail brought to him, and whatever newspapers he cared to order, including those from foreign capitals. The world had always done its utmost to spoil Lanny Budd, and his conscience gave him no rest about it; the more luxury he enjoyed, the more he hated the system of exploitation on which that luxury was based.

He spent most of his time with little Frances, on whose account he had come. He rode horseback about the estate with her; he watched with her the flocks of sheep, and fed the deer, the peacocks and lyrebirds, the swans and tame Canada geese. He listened to her play new pieces on the piano and played for her while she danced. He read to her and told her stories about sights he had seen and people he had met —but trying his best to keep away from politics. He was a romantic figure to her, and his visits were great occasions in the life of a "poor little rich girl." Her life was one of unbroken routine, but she was happy, and getting perfect training for a career as mistress of some great estate, as much like Wickthorpe as possible.

Also, he did not fail to make the acquaintance of the Honorable James Ponsonby Cavendish Cedric Barnes, Viscount Masterson, who was now half a year old, and was scheduled—"sheduled," the British pronounce it—to become the fifteenth Earl of Wickthorpe. The golden down on his head had become hair like his father's and his deep brown eyes turned to watch you in exactly the way his mother's did. He was a bond between Irma and Ceddy, just as Frances was a bond between Irma and Lanny. It was necessary that all five of these persons should be friends; so Lanny praised the noble infant's looks and signs of intelligence, and even took the time to win the esteem of the tall and severe-looking lady who had been chosen to serve as head nurse to this mite of combined aristocracy and plutocracy. Lanny would never mention but neither would he forget that J. Paramount Barnes, utilities king of Chicago, had begun life as an office boy; and here his grandson had been born a viscount, and was going to be an earl!

XV

In the evenings Lanny would read, or, if there were visitors, he would dress and go over to the castle. A week-end at Wickthorpe was an education in British political affairs, and therefore in world affairs. Men and women of various shades of opinion came; mostly conservatives, but liberals and even eccentrics were not excluded, provided they knew how to behave. Irma had made over and refurnished the castle according to Long Island ideas; some might cavil at her taste, but they soon got used to the American temperature and appreciated all the other conveniences. It was like a great private hotel used for conferences by public men and women who wanted to exchange views and broaden their understanding of events.

They treated an American art expert with great consideration; for how many men were there in England who could say that they had been guests at Berchtesgaden for a week or two at a time? Indeed, was there a single man in England who could say that he had been taken to the Führer's den on the top of the Kehlstein, reached by a tunnel and an elevator shaft seven hundred feet high? Was there a foreigner anywhere to whom the one-time *Gefreiter*—sub-corporal—had revealed his belief that Mohammed was the greatest statesman who had ever lived, and his determination to enforce German *Ordnung und Zucht* by the methods which this shepherd-prophet had demonstrated thirteen centuries ago?

Now, as never before, Englishmen and women felt pressed by the need to understand this strange disturber of the status quo, this half-genius, half-madman who had burst up from the depths of Central

European misery and despair. They discussed him in the pubs and on the street corners. "This 'ere 'Itler," or "that ole 'Itler," you would hear a charwoman say to a dustman; and in the drawing-rooms it was the same in more elegant language. The ordinary amenities in Wickthorpe Castle were suspended, and instead of a general interchange of opinions they wanted one man to do the talking. They plied him with a stream of questions. What is this Führer really like? What does he eat? What does he wear? Does he shout at you as he does over the radio? Is it true that his German is bad? And above all: What does he want, and will he really be satisfied when he's got it? How can anybody be sure he'll be satisfied? How can anybody take his word for anything?

Lanny had to be on the alert to meet such a barrage. Adi wanted him to say that he craved the friendship of England; so Lanny said it, again and again. "But on what terms?" the guests would ask. "His terms, or ours?" Lanny had to say: "I am afraid it will be on his." So then: "What are his terms? He changes them every day. If we concede anything, he takes it as a sign of weakness and proceeds to grab something else without asking. When is he going to stop?" The son of Budd-Erling had to say, more than once: "I am an art expert, not a politician or a psychologist. I can tell you what he told me, but I can't tell you what is going on in the back of his mind." Lanny had to use great care, for there were German agents all over England, and many of them in the highest circles.

XVI

Lanny had given four mail addresses to his friend Monck: the Adlon, Bienvenu, Newcastle, and his bank in London. Now he received a letter at this last address, reading: "I am sailing on the steamer *Atlantic*. The Defregger is in good condition. Your lady friend is a charming person. She is at the Excelsior Hotel. Braun."

That set a swarm of bees to buzzing in Lanny's head. This pair had got away with their risky undertaking! He wondered just what had happened? How had the woman stood it, and what was she making of it now? Had she guessed anything about the supercharger? What was she going to do with the car? And was she going back to Berlin? So many questions he would have liked to ask out of idle curiosity!

He found himself thinking of Laurel Creston in a new way. Hitherto she had been a clever writer and good company—especially as a listener to lectures on art. But now she had been put to a real test, and had stood it; now she was a comrade, even something of a heroine! Lanny thought: "She went through with it, just as if she were a man." He knew that he could never mention the subject to her, not even by the faintest hint. But would she mention it to him? Would she yield to the temptation to tell somebody about the extraordinary thing that had befallen her? Lanny found himself saying: "If she wants to learn to drive a car, I might teach her." And then: "If she wants to sell it, I could give her advice." And again: "London isn't the same as Berlin, so far as gossip is concerned. Nobody would pay any attention if I met her here."

A set of temptations almost impossible to resist. Here she was, within a couple of miles of him; here was a telephone and a book with the number of her hotel in it; all he had to do was to pick up the receiver. After all, he assured himself, Laurel Creston hadn't written anything against the Nazis—not yet. And he had been somewhat rude to her, and ought to make up for it—just by a casual courtesy, say a walk in the park. It would be a sort of joke, a sort of cat and mouse play; there was a secret between them, and both knew what it was, but she didn't know that he knew. He would be in the position of a playwright who knows how the play is going to end, but the audience doesn't know, and he has the pleasure of watching its reactions.

The hotel, whose name Lanny had never heard before, was in the Kensington district. He called it, and apparently the guest had to be summoned from upstairs; he had quite a wait before he heard her voice. "Your friend from Berlin," he said—no use using names! "What made you run away so suddenly?"

She answered: "I thought you had run first." She would never be at a loss for words.

He made a date, to treat her to a lunch in the old English style, at Simpson's on the Strand; he told her how to get there. He was in something of a glow as he listened to her voice, and when he met her he discovered that she was in the same state; she would be that way for a long while, for this had been the most exciting experience of a well-bred and well-brought-up young lady's life—very certainly the first time she had come into conflict with the laws of any country, the first time it had occurred to her to think of the police as anything but servants and protectors. And just because Lanny had been in Berlin, he would pring it back to life in her mind; she would be thinking how excited he would be if she were to tell him what she had done!

They sat at a small table in a hundred-year-old restaurant, now become modern and elegant; but a servitor still came with a small metal cart on rubber tires, or tyres in England. When he lifted the cover your eyes beheld a huge roast of beef sizzling in a pan; your nostrils were assailed by delicious odors, and if you said the word he would cut you off an elegant slice. Or you could wait for another cart with a leg of mutton almost as big. Lanny's guest was appalled by the prospect, and Lanny suggested fried smelts, better adapted to a lady's mouth. He said: "Byron expressed the opinion that a woman should never be seen eating." Then he inquired: "You know Byron's poetry?" In his mind was the thought, what a sensation if he should begin to recite:

> Eternal Spirit of the chainless Mind!
> Brightest in dungeons, Liberty! thou art: . . .

XVII

She told him, in the most casual of tones, that she had come to London on business, and was planning to return to Berlin in a few days. "I find Germany very interesting," she remarked. "I want to try to understand it thoroughly."

And that was all; she wasn't going to discuss the basis of her interest, or say anything about the underground—not to a troglodyte, a dweller in darkness, a person in whom no humanity was to be assumed. Nor was she going to say anything about his having neglected her in Berlin. No, if a gentleman does not desire the society of a Baltimore lady, she would have her tongue cut out before she would drop a hint on the subject. It is his privilege to stay away, and hers to be busy with more important matters!

Nor was she going to say a word about the car. He thought: "Maybe she has had lessons, and will offer to take me for a drive!" But nothing of the sort; she talked about the London weather, which can be bad in March, and about a concert she had attended at Queen's Hall. "Sir Thomas Beecham is a lively and volatile person," Lanny remarked.

He told her he had brought a painting out of Germany. He didn't say it belonged to Göring, for that would surely have displeased her, right now while she was in a revolutionary mood. He said: "A Canaletto; do you know him? He painted Venice in the eighteenth century." He told her about this particular example, and then said: "Have you visited the museums here?" When she replied that her visits had been brief, he suggested that the Tate Gallery was not to be missed. It was just a short walk to the Embankment and he offered to escort her. This meant another of his free lectures, for which she thanked him.

They strolled, and came to an open space where stood a lorry, and on it several men with the collars of their overcoats turned up and their hands in their pockets, it being a raw day. One was making a speech to a crowd which left barely room for the traffic to get past. He was denouncing the apathy of the British government while the free peoples of Europe were assassinated one by one. He was suspicious of the ruling classes of his own country, and thought they did not like republics, and especially not those which had a Socialist tinge, like Spain.

That much the pair heard as they pushed through the crowd. Lanny didn't offer to stop, for he had to keep away from the dangerous subject of politics. His companion asked: "Do you think there will be a war?" and he answered: "Not yet, but soon; there are always wars in Europe, you know." It was the ivory-tower attitude, and they passed on out of the noise of traffic and mob, and into the dignity and quiet of one of the world's great art treasures.

Now Lanny was at home, and could talk out of his heart. Since his friend had no special preference, he took her to the Turners. His eyes lighted up and his soul warmed as he gazed at them; his manner appeared to say that whether or not Europe went to war was a small matter compared with the fact that a man of genius had learned to put upon a piece of canvas all the marvels of the sky, the glory of sunsets, the terror of storms, the mystery of vast distances veiled by haze. He told about this odd character who had been embittered because his talents were not appreciated to the full, and who would come to the Academy on Varnishing Day and add bright reds and yellows to his canvas in order to "kill" some rival's work which had been placed alongside. Here was *The Fighting* Téméraire *Being Towed to Her Last Berth*, by a tug with a tall smokestack, through a symbolical sunset over a river. It had been exactly a hundred years ago that the painter had come and heightened the glory of that sunset because he objected to some painting which had been hung beside it for a few weeks!

"Artists are strange creatures," remarked the son of Budd-Erling; and in his mind was the thought that Laurel Creston must be thinking him a strange creature, too—a man who could be completely indifferent to the fact that the peoples of Europe might be plunging into a slaughter pit at the very hour when he was delivering a lecture on the painting of light. In his pleasure over some pigments spread on canvas he was forgetting the fact that now, as he spoke, a thousand bombing planes might be on their way to blow the paintings and the museum which held them and the city which held the museum all into the original molecules of which they had been put together!

BOOK THREE

Let Joy Be Unconfined

10

When Fortune Favors

I

LANNY called his father on the transatlantic telephone, a new miracle which had been brought in during the past two or three years; at first it had been noisy, but now it was fairly clear. The cost was high, and unless you were very rich you considered what you were going to put into your three minutes.

Lanny said: "Your friend Tiergarten is on the way"—that being the code word they had agreed upon.

"Good God!" exclaimed Robbie. "You don't mean it!"

"Expect him in a few days. He is well and happy, so far as I know." Lanny would have liked to say more, and Robbie would have liked to ask questions, but it wouldn't do. "I'm coming myself. I have a couple of picture deals to attend to and then I'll pay you a visit. How is everybody?"

Robbie had nothing special to report. Business was picking up fast; the world was coming his way. Lanny said: "Remember the precautions we agreed upon; they are urgent." This was in reference to the supercharger, and Robbie said: "Trust me." He was used to keeping secrets and didn't have to be told twice, especially not over the transatlantic telephone. Lanny asked about members of the family, and then said: "Well, so long!" He didn't even need all his three minutes.

He shipped the painting by express, and put his car in storage with the hotel. With steamer trunk, one suitcase, and his little typewriter, he boarded a boat-train. Ocean liners had become palaces in these days, and Lanny had a smooth passage, and plenty of time to think over his plans. He was on the way to see one whom he considered the most important of living men. Putting things into his mind was the nearest Lanny could come to changing the world, the present state of which was so little to his taste.

II

Arriving in New York, Lanny's first action was to telephone to his father. "Has our friend arrived?" The reply was: "I have met him, and I think everything is all right. It will be some days before I can be certain."

"Do you need me in the meantime?" When the father answered in the negative, Lanny explained: "I have a deal that ought to be attended to at once. I'll call you again in a couple of days."

That being settled, Lanny called a secret number in Washington and asked for "Baker." When he heard the voice he gave his code name and number, and the reply was: "Call back in three hours." That gave Lanny a chance to have a bath and a shave, and to read the papers and learn that his friend Adi Schicklgruber had rounded out the grabbing season by moving into Memel, a part of Lithuania at the eastern edge of East Prussia. Madrid was in the last throes of its agony, which had lasted something like a hundred and forty weeks—and not one of those weeks that Lanny's heart hadn't ached for what was happening. A grim time to be living in—and this moment the grimmest yet.

Lanny indulged in telephone chats with several friends, including Zoltan Kertezsi, whom he had called a "grasshopper." Zoltan's latest hop had brought him to New York, where he was supervising a one-man show of Jacovleff, one of his discoveries. He wanted to rave about it, and Lanny said: "See you before long; I have to skip out of town."

Promptly on the minute he put in the Washington call, and the voice of Baker requested him to fly to Washington and be on a certain street corner at nine that evening. Lanny repeated the time and place and said: "O.K." Flying two hundred miles was a routine matter, and the P.A. established himself in a Washington hotel, ate his dinner, read the evening papers, and listened to a radio in his room until the time drew near. Promptly on the second he strolled to the corner agreed upon; a car drew up, the rear door was opened, and he stepped into a vacant seat.

He gave his code number and a flashlight was turned upon his face. "O.K.," said the familiar voice. He knew nothing about the man, and the man knew nothing about him except face and voice. Lanny said: "I have sent you a total of eleven reports since I was last here. Is that correct?" The reply was: "They have all been delivered."

Lanny added: "The last time, you searched me."

"I know you now," was the answer.

"It won't hurt my feelings if you make sure," replied Lanny. "I think a lot of the Chief."

The man passed a pair of quick practiced hands over Lanny's overcoat and then under it, not omitting his armpits and trouser-legs. This ceremony over, he said: "O.K.—and thanks," and that was the end of conversation. Superfluous words were considered bad form.

They drove into the grounds of Number 1600 Pennsylvania Avenue, known to most of the world as the White House. They drove up to the front entrance, tactfully called the "social door" and serving the purposes of a "back door." Baker escorted the visitor, and the guards admitted them without question. They went up a flight and a half by a broad stairway, and Baker said "Hello" to a colored attendant who sat just outside a half-open door. He tapped, and a voice that most of the world knows over the radio called: "Come in." And so Lanny Budd entered the chamber of the man whom he had chosen for his guide.

III

F.D.R. was in bed, as always on these occasions; it was a big old-fashioned mahogany bed with a carved back. He had on blue-and-white-striped pongee pajamas, with a comfortable blue cape about his large and strong shoulders. He had a collection of legal-appearing documents on his lap, and he put these aside, took off his spectacles, and leaned over to greet his visitor with a handshake and a cheerful "Hello." Not until Baker had bowed himself out and closed the door did he speak the visitor's name. "Well, Lanny! Every time you come you bring me a bigger load of troubles!"

"That's why I come," replied the other, with a grin. He had had four sessions here and one at Hyde Park, and understood this genial great man's fondness for "kidding."

"Great guns! You sure collected a mess this time! Has the great anaconda finished his swallowing act?"

That was an invitation for Lanny to tell his story, and he went to it. He had already put the essentials into his reports; now he went over the same ground, putting in the local color, bringing to life the various personalities involved in the diplomatic battle of Europe. There was a minor battle going on inside Germany for the possession of the Führer's mind; it was between—you couldn't say the conservatives, for there were no such leaders of the NSDAP, but there were some less reckless than others. Göring and Hess were among these, and Lanny had sought them as his friends; the other crowd, of whom Ribbentrop and Goebbels were the most conspicuous, he couldn't stand, even as a matter of duty.

The "Governor" wanted to know how deep that cleavage went; would it ever become a real split? Lanny answered: "Not a chance of it. Once Hitler announces his decision, they all fall into line, like so many humble rookies. The reason for that is, not so much that they trust Hitler—many of them privately think he's a bit cracked—but they know he's managed to get the German people behind him. That is the basis of his power—that, and his luck; he's managed to get away with one thing after another, and of course every concession by the rest of the world increases that prestige, makes him bolder and his people more adoring."

Said F.D.R.: "I have the feeling that we are drifting into a frightful calamity."

"There can be no question about it, Governor." The great man had been Governor of New York State, and it had been a simple homely job compared to the one he now had, that was enough to break the back of a dromedary, so he declared.

Lanny went on: "The world needs someone to take command and put a block across the pathway of these dictators."

"I see you looking at me," replied the man in the striped pajamas. His words were playful but his look became grave. "I can only tell you that I am completely helpless. The American people are not awake to the situation and will not listen to any warning. They fear Europe, they despise it a little, because of the hateful things that are done there. They do not see the slightest reason why they should stick their fingers into the mess. Isolation is the watchword of the hour, and every smallest move I make to help our friends abroad brings a storm about my head. You saw what happened the other day when I let the French purchase a few of our military planes."

"Yes," replied Lanny, "I had a talk with Bullitt after he got back to Paris."

"Well, you can say that I should have the courage to face such storms; and I do; but I am not a dictator and have no idea of becoming one, in spite of all that my enemies say. I cannot afford to break completely with Congress, for if I do I merely render myself impotent for the scant two years of office that I have left, and if I cannot influence the choice of my successor I shall have the pain of seeing all my New Deal measures repealed and my labors brought to naught."

"I don't think you need worry about the two years, Governor. I can assure you that Hitler will force a crisis before that—unless, of course, the British are prepared to back down completely and let him treat Poland as he has treated Czechoslovakia."

"They give me very strong assurances that they will not do that; and we have all been cheered by the firm stand which Chamberlain has taken."

"God knows I hope he sticks by it," declared the son of Budd-Erling. "But his temperament is all against that, and the forces which will try to break him down again are powerful and unscrupulous. Oddly enough, it wasn't the fate of Prague which moved him to protest, but a small block of territory at the eastern tip of Slovakia which separated Poland from Hungary and gave Hitler access to Rumania and then into Russia if he wanted it." Lanny told the story of his talk with Wickthorpe and Albany on Wednesday evening and the public outburst of Chamberlain on Friday. The President chuckled, for he had a streak of mischief in him and doubtless was no ardent admirer of that stiff and lanky representative of Birmingham commercialism; he didn't love that type at home and they didn't love him.

"Lanny," he remarked, "you must get a great kick out of your job, associating exclusively with the world's headliners. How on earth do you manage it?"

"It's largely a matter of accident. My father's job brought me into contact with prominent people, and my own job helps me to keep it up. Hitler thinks he is promoting friendship with both France and America when he buys some of my former stepfather's paintings, and when he sends me to Paris and London with messages about his ardent love for those nations. I deliver the messages, and the wealthy and fashionable appeasers receive them gladly. I can only hope and pray that the damage I do is overbalanced by the value of what I bring to you."

"I think you can reckon upon that," said the President. "I have read all your reports, and I keep your facts in mind. You must understand my position—the American people have piled a man-killing job onto my shoulders. No one man can know the hundredth part of what I am required to know. Look at this, for example." He pointed to the mass of papers which he had set to one side on his bed. "I have promised to give a decision on all that tomorrow morning. And some day, sure as God made little apples, I shall have to give decisions about Europe. Most of my information comes from men who see through colored spectacles—and the color isn't Pink, believe me! The playboys of our diplomatic crowd, who meet only the plush-lined set in Europe and gather their facts and interpretations at tea parties—you know them, I am sure."

"Indeed, yes, Governor!"

"Well, a man who knows Europe as you do, and yet keeps the democratic point of view, is truly useful to me. I want you to know it and never have any doubts about it."

"That's all I need to hear," replied the P.A., fervently. "I can get along for a year on that."

IV

It was time for him to offer to depart, and he did so. But his Chief said: "No, I don't see you very often. Tell me your plans."

"I thought I would take a few weeks off, unless you have something urgent in mind. I have some picture deals to attend to—that's how I pay my way."

"You understand that I will put you on my payroll if you wish."

"There is no need of it. I get a lot of fun out of handling pictures, and it gives me a chance to travel about and get acquainted with my own country. I don't think there's anything important going to happen in Europe this spring. The anaconda has got his bellyful, and all he wants is to be let alone while he digests it."

F.D. put a cigarette into the long thin holder which he used, lighted it and took a puff or two. Then he began: "You know, Lanny, we have been having another business recession, and much as I dislike it, I can't see any other recourse but another shot of lending and spending. Congress is balking; in fact, they have got to the point where they won't do anything if they think it's what I want. They refuse to modify the Neutrality Act and allow me to distinguish between aggressor and peaceful states. They know that this impotence is one of the main factors the dictators count upon; but Congress will not act, and so I am tied hand and foot."

This appeared to be an opening, and Lanny stepped in. "All but your tongue," he ventured.

"I am afraid of using that too much. People soon get tired of hearing only scolding and complaining."

"Do you want me to speak frankly, Governor?"

"Nothing else is ever of any use to me."

"You must understand that I have a pretty lonely life over in Europe. I can't explain my conduct or ideas to anyone, and it cuts me off from all social life—except what you might call my stage career, with the Nazis and Fascists whom I despise and have to pretend to admire. So you must know that I think about you a lot; I'm all the time having imaginary talks with you, and imagining what I would do in your place. I make my reports as brief as possible, but in my imaginary talks I say a mouthful."

"Say one now!" countered the great man, with one of those chuckles which were characteristic.

"I say that you don't talk enough to the people. They are deluged with falsehood, in a thousand subtle disguises, and it's impossible for them to see through all Dr. Goebbels' tricks. What we are fighting is not just German Nazism and Italian and Spanish Fascism; it's a world-wide movement and it takes a hundred different forms. It's all over our own country. It's privilege and class domination; it's our big-business newspapers, our giant corporations which are tied up tight with the European cartels. Our people haven't the slightest idea of all that; their thinking is a hundred years behind the times."

"It will take events to educate them, Lanny."

"Events are nothing by themselves; they have to be interpreted and explained. Enough has happened already, but the people just don't understand it."

"You want me to deliver a lecture on cartels?"

"When I put myself in your place, what I do is to write a sort of open letter to Hitler and Mussolini. I say to them: 'Just what is it you want? Why aren't you willing to bring your case into court and let it be settled by fair negotiations? You are driving the whole world to a race of armaments; you are spreading uneasiness and fear everywhere, and what is it all for? What are your purposes, and what guarantees are you willing to give to the peace-loving peoples of the world, of which we Americans are surely one?' I feel quite sure that such an appeal would be approved by ninety per cent of our public."

"You think the dictators would pay any attention to it?"

"It would present them with a problem. Goebbels would rave and insult you; but that's all right, that would show the ninety per cent of our people what sort of dirty dog he is. All over this country, in the barbershops and crossroads stores, people would be saying: 'The President put fair and honest questions to them, and look how they answer; they must be crooks and they must be looking for trouble.' You can be sure nobody would be bored by such a letter, and only a few of the diehard isolationists would say that you were butting in where you had no business."

F.D.R. took several puffs on his cigarette, staring before him meanwhile; then he turned his gray eyes upon his visitor and said: "You're not the first who has had that idea, Lanny. Bill Bullitt suggested it when he was here, and Henry Wallace brought it up just the other day. Tell me: would you like to take a shot at drafting such a document?"

Lanny's face lighted up. "You really mean that, Governor?"

"I'm not making any promises. I think I told you how I work. I talk over a speech or a letter or whatever it may be with half a dozen friends, and I tell each of them to try a shot at it. Maybe I take a paragraph here or an idea there; maybe some fellow hits it just right and I use a lot of it; again, maybe something causes me to change my mind and drop the whole thing for the present. In this present case, I gather, you have the ideas pretty clear in your mind."

"Don't worry about that. I don't mind working any length of time if you'll read it."

"You may count upon my giving careful thought to it. I'm planning to leave for Warm Springs, Georgia, for a few days' rest, and if you'll get the copy to Baker he'll send it to me there. You'd better let me see you again before you go back to Europe, for I might need to ask you something."

V

Lanny went out from the presence, just about walking on air. He was going to have another chance to change the world! As had happened on a previous occasion, he was so excited that sleep seemed commonplace and unalluring. He wanted to take a long walk and think about all the things he had to say to Hitler and Mussolini—things that had been accumulating in his mind for almost a score of years, ever since the time of the San Remo conference when he had first laid eyes upon a smallish pasty-faced Italian intellectual with dark eyes and a little mustache, engaged in a political argument in a *trattoria*. One of this man's former comrades had given him a scare, denouncing him as *furfante* and *traditore dei lavoratori*, which are very impolite terms in their own language. Lanny would have liked to use them again, but of course they wouldn't belong in an open letter from the President of the United States to the Duce del Impero Romano, and holder of half a dozen cabinet posts in the Kingdom of Italy.

Spring comes earlier in Washington than in London, and this was a pleasant evening. Lanny walked from one white marble building to the next—all brightly illuminated at night. There was something like a tide flowing into his mind, a powerful tide like those that sweep into the Bay of Fundy, or Cherbourg harbor, or other places where great seas are funneled into a narrow channel. All the things that the grandson of Budd Gunmakers had been thinking about Fascism, all those that the son of Budd-Erling had been thinking about Nazism, were going to be concentrated and condensed into one masterpiece of eloquence which Franklin D. Roosevelt would hurl at the heads of the two dictators—and incidentally release to the radio and press of the civilized world.

The P.A. came back to his hotel room and sat up in bed for a while making notes so that he wouldn't forget any of his important ideas. This room was as good as any in which to work; so next morning, after a glance at the Washington papers—one of them as close to Fascist as it was possible to get without the label—Lanny settled himself at his little typewriter. All day he hammered away, and part of the night; he revised and rejected, burning up everything he didn't use. He had to do all the work himself, for of course he mustn't trust any typist.

On the second day he was satisfied, and made a clean copy. He had decided that he would pick on the Führer of the Germans, because he knew him better. Now, reading the document over, it was as if he were in Berchtesgaden, speaking his real thoughts to the half-genius half-madman in that asylum. Said Lanny:

"You realize, I am sure, that throughout the world hundreds of millions of human beings are living in constant fear of a new war or even a series of wars. The existence of this fear—and the possibility of such a conflict—is of definite concern to the people of the United States for whom I speak, as it must also be to the peoples of the other nations of the entire Western Hemisphere. All of them know that any major war, even if it were to be confined to other continents, must bear heavily on them during its continuance and also for generations to come."

Lanny went on to list the recent attacks upon three nations in Europe and one in Africa, and then wrote: "You have repeatedly asserted that you and the German people have no desire for war. If this is true there need be no war." He went on to call for "a frank statement relating to the present and future policy of governments." He invited the Führer to make such a statement to him, offering "to transmit it to all the other governments concerned and invite them to give similar assurances." Conferences would be held, in which "the government of the United States will gladly take part." He concluded with an implication that neither Hitler nor anyone else would miss:

"In conference rooms, as in courts, it is necessary that both sides enter upon the discussion in good faith, assuming that substantial justice will accrue to both; and it is customary and necessary that they leave their arms outside the rooms where they confer."

Lanny called a messenger and sent his precious manuscript to Baker. After he had called up and made sure it had been received and would be delivered to "the proper party," he burned his carbon copy, for he made it a rule never to keep one scrap of any P.A. document, either on his person or anywhere in storage. If ever his secret leaked it wasn't going to be through any carelessness of his own.

VI

Lanny didn't phone his father from Washington, because he didn't want Robbie to get the idea that he had any special business in that city. He took the first plane back to New York and phoned from there. Robbie said: "I am still awaiting a final report. Come out and see us, and I'll tell you about it."

So the much-traveling agent boarded a New Haven train to Newcastle, a couple of hours' ride along the Sound. He took a taxi to his father's home in the suburbs of the town, and just had time to greet his stepmother and hear some of the news about a large family before Robbie came in. After dinner they shut themselves up in the father's den and Lanny told his story, carefully thought out to be the truth though not the whole truth.

"I met this fellow in London about five years ago. He's a German Socialist, and I think used to be a sailor. I happened to recollect him and sounded him out. He wanted money, so I put the proposition to him. He said he'd see what he could do, and presently he wrote me a note saying that he thought he could arrange it. The next thing I got was a postcard from Holland, saying that he was on his way to London. Then I got a note in care of Rick saying that he was on his way by steamer. And that's all I know."

Robbie took up the story. "He phoned me three days ago from New York. 'This is Tiergarten,' was all he said. I had decided not to let him come to Newcastle because small places are full of talk. I said: 'I'll be in New York in two hours.' He answered: 'I'll be standing on the northwest corner of 35th and Lexington.' I drove myself in, so no one else would share the secret. When I came to the corner, there was a man with a big box tied up in burlap. He got into the car, and said: 'Drive on.' I drove, and he said: 'I had to cut the thing to pieces. I hope that won't ruin it for you.' I said: 'Not if all the pieces are there.' He said: 'I can't guarantee anything. If it isn't right, somebody has played a trick on us. Germany is full of rascality. Take the thing and test it, and if it's no good to you, dump it into the river. Meantime, I'll stay at the hotel.' I told him: 'It may be a week or two. I have to turn it over to two of my experts and they have to take it to another place to test it. I don't want to do anything in my own plant.' He answered: 'Your son told me to trust you, and I'm doing it. I'll phone you at the end of two weeks and if you need more time, I'll wait.' And that was that. He got out of the car, and I haven't heard from him since."

"He is a man who can't afford to talk much," explained Lanny. "He knows you have Nazis in your plant, and there are plenty more in New York."

"Have you any idea how he could manage this stunt?"

"Not the slightest. I know he got the gadget on Saturday night, and I had lunch with Göring on Monday before I left; he was perfectly amiable, so I felt sure he hadn't missed anything."

Said the competent man of affairs: "There is no record of a patent, so evidently he's been counting on keeping the secret."

"I have worried a little," replied the less competent son, "because when he misses it, you and I will be the first persons he suspects, and that could do me a lot of harm."

"Trust me about that, Lanny. I had my eyes on a small shop in Indiana and I bought it for a reasonable price. I have a couple of young fellows who know superchargers from nose to tail, and they put this box into their car and drove out there. They phoned me that they have put it together and are testing its performance. So far, it looks good—that's all I can say. Even if it turns out to be the real thing, I don't think you need worry about Göring; for before we get through with it, we may improve it so that he wouldn't know his own child. It'll be six months before we can be in production, and another six before Göring hears about it. Maybe he'll be at war by that time, and have other things to think about; anyhow, I'll be buying the gadgets from a concern that is entirely independent of Budd-Erling. And of course the fat rascal knows I'm entitled to the device."

"That wouldn't make him love me any better!" remarked Lanny. He couldn't say more than that, for of course Robbie assumed that he was thinking of his picture business, a small item in comparison with what Robbie stood to gain.

VII

The president of Budd-Erling had enlarged the garage on his estate, and there were half a dozen cars in it. A shiny new roadster with a large trunk in back was put at Lanny's disposal, and next morning the darling of fortune set out on a sunshiny April Fool's Day. He found that the Canaletto had arrived and he cleared it through the customs and then drove uptown to lunch with Zoltan Kertezsi and show this treasure.

It was a fine painting of the Piazetta in Venice, showing the Campanile and San Marco and the famous columns in the foreground, the Grand Canal with its gondolas, all in careful perspective, a fine sky with clear light and hard lines. There had been an uncle named Canale whose works brought high prices, and there had been a nephew who imitated him and sometimes signed his name. So there were delicate questions involved, and Zoltan gave his opinion: this was the finest Canaletto that he had ever seen, and he wondered, had *Der Dicke* failed to appreciate it? He agreed with Lanny that Harlan Winstead would almost certainly want to add this work to his collection. Zoltan offered to go along and add his confirmation, so Lanny telephoned, and next day drove his friend out to Shepherd's Corner, the unassuming pastoral name of the finest estate that either of them knew of in the western world. It was at Tuxedo Park, and behind its immense bronze gates lived a gentleman of Boston descent who had inherited a huge fortune, had accumulated all the culture of the ages, and was as desolate and unhappy as anybody could be and still live.

"Oh, why should the spirit of mortal be proud?" a poet had inquired, and this man had thought that he had the answers. His possessions included not merely ancestry and wealth, which he had inherited, but taste and fine ideals, which he had acquired. He had been educated at Groton and Harvard, and all his life had cultivated what was refined and elegant, and held himself aloof from everything noisy and common. He had built this magnificent estate, surrounded by a high metal fence with spearpoints turned outward against a hostile world. He had found himself a gracious wife, trained in his own traditions, and she had borne him two lovely daughters. Together they had spent some twenty years raising these daughters, guarding them carefully from every contact with the vulgar herd—with the result that one of the young ladies eloped with a groom on the estate and the other insisted upon a marriage equally unworthy of her high station. The proud father refused ever to see either of them, and his lovely wife pined away and died; so now this white-haired old man lived alone in haughty splendor, holding his head high and never telling anyone what was going on in his heart.

All that he had left was a magnificent collection of paintings which by his will was to go to a museum. They represented his taste, reinforced by Zoltan's over a period of a dozen years, plus that of Lanny for a half dozen. It was his quiet conviction that there was not one second-rate work in his gallery. He differed from other collectors Lanny knew in that he had no whims or peculiarities that you could cater to; if he said: "This is art!" it was because a great painter had chosen a great theme and done it justice. So now, when the Canaletto was hung in front of Mr. Winstead and he sat and studied it, Lanny held his breath. He had told Göring that he could get twenty thousand dollars for this not very large picture of Venice two hundred years ago. (It hadn't changed much in the interim.) Lanny wouldn't say who owned the painting, for that was an extraneous matter, and Harlan Lawrence Winstead was so fastidious and exacting a person that he mightn't want anything in his home that reminded him of an old-style German robber baron with beer on his breath and blood on his hands.

But works of art have no smell, whether of beer, blood, or the foul canals of an over-aged Italian city. Mr. Winstead said, quietly: "I think that a Canaletto belongs in my collection"; and that was all there was to it. Lanny explained: "The owner prefers not to be known, and has authorized me to sign the bill of sale." There was nothing unusual about that, since many of the old families of Europe considered it a sort of humiliation to part with their art treasures. The purchaser told his secretary to make out a check, and Lanny wrote a bill of sale in which he specified the name of the painter, the subject and the size; thus he earned a commission that would pay for all his traveling, and in the most elegant style.

The two experts were invited to stay to lunch. Two decorously clad servants waited upon them in silence, and having lunch at Shepherd's Corner was something like attending a church service—only the talk had to do with the salons in Paris, London, and Berlin, and with painters who were believed to be "coming on," and others who represented false tendencies. Perversity appears to be ingrained in human nature, and notoriety hunting is as common in the field of art as in literature, politics, or social life; but these three gentlemen of elegance and taste repudiated it with quiet severity. From first to last they spoke only of the graphic arts, and if you hadn't known anything else about life you might have come to the conclusion that correct putting of paint upon canvas and of pencil and crayon and pen upon paper was the purpose for which the Almighty had created a universe.

VIII

When Lanny got back to his hotel he found in his mail one of those plain envelopes which caused his heart to give a jump. It had been sent in Robbie's care and forwarded from Newcastle. It contained nothing but a telephone number, which Lanny lost no time in calling; when he heard his friend's voice he said: "Can you be at the northwest corner of 35th and Lexington in ten minutes?" That, of course, was equivalent to saying: "I have talked with my father."

Lanny drove and picked up his fellow-conspirator. "Welcome to our city!" he said, with a grin; and then, without delay: "My father is still waiting for his final report; but so far, things look good."

"That's all right," replied the other. "I haven't been to your city in more than ten years, so I'm able to keep myself entertained."

"What you have done has staggered me!" exclaimed the American. "How on earth did you manage it?"

"I'm not supposed to tell; but as a matter of fact I know very little. I had the good fortune to hit on the right man; he said he would make the try, and all I know is, I was told to leave the car at a certain place and the gadget would be taken apart and stowed in the car by seven o'clock on Sunday morning. I went there at the time set, and the man said: 'It's all there and all ready.' I took it on trust, and here I am."

"That is surely what you Germans call *Tüchtigkeit*."

Monck wanted to know: "Have you seen anything in the papers about the matter? I have been watching such as I could get."

"There was nothing in Germany before I left, nor in London. I concluded that it must have been an inside job, and that somebody was interested in keeping it quiet."

"You can bet on that. It cost quite a sum of money. I had to promise to bring in fifty thousand freimarks. Somebody went bond for me, I imagine."

"Well, you'll be able to make good—of course assuming the gadget is the real thing."

"If it isn't, I'll never be able to convince those people that I didn't get the money."

"Let us hope for the best. My father knows—and I never knew him to break his word." Then Lanny added: "Tell me about your trip."

"There's nothing much to tell. That lady is a brick—I believe that's what you Americans say."

"Not about ladies, as a rule. You had no trouble?"

"She was a well-to-do tourist and her papers were in order. She had a chauffeur, and his were in order. We went through like any other tourists. But she's different from others—she wouldn't keep the car."

"The devil you say!"

"She didn't know how to drive and didn't want to fool with it. She took it to a second-hand dealer and got two hundred and seventy pounds; she kept forty to cover her expenses in London and her trip back to Berlin. She said: 'Use the rest for the cause.'"

"Well, I'll be damned!" remarked the son of Budd-Erling. "I didn't suppose she knew anything about the cause."

"I don't think she did when she started; *aber, Herrschaft!*—she surely did when we got to London. She sat in the back seat of that car for about twelve hours altogether and shot questions at me out of a machine gun; first about the underground and how it worked—I couldn't tell her much, but I told what I could; and then about the Social-Democratic Party, how it grew and what strength it had before Hitler; and the Communists, and why we couldn't work with them; and then, what the Socialists believe, and how it would work—you know, all the things we learned thirty years ago, and take for granted that everybody knows, but they don't: who will do the dirty work, and how can there be incentives in a collectivist system, and will there be public ownership of toothbrushes. All that while we were approaching the border, and knew that the Nazis might grab us both!"

"Well, it took your mind off your troubles!" chuckled Lanny.

"It was a pleasure to answer, because she got what you said. She wanted the names of some books to read, and she wanted to write them down, but I wouldn't let her until we had got out of Germany. I actually believe she intends to get them and read them."

"Haven't you known women who get books and read them?"

"Not often; as a rule they just want to be able to say they have read them. But this is a fine girl, and you ought to see more of her."

"I thought maybe you had that in mind when you gave me her address in London. I asked her to lunch at Simpson's."

"What I had in mind," said the ex-Capitán, bluntly, "was that you might ask her to marry you."

The ex-playboy chuckled again. "I thought of that, too. But instead, I took her to see the Turners in the Tate Gallery." After a moment, thinking this might sound snobbish, he added: "What would I do with a wife, old man—jumping about the world as I have to?"

"Well, I don't see my wife very often; but she knows I'm working for the cause and not fooling with other women, and so she sticks."

Lanny answered, in a tone that no one could mistake for snobbish: "Trudi sticks by me, *Genosse*. There isn't a day that I don't think about her; and when I have a difficult decision to make, it is just as if she were with me, passing one of her stern judgments. I am sure she will never permit me to weaken in the battle against Fascism."

"You mean by that that you believe in survival after death?"

"I've never been able to make up my mind about that. But memory is a kind of survival, and a very strange thing; we only fool ourselves if we think we understand it. Does memory exist only in our minds, or does the universe have memory, too? The physicists have moved a long way since the days when you learned materialistic monism in a Marxist Sunday school. They tell us now that time may be something which our minds impose upon reality; and if that's true, it may well be that anything which ever existed exists always in some other form."

"If I tried to think about things like that," declared the serious-minded Socialist, "I wouldn't know if I was standing on my feet or my head."

Said Lanny, with a smile: "That is exactly what everybody said when Copernicus began telling them that the world was round!"

IX

The son of Budd-Erling meant to stay in New York until the matter of the supercharger had been settled; but he couldn't be seen with his fellow-conspirator because there were many Nazi agents here, and some knew Lanny and some might know Monck. The P.A. went off by himself, and thought about Laurel Creston, and the extraordinary fact that she had refused to be paid for helping an underground worker to escape from the Gestapo. Lanny did things like that himself, but he didn't expect others to do them, at least not members of what he called the "bourgeois" world. But here was, apparently, a comrade, a woman Socialist in the process of coming into being—something unexpected and quite astonishing. It was like plucking a tightly closed bud and setting it in a vase of water, then seeing a rose unfold. All the time the rose was locked up in the bud, but you didn't know it, and couldn't guess what color it would be, White, or Pink, or Red. Centuries ago there had been the Wars of the Roses in England; now there were wars of these same political colors, all over Europe, and indeed all over the world!

"Why don't you ask her to marry you?" Lanny had thought of that, and now he thought of it some more. She was going to read the books that he had read and think the thoughts that he had thought; and he might play the little drama that Rick's wife had suggested, he might ask her questions and let her explain matters to him, and educate him, just as the mysterious Herr Siebert had educated her. She would be happy to do it, and proud; she might experience toward her convert the same warm glow which Lanny now felt at the thought of her own conversion.

But then came the old objections. If he married her, would he tell her about F.D.R.? No doubt he could get the President's permission to do so. Then she would help in his work—but how? Would she give up her writing, or would she take a pen name and try to keep it secret? Very difficult indeed, for the editors who knew her work would hardly fail to recognize it under a new name. And what would she do about all her relatives and friends, who knew her as a free-spoken critic of them and their institutions? Would she pretend that Lanny had converted her, and that she had become an ardent Nazi-Fascist, an intimate of *Nummer Eins, Nummer Zwei, und Nummer Drei?* Very difficult indeed to arrange that, or even to imagine it!

No, no, it was all a dream; a pleasant and heart-warming dream, but far removed from reality. Duty, the stern Daughter of the Voice of God, called Lanny Budd. Trudi, his murdered wife, called him. Trudi wasn't jealous, and wouldn't have objected to his marrying again; but she reminded him that his work was something that nobody else could do. Hadn't he just written a speech which the most important man in the world was going to deliver? F.D. himself had told Lanny how helpful his services were, and that ought to settle the matter once for all.

Very well then, get to work. There was a job to be done right here in New York. A P.A. needed to know what the Nazis were doing in the New World. F.D. had said that he had other men taking care of that, but Lanny knew that the puppetstrings ran back and forth between Berlin and New York, and that connections he made here were useful in Germany, and vice versa. The head of the Nazi propaganda department in the New World had introduced him to men whom he had met subsequently in the Old; also, what the agents of Hitler were doing now in Mexico and Central and South America revealed what he meant to do after he had finished with Poland and the Ukraine and the Balkans.

X

Lanny consulted the telephone book and called the home of Forrest Quadratt. A year had passed since their last meeting, and Lanny said: "I have met our top friends abroad and have a lot of news." A soft, seductive voice replied: "Oh, good! Will you come up to dinner. I expect a guest whom you will like to meet—a Senator."

So Lanny drove once more to the apartment on Riverside Drive, full of books and literary trophies—for this sly little man with the gentle deprecating manner and the thick-lensed eyeglasses had been in his time a decadent poet of no slight talent and had cultivated literary friendships on two continents. He was American born, but boasted of being a left-handed grandson of one of the Kaisers; in his heart he was a Prussian aristocrat, subtle and infinitely corrupt. Having lived most of his life in America, he knew the crude and gullible idealists of this New World, and it delighted him to twist them around his fingers and cause them to do the opposite of what they thought they were doing.

He was trying it now with a United States Senator named "Bob" Reynolds, from the county called Buncombe in the state called No'th Cah'lina, a large genial gentleman in his middle fifties, wearing a black string tie along with his evening clothes. His hair was scant in front and plastered down at the sides; his nose was broad and his plump face wore an amiable grin, slightly suggestive of a circus clown's. He had been, so Lanny was told, a barker in a sideshow and a patent-medicine vendor, which meant that he had a gift of the gab and knew how to take care of himself in any company—a strange combination of rustic cunning from the "Tarheel state" with childish naïveté, helpless in the hands of the age-old and practiced subtleties of Europe.

He was a professional patriot, and one of the darlings of the Roosevelt-haters; they swarmed to him, and he put their speeches and editorial outpourings into the *Congressional Record*. He had just started publication of his own weekly, the *American Vindicator*, and had brought along some copies to show the Nazi agent, whose large mailing lists he wanted. "America for Americans" was his slogan, and his special phobia was "aliens"; he wanted to overcome "alien influence" which was seeking to undermine his native land. Apparently he didn't think of Quadratt as an alien, and when in his paper he urged members of the German-American Bund to subscribe, he was trying to convert aliens into good Americans. He had made himself the head of a semi-secret vigilante society called "the Vindicators," and provided its members with a red, white, and blue badge, a red, white, and blue feather for their hats, and a "Don't Tread on Me" rattlesnake banner. Right now he was organizing a youth group which he called "the Border Patrol," also with red, white, and blue symbols. Lanny wondered, had this bouncing demagogue got all this up out of his own head, or had some Bund members told him about the Hitlerjugend, with their daggers marked *Blut und Ehre*—blood and honor—and the parallel organization which in America they called their Jugendschaft—also carrying daggers?

The Senator had got himself elected by traveling over his state and shouting from the stump, first, that his rival ate caviar, which was fish eggs, and second, that the aliens and the Reds were trying to drag this country into Europe's wars. He was planning to run for President and to carry the nation by the same method, and turn out "that madman in the White House." He was going to Germany, to see for himself; he knew already what he was going to find there—no unemployment, and everything exactly as it ought to be. It was high time that we learned something from these "dictators." He wanted to know what Lanny thought about this, and about the *American Vindicator*, with which the Senator was as delighted as a child with a new toy. Its "masthead" showed a rising sun with the American flag on one side and the upper half of the Statue of Liberty on the other.

Lanny said: "If you will permit me to make a suggestion, sir——"

"Certainly, Mr. Budd."

"The Führer owes his tremendous political success to the fact that he had an economic program which offered hope to the 'little fellow' in the Fatherland. He promised the abolition of 'interest slavery,' the nationalization of department stores—a whole set of such measures. It seems to me that in America our friends are depending too much on a purely negative approach. They are against Roosevelt and against war; but the people want to know what they are *for*."

"You may be right," the great man admitted, slightly crestfallen. "I had such a program for my state; but how can anyone beat Roosevelt at his own game?"

"I don't know," Lanny said; "I am not an economist or a political promoter. But if you look at California you see what the people will vote for—Ham and Eggs, and other good things to eat; 'thirty every Thursday' and 'sixty at sixty'—those slogans refer to dollars, Senator, and it is an old American saying that 'money talks.'"

So for a while they discussed the possibility of outdealing the New Deal; but they couldn't figure how to do it, since the "madman in the

White House" had the United States Treasury at his back. When the statesman took his departure the host remarked, with a smile: "You spoiled his evening, Budd. He has become conservative, and can't bear to say or hear anything impolite about money. He is a friend of Mrs. Evalyn Walsh McLean, of Washington, who owns the biggest diamond in the world and wears it on her bosom at cocktail parties."

XI

The two friends of Germany sat in consultation until late in the evening. Lanny told what he had learned about the Führer's purposes, and about the attitudes of Göring and Hess and others. He was certain that Quadratt had a right to know these things, or at any rate would consider that he had. In return the one-time poet told about his work in America, its progress and prospects. They were persons of similar tastes and had many friends in common; they liked each other and foresaw the possibility of mutual helpfulness. Having revealed many valuable secrets, the son of Budd-Erling remarked: "You may do me a favor, if you will, Quadratt." He thought it was good tactics to let this man have a claim upon him.

"If I can," was the reply.

"I should like to meet Henry Ford. I understand that his wife is interested in paintings and it would be a valuable connection for me."

"He is not an easy man to meet, but I am sure that you would interest him greatly. I'll be glad to try to arrange it."

"I have other business that will take me to Detroit and I plan to motor there shortly."

The poet considered for a moment. "I, too, have business there. How would it do if you took me along? You could see Ford alone, of course."

"Oh, by no means! I have nothing confidential to talk to him about. If you wouldn't mind hearing me tell him about my visits to Berchtesgaden and my talks with the Führer——"

"No friend of the Führer would ever tire of that, Budd."

"Well then, by all means come along. I was planning to start in the next three or four days, depending upon a matter which I have to close up here. Would that be agreeable to you?"

"I'll make it agreeable. Let me know as soon as you are sure of the day."

So they parted; and Lanny drove back to his hotel, patting himself on the back and reflecting that the life of a presidential agent was just about tops for variety and unexpectedness!

XII

Lanny got together with his friend Zoltan and they passed the time very pleasantly, looking at exhibitions. This huge city had been having a wave of interest in painting; one of the big department stores was preparing to handle guaranteed old masters, and in Washington Square independent artists were showing their works and selling them at any price from a dollar up. Something worth while might come out of all that—and anyhow, it was better than getting drunk and dancing to jungle music.

Two days later there came a note from Monck, and Lanny picked him up that evening. The first thing he said was: "I've never been so scared in all my life." That scared Lanny—until the man of the underground added: "I've got a bundle of one-thousand-dollar banknotes pinned up over my heart—forty of them—and I've no idea what to do with them."

"So the old gentleman was satisfied!" exclaimed the old gentleman's son.

"All he said was: 'There you are, Herr Tiergarten, thanks, and good luck.' He didn't even say: 'Count them and make sure.' Is he used to handing out wads of dough like that?"

"He began life as a salesman of munitions, and for forty years he's been handing out all sorts of money to all sorts of people. He always knows what he wants and what he's willing to pay for it."

"I have been making my first acquaintance with what you Americans call private enterprise."

"It is a severe test of character," said the P.A. "You have pinned over your heart a bunch of capitalistic 'incentive.' In what direction is it going to lead you?"

"First, to Germany. I have to put twenty of these notes into the hands of a certain man."

"Can you get in without too much danger?"

"The country has a couple of thousand miles of border, and there are gaps between the patrols."

"Will your man be able to get rid of large American banknotes?"

"That is his problem. My promise was that I would bring them. I want to stop in Paris and give a couple of them to my wife; that will take care of her and the children for a year or two. I suppose that is fair."

"No one could object if you took it all, Monck."

"The problem is, what to do with the rest. It would be dangerous for me to carry it about, for if I have any sort of encounter with the police I couldn't explain it. My wife has no experience in handling large sums of money, and it would attract attention to her and might be the means of putting the Gestapo on my trail. If I put it in a bank under an assumed name I might have trouble in identifying myself later on."

"What do you have in mind to do?"

"I want you to keep this money. You are used to handling it and it won't attract any attention."

"That's quite a responsibility, old man. I couldn't even give you a receipt."

"Of course not. It'll just be an understanding between us—like so many others we've had. When I find a chance to use some of it for the cause, I'll drop you a note. If you don't hear from me in the course of a year, it'll be safe for you to assume that the Nazis have got me, and you can find some other way to put the money to work."

"And suppose something should happen to *me?*"

"That's a chance I have to take. You look fairly healthy."

Lanny grinned. "Last year an astrologer in Munich told me I was going to die in Hongkong within two or three years."

"Well, you don't believe in astrology and neither do I. So what?"

"I'll tell you what I'll do, *Genosse*. My father has a sealed envelope in his safe, containing my will. I'll put in with it a memo that so-and-so many thousand belong to Tiergarten. If I die in Hongkong Robbie will open the envelope, and if you show up and ask for the money you'll get it."

"I don't see any harm that can do."

Lanny added: "I'll put the money into Budd-Erling stock. If a war comes, it will shoot up to the ceiling, and you'll make some new discoveries about American private enterprise. The stock will be registered in my name and so it cannot be stolen."

"O.K. by me," said the ex-Capitán, in English. Fresh from the International Brigade, he knew how Americans talked. Now he unpinned the bunch of "incentive" from an inside coat pocket, and counting aloud, took off seventeen notes from the roll. "I'll keep one for my trip and for use in Germany," he said. "No doubt I can manage to change it here."

"Go into a smart restaurant and order a meal," suggested the ex-playboy. "Tell them you haven't anything smaller, and they'll have to get you the change." He took the notes and stuffed them into an inside pocket, but not bothering to pin them up. He was used to handling such notes, having sometimes bought a painting for as high as a hundred thousand dollars in cash.

They were in the neighborhood of Monck's hotel, and Lanny drew up by the curb. He looked into the other man's face by the dim street light, and said: "*Lieber Genosse*, we don't meet very often, and we don't express our feelings as freely as we might. We have been speaking about incentives, and I want to tell you that you have been one to me. I honor you for singleminded devotion to the cause of freedom and social justice, such as I have met only a few times in my life."

"That is a very pleasant thing to hear," replied the man of the underground. "You have said it better than I can, and I'll just tell you that I feel the same way about you. You have given up far more than I ever had to give."

"We could have quite an argument over that, *Genosse*. You have been risking your life continually during the five years that I have known you; and all the time I have been traveling de luxe all over two continents."

"You gave up one wife for the cause, you lost another *to* the cause, and you have just told me that you cannot marry a third because of the cause. That ought to count in any balance, I should think."

"Well," said Lanny, "let's leave it that way. You think I am tops and I think you are tops, and we will trust each other and do our best for what we believe in."

So they said *Auf Wiedersehen*—see you again—on a New York sidewalk, the "again" to be on a Berlin sidewalk in about three months, so Lanny promised, and added: "God willing."

11

The Trail of the Serpent

I

LANNY was motoring across the State of Pennsylvania; a land of low hills and many valleys, of endlessly changing views—dairy country, fruit country, meadows with fresh green grass and fields of newly sprouted grain. There were farmhouses tucked under great shade trees, red painted barns, orchards showing their first tints of green, little streams winding, and patches of what the farmers called wood-lots. The roads were well paved and not too curving, so that it was possible to drive five hundred miles a day without discomfort, and without paying heed to frequent April showers.

By Lanny's side sat the suave and sophisticated Forrest Quadratt, a nervous, eager talker, keeping up a flow of conversation, as if it had been some time since he had had a really cultivated listener. Always his tone was low, his attitude that of gently smiling cynicism; he knew the world of men and women and expected very little of it; he found his satisfaction in a sense of superiority to its follies and treacheries. The world was like that, and to expect anything different was to be a dupe.

Only on one subject did this world-weary esthete change his tone, and that was the subject of Germany. Here dwelt a people whose great powers had been demonstrated in every field and whose future was limitless: a disciplined people, moved by a deeply rooted race consciousness, and capable not merely of ruling but of teaching a vital culture to the ruled. Quadratt called himself an American, but he was apt to forget this in his conversation, and rarely had anything good to say about his native land. Its culture appeared to him hopelessly tainted by its Puritan origin; it was immature, crude, hopelessly naïve. The qualities of which it was most proud, individualism and reckless competitiveness, made certain that its career in the world would be short.

The World War, Lanny gathered, had been a shock and disappointment to this retired poet; it hadn't gone according to his formulas. Prior to 1917, he had labored tirelessly to keep America from coming

227

in, and after that he had given the Fatherland as much help as was consistent with keeping out of jail. But it had all been in vain, and for the past twenty years Quadratt had been scolding at history. He had written an elaborate defense of his cousin, the Kaiser, based on intimate knowledge, since he had been a frequent visitor at Doorn. As Lanny had never read this book, Quadratt told him about it: a long story, involving many personalities whom Lanny had met.

A series of great wrongs had been done, and were in process of being righted. Unfortunately, there was no way to accomplish this but by force, and Germany was accumulating the force; the ex-poet reverted to the lyricism of his early youth on this subject. It was a great hour, but one of danger, and everyone who loved and honored German culture must be active in its defense. America must be made to realize where its true interests lay; surely not in alliance with Britain, its great rival for world trade and mastery! This German-American hated the British Empire with a bitterness which he had no reason to conceal. He hated it for its arrogance, its long period of success and the self-assurance this had begotten. He hated it for its hypocrisy, its covering of greed with a coating of piety. What a preposterous thing to grab all the most desirable parts of the earth and then set up the doctrine that the grabbing days were over, that law and order were permanently established and that anybody who tried to change the status quo was a criminal! Even the Versailles *Diktat* was called sacred!

Now there had stepped upon the scene of history a man who was going to end all that, a dynamic personality, who was proving that history was fluid, not fixed by edict of Number 10 Downing Street. They talked about Hitler; and Lanny, in exchange for many confidences, told some of the secrets of the Berghof, including the retreat on the Kehlstein. Quadratt had heard about this, but could not claim that he had ever visited it; neither had he ever heard the Führer open his heart on the subject of Mohammed, the man who above all others had succeeded in impressing his ideas and practices upon mankind.

Early in their talk Quadratt had laid down as one of the fixed principles of Nazidom that they wanted nothing in the Western Hemisphere and therefore America had nothing to fear from them. Lanny had smiled and let it pass for the moment. He had learned a technique for unveiling the real opinions of intriguers; he would espouse the opinions himself, and with such eloquence that the hearer would be tempted to agree. After a while he brought up the subject of South America, and remarked that from his point of view Eastern and Western Hemispheres were geographical terms, having nothing to do with political or economic realities. "As a matter of fact," said he, "Argentina is about the same distance from New York as from Berlin, and the bulge of Brazil and the bulge of Africa have brought it about that there is more air traffic with Germany than with North America. The greater part of the population of South America is made of ignorant and besotted Indians, and what culture the continent has is Catholic and reactionary. I have always considered that South America offers the best field for German expansion, and many of my friends agree. There doesn't have to be any fighting—all we have to do is to let the Germans alone, and they will soon own both Argentina and Brazil, because of their superior organizing ability."

So after that it wasn't necessary for Quadratt to go on lying any longer. He said that all Germany wanted was free and fair opportunity. Already most of South America was covered by a network of German airlines, and they were all carrying Nazi propaganda literature, in German and Italian, Spanish and Portuguese and English; also picture pamphlets for the Indians who couldn't read. Lanny knew the shrewd little doctor who directed this work, and he said that it was the first time in history that the science of mass psychology and the techniques of modern advertising and promotion had been applied to the spreading of a political system. "To me it is one of the modern miracles, and I long ago made up my mind that the people who invented the technique and applied it were entitled to reap the benefits it is bringing them."

"Budd, I see that you are a man of discernment!" exclaimed the cousin of the Kaiser.

II

They sped past the sand dunes which border Lake Erie and came after dark to the great city of Cleveland, with its tall buildings and splendid drives. They spent the night there, and early next morning went on to Toledo and from there an hour or so to the north. The boulevard took them to the edge of a sort of plateau, and on a flat plain below them they beheld one of the great works of man: a vast expanse of one-story factory buildings, with a row of eight or ten enormously tall chimneys, painted black and standing up like organ pipes—only the music which came out of them was that of industry and commerce, not that of Handel and Bach. It was the River Rouge plant of the Ford Motor Company, goal of their long drive.

A four-lane boulevard took them to the place; on one side were acres of parking space packed with rows of cars, and a high steel bridge carried the workers across the highway to the plant gates. Visitors went in by a separate entrance; and as Lanny and his friend were ahead of their appointment they followed the procession of tourists from all over America who came each day to visit this most exciting of all their country's spectacles: the empire of the "flivver," the birthplace and nursery of the most widely known of automobiles.

Visitors were taken about the plant in open "rubberneck-wagons," and every now and then they got out and entered one of the buildings and were escorted along a gallery, looking down upon an assembly line known as "the belt." First you saw parts of cars being made and then you saw the parts being put together until the finished product rolled off and out under its own power. You saw so many that—so the story ran—you came out scratching your head to see if any of the darned little things had got into your hair. There had been a period, a decade or two ago, when the favorite amusement of the American people had been the making up of jokes like that; and some bright fellow in the promotion department had had the idea of setting all the salesmen and agents to collecting them and publishing them in a pamphlet called *The Ford Jokebook*.

Promptly at the hour set, the two presented themselves at the office. Quadratt had phoned to Harry Bennett, the great man's factotum and chief of police, for an appointment, and now without delay they were escorted to the inner sanctum, a place very hard to reach. It was simple and plain, like its owner; the room paneled in early American pine, and the owner clad in what might be called "modern American business." He was tall and spare, one of those shrewd Yankees who eat lightly and live long; he had just had his seventy-sixth birthday and was slightly withered, but still spry and interested in what came along—or, more exactly, in what Harry Bennett allowed to get near him.

III

Henry Ford, the "Flivver King"! Lanny had been hearing about him since childhood; he stood for the United States of America to all the world; there was no place where his car hadn't gone, except the tops of the high mountains and the bottoms of the deep oceans. A born machinist escaped from a farm, he had been seized by the determination to make a "horseless carriage," a cheap one that common men like himself could afford to own and run. He had come on the scene at the right moment, and the more cars he made, the more he had to make, until now he was past his ten millionth. Some of the oldest were still on the roads, and on trails in Tibet and the Andes mountains. "Tin Lizzies," they were called, affectionately; oblong boxes on wheels, as ugly as man could imagine—Henry had said that the customer could have any color he wanted provided it was black.

This was, in all probability, the richest man in the world; his fortune was estimated at somewhere between one and two billions, and he, or members of his family, owned it all. He could not endure to have stockholders, idle persons drawing income from his labors, so he had bought them all out. He was the most self-willed of men; nobody could oppose him, and again and again he had fired a good part of his staff. "Do what I say," was his life motto. He had forbidden unions in his plants, and was fighting them by every means, not excluding criminal. But the New Deal was determined to break his will and force unions into all his plants. This was the unbearable outrage which poisoned his old age, and the problem of thwarting the unions had become an obsession with him.

That was the basis of his interest in the Nazis. They had shown how to do it; they had no walking delegates in their shops and no Reds on soapboxes outside their plants; they had law and order, organization and mass-production, the things that Henry lived by and for. So, when friends of Germany came to tell him how it was done, he listened gladly, and when they asked him for jobs he made room for them. He had a grandson of the Kaiser on his staff, and one of his engineers was Fritz Kuhn, founder and head of the German-American Bund. As a result his plants swarmed with Nazis, and so did the city of Detroit and its surrounding towns.

In one of the early panics a group of Wall Street banks had sought to lend money to Henry Ford on terms which might have enabled them to take his company away from him. From that day on he had hated all bankers, and because someone had told him they were Jews, he hated Jews. He had carried on a crusade against them, and reprinted a grotesque invention, *The Protocols of the Learned Elders of Zion.* This had hurt business, so Henry had been persuaded to retract and apologize; but he hadn't really changed his mind, and that was one more reason why he admired the Nazis, and listened to their shrewd agents who whispered into his ear that what was needed for America was a pure native hundred per cent movement, combining all the other groups which were flourishing throughout the country—the Ku Klux, the Black Legion, the Silver Shirts, the Crusader Whiteshirts, the American Liberty League, the Anglo-Saxon Federation—this last the creation and pet of Henry's own editor and radio propagandist, William J. Cameron. There was a "Ford radio hour," and for some fifty minutes every Sunday evening, music lovers listened to Mozart and Beethoven, and in the middle of it they gnashed their teeth for six minutes while Mr. Cameron's rasping voice propounded a worm's-eye view of their country's social problems.

IV

"Here is where you can get all the money in the world,"—so Forrest Quadratt had said to Lanny as they were approaching the plant. Lanny had answered: "For heaven's sake don't say a word about money, or even hint at it. These very rich men are shy as mountain sheep, and you have to know them intimately before you approach the subject." The ex-poet, who had never been a rich man and had always had to live by his wits, conceived a new respect for a rich man's son who was one of the insiders and knew how to play the big-money game.

Quadratt kept quiet and listened, and Lanny listened, too; for the Flivver King was a great talker when he had what he considered the right audience. He was a genius in his special field, the large-scale production of material goods, and especially of means of transportation. Why people wanted to be able to roll at sixty miles an hour from one place to another, and what they would do at place number two that they couldn't have done at place number one—these were questions which did not concern Henry Ford. He believed in the utmost liberty, except inside the Ford plants, and each Ford-owner would drive his car wherever he pleased, and somehow a mystical principle of progress would bring it about that mankind would benefit by his journey. Henry's business was to reduce the price of the car, so that more people would be able to buy it, and thus his plants would grow in size while those of his rivals diminished.

To that end, a huge staff was engaged in every sort of research, and Henry watched and oversaw it, gloated over its progress, and enjoyed telling visitors about it. He was making everything that went into his car—and you would be astonished to hear how many things there were. All sorts of metals and combinations of metals; and plastics—he was making them out of soy beans, and couldn't get enough; and if incidentally he learned to make a hundred other things out of soy beans, that was a hundred new businesses and new ways to make money. Henry didn't care about the money, he assured Lanny; his pleasure was to make things. As it happened, the son of Budd-Erling had been hearing that from his father and his grandfather, ever since he could re-member. It was what he had heard from every great moneymaker he had ever met in all his plutocratic career—with the sole exception of Hermann Wilhelm Göring, Reichsminister and Reichsmarschall of the German Third Empire, the only one who had made bold to say: "I like money, and I mean to get every mark and dollar and pound and franc that I can."

Henry had to have rubber for automobile tires—five to each car. He was laying out an enormous plantation in Brazil, and for that he needed everything from steamships to lead pencils for the teachers who were going to teach the Indian children how to write. Also he was experi-menting with artificial rubber, a complicated matter. At the same time, he was trying to persuade Americans to appreciate and love the ways of their forefathers, and to that end had constructed Greenfield Vil-lage, made of old-time buildings, and there he was teaching children to sing the old songs and dance the old square dances. Let no one say that the Flivver King preached only hatred; he knew for a surety that he preached hatred of everything that was evil and love of everything that was good.

V

After the elderly host had talked himself out, Forrest Quadratt re-marked: "Mr. Budd is an intimate friend of the Führer's, and has been a guest in his home many times." So, of a sudden, Lanny became a personality—the Flivver King had apparently not got clear who he was, but just that he was one more person whom Harry thought he ought to receive. Now he asked about how things were going in Germany; not political affairs, which seldom interested him, but industry and its progress, and whether the people were satisfied and happy, whether they got enough to eat, and was there really going to be a *Volkswagen*, as the government had promised. In the meantime there were Ford cars available, and several large assembly plants, so that Ford was a German big businessman, well satisfied with labor conditions in that country.

"Mr. Budd's father is Robert Budd, of Budd-Erling," put in the tact-ful German-American, after a proper interval; and that was another opening for the host to expound his ideas. He had been forced to make military goods in the last war, but would never do it again, he declared. He was a man of peace, and believed that if all manufacturers would take the same stand, the warmakers would be forced out of business all over the world.

Lanny said: "I have had somewhat the same feeling, Mr. Ford. I have never had anything to do with my father's business."

"Mr. Budd is an internationally known art expert," put in the ever-helpful Quadratt. "His stepfather was the famous French painter, Marcel Detaze."

The richest man in the world didn't consider it necessary to pretend that he had ever heard of a French painter; there were swarms of them, he knew, and their names were unpronounceable. What he said was: "My wife is interested in paintings and has quite a collection."

There was Lanny's chance, which he would not miss. "So I have heard, Mr. Ford. I would esteem it a privilege if some day I might be permitted to view it."

Henry's reaction was surprising; he popped up from his chair as if he had been a youth of sixteen instead of a great-grandfather. "I'll take you now." He didn't say: "If it would be convenient." It was Henry's time for going home.

What had caused that?—the intimacy with the Führer, or the son-ship in Budd-Erling, or the art-expertness, or the combination of all three? Something had penetrated the tough shell of a suspicious elderly recluse and caused him to decide that this was no ordinary curiosity seeker, but a personality worth cultivating. "Tell Mrs. Ford I am bringing two guests for tea," he said to one of his secretaries, and took his gray overcoat and gray Fedora hat and led the way to his car which, Lanny observed, was not a Ford but a Lincoln.

On the way the host told about his farm, and the wonders he had on it, including two thousand birdhouses, electrically heated and with water supply protected from freezing. It had interested him to find out how many birds could be tempted to change their habits and remain all winter in the severe climate of Michigan. He had turned loose in his garden three hundred and eighty pairs of English songbirds, and at another time seventy-five pairs of martens. He had lived a long time in this home, and twenty-two years ago a pair of linnets had nested over the door; this morning he had counted seven pairs of these birds and wondered if any of them were descendants of the early settlers.

VI

Lanny didn't see much of the house, for they got out under a porte-cochère and went in quickly. There was a large and comfortable drawing-room, and a kindly old lady to welcome them. The small-town girl whom the young mechanic Henry Ford had married early had surely not expected to become an empress, and had never tried to learn the role. Lanny couldn't help wondering, how much did she know about the dreadful things that were involved in the building of an empire—the thirty-six hundred private police, many of them with criminal records, and the tough gangsters whom somebody had hired to slug and murder labor unionists wherever they were seeking to organize Ford workers in various parts of the country?

Lanny Budd set out to charm an elderly lady, an art which he had been practicing since childhood. He had been invited to look at paintings, so he talked on that subject. His mother had been a painters' model in Paris and he had lived among them ever since he could remember; his stepfather had sat all day happily painting scenes on the Cap, and had always been ready to explain the whys and wherefores of what he was doing. The story of Marcel Detaze, with his face burned off in the war, wearing a white silk mask and doing his best painting— that was a sure-fire hit with any audience. Lanny didn't say a word about the supply of Detazes in his storeroom, for that might look like hinting; no, he told how the painter had gone into the second battle of the Marne and never come out; and then how an elderly Polish medium had brought Lanny messages purporting to come from the spirit world. Was that really Marcel, or was it only Lanny's memories of him? Lanny had no idea what Mrs. Ford thought on this question, but there are few persons who are not interested to hear about it, especially those who know that they themselves are drawing near to that bourne from which they may or may not return.

Meanwhile they were drinking tea; and afterwards they looked at paintings, some of them good and some not so good—the sort of thing that people get when they are guided by the name of the painter rather than by the painting. For Lanny such an occasion was like a radio "quiz"; he had to be ready to speak quickly, and what he said had to be right; his professional success depended upon his ability to walk down a line and impress and even astound an art collector by the opulence of his information and the surety of his judgments. Mrs. Ford herself was hardly an authority; in the course of their talk she revealed that she was having a portrait painted by an artist celebrated in Detroit, and this artist had begun his work by taking a great many photographs of her; she was impressed by the number, and thought that was the way all great painters set about their work.

Lanny did not disillusion her. Instead, he praised what virtues he was able to find in her collection, and told interesting stories of the painters, and in what museums their greatest works were to be found. When

Lanny Budd really chose to spread himself on the subject of art he could be quite dazzling; so much so that, when he suggested it was time for them to be leaving, the Flivver King's wife inquired whether they had any other engagement, and if not, would they care to stay to dinner, taking pot luck. Lanny had no worries as to what he would find in the Ford pot, and said he would be happy to stay. Quadratt agreed; and when they had been escorted to a guest room to wash up, the ex-poet whispered: "You knocked them cold!" Lanny smiled, and put his finger to his lips. "I'll give you a chance before long," he said. They made a good team, working together like Machiavelli and his imaginary Prince.

VII

They had an enjoyable meal, old-fashioned American style—never anything foreign in the home of the Flivver King, except his wife's paintings! Afterwards they sat in the drawing-room, and while Mrs. Ford did "fancy-work," Lanny described life at the Berghof, and then at Karinhall, which was something like a fairy tale to the elderly couple. Giving his companion the promised chance, Lanny talked about Lindbergh in Germany, and how the vital ideas of the New Order were spreading in America; "the Wave of the Future," Lindbergh's wife had called it. Quadratt took the cue, and told what he had been doing to spread this wave, and of the various Senators and Congressmen who had been aiding him.

Henry, who had been silent and apparently indifferent while the talk was about painting, now came to life and asked questions; Lanny perceived that his knowledge of Ku Kluxers and Silvershirts and Crusader Whiteshirts was almost as extensive as his knowledge of soybean plastics. Nor did he assume that the propagandists of these new ideas worked for love only; he had paid money to circulate his own ideas, and realized that it would take a lot of money to re-educate a hundred million people. Quadratt declared that a great many of his friends thought Mr. Ford was the man who ought to enter the arena and defeat the New Deal in next year's presidential election, but the Flivver King shook his head; he was far too old, and had sworn off on politics after his bitter experience in running for the U.S. Senate more than twenty years ago.

They talked about Lindbergh as a possible candidate, and then about General Moseley. Quadratt said it was too bad that Father Coughlin had been born in Canada, and Henry said it didn't matter, because the case of Al Smith had shown that the Middle West would never take a Catholic. They mentioned the former preacher, Gerald Smith, as a future leader, and the host said: "He is speaking in Detroit tomorrow night; they asked me to pay for the meeting." He didn't say what his reply had been.

Lanny guessed that the old man kept peasant hours, so he excused himself early. Their car had been brought from the plant, and when they were safely ensconced in it, Quadratt exclaimed: "Budd, that was wonderful!" Praise from Sir Hubert, and Lanny replied, graciously: "I owe it to you." He knew that whenever in Europe he came upon a suitable old master, he could send Mrs. Clara Bryant Ford a telegram about it and count upon receiving a reply.

VIII

Next morning they had a day to spend; and Lanny said: "I have heard there is an art museum." Quadratt said: "I want to pay a call on Father Coughlin." When Lanny asked: "Do you know him?" the reply was: "I count him a very good friend. Would you like to meet him?"

So Lanny didn't see the Detroit Institute of Arts. His companion called a confidential telephone number and made an appointment for eleven o'clock, and Lanny drove him on the city's most pretentious highway, Woodward Boulevard, twelve miles to a town called Royal Oak. On their right loomed up a large stucco church with a tall tower, the Shrine of the Little Flower. By an odd coincidence the mayor of New York City was named Fiorello, which means "Little Flower"; but he was part Jewish and strongly anti-Fascist, so this was not his shrine.

Its creator and presiding genius was one who called himself "America's much-loved radio priest." At the time of the great depression he had come forward with a remedy for the people's ills, the abolition of the gold standard. This was no new idea to the midwest of America, having been handed down from the days of the old-time Populists. But Father Coughlin had given it a new lease on life. A radio orator with dulcet tones, he had started on one small station, begging for funds to increase his audience. Money had poured in, all in one-dollar bills, brought from the post office in motor trucks, and a hundred and fifty girls were employed in opening the envelopes.

Step by step the reverend orator had established a radio network; also he had bought a tract of land, and built this shrine, together with all the accessories—a garage to accommodate the pilgrims, an inn to lodge them, a restaurant and several hotdog stands to feed them, and souvenir shops where they could buy things to send home and prove that they had actually accomplished the pilgrimage. "We manage things better than they ever did at Mecca, or Canterbury, or Lourdes," remarked Quadratt.

He didn't say that he loathed the Catholics and all their doings; all the Nazis felt thus—but they needed the hierarchy in America, and Spanish Fascism was their creation, and Franco a devout servant of Holy Mother Church. So this registered Nazi agent contented himself with remarking that the Reverend Father was an excellent business-man; these various enterprises were owned by companies of which he and his secretaries were the directors, and it was a set-up which would have done credit to J. Paramount Barnes in his palmiest days. Quadratt knew that this "utilities king" of Chicago had been the father of Lanny's ex-wife—indeed, it was through Irma that Quadratt had met Lanny Budd.

In his early days "Silver Charlie" had been fully equipped with a popular program, and had seemed on the way to taking Huey Long's place as the American Führer. But sudden riches had had on him the same effect as on the "Kingfish," and on "Buncombe Bob" and many other mass leaders; they began to understand the rich man's point of view and could no longer bear to say anything that might hurt the feelings of those at whose dinner tables they sat. The ex-poet remarked with his sly smile: "I observe this even in myself. In my youth I was something of a Socialist, and might have made a very good rabble-rouser, but now I find I have been turned into a money raiser, and all that is left of my radicalism is that I charge the rich a good price for my services. I observe that the more I soak them the more they value me."

"Of course," agreed the son of Budd-Erling. "They value paintings in the same way, and like to pay a high price so that they can boast about it."

"The worthy Father published some articles of mine last year," added the Kaiser's left-handed cousin. "The reason I can see him any time I wish is that I made him appreciate my value."

IX

"Silver Charlie" received them in the fine home in which he lived with his mother; he led them into his study and shut the door. A well-built man under fifty, not stout, but with florid round cheeks, smooth-shaven as his priesthood required. He wore his clerical garb, black, with a white collar closed in front and fastened in the rear. Lanny had listened to him over the air—who hadn't?—and knew his peculiar Canadian accent. His manner was positive and rather abrupt, but to these visitors extremely cordial. After Quadratt had explained that Lanny Budd spent a good part of his time in Germany and knew the Führer and his associates intimately, the new visitor was listened to with grave attention.

America's much-loved radio priest was heard over the air every Sunday. His outspoken pro-Nazi and anti-democratic statements alarmed his clerical superiors, but ten million people listened to him gladly. Also, he had a weekly paper, *Social Justice,* for which he claimed a million circulation, and he had his "Christian Front," made up of fanatical followers who sold the paper on the streets and held mass meetings at which the Hitler salute might be seen and counted the days to the great Day in which they would be turned loose upon their enemies. Lanny had attended more than one of these meetings, and had taken the trouble to join up and get one of the metal crosses which the Christian Fronters wore instead of swastikas.

It was going to be a strictly Christian revolution, but a new kind of Christianity, based exclusively upon hatred of its enemies, and never mentioning love, if it felt any. It was the product of social discontent, the blind revolt of the dispossessed in the presence of wealth in which they had no share or hope of sharing. Ignorance, eldest daughter of poverty, followed in her mother's train, and this pair of harpies tormented their victims and left them a prey to any demagogue who came their way. For more than two decades the American proletariat had been besieged by the propaganda of Red revolution, and on top of that had come the renegade Mussolini and then the fanatical Adi Schicklgruber. For nearly three years the fires of civil war in Spain had kept this evil brew at boiling point; and here was one of the men who had been pumping oil into the flames. A man of hatred amounting almost to frenzy; a man who could build a church in the name of the gentle Jesus, and stand in the pulpit and rave for an hour, calling for the blood of those whose ideas he hated and feared. "Rest assured we will fight you in Franco's way, if necessary. Call this inflammatory, if you will. It is inflammatory. But rest assured we will fight you and we will win."

This orator was of Irish descent, and he therefore hated the British Empire; he hated it so that he probably did not even know that it had become the British Commonwealth. He hated the Jews, first because they had killed the Son of God, and second because they made money too fast—though not so fast as "Silver Charlie," who had bought the metal at the same time that he agitated to boost its price. He hated the international bankers and he hated the Bolsheviks, and like all the Nazis he had managed to persuade himself that the two groups were united in a conspiracy to rule the world. Goebbels told him this in a flood of propaganda, and somebody translated it for him and he put it into his paper every week, with the change of only a few words to make it sound right for Americans. This wasn't Fascism and it wasn't Nazism that Father Coughlin was going to bring into the sweet land of liberty; it was simon-pure American Nationalism, America First, America for Americans, and let us kick out Roosevelt and his Jew Deal and put an end to "the poppycock of democracy"—the holy father's own phrase.

X

Lanny had watched this poison being peddled on the streets of New York, and had talked with some of its pitiful peddlers, heirs of misery who had been raised in "Hell's Kitchen" and educated in parochial schools, and taught that the priest was God's deputy and final authority on all truth. Now a priest told each poor wretch that his half-starved and precarious way of life in the midst of unimaginable luxury was due to the fact that the Jews had got all the gold in the world and were conspiring with the "Roossians" to make a slave of him. And what chance did he have to judge whether it was true or not? He went about screaming his hate and collecting his dimes—and occasionally seizing a chance to sneak up behind some Jew as poor and unhappy as himself, and trip him up or hit him over the head with a piece of lead pipe symbolically concealed in a copy of *Social Justice*.

Here at the fountainhead of this poison, it was a P.A.'s duty to listen, and agree with everything and make mental notes to be put into a report. He knew that Quadratt had come on business, so he sat without interrupting while the other told of various books he had written under pen names and had published through his camouflaged press in New Jersey, and of new sources of information and propaganda devised by the tireless Dr. Goebbels in Berlin. Quadratt had brought along a brief case full of documents and clippings, with passages especially marked for the editor-priest. Some of this interested the latter so much that he invited Quadratt to make them into articles—on the usual terms, as he quietly mentioned.

Lanny made careful note of every word, for a trap had been set for bears, and it might be that right at this moment one of the biggest grizzlies was putting his foot into it. Some two years ago Lanny Budd had suggested to F.D. that there might be a law requiring agents of foreign governments to register their activities with the State Department; that law had been passed, and it had a lot of sharp teeth. Forrest Quadratt had registered himself, so the newspapers reported; but had he included all the different kinds of services for which he was being paid? If he had overlooked any one of them, Lanny's report might go to the Department of Justice with the suggestion that they take up the matter at once.

XI

They spent the rest of that day traveling about Detroit and its environs, meeting various promoters of the Nazi-Fascist cause. Lanny made careful note of names and activities—especially those at the Bund Camp which flourished near the city. If any of those persons paid money to Quadratt, that would be a sharp tooth in the bear trap. Roosevelt had told Lanny that he had agents keeping contact with these plotters, but he had added that sometimes a hint from a high-up insider might save a lot of wasted effort. Lanny knew that he had such an insider in his car right now.

After dinner they drove to Maccabee's Auditorium, and took seats amid a rapidly growing throng. Leading personalities sat upon the platform, and Quadratt asked if his friend would care to join them; but Lanny apologized, saying: "I have to keep to my role as art expert, and not take part in politics. You were once an ivory-tower dweller, so you will understand."

The other smiled and assented. "One learns more, anyway, by sitting among the crowd and watching them closely."

Lanny studied the faces of the men and women pouring into this hall. There seemed to be an unusual proportion of the elderly: people who obviously had worked hard all their lives, and had saved at least enough to have a suit of decent clothing, or a dress, in which to attend inspirational meetings like the present. Lanny noted their serious, deeply lined faces, and tried to imagine their lives; for this was the land of his forefathers, which he didn't know so very well. The settlers of this district had come straight from New England, grandchildren of the stern old Puritans, driving "Conestoga wagons," the Fords of that day. There had been hell-fire preachers among them, and fanatical abolitionists, whose sons had formed armies to win the Civil War.

There weren't many labor-union men in this crowd, Lanny guessed; if there were Ford workers, they were the "hillbillies" whom Henry had been bringing in by the thousands because they didn't know anything about unions and couldn't read subversive literature. Most of the audience were shopkeepers and small farmers, many of whom had sold their family farms and moved near to a town where they could get medical treatment and attend the movies and meetings; some raised chickens and rabbits, and others sat by the stove and complained of the pains in their joints.

They were serious-minded folk, and knew that there was something terribly wrong with their country; when they wanted to find out about it, the most likely guide was a preacher—their own kind, a shouting evangelist of the old-time religion. "It was good for my fathers and it's good enough for me!" Tonight they had come to hear the Reverend Gerald L. K. Smith, a handsome, burly Louisianan with waving dark hair and a winning smile when he saw fit to use it. He had joined up first with Pelley, the man who boasted of having spent seven minutes in eternity, and who had founded the Silver Shirts, perhaps on instructions there received. But Pelley had kept all the money, and Smith had moved back to Louisiana and become the associate of Huey Long, preaching the gospel of "Every Man a King." When Huey was shot, Smith tried to take his place, and, failing in that, had chosen Detroit as the future headquarters of American Nazi-Fascism.

His movement was called the "Committee of One Million," perhaps the largest committee ever formed; it needed to be, for its avowed purpose was "to seize the government of the United States." It was political, but carried on in the manner of religion—a crusade against the devil, a holy war to save America from the stinking Reds and the slimy Jews and the bewhiskered aliens and all the hordes from Europe and Asia and Africa who had sneaked into the land of the Pilgrims' pride in order to betray it; people who had no faith in Jesus Christ, and didn't understand the uses of liberty; people ignorant, dirty and degraded, dumb cattle most of them, and the few with brains the hired agents of foreign governments which wanted to drag America into their quarrels, and ultimately to destroy the faith of the Lord Jesus Christ and the country which God had founded to be its refuge and its temple.

XII

Such was the gospel of "Reverend Smith," as his followers called him. It was the whole Nazi creed of hate, complete to the smallest detail, but translated from German into Middle Western with a touch of the South. It was preaching in the style of the old-time camp-meeting, where people were used to shouting "Amen!" and "Come to Jesus!" and, when they got really going, to rolling in the aisles or "talking in tongues." When Reverend Smith got warmed up, he bellowed in a voice which put the amplifier out of business; he took off his coat and then he tore open his collar—a ceremonial of seizure by the spirit. Perspiration streamed down his face, and while he mopped it with a handkerchief in one hand he held the other aloft with fist clenched, threatening the enemies of the Lord Jesus Christ. When he finished, his shirt was soaking wet and his hair hanging limp as if he had just come out of a swimming-pool.

Here was one rabblerouser who had not yet forgotten the "poor and lowly," and was not embarrassed to have an "economic program." His heart bled for those who lived below the level of security, and he pictured for them a bright and shining Utopia, to be attained the moment the stranglehold of the Jew Deal should have been torn from their throats. Poverty in the modern world was a crime, deliberately inflicted upon the masses by the international bankers, the Jews, the Reds. Ham and eggs, thirty every Thursday, sixty at sixty—these the orator took from California; abolition of the gold standard from Coughlin; abolition of interest slavery and the breaking of monopolies from Hitler of the old Munich days.

The whole performance took Lanny back a matter of fifteen years, to the enormous Bürgerbraukeller where he had listened for the first time to a two-hour tirade of Schicklgruber. When this obscure agitator had first come onto the platform, Lanny had thought he was a caricature of Charlie Chaplin; but listening to him and seeing his effect upon the crowd, the American had realized that this was a social portent. And here in Detroit was the same thing, with few changes and all of them superficial. When Gerald Smith started pulling the tremolo stop, telling the mothers and the grandmothers in this audience how the international Jews were conspiring to drag American boys into their European wars, and picturing the horrors which would befall those boys—when Lanny heard moans and cries throughout the audience and looked about and saw women with pain-distorted faces and tears streaming down their cheeks—he grew sick in his soul; it seemed to him that some devil was engaged in making a caricature of the democratic process, reducing it to a farce, to prove that the people were incapable of thinking and must really have a master to drive them with a whip.

When Lanny came out of the Munich beerhall he had asked: "Is this the German Mussolini?" And now he asked: "Is this the American Hitler?" He asked it respectfully, of course, and with no signs of disgust. "It seems to me he has everything it takes; he understands the American masses."

"I agree with you," said Forrest Quadratt. "I am backing him for the role, and you'll be interested to know that some pretty big outfits are backing him to the limit."

XIII

Next morning they set out on their return journey, but by another route. Lanny had picture business, and his companion assented with pleasure, for he was always glad to meet rich people—who could say what might come of it? They drove a couple of hundred miles southward, and on the way they talked about the three eminent personalities they had met, and the great city of automobiles and its future. Quadratt was of the opinion that Gerald Smith had made a wise choice, for Detroit was destined to become the center of American social discontent. "Wait until the New Deal has spent the last dollar it can borrow; then you're going to see hell break loose."

Lanny agreed. The wholesale importation of labor from the South, and especially of Negroes, was bound to lead to race riots. The Nazi agent rubbed his soft moist hands together and murmured: "The American people will really have to listen to us, Budd!"

They came to Cincinnati, a sort of half-southern city on the banks of the Ohio. It was the family home of Sophie Timmons, Baroness de la Tourette, and site of the great hardware plant which had supported this red-headed and high-spirited lady in luxury ever since Lanny Budd could remember. Some of Sophie's relatives had come to visit her now and then, and Lanny knew them and had promised to call and talk about paintings. He had a portfolio of photographs to show and a list of prices to quote, and this took an evening; his Nazi friend sat by and thought that it was a high-class racket, but lacked the extraordinary future of his own. The ex-poet had seen things happen in Berlin and Vienna and Prague which made him a little dizzy. He saw himself becoming *Gauleiter* of the New York district, or even of the North Atlantic States.

XIV

Then to the east; all highways were equally good—you could hardly tell them apart. Their route took them through the Alleghenies, and it was April in the valleys, and March when they climbed, and then April again when they descended. On the way Lanny became confidential and told about the large sums he was collecting from the rich; and Quadratt was moved to emulation—his fees were not so large but were more regular. The *Münchner Neueste Nachrichten* was paying him five hundred a month as their American correspondent, and the German Library of Information in New York paid him the same as their adviser; recently they had paid him twelve hundred dollars extra as a fee for a specific "consultation." Last year, during a trip to Germany, he had collected even larger sums; for the heads of the Nazi machine understood that their collaborators had to live well and be in a position to entertain those whom they wished to enlist. "They are pouring out money," said the registered agent, "and why shouldn't I get mine?" Lanny had no reason to suggest.

They were passing through the coal districts in the mountains of West Virginia; the roads were lined with unpainted two-story shacks, built in rows of a dozen or more, sometimes all one building. Everything was smeared with coal dust, including the faces of the ragged children who stood in front of the houses, staring as the car swept by. "Mining districts are the same all over the world," remarked the ex-poet. "Imagine the idea that such people are supposed to help in ruling the state?"

The art expert replied: "Over here it is ruled by political bosses in a smoke-filled room."

This had been a delightful journey, and a close friendship had grown out of it. They took to calling each other by their first names, and presently Lanny referred to his little daughter in England; this caused his companion to ask about that celebrated marriage which the grandson of Budd Gunmakers had contracted. What had caused it to go on the rocks? Lanny replied that a man who loved music and art and books couldn't be happy with a woman who had to spend one or two million dollars every year and was concerned to make a public ceremonial of it. "Irma is in exactly the right place as the wife of an English earl," he said; and the other remarked: "I thought her an admirable woman, but a little lacking in a sense of humor."

He was moved to reveal in turn the sorrow of his personal life. "My wife is a gentle and lovely woman, but unfortunately she is part Jewish. In the beginning I thought that wouldn't make any difference, but as the years passed I discovered that the worst racial traits have a way of coming to the front with advancing age. You can understand what that means to one in my position in these times."

"I can indeed," replied Lanny, sympathetically.

"It has resulted in my two sons becoming estranged from me, and indeed going over to the enemy."

There was a tremor in the man's voice which betrayed the feeling he wished to deny to himself as well as to others; and Lanny felt a touch of pity for this perverted soul. "I can sympathize with you, Forrest. I too have Jewish relatives, and have had to avoid them for the same reasons. We have to remind ourselves that we are serving a cause, and that all humanity is more important than some individuals who happen to share our blood."

"Quite so! I have learned to put these personal troubles out of my mind. I have found that there are many charming women in New York, and some of them are always ready to provide me with entertainment. You have observed that same fact, no doubt."

"I have observed it in different parts of the world."

"The only trouble is they take it so damned seriously! I sometimes think the greatest service we Nazis have rendered to the German people is in teaching the *Mädchen* to take love-making as a matter of course."

"It certainly saves a lot of bother," remarked the much-traveled art expert. "But I wonder how you are going to patch up that problem with the Catholics."

"Oh, pouff!" exclaimed the author of *Eros Unbound*, with a sudden gesture of the hand. "We will blow them out of our way in the first week when we take power!"

12

T'Other Dear Charmer Away

I

DEPOSITING his traveling companion at the door of his Riverside Drive apartment, Lanny was so sick of Nazis and the thought of Nazis that he went to the opposite extreme, driving to the home of his half-sister Bess and her Jewish husband, Hansi Robin. They loved and trusted him, and when he said: "I am getting information about the Nazis and making important use of it," they forgave him for never going out in public with two well-known Communists. When Hansi gave a violin recital Lanny did not enter the hall with them, but bought his ticket like any other member of the audience. However, he would come to their home on the Connecticut shore and have a feast of music, and pour out his heart on the subject of the tragedy which he saw hanging over the old continent overseas.

But don't ever try to decide what was to be done about it, because then they would get into an argument! Was dictatorship necessary, as a transition stage to a collective world, or was it possible for democratic countries such as the Anglo-Saxon and the Scandinavian to socialize industry by popular consent? Marx had said that it might be possible, but very few Marxists knew that he had said it. Lenin had said that it wasn't possible, and all Communists took him for their bible, and were outraged by the suggestion that extremes meet, and that the Communist tactics had helped the Nazis to power in Germany, and that the tendency of dictatorships is to perpetuate themselves and to recognize their kinship with other dictatorships.

Oh, heresy, oh, double distillation of schism! *Anathema maranatha!* Lanny informed his relatives that Hitler at this time was persistently seeking some understanding with the Soviet Union which would leave him a free hand to deal with Western Europe. Lanny declared that there appeared to be a chance of this effort's succeeding, and the remark almost brought tears to the eyes of the two musicians. So Lanny would end such discussions by going to the piano and pounding out a Chopin polonaise.

This was a happily married couple, something not so common among modern intellectuals, plagued by a variety of novel theories. This pair had their religion—it was that, even though to use the word was to insult them. They had their art, which reached into infinity, and in which perfection was to be sought but never attained. They could earn all the money they wanted; they would do so, and then give so much to their cause that they would have to plan another concert tour. They had two lovely babies, and this was a responsibility, and a reason for their four parents to keep urging them to save something.

The two Jewish parents lived near by, and this was another home for Lanny Budd, any time he chose to visit there. Johannes Robin, one-time *Schieber* millionaire, was doing well enough as salesmanager of Budd-Erling, and had taught himself moderation in his desires. His good kind wife, whom they all called Mama, was as happy as any old woman could be who had known so much tragedy and fear. It was a wicked world, wholly beyond her understanding, and all she asked was a quiet corner to hide in with her loved ones. The fact that they were not invited to become members of the local country club—*ach, du lieber Gott,* what did that matter to a woman whose husband had been spat upon in the old red-brick police prison on the Alexanderplatz in Berlin, and whose darling younger son had been tortured to death in Dachau concentration camp? *Wenn wir nur unsere Ruhe haben!*

Truth to be told, Mama had never been happy in Germany. Making so much money, living such an expensive life, it was beyond all reason and could not but lead to trouble. All those proud rich people who came to see them had no real friendship in their hearts, and were bound to look down upon Jews and to envy them for too great success. Mama had never enjoyed their society, for she knew that she didn't look like them, and if dressmakers fixed her up it didn't become her, and what was she ever to do with her Yiddische accent? Now we have escaped, all of us but poor darling Freddi, and Rahel's poor brother Aaron; now, *um Gottes Willen,* let us live simply and not make ourselves conspicuous, and don't expect a poor dumpy Jewish grandmother with curly gray hair to dress up as if she were a queen *in der hohen Welt*. Let us send our little ones to the public school and have them learn to talk and to look as much like Americans as possible, so that nobody will hate them and nobody will want to beat them with clubs or cut them with knives or throw them into dungeons to rot and die!

But when Lanny came along, that was different. Lanny was an Anglo-Saxon, tall and handsome, but he was not like the others. He had been willing for his half-sister to marry a Jewish violinist, and had risked his life in his effort to save Freddi from Dachau. Lanny would come, laughing and full of fun; he would kiss Mama on both cheeks and tell her she was looking younger every day; he would play the piano for them—and none of that horrid jazz; he would tell them about the places he had visited and the people he had met—but never a word about the anti-Semitism which was being spread like a plague in New York and Detroit and the other great cities of this new world.

In the household lived Rahel, Freddi's widow, and their little son Johannes, who was about the same age as Lanny's daughter in England; also Rahel's second husband and their two babies. The adults of this family had learned humility in a school of suffering, and Lanny preferred them to the people who had learned arrogance in a school of success. Freddi's son was just at the age that Freddi had been when he had written his first scrawly letter to the fashionable grandson of

Budd Gunmakers, whom his father had met by accident on a railway train in Italy. He had enclosed a little snapshot, and Lanny still had that at Bienvenu, and it was astonishing how close was the resemblance of father and child. Lanny would tell about the father, and do what he could to see that Freddi's spirit of gentleness combined with courage might live on in a world which so greatly needed both.

II

A telephone call had come for Robbie Budd in Newcastle; the yacht *Oriole* had arrived at Key West, and was bound north; would it be agreeable if Mr. Holdenhurst were to call at Newcastle and make the acquaintance of Mr. Budd? Mr. Budd replied that it would be most agreeable, and added that Lanny was in the neighborhood and was looking forward with pleasure to the promised visit. So Lanny had to bid farewell to the Hansibesses, and drive eastward along the shore of Long Island Sound to meet that fate which had been revealed to him in the crystal ball.

Budd-Erling had its own wharf in the Newcastle River, made by dredging the mud of the river and depositing it behind a double row of pilings. There was depth enough for ocean-going steamers; and when the trim white yacht was carefully warped alongside, Lanny was standing there exchanging greetings with the family and guests lined up along the rail. It was a bright sunshiny day and Lanny was dressed in a gay sport suit which his tactful stepmother had laid out on his bed. Even when he is almost forty, a man needs to have things like that done for him.

Be sure that the conscientious but worldly wise Esther Remson Budd hadn't failed to find out about the persons who might be coming on that yacht. How old were they, and would it be bridge or dancing? And this Lizbeth Holdenhurst—what did she look like and how did she behave and what did she talk about? All perfectly natural and proper questions, of course, for Esther had to entertain her and must know whom she would like to meet. Esther wouldn't say: "Are you seriously interested in her?" Never in the world! She would ask, quite innocently: "What did Beauty think of her?" and: "What did you do to entertain her?"

It was a safe guess that one of the ladies on board had advised Lizbeth what to wear. When you are really a yachtswoman, there is nothing more honorific than a yachting costume, white with blue stripes on the collar and cuffs; it can be charming, if made of the best French flannel and cut exactly right, and if you have a skilled laundryman on board, who can turn it out as it ought to be, white as new-fallen snow, delicate and soft, yet without a crease or wrinkle. If you are going to have a yacht, that, too, must be right—freshly painted and varnished every year, and everything scrubbed and polished every day; those on board must likewise be scrubbed and polished, so that the turnout will be all of a piece.

Lizbeth had the right sort of things to put inside that costume: youth, health, and good nature, lovely regular features, a bright smile, cheeks that required no cosmetics, and crowning it all, soft brown hair lightly disturbed by spring breezes over the bay. Lanny had a pair of glasses through which he watched this vision slowly approaching, and he could see that traveling from one tropical port to another, going ashore and buying souvenirs, and in between times playing bridge under a deck awning had agreed with her perfectly. The same held good for her father and the half-dozen guests who were now lined up at the rail.

When the yacht had been warped close enough so that conversation could be carried on without raising voices beyond the limits of propriety, this news was verified; and when the gangplank was let down everybody made everybody else feel welcome, and it was treated as a most distinguishing thing to have been transported all the way around the world in a hundred and eighty days with hardly any incident worth mentioning. There were three cars waiting, with Lanny driving one. The visitors were whisked down the plant's main drive, and along a highway lined with filling stations and hotdog stands, and thence to the fashionable residential section of Newcastle on the heights.

There was a tree-shaded entrance, and a mansion with a wide porte-cochère, and everything as clean and shiny as a yacht. Experienced people like the Holdenhursts and their guests would need only a few glances to be sure that everything inside and out of this home was right; the servants well trained, the ladies of the household gracious and refined; Esther, gray-haired and dignified, her two daughters-in-law, leaders of the young matrons' set of Newcastle, exactly correct from the topmost wave of their hair to the tips of their open-toed shoes. Once more it was pleasant to have money, and to have had it for so long that the proper handling of it had become second nature.

A luncheon party had been prepared and distinguished guests invited. Robbie came, and his other two sons, so that a prospective investor could see in what sort of hands the future of Budd-Erling Corporation was to be entrusted. Vigorous and robust young businessmen, these two half-brothers of Lanny had been watched over since boyhood, and taught exactly what they needed to do; now in their early thirties each had a proper wife and several children, according to the Budd tradition; each was a department manager, and reported at the office at eight-thirty and stayed until five, except on special occasions like this. Both were proud of their wonderful new plant, and neither had any ideas or interests outside its proper conduct, and the payment of dividends to stockholders many of whom were fellow-townsmen and country-club members.

III

From that time on there was one continuous round of entertainments for the *Oriole* party. They were taken to drive and see the town, the river, and the harbor; then back to the yacht to dress, and there was a dinner at the country club, with dancing to the music of a boogie-woogie band. Next day they all went to see the wonders of airplane fabricating according to the latest methods, some of them of Budd-Erling creation. Then to lunch at the home of Esther's brother, who had succeeded his father as president of the First National Bank of Newcastle. They played contract, and in the evening went to dinner at the home of one of Robbie's uncles, where they met all the elder and duller Budds and were properly and respectably bored by looking at a model of an old-time China Clipper under glass, and trophies of the Far East which they had just visited and been bored by. On the following day selected Newcastlers came to the yacht and had a buffet luncheon, and afterwards played more contract. Later on the visitors were taken for a drive to see the Berkshires—which were no great shakes after you had seen the mountains of Hawaii and New Guinea and Japan and Sicily and North Africa.

During all these affairs it became Lanny's duty to entertain Lizbeth Holdenhurst; his social duty because he had introduced them, and his business duty because here was an important client, or whatever you chose to call him, and Lanny's father could use the money. Whenever there was a drive, everybody took it for granted that Lizbeth should ride in the seat at Lanny's side; at bridge she became his partner, and when there was dancing, he could not entirely neglect her, no matter how many eager swains might be on hand. They made a perfect couple, everybody agreed, and smart society in Newcastle and its environs became a conspiracy to put them together and keep them so.

The eldest son of Budd-Erling was friendly and interested, because that was his nature. He asked Lizbeth about the journey from Cannes to Newcastle by way of Dakar and Rio, the ports they had made and the sights they had seen. He told her the news from Bienvenu, which wasn't much. He told her about people he had met in Paris and London and Berlin; he discovered that she was interested in everything about the great world, but the names meant little to her without explanation; she knew titles but she didn't know personalities, and political movements and ideas went entirely over her head. She would have been greatly interested in the story of his meetings with her cousin Laurel, but caution forbade him to mention her; not even the visits to the museums, not even the short stories he had read! The less the smart world had to chatter about on that subject, the safer it would be for a presidential agent!

He was the most rigidly proper of eligible bachelors, more like an elder brother than a suitor. He told his guest about Newcastle and the people she was meeting; about Budd Gunmakers and how the family had lost it in the panic; about Budd-Erling and how his father had started it. Zaharoff and his million-dollar stock subscription made a good story, as did Zaharoff's treasure hunt, and his various spirit communications. Lizbeth had heard ghost stories as a child, but had been taught that only Negro servants believed such things; she had never heard of psychic research, and showed much more interest in this question than in the possible imminence of another European war.

Lanny Budd was a man of the world, and through all this he knew what he was doing and what was being done to him; he didn't miss the smiles and significant looks of his family and friends. All mankind loves a lover, and all womankind enjoys helping to make a match. Nor did Lanny fail to note that this girl liked to be with him and was willing to listen to him talk as long as he would condescend; she was a ripe peach hanging on the bough, and he could guess that at the lightest touch she would drop into his hand. He looked at her and appreciated her loveliness, and was not unaware of the warm currents which ran over him at the thought of her. But he had made up his mind that his job came first and the rest nowhere, and when they had finished a dance he turned her over to the next applicant instead of proposing a stroll onto the veranda.

IV

Robbie Budd took Mr. Holdenhurst into his study for a conference on business affairs; he invited his three sons, being always careful not to show favoritism among them. He gave the guest an outline of the financial set-up of Budd-Erling, and the names of his principal stockholders, including the de Bruyne family, the Countess Wickthorpe née Irma Barnes, and the estate of Sir Basil Zaharoff. He told what business the company had done and what its backlog amounted to, and exactly what use it could make of new funds. The owner of the *Oriole* asked questions, and if anyone had taken him for an idler and dilettante, that person would have changed his mind, for his questions went to the heart of the matter and showed that he understood how business was conducted and profits earned. Robbie called upon his oldest son to discuss the subject of Europe and what was likely to happen there, and Lanny could say with entire sincerity that there appeared to be every likelihood of an increasing demand for military planes.

Next morning Robbie took his guest to the plant office, and established him at the long table of the conference room, instructing his secretary that Mr. Holdenhurst was to have put before him all the company's financial statements, production records, stockholders' lists, and everything else he might call for. No secrets were to be kept from him, and he was to stay as long as he pleased. By the day's end the prospective investor was satisfied, and in the evening in Robbie's study he announced his decision. Lanny was present, and learned something new about how men of wealth take care of their possessions in a treacherous and uncertain world.

Reverdy Johnson Holdenhurst was prepared to sign up to purchase two million dollars' worth of Budd-Erling preferred stock, with which would go a bonus of an equal amount of common. He would pay for it over a period of four years in semi-annual installments. The purchase would be made in the name of forty-two different persons, including his wife, his two sons and one daughter, and an assortment of nieces, nephews, cousins and pensioners of himself and wife. The agreement would have to be signed by all these persons, and separate blocks of stock of varying sizes would be made out in their names and so registered.

That was as far as the purchaser needed to go into the matter; but he had been impressed by Robbie's frankness and explained the basis of this strange procedure, which was his objection to the income tax, and especially to the system of surtaxes in the higher brackets. This objection was a matter of principle, since the purpose of these taxes was to destroy the private fortunes upon which the progress and prosperity of America had been based. The president of Budd-Erling had exactly the same idea, so they talked out their hearts on the subject. Reverdy explained that the stock dividends would be paid to the various family members, each of whom would keep the money in a separate bank account; each was under an agreement of honor with the head of the family that he or she did not touch this money except to invest it when and as directed. If Reverdy had received all this income himself, he would have had to pay a surtax as high as eighty-two per cent, which was practically confiscation; but by this method of distribution in advance of death the surtaxes were in some cases avoided entirely and in all cases were kept to the lower brackets; moreover, in the event of Holdenhurst's dying, there would be no inheritance taxes to pay, and not even executor's fees.

Lanny wanted to say: "You are offering a high premium for somebody to poison you"; but he was afraid this effort at humor might not be appreciated. He listened while the head of the Holdenhurst family declared that so far not a single person had broken the agreement. The set-up had been arranged by a family lawyer, who handled all the details; whenever Reverdy made an investment, the whole family moved as one phalanx to the same goal. All that each had to do was to sign a check and mail it back to the lawyer. They owned stocks and bonds but did not have the physical possession of them; they had money in the bank but never touched it.

Robbie thought this a most ingenious scheme and wished he might do something like it; but all his money was "active" in his business. The other replied that some of his money was active, also—especially the yacht, which went around the world once every year. Reverdy smiled as he said this, and explained that several years ago he had had as guest a well-known authority on the valuation of jewels. Reverdy had become interested and had taken the opportunity to make a study of the subject. In the Sulu seas they had bought pearls, and from Capetown they had gone up to the diamond fields. Thus quite by accident there had been suggested to Reverdy not only a form of recreation, but a method of operating a private yacht in spite of income taxes— something which few of his acquaintances could any longer afford.

The skipper grinned as he reported that he had changed the registration of the *Oriole;* it had ceased to be a pleasure yacht and become a trading vessel. He, his wife, his two sons and one daughter owned it in partnership, and each year the father played at getting the better of diamond and pearl dealers who thought they knew it all. They were frequently in need of cash, whereas Reverdy needed nothing; so he came back from the voyage with an assortment of valuable stones locked in the safe in his cabin. There was a lot there now, and dealers would come to Baltimore and buy them, and Reverdy would make a profit. Of course it wasn't enough to cover the cost of the yachting trip—that wasn't the idea. The extremely bright idea was that the costs of maintaining and operating the yacht became a business loss each year, and thus served to reduce the incomes of father and mother, daughter and sons, and put them into lower surtax brackets!

V

"Absolutely stunning!" was Robbie Budd's comment, and he asked for the name of the lawyer who had designed the set-up. Robbie was so grateful for these confidences that he took his new friend in on a secret of his own, revealing that a couple of his bright young men had just designed a new supercharger for fighter planes, a single-gear device that operated upon an entirely new principle, and was about twenty per cent lighter than any gadget of the sort that Robbie had previously seen. He went into detail on the subject—there were gear superchargers, which were run by the power of the engine, and there were turbo-superchargers run by the power of the exhaust gases; the former were simple and light, but the trouble was, each model worked well at a certain altitude but was not so good at other altitudes. It was obvious that a fighter plane might plunge from six miles high to four miles, and still need supercharging—that is, the compressing of the rarefied air fed to its engines.

Robbie had found the solution to this problem, he declared. He was organizing what he called the "Ascott Corporation" and expected to be in production in a few months. It would be a sure thing, because the entire product would be taken by Budd-Erling, at least for the present; it would be a closed corporation into which Robbie was inviting a few members of his family and his closest friends. He would let Mr. Holdenhurst have a moderate amount of the stock, say fifty thousand dollars—of course after he had investigated the matter thoroughly. Reverdy replied that he knew Mr. Budd pretty well by now, and understood this method of getting a good thing and keeping hold of it. Robbie could put him down for five hundred shares at a hundred dollars par value and there wouldn't be any need to bother with the family phalanx—Reverdy would take this stock for himself, and if it earned too much money he might find a way to increase the business losses of the *Oriole*.

Lanny Budd went out from that conference with the realization that he had greatly misjudged the skipper of this trading vessel, whom he had taken to be a rather naïve grown-up playboy. Lanny found himself wondering, was the name of Laurel Creston included among those members of the family phalanx who were waiting, patiently or impatiently, for Reverdy Johnson Holdenhurst to decide to die? Lanny thought with amusement of the sensation he might have created if he had asked this question, and gone on to reveal the part which this cousin had played in helping Robbie Budd to develop a new type of single-gear supercharger!

VI

One day in the midst of these diversions the son of Budd-Erling picked up the morning paper, and found spread across the front page the news that President Roosevelt had addressed a telegram to Adolf Hitler, with a copy to Mussolini, inviting this pair to lay their cards upon the table and to state their purposes and demands, and the reasons, if any, why they could not co-operate with the peace-loving nations of the world. Lanny's eyes ran hastily over the text, and saw that his Chief had used a number of the P.A.'s sentences, but had changed many and added others. In offering to transmit the reply to other nations, the President had listed those on behalf of which he expressed concern:

"Are you willing to give assurance that your armed forces will not attack or invade the territory or possessions of the following nations: Finland, Estonia, Latvia, Lithuania, Sweden, Norway, Denmark, The Netherlands, Belgium, Great Britain and Ireland, France, Portugal, Spain, Switzerland, Liechtenstein, Luxemburg, Poland, Hungary, Rumania, Yugoslavia, Russia, Bulgaria, Greece, Turkey, Irak, the Arabias, Syria, Palestine, Egypt, and Iran?"

Lanny had not been consulted as to that listing, and he was dubious as to the wisdom of it; for nations which were in fear would be so greatly in fear that they wouldn't dare to admit it, and this would give the shrewd Adi an opening of which he would hardly fail to take advantage. Lanny studied the document carefully, marking the passages he could recall as his own—for he had kept no copy. He listened to the comment of his relatives and their friends, and discovered that the head of the United States government had thrown a brick into a hornets' nest. It had been a long time since Lanny had seen his father so outraged. "My God, my God, the man is mad!" he exclaimed; and the skipper of the *Oriole* took up the responses like a church congregation reciting a litany: "Stark, raving mad!"

"Can you imagine it?" Robbie continued. "He lists thirty-one countries—count them!—whose affairs we undertake to manage!" The antistrophe came promptly: "To keep them out of war!" Then Robbie: "And with us teetering on the edge of another panic, with millions of unemployed, and a national debt piling up by the billions!" Then the hater of income taxes: "And all of us being plucked like so many fat geese!"

Lanny couldn't say a word, of course; he just had to listen. Everywhere he turned it was the same: the locker room of the Newcastle Country Club resembled the Wailing Wall of Jerusalem. We were going to take on the troubles of the whole world, fight the wars of the whole world, pay the debts of the whole world—and the businessmen of the nation were powerless to help themselves because it would be twenty-one months—count them!—before they could get rid of that madman in the White House. "Somebody ought to kill him!" declared a leading citizen, and Lanny watched to see if others were lowering their voices and getting ready to carry out the threat. But no, they shouted it; they were shouting it in country clubs from Portland, Maine, to Portland, Oregon. It was their God-given freedom of speech.

VII

Adolf Hitler knew all about what was being said in America, and being the cunningest crowd compeller in the world, he set to work to make the most of this unsought and unexpected opportunity. He sent his agents scurrying; Dr. Goebbels to the Near East, Göring back to Italy, and so on, and extracted from many of the thirty-one nations statements that they were not afraid of being attacked by Germany. With the help of his advisers he prepared an answer with twenty-one numbered points, each shrewdly contrived to appeal to the golf and tennis players in the locker rooms. Then he summoned his tame Reichstag, for never would Adi content himself with telegram or cold print when he might have an audience and a radio reaching all around the world.

Surrounded by all the trappings of governmental and military power, the one-time *Gefreiter* harangued his five or six hundred deputies for two hours and a half. He told once more the history of Germany for the past quarter century: all the wrongs it had suffered and the refusal of the Judeo-pluto-democratic-imperialist nations to right those wrongs. Mr. Roosevelt wanted Germany to disarm and come into a conference; but Germany had tried that once, at Versailles, and what she had got was "the most cruelly dictated treaty in the world." Since then, the United States had expressed its opinion of the conference method by its refusal to join the League of Nations. The United States had its own method of dealing with its neighbor nations, a device which it called "the Monroe Doctrine." Said Adi: "We Germans support a similar doctrine for Europe—and above all for the territory and interests of the Greater German Reich."

Mr. Roosevelt wanted to ensure peace; all right, said the humorous Adi, he, Führer of the Germans, was busy doing it. In Czechoslovakia he had just taken control of 1582 war planes, 501 anti-aircraft guns, 2175 pieces of artillery, 785 mine throwers, 469 tanks, 43,875 machine guns, 114,000 automatic pistols, 1,090,000 rifles, and many other sorts of materials of war; thus he had made certain that these weapons did not fall into the hands of "some madman or other." Recently in the United States there had been a panic caused by a dramatic sketch over the radio telling of an army landing from Mars; Hitler had his fun with that, showing what the irresponsible democratic radio and press could do. He had another laugh, because Mr. Roosevelt had said the Irish were afraid of the Germans, whereas the Irish Premier had just made a speech saying that what the Irish were afraid of was the "continuous aggression" of England. Mr. Roosevelt had named Palestine— overlooking the fact that England was subjecting that country to "the cruelest maltreatment for the benefit of Jewish interlopers."

Said the Führer of the Germans, addressing his world opponent with elaborate sarcasm: "Conditions prevailing in your country are on such a large scale that you can find time and leisure to give attention to universal problems. Consequently, the world is undoubtedly so small for you that you perhaps believe that your intervention and action can be effective everywhere." Listening over the radio in his father's home, Lanny imagined the golf and tennis players in the locker rooms reading a translation in the newspapers and agreeing with every word of it; they would recognize it as exactly what Smith had said to Jones only the day before. "Why the hell can't we stay at home and mind our own business?"

Lanny felt a sinking in the pit of his stomach, and wondered whether he hadn't been the means of causing President Roosevelt to "put his foot in it," and to increase still further the confusion and strife inside the democratic nations. Lanny thought about those nations which had said they were not afraid, and imagined all the diplomatic wirepulling and browbeating that must have gone on. He didn't possess the gift of precognition, but he kept the newspaper clipping of the President's telegram, and in after years he checked upon it. Of the thirty-one nations which had been named by F.D.R., eight were overrun and conquered by Hitler within a little more than two years, and in two years more he had overrun and conquered sixteen, not counting Russia, of which he took a large part, and England, which he did his best to destroy with bombing planes.

VIII

Esther came up to Lanny's room one afternoon; he had sneaked off by himself and was seated in a comfortable wicker armchair by the open window, reading a book by Sir James Jeans on modern physics, a strange and wonderful subject. The stepmother said: "Can I interrupt you?"—and Lanny, who had expected this, braced himself for the shock. "Certainly, Mother," he replied; he had accumulated three mothers and one mama in the course of his active career.

He gave her the comfortable chair and took another. Esther hadn't been able to think of any indirect approach to the subject, so she began without preliminaries: "I want to talk to you about Lizbeth. Are you the least bit interested in her?"

Lanny might have fenced, and raised the question of a definition of "interest"; but he knew that would not help matters. "I think she is a very sweet girl, but I am not in love with her."

"It's really time that you thought about getting married, Lanny. Your father thinks so, and asked me to talk to you about it."

They had had this out before, more than once, but politeness required that Lanny should listen gravely whenever requested. "It's really very hard for me to contemplate marriage, dear Mother. I have to travel about the world so much, and I can't imagine myself making any woman happy."

"I wish you would take my assurance, Lanny—there are many women who manage to be happy even though their husbands' business calls them away. We in New England were a seafaring people, and we got used to the idea of women not seeing their husbands for a year or two. A woman has a child and that keeps her busy; when her husband comes back she has another child, and learns to make the best of it."

"There may be women like that, but I haven't met any that I could believe it of." Lanny, of course, couldn't give his real reasons, and this was the best he could think up.

"I wish I could persuade you to think seriously about Lizbeth. She is a sweet and lovely nature, and it is evident that she is attracted to you."

"I know," said the worried bachelor—the women wouldn't let him alone wherever he went, and it had become quite a problem. "I have done my best not to encourage it. I have been polite and friendly, but nothing more."

"I have observed that, and of course it is your right. But Robbie and I agree that it would be the most suitable match we could think of. She is the domestic type of girl; she would want to have children, and she would be happy at Bienvenu, or here with us, if she knew that you were busy with your work and would come back when you could."

Lanny's tongue was tied; he couldn't say anything about his work, which would have so disturbed the older woman as well as the younger. The nearest he could come to the subject was: "Lizbeth hasn't an idea in the world about what I am thinking."

"I know, Lanny; but she's only a child; her mind is only beginning to open to the world. I have watched her, and she listens with pleasure to everything you tell her. A girl like that builds her whole life around the man she loves. If you gave her books, she would read them; she would do anything that she thought would make you happy."

"That's what Beauty and all her women friends told me about Irma; but it didn't turn out that way. Irma knew exactly what she wanted, and went right ahead to get it."

"Well, Lanny, I can't say anything about your European world, or even about smart society in New York; to me it seems heartless and corrupt, and I would never have advised you to marry Irma Barnes, not for all her millions. But Lizbeth is different; she has been brought up at home and adores her father; she hasn't even been to a finishing school. Being on a yacht gets to be rather monotonous—so she tells me."

IX

Lanny had to listen politely and answer patiently; that was part of his job. He could understand clearly the point of view of Esther and his father; what they wanted for him was what he ought to have had—if he had been what they believed him to be. All he could say now was that he was afraid of tying himself down, of contracting obligations that he couldn't carry out. Suppose that some day he met a woman he truly and deeply loved, and found himself married to a woman he had never loved—that would mean tragedy for two women, not to mention himself. Lanny could guess that his father had told Esther about Marie de Bruyne and perhaps also about Rosemary, Countess of Sandhaven; not at the time, perhaps, but afterwards, when they had been discussing the problem of his future.

Said he: "I have been really in love, and I know what it means. If ever it happens to me again, I am afraid it will have to be with some woman who is mature, and who shares my thoughts and interests. Young girls are nice to look at and to dance with, but they seldom know anything—they don't even know what they themselves are, and I am afraid of what they may be when they find out."

Esther was afraid that if she said too much she might cause him to reduce the frequency of his visits. She asked one question which took him aback: "Tell me—may Robbie explain your attitude to Mr. Holdenhurst?"

"Good grief!" exclaimed the stepson. "Has he asked?"

"No, but we both think he'd like to know. If the mother were here, she would do the asking."

"I suppose so; but I didn't have any idea the matter had gone that far."

"Didn't it occur to you that maybe that's why he came? Newcastle isn't really such an interesting town—to a man who's just been all the way around the world."

"Well, I'm sorry if I'm such an interesting man," replied Lanny, with a touch of mischief. "I was just trying to help Robbie sell stock. I hope I didn't misrepresent anything."

"Tell me one thing frankly, Lanny."

"All right," he said, bracing himself for another shock. When people said "frankly," it was sure to be something unpleasant.

"Is there any other woman in your life?"

"No, Mother, there isn't."

"I ought to know if there is, because I'd be wasting my time."

"If ever there is, I'll promise to tell you. It won't be anything to be ashamed of."

"Well, think about Lizbeth." Esther found it hard to give up. "She's right here, and it may be some time before you meet anybody more worthy of affection."

X

Yes, she was here, and she stayed. It was the essence of the family's agreeable way of life that they were never in a hurry; if they were having a pleasant time they kept on having it. The few business details which had to be cleared up provided a sufficient excuse, if any were needed, but no one brought up the subject. The yacht had moved out into the river and anchored there, with bow pointed upstream except when the tide was running in strongly. When anybody wanted to go ashore, the launch took them. They slept on board, and when they weren't invited out to meals they ate on board; a deck chair under a striped canopy was as pleasant a place to play bridge or read a novel as anyone could find; so why worry or ask questions?

Esther had said: "Think about Lizbeth"; and Lanny had to do so, whether or no. He saw her every day and it would have been rude to avoid seeing her. She was "on the carpet," and he had been told that it was his carpet if he would have it. He wondered, how definitely had she made up her mind? Nowadays the young things seemed to know what they wanted and went after it; Lanny had been sought more than once. Lizbeth, he decided, wasn't the demonstrative sort, but who could tell what might be going on inside her? Some day he might make the mistake of holding her hand the fraction of a second too long, and before he knew it she would be in his arms.

He thought of that and resolved never to be alone with her. But even as he thought of it, his blood was telling him that it mightn't be so unpleasant to find her in his arms. It was a trap that nature had set, this infernal business of sex that wouldn't let men and women alone. The moment she came into his presence, he perceived how well the trap had been baited; she was so pleasant to look at that it made him shiver a little. How could he be an art expert and not appreciate beauty? He had told Esther that he wasn't in love with this girl; but maybe these shivers were love, and maybe the ideas with which he plagued himself were just efforts to keep from being in love.

At any rate, he was doing what his stepmother had requested—thinking about Lizbeth! He wondered what was going on in her mind. He couldn't ask, of course; that would have been walking right into nature's trap. Instead, he watched for signs; but then, if he saw one, he must glance quickly away, before she had discovered that he was looking. Was she looking, too? And was she glancing quickly away before he discovered what she was doing? That was a dangerous game to play; for what if their glances happened to meet? She would blush, and it might be possible that he would blush, and they might be at a loss for words to cover the awkward moment.

He wondered, had she taken the ladies of her party into her confidence, and were they all watching and speculating? One was a maiden lady of indeterminate age, Lizbeth's tutor in various subjects. When the yacht was at sea, there were regular study hours, but when it was in port there was a holiday. Did Miss Chisholm know that her pupil was in love with an art expert who had traveled over Europe and knew the great ones of every country? Love wasn't one of the subjects she was supposed to tutor, but maybe she had taken that on as a sideline— and out of what experience?

Lanny wondered also about Reverdy Johnson Holdenhurst, and what part he was playing in this inner drama? Had he guessed, or had he been told? Had his much-loved daughter said to him in Cannes: "Daddy,"—so she called him—"this is the man I want to marry. Please invite him to sail with us and give me three months' chance at him"? And when that plot had failed, had she said: "Please find some excuse to take me to Newcastle"? Had the father replied: "All right, I'll buy some Budd-Erling stock and make friends with the family." Was that the way things went in the modern world? Here was a man, deliberately keeping his only daughter away from her mother, the person who was naturally charged with the duty of finding her a husband. Was Reverdy Johnson Holdenhurst saying to himself that Lizbeth should marry *his* man and not her mother's man, whoever he might be? Someone who lived abroad, and not in Baltimore? Someone who could be visited by a yacht, and perhaps taken along?

XI

Lanny had assured Esther that there was no other woman in his life; and this was true, or at any rate he meant for it to be true. He had told himself that he was never going to see Laurel Creston again. But that didn't mean that he wasn't going to think about her; he couldn't help doing so, because every time he thought about falling in love with Lizbeth he found himself thinking about Laurel, too. He compared them in his mind, weighed them in the balance—and sometimes it swung one way and sometimes the other. Both were impossible, he told himself, but sometimes one seemed less impossible than the other; each served in an odd way to make him less aware of the defects of the other. It was a sort of parody of the old song—how happy could I be with either, were t'other dear charmer away!

Lanny would dance with Lizbeth at the country club, and become aware all over again of her charms, so carefully nurtured and now exhibited at this all-important moment of her life. To what man was she going to attach herself, and mold herself to his habits and tastes?

Whose home was she going to live in, whose children was she going to bear? Manifestly, these were number-one questions to a girl, and if she had picked out Lanny Budd from many others, what were her reasons, and what light did they throw upon her character and tastes? These were number-one questions to Lanny, and he gave earnest thought to them.

In Baltimore she must have met many eligible men, and surely she was meeting them in Newcastle—many who were handsome, also wealthy or certain to become so. Why had this child—so he called her in his mind—chosen an art expert, one slightly eccentric and highly uncertain? Had it been something that Emily Chattersworth or some of the other ladies of the Riviera had told her? Was it the trace of foreign atmosphere, the languages, the travel? Lanny guessed that more than anything else it was his acquaintance with the famous and great. The child wouldn't be able to judge statesmen or painters or writers or musicians, but she would have noted that every time one was mentioned, Lanny Budd knew him, and would tell funny stories about him, indicative of intimacy with and possibly a slight superiority to. She had found Lanny *distingué*—a word worn threadbare, and easy to ridicule, but Lizbeth Holdenhurst wouldn't see it that way; she would take it as the apex of desirability, the thing for which she wanted to spend her share of her father's money. A baby reaching out for the moon!

Lanny would dance discreetly, holding her not too tightly; and that made him seem dignified and aloof—as far away as the moon. But he wasn't really so; he was right here on the ballroom floor, and aware that he was holding a lovely young virgin; aware of her warmth and shapeliness, of the smile on her gently rounded face, the glances of her eyes, the state of dreamy bliss which possessed her in the arms of the man she wanted. She used a delicate and exotic perfume—and of course Lanny knew all about perfumes, knew that they were put up in fancy bottles with preposterous sexual labels and sold at fantastic prices in shops which preyed upon female credulity. He knew that hair was arranged exactly so by persons who called themselves artists, and that evening dresses were cut out of the costliest materials in such a way as to reveal exactly the right amount of the female person.

Yes, he knew all that, and in the cold light of the morning after, he told himself that it was an unworthy thing to let himself be influenced by the bodily seductions of a healthy young animal with very few brains, at least of the sort he wanted. Marriage, to be worth anything, ought to be a union of minds, because it is in our minds that we truly live, it is by our minds that we have survived and lifted ourselves above the level of the animals—however young, however healthy, and however lovely to look at!

XII

Such reflections would start him to thinking about Laurel Creston again. (How happy could I be with either!) Laurel had the brains, in fact a superfluity of them. Lanny found himself slightly afraid of them, wondering how it would be if ever that satiric energy were to be turned upon him and his worldly pretensions. Perhaps it had already happened, in the secrecy of Laurel's thoughts; and was she deciding to avoid him at the same time that he was deciding to avoid her? But no, it wasn't that, Lanny decided in *his* secret thoughts. It was that Laurel would be irresistibly driven to write stories and perhaps books; her superfluity of brains would manifest themselves in some public way, and make it impossible for a P.A. to associate with her except clandestinely—or even to explain why that must be so. And what decent woman will meet a man on the sly, and without knowing any reason for such a humiliating procedure?

No, Lanny had had all that out with himself, and it was a waste of time to go over it again. Perhaps, after all, the sensible thing was to pick out some healthy young animal, one that was especially easy to look at. The problem became even more simplified when the young animal picked him out and saved him the bother. A wife who would never trouble him with the product of her brains, but would make a home for him—and pay a good share of the expenses! One who would bear him children, and let him have them for his own, to be brought up according to his ideas. Lanny had always been fond of children, and delighted to watch them and teach them; but they had always been other people's children: Marceline, and Robbie's boys, and the Robin boys, and Marie's two and Rosemary's three; now Freddi's one child, and Bess's two, and Marceline's one. Even Irma's one was only Lanny's in a very restricted way.

But if Lizbeth had children, and he kept her respect and affection, they would be really his to control. When he went out spying he would always make one or more picture deals as a cover, and when he came back he would talk art and literature and psychic research, never politics or war. Lizbeth would be a perfectly proper wife, in the eyes of all his rich reactionary friends; even Hitler and Göring would approve her. That was a thought which sent a shudder through Lanny.

and made his whole being recoil. Suppose she admired Hitler and Göring, as Irma had done! Suppose that in England or France or wherever he took her, she picked out the Fascists to play with! She could hardly fail to do that, if she was trying to follow Lanny and to mold herself to his ideas. She would never know him, but only his role, and he would come to hate her as he hated all those poisonous people whom he pretended to admire!

XIII

The day came when the last document had been signed; also, if there had been a hope lurking in anybody's heart that Lanny Budd was going to "pop the question," that hope must have died. The skipper of the *Oriole* announced that it was time to put an end to a delightful visit. He begged that if any of the Budd family, old or young, ever came near Baltimore, they would take his home for their own. That applied to any of the other Newcastlers who had entertained his party; in short, all the amenities were complied with, and the life of the rich was dignified and serene, according to conventions elaborately contrived.

Lanny rendered the extra courtesy of coming on board for the trip down the river and out into the Sound, returning in the launch with the pilot. He stood by the rail with his friends, pointing out the sights, first of the Budd-Erling plant, then of Budd Gunmakers, then of the city. The yacht slid gently through two open drawbridges, one for the highway and the other for the railroad. Then came the inlet, with the wide blue Sound where no pilot would be needed. It would soon be time to part, and Reverdy said, not for the first time: "Come and pay us a visit, Lanny. I'm not just being polite—we'll be truly happy to have you."

Lanny answered: "It's a little hard for me to set dates, because my comings and goings depend upon the whims of clients. But I'll telephone you when I know I'm free."

"You can make it a business trip," added the other. "I am going to take my Detazes off the boat and hang them in my home and start a boom in Baltimore. When people hear what I paid for them, they will know they're good."

That was making it hard indeed for Lanny to hang back; for his friend had been in the storeroom and seen the stock of Detazes and been told that they were for sale. He said: "That is really kind of you, and I'll do my best to arrange for a visit before I go back to Europe."

"It gets very hot in midsummer, but May and June are lovely," added Lizbeth; which was certainly making a girl's attitude known to a reluctant swain.

Lanny shook hands all round, with perhaps half a second's longer shake of a soft feminine hand and half a second's longer glance into a pair of inviting brown eyes. Lizbeth had been very sweet to him, and if it hadn't been for the infernal business of sex they might have danced and played tennis and golf together and been as happy as the two babes in the woods. "*Au revoir*," he said, and not "Good-by," and followed the pilot down a rope ladder into the little launch. It darted away from the yacht's side and turned back into the inlet; the people at the *Oriole's* stern waved and Lanny waved; the distance between them widened swiftly, and parting was such sweet sorrow.

13

Where Duty Calls Me

I

LANNY was reading, for the second time, a book which he had brought with him from England, a newly published series of lectures entitled *The Philosophy of Physical Science*. Its author was a very learned gentleman: O.M., M.A., D.Sc., LL.D., F.R.S., Professor of Astronomy and Experimental Philosophy at the University of Cambridge. Lanny had always been under the impression that philosophy was a matter of speculation, but Sir Arthur Eddington now informed him that it had reached the stage of experiment, a development surely worth knowing about.

Lanny had been brought to a state of mental insecurity by almost ten years of dabbling in what was known as psychic research—or, in England, "psychical." He had seen so many things happen that were incredible, and the effort to account for them had led him into unorthodox reading and upset most of the things he had imagined he knew about the universe. His own too too solid flesh had melted and turned into empty space with minute electrical charges whirling about in it.

Still more incredibly, space had become a form of his thought, and also had become curved, while time had become a fourth dimension of space, and the universe had become circular. All this not the raving of lunatics or the phantasy of "surrealists," but a new science which called itself physics, but appeared to end up in a demonstration that the physical existence of the physical world was a matter of grave uncertainty.

Lanny had to admit himself ill equipped for the study of Sir Arthur Eddington and Sir James Jeans. He had never been to college, and hadn't even finished prep school. He had once known some algebraic formulas, but now retained only a vague memory of how they looked. However, if a learned writer would be kind enough to explain at the outset the meaning of the words he used, Lanny would read the first paragraph, and if he couldn't understand it he would go back patiently and read it again. Each philosopher and each scientist gave his own special meanings to words, but was unable to persuade others to use the same vocabulary. In a chapter entitled "The Scope of the Epistemological Method," the astronomer-knight informed Lanny that: "The term 'electron' has at least three different meanings in common use in quantum theory, in addition to its loose application to the probability wave itself." And then in a footnote the explanation: "Namely, the particle represented by a Dirac wave function, the particle introduced in second quantization, and the particle represented by the internal (relative) wave-function of a hydrogen atom."

This learned lecturer had a sense of humor, and it amused him to take sly digs at the large number of scientists who still called themselves "materialists," all unaware that "the classical scheme of physics is a punctured bubble." Someone near the beginning of the century had asked the question: "What is it that we really observe?" and thus had started us "on a path of revolution of which the end is perhaps not yet in sight." The end, according to Sir Arthur, was that: "We reach then the position of idealist, as opposed to materialist, philosophy. The purely objective world is the spiritual world; and the material world is subjective in the sense of selective subjectivism."

There was nothing novel about this "idealist" position in philosophy. When Lanny was a youth his Great-Great-Uncle Eli Budd had set him to reading Emerson, and Emerson had sent him to Plato, who had it all. An eighteenth-century Irish bishop by the name of Berkeley—which the English pronounce "Barclay"—had written a book to prove that we know only sensations, and can have no knowledge of whatever reality may or may not be behind the sensations. Dr. Samuel Johnson had answered him by kicking a stone; thus proving that it is easier to make a joke than to understand a metaphysical argument. For he didn't prove that the stone was there, but only that he had experienced a complex of sensations which he and his fellow-men had agreed to indicate by the name of "stone."

In the days from Plato to Emerson all this had been a matter of speculation. But now the physical experimenters had come along, and had granted Hamlet's request that his too too solid flesh would melt; Hamlet's flesh and Dr. Johnson's stone had been turned into electrons, and electrons were, according to Sir Arthur Eddington, not merely "the probability wave itself," but also "the particle represented by a Dirac wave function, the particle introduced in second quantization, and the particle represented by the internal (relative) wave-function of a hydrogen atom." Said the Cambridge professor, in his playful mood:

"It is pertinent to remember that the concept of substance has disappeared from fundamental physics; what we ultimately come down to is *form*. Waves! Waves!! Waves!!! Or, for a change—if we turn to the relativity theory—curves! Energy, which, since it is conserved, might be looked upon as the modern successor of substance, is in relativity theory a curvature of space-time, and in quantum theory a periodicity of waves."

II

Lanny would read sentences such as these, and then would go for a walk, or for a sail in a catboat belonging to one of his half-brothers, and would meditate upon what he had read. The ideas seemed to him of enormous importance, ultimately the most important in the world; they would form the basis of a new religion, which mankind needed most urgently. Were mind, will, and conscience fundamental to the universe? Were they forces which had some effect upon the universe? Or were they accidental and temporary products of the activity of matter—like sparks thrown off from a grindstone or a rainbow refracted through drops of water? Vanity, vanity, all is vanity, the ancient Hebrew preacher had announced, and the Greek philosopher had drawn the obvious conclusion: Eat, drink, and be merry, for tomorrow we die.

For a couple of years Lanny had been traveling about with what he called the Trudi-ghost, meaning the memory of his murdered wife, which had become the voice of duty in his soul. He had received what claimed to be communications from her "spirit," but he had never been able to make up his mind whether they were actually that, or the product of his own living memories. As Lanny had said to Monck, memory is a mystery, as great a mystery as "spirits" would be if you had decided to believe in them. Skeptics laughed at the idea that the universe, or the air, or whatever, might be full of the souls of uncounted numbers of the dead; where would they stay and what would they do? But these skeptics took it quite as a matter of course that their minds should be full of millions of memories—for the psychologists had proved that you never forgot anything you had once known or that had ever happened to you.

Where did these memories stay? In the brain cells, the materialist would reply, and think that he had said something. But how did they stay? Did each memory hide in a separate cell? The cells were changing all the time, with the wear and tear of the body; did the memory move out of an old cell and into a new one? The cells were composed of molecules and the molecules of atoms and the atoms of electrons—and electrons were waves, or curves, or "form." Was the memory, too, a form? And what made all these forms, and controlled them, and kept them and used them?

Lanny wanted to say that it was the thing he called his personality; that is, his mind, his will, his conscience. He asked one of the world's leading physicists whether or not he had the right to believe this, and the sharp-tongued scholar replied with two sentences that were like the snapping of a whip. Comparing the ideas of scientists and those of savages, he said: "We now think it ludicrous to imagine that rocks, sea and sky are animated by volitions such as we are aware of in ourselves. It would be thought even more ludicrous to imagine that the volitionless behavior of rocks, sea and sky extends also to ourselves, were it not that we have scarcely yet recovered from the repressions of two hundred and fifty years of deterministic physics."

It was a question that went to the very fundament of a man's life. If mind, will, and conscience guided the universe, a man could believe in right conduct and strive to practice it and make it prevail in the world—even though his individual consciousness might not survive in its present form. But if he was just an accident, a cog in a vast machine that had no purpose, what difference did it make what he did, and what was the use of striving, since he couldn't affect the result? What is mind? No matter! What is matter? Never mind!

Lanny had once heard Adolf Hitler utter what seemed to him the most atheistic sentence ever spoken by man, to the effect that it didn't matter how spiritual a man might be, his spirituality couldn't function if his body was beaten to pieces with rubber truncheons. There spoke what Lanny, for lack of a better word, called Satan. Satan's minions had put that doctrine into effect with Trudi Schultz; and were they right or were they wrong? Truth, honor, justice—were these real forces, real "forms" under the relativity theory? These were the questions with which Sir James Jeans and Sir Arthur Eddington were wrestling, and their answers gave Lanny Budd the courage he needed to go on living his lonely secret life.

III

The German anaconda was busy with his digestion, so not much was happening in Europe, at least not on the surface. Lanny thought that he had earned a holiday, and his relatives made this a pleasant place to take it. He played tennis, sailed a boat, and sometimes when members of the family were away he made loud noises on the piano. He took long walks, and sometimes stopped and talked with plain Americans, being pleased to discover that they did not believe all they read in the newspapers, and did not hate the New Deal so ardently as the gentlemen of the country club.

More than once he passed the public library of Newcastle, an ancient inadequate building in a small park. Lanny would think of the polite maiden lady who functioned as head of that institution, and feel a twinge of discomfort, recalling how, in the previous summer, he had driven this lady home in his car one evening; the evil contrivance known as sex had caused him to lay his hand upon the lady's hand and had caused her, in turn, to lay her head upon his shoulder. One thing led to another, as it does, with the result that Lanny was afraid he had awakened false hopes in the lady's bosom; so now he avoided going into the library. But he knew that she would know that he had been in town for some weeks, and perhaps her feelings would be hurt because he never found occasion to consult any book in her collection.

The time came when in the course of his professional labors he needed to refer to Vasari's *Lives of the Painters*. He took his courage in hand and went in, and there was the rather frail New England gentlewoman, Miss Priscilla Hoyle, seated at her desk in one of those chairs with little rubber-tired wheels and ball bearings, which can be run from place to place with a slight push. Lanny bowed as he went in, and did not stop to see the flush which spread over the lady's pale features. When he had got the information he needed, he stopped to speak to her on subjects proper for librarians. "I have been reading some new books, and when I leave I mean to turn them over to you."

This enabled the lady to conceal the reason why her heart was beating fast. "Oh, thank you, Mr. Budd! Our appropriations are so inadequate. You can't imagine how painful it is to see worthwhile books published and have to renounce the hope of them."

"I have been reading Jeans and Eddington," the visitor continued. "Have you read them?"

"I have read about them, Mr. Budd, but we don't have them."

"I will present my copies. They support the idealist position in philosophy, which you probably approve."

"By all means," was the reply. Lanny assumed that New England transcendentalism would be fed with mother's milk to persons of good family in this old-fashioned town. Really, it was a town within a town, for the descendants of ship captains and farmers still looked upon the factory people as interlopers, even after a hundred years.

Lanny went back to his father's home, and remarked to his stepmother: "I stopped at the library, and got to talking with Miss Hoyle. She seems to be a highly cultured person."

"Yes, indeed," replied Esther, a trustee of the institution; "and a most faithful soul. I don't know quite what we should do without her."

"I wondered why you don't invite her to the house. We have rather a tendency to get shut up in a narrow set, don't you think?"

"I suppose that is true," admitted the *grande dame* of Newcastle society. "I just somehow never thought of inviting Miss Hoyle. Do you suppose she would care to come?"

"She would consider it a preliminary visit to heaven," replied the irreverent stepson. "But don't do it until you are ready to make your politicians vote an appropriation for a new building, for that is what her heart is set upon."

"I suppose I really ought to do that, too. But everybody is so poor nowadays—the New Deal draws all the money out of Newcastle, as you know."

Lanny would have liked to say that the New Deal was putting the money back into Newcastle, in the form of aid to unemployed workers; but that was the sort of remark he had ceased making several years ago. His stepmother postponed the carrying out of his unusual suggestion, and he had left before she got round to it; which was just as well, for he was quite willing to have Miss Hoyle think she was going to get her new building, but not that she was going to get Lanny Budd.

I V

In the month of June the King and Queen of England crossed the sea on a visit of state. They received a truly royal welcome in Washington, with sixty tanks preceding and following their cars and ten "Flying Fortresses" overhead. It was one of the hottest of days, and that poor frail potentate in a heavy admiral's uniform with its gold lace and decorations must have suffered abominably. But it is the business of royalty in England to be both uncomfortable and bored, and this King, who was afflicted with a speech impediment and had to stop at short intervals and meditate upon the next word before he tried to say it—this Majesty had been catapulted into his job a couple of years ago, and had to learn it in action.

The royal pair were here in an effort to wipe out old scores and win the friendship of America in the grave crisis which confronted the British Commonwealth. They were, so far as one could judge through the stage trappings, quite kindly people; and of course every move they made had been studied by expert propagandists for weeks in advance. They went to the White House for a state dinner and a concert which was broadcast over the radio; all-American music for all-America—cowboy ballads, square dances, Negro spirituals, and then Lawrence Tibbett, Marian Anderson, and the large Kate Smith with her large voice singing *When the Moon Comes Over the Mountain.*

After three days of festivities Their Majesties went up to Hyde Park, where they had a picnic and ate hotdogs. They might have preferred other foods, but were trying to be democratic, and there were photographers and newsreel cameramen on hand to record them eating hotdogs and smiling between bites. Britain needed airplanes now, and before long might need ships and even warships, and if this was the way to get them, God help us to like hotdogs, and not to choke while we are in front of the cameras, or to stammer when we try to say: "Okeydokey!"

Lanny was in sympathy with the purpose for which this ceremony was being conducted; he wanted a union of the British and the American fleets, even of the British Commonwealth and the American Republic. But he couldn't help remembering a stage performance he had attended not long ago, when he had made acquaintance with the delicate and ingenious art of Angna Enters. A young woman came upon a bare stage, with only the simplest of accessories, and to the music of a piano gave little pantomimic episodes which brought a period of history before the audience. She had made Lanny think of Isadora Duncan —not because of any similarity in what they did, but because, for the first time since Isadora's tragic death, Lanny saw a woman alone on a stage and without a spoken word holding the attention of an audience through an entire evening.

Most of these sketches were of the simplest: an old-time Viennese serving maid putting on her black kid gloves and taking up her prayer-book and lace handkerchief, getting ready to go to church; then returning and putting these treasures away in a little box with loving precision and care. Or a Spanish boy cardinal, infinitely corrupt, dressed in yellow silk, taking a stroll and casting lascivious glances at imaginary girls. Only one of the episodes had been political, and that had portrayed Britannia, clad in her robes of state, sublimely haughty and unapproachable. But something frightened her, something drove her into a panic; she pulled out a tiny green flag and began waving it, casting seductive glances at an imaginary Eire; then a little American flag, then another and another, casting them here and there, pleadingly, in abject humility. It was a malicious, not to say vinegary little cartoon, but as a piece of art it was unforgettable.

Now Lanny looked at the many pictures of dressed-up royalty in the newspapers, and he knew that Britannia was in her panic, and with plenty of reason. He told himself that this was not really a King and Queen in the old meaning of those words, but two symbols of the hopes of the British people. There were three Britannias, and had been for centuries: that of the aristocracy, aloof and impervious, as they had always been in every land; that of the plutocracy, the lords of pounds and guineas, blind to everything but their profits; and that of the workers, the democracy, plus the saving minority of liberal thinkers and statesmen who had made the British Commonwealth and kept it an agency of progress. This third Britannia had pleaded the cause of the colonies throughout the American Revolutionary War; it had saved the American Union in the Civil War by keeping the British ruling classes from coming to the aid of the slave power; and now it was fighting appeasement of the dictators, and those forces at home which were Fascist in sympathy and as near-Fascist in action as they dared to be with a general election coming on.

V

A telephone message from New York—Professor Charles Alston calling Mr. Lanny Budd. It was about dinnertime, and Lanny was in.

"Hello, Lanny, this is your old friend from the Peace Conference. I may be mistaken, but I am under the impression that you and I haven't met since we parted in Paris, twenty years ago. Is that correct?"

Much practice in intrigue had made the son of Budd-Erling quick on the uptake. It took him only a fraction of a second to realize that there must be someone in the room with Alston, or else he was afraid there might be someone on the line in the Budd home, and he didn't want any such person to know that he had met Lanny two years ago and had been the means of introducing him to F.D.R. Lanny, who shared this wish and had been keeping this secret, answered, quietly: "That is according to my recollection."

"Is your father at home?" was the next question; and then: "I wonder if that is according to *his* recollection, also?"

Lanny understood then that his friend was trying to make sure whether Lanny had told his father about the meeting with Alston in New York. Lanny hadn't told anyone, so he said: "I have no doubt that his recollection agrees with mine."

The one-time professor of geography continued: "It happens that I have some information which may be of great importance to your father. I would like very much to see him."

"I am sure he'll be glad to see you at any time, Professor."

"Does he often come to New York?"

"Not often nowadays. The plant keeps him tied down."

"It so happens that I have to fly to Washington tomorrow afternoon. I wonder if he would do me the great favor to run in to town for an hour or so in the morning?"

"I don't know what his engagements are," replied the son. "I had better call him to the phone, if that is O.K. with you."

"I hesitate to call on you for a favor, Lanny, because I feel guilty, having neglected you all these twenty years."

Lanny understood that his former employer was making doubly sure that the crucial point hadn't been missed. "It's quite all right, Professor. My feelings haven't been hurt. I know how busy you have been. Everything is all right."

VI

Lanny went to the dining room, where his father had just taken his seat at the table. "Professor Alston is on the wire, calling from New York."

"Charlie Alston?" exclaimed Robbie. "Well, I'll be——" Then he stopped, because his wife was present, and a couple of her women friends. Esther permitted them to have a cocktail before dinner, but it was assumed that they never heard the word "damn" except in church.

Robbie went to the phone, and Lanny followed, in case he might be needed. He listened to one side of a conversation while two college mates who had not seen each other for more than twenty years exchanged greetings; then, with some amusement, while his father carried on a struggle over precedence. A man does not forget the impressions of his youth, and to the rich and fashionable Robbie Budd the man on the other end of the telephone wire was still a "barb," the fellow who had never been tapped for a fraternity at Yale. He hadn't helped matters by becoming a professor of geography in a freshwater college, and still less by taking up with the New Deal and being named in the newspapers as one of the "brain trust." There was nothing in this world the president of Budd-Erling hated more than the spectacle of a college professor taking a post in government and telling businessmen what to do about their affairs. The idea of being summoned to New York to meet such a man, when it was so obviously his business to step onto a train and come to Newcastle—that made Robbie swell up like a balloon-fish out of water.

But evidently the ex-professor was making it sound portentous; and deep under Robbie's bluster there lay anxiety, for, after all, these fellows were in power, and who could guess what dark secrets they might possess? It was the beginning of a revolution; but then, revolutions have been known to happen, and they are darned uncomfortable things. The end of the conversation was: "Oh, all right, I'll come." But he wasn't going to be gracious about it—no, sirree! "The Ritzy-Waldorf, eleven tomorrow morning"—and his voice seemed to say: "What the devil does a barb mean, stopping at a hotel like that?"

Robbie was too well bred to grumble at the dinner table, in the presence of his guests, but he did a plenty of it to his son later on. He wasn't going to give in one inch to the New Deal, in any manner, now or ever. Lanny stopped him with the suggestion: "Look, Robbie—suppose he wants to tell you that somebody has been getting ready to bomb the plant?"

Robbie hadn't thought of that one, and it left him staring. "Somebody?" he demanded. "*What* somebody?"

"I'm sure I can't guess. But I know that this world isn't more than a year or two away from war, and when you undertook to fabricate military planes you put yourself right up in the front trenches. Do you imagine that the angels are going to protect you?"

The president of Budd-Erling decided that it wasn't such a long drive to the city after all.

VII

Seated in a hotel room in which there might or might not be a dictaphone installed, the gray-haired little ex-geographer with the gold pince-nez wasted no time beating about the bush. Just a few words of greeting, remarks about how Robbie looked after twenty years, which was pretty good, and how Lanny looked, which was marvelous—and incidentally conveyed the idea that Alston hadn't seen Lanny in those twenty years; then an offer of a drink, which Robbie declined, having laid down the law for himself, one cocktail at lunch and one at dinner and no more. Then they were seated, and the New Deal "fixer" opened up with a battery of a hundred and eighty-eight millimeter guns:

"Budd, I'm afraid you aren't going to like this, and I don't like it either, but I want you to understand that I'm not speaking on my own initiative, but on very high authority. What I have to tell you is that your present dealings with the Nazi government are considered a menace to the safety of the country, and to put it up to you as a patriotic American that they have to be discontinued."

Robbie behaved like one of those small PT-boats when shells from the big battery go off all round it; he was lifted right out of the water and bounced around. The blood began to rush into his face in the dangerous-looking way it had, suggestive of apoplexy. "What the hell do you know about my dealings with Germany?"

"It will save time, Budd, if you assume that I know everything about them. I know that you have an arrangement by which you share ideas, and that Göring has been getting yours while you haven't been getting his; so I shouldn't think you'd be exactly heartbroken over the idea of parting company with him. I know also that he has three men in your plant, and that they are under agreement to take no part in political activities, but they are keeping that agreement no better than Nazis keep any agreement anywhere."

"If you know that they are doing anything illegal," said Robbie, in a sneering tone, "the place for you to go is to the Department of Justice."

"I am coming to an old classmate," was the patient reply. "When you have had time to think it over, I am sure you won't desire to blacken your plant and your family with scandals in the newspapers. You must realize that events are moving fast, and they are beyond your control or mine. Our country is in really grave danger, and things that were permissible two or three years ago are simply intolerable now."

"If our country is in danger, it is because we have a President who is not content to remain within his constitutional limits and let us stay at home and mind our own business."

"We could argue a long time about that, Budd. You as a maker of military planes ought to be the first man in the country to understand that staying at home and minding our own business is no longer as simple as it used to be. Let me assure you that the General Staff of the Army does not share your ideas as to what constitutes safety in a world where the range of bombing planes is being extended week by week."

"Am I to understand that you come to me on behalf of the General Staff of the Army? Or are you one of these New Dealers trying to frighten a businessman out of his right to carry on his business in his own way?"

"I am first of all a friend, Budd. I have a vivid recollection of the help which your son gave me all through the Peace Conference, and of the understanding of the world situation which he showed at that time. Tell me, Lanny, have you been abroad much during the past twenty years?"

"I have lived there most of the time, Professor."

"And do you share your father's idea that we can stay quietly at home and have nothing to fear from the Nazis and the Fascists?"

"I don't think my father is quite so naïve as he sometimes sounds," replied the tactful son. "He is anxious to have the country well armed for its own protection."

"What I object to is having this country fighting the wars of the British Empire and of France," put in Robbie, who was under no necessity of having anybody else, even his firstborn son, called upon to speak for him.

"Let me put a hypothetical question to you, Budd. Suppose that you were President of the United States, say two years from now, and early one morning you were waked out of your sleep by a phone call from the Prime Minister of Britain, and told that you had twenty-four hours in which to make up your mind whether or not to enter the war —otherwise the British fleet would be surrendered to the Germans. What would you answer?"

Lanny was startled by this question, for it was exactly the one he had invited F.D.R. to consider in his bedroom in the White House less than a year ago. Had the President passed it on to Alston and told him to use it with recalcitrant manufacturers? Or was it a question which the insiders were asking one another over the teacups in Washington —a very hush-hush question, never to get into the newspapers.

Robbie Budd, the hard-boiled isolationist, did not let it phaze him. "Your question is nonsensical," he replied. "But if it happened, I would answer that the U.S. had had enough of fighting other people's wars, and it was 'never again' for my administration."

"All right, Budd; and now another telephone call, a year later, or perhaps only six months. This time it comes from Buenos Aires. Shall they surrender, or will we help them?"

"Oh, there's no question there. I believe in the Monroe Doctrine. I would keep the Germans out of South America."

"Good God, Budd, don't you know they are all over the place? There are something like a million Germans in the Argentine, and as many Italians, and most of them working day and night for their fatherlands. They can take any country in South America any day they want to. They have a complete chain of airports covering the continent, and with a base in West Africa they can fly expeditions across and have a dozen countries under their control in half a year. They can bomb the Panama Canal out of business, and then, so far as naval affairs are concerned, they have divided us into two countries, east and west."

VIII

The two contestants could have wrangled all day over questions like that. Robbie Budd was a man who made fighter planes, and to him the proposition was simple. If you made enough of them, you could stop any bombing expedition before it got to its target. No use quoting the military maxim that the best defensive is an offensive, for Robbie had heard it, and his answer was that his offensive would be a swarm of the new B-E P11's, equipped with the new Ascott single-gear supercharger, which could get up above any bombing plane in the world. When Alston said: "You would have to have hundreds of them based at every one of our industrial centers," Robbie's answer was: "Why not? That wouldn't cost the hundredth part of what it would cost to fight the wars of the British Empire. Give me the money and let me make the planes."

It was the voice of old-time America, from the days of the Know-Nothings to the days of Henry Ford. Professor Alston, who presumably had studied history as well as geography, replied, quietly: "All right, Budd; if that's the way you feel, the problem is simple. Make fighter planes for your own country."

The other stared at him. "When have I ever refused to make them? Who wants planes, and how many does he want?"

"The government wants them, and it wants all that you can make in a hurry."

Robbie continued to gaze at the mousy little man with nose-glasses who made this extraordinary statement. In his mind was the thought: "My God, the brain trust!"—a symbol for incompetence on an astronomical scale. When he spoke, it was patiently, as if to a little child. "Listen, Charlie! You are talking to a man who has been to Washington something over fifty times, and has interviewed hundreds of the brass hats and the gold-braid admirals. They expect you to fly whenever they telephone, and when you get there they tell you that you have to submit new specifications in quintuplicate, and that the board which has to pass upon them meets next November, and that in any case the order has to be reduced from fifty units to thirty because the Naval Affairs Committee of the Senate is expected to reduce the appropriation still further."

"I know, Budd," replied the ex-professor. "I have been spending six years going round with a pair of shears cutting people out of tangles of red tape. But this time it's going to be different. May I speak to you in the strictest confidence?"

"I never gossip about my business affairs."

"This time it's more than a business affair, it's an affair of national security. I remember that in Paris Lanny used to keep his country's secrets carefully, and now I have to ask both him and his father to do the same."

"O.K.," said the father. "You can count upon us."

"The planes will be in accordance with Army specifications and will have to pass Army inspection, but the money will come from another source. You can be certain of getting it promptly; but first, you have to get the Nazis out of your plant and cancel whatever contracts you have with the Luftwaffe."

"Charlie," said the president of Budd-Erling, "I am not a noble idealist like you, trying to save the human race. I am a vulgar, common business fellow who has to meet a payroll every week, and keep several accountants working to keep records and make out social security reports and income-tax statements and everything else that you New Dealers have dreamed up. Also, I have persuaded some widows and orphans to invest their savings in my stock, in the expectation that I will be able to earn profits and pay them something to live on. My deal with Marshal Göring doesn't represent merely the cash I get—it's very little now—but it's something I can use to frighten the British and the French and the Poles, to pry orders out of them. I know that's ignoble, perhaps even rascally, but it's the way I was taught to do business by my father and the way I've been doing it for some forty years. In short, I am a merchant of death—the other fellow's death, not mine— and before I risk cutting off a considerable chunk of my income I have got to know exactly what I'm going to get to make up for it."

"You will get the money in the amounts agreed on, and at the time."

"And where will I get it?"

"It will come to you in the form of checks from the central office of the WPA in Washington."

"WPA," repeated the fabricator of fighter planes, in a tone which seemed to say: "Do my ears betray me?" There were so many of these damned letter combinations in the New Deal that nobody could keep track of them, not even their own parents. But WPA—didn't that mean Works Progress Administration, and wasn't that the double-damnedest of all damnations, which Robbie Budd and his friends at the country club had been cursing all over the golf links? By God, the relief organization! The leaf-rakers, the builders of swimming-pools and wild-duck ponds, the jackasses who had been setting fellows from Greenwich Village to painting crazy murals in post offices all over the land! *WPA!*

"Listen, Budd," said the fixer, who had no trouble in reading the thoughts of businessmen; "we have people in Congress of isolationist views who refuse to take measures for the national safety. They won't vote appropriations for battleships and tanks and planes, but they have voted large sums to put the unemployed at work; and why isn't it just as important to make jobs for the makers of battleships and tanks and planes as for those who do any other sort of work?"

"Oh, so *that's* it!" exclaimed the head of Budd-Erling. "So *that's* what's going on!"

"It has been going on for quite a while, Budd, and it's one of the best-kept secrets in the country. Don't forget that you have given your word not to talk about it."

"And so I'm going to be put on the dole!"

"You can call it that, but I think it would be better to say that you are put on your country's roll of honor. Wouldn't you prefer that, Lanny?"

Thus appealed to, the son hastened to pour a jet of oil on these troubled waters. "Ever since childhood," he declared, "my father has explained to me that the reason he stuck to making munitions in spite of all abuse was that when the time came for the country to need his services, he would be there with the goods."

"Exactly!" said the brain-truster. "The time has come, and here you are—Robbie on the spot!"

IX

Driving his father home, Lanny listened to a thorough canvassing of this unheard-of development in the life of a businessman. "I'll be handcuffed to these sons of the wild jackass," was Robbie's pessimistic conclusion; to which his son replied: "You always said that what you wanted was to be able to produce at capacity; and here you have it!"

"There's a catch in it somewhere," responded the father. "It won't work out."

Lanny had to be cautious, weighing every word. "From what I have seen in the papers about Alston, he must have a good deal of influence, and he certainly talked straight."

Sure enough, fairly early in the morning Robbie received a telephone call from Washington; a high-up officer in the Service of Supply—a man with whom Robbie had dealings in the past and not so satisfactory —this General Armisted wanted to know if Mr. Budd could be in Washington the following morning on a matter of importance. Robbie phoned Lanny at the house, interrupting the reading of Sir James Jeans. "Would you like to drive me?"—and then: "You might like to stop on the way back and pay that call on the Holdenhursts." Such a guileless parent was Robbie Budd!

Lanny consented, for he was really curious as to this unexpected development in the affairs of Budd-Erling Aircraft Corporation. They would leave at the end of the business day, have dinner somewhere on the way, and reach their destination by midnight. As an afterthought, the father said: "By the way, there's an airmail letter from Germany here, addressed in my care. No superscription on it."

Lanny knew what that meant, but his voice showed no excitement. "I'll stop by for it in the course of the morning," he replied.

He drove to the plant, and when his father's secretary gave him the letter he put it into his pocket and didn't open it until he was back in the car. In the familiar script he read: "Your friend Weinmann is going to purchase the Vereshchagin, I feel quite certain. I have one or two other paintings which I think will interest you. Trust you can come soon. Braun."

The arrangement had been that Monck was to write about paintings, selecting such as would give a hint of what he had in mind. Lanny knew nobody by the name of Weinmann, but he knew Ribbentrop, the wine salesman, and that was clear enough. Vereshchagin, the Russian, had hated war, and had made vivid its horrors in a series of paintings. Lanny did not overlook the phrase "is going to purchase," instead of "will purchase," more natural to a German writing English. The message told him that the Nazi Foreign Minister was planning a visit to Moscow, to arrange some sort of peace agreement, the deal concerning which both Hitler and Hess had dropped hints. The second sentence told Lanny that Monck had some project of his own and wanted money. The third was as near as he dared go in telling Lanny that these matters were urgent.

X

An item of news as important as this had to be taken to F.D. at once. Lanny had read in the papers that the Big Boss had gone back to the White House, and that fitted in with Lanny's plans. He drove to a near-by town, and in a pay station in a poolroom, an unlikely sort of place for anybody to know him, he put in a telephone call, dropped in a stream of quarters, and asked for Baker. He was told that the man was expected back in an hour, so he said: "Tell him to wait for an important call."

Then he took a walk, thinking about the future of the world he lived in—blacker every hour it loomed. Truly, it was like standing in the middle of a prairie and watching a "twister" approaching: a portentous stillness, and a great yellow turnip-shaped dustcloud sweeping nearer, its root reaching down, swinging here and there and picking up houses and barns and cattle, whatever caught its fancy. Lanny had never seen this sight, but had read about it. Here was a cyclone that swung over the whole earth, catching up nations and people in its deadly whirlpool: Manchuria, Abyssinia, Spain, Austria, Czechoslovakia, Albania—and now it was hanging over Poland.

Lanny went to a new place to put in his second call. He pronounced his formula, and added: "I can't come tonight. Make it tomorrow night or the next, if possible." He was told to call again at four, which fitted in with his plans. Meantime he wanted to talk to somebody, but there wasn't a soul to whom he could tell what he knew. The Hansibesses were near by, so he dropped in to tell them that he would be sailing for Europe in a few days.

The talk turned to the Soviet Union. Sooner or later Hitler was going to attack them, Bess declared, and they knew it and no doubt were doing their best to prepare. Lanny agreed with this, and wondered whether they might not become disgusted with their ally, France, and her politicians who refused to implement her treaty of alliance; also with the British Tories, who were trying to play with both sides. Might not the Soviets decide that Hitler was no worse than Chamberlain?

"You mean they might make a deal with that Nazi ape?" So spoke Bess; it was absolutely unthinkable, an obscene idea, a consequence of Lanny's associating with the rotten ruling classes, people who had no more political morals than they had of any other kind.

Said the visiting half-brother: "Doesn't it occur to you that the Soviet leaders may have heard the maxim about fighting the devil with fire?"

But no, Bess couldn't bear to hear about it, to say nothing of considering it seriously. The Communists were men of principle; they had a cause to fight for, and it was the very antithesis of Nazism; their goal was a classless society, while the Nazis were building a world of slaves.

Lanny didn't try to argue; he just sat and listened while they committed themselves hopelessly. He wondered how they would wriggle out of it, if the calamity actually came to pass. He loved them both; Hansi was a man of genius, and Bess had made herself at least a good pianist and a devoted helpmate. They had a faith, which they had built around them as a sort of armor against the cruelties and corruptions of the world. They would admit that there might be evil and selfish men in the Communist movement—yes, they had met such, it happened in every movement. But the movement itself was the workers and peasants of Russia and the struggling revolutionaries of other countries, and they were showing the way to the whole world! They were the hope of the world, and without them there would be no future! Uncle Jesse had said it, and now Hansi and Bess.

XI

Lanny put in his third call, and was told that he was to be on the customary street corner at nine on the following evening. Then he went home and packed his bags—not forgetting that he might stop off for a day or two at Baltimore. He drove his father—striking north and crossing by the George Washington Bridge so as to by-pass the traffic of a crowded metropolis. On the way Robbie talked about this phenomenon that had suddenly popped up in his pathway; Lanny had never seen him so completely at a loss, so disposed to consider the point of view of his ex-playboy son. He didn't forget that Lanny had dallied with the New Deal for years, and had never formally renounced his interest in it. With the CIO in his plant, and now the WPA becoming his paymaster, the president of Budd-Erling was like a general who finds himself surrounded by hostile forces, and can only wonder what terms they mean to exact.

And then questions about the situation in Europe, subject to such sudden and erratic changes, beyond any man's power to foresee. Lanny had never been pinned down so closely. Just what had Hitler said, and Göring, and Hess? In Hitler's recent speech he had stated that his final terms had been submitted to Poland. What were they, and how much did he mean them? If the Poles gave way, would he betray them and take Warsaw as he had taken Prague? What had the Nazis done about Skoda, and what did Schneider say about it?

Of course Robbie didn't forget the questions that all the world was asking: Was Hitler going to fight Russia, and when, and how was it going to turn out when it came? Lanny was free to tell of the hints that both the Führer and his Deputy had dropped concerning the possibility of a deal with the Soviets. This time, he discovered, the idea didn't cause the least surprise. Why not? Nazism and Communism were practically the same thing, weren't they? Why shouldn't they get together and divide Europe between them?

Lanny answered that they were alike in some ways and different in others. Both had what they called "monolithic" governments, that is, party dictatorships; but when it came to economics they were at opposite poles; the Soviets had dispossessed the capitalists, while the Nazis had given them everything they could ask for. Lanny told what Hitler had commanded him to report to the big businessmen of Britain and France—the enormous plant expansion and dividends of the great cartels under his regime. "After all," said Lanny, "what do they care who pays them the money? They turn out the goods and have a permanent market."

"Like me and the New Deal!" said the president of Budd-Erling Aircraft, with a wry face which his son couldn't see in the darkness.

XII

Next morning father and son kept the appointment with the United States Army, and found that immense institution in a mood the like of which Robbie had not seen in a period of some twenty-one years. No panic or anything like that, but a firm quiet realization that the great

U.S.A. ought to have more fighter planes. How many B-E P11's was Mr. Budd prepared to turn out in the course of the next fiscal year and what would he want for them? What arrangement was he prepared to make for changes such as might be required if a part of the product was to be taken by the British or the French government? Robbie had all the answers in his portfolio. He told about the wonderful new Ascott supercharger, and at once the Army wanted to know when and where it could be tested and how soon and in what quantities it would be in production.

Really, it was the way things happen in dreams; in that so-common dream in which you are suddenly endowed with the power of levitation, and go soaring over landscapes where formerly you had to plod your way through plowed fields and mud puddles. It was as if some mousy little gentleman with gray hair and nose-glasses had come with a pair of sharp shears and cut every single strand of red tape in this huge office building. The reason, of course, was not beyond guessing; the Army, like all other institutions under a democracy, is kept on a budget, and has to be careful how it spends its money; but if somebody comes along and says: "The WPA will pay," why then the brass hats behave like any family which is put on the dole—they proceed to spend while the spending is good. The unemployed workers of Newcastle would have jobs, the merchants of Newcastle would sell goods —and the tennis and golf players of the country club would go right on damning That Man in the White House.

Robbie Budd was busy all day, and in the evening he had a lot of figuring and dictating to do, so it was easy for Lanny to get excused; he wanted to call on an important client, he said—and that wasn't any fib. He was picked up and taken to the client in that big high-ceilinged bedroom with the dark blue wallpaper. He asked: "Did the hotdogs agree with you?" and he was answered with one of those grins which he had come to know. F.D. loved this job of his, but only on his own terms, which were that he could remain himself and have some fun as he went along. He was determined not to become stiff and formal, glum and morose, as his greatly disliked predecessor had done.

"They are very simple and friendly people," he said, speaking of his royal guests. "Everything went off very well—except that our butler at Krum Elbow slipped on a rug with a loaded tray."

"Well, I dare say that has happened in Buckingham Palace," commented Lanny. Then, being curious about Robbie's affairs, he remarked: "My father is here in Washington—being roped and branded by the Army."

"By golly!" exclaimed the President. "I hope they don't burn him too deep." The twinkle in his lively gray eyes told that he knew what was going on. Such a lot of things he knew!

XIII

Lanny understood that this was one of the busiest periods in a great man's life, for he was involved in a long and grueling struggle with Congress over the amending of the Neutrality Act. The stack of papers on his reading table seemed like a hint to a visitor, and Lanny decided to make his report quickly and take himself out of the way. But F.D. wanted to chat, and there was no stopping him. "How did you like my telegram to the Führer?" he inquired.

"It was all right, Governor; only, if I'd had a chance to revise it, I'd have left out Ireland and Palestine."

"He's a dirty fighter!" exclaimed the other, revealing that he felt the barbs which had been shot at him across the Atlantic.

"Many of the country-club set in Newcastle agreed with him; but I took occasion to sound out some of the plain people, and found that they had got the point. One old farmer said: 'Somebody will have to sit on that fellow and hold him down.'"

"Meaning me or Hitler?" asked the President; and then, after enjoying his own joke: "What is he going to do next, Lanny?"

"He's going to have his way with Poland; but first he'll make some sort of deal with the Russians, to keep them quiet. That is what I came to tell you about."

Lanny had burned the letter from Monck, having first learned it by heart. Now he recited it, and told briefly about the writer. "He is a levelheaded and careful man, and would never make such a statement about Ribbentrop unless he had got it from the horse's mouth. You know how it is with the underground—they have sympathizers in high positions, and sometimes secretaries and clerks take documents over the week-end and have them photostated. I myself have helped to get such documents out of Germany—they had come from Göring's files."

"This makes a pretty black prospect, Lanny. If the Nazis and the Soviets combine, they can just about take Europe."

"Don't read more into my message than it contains, Governor. If Monck had meant to indicate a military alliance, he would have used the name of some painter of patriotic or militarist tendencies. We talked our code over very carefully, sitting on the edge of the battle-field of Belchite, in Spain, where he commanded a company. We couldn't have a verbal code, because neither of us could risk carrying notes. It had to be painters, because that is my business. He said: "I don't know much about them, but I can look them up or have somebody else do it for me. As I read the riddle, Vereshchagin stands for peace, and it will be some sort of mutual non-aggression pact."

"But surely the Russians must know that if Hitler could knock out France, he would overrun the Ukraine in no time!"

"No doubt they know everything we know, and then some. But they will be playing for time: time to get new troops trained, time to get new factories going behind the Urals."

"From the accounts that come to me, things aren't going at all well in Russia; the people are poor, and even the commonest goods are scarce."

"Don't let that fool you, Governor. I have an uncle in Paris who is a Communist deputy, and he talks the Party line perforce, but he's a pretty levelheaded old boy, and I've had many tips from him. What he tells me is that the Soviet government allots just enough production of civilian goods to keep the population going. Everything else goes into defense preparation, and it's colossal."

"It's too bad we can't have their resources on our side, Lanny. Is there anything on earth that I can do?"

"Not much, unless you can promise aid to the Soviets in case Hitler attacks them."

"You know I can't do that. In the first place, in case of war, it would be almost impossible to get goods to Russia; and, in the second place, if I tried it, my opponents here would impeach me."

"Well, the only other thing would be to persuade Britain and France to make up their minds and guarantee support to the Soviets if they are attacked. Britain and France can't do it for the same reason that you can't—political disunity at home. The greater part of the Tories and French Nationalists would rather see Hitler win than Stalin. What they want is to have them fight each other to exhaustion; and of course that's obvious to both Stalin and Hitler—and why should they go out of their way to oblige their enemies? Hitler has said that to me in so many words. I had no answer then and I have none now; why should he?"

XIV

Once more Lanny remarked what a heavy burden this Chief Executive was carrying in hot summer weather. He offered to leave. but the

reply was an emphatic "No, I want you to answer questions." In the
six years since Franklin Roosevelt had taken office, his range of duties
had expanded to include Central Europe and all the Mediterranean
lands; he had to know their geography, their politics, and the different personalities who handled their affairs—just as he had to know the
Congressmen and Senators who were now making speeches attacking
him.

At the moment there appeared to be a stalemate between Germany
and Poland. The Führer had made his "one and only offer," and
Poland had said No. Whose move was it now? Lanny explained the
Nazi technique, the "softening up" process, the game of intimidation
which preceded every new adventure. There were more "outrages"
in Danzig and the Corridor, more screaming in the Nazi press. Maybe
the talk of a deal with Russia was just part of this process. Maybe Ribbentrop would pack up his duds and say he was going to Moscow, and
maybe that would scare the Poles so that they would give up a few
more square miles of territory.

It was the same in every capital of Europe; the Nazi agents were
working like termites, burrowing, undermining, devouring. The amount
of money they were spending was unbelievable—in France it was
billions of francs. "The French like money," said Lanny, "and most of
them take what they call an 'envelope,' then make a speech or write an
editorial or cast a vote to get another. In England it's different—they
have what Lincoln Steffens used to call 'honest graft,' meaning respectable big business. You notice perhaps that Chamberlain has been
backing out of the stand he took right after Prague. That doesn't mean
that he has been paid any money; it isn't even because he owns a big
block of Imperial Chemical stock and Imperial Chemical has $55,-
000,000 invested in the German I. G. Farben; it's that all his business
friends are tied up in such deals with German cartels, and it just isn't
cricket to hurt one another's interests. You have noticed that the Bank
of England released all the Czech gold to Hitler, by way of the Bank of
International Settlements. Chamberlain said he had found that he didn't
have authority to stop it, but of course that's just the bunk. He didn't
dare to stop it, because it would hurt business and spread alarm; it
would make Hitler angry and he would make a speech like the one he
made to you!"

"I must admit I can understand the umbrella man's point of view,"
remarked the President, with a grin. It was clear that he didn't like
Adi's method of carrying on public discussions.

XV

The Big Boss wanted Lanny to proceeed to Berlin as soon as convenient and find out what was coming next. Lanny said that had been his intention; and so at last, near midnight, he was turned loose, and set down by Baker at his hotel. He found Robbie still working with a couple of his men whom he had ordered by plane. Since Lanny didn't know anything about contract specifications and the cost of alterations in military planes, he went to bed.

In the morning he told his father that unless his help was needed, he would make reservations for a steamer to England. Robbie said: "O.K., but you'd better stop off for a while at the Holdenhursts', or their feelings will be hurt." Then he had another thought. "If you are going to Germany, I will ask a favor of you. See Göring and try to patch this thing up for me. He's used to the idea that governments control what businessmen do."

"What do you want me to tell him?"

"Say the government is forcing me to break off. Lay it on thick— they threatened to boycott me, to put me out of business; I am powerless to help it."

"That's not going to do me any good in my business with him, Robbie."

"I know. I'll make it up to you somehow. But he can't be too angry —he knows perfectly well that he's been diddling me, and he wouldn't respect me if I took it from him."

"You can't have it both ways," objected the son. "Either you're doing it because you want to, or because the government makes you."

"Well, use your own judgment. Sound him out and see how he takes it. But try not to let it be a quarrel. Kid him along—make a joke of it."

"I can see him roaring with laughter," replied Lanny, making a joke of that.

"Nobody can guess what's coming next in this crazy world," explained a capitalist who was being put on the dole. "I must never forget that Göring might come out on top, and then we'd have to do business with him again."

The opulent father took out his billfold, extracted a crisp thousand-dollar note, and said: "Take this and pay your way." When Lanny protested that he didn't need it, Robbie answered: "I'll put it on the expense account. You have earned it many times over."

XVI

Lanny drove to the nearest travel agency. It was the season of the year when steamships were crowded by schoolteachers and their pupils, by subdebs and their mamas or chaperons, on the way to put the crown on their culture. But Lanny managed to find one vacant cabin on a steamer sailing from New York in three days. That time limit would protect him against the wiles of Cupid, so he figured, and telephoned to Reverdy Holdenhurst to ask if it would be agreeable for him to stop by on his way to New York.

A couple of hours later Lanny's car drove northward on a thoroughfare which Baltimoreans oddly know as "Charles Street Avenue." He passed the old gray stone Church of the Redeemer and the famous Elkridge Hunt Club, and drew up in front of a high-pillared brick colonial mansion in the fashionable Green Spring Valley district. Rolling country with little hills and many woods and streams, beautifully kept estates, and a dignified and conservative aristocracy who considered that they had everything that anyone could want and were doing their best to keep it just so. There was Lizbeth, looking her loveliest; she was glad to see him and showed it as much as was proper for a well-bred young lady. There was the family, doing everything to make a visitor feel at home, but not urging him to stay longer, since he had stated in advance that he couldn't.

Mrs. Holdenhurst proved to be a stoutish maternal lady, revealing, as mothers do, what her daughter would become. She was self-possessed and secure in her social position, but not the severe person whom Lanny had imagined from Emily's story. She was a devout High Churchwoman, and perhaps that had had something to do with her heartbreak over her husband's defection. That had been long ago, and they had found a basis for being polite to each other. Lanny had wondered whether Mrs. Holdenhurst had different hopes for the daughter from what the father had; but there was no sign of any disharmony in this formal and well-conducted household. The hostess looked her guest over and listened to his discourses, as any mother with a marriageable daughter would do; but what opinion she formed was her secret, and it was up to Lanny to make the first move if he wanted to find out.

Lanny wasn't free to mention the humiliating WPA, but he revealed that his father was getting a contract from the Army, the biggest ever. Reverdy had got into the elevator just before it started to ascend! He wanted to know whether this development portended war in Europe, and Lanny was free to quote what had been said to him by statesmen and diplomats in the salons of Paris and London and Berlin, also the casinos and beaches and garden parties of Cannes. While he chatted away, what would a High Church matron be thinking? Speculating as to how many women he had had in his life, and whether he had one in Paris now? He had been divorced once, and from her point of view one time would be as bad as several.

XVII

It was Reverdy who appeared as the active matchmaker. He had hung the two Detazes on opposite sides of his entrance hall and had provided the right reflectors. He had shown them to one of Baltimore's leading financiers, and that gentleman had asked to be informed as soon as the painter's stepson put in an appearance. Now the banker came, a stout imposing figure looking like a cartoon of himself. He wanted to see all the Detazes and he didn't want to take the trouble of transporting his busy person across the ocean. When Lanny said that the paintings were worth more than half a million dollars and it was not the family's practice to ship them around, Reverdy put in the inquiry whether there hadn't been a Detaze show in New York. Lanny said there had been, nearly twenty years ago. "Well, why shouldn't there be one in Baltimore now?"

The upshot of this discussion was that the two gentlemen agreed upon an offer: if Lanny and his friend Zoltan would conduct a one-man show in Baltimore in the month of October, Reverdy would pay all the costs of packing and shipping the paintings, and the banker, Mr. Wessels, would store them in his vaults and keep them insured for half a million dollars. There might be other showings, in New York, Boston, Chicago—that was up to Lanny—but Baltimore must come first.

Very handsome, indeed; and maybe it was due to love of art in the bosom of Reverdy Johnson Holdenhurst—but the other works in his home failed to reveal any such abiding passion. The much-pursued Lanny Budd could not escape the suspicion that behind the whole thing was a father's practice of trying to get for his adored child whatever her heart was set upon. Now she had come to a period of life where her heart spoke with sudden vehemence; and certainly, if it had been desired to bring the son of Budd-Erling to Baltimore and keep him there, no more plausible device could have been contrived. "You are bound to have very large sales resulting from such a showing," said Mr. Hubert Wallace Wessels, president of the Shipowners National Bank and the Chesapeake Trust Company of Baltimore.

There was a tennis court on the estate, but Lizbeth preferred to play at the country club. That meant, of course, that she wanted to show Lanny off to her provincial friends—persons who had never had an opportunity to meet the headliners in the salons and casinos and garden parties of Europe. Lanny had brought the proper togs, and Lizbeth drove him in her shiny sports car, and that was the time for him to indicate some personal interest if he meant to. Instead, he told her about life at Wickthorpe Castle, and about his little daughter, a fatherly rather than a loverly topic of conversation.

In short, he was the most proper friend of the family; and after they had played tennis and drunk lemon squashes, she drove him back to her home, answering his questions about the friends he had met. After he had bathed and dressed, there was an elegant dinner party, with people eager to know what was going to happen in Europe and how it was likely to affect the stockmarket. He told them, to the best of his ability; and later, being invited to display his skill at the piano, he played one of Chopin's Preludes, very elegant and at the same time thrilling. In short, he did everything that could be asked of an expositor of ancient cultures overseas, and when he departed for New York the following afternoon, he had established himself as an eligible grass widower in the best social circles of the Monumental City.

BOOK FOUR

The Brazen Throat of War

14

The Best-Laid Schemes

I

LANNY stopped in London, just long enough to get his car and to have a chat with Rick. Everything was normal in that immense rather dingy old city. People went about their affairs, not worrying too much about the history of the future. In Fleet Street Lanny saw the advertisement of a coach company: "Don't Mind Hitler. Take Your Holiday." The social season was gay, in spite of taxation being fierce. Lanny might have entered the swim, and let his old friend Margy, Dowager Lady Eversham-Watson, or his middle-aged ex-sweetheart Rosemary, Countess of Sandhaven, take him up and find him an heiress. Instead he sat in a hotel room talking about whether it was still possible to save democracy in the world.

Then to Wickthorpe, to spend an afternoon with his little daughter, and an evening with Ceddy and Irma, and friends whom they called in to hear about "the States." There had been a hot fight going on in Congress over the issue of the Neutrality Act, which forbade the sale of arms to any belligerent, thus depriving the President of power to discriminate between aggressors and their victims. The effort to repeal the act had been defeated by a close margin—and what did that mean? What could Britain count upon from the great democracy overseas? What was the state of mind of a nation which gave advice so freely and refused any real help? "Get all you can before war breaks out," suggested the son of Budd-Erling—advice that didn't sound entirely disinterested!

Lanny found British "insiders" once more in a mood of appeasement. In the excitement after Prague the Government had signed a pact guaranteeing the integrity of Poland; and of course they would stand by their word—but that didn't keep them from urging Poland to make concessions. Anything to keep out of war! They had worked out a scheme to buy Hitler with a "peace loan" of a thousand million pounds, the biggest in history; he would agree not to spend it on armaments, he would agree to evacuate Prague, and in return he would have a share in the "development" of China and Africa—which meant colonies, of course. The news leaked, and the Government denied that anything of the sort was afoot; the consultations were "private," a way they had of treating public affairs.

The subject of Russia came up—it could never be left out. The Russians kept on demanding that France should implement the treaty of mutual defense; they wanted such a treaty with Britain also, and they wanted "staff consultations," to plan what was to be done in case of an attack. A "mission" was supposed to be going, but it was decidedly halfhearted. The Earl of Wickthorpe, who had learned to take Lanny's opinion seriously, took him into his study after the guests had gone. If Lanny was going to Berlin, would he be so good as to try to find out what was Hitler's mood, and what the rest of the world had to expect from him?

Lanny explained: "The trouble with reporting on Hitler is that his mood changes so fast; what is true when a letter is written may be false by the time it is read. As well as I can guess, the Führer is in a state of uncertainty at the moment. He's not sure how far he can go. It depends on what he thinks you mean. When you offer him a 'peace loan,' he decides that you are frightened and he goes farther."

"But, Lanny, we don't want war!" exclaimed the Foreign Office man. "People are saying: 'Do you want to die for Danzig?'"

Lanny would have liked to say: "That sounds like Dr. Goebbels to me." But he checked himself, and remarked: "Whatever they are saying, the Führer knows it."

II

On to Paris. Lanny had telephoned to Schneider, who was at Le Creusot and begged him to come there. When Lanny explained that he had business for his father in Germany, the Baron said: "I'll come up to Paris. I must hear about America. I can't understand it."

Here was one badly worried capitalist; his keen mind kept him aware of his country's peril, but his will was falling into a state of paralysis; he couldn't be sure which of several dangers was the greatest. France must at all hazards keep out of war; a whole generation had been wiped out in the last bloodbath, and another such would bring French culture to an end. But the Nazis were such difficult people to get along with! They had behaved abominably in the matter of the Skoda plant; and what if they did the same with the Schneider properties in Poland and in the Balkans—and still worse, if they made a deal with the damnable Communists! What did Lanny think was the truth about these rumors? Once more Lanny promised to find out and report.

He called up his Red uncle and invited him for a drive. Jesse, now entirely bald, and wearing no hat, was a conspicuous object, so his nephew took him through obscure streets; his beloved proletarians might recognize him, but they wouldn't recognize Lanny! The painter-deputy stuck to his story that the rumors of a deal between Hitler and Stalin were enemy slanders; but Lanny noticed that he was beginning to hedge a little—perhaps without admitting it to himself. What was the proposal which the capitalistic powers put before the Soviet Union? To give help in a defense against the Hitlerites, but without having access to Polish territory, the only route there was! Let Britain and France make up their minds which side they wanted Russia to fight on; and let them do it soon!

Lanny went to lunch with the de Bruynes. The father was away, possibly pursuing his pleasures, even at his advanced age. The two sons took Lanny to the Jockey Club, and heard the agreeable news about Budd-Erling—though of course with no reference to the dole. Stockholders like to hear about large orders, and these Frenchmen enjoyed it especially, knowing that *la patrie* had been allowed to purchase American Army planes and might get a share of this new order. The *père de famille* would call on General Gamelin as soon as he returned. Denis *fils* had just had a talk with Colonel de Gaulle, an officer who believed in the future of airplanes and tanks, and was deeply concerned over France's weak position.

The talk ranged over the problem of Europe's future, and Lanny was interested to note the beginning of a rift in the thinking of these two brothers. Charlot, the younger and more impetuous, hated the Leftists so that he seemed to have forgotten the existence of foreign enemies. Charlot renewed his feelings every time he looked into the mirror and saw the scar which he had got in a street battle with the Reds. He was still the Cagoulard, ready to overturn the government by violence, and refusing to worry about what Hitler might be doing in the meantime.

But the elder brother, like Baron Schneider, had noted what happened to Czechoslovakia, and it had frightened him. Maybe, after all, Adolf Hitler wasn't the white knight sent by Providence to slay the dragon of Bolshevism; maybe he was a German, first and last, and still believed what he had written in a book more than fifteen years ago, that German safety required the annihilation of France. The two brothers had been arguing about it, and they wanted Lanny's opinion. When that happened, anywhere in the world, the art expert sought refuge in the topmost story of his ivory tower. Who could guess what was in the mind of any man who had gained power? That was a problem for psychologists and perhaps for statesmen, but surely not for one who traveled about looking for beautiful paintings!

III

Zoltan Kertezsi was in Paris, and he agreed readily to Lanny's proposal that he should take charge of a Detaze show in Baltimore. It would be a good thing for him because his expenses there would be paid, and he would get ten per cent on whatever picture sales were made. He said that as things appeared in Europe right now, it might be wise to have the Detaze works in the United States. Even if there was war in Europe, people would still want to look at good paintings in America, and Zoltan would be glad to take those pictures on a tour and show them in half a dozen of the big cities.

Lanny had already telephoned his mother from London and told her of the project and made sure of her approval. Now, he called her again and told her to get Lanny's former tutor and old friend, Jerry Pendleton, to take charge of the packing and shipping of the paintings. Having done that job before, Jerry knew the ropes. He would have the pictures insured, and he would rent a truck and accompany the precious freight to Marseilles and see it safely aboard a steamer—better two steamers, half and half. There might be a freighter direct to Baltimore.

Beauty wanted Lanny to come to the Riviera, but he told her he had important business with General Göring. The mother said: "Do see Marceline. I am worried about her. I don't like the idea of that German." So Lanny drove to the elegant apartment near the Parc Monceau where the night-club dancer had taken up her residence. He had never seen her so blooming; and when he told her what their mother had said, she burst into poetry. "Oh, Lanny, I have never been so happy! Oh, Lanny, he is the most wonderful fellow! Never, never have I had the least idea of what it means to be in love!"

"I thought you thought you were in love with Vittorio," he had the bad taste to remark.

"*Ugh!*" she exclaimed. "Don't humiliate me!"

"Has Oskar offered to marry you?"

"I don't want him to marry me, I want him to love me. He has made the whole world over for me."

"Once," persisted the half-brother, "you told me that the next man who loved you was going to *pay*."

"Poor Oskar can't," was the reply. "He has only his salary."

There wasn't any more for Lanny to say. Once upon a time—it seemed a long time—he had warned her against a Fascist, and she had paid no attention to him. Now he was not in position to warn her against a Nazi. He felt in part responsible, having introduced her to Oskar von Herzenberg and having appeared to be endorsing him and his cause. It was more of the price Lanny had to pay for being a secret agent. He himself couldn't have a wife, and his half-sister had been thrown to the Nazi wolves.

There is a German saying: "When you are with the wolves you must howl with them." So Lanny in the wolf's den asked about the Herzenbergs, and spoke of them as his intimates. Lili Moldau was a charming actress, and the Graf was one of the shrewdest diplomats in Europe. What did he think about the present situation between Germany and Poland? Marceline replied that she refused to be concerned with the tiresome subject of politics: Oskar bored her to death with it. Lanny, thinking quickly, remarked: "It's an important subject to Robbie right now, because if there is going to be war his business will expand, and it's important for him to know so that he can put in orders for materials in advance. He begged me to find out all I could and cable him."

"I suppose that is the right way to look at it," remarked the dancer. She wouldn't need to be reminded that Robbie had been paying her mother a thousand dollars a month for forty years—and that came close to half a million if you figured it up.

"Moreover," explained Lanny, "it's important to you and me, for I have just arranged with the Holdenhursts in Baltimore to ship the Detazes there and have a show next October. That ought to bring big sales; but I'm afraid if there's a war it will be knocked out."

"Oh, dear!" said the half-sister. "I'd be glad to get some extra money! I'll tell you what—let's have a dinner party, just us five, and I'll keep quiet and let you pump them all you please."

"I won't have to pump, because I have things to tell the Graf that he'll be glad to hear, and he always talks freely in return. The only trouble is, I have a date with Marshal Göring and I have to hurry. Do you suppose you could get it up for this evening? I'll be glad to pay for it."

"I have a date with Oskar. I'll find out if the Graf and Lili can come." She picked up the telephone, and it was a date.

IV

Having time to spare, Lanny called up Kurt Meissner, to tell him the news about Robbie, and about his meeting with Emil and Emil's family. Kurt said: "Can't you come over? Otto Abetz is here, and you ought to know him better."

Lanny drove to Kurt's apartment, and met the dutiful and agreeable secretary and the devoted man-servant; also a blond, reddish-haired German of about Lanny's age. Handsome and agreeable Otto Abetz knew everybody who was anybody in Paris; he lectured at the Cinéma Bonaparte, in the Place St. Sulpice, and all fashionable society came to hear him, especially the ladies. He had a French wife and called himself "pro-French," and his purpose was to bring about a rapprochement between French and German ideas, ideals, and political affairs. He had once called himself a "Christian democrat," and apparently had believed what he preached; at any rate he had learned to look into your eyes—especially if you had a lady's eyes—and speak in a persuasive voice the most beautiful and noble words imaginable. The ladies of the *ancien régime—tout le faubourg St. Germain*, they were called—all adored him. Lanny had even heard his praises sung by his old friend Olivie Hellstein, Madame de Broussailles, a member of the Jewish banking family, whose uncle had been murdered by the Nazis, almost in Lanny's presence. Rick had a saying concerning the English appeasers, that class was more than country; here in Paris Lanny observed that it was more than race.

Otto Abetz was now Ribbentrop's man in France, and distributed money to editors, publishers and writers. Nothing dishonorable about it, for writers have to live, and if you have important ideas and want them promoted, you surely have a right to pay someone to assist you. Kurt was doing the same, and from hints that Lanny had been able to pick up in the course of twenty years Lanny guessed that Kurt's funds came from the Generalstab of the Reichswehr. Apparently all Nazi agents had orders to co-operate with one another, so Kurt and Otto were friends, and now Kurt was helping Otto to become acquainted with an art expert who was known throughout Germany as the Führer's friend and admirer.

No butter had ever melted in Herr Budd's mouth when he didn't want it to. When he met a new Nazi, he was the most agreeable person

that Nazi had ever met. He did not boast about his intimacies in the
hierarchy, but assumed that the other person would know, or would
find out. He considered what this person would most like to know,
and then poured out information in a flood. He had just come from
New York, Washington, Baltimore, Detroit; he had taken the trip with
Forrest Quadratt as his guest, and apparently it had been a money-
raising and information-collecting expedition on behalf of *Mein Kampf*
—not the book, but the cause. Two Nazi agents in Paris were eager to
know how it was progressing in these far-off great cities. They had
read of the congressional vote on the Neutrality Act, and took it as a
tremendous victory for their battle. They wanted to know if Roosevelt was actually insane, and Lanny repeated the expressions he had
heard in the country clubs, which proved that he was.

And then London. Herr Budd would tell them, in confidence—Kurt
being one of his oldest friends—exactly what the British Foreign Office
was doing and planning; what it wanted, what it feared, how it had
best be approached and placated. When two Germans thought it over
later they might realize that they hadn't learned anything especially
new; they would take that to mean that Herr Budd had failed to
allow for the efficiency of the German secret services.

The important thing was, he didn't ask a single question, or display
any improper curiosity. So, in the course of an afternoon, Otto Abetz
talked freely about various personalities who belonged to the Comité
France-Allemagne and who, when they spoke of war between the two
countries, regularly used the phrase *l'irréparable*. Lanny could tell
what Schneider and de Wendel and Juan March and Michelin had
said on this subject—and even Sir Basil Zaharoff from his grave. As a
result, he had a new Nazi friend, and the next time he came back to
Paris he might expect to receive a delicately phrased offer of remunera-
tion.

V

Returning to his hotel, Lanny dressed for the evening and played
host in a small *cabinet particulier* in one of the fashionable restaurants.
There was Seine Hochgeboren, elegant and suave, and his lady who
had studied so carefully the arts of keeping herself young; Marceline,
who, being only twenty-two, had never had to give thought to that
subject; and the blond Oskar with his pink cheeks, the left one scarred,
and his elegant Leutnant's uniform. He and Marceline spent the evening looking at each other, and Lili listened to her protector. Perhaps

she had been told to keep quiet, for the Graf wanted to find out things from Lanny, as Lanny wanted to find out things from him.

The host told about New York, Washington, and the other cities, all over again. Being a P.A. involves much boredom; it is like trolling in the ocean—you may have to wait a long time for a strike, but when you get one, it may be a five-hundred pounder. The Graf was interested in Henry Ford, Father Coughlin, and Gerald L. K. Smith; also in the country-club gentlemen and their conversation. He wasn't so crude as to ask whether the President of the United States was insane, but he said, apologetically: "Some of us found his telegram to the Führer slightly *gauche*." Lanny replied: "It made me blush."

Again London, and the Foreign Office, and what was worrying them; especially the possibility of a Russo-German entente. Speaking to an old friend, Lanny could report that he had discussed this most delicate of questions with the Führer himself, and the Führer had stated what he wanted Frenchmen and Englishmen to know regarding his attitude: that he was nobody's fool, and that no move was excluded from the diplomatic chessboard.

"Certainly not," replied Herzenberg. "The difficulty lies in what the Russians demand: the Baltic states, and Poland at least as far as the Curzon Line. We do not exactly fancy them as next-door neighbors."

"They had all that territory once," replied Lanny; "and as you know, nations, too, have memories."

"Ultimately, Herr Budd, it is a question of power. Some people can make their dreams come true, and others not."

"I don't know whether Washington is a good source of information as to Berlin," remarked Lanny, skirting a dangerous subject; "but the report there is that Herr von Ribbentrop had his bags packed for a trip to Moscow."

"It doesn't take long to pack one's bags," replied the Graf, suavely, "or to unpack them again, if the weather happens to turn unfavorable for an airplane flight. Speaking for myself, and not as an official, I should regard any sort of arrangement with the Reds as a calamity. I believe that if we are given six months more we can win a genuine understanding with France and bring about the abolition of the hateful Russian alliance."

"In that I am inclined to agree with you, Graf. You have made many friends in Paris, and it is purely a question of when they can gain power. Would you be willing for me to quote your opinion to the Führer?"

"I possess only a slight acquaintance with the Führer, and must be careful not to be put in the position of going over the heads of my superiors."

"I understand the situation, my friend." Lanny wouldn't add: "I know that Ribbentrop wants war, and you don't." Instead he explained: "I talked with Kurt Meissner and Otto Abetz, and they are equally optimistic as to the prospects in Paris. May I tell the Führer that this appears to be the general opinion of his representatives on the ground?"

"That will be quite all right, Herr Budd." Then, tempted by his fears, the old-style Prussian nobleman permitted himself to add: "It might be well if you could communicate that information as soon as possible. Lose no time, I beg you. In these times decisions are made quickly, and when steps are taken it may be impossible to recall them. There has never been a greater danger."

That was what Lanny had come to hear, and it was worth an evening and a couple of thousand francs for a *cabinet particulier* and five *couverts*. He added, with a smile: "You did me a favor once, if you remember, and I have hoped for a chance to return it."

"I do not know many persons, even Germans, who can carry a message direct to the Führer, Herr Budd." That was, in the American phrase, "buttering Lanny's parsnips for him," and it was up to him to smile graciously and assure his friend that he appreciated the courtesy.

VI

Next morning Lanny typed out a report and put it into the airmail. Then he packed up and stepped into his car, and said to his chauffeur —himself—"Berlin." He stopped at Les Forêts for a short visit with his sort-of-godmother. Emily's mind was clear, but her physical powers were failing, and it annoyed her greatly; Lanny put one arm about her and petted her a little, to cheer her up. She wanted him to stay and discuss with her the destiny of man, and whether there was going to be anything left of her when her physical powers were ended. He extracted from her the promise that she would try to communicate with him if by any chance she found herself still there, wherever it was.

Also, she wanted to know what she should do with a considerable fortune which she had managed for some thirty years of widowhood. Lanny was concerned not to have her mention that she might leave something to him. His middle name, Prescott, had been borne by her son, who had died in childhood. He told her: "Don't keep much money in France; the times are too uncertain." She answered: "Oh, God!—are the Germans coming again?"—remembering what they had done the last time.

He gave his advice: "Leave it to some scientific body in America, for some kind of research—say cancer." Then he thought of the work that was being done at Duke University, to determine whether "extrasensory perception" was a reality. He told her about it, and added: "They could use money, no doubt." Said the *châtelaine*, with a wan smile: "They might employ a medium and let me talk to her, or him, after I have passed on."

"Mediums are scarce," Lanny answered; "and money can't make them."

He couldn't stay, he explained; he had a date for the following evening in Berlin—and that was no fib. The arrangement with Monck was that, allowing a reasonable time after mailing a letter, he would come to the appointed street corner on a Wednesday evening at ten o'clock, and thereafter every Wednesday and Saturday. Lanny bade a sad farewell, and followed one of his familiar routes, up the valley of the river Oise. Then he came into the valley of the Maas, which, twenty-five years ago, the armies of the Kaiser had pounded with their hobnailed boots; Sophie Timmons, Baroness de la Tourette, had been caught in that dangerous gray flood and had to escape in a peasant's cart behind a spavined old white horse. Lively times Lanny Budd and his friends had been born into!

He spent the night in Cologne, and fell asleep to the sound of artillery and tanks rumbling under big windows. This was for him not merely the city of the perfume and the cathedral, but a place where he had suffered great anxiety, coming to meet Hansi and Bess soon after the Reichstag fire. They had been giving a concert there, two notorious Reds, one of them Jewish and the other a betrayer of her Aryan honor. Would they be allowed to give that concert, and would Lanny be allowed to drive them out of Germany afterwards? Lanny didn't know and nobody could tell him; but nothing had happened. Oh, God, if only Johannes and Mama and Freddi and the rest had come at that same time, instead of waiting a few weeks to straighten out their affairs! Lanny relived these tragic days while driving through the German Ruhr, with its ten thousand chimneys belching black smoke, all eighteen hours of the day and six hours of the night, the way it is at the time of the summer solstice. Everywhere troops were moving westward, slowing up his driving and making him hate all things German.

VII

Next morning straight on to Berlin, by one of those wonderful Autobahnen. They were the Führer's pride and hope; and who was the smarter, the one-time *Gefreiter* or the president of Budd-Erling Aircraft? Robbie said it was the greatest of blunders, because in a war Germany would run short of gasoline and rubber; Hitler should have built up his railroads, because he had unlimited coal. The answer was that he was gambling on short wars; easy little wars, one at a time, like those on Spain, on Austria, on Czechoslovakia. Would he get them? That was something a P.A. could meditate upon while rolling past a seeming-endless string of industrial towns, all with their factory chimneys smoking.

Into Berlin, and the Adlon, with anti-aircraft guns mounted on its roof and the lobby crowded with SS men. Lanny had time to bathe and shave, eat an excellent dinner, and read the papers. This last was no small part of his job, for these "co-ordinated" journals told the German people what their rulers wanted them to believe, and from them you could come pretty near to guessing what was scheduled for the next few weeks. You could wager your eye-teeth, and your eyes, too, that Germany wasn't going to war with the Soviet Union in that period, for all the propaganda against the horrendous monster of Bolshevism had vanished from the Nazi press. No more of that crouching apelike figure, hairy, snarling, with blood-dripping dagger in one hand and flaming torch in the other! Instead—since the Nazis had to have somebody to hate—you saw a smartly clad gentleman with a jutting jaw and a cigarette holder a foot long, grinning maliciously; his name was Rosenfeld and his ancestors were Jewish, which was why he hated the Aryan Germans so bitterly and sent *gauche* telegrams to the Aryan Führer!

Lanny got his car and at one minute before ten o'clock was at the appointed corner. There was no one in sight, so he drove around the block. Next time, there was Monck, just arriving; and according to his practice, Lanny drove on to a dark spot, drew up by the curb and unlatched the door of his car. A moment later the man stepped in, and away they went. Lanny had only to turn one or two corners and make sure there was no car following, then they could go on driving and talking all night if they pleased.

Monck wasted no time. "Ribbentrop hasn't gone to Moscow yet," he said. "The deal has been held up."

"The Russians want too much?"

"Very probably so. I want you to know that my information was accurate. The trip had actually been arranged. I did not bring you on a wild-goose chase."

"Do not worry; I had to come anyhow. Your news is important. Tell me all you can."

"The negotiations have certainly been going on. The decision hangs in the balance. Hitler cannot make up his mind which way he wants to jump."

"He is not alone in that, Monck. It is the same story in Paris and London."

"You understand, I cannot tell you how this information came to me. I can say that it is an old comrade who has gone Nazi, and now his conscience troubles him. He does not deal with me but with another. I feel as certain of the accuracy of the information as one can of anything human. It has been known to the underground for some time that Hitler has been making approaches to Russia, but only recently have the Russians shown interest."

Lanny replied: "I have sounded out several people, and their attitude supports what you tell me. Something is in the wind. I will get busy myself, and see what I can learn. It is the most important question in the world. Everybody to whom I mention the idea goes up into the air."

"A sad blow for the Communists in France and Britain if it happens, *Genosse.*"

"I think my Red uncle in Paris is getting his mind adjusted to it; but in America they will be bowled over."

Lanny was free to tell this friend about the Hansibesses, and about his trip to Detroit; also about Wickthorpe, and the de Bruynes, whom Monck had heard all about in Paris. Lanny said: "Don't talk about any of this, for people might guess where it comes from." The answer was: "I have never mentioned your name, nor that of anybody connected with you. I have said that my wife is getting money from relatives of hers."

VIII

They exchanged ideas about the world as they saw it: a world that was groping in darkness, in the midst of dreadful dangers, and without any clue to a way of escape. There wasn't a corner of this world safe from the intrigues of Nazi-Fascism, a fact which tormented the minds of two social idealists, but at the same time was in accord with their theories, and gave them the bitter satisfaction of seeing their prophecies come true. Capitalism was one thing throughout the world; and in every country labor was organizing, preparing to use its political power to tax big business and ultimately to take it over through the agency of the state. Capitalist resistance to this process called itself Fascism in Italy, National Socialism in Germany, Falangism in Spain. It varied slightly according to the climate, but fundamentally it was always the same; the great privileged interests, whether they were steel cartels or owners of landed estates or the Catholic hierarchy, put up the funds, and the gangsters of the "New Order" bought the weapons and did the killing. The same process was preparing itself in France, in Britain, in the United States, and all over South America; if there was any part of the world where such preparations were not under way, it must be some lonely island of the South Seas where the natives lived on coconuts and fish and had no surplus to exchange for trade goods.

Lanny said: "Tell me honestly, just how much of the underground is left in Germany now."

"I fear not very much," was the reply. "We have been stamped on with iron-shod boots. I cannot tell you what percentage of our members are dead or in concentration camps, simply because I do not know. We have learned in a school of bitter experience how to hide and be silent. I myself, if the Nazis were to get me and tear me to pieces, could not tell them the names of half a dozen persons who are active in our movement, and I only know where two of these are to be found. Yet things get done! If I ask for a forged passport, it is handed to me in a day or two; you saw that I was able to get a supercharger, and you say it works."

"My father reports that it is working very well."

"Another plan has been suggested to me. I can't tell you how far it will get, but it holds out promises."

"You want some money, I gather. I can give you foreign money now. If you want marks it will take me a couple of days to get them."

"It is a question of buying some radio material abroad; so foreign money will serve."

Lanny put a wad into his hands. "There is a couple of thousand dollars. If you need more, I will get it. It is all your money, of course."

"This will serve for the present."

Lanny continued: "I want you to know, Monck, I live an easy sort of life, but I'm not easy in my conscience. I am doing everything in my power."

"Don't worry, *Genosse*. For your comfort let me say, I have had for some time the idea that you belong to some secret service. I prefer that you don't answer; I just want you to know that that is what I believe, so I am not accusing you in my mind because you don't run the risks that I run."

"I'll tell you this," was Lanny's reply. "I was married to Trudi Schultz, and I loved her. I have not forgotten what the Nazis did to her, and I am never going to forget. Think of me as carrying out Trudi's orders."

IX

That was all Lanny had to say, and he was ready to stop by the curb when Monck surprised him by remarking: "Between us, *Genosse*, we are going to have another Trudi on our hands. That is Miss Creston."

"You don't say!"

"She has become a convert, and she means it. I am afraid she will do something reckless and get herself into serious trouble. I want to suggest that you should see her and give her a warning."

Of course Lanny wanted to know about that, and the ex-Capitán had quite a story to tell. Before he had parted from Laurel in London he had told her that he would sooner or later be coming back into Germany, and she had surprised him by exclaiming: "You have smuggled something out that you didn't want me to know about!" When he didn't deny it, she added: "I guessed that when you took the car away. You had something hidden in it!" When he asked her to forgive him she replied: "I have already done so. I wanted to tell you: I didn't know there were any heroes left in the world."

"So then we had a long talk," continued the man of the underground, telling Lanny. "She wanted to know all about our activities, and what she could write about them and what not. I told her stories, including the story of Trudi, but of course without any hint about an American husband. She wanted to know if we expected to overthrow Hitler, and I had to tell her that there wasn't a chance of it; the Nazi regime would have to be overthrown from the outside, and all we could do was to try to keep the spark of decency alight in the country, so that invading armies, whoever they were, would not think that all Germans were mad dogs. She made me promise that if I came back to Berlin I would let her see me again. I could drop her an unsigned note, and she would meet me on the street as we had done before."

"And did you tell her you were a married man?" asked the son of Budd-Erling, quizzically.

"Indeed, yes! There is nothing of that sort. I made an appointment at night, and I wondered if she'd come. She did, and we walked for a couple of hours, about as long as her legs would hold up. What do you think that woman had done?"

"Go ahead and don't keep me in suspense!"

"She had got the books I had told her about—bought them at a Red bookshop in London, and taken them into Germany in her trunk! I tried to explain the danger of it, but it was no use. She stands on her privileges as an American citizen. Fancy how far that would get her, with the fury the Nazis are in right now!"

"You mean on account of the Roosevelt telegram?"

"I mean just that. We all wonder about it. Did he really think he could make any impression on Hitler?"

"I don't know," said the suave Lanny. "It is my guess that he meant the letter for the American people—to give Hitler a chance to show himself up."

"Well, maybe so; and maybe Hitler did. All I know is, it's a poor time for an American to be caught with a copy of Kautsky's *Social Revolution and After.*"

"Is that what she's reading?"

"She had read it and got it well fixed in her mind. I was astonished; for I had looked up more of her stories in the library in New York, and while I saw she had a keen mind, I thought it would be limited by her class outlook. But no; she wanted to tell me about Kautsky's formula: 'Socialism in material production, anarchism in intellectual.' I would have expected her to be repelled by the awful word anarchism; but not so."

"What did it mean to her?" asked the amused art expert.

"I asked, and she answered: 'The Roland Park Country Club that I used to belong to.' I thought she was making fun of me, but she explained: 'I mean the free associations that people form, for whatever purpose may interest them: churches, schools, clubs, publications, anything they want, and that they run as they please, so long as they don't interfere with other people's right to form their own groups and run them in their own way. That answers the question that troubled me— I was always afraid that Socialism would mean regimentation and restrictions on personal freedom; but I realize the distinction between material things that we want standardized—matches, soap, gasoline, and so on; we want them plentiful and cheap, and we want to pay what it costs to produce them and deliver them. But ideas are different— there's no limit to those, and everybody can have all he wants, and any group of people can get together and say what they please and spread their ideas to all who want to listen.'

"That's the way it went," concluded Monck, alias Siebert. "And so you see, we have another convert. But I think you should persuade her to get rid of those Red books and keep quiet until she gets out of Hitler's power. She is too naïve and also too conspicuous to take any part in our dangerous activities."

X

In the morning Lanny called up Oberst Furtwaengler and they had one of their agreeable chats. Yes, Seine Exzellenz was fully recovered, his usual self, hardworking yet jolly. Busy days for the Air Force, many important changes, but he would no doubt find time to see Herr Budd. "How is your father?" asked the Oberst and then, "How is your family?" asked Lanny. "All well, thank you—a new baby, a boy, a future Führer, perhaps." Every German boy would hope to grow up a Führer, and ever girl to be the mother of a Führer.

Lanny phoned to the town house of the Fürstin Donnerstein and learned that she had gone to her summer place on the Obersalzberg, not far from Berchtesgaden; he would hope to go there later and collect his harvest of gossip. Also he had a chat with Heinrich Jung. Heinrich's superior had been sent to take charge of the youth of Czechoslovakia and Heinrich had moved up the ladder of authority. A wonderful system, a happy world—*heil Hitler!* A new baby was expected here, too. The master race must increase and its enemies be diminished. *Heute gehört uns Deutschland, morgen die ganze Welt!*

A return call from the Air Marshal's office; Herr Budd would be expected at three o'clock. Herr Budd wrote some letters about his picture business—commissions from the Cincinnati visit. Then he read the *B.Z.-am-Mittag*, and observed once more how Stalin had been demoted and Roosevelt promoted to the position of Enemy Number One. Poland was Number Two; there was an editorial discussing the intransigence and fanatical pride of this people. They had had the Führer's offer of friendship before them for months, and what were they waiting for? They were the sort of people who were incapable of realizing their true position in the world; they were ready to throw away their lives and their country's independence because of a crazy notion of their own importance.

Lanny entered the Ministerium with anxiety. It was not merely that he was the bearer of bad tidings; it was that he might have to hear worse tidings—that in the process of streamlining the Luftwaffe and getting it ready for defense against Poland, the Air Marshal had been counting his single-gear superchargers and had found one missing! Or perhaps his efficient intelligence service had sent him word about a suspicious activity going on in a factory in Ohio which called itself "Ascott"! But no, there was no sign of a frown; there was the usual rolypoly, his lower half encased in white flannel trousers with a broad blue stripe, his upper half in a white silk shirt—his coat with all its decorations hanging over a chair. He gave a cheerful roar, and a paralyzing clasp by a hand with thick spatulate fingers and no less than four rings on them—one, the biggest emerald that Lanny had ever seen, so big that he wondered if it had been extracted from the crown of King Wenceslaus of Bohemia.

Hermann *der Dicke* was his old self again. He had made up his mind that nature intended him to be fat, and the German people liked him that way. Lanny had written him about the price he had got for the Canaletto: eighteen thousand dollars to the Marshal's bank account in New York, and every little helped. He rubbed his hands together in a way that did not conceal the jewels. "Everything jake!" he exclaimed. "Everything Jim Bandy!" He had picked up Robbie's slang, and thought it would make Lanny feel at home to hear it; he didn't get it quite right, but Lanny didn't correct him.

Instead he listened while the great man told about some new art treasures that had come into his possession—those *jüdische Hunde* had good taste, sometimes! Göring was making addition to Karinhall—so many people wanted to come and see him! He had selected the treasures he wanted for the new rooms—no expert needed for that. As for the rest, Lanny could take them to America and sell them in his careful conscientious way. "When I meet a man I can trust, I trust him," declared Nazi Nummer Zwei.

XI

The painful revelation couldn't be put off too long. Lanny said: "Hermann, I have some bad news. I hate like the devil to be the one to bring it."

"*Was zum Teufel?*" demanded *Der Dicke*—he didn't like bad news.

"The government has come down on my father like a ton of bricks. They won't let him continue his arrangement with you."

"*Ach*, so that's it! Your Roosevelt!"

"That's it, Hermann; and my father is entirely helpless. They threaten to cut off his orders from the Army, to boycott him completely. There is no doubt they have the power to ruin him."

"*Sauerei!* What does he mean to do?"

"They compel him to send back your representatives—at least, to exclude them from the plant. They say your men have been engaging in propaganda."

"*Aber—das ist eine Lüge!* At least, if they did anything of the sort, it was against my strict orders, and I'll jail them for it."

"The government people don't offer evidence—they just say it is so, and that settles it. You know how it is with governments."

Yes, *Der Dicke* knew, but he wasn't going to admit it right now. "*Dieser elende Roosevelt!*—he is determined to have trouble with us! *Was ist los mit ihm?*"

"God knows," replied Lanny. "It is a painful thing for us."

He listened patiently while the German Air Force Commander exploded into a tirade against the President of the United States. He talked for five minutes about that "imbecile telegram" which had been addressed to the Führer. It was hard for anybody in Germany to realize that the affairs of the richest nation in the world could be in the hands of a person so crude, so utterly without understanding of the realities of European politics and the ordinary courtesies among statesmen. "What is it you say—a 'stump speech'?"

"If it's in the country," replied Lanny; "if it's in town, it's a soapbox tirade."

Göring wanted some explanation that would make Roosevelt comprehensible, but Lanny had none; that and the Einstein theory, he said, were problems beyond his powers. His family had never had anything to do with this black sheep of the Roosevelt clan; Robbie had spent a fortune trying to defeat him three years ago; this time he wouldn't be able to do so much, because of the income taxes, which were sheer robbery. Roosevelt had built up an enormous political machine, and all the office-holders and the relief clients voted for him; and so on—all the data which Lanny had collected in the locker rooms of the country club. It helped Hermann greatly, and it didn't hurt F.D.R.

XII

As soon as possible Lanny diverted the conversation to what good news he had collected: the rapid spreading of revolt against Roosevelt's policies at home and abroad; the interviews Lanny had had in Detroit, the mass meetings he had attended—he didn't mind exaggerating their number and size, for he could be sure that Göring's agents were doing the same. And then, the return to appeasement of the Chamberlain government, and what Wickthorpe and his friends had said; the confusion in Paris—Lanny named Kurt, whom he believed to be Göring's man, and praised the work he was doing. It did no harm to mention Abetz and Herzenberg, too—just to show how Lanny was circulating, and that he was too important a man to quarrel with over the question of a few airplanes.

Presently the visitor remarked: "All your people I have talked with, both in Paris and New York, are worried about the rumors of negotiations over some sort of deal between you and the Russians."

"That is a complicated question," replied Göring, "and those abroad are hardly in position to see it as clearly as we do."

"That goes without saying; but those in Paris know the situation as regards France, and they tell me with great emphasis that things are coming their way, and there is no need of anything so drastic as a deal with the Reds."

"Tell me what you have heard on that subject, Lanny."

The agent talked for a while about Schneider and the de Bruynes, about Kurt and Abetz, and about an official high in the Embassy staff who didn't care to have his name used. Friendship between France and Germany could be made, and was being made rapidly; nobody wanted to die for Danzig, and very few responsible Frenchmen were any longer concerned to keep Germany from getting back what she had lost at Versailles.

Der Dicke said: "May I talk to you confidentially, Lanny?"

"Indeed you may," replied the other. "My father taught me in boyhood how to keep information to myself."

"I am one of those who are worried about what is going on. We are western men, and we ought to stand together against the hordes from Asia."

"I have understood for a long time that that was your attitude, Hermann. The question is, what can we do?"

"I wish that you, if you have a talk with the Führer, would tell him everything you have just told me. I have said all that I can say; you know how it is, if you seem to nag, you lose influence. There are powerful forces working against us—doubtless you know what they are."

"I have a pretty good idea; and you know that I have never asked for information that you did not offer me."

"There are some close to the Führer who think that we can win quickly in the west, and have strength enough left to turn to the east.

That I do not believe, and the wise men of our Generalstab, men who have devoted their lives to the study of such questions, support me emphatically. The decision has to be made this summer—it may be made this afternoon while we are talking, and it will decide the fate of the world for our time."

"God knows, I would like to do something; but consider my position—an American, and right after Roosevelt has pulled that 'boner,' as we call it—*diese Dummheit!*"

"You have more influence than you realize, Lanny. The Führer is a shrewd man, and he realizes that his greatest weakness is his lack of acquaintance with forces and personalities outside of Germany. You represent such a contact, and he knows that you are disinterested."

"Of course I want to see him, and if I do, I'll tell him what I think. I have always done that; I should be of no use to him otherwise."

"Let me tell you that Hess has a great deal of influence with him, and sees the matter as we do. It might be a good idea to approach him through Hess."

That was a tip, of course, and Lanny said: *"Danke schön."* At the same time he smiled inwardly, observing processes of intrigue in *die hohe Welt.* Hermann didn't want to use up his credit, so let Rudi use up some of his! Hermann was afraid of "nagging," so let Rudi try it for a while!

Hermann's last words were: *"Freundschaft mit Frankreich!"* And Lanny knew that was the slogan he was to take to Berchtesgaden. Friendship with France—and, of course, its corollary: War against the Reds!

XIII

Lanny strolled back to the Adlon and sent a cablegram: "Robert Budd Newcastle Connecticut everything jake everything jimbandy Lanny." He didn't know whether it would reach his father in that form, but if it did Robbie would assume that there was a typographical error. Lanny would follow up with a letter explaining matters, and Robbie would have a chuckle.

Then he strolled over to the newsstand and bought an evening paper. Spread across half the front page was a headline: *"Abetz aus Paris Ausgewiesen!"* Rooted to the spot, Lanny read the text of a Paris despatch, telling in the Nazi style that the Jewish-plutocratic politicians who now had the upper hand in the French government had accused the well-known German lecturer and man of letters, Otto Abetz, of activities inimical to France, whose ardent friend he was. The police had given him three days in which to pack up his effects and return to Germany. It was not yet known whether the police intended to interfere with Herr Abetz's papers, but the German Embassy had taken steps to make certain that no such crime was committed. The despatch went on to quote the Embassy as expressing deep regrets at this cruel and unwarranted accusation, coming at a time when Herr Abetz's efforts on behalf of Franco-German friendship were beginning to be so keenly appreciated by intellectual and responsible elements in the country.

Lanny took a walk to meditate over that report. He had got into a position where he sometimes had trouble sorting out his real self from his role. This event would make it harder for him to meet the Führer and to gain his confidence; but, after all, what Lanny found out and how he found it out was of no importance compared to actual events in this diplomatic struggle. The expulsion of Abetz was a solar-plexus blow for the appeasers, and a sign that France was at last waking up to her peril. So, while Lanny's pretended self was embarrassed, Lanny's real self danced with joy down the triumphal way known as Unter den Linden.

"And besides," whispered the P.A., "I'll see Abetz here, and he'll be more than ever in a mood for talking!"

15

Fools Rush In

I

LANNY called the office of Rudolf Hess and learned that the Deputy Führer was in Prague, expected back in a couple of days. That left Lanny with some idle time on his hands, and it is an established principle of theology, or perhaps of demonology, that Satan finds mischief for idle hands to do. The mischief found for Lanny had to do with Miss Laurel Creston, resident of a pension not far away. Lanny recalled a childhood jingle about a boardinghouse where they had ham and eggs three times a day; but of course that wouldn't apply to an institution in Germany, where the marriage between *Schinken und Eier* has never been solemnized.

The son of Budd-Erling pictured the Baltimore lady devoting herself to the study of Karl Kautsky, intellectual leader of the German Social Democrats. Lanny had met him years ago at the school which Freddi Robin had helped to support—a shy but dogmatic old gentleman with a little white beard and spectacles. Present also had been his wife and their eldest son, all three of them active party workers, and named by their enemies *"die heilige Familie."* The father had escaped the Nazis by the surest method, that of dying; the wife was in Holland, and the son, Lanny had been told, was in a concentration camp. Twenty years had passed since he had read their writings, and now, as he looked back, they seemed to him somewhat dry; but that is the way with works which are absorbed into one's way of thinking—their contents become obvious and it is hard to bring back the thrills of first discovery.

Miss Creston was reading *The Social Revolution and After*, which investigated the question of how the organized workers were to take power and what sort of world they would build. The book had been written long before the Soviet Revolution—an unorthodox revolution, according to Kautsky-Marx, for the overturn was supposed to come in the most highly industrialized countries, and in Tsarist Russia not for a long while. Would Miss Creston understand that, or would she need to have someone explain it to her? Monck was competent, but a little hard to get hold of, and Lanny found himself in the midst of imaginary conversations in which he played the role of professor of the social sciences, very kind and fatherly. Of course there could never be any such conversations; he could never admit that he had even heard the name of Kautsky, and if Miss Creston mentioned it he would pretend to take it for a Russian name. Not Kautsky-Marx, but Kautsky-Trotsky!

Lanny had to admit that he had misjudged this pupil's mind; it was not merely clever and satirical, it was serious and inquiring. He had talked to her on a lower level than she deserved, and he found himself with a desire to correct this error. It was possible to be profound and philosophical in the field of art as well as in that of the social sciences, and Lanny in his mind began framing discourses which would assist a budding woman writer in establishing her *Weltanschauung* and avoiding the pitfalls of cynicism and dilettantism. Also, Monck had asked him to give her a warning; that was really a duty, and he must figure out a way!

II

Next mornng he telephoned the Pension Baumgartner and inquired whether Miss Creston was still there. When he was asked for his name he replied: "Just tell her an old friend from America." When she came to the phone he still did not speak his name, but said: "It's the troglodyte. I have been away for a long time." He did not say: "I should have let you know I was leaving"—he would just let by-gones be by-gones. "I met some of your friends at home," he remarked, "and thought you might be interested to hear about them."

He had noticed a little Hungarian restaurant on one of the side streets off the Friedrichstrasse. He had never entered it, but it seemed a place where he was not likely to encounter high-up Nazis. Doubtless it would have been more gracious to have offered to come in a taxi for her—he had never let her know that he possessed a car. But if she was willing to come to a restaurant, he would let it be that way. He could not afford to be too cordial.

She came, looking very pretty in a light silk muslin dress with the big flowered patterns the ladies were wearing, blue flowers on white, and blue flowers in a little soft straw hat. He ordered *Fogosh am Rost, Mohnstrudel,* and *Stierblut*—which last, bull's blood, sounds alarming, but is merely a mild red wine. While consuming it he told her about his visit home, how the *Oriole* had come to Newcastle, and how later he had stopped by at Green Spring Valley, and had inspected Uncle Reverdy's paintings and played tennis with Lizbeth at the country club. He mentioned that the uncle had become an investor in Budd-Erling; he was pretty sure the niece knew this, for he had seen her name on the list of those who had to sign checks. But she didn't mention that circumstance, so he didn't either.

In the course of the talk he remarked: "I didn't say anything about having met you."

"Why not?" she asked, surprised.

"I somehow had the impression that you were not on friendly terms with them. Your point of view is so different from theirs."

"They think that I am a trifle odd, but we have never had any disagreement. I have learned to keep my thoughts to myself."

"That is what I guessed," Lanny said. "I didn't know whether you had told them about being here, or what you were doing or thinking about affairs here." He wouldn't speak the word "Nazi" in this restaurant, but contented himself with saying: "You disapproved so very strenuously of some of my acquaintances."

"I don't go to the extreme of being embarrassed to know you," she replied, and he left the matter there. He would have to remain the man of mystery to her.

III

Afterwards they strolled and came into the Tiergarten, the great park of Berlin. They found a shady bench—one that was not painted yellow with a letter "J" on it. They sat for a while, he telling her about the proposed Baltimore showing of Detaze, and then about the other shows they had had, in New York, Paris, London, Berlin, Munich. He told funny stories about people who tried to pretend that they knew about art; one old lady who had thought that Lanny had painted all these pictures himself, and another had thought that Cap Finisterre was the artist's name, and why did he have that title? There came a lull, and Lanny glanced about to make sure there was no one near; then he began: "Miss Creston, there is something I have had in mind to speak to you about. Are you doing any writing at present?"

"Yes, quite a lot. That is the way I live, you know."

"It has occurred to me that you may be writing about the things you observe in this country. As it happens, I have known Germany for a quarter of a century, which I suspect is pretty nearly as long as you have been in the world. Consider carefully this word of advice: Don't write anything about what you have seen here until after you are outside and not intending to return."

"You mean—I might get into trouble?"

"I mean just that. You understand, I am familiar with your point of view and am speaking on that basis."

"But you must know, Mr. Budd, I don't write about politics. I don't have that sort of mind."

"You have a mind that observes the faults and follies of the people about you; and if you were to write such things here, it would be taken as political—everything is so taken, and the consequences are more disagreeable than you would find it easy to imagine."

"Really, do you believe that anybody would pay attention to my playful and mildly satirical pictures of foreign ways?"

"A lot of attention would be paid, and it might be some time before you found it out. People you met would be questioned, and might get into serious trouble. Some day you might be astonished to learn that somebody you had trusted had been set to watching you and had compiled a long list of your indiscretions."

"Thank you for your kind thought," said the lady. "It will comfort you to know that I have already considered the possibility, and have taken steps to meet it. Anything I write while I am staying in Germany will be published under a pen name."

"That does not relieve my concern," replied Lanny. "I am afraid that would only be taken as a sign that you were aware of what you were doing. It might increase the suspicion against you."

"You mean to tell me the German authorities would read a fiction story in an American magazine, and take the trouble to find out the real name of the author?"

Lanny said: "Wait!" A pedestrian was approaching—one of those old-fashioned Berlin *Bürger* who insisted upon wearing a derby hat in midsummer, with a clasp in a vest buttonhole on which to hang the hat. Lanny remarked: "They feed the lions in the afternoon, and I am told that it is a very interesting sight. We must be sure not to miss it!" Then, after the old gentleman had passed out of hearing: "They watch everything that appears in America which they consider prejudicial to their regime—and especially if it shows signs of being based on information from here. They find out who wrote it and if they can get hold of him they make it hot for him."

"In my case, Mr. Budd, the editor has agreed to keep my name secret."

"My dear lady! Did you make that arrangement by mail? Have you any idea through how many hands your letter passed before it reached your editor? Have you any information about the editor's secretary, and whom she goes out to lunch with? Your story is lively, and people talk about it. The editor's secretary meets a cultured German gentleman who invites her out, and starts talking about the story. 'There is somebody who really knows how things are in Germany now!' he says, with a laugh; and the secretary replies: 'Yes, indeed. The author is living in a pension in Berlin. Her name is Laurel Creston.' That item of information is cabled to the Gestapo, and a woman who possesses wide culture and gracious manners, and who incidentally speaks good English, comes and engages a room in the Pension Baumgartner before that day is over. She meets everybody in the place and hears what they say about you; maybe she meets you and hears what you say about Germany—of course in the strictest confidence. It might end in somebody going to a concentration camp."

"You seem to know a lot about the ways of the Gestapo."

"I go about in German social circles, and while I don't take part in such discussions, I listen and learn."

"And do you like that sort of thing?"

"Why should you ask that? I am an art expert, and am here on business. I meet all sorts of people—yesterday I spent an hour or two with Marshal Göring, and received from him a commission to handle a number of art works in America. He talked and I listened."

"And it doesn't trouble your conscience at all to know that monstrous cruel things are going on all the time?"

"It troubles me when I see a fellow-countryman getting into trouble through ignorance of what the Old World is like. So I give you a friendly warning. But apart from that I have one simple rule, I leave the politics of each country I visit to the people who live in that country, and I talk to them about the difference between good and bad taste in art, and the prices I am willing to advise my clients in America to pay for this or that particular work. On that basis I am able to go everywhere and meet everybody. If ever the time should come that I decide to retire from art experting and settle down in Newcastle or Green Spring Valley—then I might write a book, or I might tell you things I have seen and let you write about them."

IV

There he was, the troglodyte, stubborn and impermeable; he had got a safe cave and made himself comfortable in it, and was not to be lured outside by any device. Miss Creston gave up, and let him tell her about a new book he had been reading, Dr. Rhine's *New Frontiers of the Mind*. It was not the first time the phenomena of psychic research had been brought into the laboratory, but it was the latest, and Lanny asked her if she knew anything about this strange underground realm whose events you could not quite believe even after you had seen them happen. She admitted that she didn't know much, so they resumed the relationship which a man finds most satisfactory—himself as teacher and the woman as attentive pupil.

He told her about the Polish woman who had been a guest in his mother's home for the past ten years. Miss Creston had heard her spoken of, in a slightly derogatory way, a part of the queerness of the Budd household. Lanny said he was aware of that attitude; yet in the same company where it was expressed, you would find some person who had had an experience which could not be accounted for by any of the powers of body or mind as we take them for granted. People were content to exchange stories about apparitions, premonitions, mind reading, or whatever it might be, and then forget all about it. But Lanny had wanted to understand, and had tried experiments and read books, and from time to time had talked with scientists.

He told about Zaharoff and his dead duquesa, and the various other "spirits" who had haunted a munition king's séances. He told about two mediums here in Berlin who had given Irma and himself what was known as a "cross-correspondence." He told about Professor Pröfenik, an elderly mystagogue who practiced the occult arts, including the exorcising of werewolves. He told about the séances with Rudolf Hess in Berchtesgaden—for the Deputy's interest in the occult was known to all Germany, and he had founded an institute for the study of mental healing. All this was interesting to a woman writer, and proof of the fact that a man could have serious intellectual interests, even while keeping himself aloof from political subjects.

V

Lanny had had his turn, and good breeding now required that he should offer one to his companion. He asked if she had been reading anything important of late, and she answered that she, too, had been risking her reputation by taking up the study of an unpopular subject. "I have been investigating our economic system and what is the matter with it. I wanted to be impartial, so first I read a Socialist and then I read a Communist and now I am reading an Anarchist."

"Good God!" said Lanny Budd. "I hope you don't leave those books lying around on your dressing table in the pension!"

"No, I have been careful to lock them in my trunk."

"Where on earth did you get them—if you don't mind my asking?"

"I bought them in a Red bookshop in London: Kautsky's *The Social Revolution and After*, Lenin's *The State and Revolution*, and Kropotkin's *The Conquest of Bread*."

"And may I ask, have you decided which you are, a Socialist, a Communist, or an Anarchist?"

"Kropotkin hasn't had his full chance yet, but I feel pretty sure I'm going to turn out a Socialist. It seems to come naturally to an Anglo-Saxon to get what he wants by the method of majority consent."

"I am relieved to hear you make that concession," remarked the son of Budd-Erling.

"Of course there will have to be pressure," added the sociological lady. "There has never been any social change without pressure from determined groups—and perhaps the threat of revolution in the background."

"I see," said Lanny, dryly. "And where are you expecting us to find ourselves when these pressure groups have got through with us?"

"In a society without exploitation of man by man." Then, challengingly: "Does that terrify you?"

"Not especially," was the mild reply. "I figure that I have special knowledge, and there will be a use for it somewhere in the world. Perhaps your proletarian friends will put me in charge of an art gallery and let me make sure that the most important works are hung to advantage—something which isn't always the case at present."

"I'll do my best to arrange it," promised the woman.

"Assuming that you will be a Commissar, or whatever it is that the Socialists call it." He smiled amiably as he said this, so that it wouldn't have too much of a sting.

So began an interesting hour. Laurel Creston, too, had discovered a new world; not that of the subconscious mind, but that of social evolution, of the class struggle and the emerging co-operative society. She was all steamed up about it, eager for somebody to talk to; and Lanny was graciously pleased to listen. Of course he mustn't make any concessions, he must remain the troglodyte; however, he could be one of the modern, agreeable sort, who has turned his cave inside out, so to say, and made it into the most beautiful of ivory towers filled with every sort of art treasure and pervaded by delicate perfumes and sounds of music and laughter. Lanny's inquiries had to be skeptical, even mocking; enough to be provocative, but never rude.

Under the stimulation of this challenge, Laurel Creston came to life as Lanny had never seen her so far; she became the person which as a rule she kept for the hours before her typewriter. Eagerness lighted up her brown eyes and the color mounted into her cheeks which ordinarily were pale. He exasperated her by his stupidity, and she simply had to convince him, or at any rate to chastise him to her own satisfaction. God, how blind the bourgeois world could be! How self-satisfied, how arrogant in its assumption that society had been created for its sole comfort and convenience! Sometimes these people exasperate you so that you want to scream at them; but, of course, being well bred, you content yourself with annihilating sarcasm, or perhaps a *bon mot* which you carefully keep in memory and work into your next story.

VI

By this method of teasing, Lanny Budd learned how the dirty work would get itself done in a co-operative world. Machinery would do as much of it as possible, and the rest would be highly paid—precisely because there would be no other way of persuading people to do it. Wasn't that fair, when you stopped to think about it? The important point was that modern techniques could turn out wealth so fast that there would be enough for everybody who was willing to do his share of productive labor. Incidentally, the amount of dirty work could be greatly reduced by getting rid of the idlers and wasters. "You mean by liquidating them?" inquired the troglodyte, just to show how exasperating he could be. The exasperated one replied: "No, just by making it impossible for you to get any money that you do not earn."

Now and then Lanny would say: "Wait!" and would begin some remarks about the collection of animals in the zoo which gave this park its name. He would continue until some passersby were out of hearing, and then he would resume: "What was that you were telling me about personal initiative under a Socialist regime?"

One time he said: "Don't look; but I have an idea that someone is watching us. Let's take a stroll." So they got up and walked for a while, commenting on the beauty of the Tiergarten and the admirable conduct of public institutions in the Fatherland. When they came to a bench in a more isolated spot they seated themselves again and resumed their comparison of the social orders proposed by the Socialists, the Communists, and the Anarchists. Lanny said: "Don't you think it is up to you to read at least one work in defense of Capitalism?" The reply was: "Dear me! I got that in every newspaper I ever read at home—to say nothing of the conversation of my Uncle Reverdy and the other elders of my tribe."

Lanny had run into revolutionary theories at the age of fourteen, when his Uncle Jesse had taken him to meet a woman Syndicalist agitator; the Syndicalists were close to the Anarchists—at least in the Mediterranean lands. In Newcastle he had encountered a Budd Gunmakers strike and listened to the arguments of both Reds and Pinks. This had continued in the workers' school in Cannes, and at the one in Berlin where Lanny had met Trudi and her first husband. But of all this not a word to Laurel! Let her use him as a grindstone to sharpen her wits upon, and let her have the pleasure of winning every argument—but never of convincing the troglodyte!

Lanny kept thinking: "This is the way Nina told me I was to get married!" He had taken Rick's wife into his confidence to some extent, and she had suggested how a supposed reactionary might make headway with some woman of the Left. "Let her argue with you, and if you fall in love with her you can give her the satisfaction of converting you!" Nina, matter-of-fact and straightforward, hadn't seen anything funny in this; she had offered to find the right sort of girl and produce her at The Reaches—just as Beauty kept picking out the wrong sort and producing them at Bienvenu. But Nina hadn't known about F.D.R. and the critical information that Lanny was collecting and transmitting. No, it just couldn't be arranged, and Lanny wasn't playing fair with this newly fledged comrade when he allowed her to think that their acquaintance might ripen into intimacy.

VII

He realized that more clearly before that summer's day had come to an end. He strolled back with her to the pension, and it was his plan to deliver her to the door as politeness required, and then go on without attracting attention. It happened, however, that the postman arrived just ahead of them, and delivered the afternoon mail to the maid. There wasn't much of it, and the largest item was a package of magazines wrapped flat in brown paper and open at the ends. "*Die sind für Sie, Fräulein Creston,*" said the maid, and put the package into the guest's hands. Miss Creston glanced at them, and said to Lanny: "The *Bluebook*. They send me three copies. Would you like to have one?"

"Why, yes," he answered, "if you have no need of it."

"You might return it when you are through." That might be a bid or might not—for, after all, a magazine that had been mailed once could be mailed again.

Lanny accepted the loan, and walking to the Adlon, he glanced at its contents. An idea had occurred to him: a magazine would hardly send three copies unless there was a special reason. His eye ran over the table of contents and observed that the name of Laurel Creston did not appear. He noted that the first story was by "Mary Morrow," which sounded more like a stage or pen name than a real one. He glanced at it and read the opening words: "*'Bitte einsteigen,'* said the conductor of the train; *'bitte Platz nehmen.'*" Lanny needed no occult powers to guess that the scene of this story was laid in Germany. The title was "Aryan Journey."

Passing one of the outdoor cafés on the Kurfürstendamm, he took a seat at a table and ordered a lemonade with plenty of ice—these eccentric *Amerikaner!* While waiting for it he read, and one paragraph was enough for him to recognize the style of Laurel Creston. Nobody who had read her previous work in this magazine could doubt it, and the promise of an editor to keep the secret must have been the cause of smiles to the staff.

It was a story of a train trip from the interior of Germany to an outside destination. The central figure was a little Jew, who had in an inside coat pocket a small envelope containing money or jewels or something else that he wanted to hide. Apparently it had been his plan to stick it down between the seat cushions; but the compartment was filled and he couldn't find a chance to do this. His uneasiness became apparent to the other passengers, pure Aryans all. Jews were not wanted in Germany, and yet one going out was presumptuous and insulting. The Aryans watched him furtively, and observed his anxiety increase as the train neared the border; they saw beads of perspiration standing on his forehead, and were sure that he must have something very precious indeed.

At last he got up and went into the toilet. Aryans did that, and locked themselves in, but for a Jew to do it was a confession of guilt. Was he swallowing his jewels, or was he tearing up his money and sending it down underneath the train? The Aryans discussed the problem in whispers; no Jew would throw away money—they loved it too much; he would be hiding it somewhere in that tiny compartment, planning to get it after the train had passed the border. When the Jew came back they never took their eyes off him; and when the Polizei came through—SS men, always—to examine exit permits and make certain that no passenger carried more than the lawful sum of money, the Aryans reported their suspicions.

The other passengers were put out of the compartment and the terrified Jew was searched. His protests counted for nothing—they dumped out the contents of his bags and scattered them over the floor. One of the SS men was sent to search the toilet, and when he could find nothing the head man went and repeated the search. When the train came to the border station the unhappy wretch was led off, carrying the two bags into which he had been permitted to stuff such of his belongings as he could pick up in a hurry.

VIII

Lanny could see where this story had come from. The external details might have been invented, or put together from watching pure

Aryans anywhere; but the emotions of it, the accumulating sense of terror which gripped you in the first paragraph and mounted to the end—that was Mary Morrow alias Laurel Creston being driven in a motor car toward the German border and trembling in every nerve at the imagining of what might lie ahead of her. Lanny had said that the experience would "give her something to write about"; and sure enough, it had fathered a little masterpiece of the short story art! Lanny could picture her sitting down in the London hotel, dashing it off in a few hours and sending it to New York by air mail; he could picture what happened when the editor read it—he had jerked out some leading article or story which was already in type, and here was "Aryan Journey" to send shivers up and down the spines of a sensation-hungry public!

And incidentally to drive the Nazis wild! It was hard for Lanny to believe that the author could have failed to realize what offense this picture of train travel in the Fatherland would give. The *Regierung* was trying so hard to get tourists this summer, and to convince them that everything in Germany was courtesy and kindness, modern convenience combined with Old World charm! Of course they would find out who wrote that story, and who were her friends and what were her sources of information.

That settled it, Lanny told himself. He could not go near Laurel Creston again, nor must she have a scrap of his handwriting in her possession. He rolled up the magazine and addressed it with printed letters, taking the precaution to drop it into a street box with his own hands. Very rude indeed; but he would just have to leave it that way. Let her suppose that he did not desire the acquaintance of a woman who hadn't made up her mind whether to be a Socialist, a Communist, or an Anarchist.

IX

The Deputy Führer came back to town, and invited Lanny out to a little place in the country, where they could be in seclusion and talk to a late hour. This was the summer of decision. and no one knew it better than Rudolf Hess. He was a deeply worried man, and Lanny Budd was one whom he permitted to know it; he listened to all that his guest had to tell about London, about New York and Washington and Detroit, about Paris, even about Berlin. Had he seen Göring, and told these things to him? And what had been Göring's reactions? Göring had wanted Hess to "nag," and now Lanny discovered that

Hess thought that Göring ought to "nag"! After all, Göring was Number Two, while Hess was a mere Number Three!

"Rudi"—so he bade Lanny call him—was the most pro-British of any of the Nazis Lanny had met. Born in a British port, he spoke English as well as German and had read English literature. The dream of his life was an alliance between Britain and Germany to take charge of the lesser tribes without the law. Inside, he included "Amerika," by which he meant the United States and Canada. "No use to fool ourselves," he declared. "Whatever side Britain goes on, Amerika will follow. They are clever propagandists, and our people will be swept aside. That is why you and I are equally concerned—we don't want to wake up some morning and find our two countries fighting each other."

"God knows, I will do all I can to prevent it," responded the visitor from overseas—he didn't mind a little blasphemy when necessary.

"The Führer has never been outside Gross Deutschland," continued Hess—and Lanny wondered, in passing, what Mussolini, who had been Der Führer's host, would think of that statement! "At present he is being advised by men like Ribbentrop and Goebbels and Himmler, who hate Britain. They tell him not to worry about Amerika, because the fighting will all be over before Amerika can even get started to arm. They tell him that we can roll over France in a few weeks—there is plenty of time left this summer."

"What will they use for provocation?" inquired the guest.

"They argue that the Russian alliance is provocation enough—what purpose can it have but the encirclement of Germany? We would serve an ultimatum, either the alliance is canceled, or we march in three days."

"They mean to fight France ahead of Poland, then?"

"Poland does not count at all; we all know that we can take Warsaw in two or three weeks of fighting weather—in the summer or autumn."

"But the British have agreed to defend the Poles!"

"Maybe they will and maybe they won't. In any case, what can they do? If they land in France, we can wipe them out. You understand, I am telling you the arguments which are being dinned into the Führer's ears. We must find some way to counter them."

"Do you want me to see him?"

"I am uncertain about it. He is very bitter against Amerika now—that wretched telegram that Roosevelt sent him. What do you make of that?"

"It was a piece of propaganda," declared the visitor. "He was thinking of the home front, the left-wing vote."

"To us it could seem nothing but a hostile act; and there have been others behind the scenes. I don't know how much you have heard about the intrigues that are going on—Bullitt, for example, is ceaseless in trying to make trouble for us. The French have been allowed to get military planes, but we can no longer have any."

That was the cue for Lanny to repeat the sad story which he had brought to Göring. Hess apparently hadn't heard it, but would be bound to hear it soon. He took it hard, more so even than the Air Marshal, Lanny thought. "There you have it!" he exclaimed. "All these are acts of war against us. Poland, France, Britain and Amerika make one front. The expulsion of Abetz is a blow in the face, and tells us that we no longer have anything to hope for from the present French government. The Führer sees these incidents piling up—no, Lanny, I am afraid you had better not see him right now. But then, on the other hand, a little later may be too late." It was indeed a dilemma!

X

They didn't decide anything that night, except that they would put off the decision. Hess said: "The Führer is at the Berghof, and expects to stay there. I will tell him you are here, and see how he takes it. Doubtless he will have to blow off some steam; then perhaps he will feel better. You understand how matters stand, Lanny—to me he is the greatest man in the world, and also he is my teacher, to whom I owe everything. Whatever decision he makes, I follow him. But in the course of the years I have learned to know his moods, and how—I won't say to manage them, but to accommodate myself to them. The other side does that, and I have to do it better."

"I understand," said Lanny, with a smile. "Don't forget that I was at the Berghof when Schuschnigg paid his visit; also when Tecumseh or some of his spirits misbehaved themselves."

This seemed to offer an easy way to change a distressing line of conversation. Lanny remarked: "By the way, Rudi, you will be interested to know that I have been trying more experiments with Madame, and also with a crystal ball. I had a curious experience—I was shut up in my studio on the Riviera, and looking into the ball, I saw a white yacht rounding the point and passing along the shore. When I got up and went to the door and looked out, there was the yacht, one that I had never seen before."

"That interests me greatly," responded the Deputy. "It happens that I have had the same sort of experience, and more than once."

"The spirits," continued Lanny, "appear to have taken up the idea that the young lady whose father owns the yacht is the one I am destined to marry. So far I haven't been able to see it that way, but one can never be sure."

"So long as she does not take you to Hongkong!"

"Thanks for reminding me. I have never heard from that astrologer since, and I often wonder what became of him." It was a hint, but the Deputy did not see fit to take it. If the Gestapo had put the young Rumanian where he couldn't do mischief, they had from their point of view a sufficient excuse. Those who played the dangerous game of casting horoscopes did so only by the favor of Hess or some other of the higher-ups; and their horoscopes must be right!

The host called his wife in to meet this American guest. Ilse Maria was her name, and she was a mature woman, tall and lean, and, oddly enough, with stern features resembling her husband's. Gossip had it that Adi had brought about this marriage to quiet the evil gossip about himself and his Rudi. Maria shared all her spouse's beliefs in the occult, and with even more ardor; she was a Buchmanite, and also learned in Tibetan lore. Lanny, who had sat at the feet of Parsifal Dingle, was able to impress her as a person of profound wisdom.

XI

Lanny spent the night at Hess's retreat; and on their way back to town his host asked about his plans. Lanny said: "I have some art business to attend to; one deal is in Geneva, and I might drive there and then come back to Munich. How would it do if I call you up from there, say in three or four days, and you can let me know how the wind is blowing?" The other answered: "Fine!"

So Lanny went back to the hotel and packed his bags, got his car and his exit permit, and set out on the familiar *Autobahn* to Munich. Very pleasant to look at the countryside in its green midsummer dress; to see men and women busy in the fields and all the factory chimneys smoking. If only there had not been so many regiments of men tramping in goosestep, and tanks rushing about in dusty exercise grounds, and little boys with rucksacks on their backs, marching, shouting *Hoch!* and *Sieg heil!*, and singing about blood and soil and the uses of their daggers of honor. If only it had been possible to turn on the radio and listen to the lovely music of old Germany, without hearing the raucous voices of Juppchen Goebbels's propagandists scolding at the criminal *Einkreisung*.

Gradually the land began to rise, and there were foothills, and then mountain passes with the dark fir trees above and streams of clear green water rushing below. "To me high mountains are a feeling," Byron had written; and always on these trips the melodies of Heine's *Harzreise* were in Lanny's heart. That non-Aryan poet was in disgrace in Germany, and to admire his singing lines was a political offense. Adi Schicklgruber boasted that he was building for a thousand years, but if Lanny Budd had expected to be present at the end of that time, he would have put his money on Heine's simple-seeming verses to out-last the boastful slogans of the NSDAP. *Ich bin ein deutscher Dichter, bekannt im deutschen Land!*

Presently it was Switzerland, the home of free men; but a P.A. couldn't relax his precautions even here, for there were Germans com-ing and going, and many were paid observers. It was the height of the tourist season, and hotels and pensions were crowded with Americans and English, thinking about nothing more important than mountain climbing and tennis and boating and swimming in wonderful clear blue lakes; the Germans were supposed to be doing the same, but it is well known that they are a serious-minded people, with a fondness for mathematics, especially as applied to such purposes as surveying and the making of maps. When one of them finds an isolated spur of moun-tain and sits there studying with a pair of the best Zeiss binoculars, it may be that he is watching the mountain climbers among the high peaks, a favorite diversion of those who have passed the age of activity; but again, it may be that he is looking for gun emplacements already installed by the Swiss, or for sites where they might be installed by a theoretical invader.

Lanny got a room in a pleasant inn, and shut himself up with his little portable machine; it was supposed to be noiseless but he helped it out by putting a folded towel under it. He prepared a report, reveal-ing that Number One was at this moment trying to make up his mind whether to move first against Poland or France, and that in either case he would make a deal with Russia if he could get the Russian terms re-duced. This effort was being aided by the fact that Poland still refused to agree that Russian troops might enter the country to defend it against Germany, and that the Baltic states refused any form of alliance with Russia; also that the British kept delaying in sending a staff mis-sion for consultations, or even in naming the members of the mission. Having sealed and addressed this letter, the mysterious traveler moved on, and in another town stopped at the post office and dropped the letter and sped away.

XII

He headed for Geneva, where he had friends, also paintings which had been on his list for a decade or more, and for which he had found a prospective purchaser in Cincinnati. The friends were Sidney Armstrong and his wife: the husband an important official of the League of Nations, and the wife a lady who had started to fall in love with Lanny Budd, but fortunately for her had stopped. She was now the mother of two children in their teens, and a successful hostess to the eminent personalities who were still coming to the old city of watchmakers and moneylenders, to discuss the calamities which kept falling upon various other parts of the world.

It was the hundred-and-fifth time that the Council of the League had met in the course of twenty years. The Germans and Italians and Japanese came no more, for they had retired and formed themselves into an "Axis." This was fortunate, in a way—so Sidney explained—for it saved the need of listening to the scoldings and threats of these ruffianly fellows; the only trouble was, the fellows went on with their lawless conduct in Manchuria and China, in Abyssinia and Albania, in Danzig and Memel.

But in spite of everything, this earnest and hardworking official wouldn't believe in the possibility of another European war. A middle-aged and paunchy chairwarmer—so Lanny couldn't help but think of him, even while liking him—had built his very life into this League of Nations; it had become not merely his job and his wife's—it was their religion, and their home both physically and intellectually. They were living in the dream of Woodrow Wilson, who had hypnotized them in Paris two decades ago. The great horror simply could not befall the world again; at the last moment, on the very edge of the precipice, the nations would recoil, come to their senses, and return here to have their differences adjudicated in a fifteen-million-dollar temple of reason and justice!

Lanny found that the same utopian hope was not shared by the ruling class of this city of John Calvin. He dined in the home of an elderly capitalist who had been one of his clients for years, and was now glad to turn some of his paintings into American cash. Terrible times were at hand, declared Herr Fröder—he looked German and spoke German, but hated the Prussians as a brutal race, and hated the Nazis as tools of the Generalstab. To an old acquaintance he talked freely, for he wanted an art expert to go back to Germany and report that every

Swiss, whether of German, French, or Italian descent, was an armed soldier ready to fight the invaders of his country, from north, east, south, or west. Every road was guarded day and night, and stores of food had been sunk in immense watertight caissons in the icy depths of mountain lakes. Every pass was mined, so that avalanches could be loosed upon invaders, and more important yet, every one of the great railroad tunnels was stocked with dynamite and could be destroyed by the pressing of a button. So the Axis would be cut in half; Germany would get no guns from Milan and Turin, and Milan and Turin would get no coal from Germany. "That is the sort of consideration the dictators respect," said Herr Fröder. "We keep reminding them of it!"

Lanny phoned to Hess in Berlin, and the answer was: "Better to wait a little longer." That suited Lanny, for every time he entered Hitlerland it cost him a moral effort. He telephoned to Rick, who had said that he and Nina might take a holiday on the Continent. "Come to Geneva," Lanny said, "I have my car and we'll ride on the top of the world." So much pleasanter than going into an ogre's den and watching him mumble human bones!

XIII

Here came the couple with whom Lanny most liked to be, old friends who loved him and understood him, who saw things exactly as he saw them, who knew that he had a deep secret, and possibly had guessed it, but kept away from the subject. They drove through Alpine passes, and down into valleys where the lakes lay still and cold and clear. They watched the snow-capped peaks turn pink and then purple in the twilight. They drove all the way around the lake of Zurich and that of Lucerne; this was the country of the William Tell legend, and it was nice to believe it, even if it had never happened.

On Lac Léman they inspected the castle of Chillon, and Lanny would have liked to tell the legend of Laurel Creston, but of course he mustn't. He recited the sonnet, which they had once known but partly forgotten. The historians agreed with the poets that freedom is a dweller of the heights, and this trio read in their *Baedeker* of the struggles which had been waged through half a dozen centuries in these valleys. What would they not have given for a guidebook of the next ten years, so as to read what the historians would then be telling! For a ride on an H. G. Wells's time machine, around one of the curves of Einstein's space-time!

They would buy some food in the morning and at noon would

picnic by the side of some fast-tumbling stream. They would read aloud—Lanny always had several books in the car, and in the towns they could buy others, for the cheap little Tauchnitz books were still available, and Penguin books from England made up for what the Nazis suppressed. After the sun had disappeared behind the high mountains they would drive, and if one inn was crowded they would go on to the next—any time before midnight would do.

A delightful way to spend a holiday; and while they gave a lot of their conversation to worries about the fate of Europe, that didn't keep them from enjoying themselves; for nature has constructed the human animal so that his conscious mind is only a small part of his total make-up, and he goes on digesting his food and sharing the satisfactions of all created beings, even though he cannot be sure that he will be alive next year. They had no financial worries, for Lanny had earned the price by a deal which had taken him only an hour or two, and he insisted upon being the bearer of the royal purse. "Where else could I buy so much fun for so little money?" he asked; and it was literally true that for him the rarest of pleasures was to be able to speak his real thoughts.

What friends thou hast, and their adoption tried! Twenty-six years had passed since Lanny had met Rick in the Dalcroze school at Hellerau; twenty-two years since he had met Nina in London, while Rick was flying in France, soon to come near to death and to be lamed for life. In the years that had passed they had shared ideas and ambitions, hopes and fears—and if the fears had been justified more than the hopes, that was true of most men and women in the world. The collective intelligence of mankind just hadn't evolved to the point where it was equal to the problems created by modern machinery and technical processes. To believe that it ever would be equal was an act of faith.

They ran into a few people whom they knew, but most of the time they stayed by themselves, talked out the problems which troubled them, and recalled episodes which they would have liked to share at the time. Nina told about the children and what they were doing and thinking, a subject that never bores a mother. Rick told about his writings, and the play he was planning to start when he got home; about his editors, and the politicians he knew, his father's old friends who gave him information, the younger Leftists to whom he transmitted it, and the personalities of the governing world of Britain, most of whom he despised. But they were there, and they held the fate of the Empire in their hands; it was important for Lanny to add to his knowledge about them.

In return he was free to tell all that he had learned about Germany and France, and everything in America except one public figure. He could tell about the Budds and their affairs, and the way things were going in Newcastle—even about Robbie's having been put on the dole! But he forbore to mention the two young women who had entered his life, because he knew what Nina would say about each; it would be a waste of time, since he couldn't mention his job of presidential agent, which dominated his life and determined his attitude to the subject of love and marriage. In Zurich he found a bookstore which had the *Bluebook* on sale, and he bought a copy and read "Aryan Journey" aloud to his friends, saying that he believed "Mary Morrow" to be the pen name of a woman he had once met on the Riviera. They confirmed his high opinion of the story.

XIV

They had such a good time that Lanny would have liked that summer to last forever—except that it would have been such a convenience to Adolf Hitler and his Wehrmacht! Lanny felt it his duty to telephone Hess once more, and learned that the Deputy was still dubious about the wisdom of having an American visitor at the Berghof. Things were getting worse instead of better; Washington insisted upon committing one provocation after another. "You know how it is, Lanny; the Führer doesn't blame you, but the very name of your country excites him, and I am afraid it wouldn't be pleasant for you."

"I understand," replied Lanny. "I am sad about it." As a matter of fact he was the opposite, for he took it as permission to extend his holiday. "Why not drive down to Juan?" he asked. "Beauty will be tickled to death to see you—poor soul, she's been spending the summer there, missing all the fancy doings of London and Biarritz and Cowes."

Why not?—when you have a comfortable car, an expert chauffeur, and a princely purse at your disposal! "I'll drive you to Paris whenever you say," Lanny volunteered, and he telephoned to Beauty to make sure there was room at Bienvenu. There were two guest houses, but most of the time they were rented to friends. There had never been such crowds at the Riviera; it was astonishing how much money there was, and how many people showed up with bank accounts which they were prepared to exchange for bales of francs.

They drove southward from Lake Lucerne, climbing into the high mountains through a narrow pass much exposed to avalanches. This was the famous St. Gotthard, site of a monastery more than once de stroyed. When they reached the top of the grade Lanny reminded them of the verses of Heine, telling how he had come to that point, climbing from Italy, and had paused to listen to Germany snore—"sleeping down there in the tender care of thirty-six monarchs"! Heine, the rebel, had disliked the little German principalities of his time and the stuffy personages who ruled them. "What would he have said of Hitler and his Gauleiters?" wondered Rick.

The road going down was incredibly winding and full of hairpin turns. Somewhere underneath it was a railroad tunnel, nearly ten miles long; the Swiss had chunked it with dynamite, that and the other priceless treasure, the Simplon. "Be sure they are guarding them day and night," Lanny said; "the one hold they have on the Nazis."

The hot lands of Italy appeared, spreading like a panorama. The car rolled down until presently it was at Milan in the plains. When Lanny had to get somewhere, he would drive all day and night; but this was a holiday, and they stopped to look at the Brera, and at what was left of Leonardo's *Last Supper* after the restorers had got through with it. Then to Genoa, where many years ago there had been an international conference attempting to solve the problems of Europe; Robbie Budd had been there, trying to get an oil concession from the Bolsheviks, while Zaharoff stayed in Monte Carlo putting up the money and pulling the strings. In a Genoa tenement Lanny had come upon the body of Barbara Pugliese, beaten by the Blackshirts, and it was there that he had first sworn enmity to the loathesome *Fascismo*.

Presently it was San Remo, where there had been an earlier conference, and where he and Rick together had first laid eyes on an editor named Benito Mussolini, renegade Socialist taking the money of the class enemy to slander and denounce his former friends. That had been the tragic fate of the workers in all modern lands, to educate and train members of their own class to lead and help them, and then see these leaders sell out to the exploiters and become the worst of betrayers, the most cruel mockers of the people's hopes. Lanny and Rick and Nina, who had never belonged to the working class, might have said that this was none of their troubles, but they chose to be grieved at the spectacle of the vileness of which human nature was capable.

Then it was France, and the familiar highway along the Côte d'Azur. Mentone, Monte Carlo, Nice, Antibes, and then the fisher village of Juan-les-Pins, now grown into a famous resort and crowded with tourists summer and winter and summer again. The real-estate agents still begged Madame Budd—so they called her, without regard to her later marriages—to let them sell just a small corner off the estate; but she had to tell them that it was legally fixed so that she couldn't if she wished—Monsieur "Robair" Budd had saved her all worry on that subject.

The wanderers rolled into the familiar drive, and the family dogs came barking with delight. Parsifal Dingle, white-haired and rosy-cheeked, came out to greet them; Beauty met them in the drawing-room, where the glare of the midsummer sun did not advertise the awful fact that she was getting on toward sixty. There was José, the lame butler whom Lanny had met in Spain; he had helped Alfy Pomeroy-Nielson to make his escape from the Fascists, and this meant that Alfy's father and mother would give him a cordial greeting, and a most handsome tip when they departed. There was Marceline's little son, now toddling about and beginning to put words together. Soon it would be time for Lanny to begin teaching him to dance!

Lanny had said to his friends: "Beauty never misses a chance to throw a party; but you know how it is, I have made most of this Riviera crowd think that I am a near-Fascist like themselves. The Spaniards, especially, know what the Axis is doing and planning; so I can't afford to advertise the fact that I have Leftist friends." Rick's reply was: "We meet quite enough of the wrong sort at home."

So they told their hostess that they wanted to rest and not have to dress up; they went sailing and fishing, as they had done when they were boys, and when they met fashionable people they carefully kept off the subject of politics. Nina and Beauty had a baby to talk about —and really it was surprising to see how a one-time professional beauty had settled down and become domestic, to say nothing of spiritual. Until there came an engraved invitation to a reception in honor of the Grand Duke Vladimir, who since the death of Cyril was greeted as the future Tsar of all the Russias; then Beauty Budd would be like some elderly fire-engine horse which had been put out to pasture, but hears the alarm bell ring and jumps the fence and goes galloping in front of the hook-and-ladder truck.

XV

Also, there was Madame Zyszynski. Ordinarily, Rick didn't go in for that sort of thing, but for ten years he and Nina had been listening to Lanny's stories—indeed even longer than that, for it had been during the World War that Lanny had had a vision of Rick lying wounded after an airplane crash. Now Rick himself tried a "sitting"; and per-haps it was his skepticism, but the spirits passed him by, or at any rate those that came were not known to him and it was a great bore. Nina tried it, and had messages from a gray-haired old gentleman who said he was her Great-Uncle Paul; but Nina had never heard of him, and it was a question of making notes of what he said and then writing to members of her family. Lanny said he was afraid that Madame's powers might be waning; she was pretty old, and maybe Tecumseh was getting old, too—he was supposed to have lived a couple of hundred years as a spirit, but perhaps he hadn't talked all that time.

However, Lanny had learned that psychic research is a tedious business at best, and whenever he had a spare hour he would say: "I'll have a try with Madame." The one-time Polish servant would toddle down to his studio where no one would disturb them; she would sit in the easy chair which was like home, and close her eyes and go into that strange trance which the most learned psychologists did not understand. Lanny would sit perfectly silent, pencil in hand and notebook on lap, inwardly praying that the Iroquois chieftain wouldn't quarrel with him this time, and that Sir Basil Zaharoff would lay off.

But no, there was no getting rid of the one-time munitions king, who seemed to have things on his conscience. Was it that he had been so secretive in his lifetime, and was now trying to make up for it? Or was it just that Lanny had been curious about him, and that Lanny's subconscious mind was still playing with the "mystery man of Europe"? Anyhow, here he came: "that old fellow with the guns going off all round him," as Tecumseh called him. "He wants to talk to you himself. He wants you to pay careful attention."

"I always paid attention to whatever Sir Basil had to say," replied Lanny, soothingly; and then came a quavering voice which might have been that of the Knight Commander of the Bath and Grand Officer of the Legion of Honor—or might have been that of any other very old man:

"Lanny, I want you to pay a thousand pounds to a man named Ambrose Volonsky in Monte Carlo. You won't have any trouble in finding him. He insisted that I promised it to him, and maybe I did—my memory is not so good here. Promise me that you will attend to that for me."

"But," objected the son of Budd-Erling, "where am I to get all that money, Sir Basil?"

"Tell one of my nieces about it; she will pay it for me."

"But will she believe me, Sir Basil?"

There was no answer. only a great sigh. "He has faded away," said

Tecumseh. "Never have I known such an old man for worrying himself and other people. Are you going to pay that money—ha, ha, ha!" The old stone-age man burst into laughter; he had a keen sense of humor where other people's troubles were concerned.

Lanny didn't think he would ever pay that money. One of Zaharoff's nieces, when last heard of, was living in Istanbul, trying to take care of all the stray dogs of that dog-ridden city. The other was married and lived in Paris. Lanny couldn't remember her names, because she had about a score of them. He doubted if either of these ladies would remember having met him, or if they would pay out a thousand pounds on the word of a spiritualist medium. But he made note of the name Ambrose Volonsky, resolving to look him up the next time he passed through Monte Carlo. If he existed, he might have a story to tell.

XVI

A long pause usually meant the end of the séance. But Lanny never spoke first—he had learned to treat the chieftain like royalty, and permit him to decide what was to be done. And suddenly came one of those bolts out of the blue that reward the researcher for weeks of waiting. The deep voice of the "control" declared: "There is an old lady here; she has a lace collar on, and a kerchief over her head. She says her name is Marjorie, and she is the grandmother of Laurel. Do you know a Laurel?"

"Yes, I know one."

"Do you know where she is now?"

"I know where she was a month or so ago."

"The old lady says: 'I don't like what she is doing. I am worried about her.' Is she in any trouble?"

"She might be."

"The old lady says: 'You helped to get her into the trouble. You are an evil influence for her.' She wants you to let Laurel alone."

"Laurel has a special name for me. Does the old lady know what it is?"

"She says she does not want to talk to you. You got Laurel into trouble and you should get her out. She has tears in her eyes. She says that her people did not behave like that, the ladies of their family—they stayed at home and did not go gadding about the world and getting their names into print."

"That is all true," conceded the evil influence; "but Laurel was gadding before ever I heard of her. Ask the grandmother where she lived."

"She says it was an old house on the Eastern Shore. Now the roof leaks and one of the pillars of the veranda has fallen down."

"What was the name of the place?" Lanny always tried to get evidential details.

"It was called Fairhaven; the old Kennan place. Laurel was born there, and she should go back there and have the roof fixed and the piano tuned. Tell her that; if she will come here the grandmother will tell her. But you are to let Laurel alone; you should not break up families and homes the way you do. When a man is married he should stay married and take care of his own children and not other people's."

So that was that. Tecumseh rang off, so to speak; Madame groaned a few times, then opened her eyes, sighed wearily, and asked Lanny in a husky whisper if he had got anything worth while. He always told her Yes, whether or no, for that kept her contented, and she had earned that small reward. She was a good medium, and Lanny had learned that they are scarce articles, and should be cherished and indulged in their whims. Whether they are foretellers of some power which mankind is gaining, or throwbacks to some old power which mankind is losing, Lanny could never make up his mind, and there was nobody able to tell him.

But certainly they were something real and worthy of attention. Time after time it kept happening to Lanny Budd, until he could no longer doubt that the trance mind of this old Polish woman had access to anything that was in his mind, and, stranger yet, to the minds of his friends. Of course it might turn out that Laurel Creston's maternal grandmother was not named Marjorie Kennan and had not lived on the Eastern Shore of Maryland; but experience had taught Lanny that it might be so, and if it was, then either Madame had been able to reach out to the mind of Laurel Creston, or else Lanny had absorbed from Laurel's mind facts which his conscious mind had surely not possessed. This, of course, was the theory which Tecumseh called "that old telepathy"; what it amounted to was that there must be a pool of mind-stuff, like an ocean, into which the medium's mind could take a dip; and certainly that took a lot of believing.

Lanny found himself thinking about the charge that he had been breaking up homes. As a matter of strict fact, he had never broken up a home; but what he had done would seem like that to an old Southern lady who wore a kerchief and a "bertha." Very certainly she would have thought the son of Budd-Erling an "evil influence"; but how on earth would she have known that he had got Laurel "into trouble"? Lanny hoped she hadn't made any mistake as to the nature of this trouble, for he wouldn't care to have any gossip going the rounds in the spirit world. He reflected that Laurel herself didn't know that he had had anything to do with getting her into trouble; only two persons in the whole world knew that, himself and Monck. He decided that he wouldn't be in any hurry to bring the short-story writer into contact with Madame, to have that dangerous idea put into her mind!

16

Where Angels Fear to Tread

I

As WHEN a mountain is in labor, and mighty forces pent within it struggle to burst forth, the surface trembles, and quakings like sea waves rush from the center; there are rumblings and creakings, and great cracks spreading, and steam and sulphurous fumes escaping; people who dwell upon the slopes of that mountain are terrified, and hasten to their shrines with gifts to propitiate the angry gods; but many cannot believe that the foundations of the home in which they were born are crumbling, and that the vines they have planted may be buried under hot ashes or consumed by flowing lava; they mock at their neighbors who pack up their goods and leave the district; there are excited arguments as to what the gods of the mountain may intend and who or what may have offended them.

So now it was on the Côte d'Azur, the playground of Europe. People wanted to play polo and bridge, to wine and dine, to dance and gossip and make love, and to do nothing but these things; but rumors would come, of threats and preparations for war, and they would start exclaiming: "How inconvenient! How inexcusable!" Lanny would escort his mother to a reception in honor of the Grand Duke Vladimir, and talk with the Duque d'Alba and learn that Hitler was asking Spain to pay a part of her debt to him by the rushing of large shipments of tungsten, and by allowing German technicians to construct submarine pens in Spanish Atlantic ports. From a Yugoslav lumber magnate he would learn that this country had just rejected a demand from the Axis for the right to use its railways and military centers in case of war; the reserves of that small country had been summoned for maneuvers, to be held close to the Austrian and Italian borders.

And so on and so on, wherever you went in smart society. All strictly hush-hush, of course; it mustn't be allowed to get into the papers—but these were the people who had a right to know what was coming, and to get themselves and their possessions out of the path of the red-hot rushing lava. The wife of an Estonian Embassy official, sunning her shapely brown limbs on the beach at Juan, remarked to Lanny that her holiday might be suddenly terminated; her husband had written that their tiny nation was about to be sold in a deal between Stalin and Hitler. "We have our own dictators and need none from abroad," added the lady. It would serve for a *bon mot* in the summer season.

Kurt Meissner had an aunt who lived on the Riviera on account of her health; Lanny had known her since boyhood, and had kept up the acquaintance because at her home he met influential Junker personalities. Now he attended one of her *Kaffeeklatsche*, and was treated as a person of distinction because he had been received at Berchtesgaden. He listened to Prussian officials' wives scolding at the enemies of their country; he agreed amiably with everything they said, and in return had the privilege of hearing the wife of a retired Reichswehr general assure the widow of the Court-Counsellor von und zu Nebenaltenberg that there was no occasion for anxiety, for the German armies had been secretly mobilizing and there were now more than a million troops on the eastern border and as many more on the west. *Lieb' Vaterland magst ruhig sein!*

II

Rick had written an article entitled *The Folly of Appeasement*, based in part on facts which Lanny had gathered. It was about to appear, and he said: "It may attract some attention, old man, and I don't think I ought to be in your home at that time." So Lanny had to reconcile himself to the ending of this holiday, the happiest he had had in a long while.

"I suppose I ought to be in Berlin now," was his response. He couldn't tell his friend that only a few hours ago he had received a letter, forwarded from the Hotel Adlon—one of those obscure-looking letters having to do with the marketing of pictures: "You recall the Vereshchagin about which I wrote you. It has been brought to Berlin, and I am sure it will soon be sold. I have come upon a Rosa Bonheur portrait, representing a woman with a laurel crown, which I believe you would be interested to see. It is not covered by insurance so I am worried about it. I think that you could pick up some bargains here at present. I am interested in your project of a collection of historical paintings and wonder what your American friends thought of it. I know of such a work not far from the Schloss which you used to visit as a boy. Best wishes. Braun."

It didn't take any Joseph or Daniel to interpret that dream. A laurel crown wasn't bad for Laurel Creston, and the lack of "insurance" meant that Monck was still worrying about her and trying to put his worries off on her fellow-countryman. The Vereshchagin brought to Berlin meant that the deal with the Soviet Union, whatever it was, was being negotiated in Germany and was nearing conclusion. The "Schloss," of course, was Stubendorf, which was still a part of Poland, and "historical paintings" there could mean nothing but an attack on Poland. Lanny retired to his studio and wrote a report embodying these and other details which he had gathered—he sent one every few days in these busy times. Then he packed up his belongings and drove his friends to Paris.

They took the train for London, and Lanny set about his two kinds of business. Marceline was taking a holiday trip, and, perhaps not by a coincidence, Oskar von Herzenberg was doing the same. Jesse Blackless was in the country, painting pictures. Kurt had gone to Stubendorf —he paid a visit every summer and one every Christmas, thus making certain of the increase in his family. It was proper for Lanny to make a joke about this with Kurt's intelligent young secretary; as a skilled secret agent, Lanny did not overlook secretaries, and he knew the sort of jokes that went well among the Nazis. Otto Abetz was in Berlin—he had, so Lanny learned, been treated with consideration by a polite French government, anxious to avoid scandals and not curious to pry into anybody's private papers.

But the de Bruynes were in town, and Lanny spent a night with them, told what news he could safely repeat, and heard all their troubles and fears. France was one of the "have" nations, and this was one of the "*deux cent familles*," denounced by every *bistro* orator in the land. They wanted nothing more than to keep what they had, plus a normal profit, but they were surrounded by blackmailers and bandits of many sorts, and were continually having to decide which to placate, and what was the lowest price that would serve? Politicians and political associations, journalists, police agents, private detectives—all these a rich man had to pay, and all wanted more, and might be getting it from the other side.

The "have" nation was in the same position, and what money it paid concerned the "have" man in the form of taxes and imposts, loss of territories, markets, and access to raw materials. France had loaned billions of francs to Czechoslovakia, to be used in arming the country —only to see the armaments and the plants taken over by the Nazis and the bonds become worthless. Billions had been loaned to Poland, and was that to be gobbled into the same greedy maw? And then the Baltic states and the Balkan lands, all parts of the *cordon sanitaire*, so carefully and expensively built and maintained? All France was tormented by a sense of frustration, and families were rent apart by arguments as to which statesmen were the lesser scoundrels and which nations the lesser dangers. There was not much happiness left in the household of Lanny's long-dead sweetheart, and he was glad that she couldn't hear the controversies. "It is impossible to find out what France is going to do," he wrote in his report, "because France doesn't know what she is going to do."

III

On to Berlin, the place where decisions came from. Here was order and a sense of confidence, because everybody had been told his job and was doing it; he didn't have to bother about policies, because these would be determined for him. If there was hesitation and uncertainty among the few at the top, that did no harm, because these great ones kept their thoughts to themselves, and all had the comfort of knowing that sooner or later the decision would be taken, and then they, too, would enjoy the greatest of all German luxuries, which is an order to be obeyed.

Lanny arrived on a Tuesday, and couldn't see Monck until Wednesday night. Meantime, he had business with Furtwaengler, *Der Dicke's* aide. Photographs had been made of the paintings which the great man wanted sold, and now Lanny had to inspect these, and prepare descriptions, and select the most likely of his clients and write letters about the offerings. All this was quite a job, and ordinarily he would have liked nothing better than to settle down and do it without interruption; but the P.A. job came first, so he said: "Is Seine Exzellenz still cross with me?"

"Cross?" echoed the respectful young Oberst. "*Niemals, niemals, Herr Budd!* What would make you think that?"

"He must be annoyed over the severance of relations with my father."

"Seine Exzellenz is too big a man to let that interfere with his personal friendship. Do not let such an idea trouble your mind."

"I am glad to have that assurance, Herr Oberst, for he is one of the most delightful companions I know, and I would hate very much to have our cordial relations interfered with."

Lanny was quite sure that these remarks would be transmitted to *Der Dicke;* and sure enough, before the day was over, the staff member called back and announced that his chief would esteem it a pleasure if Herr Budd could make it convenient to drive out with him to Karinhall at the next week-end and see the new improvements. Of course Lanny could and would; and he didn't fail to say: "I am sure that is due to your kindness, Herr Oberst, and I hope that some day I may be able to show my appreciation." He knew what he would have to do—invite the SS officer and his wife to dinner at the hotel, and it would be a very dull occasion!

Meantime, he would employ a secretary and buckle down to work on old masters. *Ars longa, vita brevis!* Furtwaengler had revealed it as his superior's wish that Herr Budd should ship all the works to New York or Newcastle in his own name, and this was a revealing circumstance. It was equivalent to saying that the Field Marshal expected war within a very short time, and didn't mind if his art expert guessed that fact. There was also the possibility suggested that maybe the Field Marshal didn't feel completely certain that he was going to win that war!

IV

On the following evening, at the hour appointed, the confidential agent picked up Bernhardt Monck on the street. "I got your letter, forwarded to Juan," he said. "I take it to mean that there is some sort of deal on between Germany and Russia."

"My information is that it is practically concluded. It is highly secret, and some of its terms may never be known. The point is, it gives Hitler the green light so far as concerns Poland."

"What madness on the part of the Soviets! Don't they know what the Nazis will do to them, once they have a common border?"

"I am not in their confidence," countered the man of the underground. "I can only guess—they figure on getting a couple of years' respite at the least. If there has to be a war, Stalin would presumably rather have it between Germany and France-Britain than between Germany and Russia. The Nazis gave him that choice."

"Also," ventured Lanny, "he figures that Hitler will wear himself out while Russia grows stronger. Certainly it is a black day for the western world."

The ramifications of this news were extensive, and the pair talked them out in a long drive. The long-discussed Anglo-French mission had arrived in Moscow a few days previously, after long delays. Staff consultations had begun—and now, behind their backs, this deal with the enemy was being made! "Imagine their chagrin!" exclaimed Lanny; and Monck replied: "They could have flown and got there quicker. Also, they could have sent men of more importance, with authority to make decisions. The Russians were suspicious, and apparently nobody tried very hard to relieve their minds."

Lanny said: "I notice that the Nazis have announced a celebration of the twenty-fifth anniversary of the victory of Tannenberg. The people I talked to in Paris thought that was meant as a deliberate provocation of Russia. Was it meant as a blind?"

"I should say it is a pretext for moving troops into East Prussia. I'll wager the celebration will never be held; there will be war before that date."

"The twenty-seventh of this month?"

"My information is that the Reichswehr is to move into Poland on the twenty-fifth."

"Good God!" said Lanny. His hands would have trembled, if he had not clutched the steering wheel of the car more tightly. He had been foreseeing this and predicting it for twenty years, but when it came it was like the hot breath of some demon at the back of his neck. After a long pause he whispered: "The underground will not be able to do anything?"

"Absolutely not. We have been ground to powder. We shall never be able to move again until the SS has been wiped out—to the last battalion."

They drove through a good part of the night, discussing various aspects of this situation, so important to them both. Monck wanted to know if Britain would honor her recent pledge to Poland, and Lanny assured him there could be no doubt of this—any government which did not keep that word would be swept out of power overnight. So, there would be war between Britain-France-Poland on the one side, and Germany on the other. Would Italy come in? Count Ciano, Mus-

solini's son-in-law and foreign minister, was now meeting with Ribbentrop in the latter's castle in Austria. Lanny said: "I assume that he is
pleading with Hitler to wait, as he did just before Munich."

"He succeeded then, but I doubt if he can do it again. My information is that the die is cast; Hitler is going to follow his intuition this
time, and has forbidden any of his advisers to try to change his mind.
That is the way it goes in Germany now, and don't let anybody tell
you otherwise. One man decides, and the rest obey."

"I should be able to find out something in the next few days," remarked Lanny. "I am to visit Karinhall over the week-end, and I'll
meet you on Monday night unless something intervenes. Be at the
corner then and every night thereafter until I show up. I'll make it
as soon as possible."

"It's a date," said the ex-Capitán.

V

There was another subject on the minds of both this pair. "What's
this about the lady with the laurel crown?" demanded the visitor.

"*Herrgott*, Budd!—that woman is worrying me to death. She is determined to help us. You know how it is with new recruits—nothing
can check their enthusiasm. She thinks this war ought to be stopped,
that the people ought to be told before it is too late. The German
people, mind you!"

"One has to be very young to hold such ideas."

"I know it; and in times like these one needs wisdom and experience, even to keep alive. *Genosse* Laurel—so she tells me to call her—
cannot understand why we do not act in this crisis. I tell her of the
thousands who have been tortured to death and the tens of thousands
who are being slowly starved and destroyed in concentration camps.
Her answer is that this is the supreme crisis, and that whatever forces
we have left should be thrown into the breach."

"You have told her that you expect war?"

"I didn't tell her; she has figured it out for herself, from reading the
Nazi press. She says: 'They are doing exactly what they did in the case
of Prague—working up popular rage with stories of atrocities. I do not
believe that any of those things happened. I believe that the customs
disputes in Danzig are being deliberately engineered in order to provoke the Poles and work up a case. I watched the campaign over
Prague last March and I know all the signs.' You see, Budd, we are dealing with a shrewd mind, and I cannot lie to her."

"You have met her often?"

"I have met her only once since I last saw you. About two weeks ago I wrote her a note and met her in the Tiergarten at night. I have promised to do it once more, but I feel that it is a great risk. I tried to make her realize—there is surely not a pension in Germany that has not got a spy in it, reporting everything to the Gestapo. She says: 'Give me the name of some woman I can deal with—that will be less suspicious.' I had to tell her the embarrassing fact that that will be much more suspicious. If she goes out at night and has a rendezvous with a man, that will be taken as a fact of nature, of no special interest to the *Polizei*."

"What did she say to that?"

"She is not exactly naïve about sexual matters; she has lived in the smart world, where people do what they damn please; but in her inmost soul, I imagine, she stays aloof, and does not think of such things as applying to her virginal self. I made the proper apologies, of course. I said: '*Genosse* Laurel, if one wishes to take part in underground activities, it is necessary to know what the world is like, what people in pensions think if a young lady steals out into the Tiergarten on summer nights and stays for a long time without explanation. For God's sake, be forewarned, and have your story ready. It is a man, and the reason you refuse to name him is because he is a married man; that is the only excuse that might save you from a dreadful experience.' "

"And then?"

"Oh, of course she promised to comply. I told her that if we met again, I would have to see her make a number of turns in the park and make sure that she was not being followed. There might come a police whistle from somewhere in the bushes, and men would dash up on motorcycles from different directions."

"And did all that make no impression on her?"

"It frightened her, naturally, and she promised to use more care. But she still is determined to help; she is convinced that we Germans do not love liberty enough, and that an American has to teach us."

"You, the hero of Madrid and Belchite!" remarked Lanny; and added: "Not to mention the Château de Belcour!"

VI

Lanny drove in silence for a while, thinking over this problem. It seemed to him unlikely that the new comrade would try to do anything without Monck's advice; but when he said this, his friend broke into a laugh. "That shows how little you know her! She has already started, entirely on her own. Try to imagine what she has been accumulating in her bedroom in a pension!"

"Firearms?"

"Almost as bad—writing paper! She had deduced the fact that in order to appeal to the German people against an unprovoked attack in Poland, the underground would require a quantity of leaflets. What is more natural than that an American writer should purchase typewriter paper? So she goes into one store and buys a package, and then into another and buys a package and carries them up to her room and stows them in the bottom of her trunk, along with Kautsky, Lenin, and Kropotkin. It was her bright idea that if I would give her the name of a woman comrade, she would turn these packages over to her, two or three at a time, at night, and after making absolutely certain that she is not being followed. Can you beat it?"

"Trudi did much the same thing, Monck."

"Yes, but Trudi was no foreigner; also, that was in the early days, before Himmler had got all Germany organized. Today it would be suicide, as you must surely know."

"You explained that to her?"

"Indeed, yes. I gave her a lot of facts, and if she gets out of Germany alive, she should be able to do some useful writing. In my judgment, she should go now, before she subjects herself to a horrible experience. She thinks that she is safe because she is an American, and can appeal to the Embassy. I said: 'My dear lady, Germany is a country where people disappear and are never heard of again. If the Embassy makes any inquiry, they are told that the police will make every effort, and then they are told that the police have done all in their power, but that the American lady was very eccentric, and probably tied a stone about her neck and jumped into one of the canals—unfortunately there are so many that it is not practicable to drag them. Meanwhile, the lady is in a dungeon in the Columbushaus, having splinters driven under her fingernails, and the soles of her feet beaten with pieces of rubber hose, and then she is thrown into a cell which has been specially constructed of concrete so that she cannot sit down or lie down without an agony of discomfort, and there is a two-hundred-candlepower light shining directly into her eyes, and the temperature and moisture are regulated by a thermostat at the point which learned physiologists have determined to be exactly correct for reducing the human psyche to physical, mental, and moral impotence. And every once in a while a voice will be saying: 'Name the woman to whom you gave the paper and the man whom you met in the park.'"

"And what did she say to all that?"

"Well, she answered, quite correctly, that if people yielded to fear of torture, how could there be any freedom in the world, and what would become of our civilization? As I said before, she must think badly of us Germans, and especially of me as an underground worker."

"You have a good conscience, old man, and you can get along with it."

"I have faced danger when I thought it worth while; but I cannot contemplate knowing that my life and that of other comrades depends upon the ability of a foreign girl of delicate rearing to face the Gestapo's technique. I am wondering if it might not be possible for you to give her a warning."

"How can I, Monck? I cannot reveal that I know you; and what other reason can I have to suspect that she is aiding in underground work?"

"You might guess it from her writings."

"I have already done that, and have given her all the warnings that would sound plausible. She was not greatly impressed by my anxiety. She considers me a man without social conscience, and I have to let her go on thinking that."

"All right then," said Monck. "I suppose it's up to me to see her again and lay down the law. I'll tell her that the head of the underground forbids foreigners to take part in our activities. I'll have to hurt her, and make her understand that she will be on her own from this time forth."

VII

Next morning Lanny called up Hess's office and learned that the Deputy was in Berchtesgaden. One wasn't apt to find any fashionable friends in Berlin during the month of August, so Lanny decided that this was the time for him to settle down to the picture business. He spread out the bundle of photographs on the bed and began making notes of what he should say about this one and that. This Corot surely belonged in the Taft collection; this naive Italian primitive without a name might appeal to Mr. Winstead; and so on. It was like playing a game with building blocks; you arranged them one way and then shifted them into a new combination.

For a while Lanny was completely absorbed; but presently he came upon a portrait of the French actress Rachel, in a Greek costume with a wreath of some sort of leaves on her head. He could hardly be blamed if that set him to thinking about Laurel Creston and the outcome of her singlehanded war on the Gestapo. Lanny himself had been carrying on such a war for a matter of six years, and why should he have been so disturbed by the idea of somebody else doing it? Was it because the warrior was a woman, and one whose appearance pleased him especially? Or because he couldn't trust to her good luck as he trusted to his own?

Something like a little spark flashed in his mind. "By heck!" he exclaimed—and got up and began to pace the room. He knew what to do about her! Why hadn't he thought of it before? He would satisfy his own curiosity, and at the same time convey to her a warning, not from him, but from her grandmother, Marjorie Kennan—if that happened to be her grandmother's name! Anyhow, a warning from the spirit world!

Just once more, he told himself, and positively for the last time. The sooner the better, for who could guess what quantities of stationery she might be buying—enough for several volumes of her memoirs! He went to the telephone and called the Pension Baumgartner. When *Die Miss* came, he invited her to lunch in the same Hungarian restaurant. She said, quietly: "I'll be pleased to come," and nothing more. She had learned that he didn't care for chatting over the telephone in Hitler's realm.

He arrived ahead of her and sat reading a newspaper, full of denunciations of the Poles, who had arrested some Nazi customs officials trying to function in Danzig. It was the thesis of the Nazis that they had taken charge of Danzig and ran its customs office; it was the thesis of the Poles that the League of Nations had put them in charge of Danzig and that the Nazis had nothing to do with disputes between Danzigers and Poles. Just as you could "candle" a hen's egg and see a tiny red spot and say: "This is the beginning of a hen or a rooster, and some day it will be clucking or crowing in the barnyard," so you could read the news from the customs house of Danzig and say: "This is the beginning of the Second World War, and some day thirty or forty or fifty million men will be engaged in trying to murder one another." It had a tendency to diminish your interest in a Hungarian luncheon menu.

The writing lady put in her appearance, wearing the same dress with the blue flowers. Lanny arose and greeted her, and she smiled in return, saying: "How nice to see you!" She took her seat, and Lanny looked about to see if anyone was watching. They were not an especially conspicuous couple; good-looking and prosperous in appearance, but no more so than the average run of tourists. Such were here by the thousands, inspecting the wonders of Hitlerland, where not merely the trains but everything else ran on schedule, where every doorstep was washed clean and every railing dusted every day, where every barnyard was swept and no weed was to be seen in any field—to say nothing of the unemployment problem having been solved, and every boy and youth put in a neat brown uniform and taught to sing hearty songs, which fortunately few tourists could understand!

She told Lanny to order, so he called for chicken *paprikás, apfelstrudel,* and a light wine. Then, when the waiter had left, he said: "I have just come back from a business trip to Geneva and Paris."

"You take many trips," replied the lady. "Your friends must envy you."

"One comes to know all the roads, and they seem rather monotonous. I turn on the radio, and listen to music when I find the news too painful."

She wanted to know what he thought of the international situation, and he remarked that these crises came frequently, and had done so ever since he had first opened his eyes in Switzerland. He wouldn't say a word about politics in any restaurant in Germany—for waiters had a way of slipping silently up behind you, and at a signal a man would appear from nowhere, take a seat at a table close by, and start gazing attentively at the menu card.

VIII

Wait until the meal had been eaten, and they had strolled to a bench in the park. More and more Germans had taken to meeting that way, and the police had found it out; Lanny said: "I have an interesting story to tell you; but don't be surprised if in the middle of it I start talking about the animals in the Zoo. I read that there is a new baby hippopotamus."

"Also toucans have been hatched," smiled the lady. "I think that toucans are delightful." Then, after a look about her: "What is the story?"

Lanny had already told about Madame, and about the feeble spirit of Sir Basil, who interfered so greatly with efforts at psychic research. It wouldn't do to be rude to him, because that might offend Tecumseh, and possibly hurt the old woman's mediumship. You just had to submit to boredom, and after many weeks you would get your reward. Lanny's might or might not have come—it all depended upon whether Miss Creston's maternal grandmother had happened to be named Marjorie Kennan.

"How perfectly amazing!" exclaimed the granddaughter. "That was her name! What did she say?"

"Her home was on the Eastern Shore?"

"Yes; that is where I was born."

Lanny told the story, exactly as it had happened—except that he made it more emphatic that Laurel was in danger and that she should leave Germany at once. He discovered that his companion was interested in the psychic aspects of the incident, but not in the matter of her own safety. "That sounds exactly like grandmother! She was an extremely dictatorial person, and insisted upon trying to run the lives of every member of the family, and even of her friends. That is one of the reasons I left home—I wanted to think my own thoughts and make my own decisions."

Laurel Creston wanted to talk about that grandmother, and what the "control" had said about her appearance and manner; also about the old mansion—it was quite possible that the roof leaked and that a pillar had fallen; Laurel would write to members of the family and find out. A most extraordinary thing, that an old woman on the Cap d'Antibes should speak the name of a person who had died in Baltimore several years ago! Was Lanny certain that he had never heard her name mentioned by any of the Holdenhursts or their friends? Lanny assured her this could not have happened.

All very interesting; but Lanny realized that it wasn't getting him anywhere in the matter of Miss Creston's future conduct. When he remarked: "You don't take the old lady's warning very seriously?" the reply was: "I didn't let her regulate my life when she was on earth, and I can't let her do it from the spirit world."

"I found her warning impressive, and I wondered if you could be doing anything besides writing stories, that might get you into trouble in this country."

"You read the *Bluebook*, Mr. Budd?"

"Indeed, yes, and your *nom* did not throw me off the track. As a story, it is a masterpiece. I wondered what you could have experienced or witnessed that gave you such an extraordinary realization of what is going on here in Germany——"

Lanny took a swift glance, and then continued: "When it gets a little cooler we must go and see the baby hippopotamus. I saw one in the New York Zoo many years ago and they are delightful creatures; they have the tiniest little ears, and when the flies bite they wiggle them so fast that you can hardly see them. They are difficult to raise because their parents apparently do not distinguish the difference between a concrete wall and the soft mud of a river bank, and they sometimes crush their offspring." And so on, until a large stout Berliner had passed out of hearing. Then Lanny said: "I am really concerned about it, Miss Creston, because the authorities are bound to conclude that you have inside sources of information, enabling you to write with such vividness."

"Imagination is what makes us writers, Mr. Budd. It is always incomprehensible to those who don't have it."

"That is the point—it will be incomprehensible to the police. Understand, dear lady, I am concerned to spare you what might be a disagreeable experience—not merely for you, but for the people who have given you information."

"Yourself included?" inquired the lady, with a little laugh which was perhaps intended to take the sting out of the question.

"I see you won't let me be serious," he replied. "I am trying to persuade you that the *nom-de-plume* of Mary Morrow will not fool the Gestapo any longer than it fooled me. It seems to me more than likely that an investigation is already under way, to find out who is talking to you and supplying the unpleasant details about the Third Reich. If so, you can count upon it that your papers will be read in your absence from your room—and don't imagine that locks and keys will help, for they will come supplied with the means to open your escritoire and your trunk without damaging them. They will know whom you correspond with, and when you walk out into the Tiergarten and meet someone, they will know that it is because you have something to say that you don't want to have overheard."

"Really, my friend," replied the lady, "I appreciate your motives, just as I did those of my grandmother. But I say to you what I said to her: I have an impulse to write, and I want to write about the most important things I can find. I seek information, and when I find people so concerned to keep me from getting it I become more than ever convinced that I am on the right track. For your comfort, let me add that I don't plan to stay much longer."

"Ah, why didn't you say that before?" exclaimed the man.

Lanny had thought that perhaps in these critical times the *Nummer Zwei* Nazi might find it necessary to call off the week-end at Karinhall. But when he suggested this to the Oberst, the answer was that the great man rarely permitted his duties to interfere with his social life. He had trained subordinates to carry out his orders and could be sure they were doing so; in emergencies he could, like his Führer, govern from anywhere in the Reich. Lanny, who had heard both these governors bellowing over the telephone, smiled to himself.

The big six-wheeled baby-blue limousine drew up in front of the Adlon, creating excitement. Lanny's exit through the lobby, preceded by his bags, took on the nature of a royal progress; he could see the stares and imagine the whispers: *"Er geht nach Karinhall!"* It took only a minute to drive to the ministerial residence, and here came *Der Dicke*, fully restored as to both vigor and rotundity, and beaming with the fun of being alive. Why did he enjoy so much the company of an American, a decade younger than himself? Lanny guessed that it was because he liked to have his jokes returned in kind. A vigorous man gets tired of the conversation of underlings, and wants something to sharpen his wits upon. The Reichsmarschall's subordinates would not dare to make a remark that might offend him, even when they were drunk; but Lanny, without getting drunk, would return every rapier thrust, and the fat man would chuckle with delight.

Right now he was tired of politics and wanted to be the lover of art. Lanny reassured him as to the fine stuff in the shipment now on its way to New York, and *Der Dicke* told about the sixteenth-century Flemish tapestries which he was buying for the marble walls of his enormous new dining hall. He had accurate sketches of them, and wanted to show these to Lanny and get his judgment. He was buying them from the American newspaper publisher, Mr. Hearst, through a woman agent in London. "He would be a valuable client for you, Lanny." When Lanny replied that he had never had the pleasure of meeting this gentleman, the other talked about him at some length; he had visited Germany recently, and made a favorable impression upon them all—a man of brilliant mind, a typical man of the West, tall, vigorous, dominating.

"It is hard for an American to understand the National-Socialist point of view," remarked Göring; "and still harder to advocate it publicly. Mr. Hearst. I should say, does as well as anyone in his country."

Lanny replied: "I have visited several of the cities in which his papers are published, and in every one there is strong sympathy with your cause, and a movement which you may count upon in a crisis."

So they were back on the subject of politics. Lanny answered questions about American cities—New York, Boston, Washington, Detroit, Chicago; their various population groups, German, Italian, Irish, and how far these had retained their ancient feelings for the homeland and hatred of the homeland's enemies. Lanny voiced his idea that the Führer's unprecedented success was due to his shrewdness in choosing the items of a popular program, offering a hope of economic betterment to the masses; he was afraid, he said, that Mr. Hearst's lack of political success in the States was due to his having forgotten the "radical" ideas of his early newspaper career. "In those days he was all for 'trust-busting,' I am told; but now his program is purely negative, and the result is, the people read Hearst but vote Roosevelt."

"That is a valuable comment," declared the Reichsminister who was also head of the Prussian State. "I have always urged upon my subordinates that we must never forget our promises to the people and keep renewing them."

"I notice that you don't say 'carry them out,'" chuckled Lanny; and that was the sort of remark which kept *Der Dicke* amused.

X

Here was Karinhall, the magnificent estate which, if you could believe the gossips, belonged to the State of Prussia, but which Hermann Wilhelm Göring had taken over and calmly called his own. He had turned a hunting lodge into a palace, and in it he had put the lovely Emmy Sonnemann, tall blonde stage darling of the German people and now their First Lady. Lanny had made the mistake of being too cordial to her, or so his father had thought; now he would be a model of reserve, and direct all his admiration to the tiny Edda, the Crown Princess, though not yet proclaimed. She was a lovely little Nordic, and it was impossible to praise her too fulsomely. The same was true of Göring's home and most of the things in it. In a conspicuous place stood a sort of lectern of beautifully carved wood, and on it a magnificently printed and bound copy of *Mein Kampf*, like a Bible in a cathedral. A candle burned on each side of it; and Lanny remembered his talk on the top of the Kehlstein, in which the Führer of the Germans had announced the birth of a new religion, akin to that founded by Mohammed.

Lanny put on his elegant white dress suit, which had been pressed by the hotel valet just an hour before his departure and had a suitcase all to itself so that it might appear without a wrinkle. He dined sumptuously, and proposed an eloquent toast to the success of National-Socialist ideas throughout the world. Later on he was shown the elaborate colored crayon sketches of the Flemish tapestries which were to adorn the walls of the new dining hall. They represented various Nordic blonde ladies in the altogether, and to make it proper they were labeled after various virtues: Goodness, Mercy, Purity, and so on. Göring told how he had shown these sketches to the British ambassador, Sir Nevile Henderson, a tall and proper gentleman who looked not a little like his Prime Minister, and had the same first name, though he spelled it, perhaps out of courtesy, with one letter less. Sir Nevile had commented on the various ladies, and that he did not see Patience among them. Hermann considered this such an excellent *Witz* that he laughed even in the retelling.

Said the master of Karinhall: "I think the correct Englishman was a little shocked by the idea of so much nakedness in a dining room—*nicht wahr*, Lanny?" When Lanny opined that it might easily have been so, *Der Dicke* continued: "These ladies will send thrills all over me and increase my appetite—so, why not?" He added: "Of course I always think of Emmy!" He looked at his wife, then cried: "Look at her blushing!"—and burst into a roar of laughter. Not for the first time, the son of Budd-Erling imagined himself in the castle of one of those old Teutonic robber barons, of a time even earlier than the weaving of the Flemish tapestries.

XI

Sir Nevile and his puritanical traditions brought up the subject of politics again—no keeping off it! The ambassador had gone to London to report. What was he advising, and what was London going to do? Lanny wouldn't say outright: "Britain will be afraid to move," for that might have been encouraging war. He wouldn't say: "Britain will keep her word to Poland," for that might have provoked Göring to a tirade. The P.A. said: "There is a tug of war going on, and Whitehall sways this way and that. The main problem is how to control the irresponsible press."

"We have long understood that," replied *Der Dicke*. "It compels us to mobilize our armies—which is a costly procedure." He didn't say **at** any time in the course of the evening: "We are going to attack Poland." He said: "The Führer has made up his mind, and the task of dissuading him would be a hard one. I stuck out my neck the last time, and am resolved not to do it again."

The visitor's heart sank at this, for he had had the idea that Göring's purpose might be to send him to the Führer, as had happened prior to "Munich." But not again! The air commander declared: "I have to admit that the British have disgusted me, and I am not interested to hang Sir Nevile's Lady Patience on my dining-room walls. The Poles are stark mad, but a good part of that madness has been deliberately created by cunning British intrigue. They promise aid, but what aid can they mean to send?"

"It would be more proper for me to ask you, Hermann; for you are a military man, while I am only an art expert."

"Will they send a fleet through our mine fields in the Skagerrak? Or will they sacrifice part of their inadequate air force? Can they imagine getting an army ashore on the Continent in time to save Poland?"

"They have been told that the Führer desires never to face a two-front war," returned Lanny, mildly.

"It is not a two-front war when one enemy is destroyed before the other can take the field. Poland, from a military point of view, is like one of those sets which the motion-picture people build, all front, and behind it nothing. When the British realize that, they will consider seriously whether they desire to fight a long and exhausting war to no purpose."

"Then you won't bomb London or Paris at the outset?"—a bold question to ask of an air-force commander, only a few days before his planes were scheduled to fly.

But Göring believed that he had all the cards in his hands and didn't mind laying them on the table. "Of course not," he said. "We don't want war; we only want to find out what others want. Tell the British for me that we shall give them plenty of time to think it over, and to realize what they are getting themselves in for."

"I think they know it already, Hermann. Some two months ago I was shown in London a bulletin of an organization which calls itself 'The Friends of Europe Information Service.' You know about them, doubtless."

"We do not overlook anything that our enemies are doing."

"Well, this bulletin outlined the procedure which Germany intended to follow, and it was just about what you have told me." Lanny didn't say that it was Rick who had shown him this bulletin, or that Rick had had a lot to do with the compiling of it—using Lanny's information in part.

"The Führer's policy has always been open and aboveboard," declared the Führer's man of war. "All we want is to have our own returned to us. We should prefer to receive it as a gift, an act of justice; but if we have to take it, well and good. Let our foes do what they please, and we will meet them. No one will be able to say that Germany has sought war, or has ever committed an act of aggression."

Lanny would have liked to say: "Tell that to the Czechs!" But he understood that you shouldn't make jokes when you know that the other fellow has a guilty conscience.

XII

On Monday morning Lanny was returned to his hotel. He called the office of Rudolf Hess, and learned that the boss of the NSDAP was still at Berchtesgaden. Lanny had written him a note to that place and had been hoping to find a reply in his mail; but there was only silence, and Lanny realized that he was in the doghouse, along with all other fellow-citizens and subjects of Franklin Delano Rosenfeld, Dutch-Jewish, democratic-plutocratic-communistic dictator.

This was the fourteenth of August, and according to Monck, the date of the attack on Poland was eleven days off. Lanny had time enough for a trip to Switzerland to send an airmail letter to Washington. But he had already written from Paris that war was no more than a month off; and as to the exact date, he had known Adi Schicklgruber to change his mind suddenly, and he had hopes that it might happen again. If only an American psychologist could figure out some way to get hold of him and apply his arts!

Lanny called the office of Heinrich Jung, who was one of the few men able to say that he had visited the aforesaid Adi while Adi was in prison fifteen years ago. Such persons always had access to the Führer —that is, unless they were in the position of Ernst Röhm and some of his cronies, killed in the Blood Purge. Lanny was out of luck again, for Heinrich had been ordered to Nuremberg to arrange for the Youth part of the week's celebration known as the Parteitag, which took place the beginning of every September. Special attention was to be given this year to the enlightenment and inspiration of the Hitlerjugend, so Heinrich's secretary informed Heinrich's American friend; she must have telegraphed or telephoned her boss, for a couple of hours later there came a wire from Nuremberg begging Lanny to attend the magnificent series of events as Hitler's guest. If Monck's information was correct, that magnificent series wasn't going to occur; but of course the Nazis would go on making preparations, as a matter of camouflage.

Lanny bethought himself of Otto Abetz, who had come to Berlin, and now was pleased to accept an invitation to lunch at the Adlon. This agreeable conversationalist passed a couple of hours with the American playboy—for Lanny could still play playboy whenever he wanted to. Herr Abetz revealed that he was deeply grieved by the failure of his mission to France, but his love for that country was still undiminished. It didn't take Lanny long to unveil the fact that his love was confined to those French who agreed with him, and that he bitterly hated those who had invited him to pack up his valuable papers and depart from his wife's native land to his own.

Herr Abetz took his personal sorrow philosophically; he saw what had happened *sub specie æternitatis*, so he said. It was the fate of France which had been determined, and the tragedy lay in the fact that the wrong side had won. The Jewish-Bolshevik politicians had succeeded in holding the country to the policy of trying to encircle Germany, and the consequences of that were to be painful indeed for poor Marianne. Herr Abetz didn't set a date for the falling of the ax, but he said that meteorological factors on the eastern front would attend to that. Lanny ascertained that the unofficial ambassador had not had an opportunity to report directly to the Führer, but only to Herr von Ribbentrop. After that Lanny diverted the conversation to Paris; he said that in an amateur and voluntary way he would do what he could to take Herr Abetz's place. He named persons whom he believed to be the best friends of Germany in France, and made mental notes of what Abetz had to say about all of them, their honesty, their competence, and their associations. It was like calling the roll of the Comité France-Allemagne, and also of the Comité des Forges.

XIII

In the evening, the appointment with Monck. Having got his fellow-conspirator safely into his car, Lanny opened up: "I met Göring, and he didn't set a date, but he confirms your statement that Hitler's mind is closed. Göring declares that he isn't going to stick his neck out. I haven't heard from Hess, so evidently he is taking care of his anatomy, too."

"I have had further word," replied the German. "The date stands, as regards Poland, and the agreement with Russia will be announced within the week."

Monck, of course, wanted to hear the whole story of what had happened at Karinhall, and there was no reason why he shouldn't. A fascinating experience for him, to be taken into the den of that old-style robber baron, that bloody-handed bandit who had built the Gestapo and strangled the labor and Social-Democratic movements which Monck had spent his life helping to build. Now *Der Dicke* had relinquished that special job to Heinrich Himmler, who was even more scientifically and coldly murderous; but Monck hadn't yet got off with the old hate and on with the new. "Some day our time will come," he said; "and I'll be the one to get into Karinhall by the back door and empty that bastard's guts onto the marble floor of his dining hall."

But this holiday, by all the signs, was a long time off, and meantime Monck had another tale to tell. "I had a meeting with the lady from Baltimore," he said. "We spent a couple of hours in the Tiergarten, I think without attracting any special attention. We had what I could call the oddest conversation I ever heard of."

"What is she doing now?"

"She is thinking about you; she told me all about you, and asked my advice. She has taken up the notion that you must be some sort of secret agent in the pay of the Nazis, and wanted to know whether it might not be her duty to report you to the F.B.I. or somebody."

"Oh, *no!*" exclaimed Lanny.

"On my honor as a comrade! She has been listening attentively to everything you have said to her, and applying her keen mind to it. She told me a lot of things about you—things I was interested to learn."

"You didn't give her any hint that you knew me, I hope!"

"Surely not. All I admitted was that I had heard of the Budd-Erling plane. At first, she said, she had decided that you came to Germany on your father's business with Göring, which she considers infamous. But then she noted your sudden disappearance and tried to find out what you were doing in France and England. She has become convinced that the picture business is a blind, and likewise your devotion to music, literature, and art. She is certain that you are an ardent and active Fascist."

"By heck!" said Lanny. "I am a good actor!"

"You bet—none better! She has been leading you on to talk, and has noted the fact that when you go to Paris you don't meet painters, you meet public men—and the same in England. She has read about Otto

Abetz being expelled from France, and she thinks you are another of that sort."

"I had lunch with him today, and he thinks so too! But go on."

"What worries her most is that you go to America, and she is sure that you meet important public men there and bring back reports to Göring and Hitler. She wanted to know if that wouldn't be against the law, and I did the best I could, not knowing your law. I said it would be if you brought military information, but not if you confined yourself to political and business conditions, the state of public opinion and such matters. Is that correct?"

"I am afraid it is," replied Lanny. "Our country is overrun with all sorts of foreign agents."

"I think I was able to dissuade her from taking any action," said Monck. "I told her that many businessmen came and went, and collected all sorts of information and passed it on; there was nothing we common people could do about it. The funniest·thing of all, Budd—she thinks your efforts to frighten her out of Germany are suspicious."

"What would I be doing that for?"

"You are trying to protect the Nazi movement, by keeping her from finding out too much about it and putting it in a bad light before the American public. She says you made up a cock-and-bull story about her maternal grandmother having sent her a message from the spirit world."

"Oh! She thinks I made that up?"

"She says you are as clever as the devil. At first the story seemed plausible and she believed you. It was only after she went off and thought it over that she realized—you had had every opportunity to find out about her from her relatives. You went out of the way to tell her you had never told her relatives about meeting her, and she thinks that is very unlikely. Did you ever mention her?"

"I really did not; but I didn't tell her the reason—I have an idea the Baltimore girl wants to marry me, and I didn't want to set the two cousins in each other's hair."

"Well," said the ex-Capitán, with a laugh, something he did rarely, "I had the idea this girl might fall in love with you; but now she wants to land you in jail."

"The two states of mind are not so far apart as you might think," replied the experienced ex-playboy. Then, after a pause: "What should I do about all this?"

"I have thought it over," declared the other. "I think you should call Miss Creston on the phone at once and tell her that you overlooked to suggest that if she leaves Germany she should let you know her future address."

"What would that accomplish?"

"At present she thinks she ought to stay in Berlin and find out more about you. If she thinks you will get in touch with her in Paris or London, that will relieve her mind, and she'll probably go."

"Well, I'll be jiggered!" said the son of Budd-Erling.

BOOK FIVE

Ancestral Voices Prophesying War

17

Oh, What a Tangled Web!

I

EVERYBODY in Berlin was talking war. The poor, the "common" people, talked about it with fear and dismay. *"Ist es möglich, mein Herr?"* or *"Was will England eigentlich?"* They all knew that England was to blame, that England was bent on surrounding Germany, depriving her of *Lebensraum*, of the right to grow which England herself had enjoyed for centuries. The well-to-do, the influential and important persons with whom Lanny talked, discussed it as a sporting proposition, as people on the Riviera discussed various systems to beat the roulette wheel. The wheel of diplomacy was the most complicated and uncertain in the world.

Europe might be compared to a kaleidoscope, into which you peered and saw a pattern, then you jiggled it and looked again and there was a new pattern. The Great Jiggler, who lived in a retreat on the Obersalzberg, had made up his mind to make another shift in the pattern—so the insiders declared. He had decided that Britain was arming against him, and that the longer he 'eloyed the worse his position would be. He had decided that the "Colonels" who governed Poland were madmen—mad with their own conceit, hunger for glory, hatred of the *Herrenvolk*. He was going to put them in their place, close that absurd Corridor, and reunite East Prussia with the rest of the Fatherland. All that had been decided; but then, he was a man of moods, and who could tell what the next might be? So whispered various ladies and gentlemen to Lanny Budd, looking now and then over their shoulders.

Affairs with Poland had reached a position of stalemate; all negotiations had come to an end. Poland was in possession, and it was up to Germany to make the next move. The Nazis had an assortment of moves which they had tried out in several other countries. SA men and arms were being smuggled into Danzig, which was supposed to be under the protection of the League of Nations, but whose government was now Nazi. "Incidents" would occur—and who was to place the

366

blame for them, who was to know or tell the truth? The Nazis wanted to claim Danzig as a German city, but at the same time to deny Poland the right to charge duty on goods imported from Danzig into Poland. A Nazi fishing fleet went out and caught herring, and were they to go into Poland duty free? A British concern in Danzig, using Dutch capital, made margarine, and if the Poles charged an import duty on that, it became an international "incident."

Diplomats running from one capital to the next, exchanging visits, delivering memoranda. The British ambassador came back to Berlin, and had an interview with Ribbentrop's assistant, and quarreled with him, as English diplomats were not supposed to do. Shudders ran through Berlin society, and reached a presidential agent. Sir Nevile had solemnly warned that Britain meant to back Poland; he was unimpressed by the argument that the Polish Cabinet was made up of lunatics, and that this released Britain from her treaty obligations. So, then, it was to be war! Or was it? *Was glauben Sie, Herr Budd?*

II

Hilde, Fürstin Donnerstein, flew to Berlin from her summer châlet. Lanny had written her a note, and now she called him. "Do please come to see me, I am in such trouble!" Helping fashionable ladies in trouble had been Lanny's specialty since the age of three or four; so he went, and this nervous, high-strung wife of an elderly Prussian nobleman poured out her unhappy soul to the former husband of her friend Irma Barnes. Her eldest son, a sub-lieutenant just out of military school, had been ordered to join his regiment at twenty-four hours' notice. Hilde had rushed here to see him off and hadn't yet succeeded in drying the tears of parting.

"A German mother!" she exclaimed. "That is what we are made for —to part, then to wait, then to mourn!" Before the Fürstin did any more of it she got up and went to the door of her drawing-room and peered out. Then she put the "tea-cosy" over the telephone, because of her belief, true or false, that the Gestapo had a way of listening even when the receiver was on the hook. "Now, Lanny," she said, "tell me the truth and don't spare me! Is there going to be war?"

"*Liebe Freundin*," replied the American, "it is from such signs as your son's orders that we have to make our guesses. Where have they sent him?"

"It is the most sacred of secrets; I had to swear——"

"Well, then, of course——"

"*Aber*—with you it is all right. To Kreuzburg, in Upper Silesia."

"I know where it is. That is one of the districts from which a march into Poland will begin."

"We shall not be content to take the Corridor and Danzig?"

"Surely not, my dear. In war it is necessary to defeat your enemy's army, and not just to take a strip of territory."

The Fürstin began mopping her eyes again, and begging her guest's pardon. "I have fought so hard against believing this, and now it is like the end of the world. My other son will soon be of military age. Will it be a long war, Lanny—like the last?"

Most Germans were sure that the Führer's magic would work this time as it had worked over a period of six years; and it would have been very bad form indeed for Lanny to hold any other opinion. He could rely upon authorities such as Oberst Furtwaengler and General Meissner; Hilde in return would tell him what her husband said, and various diplomats and soldiers in her circle. All of them agreed upon one thing, Germany must never again get into a two-front war. The only argument that could justify the move now impending was that Poland was so weak, she was not really a front.

That brought up the question of Russia. "Have you heard," whispered Hilde, and Lanny whispered back that he had heard, and what did she think about it? The noble lady got up and opened the door again before she answered; then she said: "I really believe it. I expect the announcement will be made soon."

"Do you know what is in the agreement?"

"It is a treaty of non-aggression—that is all I have been told."

"There are no military clauses?"

"That I cannot say. You know how it is—there are secrets and then there are double secrets and triple secrets. *Aber*—I can tell you this—something you must never breathe, at least not in Germany. The way we convinced the Russians was by letting them have recordings of what went on between our *Nummer Eins* and the British Prime Minister at the Godesberg conference last year. You remember—just before Munich?"

"Certainly; I was holding my breath all those hours."

"Well, we had dictaphones planted, and recorded every word that Chamberlain said. He pointed out that the true foe of western civilization is Bolshevism, and hinted pretty plainly that that was the direction in which *Die Nummer Eins* should turn his attention. I am told that this is what decided the Russians to make a deal."

As it happened, the genial Hermann Göring had amused himself by playing one of those records on his machine for Lanny Budd not long after the Munich settlement. That had been at *Der Dicke's* hunting lodge on the Obersalzberg, where the great man had been sticking pigs. Lanny had been wondering ever since whether it was the actual voice of Neville Chamberlain to which he had been listening, or whether it was a clever imitation, a studio product. He hadn't the least doubt that an old-style robber baron who had had the Reichstag fire set in order to blame it on the Communists would have been perfectly willing to hire some renegade Englishman to play the part of his country's Prime Minister. Lanny had never doubted what use they would make of the recording; and here it was! Of course he wouldn't say anything to the Donnerstein except to thank her for a tidbit of gossip.

That was the way to console her grief; to listen to her stories about important persons and chuckle with delight. Lanny told of his unsuccessful efforts to get hold of the Führer, in the hope of suggesting a little patience to him; somebody was guarding him, probably Ribbentrop. "Oh, that odious *Emporkömmling!*" exclaimed Hilde, and began right away on his character and his career, his champagne business, his wife, his aunt from whom he had got his "von." "Rippy," as she called him, was now lord of the Fuschl Castle, in Austria; that was where he had just been entertaining Ciano—"Oh, remind me, I have a delicious story about that meeting! But first, I was going to say: Did you know that Rippy took that castle from a Jew? Just walked in one day with some SS men and put the Jew out, and that was all there was to it. Juppchen Goebbels got his magnificent place on the Wannsee in the same manner—and have you ever been to one of the entertainments he gives there? *Fabelhaft!* You would think you were back in the days of the Arabian Nights. Sometimes I wonder if we really aren't—if some day we won't wake up and discover that we have been dreaming all this phantasmagoria."

"You were going to tell me about Rippy and Ciano," reminded Lanny.

III

The P.A. had taken Monck's advice and called Laurel Creston on the telephone. "I am about to leave Germany and I don't want to lose touch with you. I hope that if you leave Berlin you will write me your new address. Juan is the best place to reach me." That was all, except "Good luck to you!"

Lanny told himself that he wasn't going to concern himself any further with what happened to her. He had given her fair warning, and now her fate was in her own keeping. He tried to work up a little irritation with a novice who persisted in attempting tasks beyond her powers and in making trouble for two veterans like Monck and himself. Surely he was justified in taking the position that his own work came first, and that he must wash his hands of the future troubles of the lady from Baltimore.

He finished his picture business, and listened to the conversation of various persons who knew what was going on in Naziland. It was time for him to make a run to the border and mail a report. He delayed, because he wanted very much to see Hitler, and his mind was busy with schemes for arranging this. He was sure that if he could see the Führer alone, and especially on top of the Kehlstein, he could get him to talking about the deal with Russia, and to reveal the "triple-secret" clauses in the agreement. But how to get to him?

Lanny felt certain that both Göring and Hess were friendly to him, and enjoyed his conversational displays. But they both knew that the American was listed in the Führer's mind as among the "appeasers"—that is, the persons who, prior to the Munich compromise of the previous autumn and the Prague raid of the previous spring, had urged him to have patience, to move slowly, to accomplish his objectives without risk of war. Right now, it appeared, the Führer was out of patience with his own patience; he was convinced that his foes did not mean to let him have his way without war, and that he was stronger now, in relation to them, than he would ever be again. He wasn't quarreling with his appeaser friends, but just didn't want to be bothered with them in this juncture.

As a matter of fact, Lanny had been having it out with himself, and had decided that he no longer wished to be listed as an appeaser. If he were able to advise Hitler how to get Danzig and the Corridor without war, would he do it? The British appeasers were trying it, but could an American anti-Nazi afford to help them, or even to seem to help them? It would mean that Adi Schicklgruber's prestige would be stepped up another notch, and by next spring he would be ready to grab Warsaw, as last spring he had grabbed Prague. Horrible as war seemed to Lanny, would it not be better to have it come while there was still some opposition to the Nazis left in Central Europe?

Lanny told himself that the line for him to take was that he shrank from this issue, he didn't feel his mind capable of a judgment, he left it to a man of destiny who had so much better sources of information than himself. Every time he had met Adi Schicklgruber over a period of a dozen years, Lanny had observed him more easily pleased by flattery, and by now there was no ecstasy of admiration that he would not have accepted from the son of Budd-Erling. But suppose that in his innermost heart he didn't really know what he wanted to do? Suppose he was a terrified little sub-corporal, confronting an issue of colossal, even cosmic proportions, and trembling in his military boots before it —what then? Uneasy lies the head that wears a crown, and surely this applies also to the heads of the courtiers who crowd about the throne.

The crowd at Berchtesgaden was, as such crowds have been all through the ages, numerous, importunate, and jealous; they would not yield easily to an outsider, trying to shove his way in. Should Lanny call the Berghof on the telephone and say, boldly: "I wish to speak to the Führer about a matter of importance"? They knew him well there, and would probably deliver his message. But what if the Führer was busy, or out of sorts? The story would go everywhere, and Herr Budd's social position would be greatly damaged; there would be many to rejoice. He might call Hess, and would hardly fail to get him; but what should he say? "I am no longer an appeaser, and don't want to talk politics to the Führer"? Should he say: "I have a painting which I should like to present to him"? But that would sound like an effort at money-making, the worst thing possible in a time of crisis. Should he say: "I have some important information for him"? But what information would it be? Hess would say: "Come and tell it to me"; and Lanny would have to have it!

IV

Every time Lanny thought of the Deputy, there was one idea that took the spotlight in his mind. *Spirits!* Hess believed in them openly, and Hitler secretly. In this vast underworld of the mind, who could tell what forces might be hidden, what wisdom exceeding that of a humble sub-corporal trembling in his military boots, and of a merchant's son from Egypt whose education had been interrupted by war, civil conflict, and political responsibility? In a crisis such as this, with the future of the NSDAP and of all Germany at stake, with the whole world hanging on one decision, Rudi would most certainly be consulting mediums and astrologers, readers of palms and tea-leaves and greasy packs of cards. Adi, too, might be doing it, but under cover, with many precautions to keep the world from getting a hint of it.

That was Lanny's ticket of admission to the Führer's retreat; that was his way to the deeps of a mystic's soul. He would offer to bring Madame from Juan for another series of sittings, and let Tecumseh report what Rudi's long-dead comrades had to advise about the next step for the Party. Things might go wrong, the spirits might not give acceptable advice—but anyhow, Lanny would get into the Berghof before war broke out, and would have a chance to touch the proper keys on the Schicklgruber organ, and learn what were his latest moods concerning Marianne, Britannia, Herr Rosenfeld, and above all, Josef Dzugashvili, alias Stalin!

Perhaps it might be wise to have something to tell Hess in advance. Lanny took the trouble to pay a visit to the fashionable Berlin mystagogue who called himself "Professor Pröfenik." Lanny had become convinced that he was a fraud; but then, there are few frauds who have set out in cold blood to make a fortune out of psychic trickery. Most of them had some gifts, and many still mixed what reality they could with their faking. This old gentleman of indeterminate origin knew the occult lore of all the ages, and in all probability he was shrewd enough to suspect that Lanny was mixing some trickery with *his* arts both social and intellectual. Neither could fathom the other entirely; but then, was that necessary in order for them to co-operate? Lanny had dropped hints in the course of a conversation and had seen Pröfenik pick up these hints and use them in a séance with Hess. The Professor must have guessed that Lanny had some purpose in permitting this, but he had no way to find out what that purpose was; it had served *his* purpose in impressing the *Nummer Drei Nazi*.

What had been done once might be done again. So Lanny made an appointment and called at the elegant residence. The old gentleman with the drooping white side-whiskers and the beautiful silk Chinese jacket welcomed him cordially. Lanny had made sure of this by always leaving an envelope with a couple of hundred marks in it. This time, he talked about world affairs, as all the world was doing, and as most of the Professor's clients wanted to do. So when the Professor retired into his cabinet and went into his trance, his "control," the one-time King Ottokar I of Bohemia, also talked about politics. His voice was clear and booming, but his words were apocalyptic. He saw four horsemen riding in the sky; he saw cities burning, walls crumbling, planes crashing from the sky—none of which was especially novel, since the newspapers were full of menaces, and Guernica, Madrid and Barcelona had set the pattern.

It was all right, because Germany was coming out on top and Adolf Hitler was going to be the founder of a party and a regime that would last a thousand years. That would serve as background, and Lanny was free to put in any details he pleased. The Professor was supposed to be in a trance and not to know what the spirit of King Ottokar I was saying, so he couldn't deny anything without admitting that his séance was fraudulent. He wouldn't want to, when he got two hundred *Freimarks* for keeping quiet—to say nothing of all the prestige at court.

Lanny took psychic phenomena seriously, and tried never to fool himself; but he took his P.A. job still more seriously, and was willing to fool any Nazi or Fascist at any time and by any means. So now he had a story; he could call Hess on the telephone and say: "I have just had a séance with Pröfenik, dealing with the present situation; really quite extraordinary, and I thought you would want to know about it. I have come to Munich on business, and I'll see you any time you say." He could hear Rudi answering: "Good for you! Come as soon as you can and call me when you arrive."

V

Lanny's program was to drive to the nearest point in Switzerland, write and mail a report, and then come to Munich and call Hess. At about nine in the morning he packed his bags, paid his bill, left his forwarding address, and stepped into his car. Then occurred one of those incidents which reveal how the destiny of a man hangs upon what seems to be blind chance. Says Goethe, in *Hermann und Dorothea:* "The moment decides as to the life of the man and as to his whole fate." Lanny had lifted his foot and was about to put it down on the starter of his car when he recollected that he had overlooked to telegraph his change of address to his mother. He left the car in care of the hotel doorman and went inside to a writing desk; he was in the act of penning the words, "Vier Jahreszeiten Hotel Munich," when one of the Adlon bellboys came to him. "Telephone for you, Herr Budd."

Lanny slipped the partly written message into his pocket and went to a booth. A woman's voice said: "Please answer Yes or No, nothing else. Do you recognize my voice?" When he answered, "Yes," the voice continued: "You gave me some advice from my grandmother. The favor I am asking has to do with that. I urgently need to see you."

Now Lanny hadn't been carrying on secret intrigues for years without learning to take hints. "I understand," he replied, instantly. "Where can I meet you?"

"You remember where we sat and talked last time—in the open?"

"I remember."

"Can you find the place again?"

"I am sure I can."

"Would it be possible for you to borrow or rent an automobile—I mean one that you would drive yourself?"

He had never told her that he had a car of his own. Now he said: "It can be arranged."

"How soon can you be there?"

"In five minutes, if you wish."

"Make it fifteen, please."

"O.K."

So Lanny didn't finish his telegram, and when he got into his car, he did not take the way to the south, but drove into the Tiergarten and began circling the spot where he had sat on a bench and told Laurel Creston about Madame and Tecumseh and the spirit of Marjorie Kennan. From the woman's tone and manner he had become certain that this was a serious matter, and he looked out for any pedestrian or car which might appear suspicious. When he saw her walking fast, he did not join her at once, but drove around behind her, scanning the drives and walks. This was one time when he didn't mean to make any mistake, and he waited until she was seated on the bench. Then he stopped his car on the drive in front of where she sat. She saw him and came; he opened the door to the rear seats, and the moment she got in he started away.

"Is somebody looking for you?" he asked, and when she told him "Yes," he said: "Lie on the seat and you will be out of sight." He had folded his overcoat to make a pillow for her.

VI

Lanny watched carefully, and made certain that no car was following. They were safe for the moment, at any rate. "Now!" he said. "Tell me what has happened."

She narrated: "There is a little square near the pension. It has trees, and benches in the shade, and I have sometimes gone there to sit and read, while my room is being made up in the morning. In the pension is a maid, a simple country girl who has become fond of me; I have given her little presents, and she has told me about life in her village. This morning she came running to the square, breathless: 'Ach, liebe Miss, die Polizei!' Three men in uniform had come and demanded to know where I was; they were searching everything in my room. I must not come back to the pension. That was all; the maid had to run back at once so that she would not be missed. I got away from the place as quickly as possible. I couldn't think what to do. I know no one in the city I could appeal to for help, or that I could trust if I did. I have no right whatever to trouble you, but I need advice so badly, and while I know how you disagree with my ideas——"

"Don't worry about that, Miss Creston. I will give you whatever advice I can. First, I must know what you have been doing."

"I have done nothing but what you know, and what you warned me about. I meant to take your advice, but I delayed. I was planning to leave next week."

"You have manuscripts in your room?"

"Quite a number."

"Things dealing with Germany?"

"Naturally. Things of the sort which you have already read."

"You must understand, dear lady, this country is on the verge of war, and they will take this sort of thing very seriously."

"You warned me, and I should have heeded you. I am terribly ashamed of being in this position."

"Don't worry too much. What I want is for you to be frank, so that I can form a correct idea of your position and be able to give you useful advice. You have letters in your room?"

"A few from friends."

"Inside Germany or out?"

"All of them outside. I have no friends in Germany, unless there be some tourists traveling."

"Have you copies of letters you wrote to friends?"

"A few, when I used a typewriter."

"You expressed opinions of Germany, and of the Nazis?"

"I wrote pretty freely."

"What else have you in your room that might interest the Gestapo?"

"Well, I have the books that I told you about."

"And others? Anti-Nazi books?"

"I have Konrad Heiden's book about Hitler, and George Seldes' *Sawdust Cæsar*—that is about Mussolini. I kept them all locked up in my trunk and I thought no one would ever see them."

"Someone is seeing them now, you may be sure, and is drawing conclusions that will do you no good. What else have you in your trunk, besides clothing and the things that ladies usually have?"

"Well, I have a considerable supply of typewriter paper. I use some of that every day."

"How much have you?"

"I am not sure; two dozen reams, I should say."

"You brought that from London?"

"No, I bought it all in Berlin."

"But why so much?"

"It was before I decided to leave. I thought that war was coming, and that paper might grow scarce."

"Imagine that I am the Gestapo, dear lady. You have to satisfy me. You have purchased about twelve thousand sheets of typewriter paper; that would hold three or four million words, which it would take you many years to write."

"You are forgetting carbons."

"Well, then, one million words."

"I am a wasteful writer. I spoil many pages. I make a great many trial copies. The people in the pension know that I write, sometimes all day, and at night. I got what paper I thought I would need." That wasn't the truth, of course, but he had told her to imagine that he was the Gestapo, and it was what she would tell them.

VII

Lanny, driving his car, kept watching in front of him, and behind with the help of his little mirror. He had left the Tiergarten, and was turning street corners frequently, to make sure no car was following. He was avoiding the main boulevards, but keeping a general westward trend, intending to get out of Berlin. His car was conspicuous, on account of its French make and license, and he had an idea that the police would be looking for it soon—for surely the servants and guests at the Pension Baumgartner would mention a Herr Budd as among the callers upon this dangerous *Amerikanerin*.

He couldn't see her; her voice came from behind him, and his voice had to be echoed from the windshield. He knew that she was frightened, and had a right to be. There was no good trying to soothe her. "Let me make it clear to you," he said; "the fact that we don't hold the same ideas has nothing to do with the case, nor does the fact that you have been foolish and refused to take my advice. It was just because I foresaw having to help you that I tried so hard to keep you out of trouble. Now that you are in, I will do what I can. You may count upon my keeping your secrets. When I take you for this ride I become your accomplice, and am in as deeply as you."

"I am ashamed and humiliated, Mr. Budd——"

"Let's not waste time in apologies and regrets. We face a situation, and I have to make sure how bad it is. It won't do any good to hide the facts from me, and then have the Gestapo confront me with them before the day is over. Have you been voicing your anti-Nazi ideas to anybody in the pension?"

"I have tried my best to keep my thoughts to myself. I wanted the people to talk to me freely, which they would not have done if I had made them suspicious. What I said was that I was not interested in politics."

"You did not show them your writings?"

"Only those about America. These pleased them greatly, I found."

"And you didn't take anyone in the pension into your confidence?"

"Not a soul. I didn't know anyone well enough."

"Did you have any persons outside whom you took into your confidence?"

"There is one man—unfortunately I had to promise never to say anything about him. I met him by accident, in a peculiar way which I cannot discuss."

"When people get into trouble there is generally some one person whom they trusted. One is enough for the Gestapo."

"I would be willing to stake my life upon the good faith of this man, Mr. Budd."

"It may be that you have staked your life," was Lanny's not very cheering comment. He had to maintain his role as stern disapprover. "Have you heard anything about this man recently—I mean, where he is, and whether or not the Gestapo may have him in their hands?"

"I have not heard anything from him or about him for several days. I am worried by the fear that he may have got into trouble."

"Have you made an effort to communicate with him?"

"I have never had any address for him. He has telephoned me, at widely separated intervals."

"That all sounds very mysterious, and leaves me in the dark. How can I give you advice on such a basis?"

"I am terribly sorry, Mr. Budd. It so happens that I gave my word of honor, and I have to keep it. I realize clearly to what an extent I am imposing on you, and I am afraid I ought to ask you to set me down somewhere before the police discover us and you become involved in my troubles."

"I have told you that I am already involved, Miss Creston," replied Lanny, still keeping his voice severe. "I am listed among your callers, and that will be enough for the authorities. It all depends upon what they have learned about you—how serious your offenses may have been. If you are known to have been giving aid to the anti-Nazi underground they will not fail to question every person who has ever spoken to you. They will probably have sent out an alarm for this car; but fortunately I left my forwarding address with the hotel as Munich, so they will be looking for me on that highway. I shall be careful to keep away from it."

"Really, I have committed a crime against you. I was in a panic, and completely without judgment. Now I want you to set me down somewhere, and if the police stop you, tell them that you have not seen me, and that your acquaintance with me was of the most casual nature."

"And what will you do when I set you down?"

"I will take a taxi to the American Embassy and ask for their protection."

"I am afraid, my dear lady, I have to advise you against that course. In the first place, it is an act of fear, and the Embassy will take it as an admission of guilt. You must understand that the Embassy has no power to protect you if you have broken German laws; furthermore, you must understand that most Embassy officials have a strong prejudice against what they call 'Reds,' and are always slow to help them. Of course, the fact that you have an uncle who is wealthy and prominent may count."

"Above all things," she exclaimed, "I must not drag my uncle into this!"

"I am afraid you will have to forget that idea, Miss Creston. You are in serious trouble, and will have to use what resources you have. Your uncle's name will mean newspaper publicity, and that may be the one thing that will save you. If you get newspaper space in America, the fact will be at once cabled back to Berlin, and the Gestapo will be much more careful what they do to you."

"Really it makes me quite sick, Mr. Budd, to realize what I have done to you and to others."

"So far," replied the art expert, "you have lived under the protection of American law, and have had a sense of security which makes it hard for you to realize the situation here in Naziland. There is really no law here—just the whims of whatever officials you happen to fall into the hands of. At the present time we have no ambassador in Berlin; we recalled him, apparently in the fond hope that it would make some difference to the Nazis. All it has done is to make them hate us more; and now President Roosevelt has been making speeches, calling them aggressors and whatnot—so you can see that an appeal by the Embassy on your behalf might do you more harm than good."

VIII

Lanny realized that he had got all the information which Laurel Creston had to give him. The gap which she could not fill was: what circumstance or event had brought about the Gestapo raid? Had they caught Monck? Lanny had no idea that the man of the underground would have named his woman helper, but they might have been trailing him and observed his meetings with her. The thought was horrid, and served to make him realize how great the woman's danger might be, and how serious the risk he himself was carrying in his car.

He did his thinking aloud for her benefit. "In the old days there used to be many ways of getting out of Germany. The country must have three thousand miles of border, including the water, and I have heard many stories about refugees and their devices. A peasant would smuggle you across his fields at night, a guide would take you mountain climbing, a ship captain would stow you away, a locomotive engineer would hide you in his cab. But now the armies have been mobilized, at least in part; I was told a couple of weeks ago that there are a million men on the eastern border and as many on the west. So now when you try to get near the border without proper papers you are a spy, and that is worse even than being the author of 'Aryan Journey.' By the way, what about your passport?"

"It was in my trunk in the pension."

"Well, the police will take good care of it. And your money?"

"I have only a few marks in my purse. The rest was locked in the trunk."

"They will take care of that, also. You must not be without some money." Driving with one hand he used the other to take his billfold from his pocket and extract a couple of notes. "Hide those away somewhere," he said, reaching back to her.

She answered: "Thank you. It will be a loan."

"I am afraid of any plan that involves trying to bribe your way out. If you know the right person, it's all right; but groping in the dark, you may find yourself dealing with a Nazi, or blackmailer, or criminal; I would be reluctant indeed to send a delicate woman out at night with a man I knew nothing about. I could not afford to go with you, for reasons of my own."

"I would not ask you to do it, Mr. Budd. I have imposed upon you too much as it is."

"You might swim the river Rhine, at its upper reaches where it is not too wide; but it is cold when it comes out of the mountains, and I don't suppose you are an especially strong swimmer."

"I am not."

"There are many mountain passes where it is possible to get across the border; but you cannot travel in the dark unless you know every foot of the way, and even in daylight you may get lost and fall over a precipice—to say nothing of getting shot if a patrol happens to see you. If you go to one of the ports, you are dealing with a rough class of men, and foreign vessels are pretty closely watched, especially in what is practically wartime. You have to figure that your difficulties are multiplied by ten, just because you chose such an unfortunate time to get into trouble."

"That was why I got in. I am so horrified at the thought of another great war."

"Your feelings are understandable, and do you credit; but sooner or later, as we live in this world, we learn the difference between what is possible and what is not. Every living creature discovers that its survival depends upon the learning of that lesson."

"Evidently I am one of the misfits," she said. He couldn't be sure from her tone whether it was irony or despair, but he guessed the latter.

"We are going to find some way to get you out of Germany," he declared. "Do not be too discouraged when I point out the difficulties. It is a maxim of military men never to underestimate the strength of the enemy; and it is only by knowing the dangers that you can take steps to avoid them. We have to canvass the situation from every point of view and choose the time and place which seem to offer the fewest obstacles."

IX

They were outside the great city of Berlin and its suburbs, driving on country roads where no one was apt to pay attention to them. Lanny kept heading west, because that was toward home, but he wasn't sure that he might not decide on some other direction in the end. He told her that this was his car, and did not offer an explanation as to why he had never invited her to drive in it; she was at liberty to think this might be the first time he had brought it to Germany. He said: "We are reasonably safe so long as we keep moving—that is, unless you are suspected of some really serious crime, so that the police of the entire Reich are combing the roads for you. We can buy food, and eat it as we drive. The thing we can never do is stop at any hotel or lodgings, for they would have to register us with the police."

"You cannot drive forever," argued the woman.

"I can drive for a longer time than you would imagine. I have driven a full day and night now and then, when I wanted to get somewhere, and I could have kept on if I had had to. Do you know how to drive a car?"

"Unfortunately, no. I am the poorest hand with machinery; I could not use a sewing machine without getting the needle through my finger."

"You will be surprised to discover how easy it is to drive a car. On these quiet roads I could teach you all you would need to know in an hour, and then you could roll quietly along for a couple of hours while I got some sleep. That may not be necessary—I am just pointing out that we can take our time and discuss the situation in detail, and not have to worry meanwhile."

"You have time to spend on this sort of holiday?"

"My time has always been my own; and certainly I cannot make better use of it than to help a fellow-countryman out of a predicament. I don't have to share your ideas in order to realize that you got into it through excess of idealism."

"It is kind of you to say that. At the moment, I cannot find any excuse for myself. I would not have called upon you if I had not completely lost my head."

"You chose an opportune moment to lose it," replied the grown-up playboy, with a smile. "In a few seconds more I should have been on my way to Munich—and what would you have done then?"

"I suppose I should have taken a taxi to the American Embassy, and from there called my Uncle Reverdy on the telephone."

Lanny Budd, who had lived among the rich all his life, remarked, with a grin: "You would have been his servant for the rest of your days. You would have had to travel about on the yacht and play bridge, or bézique, or whatever it is."

"Worse than that," replied the woman, with no trace of humor in her voice; "I should have had to promise and write proper respectable sex stories for the women's magazines."

X

They drove all that day, stopping only at a filling station, and at a grocery store in a village where they bought crackers and cheese and fruit. Lanny thought it was safe for his passenger to sit up—she could turn her face away when cars were passing. They drove at moderate speed, because they had no special place to go, and because that was the way not to attract attention. In their minds they made a round of all the borders of Germany; Lanny, who had made scores of crossings since his boyhood, could tell what they would find at this place and that—save only for the dread factor of war. That was getting worse and not better; if war actually began, their problem might become insoluble.

Lanny couldn't afford to know too much about the underground and its devices, but he protected himself by the remark: "In the old days, when the Reds seized power, it was the wealthy and aristocratic who were the refugees, and I heard endless stories of the methods they had used. Some swallowed handfuls of diamonds and pearls before they crossed the border; one of the Russian grand dukes managed to bring out three Rembrandts rolled up together, and he lived on the Riviera for years on the proceeds."

Fresh as yesterday in Lanny's mind was the story of how he had once brought a load of Detazes to Munich in a van, and had attempted to get Freddi Robin out of Germany on the return trip. He couldn't tell that, but he could say: "I have an old friend in Cannes, one of the finest of fellows; he was an army lieutenant in the World War, and he married a French girl and now has a travel bureau while she runs a pension. When wars threaten, the tourist business falls off, so right now Jerry Pendleton will not be busy. I could get him on the telephone and say: 'Take the first plane to Stuttgart,' or whatever city seemed best, and he would be here in a few hours. He knows a lot of travel people, agents and so on, and he might know somebody who would do a smuggling job for a proper price. That would be at the French or the Swiss border. Or he might go back to Cannes and have an exit permit forged for you. I have a genuine one, and he could take it and have another made. You understand that a man in his business has printing done from time to time, and he would know some old-time *poilu* who wouldn't mind playing a trick on *les sales boches*."

"Oh!" exclaimed the woman. "How preposterous that I should be tying you and your friends up in such a string of troubles!"

"It was preposterous that you should have attempted to produce anti-Nazi literature in a Berlin pension. But you did it, and now you are vindicating the poet who said: 'Oh, what a tangled web we weave, when first we practice to deceive!' Here we are in Herr Hitler's empire-sized prison——"

"Mr. Budd, you can't really admire that man!" burst out the passenger in the back seat. Since she was sitting up, Lanny could observe her distressed features in his little mirror.

"As a novelist, you would find him the most fascinating study in the world. Some day I will tell you about him; right now I want to tell about a young friend whose home is on the River Thames. He is probably peacefully punting and reciting what he calls modern poetry at this pleasant twilight hour. He is a flyer, and if I were to get him on the telephone, he would take a plane to any city in Germany. You might easily fall in love with him, for he is a charming idealist who has just been graduated from Maudlin college." Lanny pronounced it that way, and then spelled it "Magdalen," for the benefit of an American who might not understand what bad spellers the English are. "Alfred Pomeroy-Nielson is his name, and he is a bit of a Red like yourself—or maybe it is only a Pink."

"I think that is getting to be my shade."

"Well, Alfy would think it was absolutely delightful to get hold of a flying gnat and drop down into a meadow somewhere just inside the German border and pick up an imperiled damsel of his own political complexion. The only trouble is, this business of war; the border is surely guarded day and night, and an unidentified foreign plane might be shot out of the skies before it got over the North Sea or even afterwards. So perhaps Alfy would prefer to come in a speedboat—among his neighbors on the Thames are several who would bring him, and at a lonely spot on the shore they would come close at night and blink a light, and a Pink lady could wade out, swim a few strokes, perhaps—this is the bathing season, and the water will be fine. You understand, I am just imagining adventures; if we don't make any of them happen, you can use them for stories some day. The trouble about them is the one I've already talked about: if we pick up a paper and read that war has broken out, then we are sunk right there, and you will probably have to sign up for life on the *Oriole!*"

XI

Darkness had fallen, and Lanny said: "It might be a good idea if you would curl up on that seat and get a good sleep."

She answered: "I feel as if I can never sleep again until I am out of Germany."

"I understand your nervousness, but you may need all your faculties by and by. There are psychological exercises to put yourself to sleep."

"You mean counting sheep?"

"I have never been interested in sheep. I discovered that recalling poetry was a good sedative for me—I suppose because I learned to love it while I was young. Sleep comes from the subconscious, and the deeper you go the better. The most lasting impressions are those we got in childhood, and the verses we learned then are those that mean peace and happiness to us. Did you learn to say 'Now I lay me'? If so, say it now, over and over—and not mechanically, or like a modern sophisticate. Be a child, and go to sleep as a child."

"Very interesting," she said; "but let me wait until later in the evening."

They had come to the Teutoburger Wald, which lies in the center of western Germany; a chain of mountains, not high, but densely wooded. They skirted along the foothills, and Lanny said: "There should be ghosts about us tonight, for these are the mountains from which the Teuton hordes poured and destroyed the Roman army under Varus about the time of Christ. You may remember from your school books the cry of the Emperor Augustus: 'Varus, give me back my legions!' I am told that this victory is to be counted as one of the causes of the late World War, and of the next that is coming. The Franks became a latinized and civilized people, whereas the Teutons remained barbarians in their dark forests, and still cherish their belief in the holiness of bloodshed."

The same old Lanny Budd, delivering scholarly discourses, whether it was on the music, art, literature, or history of this old continent on which he had been born!

XII

They came to a glade in the forest, and some distance from the road they saw a fire burning and heard the sound of singing. Lanny stopped the engine and they listened to words of the *Horst Wessel Lied*: "*Die Strasse frei den braunen Bataillonen!*" Lanny said: "This will be an encampment of the *Hitlerjugend*, or perhaps of the *Jungvolk*, the organization of the younger boys. In the summer they go on walking tours and camp in the open. Three or four years ago the Nazis conscripted all children from the age of ten, and they have their semi-military organizations for youth training. These sound like young voices, so probably it is the *Jungvolk*."

"You seem to know everything about them," commented the woman.

"From boyhood I had a friend in Stubendorf who grew up to become one of their high-up officials, and every time I come to Berlin he fills me with more details which I have to get correct or it would deeply hurt his feelings. Fifteen boys constitute a *Jungenschaft;* three of these groups make a *Feldzug,* and three of these a *Fähnlein.* Four *Fähnlein* make a *Stamm,* and five of these a *Jungbann.* That gets you up to about three thousand, and I have to confess that my memory fails me from there up to the millions of the total. It appears that the minds of German children are especially malleable, and my friend is confident that there is not a single one among these millions who is not eager to shed his last drop of blood for the Führer."

Laurel Creston made no comment and Lanny waited until the singing had died away. Then he said: "This may provide us with a solution of the problem of sleep."

"How do you mean?"

"It is a place where we might find lodgings without a police register. At any rate, it can do no harm to try. It will be necessary for you to have another name. Will Miss Jones be satisfactory?"

She assented, and he turned into the narrow lane which led toward the encampment. When they were near, two boys of sixteen or so stepped out of the shadows and held up their hands in warning. Lanny stopped his car and engine and said, politely: *"Zwei amerikanische Gäste wollen Ihr Lager besuchen."* The reply was: *"Bitte warten Sie, mein Herr."*

They sat and listened to another song, until one of the lads returned and said: *"Bitte, kommen Sie mit."* He led them up the road to a place where a couple of other cars were parked, and when they got out he led them to the campfire. A youngish man in uniform met them, and Lanny said: *"Herr Budd und Miss Jones; wir sind amerikanische Touristen."* The man replied, in good English: "It is a pleasure to have you with us," and placed two camp stools for them.

XIII

It was a clearing in the dark forest, with tall, straight fir trees enclosing it like walls. The fire was in the center, and about it on the needle-carpeted ground sat a throng of lads from the ages of ten to sixteen. There were about fifty, so Lanny judged that it was a *Feldzug.* They wore khaki uniforms with knickers and sandals, and bandana handkerchiefs about their necks. Bright eager faces, eyes blue or gray, all turned with curiosity upon the visitors; mouths open, singing *Die Lorelei*—ignorant of the fact that the words had been written by a Jew.

Presently it was *Tannenbaum, O, Tannenbaum,* which would sound like home to "Miss Jones," because its tune had been adopted for *Maryland, My Maryland.*

The leader sat next to the guests; and after an interval Lanny took out his billfold and extracted a precious document which he used for all sorts of diplomatic purposes. It was a clipping from the *Münchner Neueste Nachrichten* of some five years ago, telling about the Detaze exhibition in that city, and recording how the stepson of the famous painter, scion of the American munitions factory, Budd Gunmakers, had taken one of the paintings to the Braune Haus to show it to the Führer, and what the Führer had said about his love of true and worthy French art. The clipping included a portrait of Lanny Budd's unmistakably Aryan features, and he had pasted it carefully upon a thin strip of parchment which could be folded and unfolded without breaking.

No Nazi could resist this magic document; it was at once an *Identifikationskarte* and a *Billet* of admission to the inner shrines of the new religion. He had tried it scores of times, and knew approximately what the reading time was, and at precisely what point the reader would come to the statement that Lanny was an old friend of the Führer, and also of Kurt Meissner, the Komponist, and of Heinrich Jung, the high-up director of the Hitlerjugend. The humble leader of this *Feldzug* sat reading by the light of his little electric torch, and when he came to this place he could no longer retain his excitement. "*Ach, herrlich! Ein persönlicher Freund des Führers!*"

Immediately he wanted to know if Lanny would talk to the boys and tell them about this marvelous friendship. Lanny said it would be a pleasure; so the leader arose and introduced the American gentleman, telling what splendid news he had to communicate. There were cries of eager delight, and when the visitor started talking they sat like so many stone images, some with hands clasped tightly. Fifty pairs of blue and gray eyes were riveted upon Lanny's face, while he told how he had visited Schloss Stubendorf as a boy and had met both Kurt and Heinrich, and how in later years, after the war, Heinrich had told him about the new movement called NSDAP, and how Heinrich had visited the Führer in prison in the fortress of Landsberg.

The narrator went on to tell how he had been taken to meet Herr Hitler in his humble Berlin apartment, and had found him playing with the two children of his housekeeper. After the Führer had taken power it had been Lanny's privilege to visit him many times; he had purchased half a dozen of the paintings of Lanny's stepfather and had put them in the guest house at the Berghof; he had done this, so he said, as a sign of his desire for friendship between France and Germany. Also he had commissioned an American *Kunstsachverständiger* to purchase a couple of works by Defregger, an Austrian painter who had painted the peasants of the Führer's homeland. The American had been a guest for weeks at a time at Berchtesgaden, and told about the life there, including the retreat on the Kehlstein. Lanny knew of only one other foreigner who had ever been taken to that mountain top, and that was the French diplomatic representative, M. François-Poncet.

To these lads a tunnel into a mountainside and an elevator shaft that went up seven hundred feet through solid granite made the most wonderful fairy tale in the world; the structure on the top, with its view of all the Austrian Alps, was heaven, the true Teutonic dwelling place of deity. When the visitor got through with his narrative they sat hushed and awe-stricken; when the leader asked with deference whether Herr Budd would do them the honor to shake hands with each of them, they came forward in a line—no pushing or crowding—and each clicked the heels of his sandals, made a stiff little bow from the waist, and solemnly shook the hand which had shaken the hand of the Führer. Fifty times and a few extra Lanny heard *"Danke schön, Herr Budd,"* and fifty times he bowed and smiled in return.

XIV

The campfire was dying, and it was time to retire. Lanny said: "What a grand spot you have here!" Rows of tents were visible by the waning firelight, and the leader explained that they moved on in the morning and a new *Feldzug* would arrive in the late afternoon. Lanny said: "I wonder if it would be agreeable if we were to camp with you tonight." The suggestion caused a wave of excitement. *Der persönlicher Freund des Führers und seine Dame wollen übernachten!* Two tents? Yes, surely, they had an abundance of tents, for on pleasant nights like this most of the *Kameraden* preferred to spread their blankets on the pine needles.

So the two visitors were escorted to adjoining tents, furnished each with a canvas cot, a blanket, and a little stand with wash basin and pitcher. Soon all was quiet, and Lanny stretched out—but he didn't start saying "Now I lay me"! For hours he lay still, going over in his mind the various mad schemes which he had outlined to Laurel Creston during their drive. In the silence and darkness they seemed madder than ever, and when he got through Lanny was just about ready to pray the Lord his soul to take!

18

Grasp the Nettle

I

AFTER a breakfast of bread and butter and hot cocoa, the *Touristen* were speeded on their way with cheers. They started west; but soon Lanny decided that it was not the part of wisdom to get nearer to the French border, so they swun toward the south. The scenery was varied and beautiful but th y failed to appreciate it; it was German scenery, and they wanted to ook at any other kind of earth. It was the morning of the 22nd of August, and Lanny turned on the radio of his car, keeping it low, and heard the official announcement of the German government that a mission headed by Foreign Minister von Ribbentrop was on the point of flying to Moscow for the purpose of concluding a non-aggression pact with the Soviet Union.

He had known that this was coming, and had found that most of the people of the "great world" with whom he talked had heard the rumors; but the non-Germans hadn't wanted to believe it, so they hadn't, and now even Lanny was shocked when he heard it published to the world. He knew that it meant war—in three days, if the statement of Monck was correct. It was the "green light" for the Nazis to take what they wanted from Poland, and to fight Britain and France if these nations chose to interfere. Lanny explained this to his companion, and they listened to the radio from foreign stations, turning it off when they were passing anyone on the road.

"This will make it very hard for you and me," Lanny said. "Precautions at the border will be doubled, and there will be no planes flying into Germany unchallenged, and no motorboats approaching the shore." The truth was, he was just about in despair as to the next step, but he didn't put it so bluntly to his companion.

"Mr. Budd," she responded, "you have been kind beyond belief, but there is a limit to my right to impose upon you. I think you ought to put me down at the next town and leave me."

"To do what?"

"Go back to Berlin and put myself under the guidance of the Embassy, and take whatever comes to me."

"I am not prepared to do anything like that—not if we have to spend a month rolling about the country camping out with the *Jungvolk*."

"Tell me frankly," persisted the woman. "What were you planning to do if you had not got my call for help?"

"I was going to Munich to attend to some picture business, not especially urgent; then I was going to telephone Rudolf Hess and offer to visit him at Berchtesgaden."

"That is really important to you, is it not?"

"It might be and might not. You saw what I was able to do last night, just by being in position to talk about these powerful persons; and it is so everywhere I go, in Europe and America. Everybody wants to hear about Hitler, Göring, Hess, Schacht—all the Nazi great ones. It is good for a meal in any multimillionaire's home in any capital in the world; incidentally I talk about paintings, and it may happen that people like Mrs. Henry Ford, or her son Edsel, realize that I offer them a chance to purchase paintings without making themselves ridiculous. One thing grows out of another, and nobody can foresee what may be the consequence of a casual conversation."

Lanny had not forgotten that this lady from Baltimore was supposed to be spying upon him, and he thought it might be an act of kindness to put her mind at rest. "You should really understand my position," he continued. "I am a lover of art, of peace and humanity. I state that fact wherever I go, and am accepted on that basis. I travel about as a sort of international errand boy, a messenger of the gods. Herr Hitler says: 'Tell your friends that this is my attitude'—and he goes on to explain how he desires understanding between Germany, France and Britain. When I go to these countries, and men of affairs ask me: 'What does Hitler want?' I reply: 'He has told me to say thus and so.'"

"But does he mean what he says, Mr. Budd?"

"The statesmen invariably ask that, and I answer: 'I am not a psychologist, and I do not read his mind. This is what he said to me, and you may take it for what it is worth.' Then, when I go back to Germany, Hitler and Göring and Hess ask me about this one and that, and I repeat what I have been told. Both sides profess to desire peace above all things, and I do what I can to encourage the idea. At this moment, you can guess that I am not very proud of what I have accomplished. I see myself as a well-meaning but somewhat futile dilettante."

II

They drove for a while, listening to the bewildered comments of the British and French newscasters at the communique from the Wilhelmstrasse. Der Führer had "put one over on them," of that there could be no question. It would take them several days to realize the implications of the act, and perhaps years to observe its consequences.

"There might be something you could do about this in Berchtesgaden!" exclaimed the woman, suddenly. "Tell me about it frankly, I beg you."

He thought for a while: "I will tell you what I had in mind, if you promise to consider it confidential, and take the promise very seriously."

"Indeed, you may count upon that."

"You must understand that right now the Führer and his entourage are making the most important decision of their careers, perhaps the most important in the history of their country. I imagine them in a state of great confusion; statesmen and generals coming and going, and steps being taken which can never be recalled. At such a time, some of them long for supernormal counsel, and Hess is one of these. I was going to offer to bring Madame Zyszynski from Juan, and see what the spirits might have to say about the future of the Fatherland."

"You really mean that he would consider such things in a crisis like this?"

"I can assure you that he takes them with the utmost seriousness."

"And do *you* do the same, by any chance?"

"I should have to deliver quite a discourse on that, dear lady. I was brought up, as you were, to think of such things as superstition and fraud; but I have been reading modern science—you remember what I told you about Jeans and Eddington. There is now a group of the most qualified physicists who tell us that time is not the fixed and absolute thing it seems to us. It is perfectly possible that what has ever been exists always, and that what is going to be has likewise existed always. So I decided to take a new attitude of mind; I am ready to believe anything if I get enough evidence, and I hesitate before I say that anything is impossible. I read a book by an Englishman, J. W. Dunne, who keeps a careful record of his dreams and finds that many of them are prophetic. I haven't had the time to try it, but I am surely not going to say that the statement is absurd."

"Such ideas would turn all my thinking upside down," declared the woman.

"Certainly, and we don't like that; we have resented it all the way from Copernicus and Galileo down to Einstein. As it happens, right now in this crisis I wasn't thinking of psychic research, but rather of international affairs. I have observed that Tecumseh and the other controls whom our elderly Polish medium brings with her are always on the side of peace and humanity. I don't know whether that is because of her nature, or whether my stepfather and I exert some influence on the communications—anyhow, they advise against war, and I had the wild thought that they might say something especially significant, and so have an influence upon Hess and others with whom he is in consultation."

"And you are failing to try it on my account!" exclaimed Laurel Creston. "That is certainly not fair!"

"Do not let it trouble you," he pleaded. "It was a rather crazy idea, and a hundred different things might have kept it from being tried out. It may be too late now, and it may have been too late then—even before you called upon me."

III

Ideas came into Lanny Budd's mind in different ways. Sometimes they came like a flash of lightning, making him start and cry out; sometimes they came in a stately way, a procession with banners and music; sometimes they came stealing quietly, like a little mouse into a room. Lanny was thinking about trance mediums and their strange ways; their personalities, the real ones and those which they brought into being when they lay back and closed their eyes. Madame was a tired old woman, and she had got a fright at the Berghof, and wouldn't like to go back there; she wasn't well, and mightn't be able to travel—certainly not alone. Lanny had been to see Pröfenik, with the idea of using him. He had visited a couple of other mediums that he had heard of, but had got nothing worth while. It would be almost impossible to do anything with any German, because of the political implications, the temptations, the atmosphere of intrigue and terror which surrounded the Führer's mountain retreat. No one who hoped to get anything, or who feared to lose anything from the Nazi *Nummer Eins* or *Nummer Drei*, would be of any use whatever in this situation.

Then came the little mouse idea, stealing into Lanny's mind; poking his tiny nose through a crack and wrinkling it as he smelled. What was the atmosphere in this place like, and should a little mouse take a chance, or should he draw back and scamper into his hole?

The woman spoke first. "I feel more than ever sure that I should not hold you back, Mr. Budd."

Lanny replied: "Wait a minute; I have something in my head."

The car rolled on, and several minutes passed before he spoke again. Then he said: "I have been wondering whether it might not interest you to visit Berchtesgaden."

"You mean the town?"

"I mean Der Berghof, the Führer's home."

"You take my breath away!" she exclaimed.

"You saw what we did last night. That was bold, you thought; but we got away with it. I have more than once acted that way, and got away with it so far. There are some verses about the stinging nettle—I don't recall the exact words, but the idea is that if you take a nettle gently it stings you for your pains, but if you grasp it firmly it remains soft as silk. I think the Nazis are like that."

"You mean that you would take me there as a guest?"

"I would think up a good pretext."

"But—with the Gestapo on my trail?"

"The Gestapo does not trouble the Führer with its problems—and especially not in a time like this. The Gestapo works in the dark, and does not let its left hand know what its right is doing. I should say that the Führer's home is the last place in Germany where it would look for an anti-Nazi writer."

"You would have me go as Laurel Creston?"

"By no means. You are now Miss Jones. Elvirita Jones, let us say. You are from New York, a large and populous city, and I met you on the Riviera."

"But what—what am I doing traveling about Germany with you?"

"I am groping my way toward an idea which I find novel and entertaining, though I must admit it frightens me a bit. Hess is always looking for a new and better medium, and I am wondering if you might not be able to oblige him."

"But, goodness me—I know nothing whatever about the subject!"

"I told you I could teach you to drive a car in an hour or two; I could make a great medium out of you in the time it would take us to drive to Berchtesgaden."

"You mean—a fraudulent one?"

Lanny couldn't help laughing. "Would that trouble your moral sense too greatly?" Then, seriously: "I have always been conscientious about matters having to do with psychic phenomena, seeking the facts and trying to understand them; but this is an entirely different matter

—this would be a ruse to try to help a friend out of grave trouble. Incidentally, you might help mankind by telling Rudi Hess that the spirit of Paul Ludwig Hans von Beneckendorf und von Hindenburg commands him to keep Germany out of war."

"I am terrified at the thought of entering that place, Mr. Budd!"

"You were terrified at the thought of the Gestapo, and you had good right to be. This could certainly not be worse than falling into their hands."

"But I am so ignorant on this subject!"

"Fortunately, I am less so. I have tried hundreds of experiments, and read scores of books. My stepfather, Parsifal Dingle, whom you may have heard of in Juan, has worked tirelessly at the subject for twenty or thirty years, and has filled me with his discoveries. I can tell you what you need to know—and be sure that we shall not approach Berchtesgaden until you can recite your lessons."

"But—how would all this help me to get out of Germany?"

"That part of it is simple. If you have convinced the Deputy Führer, anything you want in Germany will be yours. You can say that your bags have been stolen, your passport lost, and Hess will furnish you with a document that will take you anywhere in the country and let you out at any exit. Also it will be good in peace or in war."

IV

Lanny turned the car in a southeasterly direction, saying: "We might as well drive that way as any other. If we drop the plan, I can turn the steering wheel again."

"Just how does one become a medium?" demanded the passenger.

"Many scientists would be glad to know that. Apparently one does not become, one *is*. A little boy finds that he knows the answer to the arithmetic problem, not because he has worked it out, but because it is in the teacher's mind. A girl knows what her mother is going to say before the mother moves her lips; she knows that the telephone is going to ring, and who is calling. Or maybe a group of people in a mood of curiosity try the experiment of sitting in a dark room and holding hands around a table; there come raps, and the table begins to stir. Perhaps it is someone playing a joke, but again, it may be something which has baffled every scientist who has ever investigated it. Messages may be tapped out, dealing with facts that nobody in the room has ever known; the table may rise in the air, or may start to move with a force difficult to overcome. My stepfather, the most honorable of men, tells me that a group of people tried it in his home back in Iowa, and by the process of eliminating one person after another he made certain that the force came from an old woman who had been a family servant most of her life. She had had no idea of it, and was as astounded as he; the two of them laid their hands flat on the top of the table, with a newspaper under the hands so that they could not have pulled the table sideways if they had wished to. Light made no difference, and he and others could watch and see that there was no contact with the table except the four hands flat upon the paper; yet the table slid around the room with such speed that they could hardly keep up with it."

"Do you expect me to do things like that?"

"Surely not. You wouldn't know how, and I couldn't teach you. You will be a trance medium, and produce spirit communications."

"How do I proceed?"

"Let us take Madame for a model, because I have watched her most frequently. You sit in an easy chair in dim light, lean your head back and close your eyes. You may put a handkerchief over your eyes if you wish. After a minute or two you begin to breathe hard, and presently you sigh and groan as if you were in distress. Then you fall silent, and are in the trance. Nobody knows just what it is; it is like sleep, but different; apparently your consciousness sleeps, but some level of the unconscious is tapped, different from the level of sleep. You speak, but it is not your conscious mind speaking, and after you come out of the trance you have no idea what you have said or what has happened."

"What does happen?"

"You, as a fiction writer, are accustomed to imagining characters, and having them become real, and living their own lives. Apparently the medium does the same thing, in a different way. Something in the subconscious mind of Madame has created a character who calls himself Tecumseh, and says he was an Indian chieftain, but not the one known to history. He has a vivid personality, something which Madame certainly lacks. He asserts that the spirits of dead persons are appearing, and he reports what they look like and what they say; sometimes, when the séance is very successful, these spirits begin to speak for themselves; but that is something you need not attempt."

"And you believe I could carry on such a performance?"

"You have an imagination and a quick wit. You do not have to worry, because the whole affair is in your hands; nobody can keep you in a trance if you don't want to stay, and if you get into a jam you can always break it off. If I press old Tecumseh too hard he gets into a rage with me and tells me to go to the devil and let him alone. He takes offense because I speak of telepathy; he even accuses me of 'thinking telepathy' at him. You would be safe in accusing your sitter of having doubts about you, for there are few who don't, and Hess doubts at the same time that he believes. If you don't know anything more for a spirit to say, simply describe that spirit as fading out, and let some new spirit come, one you will feel safer with."

"Shall I have Tecumseh for my control?"

"By no means. Choose some personality that you know well; anybody, living or dead, whose ideas and manner of speech you understand. Give him any name you please, and let him be of any race or time; an old Negro would be good—something primitive is more impressive than an historical figure."

"It should be a man?"

"The Nazi world is a man's world. A woman medium is enough; to have a woman control, also, would be more than they would find acceptable."

"But I cannot imitate a man's voice."

"The theory is that the control uses the vocal cords of the medium. If the voice sounds like you imitating a man's voice, that suffices. It may be nonsense—I don't undertake to say—but anyhow, that is the way the game is played. This I can tell you, that America's leading psychologist of the last generation, Professor William James, gave many years to studying these phenomena; he discovered a trance medium, Mrs. Piper, a lady of high character against whom no suspicion of fraud was ever directed. Many volumes of reports of the Society for Psychical Research were filled with the records of her séances, and James's conclusion from the whole thing was this: Either you could believe that Mrs. Piper's trance mind was in communication with the minds of deceased persons, or else that it had access to the mind of any and every living person. There is another alternative, of course— you can be completely ignorant of the subject. Most people prefer that way, but it hasn't appealed to me."

V

The car was rolling through the Westerwald; beautiful mountain scenery, and many *Feldzüge* marching and singing; grown-up walking parties, also, sturdy men and rosy-cheeked women with rucksacks on their backs and staffs in their hands. No one paid any attention to the

American motorists, except for a friendly nod. Lanny decided that Germany was big, and the Gestapo not so big after all; he permitted his companion to ride in the seat beside him. When there was no one in sight he rehearsed her in the art of going into a trance and coming out again, and told her how to behave in this emergency and that.

She selected a convincing "control"; in childhood she had known an aged Negro who as a slave had been the bodyservant of her grandfather, Colonel Kennan, throughout the Civil War; had marched with him from the first Manassas to Appomattox, and had told stories of carrying the wounded officer from the field, and sharing with him a dozen grains of parched corn which had constituted a meal in the last days of the Army of Virginia. Laurel remembered this "Uncle Cicero" vividly, and could imitate his speech and his chuckling laughter. "Fine! Fine!" said the son of Budd-Erling. "You make him as real as Tecumseh! The fact that he is ignorant lets you out of anything you don't know, or that seems dangerous."

So much for the control; and now for the spirits. Said Lanny: "Your first sitter will be Rudolf Hess, and he is the one you have to convince. He believes in the idea, but is skeptical as to any new medium—naturally, he is a shining mark for pretenders and frauds. He is an intelligent man, within certain limits; he has good manners and speaks perfect English. He was born in Alexandria, where his father was some sort of merchant. He was in the army, and wounded at Verdun. Later he was fighting the Reds in Munich. Then he met Hitler and became his secretary and adoring follower. He was in the so-called Beerhall Putsch with Hitler, and then in prison, where together they composed *Mein Kampf;* the story is that Hitler talked and Hess wrote. Probably Hess did all the revising, for Hitler was an ignorant man fifteen years ago, and still is, in many ways."

"What will Hess want to hear about?"

"About the attack on Poland which they are planning, and what will be the outcome. But before you approach that you have to convince him that the spirits are there and that they are real. He will be suspicious of anything that is generally known, and especially of anything that he has told me; I will have to think up things that I know about his life and that he doesn't know I know. We had better start with something of his army days, or with the Party battles, for those are the things he is sentimental about. The idea comes to me—Heinrich Jung visited the Führer at Landsberg, and has told me about the place; he never gets tired of talking about that greatest hour of his life, and so I know all the details. Several of those prisoners have since died, and we will select one of them, and his spirit will come, and before he gets through talking Rudi will think he is back in that old castle where he dwelt comfortably for five or six months and helped to prepare the conquest of the world. You will get the atmosphere of glory, you will make him see himself in the pages of history, and he will decide that you are the most wonderful medium ever known."

"I begin to see it as a story, Mr. Budd!"

"One thing before we go any farther. This may break a writer's heart, but you must understand that I am acting to save you from what might be a most painful experience, and not to provide you with literary material. When you get out of Germany you and Mary Morrow may write about any of the experiences you have had by yourself, but not about any that I have to do with. You can see that if you were even to hint at these sacred matters—the Führer, his home and his friends, or anything concerning them—no pseudonym or other device would be of any avail; they would remember the mysterious Miss Elvirita Jones who came from nowhere and vanished again, and they would consider that I had committed one of the worst forms of sacrilege. I might not be permitted to enter Germany again, and certainly the connections I have spent twenty-five years in establishing would be severed."

"I understand your position," replied the budding trance medium. "I will consider that all this is happening in a trance, and when I wake up I won't know about it."

VI

Lanny Budd liked to talk, and here was somebody who had to listen, whether or no. He had given so many tiresome hours to the pursuit of psychic phenomena, and most of his friends regarded the subject as a bore; but this lady from Baltimore had to take it seriously! She had to be prepared for anything that might happen, so he told her of a string of incidents which had happened with Madame, who was to be her model. At the first séance with Zaharoff, not long after the death of the duquesa, there had come spirits of men who blamed him for their suffering and death. It had been more than the munitions king could stand and he had rushed from the room—something very bad for the medium.

Lanny said: "Whatever happens, never forget that you are in a trance, and must never under any circumstances open your eyes during the trance. If your trance is broken violently, you come out of it with groans and other signs of pain. Madame had foam on her lips; a bit of saliva will do, if you blow it. You are ill, you have a headache, and you are entitled to make a fuss, for the sitter has broken the rules. Ordinarily, he sits quietly, and you come out of the trance gently, about as you went in. You ask if the séance was satisfactory, but you do not ask for details. Never under any circumstances will you know what happened."

And so on, and on. It was not pleasant to prepare this elaborate fraud, but then none of Lanny's spying activities had been pleasant to him; they were a part of the war he had declared on the Nazis, and which, by all appearances, was going to last a long while.

He discussed the spirits and their behavior. They were, in disposition, very much as they had been on earth, and were generally vague about how they lived now. They were usually optimistic, and fond of saying that all was well with them. They liked to send messages to loved ones, and the messages as a rule were cheerful—but of course there might be warnings of danger. The spirits made a practice of giving little personal details to identify themselves, and their feelings would be hurt if you did not accept these. Lanny always told Madame's sitters to humor them; now he advised Laurel Creston to humor her sitters.

"At such a time as this," he surmised, "those who come to you are apt to be believers; once you give them the evidence they crave, they will be in your hands. With others, it may be a duel of wits, and you had best play safe. Let your spirits all be German, and Nazis if they have passed over within fifteen years. They must be educated persons, who would have known English in earthly life. Or you can have some other spirit doing the translating—and you don't have to identify that spirit. If Hess brings you a sitter who does not understand English, he will doubtless come along and translate. If you get into difficulty, let Uncle Cicero say that he cannot understand the spirit, who is speaking a foreign language, or speaking badly. Take things easy, and let the old Negro evade troubles with a joke—something he no doubt did in real life."

"All Negroes who live with the white folks learn to do that," said Laurel Creston.

VII

There are many mountains in Germany and they are covered with forests, which in the course of years have been tended and trained, until now the trees are in rows, like soldiers. It is a land of order and discipline, and even the wild things, animal and vegetable, obey the regulations. Lanny said: "The wild stags come to the feeding racks in winter, and they have names assigned to them, and the dates when they are to die are recorded in a book." He added, with a smile: "There may be a book somewhere with your name and mine in it!"

They were on the edges of the Oberwald, and he had begun to drive faster, because the more he thought about the plan, the more practical it seemed. If it was going to be done, the sooner it was done the better, and he had in mind to arrive at the Berghof that night. But he did not say this to his companion. He prepared her mind gradually, telling her how she would arrive and how be treated.

"There will be a great many visitors in this crisis; the most important military men, diplomats, and Party leaders. It would be a strain on you to meet them, and there is no reason why you should. I will tell Rudi that you are shy and easily upset; most mediums are like that, and he knows it. You wish to give a séance to him, and perhaps to one or two others—no more. You will be conducted in by a side door and put in charge of a maid, who will be young and good-looking—none others are tolerated. You will have to reconcile yourself to being searched for weapons."

"Oh, dear me!"

"Even the generals are now deprived of their sidearms when they enter the Führer's home. I myself have never been searched, but that is because he has known me for so long. There are several stories of attempts on his life, and one is never sure what to believe; one story seems to be generally accepted, that a girl of the underground found means to make amorous advances to Hitler, and was admitted to his presence. When they searched her they found a stiletto concealed in her underclothing."

"What happened to her?"

"That is a matter you had best not guess about. You, I take it, do not plan to assassinate him, and need not mind being searched by women. You will have a comfortable room assigned to you, and very good meals will be brought. You must take it as a possibility that your room is wired, and that someone may be listening to every word you speak, even the faintest whisper."

"All this sounds rather grim," commented the lady from Baltimore.

"It need not be. Dictaphones were invented, I believe, in our own country, and if you were playing the Wall Street game, or the political game anywhere, you would not be unaware of the possibility that some secretary or clerk might be selling your secrets. My father could tell you of many such cases."

"One thing that is really embarrassing: am I to arrive at a strange house without even a handbag?"

"That will be an important part of our scheme. I will tell Hess that your bags were stolen from the car, and he will see that you are provided with the necessities. When the time comes for you to leave, I will tell him that your passport was among the lost belongings, and so be in a position to ask him for the necessary papers."

"Truly ingenious!" exclaimed the passenger. "I begin to think you must have had a lot of experience in intrigue!" She said it with a laugh, and he judged that she would not have said it if she still harbored suspicions about him.

"My father is what is called a 'merchant of death,'" he told her, "and has dealt with some of the most powerful rogues in Europe. All through my boyhood and up to recent years, he taught me to watch them and to anticipate their moves. That is why I am not so shocked by the sight of rascality as some of my friends, who come from a younger and more naïve human society."

"America is learning fast, believe you me!"

VIII

Rudolf Hess was to be the amateur medium's shining mark, so Lanny set out to tell all he had learned about this devotee of the Führer. There would be light enough in the séance room for the medium to recognize him, and Lanny described him as a man of athletic build, wearing a simple brownshirt uniform. He had black hair and black eyebrows forming a straight line across his face; his mouth made another straight line and his lower jaw was prominent and firm; he had a heavy scar on his head, where a beermug had been broken over it, in one of the so-called *Saalschlachten*, the beerhall battles of the early days of the NSDAP. He was a fanatical man, but disciplined in his fanaticism; a man stern and grim, feared by his subordinates, but capable of warmth and even of humor among his friends.

"He is the one whom Hitler trusts most completely," explained Lanny; "he resembles one of those German shepherds which are called 'one-man' dogs. Their first meeting was on the western front in the year 1917; Hitler was a despatch rider, and Hess was a lieutenant, conducting transport to the front; we might work up a scene for the spirit of some soldier who had witnessed that meeting under the sound of the guns. Remember the most terrible scenes of battle that you have read —there has never been anything worse than Verdun."

It was quite a biography that Lanny unfolded: the political turmoil in Munich after the war, with Hess shot in the leg in battle with the Reds; then his assignment to kidnap two members of the Bavarian government as a part of the Beerhall Putsch; then his sojourn in the fortress of Landsberg, with Hitler and the other defeated and discouraged revolutionaries. Every now and then Lanny would stop, and hear his friend recite her lessons; then some new details would pop into his head. His happiest thought was of a certain Professor Heinzelmann whom he had met in Munich, and of whose death he had read in a Berlin paper just a few days ago. This old man had been a friend and colleague of Karl Haushofer, the one-time army general who had represented his country in Tokyo, and then had become professor of what he called Geopolitics at the University of Munich. Haushofer was the man who had taught Hitler and Hess their theories about the "Heartland" of Europe and Asia, the new Lebensraum-to-be of the German Reich. Heinzelmann had been in on all this, and was one of the Nazi "old companions."

"Immediately after Hess came out of prison," Lanny explained, "these professors gave him a job as assistant, a sort of clerk. So now Heinzelmann is the proper party to appear in the spirit world and tell Hess to go slow, that the time has not yet come to seize the Heartland! You might have him refer to the fact that Haushofer has a Jewish wife, which is a source of embarrassment to Hitler and all the Nazis. Also, he can mention a Bavarian nobleman, Baron Zinszollern, who sold me some paintings, and who knew both these professors well and talked to me about them. Zinszollern also died recently; so you can have him appear first, and speak about Heinzelmann, and of course Hess will ask for him and Zinszollern will try to get him, and when he comes it will be a triumph, a little drama that will roll Rudi in the aisles. I had lunch with the Baron and no doubt the professor did the same many times, so you have a meeting—we can make up a dialogue between the two that will convince the most skeptical!"

So, as the car rolled along, skirting the edge of the Black Forest, the pair composed a scene which was almost a one-act play. Lanny described the appearance and imitated the manner of a round-headed, round-faced, convivial Bavarian who hated the Prussians, yet, as a German, couldn't help being proud of their achievements. He was in the drawing-room of his palace, which Lanny described in detail, and to him came the elderly professor by the name of Andreas Heimann or

Heisemann— "You mustn't get the name too perfect," said Lanny; "you must never be glib. You grope around——"

"Uncle Cicero gropes around," reminded the other.

"Uncle Cicero complains that he cannot make out these strange names, and has to ask them to talk more slowly so that he can understand them. At first he is afraid to address them at all—they are talking together and may not wish to be interrupted. Hess will say: 'Speak to them.' So gradually you work up to a climax. It will be better if the old Negro makes mistakes, especially in the names—let him grope for them, and Hess correct him. You don't ever have to worry about your own mistakes, because you can always hide behind Uncle Cicero's; and he can always say: 'I can't make out what dey says; dey talks so funny" —anything that comes into your head, provided it is in character, the feeble yet jolly old ex-slave."

"He always complained about the pains in his joints," said Laurel Creston. "I begin to feel as if he and I might really be able to play this role."

"It looks to me as if you will have to," was the reply—"unless you can suggest some better way of getting an exit permit."

IX

It was a long drive and a long conversation; Lanny's voice became slightly husky, and in the back of his neck there was a feeling as if a needle were sticking into it. But he went on driving, eastward in southern Germany, which is the foothills of the Alps, heavily forested and cut by many streams of cold clear greenish water flowing from high glaciers melting in the August sun. The London bus company had advised the public not to worry about Hitler, and apparently somebody had given the Germans the same advice as to Chamberlain and Daladier; there were many picnicking parties in these woods and many walking on the roads; also, of course, soldiers marching, and boys and girls in uniform, and now and then caravans of military equipment. Better to draw up by the roadside and wait while these rolled by; better that a woman who was wanted by the *Polizei* should slide down in her seat and close her eyes and pretend to be asleep.

They stopped and bought food, and ate it while driving—Lanny holding the steering wheel with one hand, and reaching for food with the other. His companion supplied it to him, and found this amusing; he discovered that she was good company—she was beginning to get over her fear, and could even laugh at her plight. She took to talking

"Uncle Cicero," by way of practice; she had been raised among Negro servants and had funny stories to tell about them. In the middle of one she would stop and say: "I am talking too much. Tell me, what next?"

"If you make a success with Rudi, this is what will happen: he will say: 'I would like you to have a séance with one of my friends.' If he asks you to let it be in a completely dark room, and offers to be present so as to translate, you can be sure that the person is Hitler. This will be the most delicate of your tasks, for which you must prepare carefully. The Führer is intensely concerned with the occult powers, but he considers that it would be bad for German morale to know this; his followers must think that he is sufficient unto himself, the repository of all wisdom. You hear rumors that he consults astrologers and fortune-tellers, but very few know whether or not it is true. I promised never to mention that he had sat with Madame, so you must consider this one of the things to forget."

"I have forgotten."

"You have perhaps heard the Führer's voice over the radio, but you will hardly recognize it, for he converses quietly, even genially, and is not apt to become excited at your séance. At his first attempt with Madame he became quite wild, but that was because Tecumseh reminded him of a tragedy, the death of his niece Geli Raubal, for which he is believed to be responsible. But you must tell him only friendly and pleasant things and remind him that the world sits at his feet. The spirits can never say too much in his honor; all the spirit world, both German and foreign, rings with the glory of this great man who is making Europe over according to his vision."

"I want to tell him not to go to war!" exclaimed the woman.

"We shall come to that, but first you must have the background of his character: the spoiled darling of a young mother married to a dull and domineering old man, a petty customs official who tried to manage his home in the fashion of a drill sergeant. Little Adi Hitler, whose father changed his name from Schicklgruber, hated the old man and had a wretchedly unhappy childhood; he wanted to become an artist, but got no encouragement and no training. After his mother's death he became a wastrel in Vienna, sleeping in the public refuge for the shelterless and earning a few pfennigs by painting feeble landscapes on postcards.

"The war came," continued the narrator, "and he seems to have been a faithful soldier; but it must have been a shattering experience for one of his excitable temperament. He genuinely believes his own legend, that the army was never defeated, but was betrayed by the vile Reds on the home front. He came to Munich, destitute and at loose ends, and became a police agent, spying upon the workers in that city. You won't say anything about that period in his life, but you should understand the conditions he found in Munich, with half a dozen civil wars going on at once, and such political confusion that the historians have never been able to straighten it out. The ideas that dominated Adi's mind were patriotism, which called itself Nationalism, and anti-Semitism —since many of the Red leaders were Jews. In Munich the leader of the Communists who seized power was Kurt Eisner, an idealistic Jewish professor who wore a long unkempt gray beard, a long overcoat and a big black hat which made him look grotesque. Vengeance on these Bolshevists, and on all Germany's enemies, inside and out, became Adi's one thought, and will remain his thought to the day he dies."

"I cannot pretend to a desire to meet such a man, Mr. Budd."

"You don't need to worry; you only have to remember that deep within him he is still the frightened, lonely, thwarted child. Right now he confronts the climax of his life; he has to make a choice between two roads, one of which will lead him to eternal glory and the other to the abyss of ruin; he cannot be sure which road is which, and he would give anything in the world to have some old Teutonic god come down from Walhalla on a rainbow and tell him what to do. Barring that, he would prefer the spirit of the grim old Hindenburg, or better still, of Bismarck, founder of the first German Reich. I am afraid you had better not attempt either of those; but I will tell you of one of Hitler's earliest Munich comrades whom I happen to know about—and not through Hitler himself, or through Hess."

X

The audience of one wanted to know how in the world Lanny had got all this information, and he told her about a trip he had taken just a year ago, a raft excursion down the river Isar which runs through Munich. The host had been Adolf Wagner, one-legged political boss of Bavaria, and known as the "Führer voice," because he could imitate Adolf Hitler so well that he sometimes took his master's place on the radio. On that trip were several of the Munich old companions, and nothing pleased them so much as to tell an American visitor about the glorious old days, and the part they had played in them. "They spoke of some who had died," said Lanny, "and in your séances their spirits can mention the living and send them greetings. I can give you some names in both worlds—but above all things be careful not to mix them up!"

The narrator went on to tell about the so-called Thule Society—pronouncing it German-fashion, Toola, and then spelling it so that she would be sure to get it straight. Thule was a legendary place from which the German race was supposed to have come in the far north. In Munich in 1919 a few war-shattered Nationalists and Jew-baiters who had cultural aspirations had got together and called themselves by that name. Hess was one of them, and another was the man Lanny had in mind for Laurel Creston to use—an elderly Munich actor by the name of Dietrich Eckart.

"He was a drunkard and drug addict, and had been in an asylum; but he was also a poet and a fiery orator, and to a despatch rider fresh out of the trenches he seemed at once elegant and inspired. His statue, with wreaths, adorns the Braune Haus in Munich—a large, benevolent-looking Aryan god with an immense round head, a bulging forehead, and surprisingly small eyes. He wore tortoise-shell glasses for reading, and when he looked at you he lifted them up onto his forehead. He spoke with an immense rumbling bass voice—all that is important for Uncle Cicero, and Hitler would find it irresistible. Der Führer had to change his mind about many of those old companions, but there was no chance for disillusionment in the case of Eckart, for he died just after the Beerhall Putsch, at the end of 1923. That was before Adi's trial and sentence to prison, and the old hero can tell Cicero how he was present in spirit at the trial and in the fortress."

"Would Hitler accept political advice from such a figure?"

"I see that you are bent on giving him advice," said Lanny, with a smile. "He would think of him as a prophet and a seer; and the spirit could claim to be in touch with others of the great, and report what they said. But you must bear this in mind—Hitler had me listed among the 'appeasers,' and if you say too much about keeping out of war, he might become suspicious. It would be the part of wisdom to think first about getting yourself out of this predicament."

"I'll be guided by circumstances," replied the lady, who had a mind of her own.

XI

Shortly before sunset they were approaching the city of Ulm, which is on the upper reaches of the Danube River, and has an immense cathedral, also an art gallery; but they were not going to look at either.

Lanny said: "I believe you can do this stunt," and she answered: "I am willing to try." He said: "All right, I will telephone to the Berghof, and you can start in tonight."

"Won't we get there too late?"

"The Führer is a bad sleeper, and stays up until all hours. An appointment for midnight would be nothing unusual for him. You had better get into the back seat now and lie down and pretend to be asleep. You can recite your lessons to yourself."

He drove into the town and parked not far from a hotel where he could get a telephone booth. He had been favored with the number of the Führer's retreat, and after a couple of minutes he heard the Deputy's deep-toned voice. "Is that you, Lanny?"

"Hello, Rudi!" exclaimed the caller. "I have a find for you; a medium, a real one—the best ever, I believe."

"Oh, good!" exclaimed the other. "Where are you?"

"I am at Ulm, on a motoring trip. This is a young lady whom I met on the Riviera, and I have sort of kidnaped her, because I thought you and your friend would like to have her services at this critical moment. She has foretold the future for my mother and half a dozen of her friends, and we have never seen anything like it. I have explained to her that the affair must be confidential."

"How soon can you come?"

"I can get there between twenty-two and twenty-three o'clock, and you can have a sitting tonight if you wish."

"Splendid! I will expect you."

"Let me explain, Rudi. This Miss Elvirita Jones is a delicate person and easily upset; her work depends upon her state of mind, and she does not want to meet a crowd of people. Let me suggest that you have someone meet us at the gate, and bring her in by a side door, and straight to her room, where she can rest and freshen up. Meantime, I'll come in by the front door, and nobody need know that I have a lady with me."

"Right you are!" said the Deputy.

"You are sure we won't be in anybody's way?"

"Quite the contrary—we have all been longing for just what you have. Come ahead!"

XII

The die was cast, and Lanny drove straight toward Munich. It would be dark before he got there, and he wouldn't have to worry. He was above even the Gestapo now; if any officer were to stop him he would say: "I have an appointment with Reichsminister Hess at the Berghof." If the man would not believe him, he would say: "Come with me to the nearest telephone and call Herr Hess yourself." Grasping the nettle!

To his companion: "Now, recite your lessons. Let me hear what Uncle Cicero has to say about Baron von Zinszollern and Professor Heinzelmann." And then Dietrich Eckart. He corrected one or two errors. Seeing that she was nervous, he told her: "Remember, you don't have to be the greatest medium in the world. It will be nice if you justify my estimate of you, but if you fail, it will not be a crime. I should guess that nine-tenths of the séances I have attended have been fizzles. There are a hundred reasons—you are in a strange environment and are overanxious, the weather is not right, you have a headache—or just that the spirits are not in the mood, and you don't have to know why."

"You are being kind to me," said the woman.

"I am reminding you that our purpose is to get you an exit permit, and if you fail, they will be the more willing to part with you quickly. So take it easy, and remember how many ways there are to cover up a slip. You misunderstood what the old Negro said, or he misunderstood a German trying to speak English. If you realize that you have presented the spirit of a man who is still among the living, you say that it is his great-grandfather of the same name, and it will take some time to check that. Do not let yourself be pinned down on anything dubious; Uncle Cicero can only know what the spirit tells him, and the spirit can fall dumb, he can be angry, or weeping, or perverse—or he can just fail in his mind."

The teacher heard his pupil recite the details of life in the fortress of Landsberg-am-Lech, where Hitler had dictated volume one of *Mein Kampf* to Hess. That was the scene most apt to impress and convince the Deputy. They would create an imaginary guard by the name of Fritz; there was bound to have been one in the prison. He would say: "You wouldn't remember me, but I was there; I saw it." His efforts at English would be bad, and he would call in another spirit to translate for him. He would remark: "I come back to the room in the fortress now and then, but I find that people see me, and it frightens them." Lanny chuckled: "We may start a ghost story in the old fortress!"

XIII

They came to the city of Munich after dark, and drove through it at proper speed, obeying all the traffic lights. Nobody paid any attention to them, and when they were out in the country again, Lanny thought it safe to stop and let his friend resume her place at his side. He turned on the radio softly, and they listened to a commentator in Munich, explaining the significance of the proposed friendship agreement with the Soviet Union. The decadent French and the perfidious British had been seeking to lure Russia by promises which they were in no position to keep and had no thought of keeping; the Führer, who always kept his word, had stepped in ahead of them. The French and British purpose had been to draw Russia into war with Germany; but the Führer, who wanted only peace, had thwarted that treacherous scheme, and now it was no longer conceivable that the stubborn Poles should resist his demand for German territory to be returned to the Reich.

"You see, they are preparing the public for war," remarked Lanny.

"Oh, God, oh, God!" exclaimed the woman. "Let me get out before it comes!"

"I have been told on good authority that the time is three days off. But the Führer often changes his mind, and he might do it again—especially if *der alte Herr*, as he called Hindenburg, were to advise it."

"Radio München," said the voice; and Lanny reflected how the name of that once genial and happy city had for all time and in all languages come to stand for cowardly diplomacy and base betrayal. Would he, the presidential agent, be doing another "Munich" if he took Laurel Creston to the Berghof and helped her to unsettle the Führer's mind? No, he told himself. "Munich" had consisted in the unsettling of the minds of Chamberlain and Daladier; there could never be any harm in causing a madman to desist from his crime.

A shift of the dial, and there was a newscaster in Zurich, speculating on the hour when the German mission was to fly to Moscow. "So it hasn't left yet!" exclaimed Lanny. "We may be in time!" He said it lightly, for that was his role. A woman, face to face with a second World War, might shudder and weep; but an ivory-tower art lover would stay in his retreat and refuse to let his serenity be disturbed for a moment. Except, of course, to get a lady out of trouble!

Said this lady: "An embarrassing question, Mr. Budd. What are our hosts going to think about my traveling around Germany alone with so charming a personage?"

"I am afraid," he replied, "that Miss Elvirita Jones may be somewhat compromised; but let us hope that Miss Laurel Creston will manage to escape."

XIV

The road began to climb, and presently they saw the lights of the village of Berchtesgaden, once the haunt of the wild witch Berchta. There were streams and little lakes, and many camping parties, which they would not visit now. The road wound this way and that, and the lights of the car swung over slopes covered with dark evergreen trees. Poignant memories were brought back to the son of Budd-Erling. On just such a night four years ago he had driven over this road with two women in his car instead of one. At his side had sat Irma Barnes, his wife, and in the rear seat Trudi Schultz, his wife-to-be—though he had had no idea of it at the time. He had been engaged in smuggling Trudi out of Germany, and now he was engaged in smuggling another—both by the means of a visit to the Führer. Certainly he had never expected to repeat that dangerous enterprise!

He called his passenger's attention to a revolving light on the mountain side, sweeping over the landscape. "That is our destination," he said. "A well-guarded fortress, you will discover."

The village of Berchtesgaden was full of tourists at this time of year; it had a fine hotel, where visitors to the Berghof stopped—those who were not important enough to be put up by the Führer. Mountain climbers came, and set out with staffs and ropes; others, less ambitious, sat on rocky shelves and watched with glasses. If sometimes they turned these glasses in the direction of the Führer's retreat, that was not yet an offense, but might soon become so.

Onward and upward, to the entrance of the private road to the Berghof. Here was a barrier with blue-and-white-painted stripes, and armed SS men in the black and silver uniform of the Führer's personal guard. As the car halted, one of them flashed a torch into Lanny's face; Lanny extended his right arm and said: "*Heil Hitler!*" and the Nazis returned the salute. The visitor gave his name, and the name of his companion; the men had received notice, and all they did was to flash their torches into the car and make sure there were no other passengers. Then: "*Alles in Ordnung, Herr Budd.*" The barrier rose, and he drove on.

The road wound along the side of the Obersalzberg, close to the old Austrian border, now a border no longer. "A wonderful job of road building," commented Lanny. "It is the work of the Führer's engineer, General Todt." There were sentries along the way, but none challenged them until they were approaching the house. Here was another barrier, and the formalities were repeated. When they reached the wide drive in front of the house, they observed a sentry with a high-powered rifle pacing up and down; also a machine gun on a tripod, with two SS men beside it. A man came toward them, clad in one of the old brownshirt uniforms, the same kind that Hess wore. He was one of the Deputy's secretaries, and knew the visitor well. They exchanged their *Heils*, and Lanny introduced "Miss Jones." No one ever entered the Führer's home without being thus inspected and identified.

The secretary indicated the door to which Lanny was to drive—for what was once a modest mountain châlet had been added onto until it was like a row of houses. Lanny explained the embarrassing circumstance about Miss Jones's baggage having been missed—being careful to add that they had only just discovered the theft and had no idea where it had occurred. They surely didn't want the efficient police being notified and set to searching! "The housekeeper will take care of Miss Jones's wants," promised the secretary; and the new-born spiritualist medium stepped silently out of the car and disappeared inside the ogre's den.

19

Double-Dyed Deceiver

I

THE main reception room of the Berghof is large and square, paneled in dark wood and with beams in the ceiling intersecting to form squares. The floor at the far end is raised, and there is a great fireplace with lounges in front. The lighting is from clusters of bulbs in the ceiling, and there are many paintings on the walls—Lanny Budd's Defreggers among them.

This time, as the art expert entered, he saw more people in the room than on any previous occasion; in fact, the place appeared like a hotel lobby. They were all men, the greater number in uniform. Here and there he caught a familiar face, but many were strangers to him, and he imagined that they gazed at him with no welcome in their eyes. In time of danger men draw together and become clannish. "Who is this foreigner," they ask, "and what is he doing in our midst?" Evidently he was to spend the night, for a servant followed him with two bags.

In the company was a young physician of the Führer's staff, and he came forward to greet the visitor. Presently came the secretary to report that Miss Jones had been made comfortable, and that Reichsminister Hess was in conference with the Führer; he would be down shortly. Lanny seated himself and listened to the conversation of the doctor and two of the Führer's aides, who were discussing the orders soon to be issued for the rationing of foods throughout the Reich, and whether or not the *Herrenvolk* could be expected to thrive upon only seven hundred grams of meat per week, a little less than a quarter of a pound per day.

Hess came, and shook hands with his guest; his grip was firm and his hand had black hairs on the back. His manner was especially cordial, as if to say to the assembled staff officers and officials: "This son of Budd-Erling is all right." Then he took Lanny up to his room and shut the door. "Now, tell me about this medium."

"She is from New York," Lanny replied, "and was visiting on the Riviera. I heard reports of her powers, and after I had tried her I decided that you ought to see her at once. I won't stop to tell you what she did—you will see for yourself—that is, unless she has been upset by the journey. She is a woman of refinement and should receive every consideration."

"She knows what this place is?"

"I couldn't have persuaded her otherwise. Also, I had to tell her that you would be the first sitter. But she knows very little about you—only as much as an American would have read in the papers. Her control is an old Negro, an ex-slave whom she knew when she was a child. You know how it is—you have to pretend to believe in him, and be polite and encourage him to talk; then wait quietly until he is gone and the medium comes out of her trance. The séance need not be in complete darkness."

"All right. She sent word that she is ready. The Führer wants to see you meanwhile. You understand that he is tired and nervous—he has been holding conferences all day. The mission to Moscow flies in the morning, and he has just been giving his final instructions over the telephone. Also, we have just had word that Sir Nevile Henderson has a letter from Chamberlain which he wishes to deliver personally to the Führer. He is flying here tomorrow morning."

"I can imagine the tension," said the sympathetic visitor.

"It will be the same old story: the British will not admit our right to deal with Poland in our own way; and the Führer's mind is absolutely made up, we are going to deal with them in no other way. If I were you I wouldn't try to dissuade him, Lanny."

"Heavens, no! I'm not sure that I'd want to; and anyhow, it is not the role for an art expert."

II

The Deputy escorted the visitor to that unforgettable front room on the second story, having what was called the largest window in the world, and certainly looking out upon one of the largest views in the world. But not at the hour of midnight; the heavy velvet curtains were drawn, and the commonplace-looking man for whom the window had been built was not thinking about his beloved forests and mountains, with their legends of witches and gnomes and giants, their *Feuerzauber* and *Waldweben* and *Walkürenritt*. No, he was thinking about men, inside and outside of Germany, and their perverse determination to have their own way instead of following the intuitions of an inspired and predestined world leader.

He jumped up from his chair to greet his visitor, and shook hands more vigorously than was normal. "*Willkommen, Herr Budd, Ihr Besuch freut mich.*" He was dressed in an ordinary business suit of the color called dark pinhead worsted. With his funny little dark mustache and slightly bulbous nose he was certainly ill-equipped to be a leader of men, and there was no one of those downstairs who could not have played the role more acceptably.

To Hess he said: "Go on, Rudi, and see the woman, and tell us about it." As the Deputy strode out of the room he remarked to Lanny: "Ordinarily I am curious about such matters; but in a time like this I cannot stop for experiments. I have to follow my own inner light. When I have trusted to it, I have never gone astray; only when I let others argue with me and fill me with doubts and fears."

Adi's complexion had always been pasty, ever since Lanny Budd had first known him; now it was quite gray, and his face had deep lines of fatigue. He signed the visitor to a chair, but instead of seating himself he began to pace the floor, snapping his fingers and talking fast, pouring out his irritation with military men who insisted upon saying "if" and "but" and other qualifying words. Then he came and sat down in front of Lanny, still talking as if to convince himself; now and then he slapped his thighs to emphasize his words—another of his favorite tricks.

There was just one thing he had to make up his mind about, and that was: would Britain and France fight? That was the million-dollar question, the billion-dollar question—you would need astronomical figures to evaluate it. The Führer had the answer in his own mind and considered that he had proved it in six different tests: when he had moved his troops into the Rhineland; when he had enlarged the Reichswehr beyond the hundred thousand permitted by the Versailles *Diktat;* when he had resumed conscription in Germany; when he had taken Austria; when he had taken the Sudetenland; when he had taken Prague. Every time Britain and France had threatened to fight, and every time the generals and the diplomatic staff had said they would, but they didn't. And now, only one time more, Danzig and the Corridor; or maybe two times, for he had just announced that he must have Posen and the lost parts of Silesia; and there might possibly be a third, if the insane Poles should refuse to behave themselves and he would have to take Warsaw to keep them in order.

III

It is not permitted to interrupt a ruler so long as he wishes to talk; and Lanny was satisfied to leave it that way. But at last the Führer stood in front of him and demanded: "What do you have to tell me, Herr Budd? What will they do?"

"*Mein Führer,*" said Lanny—for in a burst of enthusiasm he had enrolled himself—"I don't believe that any man living can answer that question, and I would say, be careful of any person who claims to answer it. Neither Britain nor France is one nation, but a clash of warring factions. The decision will be taken in the last few hours, and only in the face of the latest events. I can tell you what some of the leaders of the factions say——"

"Tell me what is really in Chamberlain's mind!"

"I talked with one of his close friends a couple of weeks ago. He would sacrifice his right hand to avoid war with Germany——"

"Then why did he order conscription in Britain?"

"I do not think he would have done it of his own choice. He is the head of a party, and the pressure on him becomes more than he can resist. If you make a move, he is forced to make a counter-move."

"Germany has no aims against Britain; but Britain persists in the policy of encirclement of Germany. What else can be the meaning of an alliance with a semi-civilized state like Poland? They talk peace, but all their actions are war. By God, I have made up my mind that nobody is going to compel me to spend any more time arguing about Polish customs officials in Danzig!"

"*Dann, mein Führer*," said the son of Budd-Erling, with one of his genial smiles, "in that case I will go and purchase that property in what they call their Corridor."

Adi smiled in return, but only for a flash. His compulsions drove him, and right now the dread Four Horsemen had snatched him up and were galloping with him. "Wait until you see what happens in the next few days. You may find that the wretched Poles have compelled me to burn that house and to lay the whole district waste." Then, coming like a cry of pain: "Does anybody imagine that I *want* war? That I *like* war? I am a builder; I wanted to be an architect, and I assure you that the form of relaxation I enjoy most in this world is to design great buildings and see them arise. So far I have never destroyed a building, except for clearance purposes. If ever I am forced to do it, my heart will ache for each and every stone."

Lanny was thinking: "Madrid—Guernica—Barcelona—Valencia!" But he kept those names locked tight in his mind, and was glad that Adi didn't possess the gift of "that old telepathy"!

"But since they force war upon me—since they are determined to have it—what can I do? I said to Henderson, a few days ago: 'If I have to fight a war, I would rather do it when I am fifty than when I am fifty-five or sixty.' By the way, explain that pious and correct dullard to me—if it can be done."

Lanny said: "I have only met him casually, and do not claim to know him well; but I know his type. The upper-class Englishman is taught that it is his destiny to govern; he is taught that idea from the time he is able to understand words, and as a rule no other idea ever takes root in his consciousness. He is taught that he must govern well and honestly; and whenever his interests require that he do a certain thing, he must not fail to find moral reasons for the action. Other people may not be satisfied with those reasons, and that is what has given rise to the idea that the English are hypocritical."

That caused the Führer of the Germans to recall how Clive and Hastings had taken India. They had found moral reasons for that; and even though the rest of the world was not satisfied, India was kept. Evidently Adi had found some time for reading history; or perhaps

somebody had been supplying him with data, prior to the arrival of
the British ambassador in the morning!

The Führer wanted to know about quite a string of Englishmen.
Lord Beaverbrook, for example; he had been such an ardent friend of
Germany, and now he seemed to be growing lukewarm. Lanny told
what he had said on the Riviera. And then Lothian; he, too, seemed
to be weakening in his sympathies. Lanny explained that this noble
lord was a Christian Scientist, and therefore his brand of pacifism was
different from the Nazis'. And then the Frenchmen. Who was it that
had forced the expulsion of Abetz, and did the French not realize that
it was practically an act of war? What did Daladier have to do with
it, and more important, what part had Madame de Crussol played?
And Reynaud and his noble lady, Madame de Portes—these damned
aristocratic whores had too much to say about politics, and it was one
of the signs of the disintegration of France. Lanny had no difficulty in
agreeing.

IV

All this time there were two Lanny Budds; one a suave discourser
on international intrigue, and the other a shivering wretch, thinking:
"The séance is lasting a long time, and what does it mean?" Picturing
Rudolf Hess coming in—or perhaps Heinrich Himmler, who could
say?—announcing: "We have learned that this woman whom Herr
Budd has brought into your home is a notorious anti-Nazi criminal!"
Or perhaps, not quite so bad, but bad enough: "This woman is a com-
plete fraud, whose spirits do not know that Adolf Wagner and Karl
Haushofer are living!" Really, it was enough to produce a case of
schizophrenia, a personality split as if with an ax.

But no, the program had been well planned, and the surprises were
of a different sort. The Deputy Führer came in, striding fast, but not
forgetting his manners, waiting until his great master asked the question: "*Also, was gibt's?*" Adi addressed his former secretary in that
brotherly fashion, and Rudi was the only man Lanny had ever heard
address the Führer with the familiar "*Du.*"

"*Merkwürdig!*" exclaimed the other. "Herr Budd is right, this
woman really has the gift."

"Well, tell us about it."

Rudi began, speaking German for his Führer's benefit. "There came
a spirit who called himself Fritz; he said he had been one of the guards
at Landsberg. He thought I wouldn't remember him, but as a matter of

fact before he got through I did begin to recall him. Lanny, are you sure you never told Miss Jones about Landsberg?"

"I was most careful," Lanny replied. "I wanted this to be a real test, for me as well as for you."

"It was extremely curious. The control is an old Negro, an ex-slave from Virginia who was called Uncle Cicero. They gave them names like that, I suppose in a sort of mischief. He doesn't know any German, and Fritz was trying to speak to him in English that he said was bad. Then Fritz had to get another spirit to translate for him, so it all went rather slowly. The man described the room in which we worked, and the desk at which I sat, and how the Führer behaved and how I behaved—it was really quite striking. Some of the details were not of the sort one would expect—I know that when I was sentenced to a fortress, I thought I would be put in a cell and I certainly didn't expect a bright sunny room with a good bed in it. Fritz said he had brought us our food several times when the regular wardens were away. He told what he had brought, and what you had said and what I had said—it was really quite uncanny, hearing that from the lips of a woman who had come from New York. Quite a good-looking woman, incidentally. What is she like in her own personality?"

This to Lanny; but the Führer commanded: "Stick to your spirits. What else?"

"One very curious thing: he said he had come back to those corridors several times; but he had been seen, and it had frightened people, so perhaps it would be better if he did not come any more. I told him to come, and I would have a watch kept, and if he were seen it would be reported to me."

"Did he mention any other people?"

"He said he knew Eberhardt, and Reinach, but they did not appear. I asked him to bring some other Germans to talk to me, and presently he said there was a dignified old gentleman, whom he described in detail. The old gentleman said he was Baron von Zinszollern, and he talked to the control—his English was better, and I could notice the difference, even through the voice of the old Negro. Did you know Zinszollern in Munich?"

"I may have met him casually," replied the Führer. "He took no interest in politics, and was stingy with his money—or possibly he didn't have as much as he led people to think."

"He talked convincingly, and I questioned him about some of our friends. I named Professor Heinzelmann, and that was a fortunate thought; he said that he saw a great deal of Heinzelmann and would try to produce him, and then he did. I believe it was the most convincing thing I ever experienced in a séance. Uncle Cicero described Heinzelmann to the very life; and those two old men carried on quite a conversation. They had been friends in Munich, and they talked about dinners in Zinszollern's palace—I have never been in it, but I met him, I think at the opening of the Künstlerhaus, and I remember him very well. They argued a while about Haushofer and his ideas, and nothing could have been more lifelike."

"I would be interested," said the Führer, rather impatiently, "provided the Professor had had something to say about the present state of Europe."

"He did," replied Hess. "I said to the Negro: 'Tell him that Rudolf Hess is here, and has he any advice to give him?' The reply was that Heinzelmann was following events closely, and that it was better to take half a step forward and remain there than to take a long step forward and then have to take two backwards."

"More of those damned peace-lovers—*diese verdammten Friedensprediger!*" grumbled the Führer.

"I said: 'Ask him if Britain and France will fight.' The answer was 'They will all fight many times.' That wasn't very satisfactory, and it didn't sound at all like Heinzelmann, who was so direct and even abrupt. I asked for something more definite, but the old bore, Zinszollern, butted in, and asked if he remembered the paintings he had. They talked for a while and I didn't interrupt, because it is not advisable to try to force the spirits—it annoys them and spoils the séance. Those two voices faded away and that was the end of that act."

"Hardly worth the time it took," was the Führer's verdict.

V

However, there was another, and Hess assured them that it would be worth hearing. There had been a long wait, and he had heard the young woman breathing hard, and had thought she was coming out of her trance. "But then came a new voice, sounding like a man's but not the old Negro's. It said: 'Who are you?' in English, and repeated the question. I said: 'I am Rudolf Hess,' and the voice said: 'The Nazi?' I answered: 'Yes, and who are you?' The reply was: 'I am Sir Basil Zaharoff.' I said: 'The munitions manufacturer?' and he replied: 'The same.'"

"*Scheissdreck!*" exclaimed the Führer. "What did that old *Mischling* want?"

"That's what I wondered. I said: 'You are no great friend of ours.' He answered: 'Better than you think. You would be surprised if you knew all that I had done for you.' And he went on to tell me that he was a friend of peace. I didn't argue with him, for I was afraid it might break things up. You knew him well, didn't you, Lanny?"

"I doubt if anybody ever knew him really well. He was the most secretive of men. I only saw his reserve broken down twice in some twenty-three years that I knew him."

"Tell me, did you talk to this Miss Jones about him?"

"I mentioned him once or twice, in connection with psychic matters. I told how he had come to haunt my séance and make a nuisance of himself. Did he say anything about his dead wife, the duquesa?"

"He didn't mention her; he was busy defending himself."

"That has been one of his bad habits, ever since he entered the spirit world. In his life he must have brooded over the fact that the world hated and feared him, but he did nothing to remedy it. Now, when it is too late, he seems to want to be loved."

"He said that he had provided the nations with the means of defense, never of offense. I wanted to say: 'Nice polite little tanks!'—but of course I didn't. He said: 'I believed in the balance of power in Europe, and that it could be preserved by means of the open market for arms. I sold to anyone who had the price—it was a point of honor to me.' I remember those words," added the Deputy. "I wanted to laugh out loud."

"I have heard him say it a hundred times," replied Lanny. "My father used to say the same, when he was European representative of Budd Gunmakers. He picked up Bernard Shaw's saying about the 'Creed of the Armorer.'" To himself Lanny was thinking: "What the devil did Laurel Creston want to bring in Zaharoff for?" He decided that she must have been afraid of something, and trying to divert the conversation.

"It was an astonishingly realistic thing," continued Hess. "You wouldn't think that you could mistake a slight frail woman's voice for a man's, but I really got the impression that I was listening to that old hyena, dressing himself up in sheep's clothing. He said: 'You have no idea how I labored to protect all Europe during the World War. I disapproved of the airplane; it is a murderous and dreadful weapon; it will destroy the cities that I love, and I did everything in my power to save them. You owe it to me that the agreement was made against the bombing of the Briey Basin and the great plants there. And think what it would have meant to you if the industrial power of America had been turned to the making of bombing planes! They spent more than a billion dollars for that purpose, but they never succeeded in getting a single military plane into action in the war. Do you imagine that that was an accident?'

"I answered that I had always supposed it was American 'graft,' which is what they call their wholesale stealing. But the old rascal said: 'What would you say if I told you that I had my agents all over the country, and that I controlled the men who got those contracts and failed to carry them out?' Did you ever hear anything like that, Lanny?"

"I have heard hints of it, but Sir Basil never admitted anything to me. I will ask my father about it."

"All that is ancient history," broke in the impatient Führer. "We have new history to make now."

"*Hör' mal nun*," replied Rudi, unembarrassed. "I have something that will interest you."

VI

So came what the narrator described as the third act of this drama. "A new figure entered, speaking in his own voice, one that seemed to carry a smile. He said: 'You old rogue!' I realized that it was another man breaking into the séance; and after that it was a dialogue between those two, and the most fascinating contact with the spirit world I ever had in my life. This new man was cultured and smooth, as clever as the devil. He never raised his voice, and you could have imagined him sitting over the cognac and cigars and amusing himself with Zaharoff's efforts to look like a hero to himself. He said: 'You know perfectly well, old rogue, that you weren't thinking anything about cities. You were thinking about munitions properties. You were hand-in-glove with the Comité des Forges, and what did those buzzards care about anybody's property but their own?'

" 'Oh, so it's you, Kahn!' exclaimed the other spirit. 'A fine one you are to talk about truth and honesty—you who sought my confidence and then betrayed it!'

" 'I never talked about you until I was certain that your policy was ruining my country, and leading us into new peril. I gave you fair warning of that.'

"So," continued Hess, "I listened to a polite quarrel between two of the masters of the old world. You have a saying in English, Lanny— about thieves falling out."

"When thieves fall out, honest men come into their own."

"Well, I came into an odd lot of information this time."

"Who is this Kahn?" demanded the Führer.

"He was Otto H. Kahn, a New York banker, one of the biggest."

"A Jew?"

"Of course; one who came from Germany. His firm was Kuhn, Loeb and Company, one of the most powerful of the international bankers, and here he was, swapping uncomplimentary remarks with Zaharoff, who was probably part Jewish, also. Is it not so, Lanny?"

"I have heard it said, but was never sure. Zaharoff was born in Turkey of Greek parents; but I have heard him say that he belonged to whatever country he was doing business with."

"Did you know this Otto Kahn?" inquired Hitler.

"I met him two or three times at social gatherings. He was a person of most elegant manners, and with a sense of humor as you describe him, Rudi. What had he done to incense Zaharoff?"

"It was a little vague," replied Hess. "They were not talking for my benefit; they talked just as if they had forgotten it was a séance. I gathered that during the World War Kahn had come to Europe on business with Zaharoff, and Zaharoff had discussed frankly his attitude to the manufacture of airplanes and the efforts he was making to prevent their being used by either side in the war. Later on Kahn had reported this to a United States government investigator of the airplane scandals."

"My father gave me a lot of inside stuff on the subject," said Lanny. "There must have been a deal, for the French never bombed your Briey Basin, and you Germans never bombed Le Creusot and other munitions plants."

"The steel and munitions people were all tied up together and were making money out of both sides. Naturally they wanted to come out of it with their plants intact." That was Hess; and the Führer added, grimly: "They will find it different this time. If they go to war with me, they will discover it is in earnest."

VII

Yes, the Führer's mind was on the next war, and whether he was going to have it and how he was going to wage it. He was not in the least interested in the gossip of two elderly ghosts. Once more he indicated impatience: "*Du schwatzt, Rudi*"—you are gabbling.

But Rudi exercised the privilege of an intimate. "*Jetzt pass' mal auf und Du wirst staunen.* These two spirits were very eminent persons and their secrets are important. This Jew banker accused the munitions king of having invested money in the manufacture of war planes, and the munitions king did not deny it; all he could say was that it was later on, the times had changed, he saw there was no chance of keeping the airplane out of war, and his interest was to see that all countries had an equal chance—the balance of power. Kahn laughed at that. 'You saw where the big money was going to be made, old rascal!' That made Zaharoff madder than ever. He said: 'You put your money anywhere, for your own amusement, regardless of what it would do to society. You were the playboy of the New York money world; you even put up funds for Bolsheviks.' "

"*Herrgott!*" exclaimed Adi.

"I told you you'd be interested! It appears that Zaharoff had had a *dossier* on Kahn. The banker demanded to know what he was talking about, and Zaharoff said—of course I can't remember word for word, but it was something like this: 'You were the art lover, the dilettante! You believed in freedom of expression, and everybody having a chance to say his say! You backed a bunch of Reds in New York who called themselves the New Playwrights——'

" 'Oh, so that's what you mean!' exclaimed Kahn, greatly amused.

" 'That's what I mean!' replied Zaharoff. 'You thought it was funny, you thought it was entertainment—but it was impudent ridicule of every institution that our civilization is based on, it was murderous hatred of your class and the property rights of all of us!' The banker didn't attempt to deny it, he just laughed, and that was the way the séance came to an end. The voices faded out, and before long the woman woke up, and asked me if I had got anything worth while."

"That is really a most curious story," admitted the Führer.

"*Sieh doch!*" exclaimed the Deputy. "If there is one thing that our enemies find ridiculous, it is the idea that the international bankers and the international Bolsheviks are in alliance; they never weary of sneering at you for saying it. But here you have it, exactly as you have charged!"

"Quite true," admitted the Führer of the Germans—but not seeming as delighted as his faithful servant had expected. "Make a note of it and get the facts," he said. "Some day we may have need of them; but we're not saying anything against the Bolsheviks right now. What we have to do is to get some sleep, for I have to argue with that Englishman in the morning."

So Lanny went to his room and lay down, but it was some time before sleep came to him, even with the saying of nursery rhymes! He had been under great tension, more so than he had realized. The séance had gone marvelously, and he could find no fault with what Laurel Creston had done; but what a curious thing that she should have broken it in the middle and shied off from the Nazis to Zaharoff! Something must have caused her alarm, and he tried to guess what it could have been. Certainly it had been unnecessary, for Hess had been completely satisfied with "Fritz" and the other German spirits. Lanny tried to figure out some way that he could convey that to his friend, so that she would be reassured, and better prepared for future encounters.

He had told her quite a good deal about Zaharoff, and his behavior in séance. He had mentioned that the one-time munitions king had put a million dollars into Budd-Erling; but all that business about Otto Kahn—that was entirely new to Lanny, and he speculated about it, deciding that it might be something she had learned from her Uncle Reverdy. It was entirely possible that the owner of the *Oriole* might have been a Kuhn-Loeb client, or, indeed, that Laurel herself might have met Kahn in New York; he had played Mæcenas to many writers, musicians, and painters whose work caught his fancy. He had lived in accord with the Parisian tradition, having a beautiful opera diva for his *amie*, and having a son who became a jazzband leader. Lanny promised himself an interesting time asking Laurel Creston about these matters.

He went to sleep on the thought that he must warn her not to be too successful, or they wouldn't want her to leave!

VIII

There were rules posted on the door of the guest rooms of the Berghof. One was that there was to be no smoking in the public rooms or passageways, or in the presence of the Führer; another was that if you were coming to meals, you must appear within two minutes of the ringing of the bell. So on this morning of the 23rd of August Lanny joined a procession of generals and statesmen, many of them red-eyed and yawning, having had only two or three hours' sleep. They grumbled a bit, but consoled one another with the statement: "*Es ist Krieg*." Soon after they had got seated they learned that it was also *Sieg;* for Hess came in, snapped to attention, and cried: "*Achtung, meine Herren!*" Then: "It is my pleasure to inform you that word has just come of the safe arrival in Moscow of two Kondor planes carrying our diplomatic and military mission. *Heil Hitler!*"

There was a shout, and they leaped to their feet and shot out their arms in front of them. "*Heil Hitler! Sieg heil! Sieg heil!*" A clamor broke out, of congratulations, of exultation at this greatest of diplomatic coups. This was *Der Tag*, the day of days, for which they had been preparing, training, all the days of their lives. This was the masterstroke, which would paralyze their foes, and set the Generalstab free from that nightmare of the German military mind, the two-front war.

Lanny Budd heiled with the best of them, and no one wore a broader smile. When he said: "A great day for us," some might have wondered: "What are *you* getting out of it?" But they didn't ask. The Führer must have had a good reason for having a foreigner here at such a time, otherwise he wouldn't have been here. No one questioned what the Führer did.

After the meal Lanny said to Hess: "What time do you expect Henderson?" The reply was that he was supposed to leave Berlin in an hour or so, and should be here shortly after noon. Lanny said: "I don't suppose the Führer will have any time for Miss Jones in the meantime. If it's all right with you I'll take her for a walk and show her the mountains."

A woman whose worldly possessions consisted of one blue and white print dress and a borrowed brush and comb, could not be expected to present a very lively appearance in the morning. But *Die Miss* had been told by Hess that her work had been most interesting, and so she had slept, and with the help of coffee and buttered toast and marmalade—they had got Americans mixed up with English—she was ready for whatever came. They had brought her a morning paper from Munich, and in it she could read about the expected arrival of the British ambassador at the Berghof, and so would know that she was in the midst of great events. Also, she could read about German refugees pouring in from Poland with terrible stories of mistreatment, and thus could be sure that war was not many days off.

A maid came and informed her that Herr Budd invited her to take a walk. She was shown the way to the door by which she had entered; Lanny was there, bright and smiling, and they strolled away without attracting much attention. The guards who were all over the place would keep an eye on them, but at a respectful distance. They would walk on paths strewn with brown and slippery pine needles, and now and then would stop at some spot where the trees had been cleared away. There were vistas of timbered mountains with an infinity of green firs, and behind them still higher peaks gleaming white. Lanny would point out landmarks. In the valley below them lay Salzburg, lovely old city with a mountain stream rushing through it. Here music festivals had been held every summer in the old days; but now Austria had become the Ostmark, and the festivals were over. They had been international affairs, with Jewish artists taking part, and to the Nazi ogre in his mountain lair they had been a personal affront.

IX

Lanny said: "We can talk, but in a low voice, and only while we are moving. It will be better not to speak important names. Now and then we should stop and admire the landscape in a louder voice. You did very well last night; your audience was satisfied."

"I was afraid maybe I had been too good," she responded.

"Was that why you decided to bring in Zaharoff?"

Her reply brought him to a stop, in spite of the rules he had just laid down. "Zaharoff?" she said. "What do you mean?"

"I mean the long dialogue between Zaharoff and Otto Kahn."

"But I gave no such dialogue. I never mentioned either."

"How extraordinary!" he exclaimed. "What reason could your sitter have for making up such an elaborate tale?"

"I don't know; but I certainly know that I didn't have a thought about those two men."

Lanny persisted: "Your sitter reported a long conversation; and it was a most unlikely thing for him to invent about two dead men. It had nothing of interest to his superior." Even before he had finished the words, another idea had begun to dawn in his mind, and he became conscious of a sort of shiver traveling up and down his spine. "Tell me! Is there any possibility that you could have lost consciousness during that affair?"

"I never thought of such a thing. How could it have happened?"

"Tell me what you can recall. First, you talked about a guard; and then about a baron and a professor. Then what?"

"There was quite an elaborate scene with them; and that was all."

"Exactly what happened at the end of the scene with them?"

"I remember that I felt very much pleased. I saw that my auditor was satisfied, and I thought: 'I can do it all right; and so I am safe.'"

"Then you felt relaxed, is that it?"

"Why, yes, I suppose so."

"You were lying back at ease, with your eyes closed, and the room was semi-dark; you felt peaceful and relieved. Did it occur to you that under those conditions you might drop off to sleep?"

"I never thought of it. I was too frightened at the beginning for such an idea to cross my mind."

"What is the next thing you remember?"

"Well, I thought: 'It is time to end this. There's no use risking any more.' So I did what you told me to do; I moaned some, and then I opened my eyes, and sighed once or twice, and said: 'Did you get anything worth while?'"

"Don't you see what had happened? You had gone into a real trance."

"You take my breath away, Mr. Budd!"

"You are a medium—a good one, and they are as rare as white blackbirds."

"For heaven's sake! What am I supposed to have said?"

"I don't think there can be any doubt that you said it. Your sitter didn't know those facts, and there was nothing in them that would have advantaged him. Also, this is one matter that he is honest about; he believes in the spirits, and is perhaps a little afraid of them—more so than he would be of any man. In such matters he becomes a child."

Lanny told her the story of the scene, and she listened dumfounded; the idea that such words had passed her lips was utterly inconceivable. The name of Zaharoff had meant nothing to her until Lanny had told her about the munitions king's inconvenient habit of coming to séances and telling his troubles. As for the genial Otto Kahn, she said: "I met him once at Uncle Reverdy's and was impressed by his kindness and charm. It was some years ago, and I was quite young and romantic; I remember thinking: 'Now, if a man like that were to ask me to marry him, it would be wonderful.' But I had no ideas about his business affairs, or that he had ever met Zaharoff, or told any government agent about Zaharoff's doings."

"Is it possible that you could ever have heard your uncle speaking about these matters?"

"Well, of course I can't say what I have forgotten. I have heard reference to business matters that I never paid any attention to. I knew that Mr. Kahn was one of my uncle's bankers, and that they made important deals, but that's all I knew. I'm not sure that I ever heard he was dead. How long ago was it?"

"I'll have to look it up. We'll try to find more by the spirit route—that is, if you don't mind trying experiments."

"I'll be immensely curious. But first I want to travel—you understand."

"Surely!" smiled her companion. "I think that courtesy will require us to stay one more night and give one more séance. I suggest that this time you take pains not to repeat the mistake of last night. There have been cases of controls who talked freely about the medium they were using."

"Dear God!" said this "white blackbird," in horror. "Never fear—I'll keep pinching myself!"

X

All that critical day there were visitors coming and going at the Berghof, high officers and other personages who had been summoned on chance that their Führer might wish to consult them. He was a man of sudden moods, and they had to adjust themselves thereto; mostly they sat in the great reception room, conversing in low tones. It was easy to guess that they were anxious men, for they did not know what their country was being let in for, and were not permitted to ask. An American friend of the Führer would not question them, and still less would he intimate that he might know more than they; but when they found out that he knew key persons in London, Paris and elsewhere, they sought opportunities to draw him into their conversations.

The British ambassador was flown to Salzburg, and motored up the mountainside, arriving soon after lunch. He was the perfect type of the English upper-class man, tall, thin, with a long face and a long nose. He wore a somewhat heavier mustache than was customary—much more than Lanny's tiny one, or the two rather absurd little blobs which were the trademark of Adi Schicklgruber. Sir Nevile was perfectly tailored and just turned out of a bandbox, with a soft silk shirt, a checked tie, and a red carnation as a "buttonhole." His walking stick and Homburg hat might have been left in the car—but perhaps they were *his* trademarks. He was followed by Baron von Weizsäcker, old-fashioned diplomat who was now Ribbentrop's deputy, lending to the Nazis his elegance and worldly cunning; also by an assistant from the Wilhelmstrasse.

Conversation stopped dead in that room, and everybody stared, but nobody rose to honor the guest. Sir Nevile was smiling, as if wishing to convey the fact that there were no hostile feelings on his part; but nobody met him half-way. Weizsäcker led the way to the stairs, and up to the Führer's study; after which Lanny observed a procedure which had surprised him the first time, but which he now understood to be one of the customs of the Führer's retreat. Conversation was not resumed. It wouldn't be correct to say that anybody cocked his ears, but many heads were turned slightly sideways, and nobody tried to conceal the fact that he was waiting. Everybody knew that the door of the Führer's room would be closed behind the visitors; but also everybody knew that no door would contain the voice of Adolf Hitler very long. Pretty soon you would hear!

Then, a still more curious custom: somebody arose and went very quietly upstairs; then another, and another. Nobody was going to listen at the keyhole of the Führer's door, nobody was going to stand in the hallway with pretended casualness; what they were going to do was to enter a near-by room, and leave the door slightly ajar, and then stand behind the door, just out of sight of everybody else. Lanny's room, unfortunately, was in a distant wing, he having come so late; furthermore, being a foreigner, he could not afford to commit an indiscretion at a time such as this. He had to sit quietly where he was, and pretend to be buried in a copy of the *Münchner Neueste Nachrichten*. But he had seen to it that his seat was not far from the stairs, and he expected to get some news ahead of the newspaper.

XI

The son of Budd-Erling had heard several persons getting their dressing-down from the master of this household: first Gregor Strasser, who had later been murdered in the Blood Purge; then Chancellor Schuschnigg from Vienna, and then Dr. Franck from the Sudetenland. This time it wasn't going to be personal, for Sir Nevile was the most docile of diplomats, who said what he had been told to say and never presumed to force his own opinion upon anyone. This time he was just a special delivery messenger, bringing an airmail letter which he had received the previous evening. Nobody was going to blame him for the contents of that letter; but somebody was going to blame the British government and the British Empire and the British Jewish-controlled pluto-democratic press and the British money lords who had kept Germany poor and the British shipping and other lords who had robbed Germany of her colonies and refused to let her take any other colonies anywhere in the world.

Yes, somebody was surely going to find fault with these evil forces, and good and plenty! The storm of words was going to mount, and beat upon the door of the room, which would act as a sounding board and carry the storm down the wide stairway. Lanny couldn't make out every word, for when Adi became excited his syllables tripped over one another's heels. But he could make out what Adi thought of the beastly and degraded so-called democratic Czech nation, and how Britain had egged them on and encouraged them to make trouble for the Germans, and to compel the Germans to use force which they had been so reluctant to do. And now it was the same thing with the still more beastly and degraded Poles, whose insolent defiance of the Führer's just demands was based upon nothing whatever but the promise of British support—and what a *verdammte Lüge* that was, for the British had no way to help the Poles, and they knew it, and the Poles would have known it if they had not been a bunch of pride-maddened maniacs, and all that was happening was an effort of Britain to intimidate the Führer by a threat of war which if it came would be an unprovoked and wanton attack on Britain's part and would result in a life-and-death struggle—the German *Volk* would arise to meet it as one man. And so on and on—when the one-time inmate of the Obdachslosenheim really got going he could shout more words without stopping for breath than ever a *basso profundo* from Bayreuth or La Scala.

"You have given these Polish madmen a blank check!" stormed Adi. "They are torturing my people, they have driven a hundred thousand of them into exile already. They have even castrated some of them!" Lanny couldn't hear the Englishman's reply to this, but he heard the Führer: "There were *six* cases, I tell you! *Six* cases! I have information and I know what I am talking about. No German official dares lie to me! And it is all because of your encouragement. . . . The Poles are mobilizing, and it is because you are preparing for war, and you tell the Poles so and make it impossible for me to deal with them. . . . You British are poisoning the atmosphere of Europe. . . . You are spreading false rumors, slanders and threats. . . . Tell your Mr. Chamberlain that I no longer trust him, he is no friend of Germany, no friend of European culture. Tell him that nothing will satisfy me but a complete change of Britain's attitude. Tell him I have informed Warsaw that if there is any further persecution of my people my troops will cross the border!"

XII

The outcome was that the ambassador was to have a written answer within two hours. He was driven back to Salzburg; and meantime word spread throughout the assembled company what the British Prime Minister's letter had contained: first, an announcement of his government's determination to carry out their promises to Poland; second, their readiness to discuss all problems between the two countries; and third, their anxiety to see "immediate direct discussion initiated between Germany and Poland." Also it became known that King Leopold of the Belgians, speaking in the name of the "Oslo States," then in conference at Brussels, had broadcast an impassioned plea for peace. Lanny could see that this worried the visitors of the Berghof greatly; for they had once seen their country hated and opposed by all the rest of the world, and they dreaded nothing so much as to be maneuvered into that same position again. They dared not say it plainly, but they could hint at it in ways which men who live a long time in the diplomatic world learn to employ and understand.

But all these uncertainties were dissipated by news which came by telephone from Moscow and spread quickly through the summer capital: the Peace Pact between Germany and Russia had been signed! It was to run for ten years, and provided that neither party would commit any act of aggression against the other, and that if either became involved in war with third parties, the other would be neutral. There was no undignified cheering, but army officers and Party officials went around exchanging handshakes and beaming smiles. Even a stranger from overseas was entitled to share in this *Gemütlichkeit,* and to be taken as a member of the *Herrenfamilie.*

Lanny never found out how gossip got started in the Führer's home. Presumably there was no official gossip-starter; presumably some secretary would whisper to her trusted friend, and this one would tell two or three others, and before an hour had passed all members of the household and all guests would be murmuring: "Have you heard?" Lanny had made friends with several young members of the staff, by driving them to the Parteitag and rendering other small services. So now one of them, with a smile, relieved him of the necessity of pretending to keep the secret that he had brought a spiritualist medium to the Berghof and that Hess had had a successful séance with her the previous evening. *Höchst interessant!* And do you really believe in spirits? And just what took place, Herr Budd?

Later in the afternoon word spread that the Führer had summoned Sir Nevile for a second conference. The doctor, whose room was near his head patient's, showed his friendliness by inviting the American guest up to that privileged listening post. *"Streng vertraulich!"* he whispered, with a grin, and Lanny replied: *"Das versteht sich von selbst!"* But the little conspiracy came to naught, for the second meeting was entirely decorous—Adi didn't once raise his voice, and the British ambassador took his departure, presumably having his written reply tucked away safely over his heart.

It was a long letter, as Adi's were apt to be. There was nothing especially secret about it, and a number of the higher officers soon had read it and talked about it freely. It was just one more listing of the Führer's grievances: the "wave of unspeakable terror" which had been let loose in Danzig and the Corridor by the British support of Poland; the Führer's hopelessness of any sort of real friendship between his country and Britain; also his readiness to meet the issue of war if it came. "There can be no doubt as to the determination of the new German Reich to accept privation and misfortune in any form and at any time rather than sacrifice her national interests or even her honor." Lanny could perceive that very few even among the military men liked that way of talking; but they had hitched their wagons to the Hitler star, and now would go whirling across the heavens like a swarm of meteorites. Lanny decided that Germany might be about to plunge into another World War, but there would be no cheering and singing in the streets as there had been a quarter of a century ago.

20

They That Take the Sword

I

A STRANGE fate which had befallen this châlet, once the summer residence of an obscure Hamburg merchant, and now the center of attention of the whole world. Haus Wachenfels, or Watch Rock, it had been called; some said Wachenfeld, or Watch Field. It had been for rent, and some of Adi's rich supporters had taken it, to serve as his retreat when he was released from prison. Here he and Hess had written the second volume of *Mein Kampf;* and later, when the money had begun to pour in, he had bought it, and changed the name to Der Berghof. Thereafter it had been enlarged, year after year, until now it was no longer a retreat, but the summer capital of Germany. The world called it Berchtesgaden, that being the nearest village and post office; it was as if the wild witch had come back to life again, and there was a new Walpurgis night up on the side of the mountain, and the enchantment there wrought filled the whole world with terror.

The center of this excitement was one medium-sized pudgy-faced man who looked as if he might be the butcher, the baker, or the candlestick maker. But he had a *daimon* inside him, that drove him day and night and made him drive all other people, whether for or against him. He had built a *daimon* movement, and now it had caught him up and would have driven him forward even if he had wanted to pull back, which he didn't. He wanted to go to the end, which was the subjection of the world to that *daimon*, the making over of the world in the image of that *daimon*.

Right now he was at the supreme crisis of his career, he had the great decision to make, and he knew it; to be near him was like living in the midst of a tornado, like being in a Vulcan forge where new universes were being wrought. Telephone calls were pouring in, messages coming and going, statesmen from many capitals being summoned or seeking appointments. Newspaper correspondents crowded the hotel in the village and telephone calls were put in for Paris and London and New York. And in the midst of it all was the son of Alois Hitler, né Schicklgruber, the same frightened, angry child who had hated and feared his father, adored his fond young mother and lost her, and looked upon the great world outside with a mixture of emotions, all unhappy, because nobody cared for him, nobody appreciated him, and when he stamped his feet and clenched his fists and screamed in fury, nobody obeyed him, but some laughed at him and others cuffed him.

A great, powerful, and cruel world, having something monstrously wrong in it, and Adi's *daimon* had driven him to try to find out what it was. After many years of struggling and efforts to think, accompanied by wild surges of emotion, he had found out. It was the plutocrats, it was the Jews, it was the Allies, the enemies of Germany, of the blue-eyed, blond, and tall *Herrenvolk* with which Adi Schicklgruber identified himself, by some strange process which must have involved shutting his eyes whenever he came near a mirror. To put down the enemies and put up the *Herrenvolk* was Adi's destiny, and he had had himself portrayed as a knight in armor, riding a magic white steed which was able to gallop over continents and leap across oceans, and lead the Aryan folk to victory by land, sea, and air.

Never had his moods been more violent, their changes more sudden than right now. In the early hours of the morning, when he couldn't get to sleep, terror would seize him. Was he, the Führer, leading his people to the greatest triumph in history, or to the greatest collapse? He would summon his generals, his most highly trained military experts to a conference; and when they pointed out the dangers of the situation, the vast resources of their enemies, he would fly into a rage with them, call them cowards and mice in uniform, and send them packing. He would summon Ribbentrop or Goebbels or Himmler, men of hate and terror, men of words and dreams like Adi's own. The wild witch Berchta had taken up her dwelling in their hearts, and they saw the world not as it was but as she wished it.

II

In the midst of such agonies of mind it was impossible that Adi should overlook the possibility of supernatural or at any rate supernormal assistance. What could mean more to him than an opportunity to make contact with the spirit of Professor Heinzelmann and others of the Nazi old companions? Who could tell what heroes and elder statesmen might see fit to come in such a crisis, and give their words of wisdom to the new master of the German destiny?

The faithful Deputy came to Lanny, saying: "You understand that the Führer is under heavy pressure, and you won't expect him to be sociable."

"Certainly not, Rudi. I came for only one purpose, to bring Miss Jones."

"The Führer will wish to make a try with her this evening—that is, unless something extremely urgent should turn up."

"She is ready; and you know, Rudi, how eagerly I'll be waiting for news about it."

Lanny had seen that his woman friend was provided with newspapers and magazines. Now he advised her to rest and take things easy. He couldn't say: "Don't try to be too good," but he could say: "Don't overexert yourself," and add a little knowing smile. Also: "I suppose you will be wanting to leave tomorrow, and I'll endeavor to arrange it."

After which he went downstairs to join a distinguished company and listen to political conversation. He was careful never to ask questions or to reveal improper curiosity; but these important persons could not talk for long without betraying secrets; their very questions revealed what they were interested in and what they were uncertain about. Lanny had been meeting generals and admirals and cabinet ministers and diplomats since he was a small child, and he couldn't remember a time when he hadn't been learning the difference between important and unimportant information, and how to get the former and give the latter. He would chat with smiling casualness, and inside him be like a man who walks through a forest known to be swarming with wild Indians armed with poisoned arrows. Never in all history had there been creatures more poisonous than the Nazis, or more alert in deception and expectant of it from others. What they thought of Lanny Budd he would never know; but he was safe so long as he held the confidence of Numbers One, Two and Three.

This kind of mental warfare is wearing; so in the middle of the evening Lanny excused himself and retired to the small but comfortable guest room which had been assigned him. He stretched himself on the bed and performed a ritual which he had taught himself, of recalling every point which should go into a report, and making certain that he fixed it correctly in his mind. That done, he picked up a book, of which he always carried several on his journeys.

III

Toward midnight there came a soft tap on his door. It was Hess, and he came in, apologizing: "I hope I do not disturb you."

"By no means. I have been waiting on pins and needles."

"You understand, this is most confidential. I would rather you did not tell even the medium."

"I never do that, Rudi, because it spoils the subsequent sittings—I mean, their evidential value."

"Well, the Führer has just had a strange experience, and has been deeply moved. First there came the spirit of his father. You know he didn't get along very well with his father."

"So I have heard."

"It was astonishingly lifelike and vivid. The father knew very little English, but he had brought along a former colleague to speak for him. A strange thing, for then I had to translate the words back for the Führer. He asked his father for advice, but the father said: 'You never took my advice—you would do the opposite.' Then he talked about the Führer's mother, but wouldn't ask her to come. A strange thing, how most of the spirits that come to the Führer are persons who have in some way caused him pain. The next was Gregor Strasser, who turned against the Party and was killed in the Blood Purge."

"What did *he* have to say?"

"It appears that he is now devoted to the Party and the cause, and admits that the Führer was right. He spoke good English, and talked quite a lot, mostly about painful events—you know, the Führer is a man who has had dreadful sufferings, and has experienced treacheries which would have broken the heart of a less determined man."

"I know that well, Rudi."

"And then, the most striking thing of all—there came Bismarck."

"You don't tell me!"

"At least, the old Negro described a large magnificent man in a white uniform with an Iron Cross on his breast. He had a white mustache, and he kept raising his finger as if in warning, and kept moving his lips, but the old Negro said it was as if there was a sheet of glass between, and he couldn't hear any sounds. Now and then he would get a word, and it was German. I kept saying: 'Repeat what it sounds like to you,' and the Negro would do it. So I got the word *Gefahr!*—over and over: '*Gefahr! Gefahr!*' I said: 'That means danger. Ask him what danger he means. He will understand English.' But the Negro said he paid no attention to any words spoken to him. It was most annoying; but we got the word *Krieg*, and something that sounded like *Vernichtung*. Naturally, the Führer was greatly upset by this."

"Did the spirit say that he was Bismarck?"

"He said that name, and it is hardly likely that the Negro had heard it. But the Negro said: 'This big man speaks with a sort of cracked voice, high, like a woman's.' That does not seem to fit our Iron Chancellor."

Lanny had an impulse to say: "It happens that it does." But years of intrigue had taught him to stop and weigh his words. The less that he himself knew about Alois Hitler né Schicklgruber, and about Gregor Strasser, druggist turned Nazi and then rebel, and about Otto Eduard Leopold von Bismarck, the less chance that either Number One or Number Three would entertain suspicions of the medium. He said: "That is very interesting, Rudi. It will be something that we can check on."

"The Führer is disposed to take the séance as a warning, and naturally it has disturbed his mind. It might be worth while to consult a life of Bismarck. No doubt there are several in the library here."

"That is the sort of thing it might be hard to find in the books, Rudi; it would not be indexed. Would there be anybody in this house who can remember hearing the great man speak?"

Hess thought for a minute, then said: "Flöge will know. I will ask him."

Lanny recognized the name as that of an elderly professor of meteorology, who was here, presumably, for his knowledge about the climate on the Polish plains. "He'll be asleep by now, won't he?"

"He'll wake up when he hears that the Führer wants information. Wait, if you don't mind." Hess left the room.

IV

Lanny took time to think over what had happened, and was likely to happen. He had read somewhere about Bismarck's voice, and had supplied that detail to Laurel Creston. The same thing was true of the other details which Hess had mentioned; so Lanny concluded that the woman's plan of pinching herself had been successful. She had managed the whole thing very cleverly; the only trouble was, the story might be too good—Adi would almost certainly want more messages from the elder statesmen!

The Deputy was gone quite a while, and Lanny guessed correctly that he was reporting to the Führer. That was all right—Lanny was occupied in imagining possible contingencies and how to meet them. When at last Hess re-entered the room he made no apology, but exclaimed, with what was enthusiasm for his dour nature: "This is remarkable, Lanny! No one will ever again be able to tell me that spirits are not living and real. Flöge declares that Bismarck had a falsetto voice, entirely different from what one would have expected. It was a source of humiliation to him, and accounted for his non-success as an orator, and the fact that what he had to say was nearly always communicated in writing."

"That is really extraordinary," assented Lanny. "I don't know when I have come upon a more convincing piece of evidence. The fact that the Negro couldn't hear Bismarck's voice might mean that he has lost it in the spirit world, as a result of some complex, some psychic inhibition. He hated his voice, and now he has none, except when he makes a special effort."

"*Um Gottes Willen!*" exclaimed the Deputy, who had been taken to church when he was a small boy.

"It seems to me to suggest that the Führer should consult a slate-writing medium. It might be that Bismarck would take control and you would get astonishing results."

"A fine suggestion; but meanwhile, the Führer wants to have another sitting with Miss Jones as soon as possible. Do you suppose she could do it again tonight?"

"It would be a great mistake to ask that. She has explained to me that the effort exhausts her completely, and she never makes it except to oblige some friend."

"The Führer may be obliged to return to Berlin at any hour. Do you suppose it would be possible to persuade this lady to come there for a while? We would provide her with everything in the way of comfort."

"I'm afraid it's out of the question, Rudi. I had difficulty in persuading her to come here at all. She has engagements in New York, and I promised to drive her out as soon as she had a sitting with you and one with the Führer, if he wanted it."

"That is most unfortunate. The Führer told me to arrange to pay her whatever would make it worth while to her."

"That isn't the question, Rudi. This lady has never been paid, and would not accept money. Her people are well-to-do."

"But a present, Lanny! Surely she would let the Führer present her with a diamond ring, or even a brooch, as a token of his esteem!"

"American ladies accept flowers from gentlemen, also a box of candy now and then; but nothing more valuable than that."

"But see, Lanny—this is a matter in which I ought to have your co-operation. There are things which you and I have wished to say to the Führer, but which he would not take from us. He would take them from Bismarck, or even from Heinzelmann."

Hess was being cautious—did he think that Lanny's room might be wired? Were there factions in the Führer's household, and might Himmler, dread chief of the Gestapo, be taking measures on his own initiative? Lanny said: "You must understand, I cannot suggest such considerations to this woman, for that would be invalidating the séances. If I say: 'We are getting such-and-such results,' or: 'It is important that you stay for this or that reason'—then I am giving her suggestions, and we should never know but that her subconscious mind had taken them and was weaving elaborate fantasies on the basis of them. It is bad enough that she knows she is talking to the Führer, and has read in the newspapers that all the world is waiting for him to decide the question of peace or war."

"Well, do what you can, Lanny. At least persuade her to stay one more night and let him have another chance to speak to Bismarck. Do you know if she ever tried automatic writing?"

"I don't know, but I'll ask her in the morning. I'll take her for a walk. It wouldn't be fair to ask her to spend the whole day shut up in her room."

"Certainly not—there is no reason for that."

V

So, next morning, out in the beautiful forest, with only the squirrels and the birds for company, Lanny said: "You were a little bit too good. You have got your distinguished sitter excited, and he is demanding more."

"What did I say that was too good?" was her question.

"Well, the old-time statesman produced a powerful impression. You know, he is almost a god in certain eyes."

"I understood that. I played safe and made it hard for him to talk."

"But the words he said were so significant, in this special moment."

"Tell me, what words were reported to you."

"First, *Krieg*, several times; and he said his own name."

"That is right."

"And then, *Vernichtung*."

"What does that mean?"

"That means annihilation. Do you mean you didn't know what you were saying?"

"I had a very curious experience. I was resolved with all my will power to stay awake; and it was just as if something took hold of me and was dragging me under water. I sat pinching myself until it hurt, but I couldn't be sure that it sufficed."

"Then you don't really know whether you lost consciousness?"

"You know how it is sometimes when you are reading, and you become sleepy: you nod, and you're not quite sure whether you drop off or not; you can even read a line or two, and then miss a line, and be sort of swaying between the two states."

"Most interesting," Lanny said. "So it's possible you may have spoken words you don't remember."

"I am absolutely certain that I didn't say the word *Vernichtung*. I had decided that to say *Krieg* and to shake a warning finger was as far as it was safe to go."

"Your subconscious mind might have supplied the word, of course."

"How could it, when I don't know the word?"

"You have been reading a lot of German, and got the sense of words from the context, without having them consciously at your disposal. You know that the word *Nicht* means "not," and if you read that the Germans were afraid of the *Vernichtung* of their country you would pretty well guess what it meant."

"That might be, I suppose. If I was playing a role, I would quite probably go on with it, even if I fell asleep, or into a trance. People talk in their sleep, and I suppose they sometimes speak the words of dream characters."

Lanny told of Hess's invitation, and added: "That is something for you to think seriously about."

"It is a most dangerous thing for me to be doing, Mr. Budd. I cannot be sure of controlling myself, and cànnot guess what I might say or do."

"I know," he replied. "But, on the other hand, the world is hanging on the verge of a precipice, and it might be that you are the one person who can pull it back. You can speak words that nobody else can speak, and you can get a hearing for them."

"Have mercy on me!" she exclaimed. "What a proposition to put up to a weak and frightened woman!"

VI

They made it a long walk, looking over their shoulders frequently to make certain that their voices reached only the squirrels and the birds. They discussed the state of Europe and the problems of appeasement versus resistance. Lanny was careful to preserve his aloof attitude. He said: "I will tell you what facts I know; but the conclusion must be your own, and the decision."

"But I am involving your welfare as well as mine!"

"I will take a chance with you," he replied. "You make up your mind what you want to do and say, and I'll stay by you."

In the end she said: "All right; I will have one more sitting with the important person; but positively no more. I will go the limit on that one." She lowered her voice to a whisper. "I will let Bismarck come again, and also Hindenburg, if you can give me the data. The sitter can believe it or not, but it must be understood that he will have to be satisfied with what he gets tonight. Say that my mother is ill or anything you please."

Lanny replied: "O.K. I'll put it up to them. And now, for what you are going to say. You haven't used Dietrich Eckart, and I suggest you start with him, to get on a warm personal basis. Then give them some Hindenburg—not so easy as Bismarck, because your sitter knew him; but a few words from him will produce a tremendous impression, and perhaps prevent the war—if you want to prevent it!"

He told her in low tones the story of the grim Junker General who had commanded in East Prussia during the World War and had destroyed the Russians at the Masurian lakes. He had become a German idol—almost literally, for a huge wooden image of him had been set up in Berlin as a means of raising money for the aid of soldiers' families; pious patriots bought a nail and drove it into the statue, and before the war was over it was made of iron. After the war *"der alte Herr"* had been made President of the Republic and used by the reactionaries as their "front"; he had despised an upstart politician whom he called "the Bohemian corporal"—which was somewhat inaccurate, since the politician had never been either Bohemian or corporal. In the end he had been forced to receive this upstart, and their first meeting had been embarrassing, since one had been rattled and neither had known what to say. Lanny could tell about it on the authority of that gossip-fountain, Hilde, Fürstin Donnerstein.

"But don't use that," he said. "Tell about the breathtaking day when the upstart became Chancellor, and the old man attended the ceremony. Also, you can go back to the Osthilfe scandal, soon after the war, when the government put up funds to save East Prussian landlords from bankrupcy, and the money was misspent. The old gentleman was involved, since the grateful nation had presented an estate to him and he had passed it on to his son and the son had got his share of the gravy. The Nazis exploited this for all it was worth, so you can have the old gentleman defending himself and his family honor. That will make him real, and after that you can have him discuss the new war that is coming, and say what you please."

VII

The medium retired to her hiding place, and Lanny rejoined the distinguished company in the public rooms of the Berghof. This company resembled a flowing stream, in that the water was changed while the stream remained the same. The morrow was the day on which, if Bernhardt Monck's prediction was correct, the German armies would move into Poland. Now Lanny learned of a series of decrees which had been prepared, and were to be put into effect this night or the following day. Telephone communication with Britain and France was to be cut; airports in Germany were to be closed and civilian air traffic was to cease; the food rationing program was to go into effect. All these things meant war, the guests of the Berghof agreed.

News from the rest of the world came via radio. Last minute efforts were being made to avert the calamity. President Roosevelt felt compelled to butt in once more. He had gone on a fishing trip along the Maine coast, but now flew back to Washington and cabled a message to the Führer. He had received no reply to the one of the previous April, but even so, he was trying again; for, said he, "the cause of world peace—which is the cause of humanity itself—rises above all other considerations." He urged both the Chancellor of Germany and the President of Poland to refrain from hostile actions "for a reasonable and stipulated period," and stated that the United States was ready "to contribute its share to the solution of the problems which are endangering world peace."

Alas, he couldn't say what that share was, and to a P.A. in the Führer's home it was made abundantly clear that no Nazi wanted any of it, and that empty words were regarded with contempt. It was up to Lanny to make plain that he considered "That Man in the White House" as a Jew-lover and Bolshevik in disguise, a calamity to his country and to the world. The art expert was not short of phrases, having listened to this sort of conversation in Paris and on the Riviera, in London, New York, and Newcastle, Connecticut—wherever wealthy Americans gathered to discuss income and excess profit taxes, and the whole New Deal scheme of robbing the rich for the benefit of the bureaucrats.

War was coming, and nothing on earth could stop it—so Lanny had concluded. Could anything in heaven or hell, paradise or purgatory, limbo or Walhalla stop it? Could the spirits of Heinzelmann and Bismarck and Hindenburg, of Strasser and Eckart and the other old companions stop it? That was a problem with which Lanny wrestled at odd moments all the day and part of the night. Could it be stopped even for a few days more? Was it Laurel Creston's duty to risk her life, and Lanny Budd's to risk his job, on the chance of being able to delay it? He told himself a grim No, for he didn't believe that anything could permanently hold Adolf Hitler except a licking on the field of battle, and there was serious doubt whether delays did not help him more than they helped Britain and France.

This was a military question, and he was in a position to hear it discussed by the world's best authorities. Fighting weather in Poland was ideal in the month of September, but in October came the autumn rains and the fields were turned into bogs. So, in the consultations which were going on in the Führer's study, the military answer was "Now or never—or at any rate not until next summer." The Reichswehr men differed among themselves, but the SS fanatics were like war horses, champing at their bits and dancing on their iron-shod hooves.

They knew that everything was in readiness, and what could be holding the Führer back? When the whisper spread that it might be spirits, brought there by an American playboy and his female companion, there were glowering looks, and Lanny realized that it might not much longer be safe for the pair of them to take long walks in the forests of the wild witch Berchta!

VIII

The sun in its rounds refuses to be influenced by human hopes or fears, agonies, yearnings, despairs. It seemed to linger, but the old-fashioned gold watch which Lanny had inherited from his Great-Great-Uncle Eli Budd was there to testify that the sun went down behind the Bavarian Alps at the moment proper for the 24th of August. The crisis had grown so tense that it seemed tactful for a stranger not to be conspicuous, so Lanny retired to his room and stretched out on his bed. As an exercise in self-control he buried himself in the latest number of the *Journal of Parapsychology*.

Those fellows at Duke University in North Carolina had got so deep into the subject of "extrasensory perception" that they had invented a lingo all their own, and you had to study a glossary—to say nothing of brushing up on mathematics which you had never expected to think about since leaving school. However, Lanny knew that this is the way to impress the scientific world, to flatter them by giving them something which only they themselves can understand. Having been laughed at by most of his friends for a matter of ten years, Lanny found it pleasant to be able to hand them a publication so impressively academic in appearance—and then to watch their faces when they opened it and tried to read it!

So for an hour or two Lanny Budd forgot about wars and rumors of wars. He learned about experiments, made by the hundreds of thousands, proving not merely that telepathy and clairvoyance are realities, but also the thing which Duke called "the psychokinetic effect"—that is to say, the ability of mind to move matter without any sort of physical contact. To be sure, it is a "psychokinetic effect" when a desire causes your hand to move; but that is a sort which men are used to, and therefore think they understand. What was here in question was whether the mind could influence the behavior of dice between the moment when they were thrown and the moment when they had settled into position on a table. That had been a notion hitherto confined to persons, for the most part dark of skin, known as "crap-shooters."

To make it the subject of academic investigation and report the results in words of Greek derivation was certainly a novelty, and had taken nerve on the part of Professor J. B. Rhine.

The next article dealt with a trance medium and some of her communications; and that brought Lanny back to the circumstances of this hour, which had been set for the Führer to try an experiment with Laurel Creston. She was merely going to pretend to enter a trance; but she might slip into a real one, and, if that happened—God only knew what she might say! All the will power in the world couldn't keep that thought from leaping into Lanny Budd's mind, and it caused his heart to hit him a blow underneath his windpipe—or so it seemed, and it was certainly a most unpleasant psychokinetic effect. It suggested to Lanny that he himself was a psychokinetic construction, and not the purely mechanical object which a certain school of philosophers had been calling him for something like a century and a half.

IX

There came a tap on the door, and Lanny called: "Come in." It was Hess, with a light in his dark eyes that was not often to be seen there. "Good God, Lanny! This has been the most amazing experience! I wish you might have been there!"

"You got real results?"

"Dietrich Eckart came, and it was just as if he was in the room."

"Eckart?" said Lanny, in a tone of inquiry.

"You don't know about him? He was one of our oldest associates, a member of the Thule Society."

"I must have heard of him—the name sounds familiar——"

"He was a genius of a sort—poet, actor, orator—in Munich just after the war. Between you and me he was a bit of a bounder, but he made a great impression upon the Führer and so became the grand old man of our movement, and is now a sort of tradition. The Negro described him to the very life, and said he spoke good English, so it was possible to talk to him. Really, it was just like old times."

"What did he say?"

"He talked quite a lot about the early days, and several friends who were there. It seems that our *Parteigenossen* keep together in the other world. The Führer, of course, wanted him to talk about the present situation. It appears that Dietrich knows about it. I asked him how, and he says they can hear the radio. Imagine that!"

"It must be rather confusing to them at present."

"They wouldn't listen to the foreign stations. But here's the significant thing—all the spirits seem to have the idea that the Führer is going too fast."

"Well, you and I are inclined to agree with that, aren't we?"

"May I tell you something in the strictest confidence?"

"Everything you tell me is in confidence, Rudi—unless it is something you authorize me to repeat."

"All preparations have been completed, and for the past week the army has had orders to march into Poland tomorrow midnight."

If Lanny felt any shock he did not reveal it. "I had gathered as much from the conversation downstairs," he remarked. "I had guessed that you would prefer otherwise, but didn't feel that you had the power to change the decision."

"That is correct. But this woman has come at precisely the critical moment. The Führer didn't say definitely, but I could see that he has been shaken in his resolution."

"I trust the Führer is not going to hold the woman or myself responsible for what comes in these séances."

"Oh, of course not; he knows too much about the subject for that. It is Dietrich he is thinking about—the man who thrilled and inspired him when he was so beaten and depressed by the collapse of Germany and the triumph of the Reds."

"What did the spirit say on the subject?"

"He said: 'You can win without fighting. You can get what you want by noisy persistence. Keep on shouting, wear your enemies down, outlast them.' You understand, all this had to be got through the agency of the old Negro, and it was slow and took a lot of time. But even so, you couldn't doubt that Dietrich was there; he had been an inspired man—he came of good family, and had money, only he didn't take much care of it, or of himself."

"Genius is a strange thing," commented the son of Budd-Erling, sagely. "There have been many who could help everybody in the world but themselves."

"Exactly! But I haven't finished telling you. Hindenburg came."

"You don't mean it!"

"Just as real as Dietrich, but of course not so free-spoken. He was never a man of many words."

"What did he want?"

"First of all, he praised the Führer's work. In life he had misjudged a great German. He, *der Alte*, had been ill and tired, and badly advised by self-seeking men. But now he had renewed his powers, and saw clearly, and hailed a great Führer. You can imagine how that thrilled both of us; truly, it made chills run up and down my spine."

"I never met the old gentleman in real life," remarked Lanny; "but I heard him speak over the radio. Of course you couldn't get the effect of his voice by the vocal cords of a woman."

"We got a description of him, and it was convincing. I really believe he was there. And the important thing is, he gave the same advice as Dietrich. He said: 'Go slow, Adolf. Don't let them put you in the wrong. Germany is eternally right, and they must see it if you give them time. Force is good, but it must never be used until necessary.' The Führer wanted him to answer questions, but apparently he couldn't. The Negro said: 'It takes a lot of power to speak for such a man,' and then faded away. That was most disappointing."

"I have found it so," Lanny said, "not merely with this medium but with others. Apparently you have to wait for some sort of battery to be recharged."

"The Führer is most urgent that this woman should not leave. It means so much to him."

"I put it up to her, and she says that her mother is ill, and that she has positive engagements. I could only persuade her to come here on the promise that we would stay two days and then I would drive her home again. The prospect of war reinforces her determination."

"You can go out by way of Switzerland at any time without trouble. We can surely arrange that. Think what it means, Lanny! The Führer may decide tonight to cancel the order to the army. He has gone to his study to think it over. He didn't say, and I didn't venture to ask him; but I know that his will has been shaken. He may decide to wait, and there may be negotiations—the British may force the Poles to give way."

"I know that they have been trying to do it," Lanny admitted.

"Exactly! So it might mean the difference between war and peace. What are this woman's views on the subject?"

"I have never talked politics with her. But I don't suppose any woman wants war—certainly no American woman."

"Well, put it up to her. Tell her the fate of Europe may hang on her decision."

"But, Rudi! You don't want me to give her any idea of what has come out in the séances! That would destroy their value. With all the honesty in the world, her conscious mind could not fail to influence her subconscious."

"I can see that; but you can give her an intimation—say that the

Führer is getting communications of world significance at this critical moment. Don't say on which side, or what about."

"All right," Lanny answered. "I'll see what I can do."

X

He tapped on Laurel Creston's door, and she admitted him. She had been lying on the bed, resting, and the little print dress was beginning to look dowdy. He closed the door behind him and said: "I thought you would be interested to know that your séance was successful, and that your auditors are pleased."

"Certainly, I am glad," she replied, discreetly. He had given her so many warnings as to guarding her words.

"There is a question of when you are to take your departure. I have been asked to urge you to stay a while longer."

She looked at him inquiringly before she spoke. His eyes traveled toward the door, which put her more than ever on her guard. "Really, Mr. Budd, I don't know what to say. I have told you my situation."

"My friends are extraordinarily pleased with the results. Both of them are important men, and decisions of the greatest weight are hanging in the balance. They have asked me to explain this, and beg you to think it over. Don't be hurried; take your time."

She stood motionless, watching him, and saw his eyes moving here and there about the room. She understood that it was not idle curiosity which moved him, nor interest in her possessions—which consisted of a brush and comb on the dressing table, and what might have been a small bottle of rouge; also some newspapers and magazines which she had been reading on the bed. The room was in the new wing, recently completed; it was tastefully decorated, but rather small, with a single bed, a chair, a dressing table and a small writing table. The one window was open, and a gentle breeze blew in, laden with the scents of the forest.

He couldn't guess what might be the arrangements in this room for spying on the occupant. It was conceivable that all rooms in the building might have microphones installed, so that in case of need every whisper might be listened to or recorded. He placed the chair alongside the bed, with the back to the door, so that what he did would not be visible to anyone who might be looking through the keyhole. He didn't suppose that Hess would be spying on him, but someone else might be, and certainly it would be bad judgment to open the door and catch anybody in the act. The intimate friend of the Führer wasn't supposed to have secrets, or to suspect that he was suspected.

He seated himself in the chair and made a sign for her to sit near him. "Make yourself comfortable. This is a matter too important to be decided in a moment."

She seated herself on the edge of the bed—not forgetting that she was a lady from Baltimore, and that he was, after all, a very charming man. She sat calm and gravely erect, as a woman should if she had no interest in such things as love and romance. He had taken a little writing pad from his pocket, also a pencil, and holding both close to his body, he wrote the figure "1," followed by the words "greatly impressed." He had explained to her the significance of "Number One," or "*Die Nummer Eins,*" and why it was feminine in German, even though it referred to a man. He turned the writing toward her so that she could read it.

He wrote again; this time the figure "3" followed by the word "also." Then he added: "Army has orders to move into Poland tomorrow midnight." He heard her catch her breath. "Decision may depend spirits," he wrote. "You decide."

So there it was. She sat staring at him now, as if she couldn't believe it; he nodded his head affirmatively. She took the pencil and pad and wrote: "What do you advise?" In answer he pointed to the last two words already written.

But she couldn't decide. There were too many problems, too many dangers, too many unknown quantities in the equation. Her hand trembled as she wrote: "Please advise me."

The sheet of paper was full; he tore it off and laid it on the bed, where she could consult it if necessary. "Do you want another Munich?" he wrote; and waited while she studied this, her forehead wrinkled. At last she took the pencil and wrote: "I can't face another war." Lanny, who had been brought up in France, needed no writing materials now; he shrugged his shoulders and made a little gesture of spreading his hands apart. It meant: "Well, all right; if that's the way you feel, why do you ask me?"

She thought a while longer, with the pale skin of her forehead drawn together in two deep lines. "Why do you expect a Munich?" she wrote; and he in turn: "Br and Fr will give way before 1." They had discussed this subject, and she was familiar with his thought. "You want war now?" she wrote, and he replied: "I have 2 minds"

This was literally so. Lanny shrank from the horror as much as she did; but cold reason kept insisting that war was coming sooner or later, and the only question should be: What was the best time for Britain and France? Which side was arming the faster? Which would have gained a year from now? If Britain and France had acted a year ago, they would have had the army and air force of Czechoslovakia. If they delayed another year, they would lose the army and the air force of Poland. Those should be the determining factors to a military mind.

But not many women have such minds. Laurel Creston would be thinking: "I have a chance to postpone it; and if there is delay—even a week's delay, reason may prevail. Public opinion may be awakened, the conscience of mankind may assert itself. President Roosevelt has asked for that, and what can I do better than to trust his judgment?" The newspaper with the report of the President's action lay on the bed beside her, its German headlines staring up.

She took the pad and pencil and wrote: "I will risk one more." Then, after a moment's thought: "Only one, positively," and drew a line under the last word. He waited a while, to be sure that was her decision. She nodded her head, slowly but decisively.

"Are you ready to give me your answer?" he asked aloud—and his voice sounded startling, bold, in the long-silent room.

She answered: "I will stay until tomorrow night and give one more sitting. That must be the last, and it must be understood and agreed in advance. We will leave on the following morning."

"All right, Miss Jones. I will communicate your decision. It will be welcome."

He tore some sheets off the pad; not merely the one which had been written on, but several underneath, which might reveal the impress of the pencil. He took them into the bathroom, touched a match to them, and held them over the toilet bowl while they burned. When the flame was close to his fingers he dropped them into the water and pulled the lever.

XI

Morning papers were flown to this summer capital from both Munich and Berlin; large bundles in the present crisis, so that no important personage might lack information. Also, there were radios in the common rooms, and little knots would gather about them; it was permitted to these privileged ones to hear the evil voices from abroad— just as certain members of the Catholic priesthood are permitted to read heretical works for the purpose of refuting them. Thus on this morning of crisis army officers and Party officials gloated as they listened to British and French broadcasters worrying over the German-Soviet pact, and speculating as to its possible secret clauses. Pleasant indeed to have your enemies worried and guessing!

These personages talked freely, without paying much attention to a stranger from overseas. After all, since the army was to be on the move at midnight, and Warsaw would be taken or destroyed within a week, what difference could it make? The desire to show off superior knowledge is a common weakness, and one of the Führer's young aides remarked to the art expert that of course there had been a deal for the division of conquered Poland. The Germans had no use for the eastern half, which had belonged to Russia before the last war; and could the Russians refuse it when the Führer offered to lay it in their lap? A merry joke on the British, who had had their mission in Moscow for a number of weeks now, trying to make a deal to get the Soviets at war with the Führer! Still merrier on the solemn Sir Nevile, who had called here for his letter at the very hour when signatures were being placed upon the pact in Moscow!

All was cheerfulness that morning in the summer capital; at any rate in its early hours. Toward noon, however, Lanny began to notice a change; there was whispering, and some groups did not seem to welcome his presence. He could guess, but he couldn't be sure till after lunch, when he had a chance for a few whispered words with an SS lieutenant whom he had motored to the Parteitag a year ago. "The order to the army has been called off; we are not to move until further notice." Lanny exclaimed: "*Also! Was ist geschehen?*" But the aide didn't know. Something had changed the Führer's mind. It was for him in his wisdom to decide.

Lanny retired to his room and read the newspapers, and afterwards took up extrasensory perception again. It seemed the part of wisdom to keep himself inconspicuous, and this was still more true of his mysterious woman companion. He did not invite her for a walk that day, for it was raining; and they could not talk in her room. Anyhow, he had nothing much to say, for she had established herself as a medium and had been supplied with an abundance of local color and personal details. A skilled fiction writer would need no help from an art expert in making up words for these personages to speak.

XII

So passed a strange day and part of a night. Lanny had a brief talk with Hess, who came to his room and confirmed the calling off of the advance into Poland, and the reason therefor. The Führer had been shaken in his determination; he was wavering in his mind. Some of the older generals were glad of the postponement, but the younger men, the Nazis, were in a fever of disappointment; they had been on tiptoe, hoping soon to go to the front, and now the glory had been snatched from their grasp. Hess said: "I can't keep my own mind made up. One moment I am glad and the next sorry." Lanny replied: "I suppose I'd be the same way if I were a German. It's always easy for a foreigner to be neutral."

The Deputy explained that the Führer was tied up in an important conference that evening, so it might be late before he could visit the medium. Lanny said she understood that, and would wait patiently. "But don't fail to let me know how matters turn out, for I am deeply interested." The Deputy promised and went away.

After that Lanny had nothing to do but try to keep his mind on "critical ratios," "standard deviation," "terminal salience," "mean chance expectation," and other technicalities having to do with the proof or disproof of extrasensory perception. Under just what circumstances could a man guess the face of a card which some other person was looking at? Could he guess it before the other person had turned it up? Could he guess it while the other person was in another room? Or when he was in another city? Could he call the order of a pack of cards before their being turned? "Down through," this was called, in the glossary of the Duke experiments; its symbol was "DT"—which had had a quite different meaning in the fashionable society which Lanny Budd frequented.

Really, it was enough to give you the DTs, or the willies, or the heebyjeebies, to read of such experiments and try to realize what they meant. There were people who had called a whole series of twenty-five cards "down through" correctly. More incredible yet, there were people who had called cards before they were shuffled—that is, they had called what the cards were going to be after the shuffling had been done. That seemed like reducing the whole thing to an absurdity, and there were investigators who wanted to revise the laws of mathematical probability in order to avoid having to believe what these experiments seemed to prove. The chances against the things' having happened by accident were millions and billions and sometimes trillions.

Lanny told himself that here was something even more important to mankind than the question of another World War. Indeed here might be something which made war, or stopped it. Here was a force in the minds of men which might control their decisions without their being aware of it. Could there be more hate in the collective mind of men than love? If so, the collective mind might force the mind of a leader against his conscious will. All sorts of things might be happening to our minds, of which we had no conscious idea.

These were problems with which men would be dealing long after wars and rumors of war had been banished from the earth. It ought to have been easy to lose oneself in reading about them; but in spite of his best efforts Lanny would find that his thoughts had jumped off to Laurel Creston's room and what might be going on there. Her séance was planned to be a fraud; but suppose she had dropped into a trance again—what might be happening?

Many times Lanny had wished that he might have some psychic gifts himself. How convenient for a presidential agent, if he could read other people's minds, and see what they were doing at a distance—and even what they were going to be doing next day or the day after! The Duke experiments appeared to show that a great many people possessed traces of the telepathic gift; and now, after an all-day and half-the-night wait, Lanny decided to make another try. He put out his light and lay back on his bed, closing his eyes and concentrating his mind on the idea that his subconsciousness would receive an impression of what was going on in Laurel Creston's room. He got an impression of her lying on her bed waiting, just as he was waiting; but he hadn't the least idea that this was psychic, for it was what he had every reason to assume that she was doing. Concentrating his mind in search of a clearer vision, he fell fast asleep.

XIII

He was brought wide awake by a sharp quick tapping on his door. He started up, half dazed, then turned on his light and stepped to the door. He opened it, and faced Laurel Creston, but not as he had ever seen her before or could have imagined her; hair and clothing in disarray, face white and eyes wide with fear. He stepped aside and she entered; she made no sound, only a quick motion of the hand for him to close the door. Then, in a tense whisper: "We must get out of this house at once! The man is mad!"

"What has he done?" demanded Lanny, also under his breath.

"He tried to make love to me—to hold me against my will."

"Good heavens! Are you injured?"

"No. I threatened to scream. I said: 'You'll have to kill me!' "

"Hush!" Lanny whispered, and then: "Look." He held up one finger; then he said the word "or," and held up three fingers. She answered by holding up one. It was Hitler, not Hess.

He had noticed that there was no key in the lock of his room door, and had wondered if this was the case with all the bedrooms, to facilitate spying. He took a straight chair and wedged it under the door knob, pressed firmly between the knob and the floor. Then he signed for Laurel to sit on the side of the bed; he got his pad and pencil and sat by her and wrote: "Danger," and then: "Was 3 present?" She shook her head and he went on: "We will go. Must have exit permits. I will see 3."

She took the pencil from him. She could hardly write, because of the shaking of her hand. "Can't stay alone."

"Must go," he replied. "You fix chair." He pointed to what he had done to keep the door closed.

"Madman—will break in," was her scrawl.

"Can't fight him. Moral suasion. 3 will help."

"Will throw self out of window!"

"I will not go out of hearing. Call out and I will come."

"I am terrified. Can't control."

"No good to run. Police everywhere. Must persuade."

"Monster," she wrote; at least he guessed it was meant to be that. Her hands were still shaking, and he took them and held them in a firm grip. At the same time he smiled and nodded his head slowly, as if to say: "It's all right, it's all right."

After an interval he took the pencil and wrote some more. "I can handle. Sick man. Ashamed. He will not come my room. Positive." That was comforting, and he waited for it to take effect. He added the words: "Return soon."

She sat with her hands clasped tightly together, as if to stop their trembling, or at any rate to keep it from being noticed. Her eyes were still wild and her lips almost bloodless. "Go," she whispered.

"Don't fail to fix door," he wrote. "Don't open till I come. Three quick taps, then three more." She read what he had written, then nodded. He tore off the sheets and disposed of them with fire and water as before. Then he came to the door and removed the chair, opened the door, took a quick glance up and down the hallway, and went out, closing the door softly.

XIV

He went straight to Hess's room, which he had visited in past times. He breathed a silent prayer that the Deputy would be in, then a sigh of relief when it proved to be so. "Something urgent, Rudi," he said, as he came in.

The Nazi had taken off his coat, probably getting ready for bed. His face showed concern as Lanny asked: "Have you heard what happened?"

"What do you mean?"

"Our friend wanted the woman to stay and I guess he was a little too ardent; he has frightened her nearly out of her wits."

"*Pfui Teufel!*"

"What makes it so awkward, Rudi—you must understand that she is my woman."

"*Herrgott, Lanny!* Why didn't you tell us that?"

"Well, I didn't suppose you were interested in my sex life. I was bringing you a medium."

"You know how the Führer is—when he wants something he wants it very much."

"Certainly; and I know he's under a strain right now, and probably not quite himself. No doubt he hated to give up this medium. Was the séance good?"

"Absolutely marvelous, Lanny. Afterwards the Führer told me to go, and I took it for granted that he was going to try to induce her to stay by offering her money. I didn't dream——" Hess stopped.

"I know, it's most unfortunate, and I hope he's not going to be too annoyed. The trouble is, Elvirita has gone just about off her head, and I'm afraid I have to take her away at once."

"You don't mean tonight, surely—in this rain!"

"I'm afraid I do. It's hard for you to understand this woman's attitude, Rudi. She hadn't been sensibly taught, like a National-Socialist *Mädchen;* she is a victim of Puritan education, of prudery and sexual repression. I neglected to warn her—because I knew that if I did she would refuse to come. But I ought to have warned you; I feel guilty for not having done so."

"It is most unfortunate, Lanny. The Führer could have had no idea that she would take such an attitude."

"It is especially unfortunate because she is a medium. Such persons are nearly always ill-balanced and overemotional. This girl is on the verge of hysterics; she says she will jump out of the window if I don't take her away. I must beg you to go to the Führer and ask him to excuse her, and let us take our departure."

"It will be devilish awkward, Lanny."

"I know it, but what can I do? We don't want to have any scenes and start a lot of hateful gossip."

"No, surely not. And if you feel that way I suppose I'll have to go to the Führer about it."

"Don't let it interfere with our friendship, I beg you. It's just one of those things, and nobody's fault."

"I understand, Lanny."

"Tell the Führer not to concern himself too much about it; I know he's got his hands full right now, and this can't really mean very much to him. Tell him that I understand perfectly—he had no means of knowing what kind of girl this was, and how she would behave."

"The main thing, I feel sure, was that he hated to have the séances broken off."

"I don't doubt it, and I wish I could have arranged matters. But I couldn't have got her here except on the promise of a prompt return. Ask the Führer to forgive me, and to forget the whole thing. The girl will be all right when she gets over her fright."

So that was that; they shook hands—and then, as an afterthought, Lanny said: "By the way, Elvirita lost her luggage, and her passports were in it. I suppose she can get a *carte d'identité* in Switzerland; but we'll both need some sort of exit permit."

"That's right." The Deputy thought for a moment. "I'll get Reichenau to give you a military pass. That'll be good for anywhere in the southern district."

"Will you want to wake him at this time in the morning?"

"He may not be asleep yet. If he is I'll get his chief of staff to attend to it."

"Shall I wait here?"

"I'll bring it to your room."

XV

So Lanny went back, and gave the three quick taps on the door and then three more. The chair was pulled away and the door opened. "Everything is all right," he said, and put his finger to his lips.

He went methodically about putting his belongings into his bags. She, who had no belongings, sat gazing at the wall before her; thinking, no doubt, about the first-hand information she had obtained as to the Nazis, their manners and way of life. When there came a tap on the door, she started and looked her alarm. Lanny went to the door, opened it just enough to slip outside, and closed it behind him.

"Here you are," said Rudi, and put a small piece of paper into his hand. "Reichenau's light was still burning, so I had him make it out. I explained that you had stayed late to oblige me. I have ordered your car brought to the door."

"Thanks ever so much, Rudi. And once more—don't have any hard feelings."

"Of course not—why should I? Take care of yourself, and I hope the girl will have no hard feelings either. As a medium she's a wonder, and if you'll bring her to Berlin, I can guarantee there won't be any repetition of this mistake."

"I'll talk to her about it—a little later. I hope it doesn't come to war, Rudi, but if it does, I'll be coming in by way of Switzerland, no doubt."

"Do, by all means. The information you bring us is most useful."

They shook hands warmly and Hess went away. Lanny re-entered the room and said: "Everything O.K." He picked up his two bags and his portable. "Are you steady again?"

"I could run," she answered, regardless of discretion.

He made her put on his overcoat, over her light dress. Then they went down a side stairway, and out by the inconspicuous door through which she had entered. The car was already there, with an SS man standing beside it, regardless of the rain. "*Heil Hitler!*" said Lanny, and the salute was returned.

The man put the bags in, Lanny stepped into the driver's seat, and the passenger into the seat beside him. He started the engine, and said: "*Gute Nacht.*" The car rolled across the drive, and the barrier was lifted before them. Everything on the Führer's estate was automatic, including the men and women.

As they started down the slope of the mountain Lanny remarked: "So ends my fourth visit to the haunt of the wild witch Berchta."

The response was: "Perhaps her ghost still walks." There was a little catch in Laurel's voice, and it turned into a weeping spell. He let her alone—for he had been brought up among women, and understood that this is something necessary,

21

Auf den Bergen Ist Freiheit

I

MOTORING at night bears a certain resemblance to sitting in a motion-picture theater; on all sides are darkness and mystery, while a beam of light makes a small scene in front. If the road is straight and the hour after midnight, the show is apt to be monotonous; but if the car is winding down a mountain side, great stretches of landscape sweep before the driver's eyes; chasms open up, and tree-covered slopes magically appear, loom closer, and then vanish into nothingness. It is fascinating, but also may be dangerous, and when it is raining the careful driver will shift into second gear, so as not to have to use his brakes on the curves. "Too bad if we got away from the Gestapo, only to go over a precipice!" remarked Lanny. He thought it better to get his passenger's mind off past troubles, even by the contemplation of fresh ones.

They rolled down from the Obersalzberg, and into the town of Berchtesgaden, now fast asleep. "Here they make charming toys," discoursed the driver. "Also they mine rock salt, and I have been told that these long-tunneled mines used to provide a route of escape from the Nazis; there were entrances in both Germany and Austria, and workers who did not like the swastika would smuggle their friends through. But now that is all over, since Germany and Austria are the same."

The *Anschluss*, he went on to point out, was a convenient thing for them, since their pass was signed by General Walther von Reichenau, commander of the army forces in the southern district. "That now means Austria as well as Bavaria, so we can enter Switzerland by way of the Inn Valley—a short route, and one that takes us away from Munich and the principal *Autobahnen*. So it is safest for us."

"Tell me," said his companion, "did Hess tell Hitler that I was about to leave?"

"Oh, of course—he would have to. Hess wouldn't dream of doing

455

anything that might displease his Führer. But I don't think there is any chance that Hitler will change his mind—if that's what is worrying you. He knows you are my friend." He did not tell her of the phrase he had used, "my woman." That item of scandal, along with the others, would be shed when Miss Elvirita Jones crossed the border of Naziland. It wouldn't injure Lanny Budd in the eyes of any Nazi, and it would preclude the possibility of Adi's attempting to hold an American medium against her will.

Lanny had had a nap, he told her, and was ready for any amount of driving; she, for her part, wanted just one thing in the world, to get out of the Führer's domain. Their road wound through Alpine foothills, sometimes turning away from their goal. Rain continued to fall, but he could see clearly, and was used to driving in all sorts of weather. She didn't want to sleep, she said, but just to sit and watch the car lights playing over curtains of gray mist.

II

When daylight came they were in the valley of the Inn, which winds its way northward and eastward to the Danube, and on its way passes the village of Braunau, in which the son of Alois Schicklgruber had been brought into a world that he hated. But Lanny's course lay the other way, to the west and southward, up to the sources of the river in the high Engadine. They stopped in a village and bought food, and she handed it to him while he drove.

After that, feeling more cheerful, she turned on the radio in front of her—a Swiss station, from which they learned that Britain had signed a pact with Poland, pledging military action in the event of attack. Then they listened to a Munich station, denouncing this act of provocation, almost of war. The commentator went on to scold Prime Minister Chamberlain for statements made in the House of Commons. Then a French station—some commentator whose name Lanny didn't know, discussing what imperiled Poland would do in the event that Hitler should declare an *Anschluss* with Danzig. A strange use mankind was making of these newly contrived vibrations in a medium still unknown; all over the earth they were sent with the speed of light, carrying menaces and scoldings in a score or two of languages. The various wave lengths did not interfere with one another, but the men who used them had not learned an equal amount of tolerance.

"Anyhow, war hasn't begun," said Lanny. "Rudi told me in so many words that the army had been ordered to march at midnight; so you and I carry a weighty secret in our bosoms—we managed to postpone the slaughter for a few hours, and it may even be for a few days! This is something over which the historians may be racking their brains in years to come."

He saw that his passenger had recovered her self-control, so he added: "I wonder if it would be too painful to tell me what happened at the séance. Hess told me it was a success."

"You have a right to know," she declared. "Perhaps it was my fault that I made it too great a success. I gave them Dietrich Eckart, and they swallowed him in gulps. I suppose anything is fair against the Nazis, but really it seemed inhuman to play such a scene. Evidently Hitler adored the old orator, and he plied Uncle Cicero with questions —through Hess, of course; he would ask several questions at once, but Hess would repeat only one at a time."

"What questions?"

"First, who else was there—the names of this one and that. I was afraid it might be a trap, asking me about people who were still living. I evaded answering unless I was sure. I gave them the ones I was sure of—Heinzelmann again, and Hitler's father. I made Eckart say that old Alois was greatly honored here because he was the Führer's father. That made Hitler purr, of course."

"Too good!" was Lanny's verdict. "No wonder you got into trouble."

"I found the temptation difficult to resist. Why not say something that you knew was right, and that they would swallow? Hitler wanted to know what the spirits did, and Eckart said they talked on exalted subjects; he gave a few samples, all having to do with National Social-ism. Hitler wanted to know if there were any Jews there, and of course after Otto Kahn I couldn't say No; I said there were none allowed where Eckart was. I gave all the personal details that you had pro-vided, and I'm pretty sure both Hitler and Hess were completely satisfied."

"You managed not to go into a real trance?"

"I had my hands clasped together in such a way that my little finger was curled up, and whenever I had an impulse to feel sleepy I pressed on it until it hurt. It is still sore from the treatment."

"What did you say about the war?"

"I had Eckart and Heinzelmann discussing it. I had them agree that Germany had too many enemies and that they saw great danger ahead.

Heinzelmann asked: 'What could Stalin have in mind from a deal except to get Germany into a war with the West, so that he would have Europe at his mercy?' At the end I had Eckart talk as I imagined a Bavarian poet might, giving Hitler a warning. It must have been quite impressive."

"No wonder he couldn't bear to let you go," commented Lanny. "You must understand that from his point of view he was doing you a favor, and he must have been greatly surprised by your behavior."

Laurel made no comment.

III

The scenery of the Inn Valley is beautiful, even when rain is falling and the heights are veiled in mist. But this pair saw little of it, for Lanny had to keep his eyes fixed on the winding road before him, and his passenger still couldn't believe that there was such a thing as security in the world. Even in these Alps there were portents of war; horns would blow behind them and Lanny would draw up on the shoulder of the road while military traffic roared by. "Surely they don't plan to go to war with Switzerland!" exclaimed the woman. He answered: "They may fear that France might invade through Switzerland—or they may pretend to fear it. You can be sure the Swiss will be taking no chances."

Now and then she would turn on the radio, dialing as he suggested. They would listen to news, and to commentators in the near-by capitals. Nobody appeared to know that Wehrmacht orders to march had been issued and then canceled; but the food rationing and the restrictions on travel went into effect, and all the world took it for granted that this meant war or the threat of war—the problem was, which? A gigantic hand of international poker was being played, and sooner or later somebody would "call," and the hands would be laid on the table, and what would be found in them? The son of Budd-Erling remarked: "Some day historians will look back and observe how the fate of the world hung upon the processes of one psychopathic mind, and will contemplate with horror the idea that such a situation should have been permitted to exist."

"I don't have to wait for historians," replied Laurel Creston. "I contemplate it with horror now. I am wondering if it wasn't my duty to stay and try to control the man at any cost."

"You couldn't have stayed," was the other's response. "I would never have consented to leave you in Hitler's house."

"Not to prevent a war?"

"Sooner or later they would have discovered your real name, and then you would no longer have had any power. Also, I would have lost the power to go back into Germany, which is important to me."

"I have a tendency to forget that," she replied. "It is not very considerate of me."

"You are one of those idealistic temperaments that cannot resist the desire to save the world. I honor you for it, but at the same time I fear for your happiness. Take my advice, Miss Creston, and consider that you have done your best, and allow yourself the rest which you have earned." He said this with a smile of grandfatherly benevolence, and ventured to turn his eyes from the highway long enough for a glance at her serious, troubled face.

"My friends call me Laurel," she replied. "Don't you think that you have proved yourself a good friend?"

"My friends call me Lanny," he answered, promptly. "I hope you will be one of them from now on."

"From now on, Lanny; and I'll try to prove it. I don't know what you are doing and don't intend to ask, but I am certain in my heart that you hate those evil men we have just parted from. This is a bond between us, and I'll be prepared to stand by as a comrade."

"Well, Laurel," he smiled, "you promised that everything you saw and learned in the Berghof would be locked up in your own heart forever. I must ask you to consider my attitude toward those evil men as a part of the secret, and indeed the most important part of all. I will say this much and no more: I am under a solemn pledge, and I have to put you under the same."

"I think I understand, and you may count upon me not to hint at the subject again."

"I have to ask more than that. When you speak of me to others, do so on the basis that we have not met since that evening in the home of Sophie, Baroness de la Tourette, when you called me a troglodyte. That was helpful to me in a fashionable company, and it may be in others."

IV

A long drive through the valley of the Upper Inn, retracing the course of a swift mountain stream, still in rain and heavy mist. Lanny drove slowly, saying: "Darkness will help us at the border." When they were approaching this goal of all their thoughts, he told his friend to get into the back seat and be asleep. So he drove up to the guard station, and stepped out under the shelter, saying his *"Heil Hitler"*—always so useful—and presenting his military pass. Nothing could have been more regular, or more effective. *"Die Dame schlaft,"* he remarked, and a rain-coated guard contented himself with flashing the torchlight through the rear window of the car, without troubling to open the door. *"Eine schlechte Nacht, mein Herr,"* he remarked. *"Fahren Sie vorsichtig."* The barrier was raised and the car went on.

At the Swiss station it was a different matter. Elvirita Jones had been transformed into Laurel Creston, and had no passport or papers. Refugees from Naziland were continually escaping into Switzerland, and the Swiss were lenient with them; when an American said that his traveling companion had had her bags stolen, the lady was advised to report to the Fremdenpolizei of the district, after which she would travel to Bern and obtain a substitute passport from the American Embassy. *"Leider, meine Dame!"* said the official who made out the card. He referred to her as a *"schriftenloser Ausländer,"* but that was not meant to be impolite; it just meant a "foreigner without papers." It seemed strange to meet a man in authority who spoke German, yet was not a Nazi and an agent of terror.

Tourists had been pouring into this mountain republic by every pass and tunnel, expecting war to break out at any hour. Lanny drove, and inquired at half a dozen inns before he found rooms. When he saw his friend to her room he said: "Now you are safe, and can put all this nightmare out of your mind."

"I have no words to tell you my gratitude!" she exclaimed.

"You don't need any words," he answered. "I have had an interesting experience and it was worth while. To crown it, I found a medium, and I'd been wondering for a long time how to manage that."

Locked in his own room, Lanny set up the little portable. That was always his first duty, and it had been delayed too long. He wrote what he had learned in the Berghof concerning the secret clauses in the Russo-Soviet treaty. He wrote that the army had been ordered to move at midnight of the twenty-fifth, but that Hitler had consulted the spirits, who had unsettled his mind, and no one could be sure how long it would take to get settled again. He wrote about Sir Nevile's visit, and the efforts which Britain and France were making to hold Poland back. It was a long report, with items picked up in Berlin as well as the Berghof. Lanny double-sealed it as usual, put the envelope under his pillow, and slept the sleep of a good and faithful P.A.

V

In the morning the clouds had blown away, the air was washed clear, and the Alpine peaks were shining like Christmas cards with tinsel on them. They breakfasted in heavenly peace, like two soldiers who have been through a battle and escaped unscathed. They continued on their journey, and the contrast of the scenery with what it had been on the previous day made them feel that they had escaped from the caverns of Niebelheim into the bright land of freedom. When they were far enough from the border not to fear attracting attention, a lady wearing a man's overcoat emerged from a car and entered a shop, explaining that her traveling bags had been stolen. An odd sensation to be without so much as even a toothbrush in the world! It was a revelation as to the complications of civilized life—to discover how many things you had to have.

Laurel Creston, a considerate person, stopped only for the real necessities. Lanny had told her that he was bound for Paris upon a matter of importance—not saying that it was to find out what the French would do in the event that Hitler should declare Danzig a part of his German Reich. He asked about her plans, and drew from her the fact that she had been too greatly upset to make any. Poor little woman, she had been trying gamely to achieve her independence, and had succeeded, but now her affairs had been knocked galley-west; not merely all her clothes were lost, and the money she had had in her trunk, but her manuscripts, except for those of which copies had been mailed to editors.

"The first thing," Lanny suggested, "is to cable each of those editors to hold the manuscripts until you send a new address. The next thing is to be frank with me and tell me how you are fixed for money; I have more than I need, and there's no reason for you to worry."

"I have money in the bank at Baltimore," she assured him, "and I surely don't mean to impose on you any further."

"Put it this way," he replied. "I have discovered one of those white blackbirds, a good medium. I hope to experiment with her and to learn a lot. Peace of mind is necessary to her work, and it is to my interest to see that she has it."

"When do you wish to try an experiment?"

"Ordinarily I would say as soon as you feel fit. But I have some matters pressing upon me. I have to go to Paris, from there to London, and then possibly to New York—it depends upon the war. In any case

I ought to be back in a month or six weeks, and then, if you are free, I will come wherever you are."

"Perhaps it might be a good idea if I stayed in Switzerland for a week or two, until I get myself together and make some plans."

"I have an idea," Lanny said. "My mother's home on the Riviera is a lovely spot, and there is an abundance of room there. My mother is a hospitable soul and would be delighted."

"But I barely know your mother, Lanny!"

"In that playground of Europe people drop in and drop out again, and nobody bothers about where they have come from, or what they are doing, except having a good time. The important person in this case is my stepfather, who is the most uniformly kind human soul I have ever known, and a devout student of the occult. To him you would come as a messenger from heaven; he would find out all about your psychic powers and help you to develop them. He is another kind of white blackbird, a genuine saint, and you would find him a welcome contrast to the Nazis."

Lanny talked about Parsifal Dingle, his healing powers, and the extraordinary impression his persistent kindness had produced upon even the most worldly on the Côte d'Azur. The stepson had already told about Madame, and about the monastery of Dodanduwa in Ceylon, whose monks had appeared in the old woman's trances. He said: "It will be interesting to have you sit with Madame and then Madame with you, and see if you get Tecumseh or Claribel, and what Madame might get from you. Parsifal would be delighted with such an opportunity and would make elaborate records, which might perhaps be published by the Society for Psychical Research in London or New York."

"All this sounds very interesting," admitted the woman. "How would you arrange it?"

"I can stop in the next town and get my mother on the telephone. It is my duty to call her every now and then and let her hear the voice of her only son. I can tell her about you, and, if you wish, you can hear her voice, telling you that Bienvenu means 'Welcome'!"

VI

However, things are rarely that simple in the *haut monde*. Before they reached the next town, Lanny remembered that Laurel Creston had once called Beauty Budd's son a "troglodyte," and in Beauty Budd's hearing! Beauty in return had called her conduct "insolence"—not to her face, but driving home with Lanny and Marceline. For things of that sort Beauty had the memory of an elephant; and besides, it had been only a year ago. Also, there was all that smart crowd to be considered—so free and easy in their manners and morals, and also in their conversation. What would be said of an anti-Nazi fiction writer turning up at the home of a woman whose son was a friend of the Führer?

Motoring through mountain passes and alongside sparkling blue lakes, Lanny entered upon a carefully worded explanation. "I have admitted to you the fact that I do not like the people of the Berghof, and that is a secret I have not entrusted even to my mother or my father. The reasons I am not free to reveal; I can only tell you that when I am in the company of the idle rich, I take the attitude that I am an art expert, turning my specialized knowledge into money—something they respect me for. When I meet Nazi-Fascist sympathizers, I give them to understand that I am one of them, and when they hear that I have visited the Berghof, they talk freely in my presence. This is a matter of the utmost importance to me, and I must never permit anything to interfere with it."

"I understand, Lanny, and you may count on my keeping your secret."

"What I have to ask is that you will keep some of your own secrets, also. It would not do for an outspoken anti-Nazi to be a guest at my mother's home; it would cause gossip, and interfere with my intimacy with Juan March and the Duque d'Alba and Lord Londonderry and Lord Beaverbrook and the rest. You can write what you please, of course, provided you keep it locked up—the police will not raid Bienvenu. You can publish it under the name of Mary Morrow, provided you don't talk about it. But in your conversation I would ask you to become a lady troglodyte for the time being. You are a writer, interested in human nature, and bored by political questions. Could you do that?"

"But I have already talked to friends on the Riviera!"

"That was a year ago, and you can say that you have come to know Europe better. The wealthy take it for granted that people have eccentric notions when they are young, and as they grow up they acquire what is called common sense. As it happens, you have a perfect cover; you have suddenly discovered that you are a medium, and are greatly excited about it. Parsifal has invited you to come to Bienvenu for some tests, and you and everybody else are so curious about the results that nobody bothers you about politics."

"Suppose I never go into another trance, Lanny. Suppose it happened that one time, perhaps because I was frightened."

"Even so, you have your story. You were in a pension in Switzer-land—I wouldn't say anything about having been in Germany, because that might cause questions to be asked and inquiries to be made. Just wipe all that off the slate. I'm certain that it wouldn't do you any good to try to get back your money or other property from Berlin; the money has been stolen, and the clothes are being worn by the mistress of some Gestapo official. You would only bring troubles upon your head—investigations, and possibly publicity."

"I have already made up my mind as to that. It is forgotten."

"All right then. You were in a pension in Bern, let us say, and the people were dabbling in psychic matters and you went into a trance; afterwards they told you what you had said—make up some story, not Uncle Cicero, of course, for he is dead along with Miss Jones. You remembered what you had heard about Parsifal Dingle's interest in the subject, and you decided to come and put yourself in his hands and see what use could be made of your gift. That is all consistent, and will give the playboys and girls so much to talk about that they won't ask what you think about Hitler or Roosevelt."

"All right," said Laurel. "I will follow that role. Incidentally, Lanny, I perceive that you must have been making up roles for quite a while."

"Since about the age of four," replied the grandson of Budd Gun-makers, a bit disconcerted by her shrewdness. "I used to sit as still as a little mouse and listen while my father was telling my mother how to persuade the Duchesse du Diable to invite the Ruritanian Minister of War to a luncheon, so that my father could sell him a thousand light machine guns."

VII

That evening, which was Sunday, they arrived in Bern, and from his hotel room Lanny got his mother on the telephone. "Oh, Lanny, where are you? And what are you doing?" Before he had time to answer the second question, she rushed on: "Are we going to have a war?"

"I don't know, darling."

"Oh, I can't live through another war! I refuse to stand it!" And then: "What has got into the world? It seems that everybody has gone mad."

He waited while she poured out her feelings. He had been through World War I with her: Marcel's desperate injury, his disfigurement, and his final disappearance; then all the *blessés* and the efforts to help them;

then Kurt's peril as a German agent in Paris, and her flight with him—yes, Beauty had had her share of war, enough for one lifetime. "Oh, Lanny, you wouldn't get into it, would you?"

He told her No; America would surely keep out this time. He told her he was going to Paris and then to London, and would call her from there. He added: "I have just had an interesting experience: I have discovered a medium, a young woman who beats even Madame, I think. Parsifal will be crazy about her."

"Lanny, are you getting into another horrid affair?" demanded a mother to whom love had always stood as Number One among human phenomena.

"Nothing of that sort, old dear. She's a perfect lady, and very self-contained. She's a niece of Reverdy Holdenhurst."

"Oh!"—a large and voluminous syllable. Then: "Where did you meet her?"

"I met her at Sophie's, and so did you. Do you remember the woman writer who called me a troglodyte?"

"*That* woman, Lanny?"—a tone of dismay.

"She has changed her political ideas, and admits now that I am right. So that's all ancient history and you must forget it. The important thing is that she has discovered that she's a medium, and produces most important phenomena. Do you remember Otto Kahn?"

"Yes, of course."

"Well, I have just listened to a talk between him and Sir Basil in the spirit world, the most convincing thing you could imagine. Parsifal will be enraptured, and will want to try her and Madame together. I want you to invite her as a house guest and let him make a series of tests."

"But why don't *you* come, Lanny?"

"I have a picture deal on—I'll tell you about it later. Take my word for Miss Creston—you will find her an acceptable person, and all our friends will be crazy to have sittings with her." He went on in that vein for a while: a medium would be a social distinction—especially when she came from an old Baltimore family, and had promised to behave with propriety.

"Lanny, have you got yourself mixed up with her?" demanded the mother, who had become so regardful of the proprieties in her near sixties.

"Nothing of that sort, I give you my word. She is a prudish person, I believe, though I haven't made any inquiry. She is staying at a hotel here; she heard a lot of talk about psychic phenomena and became interested; then she tried an experiment, and made the discovery that she went into a spontaneous trance and didn't know what she had said in it." An interesting example of how to walk on a tightrope of fact over an abyss of falsehood!

Beauty said: "All right, of course; send her." And then: "Oh, something ought to be done in this dreadful crisis. Can't you talk to some of the influential persons you know?"

"I expect to talk to Schneider tomorrow evening. I've been doing all I can."

"Lanny, what people need is a moral rebirth; we are frivolous and heedless and selfish people. We ought to learn to love one another, and teach our children a religion of service."

"Yes, old dear," said the dutiful son. He knew that this was Parsifal Dingle speaking through Parsifal's wife. For something over twelve years Lanny had been watching the change in his mother's vocabulary, and he found it touching, but at the same time he couldn't restrain a smile at this so unforeseeable development in a one-time "professional beauty."

VIII

Lanny and Laurel parted that night, because Lanny wished to make an early start next morning. She would go first to the shops to get herself a presentable costume, and then she would apply to the Embassy for her papers; this, presumably, would require inquiries of Washington and involve delays. Lanny put into her hands most of the money he had with him—he could get more in Paris, he told her. She tried to thank him for his many bounties, and there was a little unsteadiness in her voice. He hastened to tell her that it was nothing, he was happy to have served her, it was worth a lot of trouble to find a new medium. He put it on that basis, because he knew human nature as well as his mother did, and he feared the sort of scene his mother had feared. He couldn't afford anything of the sort in the midst of a world crisis.

He stepped into his car, on a bright fresh morning with traces of winter beginning in these high regions. He passed around the long lake of Neufchâtel, and through the Jura mountains into France; another of his all-day drives, with only one stop for a bite of lunch and a fresh supply of *essence*, as the French call it. He had telephoned Schneider, setting an hour for arrival and promising to come directly to the Baron's home. The Baron was the one who would know what was happening in *la patrie,* and would part with his information in exchange for Lanny Budd's.

Meantime, turn on the radio and catch up with events. Having watched this new force in human affairs from the days of its infancy seventeen years earlier, Lanny knew the stations of Europe, their designations and wave lengths, their voices and their official minds. From Switzerland and Holland you could get facts; from Britain, facts, but carefully filtered; from France, a mixture of facts and falsehoods always colored by propaganda; from Germany, falsehoods with now and then a few facts to lend plausibility, and everything for the promotion of National Socialism. You listened to it because, with practice, you could learn from lies as well as from truth; what the Nazis wanted their people to believe revealed surely what they were up to.

Hitler, in Berlin, had provided a plane to fly Sir Nevile Henderson to London. Evidently, he had some new proposal; the Hearst papers in America published what they claimed was the substance of it. The French papers reported rumors of an exchange of correspondence going on between the Führer and the French Premier. The British BBC announced that Chamberlain would address the Commons on the morrow. The Nazi stations broadcast more stories of torturing and castrating of Germans in the so-called Polish Corridor; the Swiss stations reported denials of the charges by Warsaw. Each hearer believed what he chose.

IX

The Baron had delayed the dinner hour, awaiting his guest. Impeccable French *politesse* forbade him to press questions upon the guest until he had eaten; but when they retired to the study, Lanny paid for his meal by laying bare the mind of Adolf Hitler, his Deputy, his household, his military and official staffs. An incredible thing, that a man of this lowly origin and disordered mentality should have accumulated such power, should have subjected seventy million of the world's most progressive people to his volcanic will. Schneider couldn't believe it; few in France could believe it—skeptical, libertarian, individualistic France! The Baron listened, as if to another of the Arabian Nights' Enchantments. There had been some two or three thousand of these nights already, and not all the magic of the East or the psychic research of the West enabled one to guess how many thousands more there would be.

Schneider's questions revealed the state of his own mind. The German-Soviet deal had completely floored this man of great affairs. He took it as a complete vindication of his position, that the Franco-Soviet alliance had been utterly worthless, a trap for his country; but now that he had been proved right, he was not happy, but on the contrary in a state of utter confusion. Poland was a broken reed, and the whole of the Balkans was so much grain, ripe for the Nazi-Soviet harvester. The *cordon sanitaire* was gone, and France and Britain faced the barbarians alone.

The munitions king was in such a state of distress that he even wanted an American expert to tell him what to do. At this late hour he hadn't made sure what part airplanes were going to play in war; what trust he should put in the word of half a dozen elderly French generals, who declared the Maginot Line absolutely impregnable, the French army the finest the world had ever seen, and alarmist talk about air power merely enemy effort to frighten Marianne into giving way to the dictators. "Tell me frankly, Mr. Budd, what will satisfy Hitler?" And of course Lanny had to say: "I fear that question is beyond the power of the Führer himself to answer. His appetite grows with what it feeds on."

Said the Baron: "Many of my associates have become convinced that if we grant his demands for parts of western Poland, we shall simply see in Warsaw what we saw in Prague. Then, they say, it will be Alsace and Lorraine."

"I have never heard the Führer mention those provinces," replied the American. "His grievance against France is that its press is irresponsible, it insults him and makes ideological war upon him."

The Baron shrugged his shoulders. "*My* papers surely do not insult him. But what can we do about the others?"

Lanny wanted to say: "The Führer will tell you." But he knew it was no time for a jest. In reality, Schneider needed no telling, for he had backed the efforts to overthrow the Third Republic, and the first proposal of the Cagoule had been to suppress the newspapers of the Left. But that effort had failed so ignominiously that the munitions king no longer referred to it, and perhaps considered it a mistake. What had happened at Prague, and to the value of his shares in the Skoda plant, had caused him to shrink back, and to talk about the need of solidarity among Frenchmen.

Having answered many questions, Lanny had the right to ask some. "What is this I heard over the radio about an exchange of letters between Hitler and Daladier?"

"I have seen copies of them," replied the Baron. "They represent one more effort to persuade Hitler to listen to reason; but I fear it will be futile, for Daladier says that the government will stand by its pledges to Poland, and of course that only serves to provoke Hitler."

They talked about this *premier de la république française*, who had been born the son of a baker and had begun his career as a humble *lycée* teacher. That he was a crude fellow who smelled of absinthe and talked with a cigarette stuck to his lower lip did not trouble the Baron so much as the fact that he was weak of will and shrank from stern action in any crisis. "He is still a Leftist at heart," was the way the munitions king put it. "He promises firmness, but then he goes off by himself and thinks what his old-time associates will say about him, and he begins to wobble again."

"He has to make a decision now," opined the American. "Hitler demands it."

The other reflected. "It occurs to me, Monsieur Budd, that it might be a good idea if you were to tell Daladier the things you have just told me. Would you be willing to do so?"

"Certainly, if you think it would be of interest to him."

"I doubt if there is anybody else in France who has talked with Hitler within the last two or three days. And it might be that you could drop a gentle hint that the government might put more pressure upon Poland to make concessions and get us by this bad corner."

"I am afraid I do not feel myself competent to give advice, Monsieur le Baron. I know what the Führer has said to me, and what he has told me to say to others. But when it comes to deciding policies, I find myself too humble."

"It would be a good thing for *la patrie* if some of her statesmen would take the same view of themselves. In any case, I think it might be good for 'Dala,' as his admirers call him, to hear your report. I shouldn't care to approach him, but I know someone who could do it with propriety, and with your permission I will make the suggestion."

X

So it came about that Lanny spent the night in Schneider's home, a privilege which highly placed Frenchmen do not readily extend; and in the morning he drove to the War Ministry in the rue Saint-Dominique, where the French executive insisted on living and working—to the displeasure of many who thought that the elderly and conservative generals had far too tight a hold upon him. An old, gray, sad-looking building of four stories, dark inside, also, with large rooms done in mahogany, and everywhere the inevitable thick red carpet.

Lanny arrived on the dot as was his custom, and was not kept waiting, even on this most crowded of days. He was escorted into the presence of the stocky and stoutish figure whom he had heard bellowing once or twice in the Chamber of Deputies. "The Bull of Vaucluse," he was called, but some wit had said that he was now the "Cow of Vacillation." He had a bull's neck, a dull brownish complexion, and kindly, tired eyes—there were few statesmen in Europe right now who were not on the verge of exhaustion. Ordinarily his manner was said to be sullen and his expression glowering; but he chose to present a different aspect to the son of Budd-Erling, holding out two hands to welcome him, and saying that he had met the father and heard of the son.

The Premier's breath revealed that he had started the morning with what the Americans call a "bracer" and the French an *apéritif*. While he listened to his caller and plied him with questions, he lighted one cigarette after another, and contrived somehow to make them stick to his lower lip when he spoke. Lanny was no snob, and didn't object that this was a man of the people, still having traces of a Provençal accent, and not very tidy in his personal appearance. In his speeches "Dala" talked about his "democratic conscience," but Lanny could not forget that he had condoned the murder of the Spanish people's government, and then had come to Munich and helped to wipe the Czechoslovak republic off the map. Now it was a question of Poland, no republic, but a dictatorship of the "Colonels," the landlords, and the priests. "Do you want to die for Danzig?" the appeasers were screaming in *Gringoire*—even now while millions of Frenchmen were being mobilized and sent to the border. Lanny would have liked to say: "Make no mistake, Monsieur le Premier, you will have to fight the Führer sooner or later." But of course his role didn't permit that.

What he had to say was: "I am a lover of art and a friend of peace. I have known Herr Hitler for many years, and this is what he tells me." Then followed one of Adi's discourses on his respect for western culture and his abhorrence for that of Asia—all parts of that continent, Tartar and Mongolian as well as Semitic. This could not have been very new to Daladier, who had just received two of Adi's long communications, pouring out his grievances. "The Macedonian conditions prevailing along our eastern frontier must cease. I see no possibility of persuading Poland, who deems herself safe from attack by virtue of guarantees given to her, to agree to a peaceful solution."

What the man of the French people wanted was to ply Lanny Budd with questions concerning the man of the German people, to whom he had appealed as one front-line soldier of the last war to another of the same. What kind of man was he, *au fond;* what did he really want, and where would he stop, if anywhere, and could anybody trust him—save possibly his own Party members, and the General Staff of his army?

Lanny had to bear in mind that every word he spoke would go back to Berlin, and with magical speed; for Dala's Foreign Minister, Georges Bonnet, was the most ardent of appeasers, and Bonnet's wife had been the intimate friend and confidante of Otto Abetz. Lanny said: "No, Monsieur le Premier, I am certain that the Führer is not bluffing. I don't think that he wants war, but he wants Danzig and the Corridor, and is determined to have them before the fall rains. The night when I left Berchtesgaden he was hesitating; but now he is in Berlin, and may be seeing a different set of advisers, and for all I know his army may have orders to attack Poland tonight."

XI

As soon as he went out from this bewildered and unhappy presence, Lanny got Kurt Meissner on the telephone. Take no chances of being misquoted, or of seeming to have anything to hide! "Hello, Kurt," he said. "I have returned from a visit with *Die Nummer Eins*, and have just this minute had a talk with *Le Numéro Un*." Kurt's answer was: "Excellent! Come and have lunch."

So Lanny drove to the fashionable apartment near the Parc Monceau and made himself solid and safe by telling Kurt and his agreeable secretary all about his visit to the Berghof—but of course without mentioning either Laurel Creston or Miss Jones. That was the Führer's secret, and if it leaked it wouldn't be Lanny's fault. He left it to be supposed that he had gone for the purpose of conveying to the Führer what he had learned in Washington and New York, Paris and London. He was free to say that the Reichswehr had had its marching orders for two days ago—doubtless Kurt knew that by now, and may have known it earlier. Lanny reported that the Führer was hesitating, and the Premier was hesitating—a safe report to make about the head of any government in Europe that 29th day of August 1939. In his role of friend to all the great, Lanny would chat freely, and his host, cordial but cautious, would reveal more than he realized.

This day Prime Minister Chamberlain was addressing the House. Radio microphones have never been admitted to that sacred place, but soon afterwards the BBC broadcast a summary of the speech. The Prime Minister rebuked the Hearst press for having "invented" an alleged text of his confidential reply to Hitler; he went on to reveal that the argument had been narrowed down to a question of procedure. The British government insisted that the issues between Germany and Poland must be settled by negotiations and not by force.

Poland was willing; and would the Führer refuse? What the British government had in mind as a final settlement, Chamberlain did not say, and perhaps did not know. Was it to be another Munich? Or was it to be "a corridor across the Corridor," a device much talked about? Lanny said: "I am going to London soon, and if I learn anything of importance I'll get word to you."

He returned to the home where he was a guest, and made a report to his host. That duty done, he shut himself in his bedroom and wrote a quite different report to F.D.R. It would almost certainly arrive too late, but his duty was to send it, even so. He dropped his letter into a mailbox, and then went to keep an engagement with his Red uncle. He was curious to investigate the Party line of the French Communists, vis-à-vis Ribbentrop's recent visit to Moscow, and the photographs which had appeared in the capitalist press of the world showing the Nazi champagne salesman and the somewhat shorter Red chieftain standing side by side and beaming.

Lanny would have enjoyed being here a week earlier, to catch his uncle with his revolutionary pants down, as the saying is. But by now the deputy had had time to think, and to consult his comrades; by now the Party line had been fixed and the arguments standardized. There was no difference, moral, political, or social, between the capitalist democracies and the Fascist states. Britain, France, and America had been doing all in their power to get the Soviet Union into a war with Germany, and the Soviet Union had shrewdly forestalled them. There were no military clauses and no secret understandings, and the pact was a contribution to the cause of world peace.

"So now you are a pacifist!" exclaimed Lanny.

"The Communists have always been pacifists as to capitalist wars," declared the baldheaded old warrior. "But if capitalist states want to fight one another, we surely have to let them."

"The deal is for ten years," said the skeptical nephew. "Do you think it will actually last two?"

"You can be sure that whatever the time, we shall be using it to make our Soviet land secure."

"God help you, Uncle Jesse, if Hitler finishes off Poland and has a common frontier with the Soviet Union! He will start marching some midnight, and won't stop till he has reached the Urals."

"It may be you are right," was the reply. "If that happens, we shall retreat to the Urals, and start to beat him from there."

XII

Several millions of the young men of France were being put into uniforms and shipped away to the eastern border; it would cost several billions of francs, and that was a terrible thing for the taxpayers; they cursed the Nazi fanatics who were making it necessary, and cursed still more heartily the politicians who had failed to settle these matters in a sensible and orderly way. Lanny Budd, who remembered from boyhood the scenes in Paris at the outbreak of the First World War—the marching, the singing, the mad cheering—now saw the men crowding to the railway stations, dull and listless, just as they entered the factories for tasks in which they had no interest. Spectators paid little attention to them, and authorities who had the duty of conducting propaganda and working up enthusiasm had apparently realized the hopelessness of their task. Marianne had been asked the question: "Do you want to die for Danzig?" and she wasn't interested enough even to reply.

The life of the rich went on, just as if no danger had ever been in the world. Smart ladies descended from their limousines in front of the jewelry shops on the rue de la Paix, and toddled in on heels four inches high. Instead of thinking about war or peace they thought about blue fox furs and hair-dyes to match, green rouge, purple lipstick, and a choice of fantastically named perfumes. A night of pleasure was more important than their country's honor, and an invitation to a *chic* affair of more concern than the peace of the world.

Marceline Detaze, daughter of a famous painter and a professional beauty, never had to worry about her social position in Paris. She was dancing at one of the expensive night spots and acclaimed with unfailing ardor. But when Lanny called her on the phone he heard distress in her voice. "Oh, tell me! Is there going to be war?"

"Nobody can say," he answered. "It's touch and go." He thought: for the first time that he could recall in his half-sister's twenty-two years on earth, she was showing interest in a question of general concern.

But no, it wasn't that. "Oh, Lanny, if Oskar goes, I have to go, too. I'm just not going to lose him."

"But, dear," he objected, "if there's war, he will be called to the front, and you won't see him in any case."

"He can get furloughs; and it surely can't be much of a war with Poland!"

Lanny thought this was serious enough to go and see her. In her elegant but somewhat over-furnished apartment he explained: "If there is war, it will be Britain and France against Germany, and it may last a long time. If you go to Berlin, you will make it impossible to come back to France—perhaps for years."

"Oskar assures me I can get engagements to dance in Berlin."

"That I don't doubt; but it will be taken as a political stand, and you will be hated in Paris, and will not be allowed to return. You will have branded yourself as a Nazi."

She stared with astonishment in her lovely brown eyes. "What nonsense, Lanny! Nobody hates the Nazis—at least, nobody who counts."

"That may be true today; but it will change instantly if there is war. Believe me, I watched it the last time, and I know that when people get to fighting they hate one another—how else can they fight? Atrocities are committed, or at any rate they are told about and believed." He had to be careful, for he could be sure that what he said would be reported to Oskar von Herzenberg, perhaps before the day was over. She was dressed in a lovely peach-colored *peignoir*, her hair dressed and her face made up, so he guessed that she might be expecting a visit.

"Listen, dear," he said, tenderly—for she was his "little sister," and he had taught her to dance at the same time that she was learning to walk. "I am an American, and regardless of my feelings I intend to be neutral in the war if it comes. You are half-American, and it will be wise if you keep that half to the fore in this unhappy time. If you go to Germany it will be taken as a repudiation of France, and you will not be able to get an engagement in this country for ten years at the least. You will not be happy in Germany—they are a different kind of people, and they aren't going to have as easy a time as they expect."

That was as far as he could go; and he saw that it wasn't going to do any good. Marceline had always had her own way—she had been brought up to it, and since her unhappy marriage she had become hard-boiled. She didn't really love this son of a Prussian nobleman; she was thrilled by him because of his high position, his elegant manners to her and arrogance to others, and the sense of power that radiated from him. He was a Nazi, and the Nazis were on the way up, they were going to rule the world. Lovely, gay, self-willed daughter of pleasure, Marceline was going to be one of the court favorites, a Pompadour or a du Barry.

"Has he asked you to marry him?" inquired the proper half-brother.

"*Mon dieu*, no! I wouldn't if he did. I mean to be free, and nobody is going to tie me down."

XIII

The lovely and intelligent daughter of Baron Schneider was married to a man who was active in his father-in-law's vast affairs, and whom Lanny had met in the days of "Mister Irma Barnes," who had leased the palace of the Duc de Belleaumont and dived over his head into the social swim. Now the daughter wanted Lanny to join them at a dinner party they were giving at the ultra-fashionable Trianon Palace Hotel in Versailles. *"Tout le monde* will be there," she declared; whereupon Lanny told her the favorite story of his friend, Sophie de la Tourette. The president of her Cincinnati hardware company had brought his new wife to the Cap on a honeymoon tour, and this lady had social aspirations and wished to know people of importance. Very earnestly she inquired: "Who is Toola Maud?"

This party took place while Poland was decreeing mobilization, and while Sir Nevile Henderson, having flown to Berlin with Chamberlain's reply to Hitler, was summoned to the Chancellery to receive Hitler's reply to Chamberlain. That day the Nazi press had reported five more Germans killed in Poland, and Adi, having created a press to fool the rest of the world, was now permitting it to fool him. He shouted his grievances at the British ambassador—but the sounds didn't reach to an ornate luxurious restaurant, where the wealthy and famous crowded together in promiscuity which would have shocked a Grand Monarque who had built Versailles as the most exclusive of royal residences. This famous old hotel stood on the edge of the park, so that really the park was its garden. Honeymoon parties came here by tradition, as in America they went to Niagara Falls.

Tonight Lanny encountered the American ambassador, Bill Bullitt, rich Philadelphian, who had agreed with him in disapproval of the treaty of Versailles, and after it had been signed had joined him at Juan, "to lie on the sand and get sunburned and watch the world come to an end." Here were editors, writers, motion-picture stars—and also the statesmen who held the destinies of France in their keeping. Here, surveying fastidiously a tray full of hors d'oeuvres, Lanny observed the Foreign Minister, Georges Bonnet, lean, long-nosed, his complexion sallow, almost green; he was the ardent advocate of *le couple France-Allemagne*, ready to give the Führer anything he chose to ask for; his wife, Odette, who sat by his side, was the friend of all the Nazi agents.

At the next table, toying with a large half *langouste*, sat dapper little Paul Reynaud, Minister of Finance. He plotted incessantly to replace

Daladier, and was egged on by his *amie* of twenty years, the Comtesse de Portes, one of those political ladies who pulled the strings and made French public figures dance. There wasn't much secret about Hélène, for she had a shrill voice and a violent temper, and when she became excited she shouted so that all the restaurant could listen, and did. A lean, neurotic woman, with few of the charms which are supposed to aid in seduction, she had ambition and a driving will, and had never wearied in the determination to drag her lover from his Leftist associations into the paths which led to prosperity and power in France. In this crowded place she scolded at "Jewish warmongers," in tones which these gentlemen were meant to hear. She loathed Bill Bullitt, and expressed her feelings in tones which he corld hardly ignore. Sitting at the next table Lanny observed a man diligently making notes, and the lady at Lanny's side whispered that this was the correspondent of DNB, the official German news agency. It was that easy to obtain secrets of French politics!

The lady who whispered was charming and soft, golden-haired and blue-eyed like a doll; she was Jeanne, Marquise de Crussol, who had been "Dala's" lady friend since the death of his wife some years ago. The lady seemed amiable and harmless, but Lanny knew that the Premier's old-time friends deplored the attachment, saying that the lovely marquise was the means of introducing him into reactionary circles and modifying his thought without his realizing it. "If a woman of delicate rearing takes up with a 'Bull of Vaucluse,' it is because she is in love with power, and if she does not make use of it, be sure that her friends do." Thus had spoken Jesse Blackless, implacable friend of the proletariat, who for many years had been baiting that bull in the arena known as the Chambre des Députés, and had many times made the public declaration that it was the influence of these "aristocratic harlots" which made it all but impossible for a man of the people to remain faithful to the creed and the cause of his early years.

BOOK SIX

Let Slip the Dogs of War

22

Mournful Midnight Hours

IT WAS on Thursday, the last day of August, that Lanny Budd set out from Paris to Calais. One of his friends pointed out that if he was in France when the war broke out, there would be a good chance of his car's being commandeered. Evidently others had the same idea, for the Channel boat was so crowded that he had to line up and wait for a third boat. Meantime he ran his radio, picking up fresh items of news, and people gathered to listen—he had quite a congregation, both on the quay and on board the tightly packed boat. Everybody's fate was involved, and everybody knew it; English reticence broke under the strain, and strangers discussed what they had heard and what they feared.

Lanny's first action in the town of Dover was to telephone to Wickthorpe at the Foreign Office; his lordship was certain to be there, day and night, in this crisis. Lanny spoke the words which had been a passport everywhere in Paris: "I was with Hitler last Saturday; and yesterday morning I talked with Daladier." Ceddy's reply was: "Oh, good! Will you come and tell us about it?"

A couple of hours later the P.A. was sitting in one of the commodious rooms of the big gray smokestained building in Downing Street, with Ceddy, Gerald, and another of the staff. All the Englishmen were haggard and exhausted, having had nothing but catnaps for the past three nights; even so, they were polite Englishmen, and now and then while they plied Lanny with questions they would ask: "Do you mind?" The questions were the same as Schneider's; in London as in Paris, people were trying to understand that madman in Berchtesgaden: what was the matter with him, what did he want, what would satisfy him—if anything!

Lanny talked freely, having about decided that he had paid his last visit to the Berghof, and wishing to help England if he could. His friends had heard Sir Nevile Henderson's detailed account of the

Führer's behavior in the Berghof; and now to hear that Lanny had been in the building at the time and to have him repeat many of the Führer's wild phrases was definitely convincing. That very morning, in the "wee small hours," Sir Nevile had had another rumpus of the same sort—only this time it had been with Ribbentrop, and the place had been the Chancellery in Berlin. The ambassador's report on the affair, telegraphed in code and now typed out in English, lay on the table while Lanny talked, and Gerald Albany picked it up and read a few sentences aloud.

Propositions and counter-propositions had been going back and forth between London and Berlin for more than a week, and this morning the ambassador had gone to the Chancellery, taking Chamberlain's reply to Hitler's reply to Chamberlain's reply to Hitler's reply—so on to the fifth or perhaps the tenth power. He had found the champagne salesman in a fury, for the Führer had demanded that the Poles should produce a plenipotentiary in Berlin by midnight, and no such personage had appeared. Ribbentrop seemed to have the idea that Henderson had deliberately delayed his own appearance until after midnight, despite the fact that the polite Englishman had telephoned, explaining that his government's reply had come in code, and that he was waiting to have it decoded. Evidently the champagne salesman had decided to imitate the manners of his master, for he had used language which the Englishman had felt it necessary to rebuke. They had wrangled over the question as to who was to blame for the Polish mobilization, and whether Germany could have expected to mobilize without having Poland do the same.

II

The Foreign Office men admitted themselves completely "stumped," and were reduced to asking an American visitor what he thought this behavior could mean. Ribbentrop had produced what he said were the final terms for a German settlement with Poland. They consisted of sixteen points, elaborately and precisely set forth, and the champagne salesman had proceeded to read them aloud as fast as his lips and tongue could move—which was faster than the mind of an Englishman could take in German words and sort them out from the oddly inverted German arrangement. Henderson had protested, whereupon Ribbentrop had thrown the document onto the table, declaring impatiently that it was all out of date anyhow; the Poles had failed to send the plenipotentiary as required.

The demands, as published later that day in the Berlin newspapers, were not unreasonable, and there might have been a possibility of persuading the Poles to accept them. But what was the purpose of presenting them in that extraordinarily rude and self-defeating way? Could it be that Hitler, with his bombing planes ready to fly and his tanks ready to roll, had devised a trick, so that he could say to the world: "You see what reasonable plans I suggested, but the Poles would not consider them and the English would not even transmit them?" Here sat three honorable gentlemen, public-school men carefully trained to the public service, and they contemplated such a possibility with blank dismay. "What do you think, Lanny?"

The answer was: "Nobody may ever know. It may be a stupid plot, and it may be just that the Chancellery is a madhouse, with factions pulling and hauling, and going to any length to have their own way. Göring and Hess and perhaps Weizsäcker want a rational settlement; they prepare sixteen points and persuade the Führer to approve them—and then in comes Goebbels raving, with another story of some Germans being castrated in the Corridor. Ribbentrop comes and insists that the terms are nonsense, the Poles are being egged on by the British, and wouldn't keep any agreement. 'Let me present them,' he says, 'and see what Henderson's reaction is.' He comes back to Hitler and says: 'I presented them, and Henderson pretended that he couldn't understand them. He came late on purpose because he wanted to defy you by waiting until after the deadline you had set.' Something of the sort would be my guess."

The proper and reticent Gerald Albany surprised Lanny greatly by his response to that explanation. "What a louse!" said he.

Lanny didn't say anything about the spirits of Bismarck and Hindenburg, Heinzelmann and Eckart and the other old companions. But in his secret soul was the whisper: "Adi came out from under their influence, and Ribbentrop got him again!" He could not repress the thought: "Oh, God! Should we have stayed, even at the risk of our lives?"

It was too late, and no use to worry over it. He could only wait and see what happened; and likewise his friends of the Foreign Office sat there, paralyzed, helpless. The whole British government, the whole British Empire, was in the same condition; they had lost what the military men call the initiative, and could only wait for a one-time inmate of a home for the shelterless to tell them what was going to happen to them next. Polish reports came in that German patrols had already crossed the border at several points. Was it true? Nobody could know what to believe any more!

III

The officials talked about the efforts they had been making all that day, first to get the text of the sixteen points through a friend of Göring's, and second to persuade the Poles to get in touch with Berlin and indicate their willingness to negotiate on the basis of the German demands. The Polish ambassador had been to see Ribbentrop, and Ribbentrop had asked, what had he come for and did he have full powers to negotiate? Lipski, the Pole, had replied No. Did his government accept the sixteen points? Lipski's reply was that the text had never been submitted to him or to his government; he had just seen it, published in extra editions of the Berlin papers. What sort of way was that to carry on diplomatic negotiations?

While Lanny sat talking with this unhappy trio—diplomatists reluctant to turn their business over to the military men—there came a messenger with a despatch from Sir Nevile in Berlin, reporting that Lipski had again seen Weizsäcker at nine-fifteen that evening and had been told that the Führer had been waiting two days for the arrival of a Polish plenipotentiary, and now he could only assume that his proposals had been once more rejected. The Englishmen looked at one another blankly. "That means he is going to war!"

They talked for a while about the German army. Who had been at the Berghof while Lanny was there? General Keitel, the Chief of Staff? Lanny said: "Yes. He is one of the Nazi favorites, and I didn't cultivate him." And Brauchitsch? "Yes. He is an old-line Junker, and a pal of my friend, Emil Meissner. Reichenau was there, and gave me a military pass to come into Switzerland."

Did Lanny know what was the attitude of these men to the question of war? He knew they were divided in their counsels, but agreed that it was now or never. They had a couple of meteorologists with them— one of them an elderly professor who had known Bismarck and talked about him. Military strategy was decided by the weather men these days, and they warned the Führer that this sunshine and dryness on the flat Polish plains would not last forever.

And then the question of France, and the attitude of the French politicians. Lanny said that France was in the same plight as Germany —she had a louse as Foreign Minister; there was no appeaser in Paris more tricky and more probably corrupt than the sallow and long-nosed Bonnet. The three Englishmen didn't say Yes, nor did they say No. They asked about Daladier, who had just written to Hitler that *la patrie* would stand by her pledge to Poland. Had he said a single word to Lanny which might indicate a weakening on this point? Lanny repeated carefully every word he could recall of the Premier's utterance. He saw Ceddy look at Gerald significantly and then turn to the third man. "Don't you think it might be worth while for the P.M. to hear this?"

They all agreed, and Lanny said: "Naturally, I'd be very glad to meet the P.M., if you are sure I wouldn't bore him, and if it isn't too late." It was just after midnight, and the date was the 1st of September. The Englishmen were sure that nobody would go to bed that night; they might doze for a bit on a sofa, but all would be "on call."

IV

His lordship left the room to telephone, and came back to report that the head of the government would be happy to hear Mr. Budd's story. It was just across the street and the evening was pleasant; Ceddy and Gerald walked with him—they were glad to get outdoors, and away from the radio and a hailstorm of despatches for a bit. Downing Street is a dead-end street, only one block long. At Number 10, the Prime Minister's official residence, the two policemen on guard knew them and admitted them with a "Good evening, sirs." Quite a contrast with the Berghof!

Lanny was escorted into the "Cabinet room," which was on the ground floor, at the rear, with windows looking out onto the park. A long green baize table pretty nearly filled it, and at the head of this table sat the "man with the black umbrella," whom Lanny had met only casually but had seen in a hundred cartoons in newspapers of a score of cities. There had just been a Cabinet meeting, and apparently the head of the government had remained sitting in his chair, brooding over his tragic impotence and the failure of his career.

Gerald Albany waited outside the door. Wickthorpe, who had known Lanny longer and had made the suggestion, escorted him into the room and introduced him. Being a man of perfect tact, he did not linger, but withdrew promptly. The Prime Minister rose politely and shook hands with his visitor, then said: "Come with me into the small sitting-room, where we can be cozier."

Neville Chamberlain, tall and lanky, was more powerfully built than would have been guessed from his photographs. He was in his early seventies, but his hair was still dark, except for a striking white lock in front. His most impressive feature was a pair of large dark piercing eyes. He wore an old-fashioned wing collar and a large black tie, and had no pretension to social graces; he was a plain businessman, and it was over a businessmen's Britain that he presided. They had chosen him because he was exactly their type and they could be sure of his every reaction and word. No nonsense, no imagination, no extravagance of hopes or fears. There had always been an England and always would be, and its motto: "Carry on!" There had been difficulties, and would be more, but nothing that sensible businessmen couldn't settle by talking things over and making concessions—but of course never any more than necessary.

Just now he had come to the most trying moment of his life. He had had little sleep, and his face was lined and haggard. Lord Wickthorpe had said to him over the phone: "The son of Robert Budd, of Budd-Erling Aircraft. I have known him since we were boys." That was enough, and the P.M. wanted to hear every word of Lanny's many-times-told tale of the mountain home of the wild witch Berchta. Chamberlain had been taken there a year ago, on his first trip which had initiated "Munich"; later, at Godesberg, the Führer had expressed a wish to take him again and show him the retreat on the top of the Kehlstein. "Extraordinary man!" said the Prime Minister. "He had told me with great emphasis that the settlement of the Sudeten problem could not wait another day; then, an hour later, he wanted to drop everything and fly me two or three hundred miles in order to see a tunnel in the interior of a mountain!"

"He is a man of impulses," replied Lanny Budd; "and some of them are of hospitality."

"He actually succeeded in making me think that he liked me," said the Prime Minister. "Do you suppose that is possible?"

"Shall I tell you what he called you?" inquired the other.

"By all means."

"He referred to you as 'that good old man.'"

"Incredible!"

"At that time you had given him what he wanted."

"So now, I suppose, I am a bad old man."

"I fear that you are, sir."

"I will tell you, Mr. Budd, I am an unhappy old man. I confront tonight—or shall I say this morning—the failure of my dearest hopes. I am expecting word that the German armies have invaded Poland in force."

"I think that you should get it about dawn, sir."

"Well, I am not given to extravagant language, but I really can see **no** limits to the calamity; it may mean the end of our civilization, **and** I cannot imagine what will come after it."

V

This was the old man whom the young Leftists had been damning up and down and all around. But it was usually hard for Lanny to dislike anybody whom he knew personally, and he found Neville Chamberlain a warmer and kindlier person than he had imagined. Perhaps it was the special circumstances of their meeting, when everything had been done and there was nothing to do but wait; when no word could any longer have any effect, and so it was permitted to speak frankly, as a man might speak before the Judgment Throne. This American, who had been to all the places and knew all the persons involved, might well serve as posterity; the Prime Minister of Great Britain entered his claim: "No one will ever be able to say that I did not do everything in my power to avert this calamity."

"Assuredly not," Lanny replied. "If they have any fault to find, it will be that you tried too hard."

"I would rather it stood that way, Mr. Budd. This war, if it comes, will be such a ghastly thing. I was resolved not to have it on my conscience."

Lanny's thought was that it might be a ghastly thing to have on one's conscience the downfall of the Spanish democracy and the Czechoslovak republic, both of which would have been stanch allies of Britain now. Still worse would it be to have the defeat of Britain in this war laid to one's account. But these were not words which could be spoken by a foreigner. It would be for the British themselves to decide the proper mood in which to wage this war, and the proper statesman to voice it. That Chamberlain himself was not without his uneasiness as to the outcome was made plain by his questions concerning the strength of the Luftwaffe. How much had the visitor managed to learn about it?

"They talk about it freely, as you doubtless know," Lanny replied. "They have talked to Lindbergh, to Lothian, to Beaverbrook. In my case I have found that they are not always consistent. I have suspected some of trying to keep the facts from me, and others of trying to frighten me—or rather to have me go out and frighten influential friends in Britain and France. My father has made it his business to know, and he is convinced that they have a stronger air force than Britain and France combined. That refers to matériel; the quality of the personnel can only be determined in the tests."

This tired old man gave no indication that he would welcome any tests. He looked depressed, and remarked: "We have generally done badly at the beginning of our wars; we manage to do better later on."

Lanny had on the tip of his tongue that in the case of air warfare, there might not be any "later on"; but that, too, was not to be voiced by an outsider. He contented himself with saying: "It is my father's opinion that you will be strained to the uttermost; and the same with France."

The P.M. wanted to know about those Frenchmen with whom his caller had talked. He could, of course, have called Daladier on the telephone, and no doubt had done so in the course of this critical day; but what the Premier had said informally might be more revealing. Lanny said: "I think, sir, the Premier feels just as you do about not having this war on his conscience; but he fully intends to stand by his pledge to Poland—as I am sure that you do also."

Was that a gentle suggestion? Or was it a delicately phrased inquiry? The P.M. apparently did not care; he responded promptly: "We shall have to do that, unquestionably."

That was what Lanny was here to learn, and as soon as he had heard the words he wanted to get away and put them on paper and get them into the airmail, which had recently been established by Clipper across the ocean. Every minute was precious, because if war came, censorship of mail would go into effect and secret communications might no longer be possible. He talked for a while about Bonnet and Reynaud and Schneider; then, at a pause, he said, gently: "You look tired, Mr. Prime Minister; am I keeping you from your rest?"

"It will be hard for any of us to sleep tonight," was the reply.

"I can tell you this with some assurance," replied the friend of the great; "there is very little chance that anything will happen until dawn. I have heard some of the Führer's aides discuss the subject, and they agree that the bombing planes will fly according to the almanac; they will leave their fields so as to arrive over their targets at the first moment of visibility."

"Poor Warsaw! Poor Warsaw!" exclaimed the sad old man.

VI

Lanny drove to his hotel and wrote his report and dropped it into an outside mailbox. Then he took a chance and called the hotel where Rick always stayed when he came to town. Lanny had wired from Paris saying that he was coming, and now he found that his guess was correct: Rick couldn't stay in the country at a time like this, and he couldn't sleep on such a night. He had just mailed a letter to one of the afternoon newspapers, urging the British people to be on the alert to see that an appeasing government didn't force Poland into another "Munich," and that they didn't welsh on their agreement in the event that Poland stood firm.

Lanny said: "Let's take a drive, and listen to the radio in the car." So they drove out Hampstead way and into the country. A year ago in all the parks of London rows of trenches had been dug to serve as emergency bomb shelters, and these had been allowed to stay till the next "Munich," so dreaded by all the popular forces. Now on the undulating stretches of Hampstead Heath they found gangs of men working by torchlight, digging foundations for anti-aircraft guns. "That doesn't look like appeasement," opined the American, and told his friend what he had just heard from Chamberlain's own lips.

But Rick was not to be comforted; he insisted that he wouldn't trust Neville and his gang as far as a lame ex-aviator "could throw a bull by the horns." Right now the appeasers would be working like eager beavers to break down the nation's will and betray the nation's honor. "Don't you see, Lanny, if we fight Hitler we shall be helping Stalin? That is the way Stalin has willed it, and not to let him have his way is the first thing our reactionaries think about."

They listened to the radio, on which they could get Paris and Brussels and Amsterdam, and Berlin when there wasn't too much static. Even in these early morning hours the war of news and opinion was going on with furious energy, each side telling its story and arguing its case. The sixteen points were read and discussed, and the question whether or not they had ever been submitted to Britain and to Poland, and whether there had been an ultimatum, and who was to decide what constituted one, and who was to blame for its rejection. How many Germans had been murdered by Poles in the Corridor and how many Poles by Nazis in Danzig? How many Germans had been castrated— the Nazis talked incessantly about this crime, for they were racial fanatics, and the glory of every Nazi was his power to bring more

Nazis into the world. Correspondents and commentators who had not slept for a couple of days and nights told what they had seen and heard, and what they thought it meant. Everything turned upon the all-important question: Did it mean war? What were the German intentions and how were they going to be made known, and when, and where? The Germans, if they struck, would surely bomb Warsaw. Would they also bomb Paris and London?

VII

"What are you going to do?" Rick wanted to know. "I mean if it's war."

"I haven't made up my mind," replied his friend. "I am supposed to help Zoltan run a Detaze show in Baltimore and other cities. I could get out of that, but have another obligation in America, which I have to attend to and to get released from for the future. Then I believe I'll volunteer in the British army, if they'll take me."

"You mean, as a private?"

"I'm not fit for anything else, with no training."

"That's a pretty rugged job, Lanny."

"I know; but I'm fairly fit, and I could toughen up if I had to. What is the age limit?"

"I don't know what it'll be now—well over forty, I'm sure. But it would be a great waste of your talents."

"What else could I do?"

"Good God! Put the proposition up to Ceddy, and he'll arrange for Intelligence to take you on in no time. A man who speaks French and German like a native, and can go into Germany by way of Switzerland —he could have anything he asked for."

"Well, I'm not so sure the Nazis will welcome me any longer. However, we'll see. I'll have to have an argument with Robbie, I know, for he'll want me to help him, and he'll argue that airplanes are important."

"He'll be jolly right, too. But come back here before you decide, and by that time we'll know more."

"And you, Rick?" inquired the American.

"What can I do, with a game leg? I'd like to help in the Ministry of Information or some other propaganda work; but I doubt if they'll be taking on any Leftists."

"Surely, Rick, they'll want national unity now!"

"No doubt; but it'll be unity for *their* Britain, not for ours. I fancy

I'll have to go on free-lancing it. We have wild men on our side who'll need some whipping into line, and maybe I can help with that. This tight little island is in for a tough time, old man. What do you think are the chances of our getting any help from your side?"

"That's one of the things I hope to find out. In general, I'd say, the worse things get, the more help you can expect. We'll do what we absolutely have to, no more. Tell me, what is Alfy doing?"

"Alfy has joined up with the Air Force, and if it's war, he'll be in one of the first flights."

Lanny had an impulse to say: "Poor Nina!"—but he knew that wasn't English. Chamberlain would say: "Poor Warsaw!" but never: "Poor London!" You were sorry for other people, but for yourselves you said: "Carry on!" or "Never say die!"—or, shortest and therefore best of all: "Cheerio!"

VIII

At four o'clock in the morning the Nazi Gauleiter of Danzig issued a proclamation announcing that his city was a part of the German Reich. At a quarter to five o'clock a German cruiser opened fire upon the Polish port of Gdynia, near Danzig, and one hour later German troops all around the German borders of Poland started their march—some seventy divisions altogether, more than a million men. At the same time the Luftwaffe took off from its carefully prepared bases, and showers of bombs fell upon Polish airports, oil depots, and communication centers. The German espionage had been so perfect that they knew exactly where to strike, and the greater part of the small Polish Air Force was destroyed on the ground. The German Panzer divisions swept forward with such speed that the Poles never got a chance to complete their mobilization. It was like a swarm of stinging wasps swooping down upon some large slow animal, blinding it, paralyzing its nerve centers, and leaving it a mass of helpless flesh. From the Nazi point of view it was glorious, and from the point of view of military science it was something new in the world.

Needless to say, Adi Schicklgruber wouldn't do a thing like that without issuing a manifesto; and of course he would say that he was attacked. He told his Reichswehr: "The Polish state has refused the peaceful settlement of relations which I desired, and has appealed to arms. Germans in Poland are persecuted with bloody terror and driven from their houses. . . . In order to put an end to this lunacy, I have no other choice than to meet force with force from now on." He appointed a Ministerial Council for Defense, and put Göring at the head of it, with five other members, including Hess and General Keitel. Then he summoned his tame Reichstag, and once more the world heard his bellowing voice, proclaiming his own innocence and the wickedness of his foes. Said Adi:

"I desire nothing other than to be the first soldier of the German Reich. In evidence of this I have again put on that old coat which was the most sacred and the most dear to me of all. I will not take it off until the victory is ours or—I shall not live to see the end. If anything should happen to me in this struggle, my first successor will be Party Member Göring. Should anything happen to Party Member Göring, his successor is Party Member Hess. It will be your duty to follow these men as Führer with the same blind loyalty and obedience as you follow me."

In *Mein Kampf* this master orator and statesman had laid down the rule that when you told a lie it should be a big one, as that was easier to believe. So now he told "his" deputies—"*meine Herren*," he called them: "Last night for the first time Poland opened fire on our own territory, this time with regular troops. From five forty-five this morning this fire has been returned"—and so on. He told them, truthfully—since falsehood must always be mixed with some truth—that he had spent more than six years in building up the German armed forces, and that "during this time more than ninety billion marks have been devoted to this purpose." The statesmen of the democracy must have shuddered as they heard that figure, equal to more than thirty-five billion dollars, or, as the British would have said, nine thousand million pounds. Where was the statesman who would have dared to ask any parliament, congress, or other legislative body to vote such a sum for armaments?

It was going to be real war—that is, if the democracies saw fit to take up the gauge. Said the one-time sub-corporal: "As a National Socialist and a German soldier I enter this struggle with a stout heart. My whole life has been nothing but a constant struggle for my people and its resurrection and for Germany. This contest was inspired by one single doctrine of faith—the belief in this people. There is one word that I have never learned—capitulation."

IX

What were Britain and France going to do about it? The world waited for the answer; and a lame playwright-propagandist who distrusted his government spent his day stumping about Fleet Street, visiting editors whom he knew and begging them to be uncompromising in their demands that Britain should honor its pledges. This wasn't a job for an American, a man whose government had only fine words to offer. Lanny decided that he had done his part, and would visit his little daughter and make up for lost sleep until the decision was made known. In the hotel he had met a woman official of the A.R.P.—that is, Air Raid Precautions—who told him about the evacuation of children from London. He had the thought to do his bit, and was put in touch with the Fulham district. The whole matter was handled through the school system, and Lanny loaded his car with a teacher and two little tykes in the seat beside him, and half a dozen more tykes packed into the rear.

They were children of the slums, and their best clothing was none too good. Later the vermin would show up and fill the country people of Britain with horror, and with a realization of how their "other half" lived. But the youngsters were full of energy and Cockney conversation, and to the son of Budd-Erling a source of education as well as amusement. Most of them had never seen a cow, and as they gazed out at the countryside they exclaimed with wonder at these immense and alarming creatures. When Lanny inquired how they had thought milk came into the world, their answers varied; some said: "Out of bottles!" and others said: "Out of tins!" He delivered them safely to the Wickthorpe village schoolhouse, as per instructions, and then he stopped at a "chemist's shop" to buy disinfectants for his car. In memory he was carried back three years to the time when he had evacuated a family of Spanish peasants from a fighting zone.

He had telephoned Irma to make sure that he would be welcome; so here was Frances, playing on the smooth green lawn in front of the castle and keeping watch for him. What a contrast of life on one little island! His daughter wanted to rush into his arms, but he had to bid her wait until he had had a bath. He explained that there had been some very dirty people in his car; and of course that was a novel idea to a poor little rich girl, and aroused her curiosity. He was pledged never to trouble her mind with any of his Pink ideas, but how could he explain this episode without some trace of "class-angling"? He thought it wiser to have Irma present when he told the story, and let her be the one to explain why there had to be such very poor children, and why they couldn't at least keep clean!

X

The itinerant father had a lot of sleep to make up for; and in between times he read the papers and listened to the air waves. Chamberlain had made a statement in the House, telling of his long struggle to preserve the peace of Europe, and how little encouragement he had got. Even now the poor man couldn't give up his hopes; he had sent a communication to Hitler, proposing that he should cease his attacks on Poland and withdraw his troops from the country as a preliminary to negotiations. That might have seemed an absurdity—until you learned that Bonnet was busy in Paris, and that he had got Mussolini helping him! Musso didn't want war; he was afraid his Axis partner might ask for help, and Musso alone knew how wretched his army was.

It was another Munich in the making, long after the twelfth hour had passed. They were going to persuade Hitler to stop his armies where they were, and keep the western parts of Poland which he had seized, and persuade the unhappy Poles that they were already licked and that there was no such thing as honor in the world, because there wasn't any in the hearts of Bonnet and Laval and Musso and the rest of the conspirators. They were laboring frenziedly in Paris and Rome and Warsaw and Berlin—and also in London; Lanny needed only one or two hints over the radio to guess what was going on. He had to be careful with his tongue, for Wickthorpe Castle was a center of appeasement activity, and its mistress, his former wife, remarked: "Surely the Poles cannot be held entirely blameless! They are the most unreasonable people I have ever tried to deal with."

Lanny remained the art expert, who had seen and heard a great deal but wasn't especially interested in it and didn't consider himself competent to express opinions. Also, he was the devoted father, who liked to play the piano for his little daughter, and dance with her, and ride horseback while she rode a pony, followed by a groom. "Why don't you come to see me oftener, Papa?"—and then: "Why do you have to go so soon?" He tried to make the picture business real to her, telling about great artists and their work, and explaining the paintings in the castle, mostly the ancestors of her stepfather.

Also he had to meet and be polite to Fanny Barnes, his former mother-in-law. Residence in the shadow of an ancient castle had made this large majestic lady more English than any Englishwoman; she regarded Hitler as an ill-bred person, and couldn't understand how Lanny could desire to associate with him. Weren't there enough people of good breeding willing to buy paintings? Also, there was Fanny's brother, "Uncle" Horace Vandringham, derelict stock-market manipulator and pensioner of his sister. Horace was developing bags under his eyes, and his shoulders were bowed, but he couldn't give up his ambitions; he whispered confidentially to the son of Budd-Erling that a hint of what was really going to happen in Europe would be deeply appreciated, and that anybody who had some ready money could make a killing on the New York market right now. Lanny explained that what little money he had was invested in his father's business; whereupon Horace smacked his lips and exclaimed: "Your father must be a happy man right now!"

XI

The efforts of the appeasers failed, because of the psychological fact that when a lion has tasted blood he cannot be persuaded to withdraw from his prey. It was on Friday that the invasion of Poland began and it was Sunday when Prime Minister Chamberlain announced in the House that his proposals to Hitler had been left unanswered, and that Britain therefore must fulfill her pledges to Poland. Daladier made the same announcement as to France; and Lanny, with a heart full of relief which he must not show, joined the guests, the servants, and the tenants of the Wickthorpe estate in listening to a radio address by the King, delivered in that phrase-by-phrase, almost word-by-word enunciation which was made necessary by his impediment. "In this grave hour, perhaps the most fateful in our history, I send to every household of my people, both at home and overseas, this message, spoken with the same depth of feeling for each and every one of you as if I were able to cross your threshold and speak to you myself."

The address was a solemn committing of the British cause to God; and after that, the die having been cast, it was proper for Lanny to say to his ex-wife: "I am going up to town the first thing in the morning and arrange for passage to New York. I have promised to attend a Detaze show in Baltimore, and then I have in mind to come back and enlist in the King's forces."

Irma's answer was: "Don't be absurd, Lanny. You are a gentleman, and gentlemen don't enlist, they apply for commissions."

"But I don't know anything about fighting, Irma!"

"It would take you no longer to learn to be an officer, and then you might have a career. Ceddy would arrange it for you gladly. Promise me that you won't do anything without consulting him. It would be false heroics, and people would take it as reflecting on us; they would be certain that we must have quarreled, or something." It was a complicated world, and you found it out when you married an heiress and brought a little rich girl into the world, and then became a sort of left-handed lord of a castle!

Lanny said: "All right." He wasn't clear in his own mind, and couldn't be until he had talked with F.D.R. and been released from his obligations.

XII

As it turned out, getting to America wasn't any longer the simple matter of putting down some banknotes on the counter of a travel agency. Half the Americans in London had suddenly decided that they wanted to get home, and boatloads more were being dumped onto the British Isles from all the northern and western ports of the Continent. Lanny applied at several places and was told that everything was sold out for two months ahead. As grandson of Budd Gunmakers he had learned in boyhood that you didn't give up under such circumstances; you took thought and availed yourself of the thing known as "privilege." You went to some friend of your family and got introduced to the president of the steamship company; or you consulted your banker or your family lawyer, and a quiet word was spoken, a button was pressed or a wire pulled.

Lanny might have got word to President Roosevelt, but that would have involved revealing his secret. He might have applied to Ceddy or Gerald and asked a favor in return for the information he had brought; but he hated the idea of troubling either of those harassed men. He attempted to telephone his father, but discovered that all transatlantic wires were stopped except for government business.

What he did was to pay a call on Mr. Stafforth, of the legal firm of Stafforth and Worthingham, who had been his father's London solicitors for the matter of thirty years, and who had once before aided Robbie's son, by telling him how he could get married to Irma Barnes without waiting for the banns to be posted and read in church for three Sundays as required by English law. This legal gentleman was tall, baldheaded, stoop-shouldered and wrinkled, but still alert, and he listened respectfully while an American whom he had known from a youth explained that his father was now making the fastest fighter plane in the world for the United States army, and that the British army was secretly getting a part of this product; that Lanny had been on the Continent getting for his father information of a character so confidential that it could not be trusted to cable transmission. Surely Mr. Stafforth wouldn't need for Lanny to emphasize the importance of the airplane industry to the British Empire in this crisis; and Mr. Stafforth replied that he had no such need.

"Would you like to fly?" he inquired; and Lanny replied that nothing would please him more, but he had been told that the Clipper service, which had been inaugurated a few weeks ago, had been booked some months ahead, even before the threat of war had come to a thunderhead.

"I think they may perhaps have reserved a few accommodations," replied the Englishman. It was a long sentence for him. "I'll ring you at your hotel within the hour."

"If it costs anything extra, I'll of course be glad to pay," put in the scion of privilege.

"I don't think it will."

Lanny went back to the Savoy, which, like all the big hotels, was something of a madhouse. In the latest extra newspaper he read that the Germans were sweeping over Poland and claimed to have put out of business every airfield in the country. Of course that might not be true. The Poles were calling for help, but how could Britain or France get fighter planes to Poland, and where would they land if all the bases were destroyed or in German hands?

The telephone rang, and it was Mr. Stafforth. "There is a place reserved for you on the Clipper tomorrow morning, Mr. Budd. You are to call at the office at once and make the payment. No extra charge."

"Oh, thank you so much!" exclaimed an impulsive American.

"Not at all; a pleasure. My compliments to your father." A lawyer to the rich knows exactly what to say, and how to take care of himself in a world where the race is usually to the swift and the battle to the strong!

XIII

Lanny went and paid his money and got his ticket—no questions asked. Then he hunted up Rick, and they had lunch together in a quiet place where nobody knew them. Rick was so relieved that his country's honor was safe that he had almost forgotten the possibility that his country's military position might be unsafe. England had always won her wars, except those two unnecessary ones with Lanny Budd's homeland. The less said about them the better; they had really been civil wars, family arguments, and not the same as fights with Spanish and Dutch and French, Russians and Germans and whatever else had come along through the centuries.

Later in the day, after a lengthy wait, Lanny succeeded in getting his mother on the telephone. He was curious to know what had been happening to Laurel Creston and her newly discovered mediumship; but he wouldn't make the mistake of calling Laurel—no, indeed! Beauty Budd must be first in that household. Lanny told his plans, and promised to deliver messages to Robbie and others. "Oh, the poor Poles!" exclaimed the mother. But she wasn't worried as to herself; the Germans would never get to Juan, and if they did they would be polite, for Beauty had so many influential friends in Berlin. She was going to stay right at home and practice holding the thought of universal love, in the certainty that ultimately it would spread to other minds and mankind would abandon the insanity of war.

Casually Lanny added: "By the way, how is Miss Creston getting along?" So he learned that her performances were quite remarkable, and that Parsifal was deeply interested. No time for more, because there was a limit imposed on long-distance calls. "So long!" Lanny said. "I'll cable you from New York."

He decided that the days of luxurious motoring were at an end, so far as the old continent was concerned; a terrible thing to contemplate, having to travel on trains, like hoi polloi, but so it must be. Lanny might have shipped his car to Robbie, or put it in storage at the castle; but he had been deeply moved, and decided that he would rather do his bit for England and provide an extra staff car for the expeditionary force which no doubt was getting ready. He wouldn't make the gift himself, for that might attract attention, and there were no doubt many Nazi spies in England. He gave Rick a bill of sale for the car, and told him to make the gift in his own name.

XIV

An interesting experience to be in London those first days of war. The authorities had not been so completely asleep as outsiders had thought; the streets were full of constables, the new ones still in "cits" but wearing armbands, and all with "tin hats." There were swarms of new firemen in dark blue uniforms, and great numbers of taxicabs now had trailers, supplied with pumps, hoses, axes and rope ladders. Every block had its air-raid wardens, and here and there you came upon trucks loaded with sand and empty sacks, and volunteers eagerly working to fill the sacks and pile them against the sides of public buildings and monuments.

Lanny pitched in and helped for a while, because it was a way to meet the people and hear what they thought. In the last war the cry had been: "Are we down'earted?"—but this time nobody appeared to think of that possibility. What they thought was: "That ole 'Itler has gone and done it now, and this is goin' to be the end of 'im." Everybody was comforted by the presence of great sausage balloons in the sky, many hundreds of them all over the city. They were held by steel cables which were supposed to keep enemy planes from diving low and taking accurate aim; they shone like silver in the sunshine and waved slowly in the breeze as if they were dancing a sarabande.

Most of the people had been provided with gas masks, which were of all sizes, some even for infants. Many people expected that ole 'Itler to use poison gas at the outset, and there were even reports that he was doing so in Poland. Lanny, who was leaving so soon, didn't bother to get a mask; he guessed that Göring wouldn't spare any planes to bomb London until he had finished with his Polish objectives, and perhaps not until he had given the appeasers time to do their undercover work in Britain and France.

Strange it was when night came, to see a great city completely "blacked out." Every place of amusement was closed, and Piccadilly Circus was as quiet as the village of Wickthorpe. The busses had faint spots of light, and pedestrians carried shaded torches; the traffic signals were dim red and green crosses. After you had bumped into a few lampposts and railings, and had dashed across a couple of thoroughfares at the risk of your life, you decided that this would be a good night to shut yourself in your room and read a book.

XV

Next morning the scion of privilege packed his bags and took an express to Bristol. From there a plane flew him to a tiny village on the west coast of Ireland, known as Foynes. There on the water lay the great two-decked silver airship known as a Clipper. A launch took him to it and he found himself in a spacious cabin with comfortable chromium and leather seats and all the comforts of home. Presently the engines began to whir and the great contraption slid over the water and rose into the air. Higher and higher, until the gray Atlantic below looked like a vast sheet of paper with tiny wrinkles on it. It was so quiet in the cabin that you could chat with the other sons and daughters of

privilege; or you could ring for drinks, iced or hot, or cards, or check-
ers—anything within reason, including a can to vomit in if the weather
was rude and the vessel was rocked too violently.

Rough or smooth made little difference to the powerful engines, or
to the trained pilot and his navigator. Once the Yankee Clippers had
rounded the horn to the China Seas, and now their namesakes would
sail through all the airs of the world. They had come in the nick of
time, and were destined to a burst of development such as Tennyson
had dreamed:

> For I dipt into the future, far as human eye could see,
> Saw the Vision of the world, and all the wonder that would be;
> Saw the heavens fill with commerce, argosies of magic sails,
> Pilots of the purple twilight, dropping down with costly bales;
> Heard the heavens fill with shouting, and there rain'd a ghastly dew
> From the nations' airy navies grappling in the central blue.

23

Two's Company, Three's a Crowd

I

LANNY had taken it for granted that he would have to wait a
while before he could see the "Governor" in this crisis of world history. He pictured the great man as besieged by a hundred problems,
and when he got Baker on the telephone from New York he said:
"Tell the Chief I am at his disposal. I'll wait here or in Washington,
as he prefers." But when Lanny called the second time he was told:
"You are wanted at once. Take the first plane and report." Lanny suggested that there might be difficulty in getting a plane, and the reply
was: "I will arrange it. Go to the La Guardia airport and say it is government business and give your number."

War was going to make a difference in America! Lanny had no
psychic powers and could not foresee the word "priority," but he
recognized the phenomenon as soon as he met it. At the airport on

Long Island he spoke the magic words and was referred to a special desk. There he said: "Reservation to Washington; number 103." An envelope containing his ticket was handed to him, and when he asked the price he was told that it had been paid for. Half an hour later he was in the air—reading comfortably, in the latest New York "extra," reports of the annihilation of cities and the machine-gunning of civilians in flight and of peasant women working in the fields. War was making a difference in Europe, also!

That night Lanny was taken by the familiar route, and found the great man in his high-ceilinged bedroom full of gay prints and family photographs. He appeared tired, but ready as ever for a chat. Lanny's reports had been deliberately made bare and emotionless, but that didn't have to be true of his conversation. He had come right out of the heart of the thunderstorm, and the pattern of every lightning bolt was impressed on his mind. First Berlin, then Berchtesgaden, then Paris, then London—the President wanted to hear about each place and how the people had behaved and how the leading characters had looked and what they had said. He might be ever so conscientious and bowed down with responsibilities, but he would not lose his sense of drama, and this was the greatest show yet enacted upon the stage of history.

After he had got the facts, he wanted opinions. Poland was lost, of course; the British and French would be blamed for not helping, but that would be silly, because they were powerless. Would Hitler attack them as soon as he had finished Poland? Lanny didn't think so. Hitler would give his Fifth Column every chance to work; he didn't want to fight France and Britain the least bit, and he would argue with them publicly, and tempt and cajole their statesmen behind the scenes. From his point of view it was crazy of France and Britain to insist on fighting over Poland. Said Lanny: "Adi is at a disadvantage because he doesn't understand moral sentiments. He is like a boor in a drawing-room, who doesn't realize how he shocks people by bad manners."

Said F.D.: "He has surely shocked me!"

II

A P.A. had no right to ask questions, but the President chose to tell him things, and wanted his advice; he wanted everybody's advice in this unprecedented crisis. He had proclaimed an embargo against the warring nations, as the law required, but he believed that it would now be possible to persuade Congress to repeal that ill-advised enactment. He said, more than once: "We are not going to get into this war." He had said it over the radio, and Lanny had heard snatches of the speech at Wickthorpe. Now F.D. added: "I hate to be a Pollyanna. What do you think?"

Lanny replied: "I was satisfied with your statement that we would be neutral in action but didn't have to be neutral in thought."

"I am getting the devil for that, of course. They say I have reversed Wilson's policy."

"You have had more provocation than Wilson. Hitler is a far more dangerous man than the Kaiser."

"Exactly! Between you and me, we shall have to act on the conviction that the British fleet is a bulwark of the Western Hemisphere."

It was what Lanny had been urging, ever since his first meeting with this great man; but he was too tactful to mention the fact. "We can afford to wait," he ventured. "Hitler will give us plenty of provocation, and all you will have to do is to point out to the people the meaning of his actions."

The embargo proclamation, issued that day, declared a "limited emergency." The President smiled as he told how this had troubled the lawyers, who had never heard of precisely such a formula. He was going to put up funds to bring Americans back from Europe in a hurry, and he was going to "increase the armed forces"—to Lanny in the privacy of his bedroom he added: "Good and plenty, you can bet!" He told about the arguments which had occurred over the question whether or not he should include Canada in the embargo. If he did, it would hurt Canada; if he didn't, it would hurt the feelings of the British government. F.D. chuckled as he told how he had telephoned the Canadian Premier, and the reply had been to let the British do the suffering! But a couple of days later the President changed his mind and included Canada.

III

"Really, Governor," protested Lanny, "I am taking an awful lot of your sleeping time."

"The most important thing hasn't been settled. What are you planning to do now?"

"I thought that if you would release me, I'd try to get into the British army."

"You don't tell me! What put that into your head?"

"Well, that's the way I feel. I want to do something."

"But you are doing something for me!"

"I don't see how I can be of much use now. I doubt if the Germans will let me in, and even if they do, the French would hardly let me return from Germany to France."

"Even in Britain and France, your usefulness would be greater now than ever. You can keep in touch with the appeasers, and find out what the Nazis are proposing to them. You might even go into Switzerland and meet some of the Germans there."

"But I could no longer mail you reports; the French and British censors would surely stop them."

"We might take Bill Bullitt into the secret and let you report to him."

"I have every confidence in Bill, but very little in an embassy. It is always surrounded by spies, and there are secretaries and telephone operators and servants and what not. In wartime I can't afford a slip."

"You can use your code name and number and mail your reports to Bill in a double envelope. He can forward the inside envelope to me in a diplomatic pouch without knowing who is the writer."

"That might work for a while. You'd have to make the same arrangement with somebody in London."

"Joe Kennedy is a terribly pessimistic soul," remarked the smiling President. "He takes his ambassadorial duties hard, and is certain that this is the end of the world. He called me on the telephone just after the British decided to enter the war, and I almost saw his tears. Do you know him?"

"I have met him at two or three social events, but only casually."

"The Irish are goodhearted, but emotional. I had to pat him on the back—at three thousand miles' distance." Then, with a sudden change of mood: "All right, Lanny. Can it be considered settled?"

"Of course, if it's orders."

"It's orders of the most urgent sort—unlimited emergency. When you are in France you will mail your reports to Bullitt, marked personal, and when you are in England you will mail them to Kennedy. Perhaps I had better include Harrison, in Bern. I will instruct all three that when they receive an envelope containing a sealed letter marked 'Zaharoff 103' they will seal it in another envelope marked 'Personal for the President' and send it by diplomatic pouch. There is only one other trouble I can foresee, and that is your passports. We are going to make it hard for Americans to travel in the war zones, and if I should give the State Department orders to show special favors to you, that would be a give-away."

"I'll make a suggestion," volunteered the agent. "My father's business can serve as a cover. If the embargo is lifted, he will be having a lot of business with France and Britain. I doubt very much if he will wish to travel; he will be busy, and the British and French will come to him. But by giving an order applying to both of us, you will make it appear that I am his agent and not yours. That would look right even to the Germans, if they happened to get word of it. My father's dealings are with the War Department, and you could drop a hint to the right man there; doubtless the State Department issues passports when the War Department requests it."

"Excellent!" said F.D.R., and made a memo on a pad. "See me again when you are ready to leave."

IV

While waiting in New York Lanny had telephoned his father, also Zoltan Kertezsi, who had made an early escape from the war. The Detaze show in Baltimore was scheduled for early October, but it seemed to Lanny hardly conceivable that anybody would be interested in looking at paintings with the world in its present mess. But when he got Reverdy Holdenhurst on the telephone and voiced that idea, the sponsor replied: "Don't worry. In a couple of weeks people will have got used to the war, and be ready for something new."

He urged Lanny to stop off on his way back to New York; and Lanny strongly suspected that this was the purpose for which the works of Marcel Detaze were being made known to the Monumental City. The guest took a morning train, and Reverdy's car met him at the station and drove him out to Green Spring Valley, this time by a different route, around Druid Hill Park. The chauffeur, acting as cicerone, pointed out the estate of this or that eminent family, some of whom Lanny had met on his last visit. "Miss Lizbeth's début party is set for the evening before the show opens," remarked the man; he added, American fashion, "Bunching our hits."

The smart folk were coming back from seashore and mountains, and the social swirl was getting into motion. In between listening to the horrors of war on the radio and seeing pictures of them in the papers, Lanny Budd enjoyed pleasures with Lizbeth Holdenhurst and her friends. It was the same sort of people and the same life that he had lived on Long Island ten years ago. The "smart sets" in American cities had become as standardized as the breakfast foods and the soaps; they patronized the same costumers, played the same games, spoke the same slang, and danced to the same jerky growling jungle tunes called hot jazz, then swing, then boogie-woogie—the more the name changed the more it remained the same thing. The smart folk were shocked by the tragic fate of a nation concerning which they had vaguely romantic ideas, but it seldom occurred to any of them that this was going to make any difference in their routine of play. They talked about parties past and present, about places to dine and dance, about personalities and possessions and love affairs and quarrels. They talked about Lizbeth's coming-out party and the Detaze show, and with equal interest about Panzer divisions and Luftwaffe and the unpronounceable names of Polish towns—all this in between a round of golf and one of drinks.

Among these children of privilege—third and fourth generations for the most part—were men of handsome presence and agreeable manners. They had family, they had money, they wore properly tailored clothes and had been to Princeton or the University of Virginia; they were in every way suitable as husbands, and they were on the job, ready to squire the daughter of the Holdenhursts wherever she wished to go. Why should Lizbeth have picked out a comparative stranger and fixed her thoughts upon him—as so evidently she had done? Lanny, pondering the problem, decided that it was because of his strangeness, the differences which set him apart. He had traveled all over Europe, he had been a guest in palaces and courts, he had had romantic adventures about which Lizbeth must have heard at least rumors on the Riviera. Right now, with everybody talking about the war, he could remark: "I was in the Führer's home less than a fortnight ago, and he said thus and so." Straightway the people in a drawing-room would gather about him; or, if it was in the dining room, other conversation would cease and the guests would ply him with questions as to what Hitler and Hess and the rest of them were really like and what they meant to do to the world.

It was natural that Lizbeth should have decided that this was a distinguished man. She was "throwing herself at his head"—something against which all mothers and aunts warn all girls. Men do not like to be "run after"; but Lizbeth could not see what else to do, since Lanny made it evident that he didn't mean to run after her, but treated her with the same friendly courtesy he showed to her parents.

As a matter of fact he wouldn't have especially minded being run after, because if he took a wife he would want her to be in love with him; she would have to be, to stand his peculiar ways. Though he did not let anybody know it, he was strongly attracted to this girl, who was not merely untroubled and lovely to look at but genuinely sweet and unaffected. By all the books, she ought to have been spoiled, for she had had everything she asked for all her life. The effect had been to keep her somewhat immature; she had never had to make decisions for herself, except small ones—whether she would go to this party or to that, buy this dress or that. How would she behave when it came to a major issue and she discovered that she couldn't have what she wanted? Would she fly into a temper and throw her hairbrush across the room? Or would she dissolve her make-up in tears of frustration? Lanny, who had known so many fashionable women and had disappointed more than one, recollected scenes and wondered what might be happening offstage now.

His conduct, from the feminine point of view, was really exasperating. When she drove him to the country club to play tennis, he offered no playful caresses with hands or eyes; he talked to her about the great world in the manner of a kindly teacher, or perhaps an uncle. He would dance with her, pleasantly and coolly, just as he danced with other girls. He didn't invite her for a stroll in the wooded glen which ran through the estate; instead he offered to play the piano for her friends, and then he would discuss the music. Didn't he have any romance in him? Or was he in love with some duchess overseas—and if so, why didn't he talk of his infatuation, of his interest in love, after the manner of the younger set who had few secrets from one another?

V

What was going on in this visitor from overseas was a war between two parts of him, an ambivalence he had known about since boyhood. "I feel two natures struggling within me," the sculptor Barnard had entitled one of his works. There was one half of Lanny Budd—possibly a little more than half—which wanted to quarrel with an evil social order and to make sacrifices in the cause of truth-telling and justice; and there was another half, or near half, which liked to live in a well-appointed home, enjoy well-cooked food, be waited on, have a properly tuned piano—a long list of things which the world does not allot to its heroes, saints and martyrs. "No man can serve two masters: for either he will hate the one, and love the other; or else he will hold to the one, and despise the other. Ye cannot serve God and mammon."

Lanny had experienced this inner conflict through both of his marriages. Irma Barnes had been luxury and worldly prestige, while Trudi Schultz had been heroism and devotion to a cause; and neither had satisfied the husband entirely. He had called Trudi the incarnation of his better nature, and he had tried his best to keep her from knowing about his other half. It had been in vain, for she had understood him thoroughly, and had feared his worldly half, and had said, in the clearest way, that he would never be able to love her completely, because she had none of the graces he was used to in women, and because she neither could nor would move in that "great world" where he had spent most of his life. Perhaps that hadn't been a good suggestion to give a husband, but Lanny knew in his heart that this was the truth, and in trying to change himself he was always under a strain.

Now again it had come about that this ambivalence was embodied in two women, both of them out of the same world, indeed the same city, the same family. One reason why Lanny never made love to Lizbeth was that whenever he was with her he spent part of his time thinking about her cousin, comparing the two and trying to make up his mind which of them would make him the sort of wife he ought to have. This was interesting as a psychological exercise, but hardly conducive to romance, or even to flirtation. But Lanny, who was expecting his fortieth birthday in a couple of months, figured that he was past the age where he could be excused for stumbling into a love affair by accident.

He had practically told Laurel Creston that he was a secret agent of some sort. If he asked an anti-Nazi writer to marry him, it would have to be on the same terms as with Trudi: a closely guarded secret, with clandestine meetings at widely spaced intervals. As matters stood at present, Laurel could stay at Bienvenu and be absorbed in mediumistic experiments without anyone giving much thought to her or digging up her published stories. But if she were to marry Lanny, or appear to be thinking of it, the case would be quite different. Everybody on the Cap had been interested in the loves of Beauty Budd and her son and had talked about them for a quarter of a century. They would get busy on this latest comer and rake up every scrap of information about her—including the fact that a little more than a year ago she had publicly described her future husband as a "troglodyte."

Ordinarily this would have served as a tidbit of gossip, but not in this time of suspicion and raging hate, of civil war on the Riviera as everywhere else. There were British and French who were loyal to their country, and others who were loyal to their class, and took Nazi-Fascism as their protector against the Red menace. There were the paid agents of Hitler and Mussolini and Franco, laboring by bribery, blackmail, and every sort of device to break down the morale of their enemies. They trusted nobody, not even their own fellow-workers; they were jealous of everybody, most of all of their fellow-workers. The son of Budd-Erling would have been naïve indeed if he had expected to go among such people and not have every circumstance of his life gone over with a fine-tooth comb and studied under a microscope.

VI

So Lanny's thoughts would come back to Lizbeth, and go the round all over again. Here was an alliance in which the most suspicious enemy could find no political speck or blemish. Marriage with the daughter of the Holdenhursts would establish a near-Fascist as a member of the right class, holding the right ideas and living the right life. She was not merely the "lovely young thing" a man of his age might rejoice in, to find respite in as in a rose garden or an exquisite piece of music; she was an embodiment of all the graces his worldly life required. The trouble was, his young bride would see so little of him; and how long would it be before she began to wonder why he persisted in taking long journeys and not asking her along? When *she* had so much money, why did *he* need to be peddling pictures? Lanny could hear the very words—because Irma Barnes had said them all.

Could he take Lizbeth into his confidence, even to a partial extent? What would his ideas mean to her except something abnormal and terrifying? Could he take on the job of educating her, away from all the ideas, the basic instincts of her class? She seemed so pliable, natural and straightforward; but that was because she had everything she wanted, everything made to order for her. She was like a stream flowing smoothly over a pebbly bed; but set a big rock in the middle of that stream, and see what a surging and splashing, a boiling and bubbling there would be! Lanny had seen it and heard it with his first wife over a period of six years, and was filled with a dread of it.

Yet another dread—he had discovered the ability of women to suffer when their desires were thwarted. He found himself thinking: "This girl is going to be unhappy!" He knew the symptoms: a catch in the voice, perhaps a trace of anger in the eyes, or a pleading look. It must seem to her unkind, even insulting, that this attractive man went on treating her like a kind teacher or an uncle. Did he suppose that hands were made only for piano-playing, and lips only for talking about the increase in emotional content of the music of Beethoven over that of Mozart? Some day she was going to break down—and then what the devil would her teacher do?

He decided that he was dawdling here, and that the world needed him. He explained to Reverdy that he hadn't yet seen his father, and that he had a lot of picture business which would require traveling. He would return to Baltimore for the début party and the opening of the show. His host said: "Right afterwards we are going to start on our cruise. Wouldn't you like to come along?"

Lanny had been wondering about this, and was prepared in his thoughts. "Aren't you disturbed by the dangers of war?" he demanded.

"We are going by way of the Panama Canal to the South Seas. We may come back that same way—or by the Cape of Good Hope. We won't attempt to enter the Mediterranean."

"The Germans had raiders all over the South Seas in the last war," cautioned Lanny. "They are pretty certain to have them in this one, and perhaps long-range submarines, too."

"I am taking every precaution," explained the other. "I am having a large American flag painted on each side of the *Oriole*, and I will keep these illuminated at night. Also, I'm having the registry of the yacht changed back from a commercial to a pleasure vessel. That will cost me money, but avoid the possibility of trouble."

"I hope so, Reverdy. I wish I could go with you and see the half of the world I have missed; but I have commitments to my father and others. Remember, I have a mother in France and a daughter in England."

"We shall all of us be sorry," was the response. "We should have enjoyed your company." A proud and somewhat formal Southern gentleman couldn't say more. He knew the meaning of what he had heard. In modern language it was: "Nothing doing!"

VII

Zoltan was in New York, and eager to see his friend and business associate, and to hear the news. Right now, with Polish cities falling into dust and rubble and Polish men, women, and children having their lives wiped out by the thousands every hour, the "good European" was in a depressed mood. "My native land is going Nazi," he said, "and the Continent is *kaput*. I've made up my mind to settle down in New York and apply for American citizenship. I've made all the money I need, and I'm tired hearing cries of hate."

Lanny, also heartsick, replied: "I'm afraid you will hear them in New York. There is going to be a fearful controversy over America's part in this war. But I think your decision is wise. Travel to Europe will become difficult as well as dangerous."

"What are you planning for yourself, Lanny?"

"I am in a privileged position. Our government won't consider that we need old masters, but it will be certain that Britain and France need fighter planes. So when the embargo is lifted it should be easy for my father and me to get passports. If there is some business you want transacted, I'll be glad to help you, and meantime you can sell Detazes in America. Keep the prices high!"

"Let's go over the schedule," said the Hungarian.

VIII

Lanny arrived in the middle of the afternoon, and took a taxi to his father's home. The butler said: "The Library Board is meeting in the library, sir." Lanny might have been puzzled by that if he had not known the circumstances; the Library Board was the governing body of the Newcastle Public Library, and Esther was a member. They met once a month, and she no doubt had invited them to meet at her home as a social courtesy; afterwards they would have tea, and continue their plotting to persuade the Town Council to vote funds for a new building.

Lanny went upstairs to the attic room which had been his ever since the spring of 1917. In that year a pair of mocking birds had built their nest in a cherry tree just outside the window, something which was unusual in Connecticut. Now the birds were gone, but his books were still on the shelves, and nothing had been changed between World War I and World War II. Lanny washed up, and, noticing his old golf clubs hanging in the closet, thought it would be fun to run out to the country club and stretch his legs. But then he realized that Esther would be expecting him to meet her Board members. It would be a bore, but he was always careful to show courtesy to his stepmother, knowing what a difficult relationship this is.

He went downstairs and passed the double doors of the library, in which half a dozen ladies and gentlemen were seated. He went on into the new sunroom, planning to read a magazine. Entering quietly, he stopped, for at one of the windows he observed a woman sitting, directly in front of a panel of rose-colored brocade by the French windows. The rich brown of her softly dressed hair was accentuated by the background of the room. The shadows interspersed by the afternoon sun were rosy, and the pale blue dress she wore was splashed with the color of red roses; there was, by chance, a basket of coral roses on the table behind her. She was absorbed in reading a book, and not aware of his entrance, so he was at liberty to look at her.

There was something vaguely familiar in her features, delicate and sensitive, but at first he didn't recognize her. She was—how old? Not as old as himself, and perhaps considerably younger. Was the warm color in her cheeks her own, or did it come from the sun shining on the rose-colored objects? Lanny, with the eye of an art connoisseur, appreciated a fine composition, and wondered if it had been made by chance or by design. A ladies' man since childhood, he knew the ladies' arts, and would not fail to wonder whether this one had known who was coming, and had placed herself with the right background. Or had Esther told her where to sit?

Don't blame him for such thoughts; for every woman he knew was up to these tricks, and despite all envy, hatred, and malice they aided one another. All good women were busy finding wives for the unattached men of their acquaintance. Lanny had wondered, was it because they felt that men must have wives, or the other way around, that women must have husbands? Perhaps it was a reciprocal need, of which women were fundamentally, biologically aware. It was no second-class matter to them; it took precedence over all other matters, even a man's duty to the world, even his duty to God. They justified this by declaring that if a man could not be true to a good wife he could not be true to God. Psychologists called this "rationalizing," but the women considered it entirely rational, and apparently God was with them—for women managed to live longer, and to inherit the money. Lanny had read that they now controlled seventy per cent of the property in America, and certainly it was true that a majority of the clients on Lanny's list were rich elderly widows, who lived their own lives and had no doubts about the irresponsibility of the male animal.

IX

Did some obscure sixth sense warn the woman there in the sunlit corner that someone was gazing at her? She looked up from her book, and at the same instant Lanny realized who she was—the librarian whom he had taken for an automobile ride on a moonlit midsummer's night a little more than a year ago! Miss Priscilla Hoyle, of the Newcastle Public Library, daughter of the Puritans and prim official of a proper small town—but what a change in her! When last he had seen her, in an ancient and rather dingy place of employment, she had been pale and bloodless, or so he had thought; subdued and unobtrusive, a virgin in the temple of Minerva, goddess of wisdom; a lady of an age, or appearance of age, which had not changed for a decade and might not change for another. Or so he had thought.

But now she had color in her cheeks, or at any rate on them; now she wore a delightful little toque of red roses, and a dress to harmonize with the saucy headpiece. To Lanny's expert eye it was apparent that the dress had been made at home; but even so, it was somewhat elegant and decidedly gay; he wondered, was that the way the town librarian was supposed to get herself up for the monthly meetings of the Board? Or was it only for special occasions, when the meeting took place at the home of the town's "first lady"?

This was a woman whom Lanny had kissed and wished he hadn't; but he was much too well bred to show any trace of embarrassment. "Why, Miss Hoyle!" he exclaimed. "A pleasure!" When she answered by speaking his name, he inquired: "May I join you?" Since it was his father's home, she couldn't say less than "Of course." She closed her book, as a sign that she was prepared to give him her attention.

Drawing up a chair, he inquired, pleasantly: "Doesn't the Board require your advice?"

"Just now they are discussing the appropriation for new books, and I fear they will not give me what I have asked. I didn't want to embarrass them by my presence."

"You are far too polite," he countered, with a smile. "You should stay there and shame them."

"I am saving my credit for the more important purpose—the new building."

"I promised to help you with that, dear lady, and I talked to my stepmother very earnestly about it."

"No doubt that was the reason she invited me to lunch some time ago. She gave me a full hour of her time and was very gracious. Our book-reading public is in your debt."

All very conventional and proper, here in bright afternoon sunshine—and with the Board members in the next room. Quite different from the privacy of a motorcar on a moonlit midsummer's night, when fairies and witches and other creatures are abroad and strange impulses stir in the hearts of men and women. It had been on the banks of the Newcastle River, at a spot favored by picnickers in the daytime and by petting parties at night. Almost exactly twenty years previously Lanny had kissed another girl there, and at that age it had been easier to excuse himself.

What was going on in the minds of this pair while they chatted politely about cultural conditions in the city of the merchants of death? Lanny's mind was pervaded by surprise. He couldn't take his eyes off his companion. He kept thinking: "Why she's really a lovely woman!" And then: "What a difference it makes when they use their arts!" Then, horrid thought: "I wonder if she knew I was expected this afternoon! She must have known that I was likely to show up." And so there started a panic in the breast of this much-sought widower. "Good Lord, is she expecting me to follow it up?" A truly distressing idea, to a man who was just congratulating himself upon having escaped from one entanglement! Wasn't there any part of the world where a man could be safe from women?

X

What was going on in *her* mind? It was something she was going to allow him to guess about—that being the way of a maid with a man. Suddenly she surprised him with a question: "Tell me, Mr. Budd, do you believe in God?"

There had been a time in old New England when this question had been widely discussed in the best social circles, but nowadays God had been replaced by sex as a topic of polite conversation. Lanny felt it necessary to fence. "You mean the Old Testament God? Jehovah of the thunders, Lord God of battles?"

"I mean a purposive, creative Intelligence," said the librarian.

Lanny stayed on the defensive. "Why do you ask me that?"

"I have been impressed by the books which you donated to the library—those of Jeans and Eddington."

"Oh, I see. Those books surely give one a lot to think about."

"I should be interested to hear your thoughts, Mr. Budd."

Lanny ventured: "Whenever I try to think about God I run into contradictions, and begin to suspect the limitations of my own mind. You know the argument of John Stuart Mill, that God cannot be both all-powerful and all-good, or why would He permit evil in the world. This war, for example."

"But this war is made by men, Mr. Budd."

"Yes, but the men were made by God; and surely, if you or I had been consulted in the making, we would have put less hatred into their hearts."

"You and I can choose between hate and love in our own hearts, can we not? Without this right to choose we would be mere cogs in a wheel. Without evil we could have no freedom. Until recently modern science has required me to believe that the universe had been wound up like a clock and would go on running mechanically, regardless of anything I might do. But now modern physics permits me, even encourages me, to believe that this is a mental universe, and that my choosing between good and evil may be a part of the process which constitutes God."

"I see that you have really read those books," remarked the man. He added, gallantly: "I feel sure you are much better equipped than I to understand them."

XI

This highbrow conversation was interrupted by the breaking up of the Board meeting. The door from the library was opened, and Esther Remsen Budd came in. Did she feel any surprise at the tête-à-tête which she discovered in her sunroom? Had she felt any trace of suspicion some time ago when Lanny had suggested that she ought to cultivate the acquaintance of the librarian of her home town whom, naturally, she would know more about than her migratory stepson? She was the most self-contained of women and would never reveal an emotion unless she had weighed it and decided to do so. She invited the couple into the library to have tea, and presented her stepson to the members of the Board, several of whom he already knew.

Lanny found himself seated next to a magnificent stoutish lady, Mrs. Archibald Fleury, wife of the leading surgeon of the town, who had been known to charge members of the Budd family as much as a thousand dollars a shot. Both husband and wife belonged to the country club, and Mrs. Fleury was a past-president of the Clionian Society, and considered herself an authority on many subjects. Said she: "Miss Hoyle, I notice that your list of proposed purchases include a work on 'hypnotherapy.' We were all puzzled as to why you should think such a book needed in our library."

"We have had a number of applications for it," replied the librarian, with proper meekness; "I suppose for the reason that there have been articles in the magazines about the use of hypnotism in the treatment of various mental ailments."

"My husband says that the idea was given a very thorough trial a generation or more ago, and has been discarded."

"That may be, Mrs. Fleury; but sometimes it happens that old ideas are revived in the light of new knowledge."

"The Board decided to strike that item from the list," announced the great lady, and the humble employee bowed her head and held her peace.

It really wasn't any of Lanny's business, and no one had asked him to butt in; but he had been inclined toward self-assertiveness from boyhood up, and the years had not tamed him. "You have brought up an interesting subject, Mrs. Fleury," he remarked. "I should be glad to buy the book for my own reading and then donate it to the library, if there would be no objection."

"Certainly not, Lanny"—she had known him from his youth. "We are not exercising any censorship. It is merely a question of the wise use of our limited funds."

"My stepfather in France has quite a library of books on subjects having to do with the subconscious mind," persisted the interloper. "I read several books by English and French physicians dealing with hypnotism. They may have been discarded and forgotten, but they ought to be of especial interest to your husband, for they contain well-authenticated cases of the use of hypnotism as a substitute for anæsthetics in surgery. I remember one extraordinary case of an operation performed by Dr. Esdaile, an English surgeon in a government hospital in India—the removal of a tumor from a man; it weighed more than a hundred pounds and had to be lifted out with a sort of improvised derrick; yet the hypnotized patient felt no pain whatever."

The wife of Newcastle's great surgeon did not take kindly to the idea of receiving instructions from a layman. Said she: "People were more credulous in those days—even members of the medical profession. Nowadays we should find it hard to believe that a man could carry a hundred-pound tumor."

"He didn't carry it, Mrs. Fleury—he just lay still with it. He was an ignorant peasant and had no idea what else to do. His relatives brought him food, and of course they fed the tumor at the same time."

"I never knew that you were interested in hypnotism," put in Lanny's stepmother, bringing a few drops of oil to these troubled waters.

"I have watched many experiments with it, and learned to practice it—not as a parlor trick, but as an important aid to the study of the subconscious mind. I can understand why the doctors have dropped the technique, because it requires special training and takes a lot of time and patience; giving pills is much simpler. But really, Mrs. Fleury, you would be astonished if you could see what can be done, and how many problems can be solved. I could hypnotize the members of this Board, with their consent, and tell them that they would accept the judgment of their librarian about books, and they would do it with entire contentment of mind."

Nothing could have been more amiable than the manner of this offer, but for some reason it failed to appeal to a fashionable surgeon's wife. "No, thank you," she said. "I doubt if any of the Board would be interested in giving up their own judgment."

"We do cherish our egos," laughed Lanny; "even when they are opposed to proven facts."

"Never mind," interposed the librarian, hastily. "It's my ego that's out of order in this instance."

"Well then, we might try it the other way," suggested the visitor from *outre mer*. "I might hypnotize Miss Hoyle and tell her that she would always be pleased with the decisions of her Board."

"That would be much better," agreed the surgeon's lady, forced to smile.

XII

The guests were taking their departure, one by one; and Lanny stood with Miss Hoyle in the music room, showing two paintings by Arnold Böcklin which he had sent his stepmother from Germany many years ago. They were the kind of art which Esther appreciated because they dealt with ethical concepts, and she was an ethical person; they were symbolical, and while she wasn't sure what the symbolism meant, she was certain that it must be profound. A woman's figure with bowed head and long black veils, with Italian cypresses in the background painted very dark and mysterious—that might mean any kind of sorrow, and you could take it for your own. On the opposite side of the room was a youth, with face uplifted in a shaft of sunlight, and about him were meadows full of flowers; that was joy, or perhaps it was young acceptance of life, while the other was the regrets of maturity. You could have it your own way, for no "book" had been provided.

Lanny had discovered that his present companion was another ethical person, and he guessed that she would begin speculating about these paintings. While they were in the midst of it, Esther came and they agreed that since they were beautiful, it didn't matter so much what they meant. Lanny decided that the two ladies had much the same kind of minds, and that his was different; which was only natural, since they had been raised in a grown-up Puritan village and he in the playground of aged and corrupt Europe.

When the librarian was ready to leave, the hostess remarked: "My husband has just telephoned that he is tied up in a business conference and will not be home for dinner. Wouldn't you like to stay and take his place, Miss Hoyle?"

The librarian made no effort to conceal her pleasure. "Oh, thank you, Mrs. Budd!" she said. "You are too kind!" Lanny didn't say anything; but his thought was: "What the devil!"

A suspicious and much-hunted male, he didn't for a moment believe that Esther was concerned about an empty place at her dinner table. Could it possibly be that she was interested to throw her stepson together with an employee of her Library Board? Through Lanny's mind flowed a whole stream of imaginings about what could be flowing through Esther's. She had given up hope of ever interesting him in any of the town's best "catches," and said to herself: "All right, maybe it's a bluestocking he wants. After all, he earns enough money for two. It would rather shock people, but they'd get over it; she has fine manners—and everybody's talking about 'democracy' these days. We could easily get another librarian."

Something of that sort; and Lanny had the feeling of being nudged and ever so gently guided. He had seen a motion picture of the trapping of a herd of wild elephants in a great stockade. Two well-trained female elephants were introduced among the terrified captives, and they would single out one of them and place themselves on each side of him, then shove him and impel him to a place where ropes were ready to bind his legs and render him helpless. These trained ones were always females; and he could imagine that the sounds they made were elephant language, and bore a close resemblance to the words he had heard from his mother and his stepmother, from Emily, Sophie, Margy, Nina, Bess, Rosemary, and other ladies elderly or middle-aged.

XIII

At the dinner table Lanny told the story of his recent travels. An interesting story, for, after all, who was there in the town of Newcastle, or for that matter in the state of Connecticut, who could say that he had talked with the masters of Europe on the verge of war? His audience was all of one sex: the mistress of this home, her secretary, and an elderly cousin who relieved her of the burdens of housekeeping; also, two visiting Budd ladies, and the librarian of the Newcastle Public Library. Of the half-dozen, none was more obviously absorbed than the last; she missed no word, and her questions were to the point, with the result that Lanny said to himself: "This is a really intelligent woman!"

And of course he didn't fail to tell himself again that she was surprisingly pretty. Had she gone and got herself a "permanent," or were the soft waves of her dark brown hair really permanent? Her neck showed no trace of those cords which betray age in women, and which caused our grandmothers to invent the band of soft velvet known as a "dog collar," often weighted down with costly jewels, telling the world that if we're no longer young, at least we have got the stuff, the mazuma, the spondulix, and that is what talks, and makes the mare go, and pays the piper and calls the tune.

Lanny had had this pretty woman on his conscience; not heavily, but enough to register in the scales. Now, while the others expressed their ideas about the war, and how wicked it was, and how it ought to have been prevented, Lanny thought: "Of course I shouldn't have laid my hand on hers in the car; but how the devil was I to guess that she would lean her head on my shoulder? Maybe she had never been kissed before in her life; and maybe she thought I would come back—but, good Lord, doesn't she know that I've been traveling?" So it goes in the minds of much-hunted widowers; and most of them say, let the woman look out for herself; but Lanny was tenderhearted, a regular softshell crab, who thought that women get a harsh deal from life and he didn't want to make it any worse.

Esther had put him in his father's seat at the head of the table, and this lady as the guest of honor at his right. He had every chance to look at her, and she behaved with the utmost decorum, not flashing him any signals, but really concerned with the history of the world, now being manufactured so rapidly and coming to all thinking people by radio and the newspaper page. It was something transcending in importance the fate of any individual, and to realize that was a matter of propriety. At the foot of the table sat the serious-minded mistress of this elegant but slightly austere home, and Lanny addressed her most of the time, and so did her town librarian—not forgetting the new building.

It was the same in the drawing-room, for a polite hour or so. Then, after the other ladies had withdrawn, Esther said: "Lanny, will you drive Miss Hoyle home?" That could mean only one thing, the world being what it is and ladies and gentlemen being what nature has made them. Esther might with propriety have said: "The chauffeur will take you home, Miss Hoyle." Instead, she chose to say: "You may have your chance"—and to Lanny: "If it's what you want, it's all right with me." Of course she didn't speak either of those sentences, but they were what her action meant; and neither of the two would fail to know it.

XIV

So there they were, in a car, the same in which they had had their innocent yet dangerous petting-party. What would happen this time? Would Lanny drive the lady properly and directly to her home, only a mile or so away? Or would he meander, and proceed slowly? If he went to the wooded point by the river bank, it would be symbolical, and Miss Hoyle had indicated that she liked symbolism in art. The weather was cold, but not unpleasantly so, especially in a closed car.

Little shivers were running over Lanny Budd. He was afraid of what he might do—and with good reason, as it turned out. He had been looking at an attractive woman for several hours, and now suddenly she was available. Automatically his hand went out, and did what it had done on the previous occasion—laid itself gently on hers.

But the next development was not according to the book—at least, not Lanny's book. The lady's hand was withdrawn, not suddenly or violently, but, as you might say, with delicacy and consideration. It moved, and in the dark Lanny couldn't see where to. There fell a pause in the conversation.

"Have I offended you?" he asked, considerately.

"No," was the reply. "I do not take offense so easily. But I try not to make the same mistake twice."

"You are sure it was a mistake?"

"Aren't you, Mr. Budd? I gathered as much, from the fact that you didn't return."

"I admit that I didn't behave very well," he replied, humbly. "But I have been traveling——" He stopped, as a sort of admission that it wasn't a very complete excuse.

Suddenly she laughed. "Would you like me to tease you?" she inquired. "Are you familiar with the art known as coquetry?"

"I have observed it in action," he replied, in a tone more serious than the question called for. He had been taken off balance.

"I would let you have my hand, and then withdraw it and let you search for it. By and by I would let you kiss me, but not so freely as I did on a previous occasion; then suddenly I would begin to laugh, and make a joke of the situation. I would make it impossible for you to be sure whether you had gone too far or not; I would have you bewildered, and at the same time possessed by curiosity. What sort of woman am I, and what do I mean, and how far will I go? Do you think you would care for that?"

"Frankly, I can't imagine that I would, Miss Hoyle."

"No man can imagine it; but it happens to them all the time. Maybe you are no different from the other men: you do not develop your full powers except in the pursuit. Maybe that is the way to rouse and stimulate you; the woman who is too easy to attain, who throws herself into your arms, inspires you only with boredom and repugnance. Can that be true of one so cultivated and gracious?"

Lanny was greatly embarrassed. "Dear lady," he said, "I see that I have caused you pain."

"Some pain, dear gentleman, I do not deny. But perhaps that is the only way we women can learn about men. What you have done is to make me into a good and earnest feminist. You have caused me to think hard and truly about the lot of my sisters in a man-made world. I am quite on fire with the realizations that have come to me."

"You mean that I have taught you to hate men?"

"Not at all; you have taught me to love women. I do not blame either sex, because I know that nature had put these differences into our hearts. But it is a man's world, and the lordly creature condescends to notice, and then walks out when he is bored."

"You make me aware of having been most inconsiderate, Miss Hoyle," said the scion of the Budds, with surprising humility.

"I do not want to embarrass you, and I am not coquetting, but speaking out of newly acquired wisdom. You are not the sole cause of the transformation in my mind. I will entrust you with a confidence, if you promise to respect it."

"Most certainly."

"When you departed and did not return, I was terribly humiliated. I felt that I had been the toy of a moment. But I am not a toy; I am an adult woman."

"I was away because of urgent duties, Miss Hoyle."

"The postal service was still working. But that is not what I am speaking of. I broke down and confided in my mother, who is a wise and kind woman, and was beautiful in her time. She told me the secret of her life—that my father had deserted her for another woman. This was when I was a small child, and I was told that my father was dead, and I always believed it. So you see, you are not the only man who exercised his privilege to sample and reject too casually. Sex cannot be casual. A woman may give the best she has, but when she reaches the age when her charms begin to fade, she confronts with terror the possibility that the man will feel the need of fresh stimulations, and will leave her with an empty heart and perhaps an empty home. What do you, as a man, suggest as a remedy for this form of tragedy?"

"I don't know," admitted the son of Budd-Erling; "unless you women stand together, and succeed in teaching men some ideals of loyalty."

"The feminist movement got off on the wrong track," said the town librarian. "It took up the foolish notion that women should imitate the casual relationship between the sexes which men have always found to be to their advantage."

XV

This turned out to be a long drive, and for the driver a stimulating experience, the exploration of a new type of woman soul. He had met a number of "feminists," especially in his youth, when they had been raging. Rosemary, granddaughter of Lord Dewthorpe, had been one, and she had had her solution of the sex problem, which was to take it in masculine fashion, as a biological necessity, and never let it worry her. Trudi had been a feminist, too, but had never called herself that, because the abolition of economic servitude had seemed to her so much more important. Trudi had believed in love as a partnership in working for social justice, which would solve all problems.

But Priscilla Hoyle believed in love as a spiritual expansion, a means of escaping from the limitations of the individual ego; as she explained it to Lanny he wondered if he had not been missing something all these years that he had spent in the playgrounds of Europe. He thought of the five women he had loved so far, and decided that the one who had come nearest to agreeing with Miss Hoyle was Marie de Bruyne; she was the one who had given him the most, over a period of six years. Lanny was deeply touched by this memory, and ventured to lay his hand on his companion's once more—this time in brotherly kindness.

But again she drew it away, saying: "Let us not play with fire."

"Are you quite sure that I couldn't add anything to your life?" he inquired, and she answered, without coquetry: "I am quite sure that you could, but also that you wouldn't want to for very long. I have thought it over and realized the gulf between us. Your world and mine are like two billiard balls which touch but never come together. You have your habits and tastes, your friends in your *grand monde*— and what could I give you? A few hours of pleasure, of thrills, perhaps, and then you would know that you had made a mistake—and I would know it before you did; indeed, I would know it before I started, and I would hate myself and you for such conduct."

So there it was; she turned him down. For him it was a novelty, and just a little humiliating. To be sure, Gracyn had turned him down, for a thirty-thousand-dollar start on Broadway; Rosemary had turned him down to become a countess, and he suspected that Irma had done the same. But all three of these women had been his for a time, whereas this woman wouldn't even let him kiss her again. She suggested that it was getting late, and that her mother might be worried, and his stepmother, also.

So he drove her to the modest cottage where he had delivered her once before; and when she got out there came an unexpected flash of humor. She gave him her hand, and said: "If you were in France now, you would know what to do—*n'est-ce pas, monsieur?*" So he kissed her hand, gently and respectfully, and it seemed to him a quite lovely hand, which he hated to let go.

Lanny drove away experiencing pangs of conscience. Here, it seemed to him, was a woman whose personality embodied those ideal things which he craved. It pleased him not at all to have her thinking that he considered the town librarian as his social inferior; but he was not at liberty to give her the slightest hint of his democratic sentiments. He had to tell himself once more that a presidential agent was something less than a man, and could never be a satisfactory husband. Incidentally, he reminded himself of a basic principle having to do with the motorcar—that when the car is in motion, the driver should keep his two hands firmly gripped upon the steering wheel.

24

A House Divided

I

WHEN Lanny Budd had last visited the town of his forefathers it had been like all the rest of the nation, a jumble of contradictory opinions, but almost to a man united on one slogan, which was: "Never again!" If Europe chose to plunge into another war, that was Europe's privilege; but the good old U.S.A. was going to keep out, and any man who suggested otherwise was a public enemy, and probably a paid agent of some foreign interest. Everybody in Newcastle had agreed on that, from the president of Budd-Erling to the bootblack on the corner of Dock and Main streets. "America is going to keep out of the next war!"

But now, in a few days, what a sea change! The government had placed an embargo upon the export of arms, ammunition, and implements of war to all the belligerent nations, and to the town of Newcastle that was like clapping an extinguisher upon a candle. The principal support of the town was the century-old and constantly growing industry of Budd Gunmakers. After the last war its immense plant had been converted to the making of everything from frying pans to elevators; but in recent years the gunmaking had been resumed and had become once more the principal industry of the town. Large shipments had been going to both Britain and France—and now down had come the extinguisher! One ship, heavily loaded, had passed out of the river and into the Sound, and was passing Montauk Point when a government cutter had come racing after it, flashing signals and ordering its return. Now those goods were back in the company's warehouses, and half a dozen departments of the plant were shut down, and their workers sitting at home, waiting for their relief applications to be acted upon by the WPA.

It wasn't so bad with Robbie Budd, because he had a backlog of U.S. government orders. But a part of those planes had been destined for Britain and France, and now they wouldn't go, and Robbie had sent a telegram to the War Department, demanding to know if new orders would be placed, otherwise he would cut down his operations from three shifts to one. Several telephone calls per day were following up that notice—brass hats being what they were, and no bureaucrat being capable of making a prompt decision about anything.

It was not merely the workers and the executives of Newcastle who had been living on French and British money; it was the grocery and department-store employees, the doctors and lawyers and bankers, and likewise the farmers for miles around who brought their products into town to feed this population. The extinguisher cut off their supply of financial oxygen; and according to the principles of economic determinism they all began to think hard and to revise their ideas about the world they lived in and the policies of their government. Arguments went on in every home and on every street corner, and the confusion in one small city became many times confounded.

The old New England stock was what its name implied in its speech, manners, and sentiments; it believed in free institutions and disapproved of the Nazis, except as they might be needed to hold down the Communists in Russia. Now that the Nazis had made a deal with Russia, the old-time New Englanders had no further use for them, and argued vehemently that the so-called "Neutrality Act" favored Germany, which couldn't get any American goods anyhow. Their arguments were supported by the Poles, who had their share of the town's immigrant population. It was opposed by the Irish Catholics, whose greatest pleasure in life was inflicting harm upon the British Empire. The Irish all turned into fighting pacifists, and were joined by the Germans and most of the Italians, also the French-Canadians, who were Catholics before they were French.

II

Lanny listened to this babel of opinions, and compared the home-town of his forefathers to a mess of eggs which had been broken and dropped into a frying pan and beaten up, but had not yet begun to solidify into an omelet. However, there was a hot fire under the pan, the hottest ever built in this world. All day and half the night the people of Newcastle heard by voice and read on the printed page the horrible details of the destruction of an unoffending nation in a period of eighteen days: armies being slaughtered and driven in rabble rout; cities turned into blazing infernos or heaps of rubble; fleeing civilians bombed and machine-gunned on roads; invading barbarians bringing with them whole trainloads of scientists, especially educated for the wiping out of a national culture. On the streets of this small New England city men stared at one another and exclaimed: "My God, what does this mean to us? And what will it mean if they do it to France and England? Maybe this Neutrality Act was a mistake after all!"

Few of them were willing to abandon their determination to keep out of the war; but they became ingenious in figuring out devices whereby they might sell Budd Gunmakers and Budd-Erling products without incurring risk—or at any rate not too much risk. Britain and France had plenty of ships; why not make them come in their own ships and get the goods, and thus reduce the chances of mishaps at sea? We could give Germany assurances that American ships would carry only non-war goods; such ships would be plainly marked, and so there could be no excuse for torpedoing them. And then there was the question of credits, whereby we had got so badly stuck the last time. Britain and France had plenty of gold; also they had the securities of American corporations, to say nothing of railroads in the Argentine and other properties all over the world. Why not make them turn these over? Put the selling of munitions on a strictly cash-and-carry basis, thus combining the saving of civilization with a sound business deal!

Such had become the orthodox opinion among the well-to-do in Newcastle; and the unorthodox would cry: "Aha! The same merchants of death, planning to turn human blood into profits!" These eccentric persons apparently had the idea that the manufacture of munitions ought to be carried on at a business loss; or did they think that profits ought to be permitted only to Nazi merchants of death? The orthodox would ask with bitter sarcasm, and the fat would be in the fire. The arguments would continue until the arguers were no longer on speaking terms, and perhaps that would continue for the rest of their lives—such being the custom in New England feuds. There were elderly Budds who had not entered the same room at the same time for more than half a century—family funerals alone excepted.

Word spread with the speed of lightning—over the telephone—that Lanny had been in Europe, and had talked with Hitler and Daladier and Chamberlain. So everybody wanted to meet him and hear his story. They wanted not merely his facts, but his opinions; and this was awkward for a P.A., who couldn't expect anybody to believe that he was wholly absorbed in the marketing of old masters at a time like this. He had to get a new "spiel"; he would say: "The problem is so complicated, I really don't know what to think. We shall just have to wait until the situation clarifies itself." That sounded like a statesman and impressed the judicious. The others were satisfied to tell Lanny what *they* thought.

III

One who had the right to know everything was Lanny's father, and their conference in Robbie's study was not so different from the one they had had in the Hotel Crillon a quarter of a century ago. Robbie could never give up the dream that his firstborn might come into the business and help him. Manifestly, Lanny couldn't continue his migratory habits in submarine-infested waters; and what could be more important to a patriotic citizen than to see his country abundantly equipped with fast and deadly fighter planes? These were weapons of defense, since their range was short and they had to be based at home; therefore they deserved the admiration and respect of every pacifist, humanitarian, idealist—whatever it was that Robbie Budd's firstborn called himself at the present alarming moment.

Lanny couldn't very well insist that he planned to go on risking his life at sea or in the air in order to add a few more old masters to American collections. Robbie would have said: "How do you expect to get passports?" If his son had replied: "I want you to tell the War Department that I am aiding Budd-Erling abroad," the father would hardly have judged that a proper request.

Lanny would have to take his father into his confidence, at least in part. Since Robbie himself was working for the government, it could hardly trouble him to know that his son was doing the same. Lanny said, very gravely: "What I am going to tell you is not to be mentioned to a soul, not even to Esther. I am under a promise myself, and it is a serious matter. The information I have been gathering in Europe during the last couple of years has been turned over to someone in authority, and is being made use of in an important way. I have just offered to quit, and have been asked to continue. The request was put in such a way that I couldn't refuse. More than that I am not free to tell, and you must never give the slightest hint of even this much."

"That's a pretty serious matter," was the father's comment. "Are you planning to go into Germany in wartime?"

"I'll be guided by circumstances. The secret has been well kept, and I think I'll be all right."

"May I ask, are you being paid for this?"

"I was offered expense money, but I said I didn't need it, and I've never taken any. Let me tell you, for your comfort, I'm not getting or sending military information. I'm really a sort of friend of the court; Hitler tells me what he wants said to the British and the French and ourselves. I say it, and they tell me what to reply, and I reply it."

"There won't be much of that going on, now that they're fighting, Lanny."

"I'm fairly sure you're mistaken in that. My guess is they'll go right on talking, even while they smash one another. The war's got to end sometime, and meanwhile, both sides will be developing ideas. Each country has its friends in the enemy country, and they're not going to lose contact. It may be that you yourself will have something you'd like to have said to Göring; you can be certain that Schneider will have, and also that Göring will be glad to hear it. Surely you don't suppose the cartels will stop discussing deals back and forth—or that their messengers will be in any danger!"

"No, I suppose not, if you get backing of that sort—and if you don't carry any papers that would incriminate you."

"I carry no papers except my passport, and those concerned with my picture business, which serves as a cover. Everything else I carry in my head, and I have never put a line into the mail inside Germany."

"You can't put it into the mail in Britain or France now, on account of the censorship."

"That has all been provided for. I am not at liberty to say how, but you can be sure that nothing ever bears my name, or anything that could identify me. I am careful to use a different kind of paper and envelopes for each report, and I never make carbon copies, or carry any envelopes or paper similar to the kind I have used in mailing a report."

"All this interests me greatly, of course," said the father. "I have had some vague idea of it, but I didn't want to butt in."

"I made a promise, and I had to keep it," responded the son. He added, with a smile: "I have never made any report on your business, or anything that would concern you. Now that you are working for the government we are in the same boat. I have arranged that both of us are to have the privilege of traveling into the war zones whenever we wish. That is to be handled through the War Department, so that the airplane business will serve as my cover. If orders had been given to the State Department it would mean marking me as a government agent, and a lot of people would know about it; but if I'm representing Budd-Erling, that is what the Germans and everybody else would expect. I felt sure you wouldn't mind my making use of you in this way. My information will really be of use to you, and there's no reason why I can't represent you in negotiations in London and Paris."

"I don't think I'll be needing that," replied the president of Budd-Erling. "They will be coming to me for what they want. But of course it's all right for you to travel as my son, and to ask questions and bring me any news you get. I rely upon your discretion, now as always."

IV

Hansi and Bess were about to set out on a concert tour, this time over the United States—no more Europe for God alone knew how long. Lanny went to stay with them, and drove them in to the city for a concert in Carnegie Hall. They played the César Franck sonata, which Hansi had played, with Lanny accompanying, at Sept Chênes, Emily Chattersworth's estate near Paris; Bess had listened, open-mouthed with wonder, and that had been the beginning of their headlong love. Some fifteen years had passed, and they had played this composition in public a couple of hundred times, by their own estimate. To them it had secret meanings; and to Lanny, who knew every note of it, and shared all the secrets, it was gracious and yet sad music, and becoming more so.

This decade and a half of the Hansibesses had been years of stress and suffering for all humane and sensitive persons. Through it all this couple had worked and striven, having as their goal not merely the perfection of art, but the perfection of mankind—a stubborn material, less easy to shape and control than the vibrations of violin and piano strings. The world orchestra had refused to play as Hansi and Bess had dreamed; not brotherhood but raging hate, not trust but villainous intrigue, not peace but war, had been the program this orchestra had rendered. The couple had struggled on, firm in the faith that they knew the way of redemption for mankind. "Arise, ye prisoners of starvation, arise, ye wretched of the earth, for justice thunders condemnation, a better world's in birth!"

So they had believed and so they had preached for fifteen years in perfect unison; but now, it appeared, even their harmony was being jangled. Bess was still the loyal Party member, determined, even fanatical; nothing the Party might do would ever shake her confidence, she would go on reciting the closing prophecy of the Communist hymn: "The international Party shall be the human race!" But Hansi, alas, was not so staunch; Hansi, gentle, kind, unwilling to hurt a fly, was tormented by the spectacle of his beloved Soviet Union playing what seemed to him the dreadful game of *Machtpolitik*. The deal with the Nazis, and the partition of Poland which he now saw going on, troubled his conscience, and he could not keep from voicing his anxiety. This musical pair were going to tour the three million square miles of Bess's native land and Hansi's adopted land, arguing about whether the end justifies the means, and what end, and what means, and where are you going to draw the line if you once admit the Jesuit doctrine that it may be necessary to do evil in order that good may result? The time would come before their tour was over when they would have to agree to read newspapers and listen to broadcasts and never to speak to each other about what they had learned; never to discuss events which they both considered the most important in the history of mankind.

All through the leftwing movement it was like that. Ralph Bates wrote: "I am getting off the train"—and his sentiments were echoed by thousands; everybody was arguing furiously, and marriages and life-long friendships were broken. Some lost their faith and never regained it; some died brokenhearted, and some took their own lives. Verily it was, as Trudi Schultz had said, "a bad time to be born"!

V

Lanny moved into New York, and went to call on his friend Forrest Quadratt, in the latter's Riverside Drive apartment lined with books and autographed photos and sketches. He found this registered Nazi propagandist in a state of feverish activity, working, so he declared, twenty hours a day. For this was the crisis of his labors, this was the hour of decision for the American people. The villainous conspiracy to repeal the Neutrality Act would mean, if it succeeded, the absolute certainty of America's being drawn into the war. Manifestly, Germany would never consent to so-called neutrals serving as sources of muni-tions supply for her enemies; manifestly German submarines would have to attack all vessels going to Britain and France, for in these times all goods were war goods. When shooting was going on, the way to avoid getting hurt was to stay away from that neighborhood—wasn't that plain to every sensible man?

Lanny Budd, son of a merchant of death, made haste to agree with this opinion; he told of his bitter arguments with his father, and how he had left his father's home, perhaps never to return. Forrest Quadratt clutched at him eagerly, wanted him to make speeches in drawing-rooms, to send telegrams to Congressmen, to raise funds among the rich whom he knew. Lanny said No, he had never made a speech; his talent lay in consultations with important persons, in quiet words dropped here and there like seeds in soft and well-watered soil. He talked about Schneider and the de Bruynes, about Daladier and his marquise, about Reynaud and his Hélène, about Marceline and her young Herzenberg, about Kurt Meissner and Otto Abetz.

Lanny didn't say: "I was in the Berghof the week before the war broke out." No, nothing so crude. He would say: "The world will never know how long the Führer hesitated, and how reluctant he was to take the fatal step. I pledge you my word, I saw sweat of agony on his forehead while Keitel and Brauchitsch were pressing him for a de-cision, on account of the bad weather due in Poland next month." Then, of course, Quadratt would start asking questions, and would drag the details out of this art expert who seemed so completely unaware of the importance of what he had to reveal. If the German propagandist could have had his way, he would have produced the son of Budd-Erling on a platform in Madison Square Garden, and had him tell that story to twenty thousand true American patriots, whom Quadratt could assemble by means of the innumerable organizations which he and his friends had established and financed in and near New York.

Having heard this most inspiring story, he talked freely in return. All true American patriots were working day and night like himself to keep the Neutrality Act on the statute books. They were calling meetings all over the country, and preparing to send out literally millions of congressional speeches through that happy franking privilege which they enjoyed; before they got through they would cause telegrams by the tens of thousands to come flooding in upon those Congressmen and Senators who had not heard the people's voice or who refused to heed it. Only yesterday evening Quadratt had stepped from an airplane after flying to Detroit to present a new idea to Father Coughlin. It was the mothers of America who would suffer most in the event that America was dragged into a foreign war, and it was the mothers of America who were going to appeal to Congress to save their boys from this ghastly fate. Mothers' organizations were going to spring up spontaneously all over the land, and embattled mothers were going to descend upon Congress the moment it assembled. This master propagandist smiled slyly as he pictured the screaming and wailing he would create in the offices of those statesmen who dared to support the administration program.

Of course Lanny didn't have to assume that everything Forrest Quadratt told him was strictly and literally true; one didn't have to assume that concerning any Nazi. But there could be no doubt that within this small head and behind these thick-lensed glasses there operated a cunning brain, almost as capable as that of the crooked little Doktor Juppchen in Berlin. Quadratt had, so he claimed, a mailing list of a hundred and fifty thousand names, and seldom a day passed that he didn't write a speech for some Senator or Congressman to deliver. Then it would be printed as part of the *Congressional Record*, reprinted at a nominal cost by the Government Printing Office, and mailed out to these names, and to other lists supplied by Nazi or near-Nazi organizations scattered all over the country. In addition, Quadratt had a string of pamphlets in his own name, and various books published under pen names; the multiple author showed Lanny a row of them, and it was really funny. Quadratt is the German word for "Square"; but when this German-American crusader resorted to camouflage, he chose the most fashionable English names that ever came out of Ouida or Marie Corelli, and always three of them in a row—Percy Montmorency Raleigh, or Cecil Northumberland Oglethorpe. Lanny couldn't keep from laughing, and his friend joined in, taking it as a compliment to his sagacity.

VI

Driving one of his father's cars, and with General Göring's paintings and others carefully wrapped and stowed in the back seat, Lanny set out on one of those tours by which he earned his comfortable living. He went first to visit his friends the Murchisons in Pittsburgh, driving through the Allegheny mountains at the most agreeable time of the year, when frugal Mother Nature was drawing back the precious chlorophyll into the twigs of the trees and turning the leaves bright yellow and red and orange. When he arrived in the great steel city he did not have to put up at a hotel or to hire a salesroom; he hung his wares in his friends' drawing-room and they invited their friends to see them, and it was not a commercial but an artistic occasion. Lanny used no pressure, but talked instructively about the old masters who were represented, and left it for his auditors to grasp the fact that this sort of opportunity came rarely in a lifetime.

The prices were staggering; but then, what was money to a steel man or a steel man's wife at this moment, when the two richest nations of the Old World were bidding for everything they had or could produce? The Pittsburghers had got over the brief flurry of concern which the embargo had caused; it was bound to be repealed—they had their lobbyists in Washington, and these competent gentlemen had already reported what they would be able to do. The pro-Nazis, reinforced by the Reds, would raise a terrific clamor, but would not be able to check the new tide of prosperity that was flooding into America. What did Mr. Budd think about it? The old masters from Florence and Seville were forgotten while Mr. Budd told what Hitler wanted and what England and France would be able to do.

Lanny's next hosts were Margy's whisky relatives in Louisville, and after that Sophie's hardware relatives in Cincinnati: and after each visit his load was lighter and his purse heavier. From there his route was Cleveland to Detroit to Chicago, all of which cities had had their cultural opportunities increased by him in the past. When he reached the great metropolis of the porkpackers he had only one painting left, a charming Breton child in a quaint seventeenth-century costume. He had saved this for old Mrs. Fotheringay, whose mansion on the North Shore Drive was a sort of silent kindergarten. He had written her about this work of an unknown master, and whenever he got an offer for it he wrote her a playful note, just to keep her on the *qui vive*. When at last it was safe on her walls she considered that he had done her a great favor, for which the writing of a check for seven thousand dollars was a return hardly worth mentioning.

Incidentally, Lanny carried with him several examples of the work of Marcel Detaze. These were not for sale, at least not at present; they were going back to the Baltimore show, and Lanny told about this, and about Zoltan, and Zoltan's project of bringing these paintings to other cities. If any city was to share this cultural opportunity, it was up to some of its citizens to form a group of sponsors of sufficient dignity and prestige. There is an art of painting, and there is an art of presenting paintings to those fortunate ones who have the money to buy.

There was keen rivalry among American money princes. They didn't want just to have wealth; they wanted to be known to have it, and to be making intelligent use of it. If capitalist Holdenhurst and banker Wessels of Baltimore had got their names and pictures in the *Sunpaper* by patronizing the works of a Frenchman dead in defense of his country's liberties, why shouldn't whisky distiller Petries of Louisville and hardware manufacturer Timmons of Cincinnati do the same? Just a few telephone calls or a few orders to your secretary and the trick was done. Paintings insured for half a million dollars would be brought to your city in a big truck, and your friends would gather to look at them and thank you for the privilege, and if a few chose to buy, all right, it was a sound investment. You couldn't eat your cake and have it, but you could look at your masterpiece and have it all your life!

VII

Lanny took the opportunity to renew his acquaintance with several of the important persons whom he had met with Forrest Quadratt. He paid another visit to the Ford home, and heard the richest man in the world pledge his fortune to the keeping of his country out of this most devilish war. Once before, the Flivver King had declared he would never make any sort of war goods, and he had been forced to break that resolution; but this time, nothing was going to change him, so he vowed. Incidentally Lanny met his son Edsel, a quiet, subdued fellow who did what his dominating father wished. His mother wanted him to have culture, so he had begun an art collection in a timid way. He took Lanny to see it, and it was one of the times when the grandson of Budd Gunmakers had need of all the tact which he had acquired from a lifetime of association with diplomats.

Very gently he told this middle-aged man who was still a youth in mind that the acquiring of a great art collection was one of the most difficult achievements in the world. Many who offered themselves as advisers were incompetent, and many of the dealers were the shrewdest of rascals. Lanny quoted the saying of the great art authority, Dr. Bode, that Rembrandt had painted seven hundred paintings during his lifetime and that ten thousand of them were in America. Lanny added that even when old masters were genuine they were not necessarily good, for there were few painters who had not done mediocre work now and then. Having planted these little seeds, Lanny produced his Detazes, and delivered one of his suave lectures on the difference between sound art and fraudulent. When the evening was over he had given Zoltan's address and obtained the promise of both Edsel and his mother to sponsor a Detaze show in Detroit during the winter.

Also, Lanny drove out to the village which had become famous all over America—Royal Oak, named for a reason which nobody seemed to know. He wanted to have a worthwhile report to make to Forrest Quadratt, so he listened for an hour while "Silver Charlie" poured his rage upon those servants of Satan who were planning to repeal the wise and righteous Neutrality Act in the cause of their filthy, bloodstained profits. The Shrine of the Little Flower and its adjoining offices were swarming like a hive of bees, and some editor employed by the fervent Father was taking the mental poison of Josef Goebbels in Berlin, paraphrasing it in the American idiom, and sending it out every week to the half-million readers of *Social Justice*. When his enemies pointed that out, it didn't worry the man of God in the least. A strange kaleidoscopic moment of history, when the Nazis had stopped fighting the Communists and the Communists had stopped fighting the Nazis! But Charles Edward Coughlin, whose forefathers had come from Ireland, had one pillar of fire to guide him, one principle which could never fail —whatever hurt the British Empire must be pleasing to God.

Incidentally, the usually tactful Lanny Budd pulled what came near to being a "boner." He remarked: "Quadratt told me about his recent visit to you. That was a wonderful idea he suggested."

"What idea?" demanded the reverend propagandist.

"The idea of appealing to the mothers of America."

"Did he tell you that was his idea?"

Lanny saw the puddle in his path, and sidestepped it. "I got that impression, but of course I may have been mistaken."

"Well, it wasn't his idea. I told him I was planning to do it, and he offered to write some of the copy for me—always for a good price. He is a clever chap, but don't let him give you the notion that he is in command of the battle to save America."

VIII

Returning from Chicago, Lanny found the highway blocked by a paving job, and, making a detour, he came upon a sign: "*Welcome to Reubens: A Friendly Town.*" A memory stirred. "Reubens, Reubens? Where have I heard of Reubens, Indiana?" Across some fields he saw a two-story brick factory of considerable size, and running along the top of it in large letters: "Bluebird Soap Is the Housewife's Delight." So Lanny didn't have to search his mind any longer; memories came pouring in: memories of a trim white yacht that looked as if it had just been scrubbed with kitchen soap, both inside and out; memories of the blue Mediterranean and its so varied shores; of Naples with its lovely bay full of stinks and its ancient streets swarming with beggars; of the Isles of Greece, where burning Sappho loved and sang; of the ruined temples and the shepherds with their conical huts built of brush; of Marcel Detaze painting his pictures, and the fashionable ladies and gentlemen playing bridge and dancing on deck, bored by five thousand years of history.

Moved by this return to boyhood, Lanny stopped at a filling station and inquired: "Can you tell me if Mr. Ezra Hackabury lives in this town?" The answer was: "Sure thing. Take the first road to your right and drive about half a mile." Lanny said: "Is it *old* Mr. Hackabury?" and the man replied: "He's plenty old, all right." As the visitor drove, he figured—Ezra must be seventy-five at least; and would he remember the little boy whom he had taught to pitch horseshoes, and with whom he had climbed the hill called the Acropolis?

Back from the road was a two-story frame house of modest size, set in the shade of maple trees now turned scarlet and yellow. The house, white-painted, was in the style of our forefathers who had invented the scrollsaw and discovered the possibility of cutting out innumerable curlicues of wood and nailing them onto porches and cornices and gables. Keeping these clean and freshly painted cost a good deal, so they were a sign of elegance, and ladies who dwelt in them expected their husbands to dress up to match the houses, and never to be seen outdoors without their coats on.

But Ezra, twice a widower, didn't have to please any woman. He could put on a blue denim shirt and overalls and go out and rake up the maple leaves from his own front lawn whenever he felt like it. That was what he was doing this afternoon of Indian summer, and the smoke of the burning went up in a tall column in the still air and wavered over the green-shingled roof of the house. He was a big man, but no longer florid as Lanny remembered him; his skin was wrinkled and his cheeks hung in pouches, but there was still the bright twinkle in his eyes. He was the homely, shrewd Middle Westerner, who had once been persuaded to turn yachtsman and had hated it, and now was back on the prairie which he loved.

Lanny got out of his car and came to him, saying: "How do you do, Mr. Hackabury?"—and then waiting, with a little smile of mischief.

The soap manufacturer stopped his work and looked at the visitor. It was somebody he was supposed to know; somebody very well dressed, and with a good car, and a look that said: "See if you can guess!" All right, if it was a game, he would try; he studied the quizzical face, and found something familiar, but it must have been a long time ago—or was he getting old at last? When the visitor said: "I didn't have a mustache, and I was only about so high"—indicating his chest—the memories came to life, and Ezra exclaimed: "Jiminy crickets!" and "I'll be durned!" and other phrases from the days of the scrollwork style of architecture.

IX

What a time they had, going back twenty-five years—nearly twenty-six, to be exact. Pitching horseshoes at Bienvenu, and then the long motor ride to Naples, and the cruise of the yacht *Bluebird*, and the little cakes of soap that Ezra had been accustomed to give away to beggars and peasants who didn't know what it was. Lanny had thought the old man might perhaps not wish to recall the tragic bust-up of his marriage which had taken place at the harbor of Piraeus; but not so, for time heals all wounds that do not kill. "Whatever became of Edna?" the soapman wanted to know.

"She married her Captain, and I met them a few times in society."

"I expected she'd be asking me for money, but she never did."

"They got a good price for the yacht which you left behind, and no doubt he made her take care of the money. They were living at

Brighton the last I heard. No doubt the army will have taken him back and given him some desk job."

They talked about the war for a while. Lanny didn't say anything about his adventures abroad, for that would have been a long story and he was tired of telling it. He spoke of the business of collecting old masters, and of the work of Marcel Detaze, who was becoming an old master, perhaps was one already. The soapman knew nothing of this development but remembered the painter vividly; Lanny told of his tragic fate in the war, and didn't forget to mention that he and Beauty had been duly and lawfully married, for he knew what Reubens, Indiana, a friendly town, thought on the subject of French artists and their morals. When he mentioned that he had some of Marcel's works in the car, including one which had been done on the *Bluebird*, the old gentleman wanted mightily to see them, and called a servant to bring them in and unwrap them.

So they had a little one-man show; but Lanny didn't deliver any spiel or try to make a sale. He just enjoyed talking about Marcel and his ways—how tireless he had been in sketching ancient ruins, and shepherds and peasant children and all the sights of the Mediterranean shores. When weather permitted he would sit all day on the deck of the yacht, painting in bright sunshine the bright pictures which were among the world's treasures. "Who would have thought it!" exclaimed the soapman. "I bought two of them, but they went with the yacht, and I forgot all about them. What would one of these paintings bring now?"

"They vary considerably. These are choice examples and will bring fifteen or twenty thousand dollars each."

"Jehoshaphat!" exclaimed Ezra. "That beats the soap business! And to think we saw it in the making and had no idea of it!"

"A lot of hard work went into the building of his reputation; but once it's done, then you're on easy street."

"Too bad Marcel couldn't have lived to see it! But as I remember him, he didn't care a thing about money. All he wanted was to paint."

"If he'd been here, he'd have been sitting out there painting your maple trees, and making magic out of your fire and its gray smoke spreading."

The older man reflected for a space, and then said: "I'd like to own one of those paintings of Greece, just to remind me. You know, I'm a plain old fellow, but I didn't fail to see something pretty over there, and I had some happy hours in spite of the troubles."

Lanny replied: "The show will be coming to Cleveland and Detroit and Chicago. When it's over, I'll be happy to present you with one of the works."

"Nonsense!" exclaimed Ezra. "I couldn't accept such a gift."

"Don't forget that you gave me many happy hours, and also my mother and Marcel. You made it possible for many of these paintings to exist."

"That's true, and I'm glad to be told it. But I have money, and there's no reason why I shouldn't pay what anybody else would. I'll tell you what—let me know about the shows, and I'll come and pick out half a dozen that I like, and hang them in this house and leave it to the town for an art gallery. I'll do it, if it's only to spite my heirs."

"You don't get along with your heirs?" inquired the visitor, amused.

"I have three sons who run the business, and I get along with them fairly well, except for the in-laws and the children. The longer I live the more I decide that it's the women who make the trouble in the world. If I give a stick of furniture to one of my daughters-in-law, the others go wild with jealousy. And as for the children, who is going to make them work when they don't have to? If I should pay twenty thousand dollars for a painting, they would never think about anything but getting to own it, and they'd tear it to pieces in the squabble."

"Don't let them do that!" said Lanny, entertained, as he had always been with Ezra Hackabury.

"If I had my life to live over again," reflected the creator of America's favorite kitchen soap, "I wouldn't work so hard to make a pile of money for other people to waste. I'd take time off to pitch horseshoes, and maybe even to look at an art show."

"How often I have heard remarks like that!" remarked the son of Budd-Erling. It had become a sort of theme song of the rich; they expected so much from their money, and somehow or other they were nearly always cheated.

X

When Lanny Budd got back to New York, the President had summoned Congress into extra session and asked it to modify the Neutrality Act to permit American munitions to be sold to belligerent nations for cash and transported by them in their own ships. A furious debate was under way, for both sides knew that the issue was crucial; the destiny of America and indeed of the world would depend upon the decision. If you were willing to see Nazi-Fascism prevail in the world, you had to defeat this measure; if you wanted democracy to survive, this was the way to keep the strangler's hold from its throat. There were two armies marching on Washington, the pros and the cons, and every legislator was under siege.

Lanny called Forrest Quadratt and said: "I have just come back from seeing Coughlin and the Fords." The reply was: "Would you come to dinner at Miss van Zandt's? She would be delighted to have you, and you would meet Ham Fish."

Lanny agreed to come if invited, and an hour or so later a messenger brought a handwritten invitation to his hotel. It being a pleasant evening, he walked down Fifth Avenue, watching the traffic which had become so great that it was self-defeating—you could get to your destination faster on foot. The lower avenue wasn't so bad, for the dressmaking trade had emptied its lofts and offices and the streets were nearly empty. Miss Hortensia van Zandt was one of those stubborn old residents who had refused to give way to commercialism; she still clung to her brownstone house and hated the invading hordes who had destroyed the dignity of her neighborhood. In years prior to that it had been a Dutch farm, and Miss van Zandt's grandfather and her father had refused to sell a foot of it; she herself had honored the tradition, with the result that her agent collected enormous rentals from tall office buildings crowded together where once a herd of Holstein cows had peacefully grazed.

The mistress of this fortune was tall, thin, white-haired, and clad in a long black silk dress; she lived as she had in girlhood, when her lover had been killed riding to hounds in the wild country called the Bronx. Year after year she had watched first the publishing business and then the clothing business invading her neighborhood and driving the decent people uptown. Her forefathers had fought the Red Indians, and now she was fighting the Red Jews; she regarded their headquarters in Union Square, half a dozen short blocks away, as a hostile fortress, and fully expected the day when the hate-maddened creatures would come forth with arms in their hands to expropriate her family mansion and turn it into a free-love center. She gave large sums to avert this calamity, and her home was a gathering place for every sort of person who knew or pretended to know how to crush Bolshevism.

Her dining room was paneled in dark walnut and lighted by old-style chandeliers with dangling crystal prisms. There was a huge sideboard with an elaborate silver "service," and they were waited upon by an elderly man in black knee breeches and pumps. At the table sat two other ladies, one a cousin even older than the hostess, the other an elderly secretary; to keep them company were three gentlemen, a left-handed grandson of a German Kaiser, a left-handed grandson of Budd Gunmakers, and the eminent statesman known as Ham Fish.

It was a peculiar name for a man to carry, and Quadratt reported the man's remark—that he had lived with it for fifty years and heard all possible jokes about it and didn't think they were funny. He was properly known as the Honorable Hamilton Fish, Jr., Congressman from the Twenty-sixth New York district. He came of an old family of landowners in the Hudson River Valley; his father had been Congressman before him and his grandfather had been in the two cabinets of President Grant. A big six-footer who had played football with éclat at Harvard, he was heavy-featured, with beetling dark eyebrows. Lanny had been told that he was stupid; now, watching him and listening to him, the P.A. decided that Ham knew exactly what he wanted and was fighting for it with energy and ability.

He had wealth and he believed in wealth and its right to rule the world. He believed that men of wealth were trained for management, and that the greedy and ignorant mob had to be forced or tricked into obedience. In short, he was an old-style English Tory transported to Dutchess County, New York, where his forefathers had established an eighteenth-century "rotten borough." The three counties which composed the district were agricultural and their towns were small; the wealthy farmers, many of them "gentlemen farmers," meaning that they did no work, were all Republicans, and they put up the funds and maintained a smooth-running political machine. The "courthouse crowd" knew how to see to the getting out of the voters and the counting of the ballots, and so Ham was serving his eleventh term in the House. Oddly enough, his district was Franklin D. Roosevelt's own, containing the village of Hyde Park. "That Man" could carry the United States of America, but he could never carry Dutchess County!

In a pluto-democracy, politics is the art of outwitting the voters, so the Honorable Ham would never say that he hated the labor unions and proposed to keep them down. What he said was that the Reds were plotting to seize America. Some fifteen years ago he had got himself appointed chairman of a committee to investigate the Communists. His definition of this word was rather vague, and included everybody who proposed any sort of change calculated to reduce the gulf between the rich and the poor. Ham had traveled the breadth of America putting such persons on the witness stand and browbeating and ridiculing them in his heavy-handed way. He had expected to become President on the basis of that public service, and it was a source of infinite annoyance to him that his Democratic constituent, the Squire of Krum Elbow, had managed to shove in ahead of him.

XI

The patriotic Congressman had an interesting story to tell to the guests at this frugal dinner. He had just come back from a visit to Europe, in the course of which he had called upon the leading statesmen and told them his views. He had publicly stated his belief that Germany's claims were just, and had recommended a thirty-day truce in which the quarrel with Poland might be adjudicated. Now, of course, the stubborn Poles were paying the penalty for having refused the advice. Ham had been a guest of Ribbentrop in Schloss Fuschl, which the wine salesman had expropriated from a Jew—but perhaps Miss van Zandt in her Schloss Fifth Avenue was not aware of that detail. Fuschl was not far from Berchtesgaden, and Lanny said: "I was there only a couple of days after you left." But Ham did not follow up this lead; perhaps it would have detracted from his own prestige, and he needed all he could get right now. It was a time of desperate peril, which the humorless and heavy-featured ex-fullback had been predicting for a long time.

"If Roosevelt succeeds in driving this bill through, we shall find ourselves in the war inside of a year," he announced, and the three old ladies shuddered as one. They had hastened to join and support the various "mothers'" organizations, even though they had no sons or grandsons to be saved. Ham told of another organization which he and other Congressmen had formed, and which they were calling by a large name: National Committee to Keep America out of Foreign Wars. A curious circumstance which Lanny had unearthed in Detroit—the Communists were joining this committee! They, too, had become pacifists all of a sudden! But of course he wouldn't mention this; he would listen respectfully while the Honorable Ham told of the speech he was going to deliver in the House and of the radio talk he would like to give if the money could be raised. He delivered a good part of both between the bouillon and the coffee, and the rest in the upstairs drawing-room with old-fashioned horsehair sofas and "what-nots" and a coal-grate fire to keep the autumn chill out of the bones of three elderly spinsters.

The Kaiser's grandson sat by, accompanying the orator like a drummer accenting the rhythms of a saxophone, nodding and smiling approval of every sentence, and now and then ejaculating "Good!" or

"Exactly so!" or something of the sort. Quadratt knew just what it cost to have speeches printed by the Government Printing Office, and he explained that the saving of America was purely a question of whether or not the Congressman's golden words could be placed in the hands of a sufficient number of voters. When Miss van Zandt wrote a check for five thousand dollars, the German-American seemed as happy as if it had been payable to him personally, instead of to the Committee with a name so long that the secretary had difficulty in getting it into the space on the check.

Quadratt had "got his" only a few days earlier, so he whispered to Lanny. He had already mentioned how he had paid money to Fish's secretary in Washington, a man named Hill, to ship out Nazi literature under Fish's frank. Lanny embodied this fact in a report to F.D.R., suggesting that this might come under the recent law requiring foreign agents to register their activities with the State Department. Lanny added: "A grand jury ought to try to find out whether Fish knew anything about this." But he didn't venture to ask Fish himself!

25

On with the Dance

I

ZOLTAN was in Baltimore, arranging the details of the Detaze show. On the day before the opening Lanny drove there and put up at the Belvedere hotel—the largest and most fashionable, though its abundant gilded carvings were tarnished and dingy. You wouldn't call attention to the fact, because Baltimoreans had held all their swanky cotillions there, and were sentimental about it.

Lanny had decided that it would hardly be decent to trouble the Holdenhursts on the day of the début party. But when he telephoned, Reverdy insisted that he should at least come to dinner—they would all have to eat, and one more plate wouldn't matter. As a matter of fact they were most of them too excited to eat, for they had only one daughter, and she would make only one début.

Lanny went, and found the house turned into a flower garden. After dinner they all retired to array themselves, and just before they went downstairs again the father escorted Lanny to his wife's boudoir, where Lizbeth was standing in the middle of the floor, wearing a white tulle dress lightly touched with tiny silver sequins; both full and floating, yet by the designer's art folding into a clinging, cloudy mist.

It was as if Reverdy said: "Did you ever see anything to beat it?" And Lanny in his heart had to admit that he seldom had. Aloud he said: "Lizbeth, you are the prettiest thing ever!"—and she blushed and trembled so that it almost went to her knees.

A great occasion for her, almost as important as a wedding, in fact the first step toward a wedding. It was a leading family producing their most precious treasure and saying to their world, and to all Baltimore through its *Sunpaper:* "Here she is, 'finished.' She is ripe and ready. Come look her over and make up your minds about her."

The eligible swains would come, not merely from this city but from others. They would inspect the home and the service and sample the foods and wines; they would look over the débutante, her expensive sophisticated dress from New York, her proper hair-do, her make-up, her modest jewels; they would dance one or two turns with her and hear a few intelligent words in her soft refined voice. They would decide that everything was as right as right could be, and if they thought there was any hope for themselves they would seek further opportunity.

In that large throng, almost a crush, there was nothing to make Lanny Budd conspicuous. He would have his minute or two of dancing with the débutante, and would not overlook the mother and other ladies of the household. He would learn from Zoltan, who had been invited to the party, that everything was ready for the next afternoon, and he would take occasion to thank Reverdy and the banker for their courtesies in this matter. Later on he would be drawn into the smoking-room by gentlemen who wanted to ask him what was going to happen next in Europe, and were Britain and France going to send aid to Poland, and why had they promised it if they knew they couldn't send it?

Also, there were ladies, mostly matronly, who wanted to know about the French painter about whom they had been reading so much in the papers of late. They didn't know that a skilled publicity man had been at work for the past month to bring that about, and Lanny didn't tell them. He delivered an agreeable discourse—one of a score which he could have said in his sleep, and perhaps did. He pointed out the two examples which Reverdy had hung in his drawing-room, and which would be taken down next morning and transported to the showrooms, marked with their owner's card.

The music thumped and the champagne flowed and never could you have guessed that there was anything wrong anywhere in the world. It was a magnificent and costly occasion—and all for the purpose of telling the world, including Lanny Budd, what an important young person the Princess Lizbeth was. Lanny understood this, and sought the honor of a second dance with the heroine of the occasion, and paid her one or two more compliments; he ate his plate of terrapin stew, drank a sip or two of wine, and at three o'clock in the morning excused himself and drove back to his hotel.

II

The one-man show proved to be as exactly as "right" as the one-girl party. Zoltan had found a high-class press agent and supplied him with a mass of copy, biographical as well as critical. No painter had ever a more moving story, and in the course of years Lanny and his associate had learned exactly how to exploit it. Zoltan had paid for the right amount of advertising space in the papers, and therefore was entitled to a certain amount of reading space, and could get more if the copy was impressive. The critics were provided with reprints of what had been said about the paintings in Paris, Berlin, Munich, London and New York. They were informed that there was a Detaze in the Luxembourg and one in the Tate, six in Adolf Hitler's home in Berchtesgaden and two in the Holdenhurst home in Green Spring Valley.

Thus the public had every opportunity to realize that a great art event was taking place in their city. These master works had been brought to America in order to keep them safe from the chances of war; and thanks to the enterprise of two leading citizens, Baltimore was being favored with the first opportunity to view them. "Everybody" came; and there was Zoltan, correct with morning coat and pin-striped trousers, and a silk bow tie lending a Bohemian touch. His slightly rebellious gray mustache was newly trimmed, and his manners were foreign but not too much so. There was the painter's stepson, whom "everybody" had already met or heard about; and there were members of the two great families who had espoused this painter, and by now were not quite sure whether they shone in his glory or he in theirs.

The prices of the paintings were not marked on them, for that would have been vulgar. You would have to go to Zoltan or his clerk, who would consult a typewritten list in which the works were priced by number. When you learned that a Greek peasant boy was expected to bring twelve thousand dollars, you would go back for another look and discover virtues you had missed at first. Then it would occur to you that it would be a story to tell, and that your friends would be just as much impressed as yourself. You would start to figuring—what was there you had intended to buy that you could just as well get along without for a month or two? So it was that a dozen numbers were checked off as sold; and Lanny began to worry, as he always did —for he had guarded these paintings for a long while, and wondered if it wasn't his duty to persuade his mother to donate them all to one great museum. But Beauty always needed money, and so did Marceline—and so did the underground!

III

A pleasant holiday in this lotus-land on Chesapeake Bay! It was the time of year when it seemed "always afternoon," as in Tennyson's poem, and the dwellers in this land "smile in secret," not exactly "looking over wasted lands," but reading about them in their newspapers:

Blight and famine, plague and earthquake, roaring deeps and fiery
    sands,
Clanging fights, and flaming towns, and sinking ships, and praying
    hands.

Lanny met charming and cultivated people, and was invited to dinner parties where he was a feature, because he could tell so many "inside" stories about Europe, going back to the last war which we had won and the peace which we had bungled. Would things have been any better if we had joined the League? An interesting speculation, but remote from the dinner tables of the American rich; Europe seemed to them in very truth "a lamentation and an ancient tale of wrong." Apparently it had never occurred to any of the persons Lanny met that the foundations of their social system might be cracking.

So many people wanted to see the paintings that the show was being continued for a third week. But Lanny couldn't stay longer, for it became evident that the legislation being shaped by the congressional committees was going to forbid Americans to travel on the ships of belligerent nations and forbid American ships to enter the ports of such nations. These provisions would make it difficult for a P.A. to return to Europe without revealing his status to somebody. Lanny decided that he had better go while the going was good.

IV

He announced his decision to Reverdy, and as a result was invited into the yachtsman's study and the door was closed, somewhat portentously. Lanny guessed what was coming, and it was none the less embarrassing because it was conducted with so much tact and consideration. Reverdy wanted to tell his younger friend what this friend already knew but had to pretend not to know: that there was a split in the Holdenhurst family, symbolized by the fact that Lizbeth spent half of each year under her father's care and the other half under her mother's. This made the disposing of her future a complicated matter, and the father begged Lanny's permission to have a heart-to-heart talk. Lanny granted the request with grave courtesy, realizing that this scene would call for all the training he possessed.

"You, too, have a daughter," said the host; "so you will be able to understand what is in my heart. The unhappy circumstances of my life have caused me to center my affections upon Lizbeth. Many people have said that I was trying to spoil her and maybe they were right, but I do not think I succeeded, because she is fundamentally so good and kind. What I want is to see her happy; and, as you know, that depends most of all upon the man she picks out. Nothing torments a father more than the thought that his dear one may make a wrong choice. In these days the parents don't have much to say about it; you watch and wait, wondering what fate will hand out to you—because, of course, if she blunders, you are going to help pay the penalty, you are going to suffer every pang that she suffers."

"Long ago," remarked the well-read Lanny, "I made note of the saying of Bacon, that 'He that hath wife and children hath given hostages to fortune.'"

"Precisely so; and we do not know what fortune will demand of us; we can only sit and watch while the die is thrown. I observed that Lizbeth was greatly impressed by you from the first time she met you, and I was pleased, because I, too, admire and like you. Now I have decided that it is the part of wisdom to talk to you frankly about it, and I hope this will not be displeasing to you."

"Not at all," replied Lanny; "on the contrary, I am glad to have the chance to let you know exactly my position."

"Let me say this, Lanny: I understand that a man cannot be asked to change the impulses of his heart. If Lizbeth does not seem to you the woman you want, that is something nobody can blame you for."

"Let me answer without delay. Lizbeth seems to me one of the loveliest girls I ever met. I have thought about her a great deal. It would be foolish to deny that I have observed her interest in me. I hope you know that I have been careful to do nothing to encourage her feelings. I have been a friend; and many times I have wondered if I ought not to keep away from your home."

"Your attitude has been blameless, and that is one reason I venture to bring up the subject. Are you in love with some other woman?"

"No, it's not that. But I have thought the matter over, and I do not believe that I could make Lizbeth happy."

"Why do you feel that way?"

"I am twice as old as she is, and I have acquired habits and ways of life, interests and obligations which are foreign to her. I have to travel a great deal, on my own business and my father's. I have to pick up and leave at an hour's notice, and have no idea when I can return. I tried marriage once on that basis, and made one woman unhappy. I took a vow I would never try it again."

Lanny might have gone on and said: "I have work to do which I am not at liberty to tell even my best friends about." But he couldn't say that; he must not make himself a man of mystery, and spread the suspicion that he was something else than the dilettante he pretended to be. This made matters difficult, because the master of Briarfield and skipper of the *Oriole* couldn't for the life of him see why a dilettante couldn't make a proper husband for his darling daughter; in fact an elegant and cultivated and at the same time wise and kind dilettante was exactly what he was looking for, and thought he had found in the son of Budd-Erling. He was so sure of it that he was willing to overlook an ex-wife and a half-grown daughter in England!

V

Everything was so exactly to his taste that the head of the Holdenhursts questioned and hinted for quite a while. He painted an alluring picture of life on board a private yacht with most of the water surface of the world as your playground. You knew when the typhoon seasons ended and where the mosquitoes were and where they were not. You had a good library, and a radio with an aerial which would catch the voices of all the world bouncing up and down against the Heaviside layer. You had a piano, and no end of recorded music. You could dance, or play cards, or stop the vessel and enjoy a swim. Lanny had known all this in boyhood, and in those days he had learned "The Lotos-Eaters" by heart:

> Let us swear an oath, and keep it with an equal mind,
> In the hollow Lotos-land to live and lie reclined
> On the hills like Gods together, careless of mankind.

In those ancient days the sea had been full of perils and the mariners had dreamed of delights on shore; but now modern science had made the sea a playground for the fortunate ones and they could travel and dream at the same time. When they got tired of change, here was this elegant estate which would be Lanny's home—Reverdy was lavish in the offering of bribes. He would build a separate study for his son-in-law, and some day the whole place would be Lizbeth's. They would have servants to wait upon them, and every desire of their hearts gratified. Anything in the world, to avoid disappointment for a daughter who so far in life had hardly known what the word meant.

Really, it became embarrassing. Lanny realized that Lizbeth must indeed have set her heart on him, and that she must have told her father so. All that the visitor could say was: "I am terribly sorry, my dear friend, but it would be a mistake. I have obligations which I cannot in honor escape." Reverdy would doubtless be guessing that there was some other woman, perhaps a married woman whom Lanny was not free to name or to hint at; and Lanny would let it stand that way.

At last the father said: "Your decision will make a change in my plans, for I cannot answer my wife's argument that Lizbeth ought to stay here this winter and take part in social life."

"That will indeed be hard on you," replied the other, sympathetically.

"I will invite other members of the family on the cruise, and Lizbeth will be left in her mother's charge." He didn't say, but Lanny could guess the rest of his melancholy reflections. It would be his wife and not himself who would have the influencing of the daughter's marital choice; the lucky one would be some alert and successful businessman of Baltimore, and no "mild-eyed melancholy Lotos-eater" to go wandering on a yacht!

"Come and see her when you return to this country," said the father. "You might think it over and change your mind." It was so hard to give up what he wanted!

VI

The President had gone to Hyde Park for a week-end, something he did now and then when the pressure of Washington affairs became too great. Lanny called Baker at a hotel in Poughkeepsie and said: "Zaharoff 103 is about to leave. Does anyone want to see him?" The order was to call later, and when he did so he was told that he was to walk past the hotel at ten that evening. He had to pack up his things in a hurry and drive fast through a cold autumn rain.

When he came to the "Skyway" leading to New York he did not enter the city, but continued up the Hudson River Parkway, formerly the Albany Post Road, a drive of eighty miles or so in country made famous by the Revolutionary War and by Washington Irving's legends. Arriving on schedule, as he always did, Lanny parked and locked his car, and was picked up and driven to Krum Elbow, the estate which belonged to the President's aged mother. It was here the P.A. had come for his first interview and received his assignment. But this time he did not enter the grounds by the regular gate, where army men were mounted in a guard box; he was driven by what appeared to be a woodroad, through a grove of fine trees of which F.D. was very proud —when he voted, he gave his occupation as "tree-grower." When they approached the house they met a soldier on guard and slowed up while he flashed his torch into Baker's face. When he said "O.K.," they drove on.

Newspapermen were not permitted to swarm about this "summer capital," but stayed in Poughkeepsie, and received every day a list of the President's visitors. Needless to say, the name of Lanny Budd would not be on that list; he judged that not even the members of the family knew of his visit. He was taken by a rear stairway to the President's bedroom. This handicapped great man had no legs that he could stand on without steel braces, and these hurt him; so when he had work to do in the evening he retired early. The only time Lanny had seen him out of bed was on his first visit, which had been in the afternoon, and the caller had been received in the library of this fine old house.

The bedroom was large and cheerful, done in chintz; Lanny had seen pictures of it, and of most of the other rooms, at the time when the King and Queen of England had come visiting. Now there was a grate fire burning, and this large man with the powerful shoulders had his blue cape around him—one of his weaknesses being susceptibility to colds. He was grinning cheerfully, as he never failed to do, and his

long cigarette holder was cocked at an angle which was a challenge to
his foes. He always had some funny greeting, a new story, a nickname
for everybody he knew. Henry Morgenthau, Secretary of the Treasury and a neighbor here in Dutchess County, was a serious-minded
gentleman, so he was Henry the Morgue; Harry Hopkins was Harry
the Hop and Thomas Corcoran was Tommy the Cork. It didn't require much genius to predict that the present visitor would be Lanny
the Bud, and he had stopped at a florist's and put a pink rosebud in his
buttonhole, to identify his political complexion.

"Well, Governor," he began, "it looks as if Budd-Erling would be
able to go on making planes."

"I hope your old man is satisfied," responded the other, with a smile.

"I talked with him on the phone this morning, and he seemed to be.
But I can't say that I am. If the amendment goes through in its present
form, we shall be abandoning every principle of the freedom of the
seas for which we fought last time."

"I know, Lanny; but apparently it's all that public sentiment will
stand for at the moment."

"Is it really public sentiment—or just pressure groups, small but
noisy?"

"We have very few Congressmen and Senators who represent the
public," was the reply. "Most of them represent the interests which put
up their campaign funds last time and are expected to do it next time."

"Be careful what you say, Governor! Somebody might be tempted
to quote you!" They jested back and forth; so a man who was burdened with the fate of a hundred and thirty million of his fellows kept
up his courage and spirit.

VII

Lanny had come for instruction, and presently he began getting
them. F.D. had received many reports as to what was coming in Europe, and they were highly contradictory. Since the collapse of Poland
there had come a lull; and how long was that going to continue? Was
Hitler meaning to wait out the winter? Was France planning to attack?
Or were the appeasers going to have their way, and turn this war into
an armed truce? Most important of all, from the President's point of
view, what were the cartels going to do? What plans were they working out behind the scenes?

A peculiar situation confronted the steel interests of France, the
Comité des Forges, the real governing power of the country. They

had the iron ore in Lorraine, but the coking coal came from the Ruhr. So they were dependent upon their German colleagues, and neither could get along without the other, neither could harm the other without suffering equal harm. That situation seemed to call for a compromise, unless, of course, it was the Führer's idea to seize Alsace-Lorraine, something he had always firmly disavowed. Now he might consider that France's declaration of war canceled all promises; but what would the steel men be thinking, and what would their secret messengers be carrying back and forth across the line? Would they be sparing one another's properties, as in the last war; or would it be "all out," as Hitler had threatened? These questions would determine American policy, including that of Budd-Erling.

The P.A. said that he would do his best; and he was pleased to be told that what he had done so far had won good marks. "Apparently," said F.D., "people lie freely to those they know to be government officials, but sometimes they tell the truth to their friends."

"To separate truth from falsehood is a subtle art," explained an experienced listener. "It always depends upon circumstances, and I think I have fooled myself as often by being too skeptical as by being too trusting. Even a man like Papen speaks the truth now and then, if only to rest his mind."

They had agreed upon some code names, and F.D. had the list in a portfolio which was always at his hand. Lanny, of course, had to have it in his memory, and they checked over it, and added a few names. Abetz would be "Bonaparte," because he had lectured in Paris in a theater of that name, and Daladier would be "absinthe," because of his breath. The President said he had made note of Lanny's suggestions concerning Quadratt and Ham Fish, and, by golly, he would make these persons as uncomfortable as he could. Finally, an important detail, he told Lanny how to get his passports; his father was to call a certain man in the War Department, and whatever he asked for would be furnished without his having to come to Washington. Lanny would have passage on the Clipper, believed to be safer than the liners.

That was all, and they parted with a warm handclasp. F.D. pressed a button, and his Negro valet escorted Lanny down the back stairs and turned him over to the waiting agent. He was taken out by the wood-road and returned to his car, in which he drove, long after midnight, back to New York.

VIIı

The car was Robbie's, and next day, or rather later in the same day, Lanny drove it to Newcastle to say his farewells. He couldn't tell Robbie what he was going to Europe for, but he could offer to do errands, and it turned out that what his father wanted was for him to interview Schneider and de Bruyne and de Wendel, and find out the very things which "That Man" wanted to know. Incidentally Lanny made the discovery that Robbie's opinion of Roosevelt had undergone a sudden and surprising change. The man whom he had hated and despised so heartily for seven years had become a far-sighted statesman, doing his best to persuade a purblind Congress to let French and British freighters come into the Newcastle River and carry Budd-Erling fighter planes to the places where they could be of use!

"The bill is certain to pass," Lanny reported; and the father replied: "The British and French have known it for a week or more, and they both have representatives here now."

Rare indeed is the fortune of a man who likes to make money, and who suddenly discovers that it is his social obligation to make enormous quantities. Such had become the position of Robbie Budd, and he made no bones about revealing how much he enjoyed it. He was not given to introspection, and didn't waste time examining the basis of this satisfaction. He had his formulas, prepared in youth and built into the very structure of his mind. Money made the mare go; money was power to do things, and he had got that power and was using it. He had foreseen the future of airplanes, and now he had them to sell, and was charging all he could get—because more money meant more power to make more planes.

Something like this had happened once before, twenty-five years and three months ago, when Robbie had been representing Budd Gunmakers in Paris. That time Robbie had had to send cablegrams in code and take the orders of his stern old father; but this time Robbie himself was the boss, and people took *his* orders. The town of Newcastle near the mouth of a small river flowing into Long Island Sound had suddenly become a place of importance to London and Paris. Persons who wore gold braid and bore titles got themselves flown to the Budd-Erling airport, put up at the swanky Riverside Inn, and asked for conferences. They wanted fighter planes, and Robbie showed them his schedules and revealed that he had orders it would take him six months to fill. His plant was working twenty-four hours a day and couldn't make any more hours.

So then the visitors wanted him to expand the plant; and how quickly could he do it? Robbie told them the story of what had happened to the family property in the last war. His father had refused to expand, until the United States government had put it up to him as a patriot and practically forced him to do so; then, the moment the war was over, orders were canceled and the concern left to sink or swim as best it could. The result was, a Wall Street syndicate had taken Budd Gunmakers, and Robbie Budd had learned a lesson that he wasn't going to forget.

Budd-Erling Aircraft would remain a little plant—that is, little according to modern standards; it had some bonds outstanding, and would issue no more. If any government—British, French, or American— wanted more planes, it could build a new and larger plant adjoining Robbie's property, or Robbie would have it built for them, using their money. They could equip it, or Robbie would equip it, with their money. Robbie would run it and build planes for them, at a fair profit. When the war was over, Robbie would have an option to take the plant over at one-half cost, and if he had the money and thought it advisable, he would exercise the option; otherwise the government would have the plant and could do whatever it pleased.

A heartbreaking proposal to the British, and to the still more frugal French. They wanted American capital to finance production for them —that was the established way, and this war was going to cost them huge sums, perhaps everything they had. Robbie said: "If you can get American capital it's O.K. by me; but that's not my job, and I'm not telling any of my friends to gamble on this war."

So the visitors replied: "It's all off. Sorry." But then they went back to their hotel and had long telephone talks with London and Paris, and London and Paris told them to go back and plead and argue some more. So it went, until Robbie told them that it was every nation's privilege to lose a war if it wished. That hurt their feelings, and Robbie said he was sorry, but he had been dealing with governments all his life and found them lacking in foresight and tangled in miles of red tape; only when they were in trouble did they have any use for the manufacturer, and it was necessary for one manufacturer to state plainly that their troubles were theirs and not his. So matters stood when Lanny arrived in Newcastle, and so they remained when he left.

IX

The same Clipper which had brought Lanny across the sea took him back again. It was the beginning of November, which in England is a month of rain and fogs with twilight in mid-afternoon. Now there was the blackout; you carried a tiny pocket flashlight, and getting anywhere became such a problem that you marveled how a city's life could go on. The war was two months old and the expected bombing hadn't yet come; but it might come at any hour, and everybody was supposed to carry gas masks, but had got tired of it.

Lanny found the Cockney his usual cheerful self. He and his forebears had lived on this foggy island for a long time, and had got used to having a million chimneys pouring black soot into the atmosphere he breathed. A few troubles additional didn't make much difference to his spirit. The general sentiment was that ole 'Itler 'ad gone and put his foot in it this time. The army was being transported to France and lining up along the borders of Belgium and Holland—familiar ground to Britishers, who had fought there in the last war, and in the days of Napoleon, and in those of Queen Mary, who had had Calais written on her heart.

Lanny went first to Wickthorpe, for him a place of business as well as pleasure. No war was going to cause Englishmen to give up their week-ends, which were really the time for conference and quiet discussion. The formula "business as usual" included the business of gracious living, and no fear of bombing planes would ever keep an Englishman from dressing for dinner. The tone of social gatherings would become serious, of course, for everybody knew that England had taken on the most difficult task in her history, and few ventured to guess how many years it might take to complete it. Certainly longer than the four years and three months of the last time!

X

Lanny's first talk was with Irma, and he discovered that she was accepting her role with the quiet dignity which became her station. He wondered, but forbore to ask, what was going on in the depths of her heart. Would she ever look back and wish that she was in her own palace on Long Island, safe from dangers and inconveniences? Maybe so; but she was proud, and not even her mother would be permitted to hear a complaint. She had made a failure of one marriage, and must surely not repeat. Having made over this ancient building, equipping it with modern conveniences and the fanciest plumbing gadgets, she was distressed to think what one large bomb might do to them; she asked Lanny—would the Germans waste even one bomb on a residence which was not a military objective?

She had saved this estate from being split up and sold—the fate of so many others in these days of taxation inspired by Leftist theorizers. But now a new form of desecration had fallen upon the place: a great part of the beautiful grounds had been plowed up and harrowed, and in the spring would be planted with potatoes, cabbages and Brussels sprouts. The word had gone forth that Britain must become self-sustaining in the matter of food, and now, as always, it was the duty of the ruling class to set a prompt example.

The most serious trouble confronting the mistress of this demesne was the children who had been evacuated from London. The carful which Lanny had brought had been followed by scores of others; they had been quartered in the village, and a spare building on the estate had been turned into a school. Some of the youngsters were quiet and decent, but others were little savages. The problem of keeping them physically clean was almost too much for the people of this staid community, where nothing of importance had been changed in a hundred years. Lanny heard about the widow of the former parson of the village who, in course of her Christian duty, had taken two of the most verminous slum lads into her home. She had escorted them to the bathroom, and turned on the water and told them to strip, then had decorously left the rest to their understanding, which was incomplete. A maidservant, listening at the door, heard one of them say: "Wot's up now?" The other replied: "I think the old bitch is going to drown us."

The refugees at the castle couldn't very well be kept behind bars, and the more adventurous presumed to wander over the estate. This presented another problem for a mother of an heiress. To little Frances they were objects of intense curiosity; she asked endless questions about them, she watched them whenever she could, and they watched her. Irma was conscious of a powerful force drawing children toward one another; they were little gregarious animals, knowing nothing about class distinctions, good manners, or decent language; they were not shocked even by vermin, but rather curious about them, as another kind of gregarious animals.

Lanny said: "The war is making a lot of changes in the world, Irma. The fathers of these children will be in the same trenches with our friends "

"Oh, but the words they use, Lanny!"

The ex-husband felt impelled to point out that words are artificial and conventional things; one sound is no more inherently wicked than another, and is not made wicked by taking away one consonant and substituting a different one. When Irma exclaimed that she couldn't bear to have a child's mind defiled, Lanny replied: "They are words the common people have been using for a thousand years, and that makes them interesting to students of language. You have learned them, and have managed to survive, and you might as well make up your mind that Frances will learn them sooner or later, and she, too, will survive."

He was afraid to say anything more, for Irma might take this as an echo of his former "radicalism," which he wanted her to believe he had entirely outgrown.

XI

The guests came to Wickthorpe by train now, and were met at the station by whatever number of cars were needed. When they had bathed and dressed they came down to the great hall where they had whiskies and soda, or American cocktails if they preferred. They listened to the latest news over BBC, and then went in to dinner, which was served by maids—another wartime revolution, since a quarter of a million men had gone overseas and a million more had been drafted and were now being marched over all the roads of England to toughen them. The dinner tables were still provided with New Zealand mutton and Argentine beef, but that was going to grow scarcer and be rationed before the history of England had unfolded much further.

In serious tones the ladies and gentlemen discussed the state of their world, and sought information from those who were reputed to possess it. One who had left New York only a couple of days ago could be sure of being heard with close attention. Word had just come that the Congress had passed the bill revising the Neutrality Act, and it was known that the President would not delay to sign it. This made for good digestion, and for pleasant remarks about "hands across the sea." It was of especial importance to Irma, née Barnes, who had had the foresight to invest a chunk of her fortune in Budd-Erling Aircraft, and now could have the pleasure of helping her adopted country and at the same time increasing her private income. However, it wouldn't do her much good; she would have to pay income taxes both in America and in England!

What a P.A. was interested in was the attitude of these people toward their allies and their foes. Most of them had been appeasers, for that had been the tone of Wickthorpe, and if you loathed the Nazis, you preferred putting your feet under some other dinner table. Now a number of the guests had changed their minds; they said that Britannia had put her hand to the plow, and must go to the end of the furrow. Others had decided to "pipe down," and no longer sang the praises of the Führer as a bulwark of order and future liquidator of Bolshevism.

Ceddy was one of these, and his wife followed his lead, as a wife has to do if she wants her man to have a career. But when Lanny was alone with them he discovered that his lordship was a man convinced against his will, and that his wife was not convinced at all. Both considered this war the greatest blunder in British history, and a source of satisfaction to no one but Josef Stalin. That bloody-handed tyrant had planned it, and now was going to sit on the sidelines and watch the capitalist powers fight one another to exhaustion. Already he had got half of Poland, and before it was over he would have the whole of Central Europe, and perhaps the Balkans, who could say?

The pair talked to Lanny as a member of the family. He told them that he agreed completely, and so did his father, who hated the profits which the government forced him to make. Lanny was going to France, to get into touch with persons who held the same opinions there, and he hoped before long to make contacts by way of Switzerland with the friends of peace in Germany. He knew that neither Göring nor Hess had wanted this war, nor did they now want it fought to a finish. It was only a little group of rabid Anglophobes who had persuaded the Führer into the deal with Russia, the real foe and the real dread of the German people.

Interesting indeed was Lanny's account of his meetings in New York and Detroit and Chicago with influential Americans who had this same point of view and were standing by it in the face of bitter opposition. Irma took her ex-husband into her confidence and explained that she and Ceddy could no longer speak with entire frankness in a mixed company, but they had a few special friends who shared their lack of enthusiasm for the coming slaughter, and would Lanny talk to these? This was what Lanny was in England for, and presently he found himself in the center of a group of irreconcilables whom Rick had described in his formula: "Class is more than country." There were many of them in England, some in high positions, including members of the Cabinet. Ceddy reported the P.M. as being with them in his heart, although for reasons of state he could not admit it. "The first move ought to come from Hitler," declared his lordship. "He holds all the cards now."

"Yes, but he has a common border with Russia," declared the son of Budd-Erling, with a little smile which the other members of this company understood. It was an unwritten assumption of European statecraft that when two great powers had a common border, they were bound sooner or later to fight over it. The problem was, how to get Russia into this war, and to get Britain out. Lanny listened, and thought to himself that with a Prime Minister and part of his Cabinet in this state of mind, the British Empire was going into a slugging match with one hand tied behind its back.

XII

In these ticklish times, with so many people keeping watch, a presidential agent had to be careful whom he talked with. Lanny returned to London, and from there phoned to Rick, not giving his name, but saying "Bienvenu." He asked Rick to meet him at a small hotel where neither of them was known, and there they shut themselves in a room and told their hopes and their fears. Lanny wouldn't name Roosevelt, but could say: "I had a talk with my boss, and I'm not allowed to join your army. I'm to go on watching the appeasers and reporting." He added, with a wry smile: "I'm never allowed to do anything that will make me uncomfortable."

"The appeasers will make you uncomfortable before this war is over, damn their souls," replied the Englishman.

He was in a state of acute anxiety concerning his country's plight: the lack of preparedness, the lack of realization of the danger, the lack of spirit for the fight, in some cases amounting to downright treason. Rick wanted to make a clean sweep of the men who were directing the foreign policy of the Empire; he called the roll of them, and gave their records: what sort of fellow was this or that to be in charge of a war on Fascism! Lanny told of what he had heard at Wickthorpe, and the lame ex-aviator figuratively speaking wrung his hands. "You see! Absolutely putrid!"

However, they were able to find a few spots of silver in these dark clouds. There was the new First Lord of the Admiralty—or rather the old First Lord brought back. "Winnie is a fighting man," Rick admitted; and Lanny smiled to himself, thinking what strange bedfellows this misery had made. For Winston Spencer Churchill was a Tory Imperialist *pur sang*, and one who did not feel it necessary to apologize for his creed. Lanny told of their talks by the swimming-pool of Maxine Elliott, where few things had been hidden, whether of the body or the mind. It would be a long time before "Winnie" would again be found lolling in Riviera sunshine, his pudgy form in a red bathrobe and his bald head protected by a floppy straw hat. "Good old Winnie" would stay in dark and smoky London, spilling cigar ashes over his weskit, and studying the wall charts on which the position of British men-of-war was marked. Already the enemy had torpedoed one of his best battlewagons, the *Royal Oak*, in Scapa Flow, a shelter north of Scotland where the main fleet had been wont to rest. Now the fleet had moved to a place which few knew and none told.

The blockade of the Nazi power had begun. It was a kind of warfare which operated in silence and secrecy; most of the time it was nothing you could see or measure, and it was very slow—Rick talked of five years, perhaps ten. All over the seven seas the German vessels would be hunted, and now and then one would be captured or sunk, until in the end not one would be left. It would be like a strangler's hold, applied little by little, reducing the air and the blood supply of the victim and bringing his powers of resistance ever lower. The German submarines would be hunted, and the ships which brought them fuel, and the German raiders which would sneak out to prey on British commerce. Right now there was a cruiser reported operating off the coast of Africa; a few weeks later, off the coast of Uruguay, this *Admiral Graf Spee* would find her resting place on the sea's bed.

XIII

Alfred Pomeroy-Nielson, grandson and namesake of the baronet, had joined the Royal Air Force. He was a trained flyer, and had what few Englishmen could claim, experience in actual combat. Men who had gone to the aid of the Spanish people's government were looked upon with deep suspicion by the military men of all "capitalist" governments, and Alfy had a tragicomic story to tell of his efforts to have a part in the defense of his native land. He came to see his old friend Lanny Budd in the same way that his father had done, for he was one of those who shared Lanny's secret. He considered that he owed his life to the help Lanny had given him in Spain, and while he did not talk about it, he would be on the watch for a chance to repay that debt.

Alfy was now twenty-two, and had got all the learning he wanted at Magdalen College, more than would ever be of use to him, so he said. He was tall and spare, with his father's thin face, but with brown hair and eyes from his mother's side. Serious and conscientious, he was in this war as a crusader on behalf of freedom; he said it was one of those decisive struggles, as when the Greeks had defeated the Persians at Marathon, and when the hordes of Attila had been defeated on the plains of Northern France. If these modern Huns who called themselves National Socialists were beaten, it would mean the greatest leap toward democracy yet achieved; on the other hand, if they should win, it might mean the end of the democratic dream for all time. In that spirit the baronet's grandson was fighting the Fascist-minded inside the R.A.F.—and there were a lot of them, some high in authority. They paid him back by denying him the command to which his experience entitled him, and by sending him on the most dangerous missions, from which he was at liberty to return if he could.

So far it had been mostly scouting, all over the surrounding waters and the enemy's land. Wilhelmshaven had been bombed, but mostly it was leaflets that were being dropped upon the enemy. A tragic thing to an airman, to have to watch the destruction of Poland, and to be helpless. Göring's Luftwaffe had done what they considered a fine job there; but so far they hadn't carried out their threats to bomb English cities. They had made several attempts on the fleet, but without much result, and they had lost more planes than they had shot down. Alfy said: "Here's one thing to learn; they are going to lie, so don't ever worry over their claims."

"Perhaps their airmen are too optimistic," suggested the other, with a smile.

"All airmen are," was the reply. "It's the business of HQ to pin them down and get the facts. We know what we've lost, so we realize that the Nazis have a system. Whatever they get, they claim double."

Alfy wanted to know about the progress of Budd-Erling, and Lanny was free to tell him, and didn't mind if Alfy passed it on to his superiors and got some kudos out of it. Alfy had flown one of last year's Budd-Erling models, and reported that it was better than the Messerschmitt, but not so good as the Spitfire. "Thank God we had men in the force who were on their toes!" he said. Lanny could assure him that Robbie's most recent model was both faster and more heavily armed; also, that it had a single-gear supercharger that was a whiz, though he couldn't drop the smallest hint of how that marvel had been achieved. He could report that the plant was working day and night, and there was a good chance of its being enlarged.

Thus they talked "shop." It was important to both of them, for Robbie would be glad to hear what a fighter pilot had learned of his own and other planes in actual combat, the one test that really counted. Alfy, for his part, could deliver to his superiors a set of facts. How many planes was Budd-Erling actually turning out at the present time? What was their actual top speed, and would they be able to carry heavier guns, as the British were already putting into their "Spits"?

Lanny wouldn't ask what the British production was, but he knew that the Luftwaffe outnumbered the British and French air forces combined, and Alfy admitted that this was the fact. "But our men are better than theirs," he declared, and stuck by this. "Nobody can tell me that a dictatorship can produce the same grade of men as a free land."

"I assure you," countered Lanny, "Göring's men haven't the slightest idea they aren't free. They believe in Germany, just as you believe in England. They believe in their leaders, far more than you believe in yours. At this moment they are not troubled by such doubts and fears as you have revealed to me."

"I know," said the Englishman; "but we're only at the beginning of this war. Already they are lying; and don't you know that the knowledge of that is bound to spread, and to eat into their faith and their fighting spirit?"

"I hope you are right," said the American. "But you will have to prove it to them."

BOOK SEVEN

The Winds Blew and Beat upon That House

26

Time Ambles Withal

I

TRAVEL between Britain and France was not encouraged in wartime; but Lanny consulted his friend Ceddy, pointing out that he had brought worthwhile impressions of opinion in America and might do the same for France. He might travel into Switzerland, ostensibly on his father's business, and contact some of the Germans who would be swarming there; he might even receive an invitation to Berchtesgaden, or to meet Hess in some inconspicuous place. The Deputy Führer had no more real stomach for this fight than Lanny or Ceddy; and who could say what concessions he might have to propose?

His lordship jumped at this suggestion, saying that he would not merely see the path made smooth for Lanny, but would tip off the French to do the same. However, Lanny said: "Better not, because I don't want to acquire the status of an official person. Denis de Bruyne and Schneider are both interested in Budd-Erling, and will surely have the necessary influence. It will be much better for me to travel as my father's son."

"Righto!" said the Foreign Office man.

A plane sat Lanny down at Le Bourget airfield, as it was doing for others who had large quantities of goods to sell, or who spoke for men of that sort. Goods were needed in war, even more than in peace, and money which made the mare go did the same for the bombing plane and the tank. Lanny put up at the Crillon; and as soon as word spread that he was in town, important persons wanted to see him, and learn what was going on in Washington and New York, and even Newcastle, Connecticut.

Baron Schneider, first of all. He invited Lanny for lunch, and kept him most of the afternoon. How many planes was Robbie turning out now, and was he going to enlarge his plant? When Lanny said probably not, the Baron suggested that he might be able to find a way to assist. These big fellows would rarely say straight out: "I will put up the money." It was a matter for circumlocution, something evasive and devious. Frenchmen who had had money for generations would prefer you to assume that it was all tied up, and that they would have to go to a lot of trouble to find someone to oblige you. When Lanny said that his father was unwilling to borrow more money, that, too, was taken as part of the game, and meant that he wouldn't want to pay quite so much for it. No bonus of common stock from now on!

The munitions king was almost schizophrenic in this crisis, a man divided in his mind and unable to bring the two parts into harmony. He wanted France to be defended, but at the same time he didn't want her to be attacked. To him this conflict was a nightmare dreamed by a homicidal maniac. There was bloody Stalin, sitting on his far-off throne and chortling with glee. He had got everything exactly as he wanted it—the prosperous, property-respecting nations tearing at one another's throats, while he, the expropriator, armed himself and prepared to loot Europe, or to rouse its proletarian hordes to do the job for him.

The master of Le Creusot wanted fighter planes made, because these could be used for defense; he wanted the French government to buy such planes, and he wanted to arrange for Lanny to talk with General Gamelin and General Weygand and Admiral Darlan and tell them what miracles the Budd-Erling plane was now performing or about to perform. The Baron himself was growing more and more worried about the part which aviation was playing in this war. No polite, well-ordered war, like those in the past, but blind, indiscriminate destruction, with loads of high-explosive being dumped in the night upon cities, and not sparing the palaces of industrial magnates, or the headquarters of elderly, distinguished generals and admirals! Not sparing steel mills and coal mines and munitions factories and railroads—the enormous complicated structures to which the Baron and his father and his grandfather had devoted their labors, their thoughts, and their hard-won capital!

Somebody ought to stop it! And here was a man, young, energetic, persuasive, *un homme de bonne volonté* if ever there was one. A citizen of a neutral country, he was free to travel in Europe. Why couldn't he go now to Berlin by way of Switzerland and make the Nazis realize what a mistake they were making, and persuade them to accept a compromise? Poland? What was the use of talking about Poland any more? There was no Poland; and did any man in his senses imagine that France and Britain could conquer Germany as she now was and set up Poland as she had been? Had not General Gamelin told them that the next war would be fought behind concrete, and that the first army which came out from behind the concrete would be annihilated?

Lanny said that he would be very happy to meet the French military men and talk fighter planes to them, that being his father's business, and incidentally the Baron's. But as to making proposals to Germany, that appeared to be a job for the diplomats. Schneider replied that he had tried the diplomats, the best he could find, and they had failed. Lanny replied: "It seems to me that before anybody approaches Hess or the Führer, Frenchmen ought to make up their minds what they are willing to concede. At present there appears to me a chaos of opinion in this country, and much the same in Britain." The other admitted mournfully that such was the case; only the Nazis knew what they wanted, and they proceeded to take it, without any regard for the established courtesies and conventions of Europe.

II

The melancholy days had come, the days of cold and rain and little sunshine in France, of fear and uncertainty in the souls of Frenchmen. There was the blackout, though not so bad as in London; street lights were painted blue. You carried a gas mask wherever you went, and kept in mind the whereabouts of the nearest shelter; indoors, you were warned to stand with your face to a wall, on the theory that you would rather have glass splinters in your back than in your eyes. When the weeks passed, and the months, and no bombers came, you gradually relaxed these precautions; but you could not escape the inconveniences, the shortages, and worst of all the doubts and breakdown of spirit.

The average Frenchman didn't want war, and could hardly believe that he had got into one; he could find so many reasons for not fighting, and lived in the hope that somehow "they," the superior powers, would find a way to get him out of the mess. A great part of the newspapers which he read opposed the war, or at any rate put the blame for it upon the groups in control of the government. Even the Socialists couldn't make up their minds how far they wanted to go, or in which direction; their paper, *Le Populaire*, solved the problem by dividing its editorial page in halves, one "hard" and the other "soft," one for putting Hitler down and the other for making some sort of compromise with him.

The position of the Reds was even more unpromising for the future of France. The Communist Party had proclaimed that this was one more capitalist war, and that the fatherland of French workers was the

Soviet Union. The government replied by outlawing the Party and throwing hundreds of its leaders into jail. The effect of this was to deprive Lanny of one of his sources of entertainment as well as information; for Uncle Jesse Blackless disappeared, together with his wife. The police raided his tenement rooms and seized his papers and put a seal on the door. His nephew might perhaps have found him if he had made inquiries in the right quarter, but he couldn't afford to advertise his Red connection. He guessed that Jesse would make his way to Moscow—and this guess proved to be correct.

III

It was a matter of no slight importance to *la patrie* that its most important political party, with several million adherents, had gone "underground" and was opposing the national effort. The Reds were the most tireless propagandists, and wherever in the factories a worker grumbled at the 72-hour week, there would be a "comrade" to whisper: "This is one more capitalist war." Wherever in the trenches a *poilu* complained of monotonous food and two-and-one-half cents a day compensation, there would be someone to direct his bitterness against those *sales cochons*—not the boches, but the politicians at home.

And of course the enemy agents were at work day and night. Those of German nationality had got out, but they had established an elaborate machine and put Frenchmen in charge. Lanny knew who many of these persons were, and he knew that the money was pouring in by way of Switzerland, Belgium, and other neutral countries, including Lanny's own. The Bank of International Settlements in Zurich was still functioning, and the businessmen were still insisting that "business as usual" was an honorable motto. The French reptile press was still getting its "envelopes," and there were even papers which had no circulation, but were printed in large editions and given away. Needless to say, these were all humanitarian in tone, emphasizing the fact that war is a very evil thing, and that mothers love their sons and do not like to have them slaughtered for the benefit of *les bellicistes*, the warmongers, mostly political adventurers and merchants of death.

In the early days of the attack on Poland the French troops had advanced toward the Saar valley, using the ingenious device of a herd of pigs driven before them to explode the mines. The Germans had fallen back without resistance; and after Poland had been cleaned up, the French had thought it over and realized that they were outnumbered, and that to attack the German fortifications would be very costly.

General Gamelin was in command, and he remembered his own warning, and drew back into the security of his Maginot.

The Germans had called their sweep into Poland a *Blitzkrieg*, and now the public in France and Britain gave a name to their own kind of warfare; it was a *Sitzkrieg*. Half a year of it would fix firmly in the minds of soldiers the idea of resting comfortably and letting the enemy have the troubles and shed the blood. After all, there were worse things than sitting in a casement playing cards and smoking cigarettes, and arguing about who was to blame for the war and what was the best way to get out of it. The mail came, and the newspapers; also, a variety of other literature turned up, no one was sure just how, but it was passed from hand to hand and caused amusement and discussion. Lanny saw samples; for example, a leaflet with a picture of a British Tommy, and underneath him the question: "Where is your wife?" When you held the leaflet up to the light you got the answer, for you saw a naked woman in the Tommy's arms. That might start uneasiness in a poilu's mind, for it was well known that the British army had taken over a good chunk of Northern France. They hadn't done any fighting to speak of; and now and then there would be a leaflet asking, who was going to get the English out of France, and when? Had they not taken French ports in past wars and kept them? Who had not heard the phrase, *perfide Albion?*

IV

Lanny learned more about this underground literature when he went out for his week-end at the Château de Bruyne. Both sons were gone; Denis *fils* was a staff officer at a headquarters near the Belgian border, and Charlot was an officer of reserves behind the Belfort fortifications. The elder brother had made up his mind that the war had to be fought, whatever the political outcome; but Charlot was still the Fascist rebel, completely untamed; he was bent upon appeasement, and if that was impossible he wanted a Hitler victory, as a means of putting down the labor movement and putting the Right people in control of France. That was a pun which was valid in the French language as in English; you spoke of *les hommes du droit*, and you meant that the people of honor and decency were those of your own political way of thinking.

Robbie Budd had written to his business associate, saying that Lanny was to serve as a wartime messenger between them; so Denis talked freely, expounding his carefully considered ideas. Civilization in France must be saved by the same method which had been used in

Spain; the corrupt and vicious "Third Republic," a creation of mob violence, must be overthrown, and a Catholic dictator like Franco must take charge of the country. This war now under way was not a foreign but a civil war, as in Spain. Hitler and Mussolini had helped there, and would help here, that being the only way the job could be done. The fact that Hitler had made a deal with the Reds meant nothing except that he wished to have his eastern frontier safe for the duration. The Führer was the implacable foe of Bolshevism, and would not delay to put it down, the moment his hands were free. Denis had received personal assurances of this, from Kurt Meissner and Otto Abetz and Graf Herzenberg and other Germans of culture and tact who had been making their homes in Paris.

What especially interested Lanny was Denis's revelation of his younger son's activities. Charlot's army post was close to the Swiss border, and this was no accident, but had been planned. Some five hundred officers had been involved in the Cagoulard conspiracy of a year or two ago, and many of these were now conniving at the smuggling of German-printed leaflets and pamphlets across the Swiss border and their distribution to the troops. Said Denis: "The Reds have had their 'underground' in Germany and have been sending in literature from France for the past six or seven years. Now we have taken a leaf out of their notebook."

A dangerous business in wartime, Lanny opined; but the father said, No, they had grown too strong to be prosecuted; they had too many friends in Parliament and in the Cabinet. The authorities had arrested Marcel Déat for circulating anti-war literature but hadn't dared bring him to trial. Several high-ranking generals were sympathetic to the rebels, including Marshal Pétain, who was now in Madrid as French ambassador, trying to work out with the German ambassador there the terms on which this idiotic war might be brought to an end. Once that was done, the overthrow of the government would be easy.

V

Lanny gave close attention to this suave and elegant Frenchman, a member of whose family he had been for almost two decades. Denis was past eighty, aged and shrunken, his face lined with care—but still no one ever saw him that he was not a model of the tonsorial and sartorial arts. He had greatly increased his wealth since Lanny had known him, and apparently his public standing had not been injured by some months of martyrdom in prison. Lanny wondered, had age diminished his interest in his peculiar sexual pleasures? He would make reference to the affairs of other men, and his bright dark eyes would twinkle and the lines about his mouth deepen into a grin. He had taken these pleasures as his right, just as he took his wealth, and his position as the head of one of the "two hundred families" which governed France. An odd thing, he knew that these families existed, and would talk about them freely, but he took the phrase as an insult, a device of hated class enemies, moved by the basest impulses of envy and greed.

Denis de Bruyne had broken the heart of his gentle-souled and lovely wife, and then left it for Lanny Budd to repair the damage to the best of his ability. When Marie had told her husband that she had taken a lover, he had been upset, but not for long; as a sensible French-man of the world he had come to the conclusion that it was better for the mother of his sons and keeper of his home to be cheerful and con-tented rather than glum and resentful. So he had accorded to the good-looking young American the status of an honored guest, and little by little, of a friend. Such a relationship was difficult for an American to imagine, but the French had a name for it, *la vie à trois*—life in threes— and there were numerous instances of it in the history books, notably Anatole France and his *amie*, Madame de Caillavet.

Lanny looked back upon those years, first as a lover and later as a sort of supplementary widower and foster-father to the sons. He hadn't been able to do for them what he would have wished to do; but then, he reflected, Marie wouldn't have liked it if he had. She had been Catholic and conservative, and if she had lived, he would have had to keep his dark secret from her. When she died, he and Denis had walked side by side at the funeral, both of them sartorially and socially cor-rect; they had spoken words of proper grief, but Denis had spoken no word of remorse, and in the years of friendship and business associa-tion which had followed, Lanny had never heard from the aging man one word of personal emotion—grief, fear, shame, despair, even depres-sion. Anger, yes, and of the bitterest sort, but always political, having to do with the protection of his fortune and the social mastery it gave him.

Such was the "polite" world, in which the conduct of human beings had been rehearsed for centuries, and all actions, all gestures conven-tionalized and fixed. In such a world, morals tended to become man-ners, and nobody asked what was going on in your soul, they only asked that you should behave according to their expectations, and not trouble them with your troubles. They didn't even ask if you meant what you said; on the contrary, they were apt to take it for granted that you didn't, and that you would be somewhat *bête* if you did. All the world was a stage, and men and women played exalted and dignified roles upon it; what they were in their hearts, and what they did when they retired to their dressing rooms, were matters upon which you did not intrude.

Marie had told Lanny that her husband was one of those unfortunate men who "had to have virgins." In the years that had passed Lanny never once asked where he got these virgins, or what he paid for them, or what steps he took to make sure he was getting what he paid for. He knew that Denis was a Catholic, and bringing up his sons to be the same; but never would Lanny ask how he reconciled his practice with his creed, or what he said in the confessional. Lanny knew that Denis's creed damned Lanny Budd, a Protestant, to eternal fires; but it would have embarrassed Denis to have that referred to, so Lanny didn't.

Before a log fire in the drawing-room of this ancient red stone villa called a château, they talked about the activities of the British fleet, which Denis rather resented, because it made more difficult the program of appeasement upon which he had set his heart. They talked about the personalities of the political and financial and social worlds, for the code of *politesse* did not forbid gossip but made it, on the contrary, one of the social enjoyments. If it chanced that one of the persons you were talking about dropped in for a call, you changed the topic without embarrassment. Lanny would listen, and if he found that the new caller was one who hated the Germans and wanted to win the war, he would guard his conversation and avoid embarrassing his host.

VI

Lanny returned to Paris and took his place in *la haute société*, the people who knew what was happening because they made it happen. Men were scarce, and he was invited to receptions and dinners and dances. He was still remembered as the husband of a great heiress, and it was assumed that he would be looking for another; meantime, there were many lonely ladies looking for consolation. This war, which few wanted and none knew how to get out of, had unsettled the smart world and brought the women to a state of hysteria. Never before had Lanny found it so difficult to keep them talking about public questions; never before had he had the experience at a dinner party of moving his knee to escape the pressure of the lady on one side, only to discover that he had encountered the pressure of the lady on the other side. He made note of the covers of magazines and the posters on the kiosks, and thought that never had he seen so much of what the French called *la belle poitrine*, and what current American slang knew as "cheese-cake"—meaning the semi-nude bodies of young females. He had the idea that it heralded the downfall of the nation or social class in which it prevailed.

Lanny observed the working out of the French governmental custom whereby a new member of the Cabinet celebrated his triumph by choosing one of the *ingénues* of the Théâtre Français or a *chanteuse* of the Opéra as his *amie*. It was the way these young ladies made their careers—both the great institutions being under government control. Of course each lady had to have furs and jewels to correspond to her new station, and that was why French politicians were so eager in collecting "envelopes," and why so many popular leaders turned into reactionaries. Public policies were determined by ladies ardently promoting the careers of their chosen statesmen, and hating those ladies who espoused the measures of rival statesmen.

In *la belle France* in the midst of dire peril and supposed to be getting ready to fight for her life, the head of the government was enjoying the friendship of that lovely blue-eyed daughter of a sardine-canning magnate and wife of a French marquis named de Crussol. The Premier's most active rival for the place of honor was a lawyer who had chosen a wealthy contractor's daughter married to a comte named de Portes. So the Marquise Jeanne and the Comtesse Hélène hated each other and denounced each other in public, and wherever one favored a man or a measure the other automatically labored to keep the measure from being adopted and the man from being promoted. The situation was complicated by the fact that Hélène de Portes was an ardent appeaser, while her lover, Paul Reynaud, was attacking Daladier for his lack of ardor in the conduct of the war. Hélène, tall, aggressive, hollow-eyed and singularly unattractive, would announce at a dinner table that she intended to change her lover's views. "*Vous verrez! Vous verrez!*" You shall see!

At present, smart society in Paris was repeating what it considered a delicious anecdote concerning these two rivals. Hélène wanted to marry her Paul, but the French law forbade her to do so until three years after a *separation de corps;* this law might be rescinded by the Minister of Justice as an emergency measure, but this Minister was Paul Reynaud, and it wouldn't look just right for him to take such action in his own favor. So Hélène swallowed her pride and went to her hated rival, the friend of Edouard Daladier. All the world knew that "Dala" wanted to get rid of Bonnet, his pro-Nazi Foreign Minister, but didn't dare because of the votes he commanded in the Chamber. So now, said Hélène: "Why doesn't Edouard take the post of Foreign Minister himself, and put Bonnet in the post of Minister of Justice, where he will be less harmful? He can make my Paul the Minister of Finance, which will satisfy Paul, and Daladier will no longer have to fear him as a rival."

The Premier found that an excellent scheme, and made the shifts; whereupon Hélène went to call on Odette, wife of Bonnet, saying: "Daladier was determined to get rid of your husband, but I persuaded him to make him Minister of Justice instead. Now your husband may do me a favor in return, by changing the divorce law so that I can marry Paul at the end of a year?"

So it was that cabinets were formed and laws were made in *la grande nation;* and so it was that no pro-German could be punished, because the Minister of Justice was one of them. Indeed, the wits of Paris had a saying—that Georges Bonnet was in the service of every government in Europe except the French!

VII

Kurt Meissner and his entourage had gone back to Germany; so had Graf Herzenberg with his—and that included Marceline. She was dancing at one of the more expensive night spots in Berlin, and that circumstance had been noted by the Paris press, with comments according to their politics. Lanny found the circumstance convenient, for it helped to establish him as an appeaser, and gave him a topic of conversation leading in the direction he desired. Chatting with the very elegant mistress of one of the steel kings, Lanny would defend the right of his half-sister to do what she could to maintain cultural relations between the two greatest peoples of Europe; the lady would agree, and in return Lanny would agree as to the right of the steel king to ship half a million tons of Lorraine ore into Belgium every month—even though it was finding its way into Germany. *Les affaires sont les affaires!*

Lanny celebrated his fortieth birthday by a flying trip to Madrid. He landed at the same field where he had left Alfy three years ago. He passed through the streets where he had driven Raoul Palma, at a time when artillery shells were crashing and hostile planes, including a few Budd-Erlings, were dropping bombs. It was almost unendurable pain to see this great city, so dreadfully wrecked and with no efforts at restoration. Generalissimo Franco was a soldier, a crusader for Christianity as he conceived it, but he was a poor administrator and no economist; his only conception of government was to kill all the people who did not agree with his ideas, or at least to shut them behind bars and feed them very badly. Carpenters and masons, steelworkers and miners, were dead or dying by the thousands, and did not contribute to the restoration of the shattered cities of Spain.

Lanny's errand was to interview Marshal Pétain, ambassador of France in Madrid. Lanny had come at the suggestion of Denis de Bruyne, and brought the highest credentials. The hero of Verdun was now eighty-three, a wrinkled little figure wearing his uniform and decorations; his body was feeble, but his mind still operated within the narrow limits of his ideology. He received the visitor in the splendid palace which was both his residence and headquarters—Lanny thought of it that way, rather than as an office, there being so many military uniforms about. It was the same all over the city, a concentration camp rather than a center of industry and trade.

Henri Philippe Benoni Omer Joseph Pétain took a paternal attitude toward the people of France; he loved them, and knew what was good for them, and had been divinely appointed to tell them what to do and see that they did it. The old gentleman was as pious as Franco himself, and according to the same creed of Holy Mother Church. He was the well-nigh unanimous choice of the factions which sought to overthrow the evil, atheistic Republic; the Croix de Feu, the Jeunesse Patriote, even the Cagoulards operated in his name, and looked to him to take charge and rule. Like Franco they had a hanging list, or shooting list— or perhaps they would bring out Madame Guillotine again, if there was time. They would make a clean sweep of all republicans, the democrats, the Socialists and Communists, Syndicalists and Anarchists, atheists and Freemasons, and *la patrie* would once more become pious and happy, as she had been two centuries ago.

The old hero talked freely in his quavering voice. He was filled with a sense of destiny, the consciousness that the fate of Christian Europe hung upon the negotiations he was carrying on with the German ambassador. Matters were urgent—for of course the Führer could not be expected to wait indefinitely. The Germans were being fair, even gracious; they were not standing upon formalities or prestige. France didn't have to sue for peace, didn't even have to propose peace; all that was wanted was that sensible men should settle the basis upon which two great powers were to live together in future. Britain was not excluded; on the contrary, the same fair terms were being offered to her, here in Madrid and through other channels. The integrity of the British Empire would be guaranteed forever, and all that was asked was recognition that Eastern Europe constituted Germany's sphere of influence.

Lanny had his own story to tell; he was a personal friend of the Führer and of his Number Two and Number Three. He mentioned his recent visit to Berchtesgaden—nothing about the spirits, of course, since Holy Mother Church calls them creatures of the devil. *Retro me, Satanas!* Lanny's story warmed the chilly heart of this military patriarch, and he talked to the Franco-American agent as if he were a son, introduced him to several of his advisers, and gave him the entree to the Franco-German-Hispano junta which was pouring Nazi-Fascist propaganda into the Spanish and Portuguese Americas, as well as the United States.

VIII

So when Lanny flew back to Paris, he had a real report to make. He had been mailing them about twice a week to Bullitt—without Lanny's name, of course. It was quite amusing to meet the ambassador at a smart reception, and to be coldly rebuked for his pro-Nazi sentiments, rumors of which had reached Bullitt from several quarters, he said. Lanny smilingly denied that he was pro-Nazi—he was an art expert and lover of beauty, also he was looking out for the interests of Budd-Erling Aircraft, which played no favorites, but sold to those who had the cash. "A merchant of death, eh?" said the wealthy Philadelphian. He had grown rotund and partly bald, but in the old days he had been quite a "radical," and had written a novel about the ruling class of his native city in which leading personalities had believed they could recognize themselves.

This *rencontre* amused Lanny, but also it saddened him, for he was decidedly lonely, and now and then became sickened of his job. It was literally true that he hadn't one real friend in this great city of pleasure, *la ville lumière* as it was pleased to call itself. There were old friends here who agreed with his secret ideas, but he was not at liberty to go near them, even privately. He had to associate with those he distrusted, and to see their influence spreading and hear their anticipatory gloatings. Even Olivie Hellstein, daughter of the great Jewish banking house, with whom Emily had tried to make a match for Lanny. Just think of it!—he had seen Olivie's Uncle Solomon, the Berlin banker, being whipped on his naked back by Göring's thugs in order to extract a ransom from him; Lanny had come to Paris and told the family about it, and had witnessed their horror and grief; yet now Olivie, Madame de Broussailles, and most fashionable of matrons, wasn't at all sure that it was desirable to see Nazi-Fascism go down to defeat! It would almost certainly bring revolution in Italy and Spain; and had you thought how it would set up the leftwing politicians of France? Lanny recalled again Rick's saying that class was more than country; indeed, it was more than race, it was more than religion, or whatever you chose to call that which distinguished a Jew from a Gentile.

By way of consolation, Lanny paid a duty call upon Emily Chattersworth. He went by train, and was amused to realize that it was the first time in his life that he had traveled to Les Forêts by that mode. Emily's health was failing, she told him, and she dreaded the trip to the Riviera, but all her friends were worried because her home lay in the path of the Schlieffen plan for the invasion of France. What did Lanny think? He told her of the negotiations going on, and that he was sure Hitler would not move until spring. The French army believed itself the best in Europe and would surely fight hard; more than that, who could say? Lanny advised her to go now, because when the fighting got hot, her cars would be commandeered and her château taken as a headquarters or a hospital.

He told her that he talked with Beauty now and then over the telephone. Emily had done the same, and wanted to know, what about that "spooky lady" he had sent to Bienvenu? Lanny said there was nothing spooky about her, any more than about himself; he was surprised that Emily hadn't read her very lively stories. No, he wasn't in love with her, and had no idea of being; but she had developed mediumship, and Lanny had been sure that Parsifal would be interested to experiment with her. Parsifal had been sending Lanny copies of his notes on her communications; there had appeared what claimed to be the spirits of members of her family from Baltimore and the Eastern Shore of Maryland; also some of Parsifal's relatives in Iowa. Both places were a long way from the Cap d'Antibes, and it was all very strange and fascinating. At present Parsifal was trying the experiment of hypnotizing Laurel, and Lanny could hardly wait for a chance to witness this. He had promised his mother that he would surely come for Christmas.

IX

Lanny hadn't talked with Laurel over the telephone. His mother would have been bound to know about it; and many as were the virtues of Mrs. Beauty Budd Dingle, she had one weakness, which was that she demanded to be first in the mind of her precious only son. She had been willing to make way for Irma Barnes, because Irma had been so incredibly rich, and because she had been Beauty's own selection. But the mother had been grudging in her concessions to Rosemary, and to Marie, and most of all to that mysterious German woman whose presence in Paris she had guessed but whose name she had never heard. Lanny didn't want anything of that sort in the case of the author of "The Troglodyte"; so when he wrote a polite note to congratulate Laurel upon her success as a medium, he was careful to write a longer letter to his mother, and to fill it with interesting gossip and declarations of affection.

Laurel answered, in the same tone that he had set. She, too, was amazed by the things which had come out of her subconscious mind, and was grateful to Mr. Dingle for his instructions and to Mrs. Dingle for her hospitality and unfailing kindness. She was going on with her writings, and hoped to make good use of her experiences. She was distressed by this dreadful war, and hoped that Lanny was not putting himself in any danger. That was all; discreet and carefully phrased, and Lanny, who was used to writing that way himself, read the phrases over several times, and realized that she was telling him he could trust her, and that no matter who might read her letters, whether in Bienvenu or Paris, the person would get no hint concerning Berlin or Berchtesgaden, or the misadventures of Miss Elvirita Jones.

So when Lanny arrived at his mother's home, a couple of days before Christmas, everything was exactly right among all the parties concerned. Laurel had managed to win Beauty's trust, and had turned herself into a New Thoughter, saying her little prayers several times day and night to keep herself in tune with the Infinite. How much she meant of it and how long she would keep it up after she had rejoined the smart sophisticates of the New York magazine world were questions Lanny did not ask. When you are in Rome, do as the Romans do —unless it is the Romans of Il Duce's Nuovo Impero! Lanny had carefully explained to Laurel that the way to get along with the spirits was to believe in them and accept whatever they told you; and certainly it could do no one any harm to agree with this white-haired and pink-cheeked old gentleman who practiced kindness to everyone he met, no matter how cynical and even cruel they might be in their hearts, and who was patiently investigating Laurel's subconscious mind and providing her with elaborate typewritten notes concerning it. "Why," she exclaimed, "in New York people are going to psychoanalysts, paying ten or twenty dollars per hour and not finding out nearly so much!"

X

This place had been Lanny's home ever since he was old enough to remember anything. Here he had learned to dance and to read and to play the piano. Down on the tiny beach he had made friends with the fisherboys and learned to swim and sail a boat. Here he had lived through most of World War I and here he had helped to bring Marcel, crippled and defaced. Here was the studio where Marcel had painted, and where Lanny now had his library, and his piano, badly affected by the sea air. Here, it seemed to him, he could have passed all his days in serenity—if only it had been a world in which a man's conscience would permit him to enjoy that luxury.

He had so many happy memories of this villa, built around an inner court, bright with flowers and populated by bees and birds. Always there had been dogs, and nearly always a child learning to toddle or to dance: first Lanny, then Marceline, then Frances, then Freddi Robin's little boy, and now Marceline's darling, now two years old, lovely as both his parents had been, and happy as the day was long. He had no memory of his mother, and did not know that he had been deserted in favor of a handsome and arrogant Junker's son. Lanny would take his tiny hands and hum a tune and teach him little steps, and it was like teaching a bird to peck or a fish to swim. Marcel Detaze—he was going to carry that name out into the world again, and what was he going to do with it?

The Riviera was crowded as Lanny had never seen it that he could recall. So many people wanted to get away from Paris and the bombs that were expected! They offered fantastic rentals, but Beauty had resisted temptation and leased the Lodge to Margy and the Cottage to a cousin of Sophie's at the old rates. Now there was a dowager and her granddaughter begging to inhabit the second studio, the one which had been built for Kurt and his piano. Beauty was always in need of money, because she could never resist lovely things in shops, and also because she was kindhearted, and was victimized by people in trouble —often perfectly worthless people preying on the well-to-do. Lanny was able to give her the cheerful news that she was going to have a lot of money to tide her over the war—and it would be dollars, not francs, which already were down to two-and-a-half cents. The show in Baltimore had been a success, and now it was in Pittsburgh and presently would be in Cleveland.

The first thing Lanny had to do whenever he came home was to tell

Beauty his adventures: every single person he had met and everything that person had said—Robbie and Esther, Hansi and Bess, Johannes and Mama, Reverdy and Lizbeth, Irma and Ceddy, Frances and Fanny, Rick and Nina and Alfy, Denis and Emily and Olivie, and so on and on. When he thought he was through, she would start asking questions and discover that he had left out the most important details. She would tell him about Sophie and Margy and Maxine and other friends here on the coast, and list the celebrities who had arrived; Lanny would make notes in his mind, that being part of a P.A.'s job.

Only after Beauty was satisfied was he free to turn his attention to his stepfather and Madame and the new medium. They, too, had stories to tell, and a mass of new records to present; Lanny thought it the part of wisdom to hear the tale in front of the fire in the living room, so that his dear mother could be a part of it. Never would he take Laurel for a walk alone, for if he did, right away he would hear: "Lanny, are you going to fall in love with that woman?" Beauty had had full opportunity to study the woman, and couldn't find any real fault except that she wasn't an heiress, and why shouldn't Lanny make real use of his opportunities? Beauty had dragged out of him the story of his talk with Reverdy, and it almost made her weep. "Lanny, where on earth can you expect to find anybody better than that lovely girl?" His excuses fell flat, for he surely couldn't expect to go on traveling, now while the seas were swarming with U-boats; and anyhow, Lizbeth could live here, and Beauty would take care of her, and she would never have a care in the world.

XI

The three psychic researchers had been conducting experiments day after day. At first Madame had been peeved, fearing that her status in the family would be impaired; but Laurel had managed to win her confidence, and now she was reconciled. They were trying "cross-correspondences"; that is, to find out if Madame's "spirits" could give half a sentence while Laurel's "spirits" gave the other half; or if one could give some facts about a certain matter and the other give facts that fitted. It was like asking for the parts of a jigsaw puzzle; and the only person who knew the whole picture was Parsifal, who had composed it. The least this proved was telepathy, the ability of the two mediums to dip into the mind of the experimenter when they were entranced; it might even mean that at a certain level all three minds were one. Having proved this to his satisfaction, the old gentleman had set out to

eliminate telepathy as an hypothesis. He would set the "spirits" a problem such as this: "The second bookcase to the right of the door of
Lanny's studio, the third shelf from the top, the seventeenth book
counting from the left; give me line 11 of page 272. Parsifal himself
didn't know what the book was, to say nothing of knowing what was
on a page whose number he chose at random. If the medium could give
him that, it would have to be some form of clairvoyance. After they
had done it a few times, Parsifal took to inviting Madame to give one
half the line, and Laurel in the next room to give the other half.

The Baltimore lady had developed several "controls," the most
favored being Otto Kahn, the New York banker who had been taken
from the scene of his profitable activities some half-dozen years previously. In the spirit world he was, as he had been in real life, a super-
intelligent person, and took great pleasure in demonstrating his ability
to meet any challenge put to him. He listened while Madame's "control," Tecumseh, told about himself and his circle of friends; then the
banker announced that he would make it his business to seek out this
old-time Amerindian in the "spirit world." Presently he announced that
he had succeeded, and had made friends with him; after that it was like
two radio stars who appear as guests on one another's programs.

It amused an international sophisticate immensely to pretend to stand
in awe of a stone-age chieftain, and to treat him with all the ceremony
his rank required. Tecumseh had never had anything to do with bankers, and couldn't be expected to understand that a senior partner of
Kuhn, Loeb and Company had been a ruler of another and far more
powerful sort. He accepted the white man's homage, and took seriously every compliment that was paid him. On that basis the pair were
good companions, and Otto was always tactful in pointing out any
error which Tecumseh's spirits might make. Otto knew his Shakespeare, and would quote Owen Glendower's boast: "I can call spirits
from the vasty deep." He would paraphrase: "And they will come
when I do call to them"—and sure enough, here they were!

Lanny had read a lot about cross-correspondences in the proceedings
of the British Society for Psychical Research. There were cases where
part of a sentence had been supplied in England and the other part in
Australia. The experiments had been made over a period of half a century, by well-known scientists, writers and clergymen, and the records
stayed on the library shelves and gathered dust. Lanny wondered, did
anybody ever open the books? Did the scientific world ever pay any
attention to what had been so carefully proved? "Spooks!" said the
skeptics, and you were considered to be dim-witted if you stooped

even to know about such things. Lanny reminded himself that the ancient Greeks had known that the earth was round and that it moved; but the learned world had chosen to forget it for a thousand years or more, and had shut Galileo in a dungeon and forced him to recant the heresy. *Eppur' si muove!*

XII

Lanny had written to Parsifal, suggesting that he should hypnotize these mediums, to see if an induced trance would tap a different level of consciousness from a spontaneous trance; also, whether they might be brought into *rapport*, each with the other. Parsifal had been doing this, and now it had become a regular show, which Beauty's friends clamored to be allowed to see, but which Beauty's husband wouldn't let them see unless they had qualified themselves as serious students of the occult. Lanny was so established; and now he sat in the living room of his mother's home, together with his stepfather and the two mediums. The only other guests were Sophie and her husband, Mr. Armitage, who had been an engineer and was a thoughtful man, glad to be able to go out with his wife to some place where it wasn't, as he said, "just gabble, gobble, git."

Very interesting to see Parsifal Dingle applying his doctrine of universal benevolence to the technique of hypnosis. He made no elaborate passes, no effort to be dominant and impressive; he simply told his subject to gaze steadily into his eyes while he murmured gentle words about sleep. Under this soothing influence both women had learned to pass into the trance in a few seconds, and to come out again under a quiet word of command. This was convenient, because he could repeat an experiment many times and vary it at will; they were never under any strain, and never knew what they had said or done in the hypnotic sleep.

The subject would sit staring in front of her with open eyes, not moving or speaking unless she was told to. Parsifal would bid her raise an arm, and would tell her that the arm would stay there without fatigue; it would stay, apparently for an unlimited time—he hadn't tried to reach the limit. Lanny thought of Adolf Hitler, whose boast it was that he could give the Nazi salute to a whole army of his troops passing by, and never once have to lower his arm! Perhaps Adi had hypnotized himself—who could say?

Parsifal would comment: "You will have no feeling in your arm," and he would take a needle and touch it to the woman's skin and she wouldn't know it; he could have driven the needle through the arm, and she would not have winced or bled. He would tell Laurel that her mind would be divided into halves, and that her right hand would write answers to questions which were whispered into her right ear, while her lips would reply to questions whispered into her left ear. This she would do with speed, and without any sign of confusion, or of weariness afterwards. He would give her post-hypnotic suggestions, of things she would do when she came out of the trance; not the stunts with which stage performers bring laughter, but serious experiments to find out how far her normal consciousness could be inhibited. Parsifal told her, very impressively, that she would not recognize Beauty Budd when she saw her. Then he terminated the trance, and asked Laurel where Beauty was, and Laurel wandered about the room, very much confused, looking from one woman to another, and unable for quite a while to make up her mind which was her hostess.

XIII

But to Lanny the most fascinating experiments of all were those in "age regression," which he had read about in one of those old "discarded" books by a Dr. Tuckey, and which Parsifal had repeated with great care. He would put Madame to sleep and tell her that she was five years old, and then give her pencil and paper and ask her to make a picture of a man. This old woman, stout, flabby, and approaching second childhood, would go back to her first. She enacted to perfection the role of a tiny child, shy, hesitant, but conscientious and anxious to please. She grasped the pencil as if it were a stick, and put her eyes close to the paper as a child does. Two crudely drawn circles, a small one on top of a large one, and four projections from the large one—that was a man. She not merely acted a child, but thought and felt a child; everything that had been in her mind then was in it now, and everything that had entered her mind since was blotted out. Lanny had read in many psychology books the basic principle that no memory is ever lost; but to see that principle in action was something uncanny, astounding, like taking a ride in an H. G. Wells time-machine.

This peasant child knew only her native language; and Parisfal had gone out and found a Polish refugee, earning his living as a café waiter, and brought him to the house to translate. The child was afraid of her father, who got drunk and beat her; also she was afraid of snowstorms, having been lost in one. When Parsifal told her that she was twelve years old, she could draw a much better man, and she was happier, because she had her calf, the precious pet named Kooba about which she had told Lanny many years ago. Parsifal would accumulate a mass of notes and amaze her in her waking state by recalling things about her past which she had forgotten.

And then Laurel Creston. A curious contrast between the life of a peasant child in the Austrian part of Poland under the rule of the benighted Habsburgs, and that of a landowner's daughter on the Eastern Shore of the proud "Free State" of Maryland! At the age of five little Laurel had been taught how to hold a pencil, and to sit very primly at a table and speak with proper manners; she had three lovely dollies, also a French governess. But oddly enough her life was blighted by the same curse of alcohol which plagued the Polish peasant child; her father was a "drinking man," and she had seen him in a condition which frightened her, and had seen her mother in tears. She did not know any person in the drawing-room of Bienvenu, not even the kind old gentleman who was asking her questions.

When the two women were taken back to childhood at the same time there resulted amusing scenes, for not only did they not recognize each other, but each found it incomprehensible that the other should claim to be a child. When Parsifal told them they were fifteen, Madame was a kitchen maid in the city of Krakow, and Laurel was at boarding school in the Roland Park district of Baltimore; they were both old enough to know the date, and Madame said that it was 1890, while Laurel in a polite but positive manner declared that it was 1923, and that a gentleman from Vermont by the name of Calvin Coolidge had recently become President of the United States. Both the women were in a passive state of mind, and did not address each other, but replied only to Parsifal's questions.

Incidently this told Lanny something he had wondered about—that Laurel Creston was thirty-one years of age. He didn't say anything about it when she came out of the trance, for it was her secret if she wanted to keep it. He thought her courageous to trust anybody to delve into her past life. Aloud, he commented upon the light which these tests threw upon the technique of the Freudians, whose rise to prosperity he had watched during his lifetime. He had known people to devote years to recording dreams and reciting them, and listening to fantastic interpretations of them; if you had the money you could spend many thousands that way, and perhaps it kept you out of mischief—but Lanny had never yet known a person who had been cured of anything by it. Here, by this simple method of hypnotism which the doctors had "discarded," you could have the early mind before you, and live with it and question it as long as you pleased.

> Backward, turn backward, O Time, in your flight,
> Make me a child again just for tonight!

27

With Hell at Agreement

I

THE Côte d'Azur was almost as favorable a place as Paris for the activities of a presidential agent. The appeasers swarmed there, and Cannes was a sort of half-way station between Italy and Spain—two nations which called themselves neutral, and whose citizens therefore could come and go freely, carrying out the errands of the enemy. Smart society buzzed with gossip concerning the doings of Serrano Suñer and Señor Juan March, of Count Ciano and General Balbo, of Charles Bedaux and half a dozen English lords who came visiting and intriguing.

What part was Mussolini going to play in this war? He was one-third of the "Axis"—Japan having been taken in. Lanny's friends on the Riviera agreed that Il Duce was bound to have a share of the spoils, and you could pretty nearly tell how the war was going by his attitude. Bedaux reported that the Germans didn't want him in, Italy being far more useful as a neutral; Britain and France were reluctant to interfere with her trade and she could ship arms to Germany and get coal in return. Britain sought to buy arms from her, but Mussolini wanted too high a price, and went on bringing German coal in Italian ships; the British were threatening to stop this traffic and the argument was growing hot. A division of the French army was at Mentone, ready to block the road along the Riviera, and troops were guarding all the passes through the Alpes Maritimes. Taking no chances!

And Franco—what was he going to do? He was bound to the Axis by ties of gratitude, also by a debt in marks and lire which it might take him several lifetimes to pay. His ships could carry copper and iron ore and mercury to Italy, and he would hold over the Allies the threat of seizing Gibraltar. Would he dare? Lanny cultivated his Spanish friends and picked up the gossip that fell from their dinner tables. They considered that the Führer had compromised his cause by his deal with Red Russia, and thus Spain was no longer bound by her signature to the Anti-Comintern Pact. Their country, like Italy, could be more useful as a neutral; they whispered concerning U-boat bases on the Bay of Biscay, Spanish vessels smuggling fuel to U-boats at sea, and radio stations set up by their German friends in Spanish and Portuguese harbors.

Then, too, there was news from the Near East, the Balkans and Turkey and the Arab lands. Couriers came by ships, and messages by secret wireless; it was all supposed to be hush-hush to the last degree, but somehow things leaked, and if you went to the right social gatherings and helped to get the right persons drunk, you could pick up surprising information. Lanny was kept busy writing reports, so many that he became uneasy about mailing them to the American Embassy in Paris. He took to addressing them to an inconspicuous "Mr. W. C. Bullitt, 2 rue Gabriel, Paris." He never mailed one in Juan, but drove into Cannes and dropped them into some inconspicuous box; now and then for one of special importance he would visit the larger city of Nice.

II

Outwardly it was a gay life the son of Budd-Erling lived. All his friends were glad that he had become what they called sensible, and was enjoying himself as his wealth and family position entitled him to do. World events made little difference to the expatriates of the Riviera; they had come here to get away from care, and they stayed away. Business was booming at home and money was plentiful; they spent it on elegant pleasures, and resented even the slightest inconveniences. The *Sitzkrieg* was something far-off, to be read about in the papers and discussed over the "apéro."

What fighting there was took the form of scouting, mostly on dark nights; some of the poilus earned their two-and-a-half cents a day by donning black leather suits, well greased to make them slippery, and stealing out in front of their Maginot Line, armed with knives which they had sharpened to razor keenness. They would surprise an enemy outpost and slit the throats of a few *Fridolins*, as they were calling the boches in this war; meantime, somewhere else along the line, some *Fridolins* would be doing the same to a few poilus. It was like the Indian fighting which had gone on in America for a couple of centuries, and which Europe knew from the *Leatherstocking Tales*, and saw now and then in the cinema.

The only way that war could come to the Riviera was from Italy; and why worry about that? The Italians were here, some in uniforms and some in sport suits; they were charming fellows, glad to help out at a dinner party or on a dance floor. To be sure, they demanded Nice as a part of their birthright, and suggested that they might have to take Cannes and the Cap for greater security; but what difference would that make to American residents, or even to British and French? They were gentlemen, and would conduct themselves as such; they would put down the Reds, and the trains would run on time, which they surely were not doing at present. The Italians were tireless in giving assurances to their friends; and every evening you could hear the voice of the American poet, Ezra Pound, speaking in English from a station on the Italian Riviera, ridiculing the idea that the ignorant rabble was fitted to govern any country, and hailing Fascism and its "corporate state" as the form of the future society.

III

The psychic experiments continued, and Lanny had opportunity to become further acquainted with the mind of Laurel Creston. It was, he discovered, both receptive and keen. He had known few intellectual women in his life, the ladies of his circle having been interested in only one branch of learning, which might be called applied psychology, though commonly it went by the less pretentious name of gossip. This science had to do with what was going on inside the minds of the other ladies and gentlemen of their acquaintance, it being necessary to the life of gregarious creatures to know which way the flock is going to fly or the herd to run.

Laurel had been interested to find out all she could about the world she lived in, and now she was finding out about her own instrument of investigation. What was her mind, and how many minds had she? What were these trances into which she fell so easily, and where was her conscious mind at the time? She wished she might have had two minds, one to sit and watch while the other entered the trance. As it was, she would ask questions, and study Parsifal's notes, and pounce on this point or that, and suggest new tests to settle some uncertainty.

Also, she began digging into the library which Lanny had accumulated on the subject. It was a small library, but some of the books were not small. She read the Myers tome, and the two volumes of Gurney, and Janet's two on *Psychological Healing*, something like twelve hundred pages. Laurel studied them, one by one, and had some of the experiments repeated on herself. She read Osty and Gelet and William MacDougall, and her wonder grew that the scientific world should remain so indifferent to the universe hidden in the subconscious mind of man. She wanted to write on the subject; and Lanny said, "Go to it; but the popular magazines won't be interested, and if it's a book it won't sell. Psychic research is a form of self-indulgence of the well-to-do."

Said Laurel: "I can earn my living writing fiction, and it has never taken all my time."

She would take a pad of paper and a pencil, a steamer chair and a cushion, and find herself a sunny spot on the grounds of the estate; then no one would see her again until lunchtime. She never told what she was writing; Lanny guessed it was some anti-Nazi stories which she would publish under a pen name after she had left here. She excused herself from social affairs, and the few people who met her thought of her as one more of the queer people who had been turning up at Bienvenu ever since it had started: painters, poets, musicians, dancers, religious healers, mediums, even ghosts—so they said. Lanny understood that the new medium was carrying out the request which he had made of her in Switzerland, and was impressed by the strictness with which she kept the bargain.

IV

Laurel Creston couldn't have been in any doubt as to what Lanny himself was up to. He didn't talk; but when he went to have lunch with Juan March, or dinner at the California home of the Duke and Duchess of Windsor, Beauty would ask whom he had met and what they had said. Laurel never asked questions, even when she and Lanny were alone. That was rarely, because she avoided it, and the experiments were always shared by Parsifal. The lady from Baltimore, no amateur in applied psychology, was aware of the mistress of this household watching everything that went on.

More than once the mother asked: "Lanny, are you falling in love with Laurel?" and he would reply: "No, old dear, not in the least. I am interested in her work." Then came a time when Beauty surprised him with a different remark: "Lanny, I've been thinking it over, and I wonder if Laurel isn't the sort of woman you ought to marry. She's interested in all the things that you are; and I suppose you'll never be happy with anybody but a bluestocking."

He gave his usual provoking answer: "I'm not planning to marry, darling; I'm getting along very nicely right now—and so is Laurel, so far as I can see."

"A man never sees very far into a woman's heart," was the mother's reply. "No woman remains an old maid if she can help it."

You would have had to know the mistress of Bienvenu to realize what a condescension this represented on her part; it was the first time in Lanny's love life that his mother had ever recommended a girl or woman who wasn't at least moderately rich. It was a triumph of Parsifal Dingle's ideas over those of the *beau monde*, the *grand monde*, the *monde d'élite*. Lanny was amused, but also touched, and somewhat troubled—for he had been less than frank when he said that he wasn't in love with Laurel Creston. What he was doing was scolding himself for getting mixed up with this infernal business of sex once again. He had thought it absurd to be half in love with two women, and now, apparently, he was one-third in love with three! Laurel, he admitted, had turned out to be a lovely woman; but so had Lizbeth, and so had Priscilla Hoyle, to his great surprise. How happy could I be with one of them, were t'other two charmers away!

V

It is an old saying, that propinquity is the major part of love; and right now Laurel had the propinquity! The lonely widower confronted daily not merely her charms but her mind, and more important yet, her character. She was honest, she was straightforward, she was concerned with the search for truth. She was, very certainly, the woman whom Trudi would have picked out for him; and the Trudi-ghost was still the most important single influence in Lanny's life. The Trudi-ghost was conscience, and stood watch over his choices. It said: "The cause comes first. The cause is everything. The cause is the future—all mankind, long after you and I are gone and our very names forgotten."

Daily he went over the same round of thoughts: "What would I do if I asked her to marry me, and she consented? Where would I hide her, and how would we live?" It was the old problem, to which there was no answer. Keep her in Bienvenu, as Beauty had in mind? As a spiritualist medium, she was a freak, to whom the smart world paid no attention except to smile; she was one of Parsifal Dingle's whims, and Lanny was not held responsible. But as Lanny's wife she would be the future mistress of the estate and a personage; everybody would want to meet her, and gossip about her would spread through the smart world. Would the Nazi agents overlook a man who had been the Führer's guest so many times, and made it his *carte d'entrée* into Nazi circles on the Riviera, and in Berlin, Paris, London, New York? Undoubtedly they would have checked his story in Germany; and how long would it be before somebody would begin asking questions about the mysterious medium who had been at the Berghof and subsequently had vanished off the face of the earth?

No, it was obvious that if Lanny wanted to have Laurel for a wife, he would have to hide her. But where? Certainly in no place frequented by the people from whom he collected information. She would have to stay in an obscure apartment, and never appear in public as his wife. Trudi had done that, but would Laurel be willing to do it? And how about her anti-Nazi stories, and magazines and checks coming from abroad? A clandestine life had been possible in peacetime, but now the war multiplied its difficulties. Lanny could think of a hundred slips that might be made—and one would be enough to ruin his work.

Laurel spoke of returning to New York after the psychic work had been completed; and that started Lanny on another set of imaginings. He could get a car and they could have a delightful honeymoon through the Southern states. But then where would they live? Take an apartment in some unfashionable part of New York, and have Laurel rent a post-office box under her real name? But how long would it be before her literary friends would become curious about a woman writer who never invited anyone to the place where she slept? Would she love him enough never to see anybody, even when he was in Europe for months at a time? Suppose she were to fall ill, or to meet with an accident.

Or suppose her writings became so successful that the Gestapo would order its agents in New York to track her down and find out who her associates were, and where she got her strikingly correct information? Any data the Gestapo really wanted it would get; and Lanny must never for a moment forget that they had Laurel Creston on their wanted list in Berlin. They had her writings to date, including a lot of unpublished manuscripts; and they had plenty of men who knew the English language, also the art of letters, and were capable of comparing the writings of Laurel Creston with those of Mary Morrow, and of any other pen name she could invent.

Forrest Quadratt, for example! Put half a dozen short stories into his hands, and he could very soon say whether they were written by the same author. And with a suave personality and unlimited funds, how long would it take him to plant an employee in a certain magazine office, or to take a publisher's secretary out to dinner? Once they had spotted Laurel and her post-office box, how long would it be before they had her telephone tapped and a dictaphone in her apartment, and had the name and record of the gallant who came to visit her now and then, or who met her on street corners and drove her to some roadhouse in Jersey?

VI

The weeks passed, and the psychic wonders multiplied, and so did the reports of P.A. 103. From the Italians he learned of the bitter feud between Ribbentrop and Ciano, promising no good to the Axis. Mussolini's son-in-law charged that the champagne salesman had promised him three years in which to get Italy ready for war, but now he had broken the promise and gone ahead to grab everything in sight. Italy was dreaming of Nice and Corsica and Tunisia, but wasn't yet strong enough to take them, and now feared that the Führer meant to grab Tunisia himself. Italy would fool him, all the Italians agreed. The moment France showed signs of breaking, Il Duce would leap in—and he was nearer.

As for Spain, she would almost certainly move if Italy did, and would take Tangier. As for Gibraltar, the understanding was that Italy was going to bomb it for her, and in return would have submarine bases on the Spanish coast. The British Mediterranean fleet would be reduced by this means, and then Mussolini could supply munitions and a Spanish army could invade the Rock from the land. The salons of the Riviera appeasers buzzed with talk of these enterprises. Realizing that they couldn't get their way at home without outside help, many Frenchmen had come to the opinion of Denis de Bruyne, that the will of their political enemies had to be broken by military defeat.

Russia had gone to war with Finland, claiming that that little country was in the hands of the Fascists and was being fortified and prepared as a base for an attack upon Russia. At first the Red armies did very badly, and all the world of fashion rejoiced, and became ardent in sympathy for a little nation struggling for its liberties. In the Scandinavian lands, in Britain and France, even in far-off America, there arose a clamorous demand for aid to the Finns. The Rightists found this a heaven-sent chance to attain their goal of war upon the Soviet Union. Three years ago the cry of airplanes for Republican Spain had enfuriated them, but now they set up their own cry of airplanes for Finland—even though France hadn't enough to defend herself against the foe at her gates.

It became Lanny Budd's duty to take the Blue Express, the night train to Paris, and to revisit his Rightist friends. He found a small civil war going on in Paris, between Daladier and his lady on the one hand and Reynaud and his lady on the other. Jeanne de Crussol wore her Premier out with stories of the intrigues of Hélène de Portes, and with demands that her adored Edouard should get rid of some Cabinet member who was on Reynaud's side, or some general who had dared to lunch with the Minister of Justice. Daladier had been created a dictator in the war emergency, but he wasn't a very good one, because his liberal conscience plagued him; he found it hard to make up his mind, and rarely did so until it was too late.

So it was going to be with the problem of Finland. "Dala" thought that something ought to be done, but he couldn't bear to be the one to do it. If an expedition was sent, it would have to go by way of Norway and Sweden, and Germany would probably attack those countries, and it would mean real and terrible fighting. The Premier had been making speeches in which he promised to avoid the shedding of French blood in reckless adventures; and in this he had the support of old General Gamelin, who wanted to stay behind his fortifications.

What they did was to organize a force of volunteers, both British and French, supplied with arms from both countries, and they sent this through Sweden with German connivance. It was supposed to be the most closely kept secret in the world, and the censors wouldn't permit the publication of a word; but Lanny's important friends knew about it, and some of them were supplying the planes and tanks. He was able to send his Chief a schedule of the supplies, and an account of what had gone on at the meeting of the Supreme Council on February 7, in which the problem of Finland had been the topic of discussion, and in which, characteristically, they had decided to postpone their decisions.

"Too little and too late" was the formula. The Russians settled the matter by bringing up fresh troops, and beginning a determined assault upon the Mannerheim Line, named after the Finnish baron who was in command, and who had earned the adoration of the Rightists all over

Europe by his slaughter of the Finnish Reds after the First World War. He had a German name and German training, and it was upon him that the Soviet hatred was centered. Now the news grew worse and worse, from the point of view of the fighting pacifists who were Lanny Budd's friends and informants. At the beginning of March, just when the British and French had made up their minds to act, and had got ready fifty thousand troops from each nation, word leaked out that the Finns were in Moscow suing for peace.

VII

Lanny went back to Bienvenu, and to more efforts to investigate the underworld of Laurel Creston's mind, and Madame's, and Parsifal Dingle's, and his own, at a point where they appeared to be all mixed up together. At any rate, Laurel in trance was able to tell any of them about things they had done or said, and so did Madame in her trances. Why one woman had to find it out through the mind of a deceased international Jewish banker, and the other through the mind of an Amerindian chieftain, was one of the mysteries of this unendurably mysterious universe.

Otto Kahn laughed when you asked him about it; he was far too urbane to become irritated, like Tecumseh, at the suggestion of "that old telepathy." He said that of course he understood how impossible it was for anyone to believe in spirits; he would have taken exactly that attitude himself. But here he was, and he knew he was here, much as it embarrassed him to say so. Why was he here? Well, that was a difficult question. He countered with another: Why had he been on earth? And how did he know the things he revealed? Well, how could any spirit explain it to an embodied being? Things came into his mind, just as they had done on earth—for example, the idea of being an art patron, or of taking an interest in a beautiful diva at the Metropolitan.

When these remarks were reported to Laurel Creston after the trance, she said it was exactly as she remembered that genial man of high finance, conversing in her uncle's Baltimore home. Could it be that there was another storyteller in her subconscious mind, making up Otto Kahn, in combination with herself and Lanny Budd and Parsifal Dingle and their circle of friends? Surely this was one of the most fascinating problems in the world! Dr. Morton Prince's "Miss Beauchamp" had had five separate personalities in her, and if you could have five, why not five million, or for that matter all the people who now lived on earth or ever had lived there? When they asked that question of Otto Kahn he replied: "Well, why not?"

These fascinating inquiries continued; and meantime the sun maintained its ancient practice of rising a minute or so earlier each morning, and spring came back to the Riviera. The fig trees put out their buds, the stems resembling long gray candles with a bright green flame at the tip. The tulips and narcissi spread their colors in the court and the white jasmine flowers filled it with their delicate perfume. The birds built nests in the vines, and the bees filled the air with the sound of their visitations. A little human bee buzzed and a little human bird sang in that court, and Lanny marveled once more to see life renewing itself, so full of eagerness and trust, so delightful in its beginnings—and oftentimes so sad in its endings.

The warmth spread northward, and the buds and flowers came out all over Europe. It brought joy to the children, but to the adults only fear, for they knew what the lengthening of the days and the drying of the ground mean in wartime. In far-off Washington, Senator Borah had referred to this as a "phony war"; perhaps he had been trying to defend himself, having solemnly assured the country in the previous summer that he knew upon reliable authority there would be no war in Europe that year. The phrase "phony war" had caught on all over the world; it pleased people who were expecting sensations, and could not enjoy their breakfast without the slaughter of ten thousand of their fellows. Lanny heard Americans using the phrase on the Riviera, and he wanted to cry: "Idiots!"

He knew that for seven years Adolf Hitler and his able executives had been getting ready for what they were going to do this spring and summer and autumn. The whole industrial power of one of the three or four greatest nations on earth had been turned to the manufacture of deadly weapons. "Guns before butter," Göring had said—and be sure that he meant it with all the power of his driving will. Now, at the end of the eighth winter, the armies were lined up at the frontiers, the men trained like athletes for a race, the plans completed to the last scratch of a pen. The planes were in their underground hangars; the tanks hidden in the forests, or in fields, camouflaged as haystacks or sheds; the shells piled in rows like village streets. From the factories were pouring rivers of new planes, new tanks, new shells, everything that could be used in war, and very little else—just enough to keep life going in eighty million Nazi robots, plus the slaves they had already taken, and the millions more for whom they had the pens already constructed.

VIII

Such was the promise of the spring of 1940 on the old continent of Europe. The only question was, where would Hitler strike, and on what day? It was Lanny Budd's business to find that out, and he met many persons who were eager to tell him; but it was like a diagnosis by many doctors or a horoscope by many astrologers—they did not agree. The place to find out was Berchtesgaden, and Lanny thought of going there by way of Switzerland, but he kept hesitating, because he couldn't offer to bring Miss Elvirita Jones again, and he thought it the part of discretion to let the memory of that lady grow dim. But meantime, the hour of decision was drawing near. Lanny considered the possibility of visiting Switzerland, and from there writing Hess an offer to bring Madame Zyszynski for a second visit. To be sure, Poles were not exactly honored in Germany at present, and they would probably search her to make sure she didn't carry a dagger or a capsule of poison; but their curiosity might overcome their repugnance, and if she could produce the spirit of Paul Ernest Ludwig von Beneckendorff und von Hindenburg as she had done on her former visit, they would grant her the status of an honorary Aryan.

It would be a risky venture, for he could never know but that the Gestapo had already dug up the truth about the much-wanted Laurel Creston. Even so, he had about made up his mind to chance it, when the fates were kind and presented him with another solution of his problem. There came in the mail one of those undistinguished envelopes which for the past few years had been making sudden changes in Lanny Budd's plans. This time the envelope bore a Swiss stamp, also the seal and number of a French censor. It was written in English and addressed very formally to M. Lanning Prescott Budd, Connoisseur d'Art, Bienvenu, Juan-les-Pins, Alpes Maritimes, France; the honorific title being, of course, for the censor's benefit.

Beauty was in the room when José brought this mail. While the mother looked at her own—mostly bills, alas!—Lanny slipped the letter into his pocket and pretended to be absorbed in opening up the *London Times*. After a while he got up and went to his room and shut the door, where he opened the letter, and read:

"Dear Sir: I have been keeping a lookout for paintings which might be of interest to American collectors, according to your recent suggestion, and this is to inform you that I have come upon a Werner here

in Geneva which seems to me important, and which you might care to inspect upon your next visit. My employment keeps me busy and does not allow me much time, but I am so fortunate as to get Tuesday and Friday afternoons off. I use these to work in the excellent public library of this city, hoping to increase my knowledge of the fine arts so that I can be of service to an eminent authority such as yourself. Not being sure where you are at present, I am sending a copy of this letter to you in care of your daughter in England, and also one in care of your father at the Budd-Erling Aircraft Corporation in Connecticut.
                                        "Respectfully, Brun."

Lanny read this letter several times, and studied every phrase, knowing that Bernhardt Monck had done the same. The compliments, of course, were for the censor, also the mention of Budd-Erling. The significant word in the letter was the name of the painter; Anton von Werner had painted military scenes of the Kaiserzeit, and incidentally was a favorite of the fat Feldmarschall. No doubt Monck had looked him up in the excellent public library of Geneva. What he was telling Lanny Budd was that he had important news about the plans of the German army, and that Lanny could find him in that library on a Tuesday or a Friday afternoon. Incidentally, he had left one letter out of his name, which made it French instead of German; this also for the censor, an important person in the life of secret agents.

IX

Lanny wouldn't waste time in hesitation. The day was Monday, and this was a time of "spot news"; what was alive today might be dead tomorrow. He told his mother: "I have a letter from a man in Geneva who thinks he has a worthwhile painting, so I'm taking the night train." Beauty may have had suspicions, but it wouldn't do her any good to voice them.

When Lanny told Laurel Creston of his plan, she said: "If you are gone for any length of time, I may not be here when you return. I have matters that I must attend to in New York."

Lanny responded: "I shall miss you. But if you must go, it will be the part of wisdom not to delay."

The American State Department was urging all Americans to come home, and had chartered a number of liners to bring them. The vessels had the American flag painted on their sides, and it was hoped that the U-boats would not be impolite to them. One would be sailing from

Marseilles in a few days, and Lanny's old friend Jerry Pendleton would try to get accommodations for Laurel. It wouldn't be a stylish crossing, but it would be the same New York harbor into which the vessel would crawl, and the same Statue of Liberty she would pass. Americans appreciated that harbor and statue in these days of spreading calamity.

So the pair bade each other farewell. "You have taught me a great deal," said the woman, "and I shall never cease to be grateful to you. I hope we may always be friends."

"Indeed, yes," was the reply. "May I write to you?"

"I hope you will. I don't know what my address will be, but I will write you to Bienvenu. Also, you can always reach me in care of the *Bluebook*. They have accepted another story." She didn't tell him what it was about; but she did say: "I want you to know that my eyes have not been shut while I have been here. I think I know what you are doing, and I honor you for it. Be sure that I will never drop a hint of it to any living soul. Take care of yourself and good luck to you."

"Thank you," said the P.A. "I, too, have thought a lot about you, and am grateful for what you have done, and for what you have just said." All very formal and proper, but there was deep feeling behind it, and Lanny could imagine that there might be tears in her eyes—after she had gone to her own room. The devil of it was, he couldn't know whether or not she cared for him without making some approach to the subject, and that would be like trying to find out if a gun was loaded while having it pointed at your heart.

X

Lanny visited the Swiss consulate and got his passport visaed, giving as his purpose the purchase of paintings. He put his belongings into a couple of bags, including a file of correspondence having to do with his profession—this on the chance that anybody might search the bags in his hotel room. He drew some thousands of dollars out of his bank in Cannes, something he could do without attracting attention, since it had been his practice over many years. He took the notes to the travel bureau of his one-time tutor, who handled sums of money from all over Europe. Lanny said: "I want all the Swiss francs you can get me, and don't mention me, because I don't want to advertise the fact that I'm padding my coat with them." Jerry grinned, recalling how, in the old days, Beauty Budd had insisted upon his going along with Lanny, guarding a couple of million francs with a gun.

The train wound its way up the valleys of the French Alps, and next

morning the passenger stepped off in the Cornavin station of the old
city which he had been visiting off and on ever since the end of World
War I. He had bought pictures here, and after he had put up at the
Hotel Beau-Rivage he set out to regularize his position by visiting the
dealers. He wanted to satisfy the agents of various nations who swarmed
here; for this was not merely the home of the League of Nations, but
a sort of clearing house for the spies of all Europe. The government
was sternly determined to preserve the country's neutrality, and leaned
over backwards in its effort; but of course there were plenty of individuals looking for a chance to make money, and some were making
it from both sides.

After lunch, Lanny set out for another stroll, this time to the public
library, which is in the University building. He went as a tourist, observing the spacious Promenade des Bastions, and the park which it
bisects; when he ascended the steps of the building, the largest in this
venerable city, his mood was that of an animal trainer entering a cage
full of wild beasts. He did not have even the advantage of the trainer,
who knows his beasts; here there was no way to tell a lion from a tiger,
a hyena, or a jackal, or any of them from a respectable watchmaker
or moneylender. There would be earnest students here, many of them
refugees; for this was the native land of freedom, this had been a sanc-
tuary through four centuries of varied oppressions. Voltaire had made
his home in a near-by village, from which he had sent out the books
which had overthrown the *ancien régime*. Rousseau had been born
here, and Lenin had studied in this library. No doubt among the
present-day students, men and women, were some who were mewing
their mighty youth and preparing to change the future of the world.

Lanny had no time to inspect ancient Bibles, or the manuscripts of
John Calvin, or books which had belonged to Bonnivard. He strolled
into the reading room and pretended to be looking for a book on Swiss
painters; having found it, he sat down and read, only now and then
darting a quick glance about the room. He was searching for a familiar
close-cropped German head, for the back of a neck which went up
straight and solid, for a torso which was not that of a student but of
a sailor and fighting man. No doubt Monck would place himself where
he, too, could keep a lookout; he would know what he was looking
for, and quite possibly he would know some of the lions and jackals.

The man of the underground came in by the main entrance, and did
just what Lanny had done, selected a book and sat down to consult it.
They exchanged one quick shot of the eyes; and after a while Monck
got up and strolled out. Lanny waited a brief interval; when he went

out, his friend was standing on the steps, looking out over the park. Lanny didn't even glance at him, but strolled by; he knew that the other would follow, and he turned several corners, so that his friend could have a chance to make certain that no one was on their trail. Their meetings in Germany had always been under cover of darkness; Lanny knew there must be some special reason why Monck had specified afternoon. Perhaps he was employed in the evenings, or perhaps the library wasn't open then. Whatever this experienced man of the underground did was bound to have a reason, and it was Lanny's part to conform.

They were in one of the back streets, and he stopped to look at the contents of a shop window. Presently his comrade was standing beside him, and whispering out of the side of his mouth: "Can you meet me tonight?" When Lanny replied in the affirmative, Monck said: "I will be in front of the Reformation Monument exactly at ten o'clock." Lanny replied: "O.K.," and the other passed on.

These elaborate precautions meant real danger, Lanny understood. The one-time organizer of the Social-Democratic Party, the one-time Capitán of the International Brigade in Spain, might be known to the Nazi agents here, and was sparing Lanny the risk of being seen with him, even for a moment. Lanny was anxious to be spared, and only hoped that Monck wasn't going to ask him to smuggle out any documents in wartime. Or to tell him that *Der Dicke* had found out who had stolen his supercharger! Or that Hess had learned who it was that Lanny had brought to the Berghof!

XI

The visitor stepped into a taxicab and was driven to the right bank of the city, and out to Ariata Park, site of that magnificent structure with the square gray columns, the Palace of the League of Nations. Here, in a private office fit almost for the president of a steel cartel, sat his old friend Sidney Armstrong, a good fellow, an earnest soul, and the prototype of all bureaucrats. He was delighted to see this fellow-countryman and had all the time in the world to talk to him; in fact, he had so much time that he was embarrassed and saddened about it. Nobody came near him any more, nobody asked his advice; the world was going to run itself, in its own cruel and destructive way.

Lanny Budd had been, as you might say, one of the *accoucheurs* of this great organization, or at any rate an assistant, a nurse who came running with the hot water. the basins. the sterilized towels. He had watched its growth from the vantage point of a member of the family, one who was taken into the nursery and shared its secrets: this over a period of twenty-one years, with few in which he had not eaten a dinner in Sidney's home, and listened to the inside story of how hard it was to restrain the evil passions of mankind. Now, had he come to attend the funeral of this bright dream of the president of Princeton University, who had quite literally given his life for it?

Really it seemed so. In this desperate crisis there had been no meeting of either Assembly or Council since December. Then they had taken their one really decisive action, expelling the Soviet Union for its aggression against Finland. A Chinese delegate had been heard to exclaim: "We never got anything like that!"—referring to the period of eight or nine years during which the League had been refusing to take the same action against the Japanese invaders of Manchuria. It was decidedly unfortunate, for it seemed to line the League up as anti-Soviet, something which Sidney insisted was not so.

Anyhow, it was evident that the end was near. The precious archives had been packed up and shipped to France, a big country, better able to defend itself. The staff had been reduced to eighty-nine persons, and they had all been moved into one wing, where they made pathetic efforts to keep up a pretense of their former activities. Seven hundred periodicals came from all over the world, and all were read and indexed. The magnificent library of three hundred thousand volumes had to be left where it was, because of its enormous weight; but every window in the three-sided palace had to be covered with blackout paper, a regulation of the city of Geneva.

The worst trouble was the shortage of money. What nation was going to pay its quota to a temple of peace in the midst of ever-spreading war? The members of the staff had been given their choice, of resigning, effective in one month, or of staying on subject to a day's notice. Sidney was staying, because where else could he go and what else could he do? He was forty-eight, and had spent exactly half his life at this task or getting ready for it—he had been one of President Wilson's experts, chosen in the year 1916 to prepare plans for this great undertaking. Now, after having had charge of a large staff of clerks and secretaries, and having in his imagination given orders to diplomats and statesmen and generals of the whole world, he contemplated the prospect of having to teach a class in some obscure home college.

XII

The son of Budd-Erling was taken to dinner to meet the charming lady whom he had had a chance to win, only it had been in the days when he was in love with Marie de Bruyne. There were two children who tried dutifully to share in the family sorrow, but couldn't quite manage it because the death of the League would mean their return to America, a fabulous land which they knew only from the cinema and the illustrated papers. Lanny did not diminish their curiosity when he told about millionaires who wrote checks for one or two hundred thousand dollars to pay for old paintings, and about a great factory, brilliantly lighted all night, from which deadly fighter planes came rolling, a new one every two or three hours now.

After a frugal meal—"We are learning to economize," said the father —they sat and talked about the prospects of the world. Lanny couldn't tell his real opinions and didn't want to tell his pretended ones, so he listened, which suited his friend perfectly. Living in this tiny land, composed of squeezed-up mountains, and surrounded by belligerents or would-be belligerents, Sidney Armstrong met all kinds of people and heard contradictory opinions. He tried to keep what he called a "sane and balanced point of view," which was that this war had reached a stalemate, and was going to result in some kind of truce, with a return to the League as arbitrator. Manifestly the French weren't going to do any fighting unless they were forced to. The British couldn't, for how could a whale fight an elephant? And as for the Germans, what had they to gain by forcing the issue? They had got what they wanted, and all they had to do was to consolidate their gains and stand pat.

So spoke Sir Oracle, and no dog barked. Lanny didn't say that he had been in Germany recently and was quite sure that Hitler and Göring and Ribbentrop had other ideas. He was content to tell about meetings with British and French statesmen, and with various personalities on the Riviera who had much the same ideas as the League official. Sidney told of Germans and Austrians who had been here and what they had said; Lanny made mental note of the names, for he understood that few would come in these days except Nazi agents and favored businessmen.

"I suppose the German underground has its agents here, also?" he remarked, casually.

His friend replied: "The German underground is a myth. Whatever there was of it has been wiped out by Himmler."

"But don't you have refugees here?"

"Yes, but they are quite inactive. The police watch them closely. You can hardly imagine how determined the Swiss are to preserve their neutrality in this war; and naturally they are most afraid of displeasing the Germans."

The host turned on the radio, a habit which few social groups could escape in these times, for while you were drinking your coffee or your liqueur, the whole British fleet might be sunk, or Paris or Berlin bombed out of existence. What the family heard was a broadcast by Winston Churchill, appealing to the various neutral states and pointing out to them that they were being forced to supply a power whose victory would mean their own enslavement. That seemed like a reply to Sidney's idea that there could be peace for anybody in Europe while the Nazis remained. The First Lord of the Admiralty was a fighting man, and it was hard to imagine him remaining in any government which consented to a truce or even a stalemate with the nahsty Nahzies. His first lordship pronounced the "z" in English fashion, and this seemed to emphasize his contempt, as if he didn't grant them even the right to choose their own appelative.

The vile ones had sunk two Norwegian merchants ships that day, and had made no effort to aid the helpless seamen. That made close to a hundred Scandinavian vessels sunk in defiance of civilized practice. Yet the Nazis demanded of these small states the most rigid compliance with "neutrality" as the Nazis chose to understand it. Their armaments industry was dependent upon the high-grade iron ore which came from northern Sweden, and was brought by rail to the Norwegian port of Narvik, and from there transported southward along the coast, keeping within the three-mile limit which was supposed to constitute Norwegian waters. The British were demanding the right to mine these waters, and Churchill declared that this was the most important leak in the British blockade of Germany. The Nazi press broke out in furious abuse of the First Lord, and threats as to what they would do to the Norwegians if they yielded to the British demands.

Sidney Armstrong, a man of precedents and of vast learning about them, discoursed on this subject: how the Norwegians themselves had mined these waters during the last war, and what the authorities on international law had written on the subject. He still couldn't bring himself to realize that all this learning had been in vain, and that none of these "laws" counted. The Nazis knew no law but their own will "It is, of course, a crucially important point for them," admitted the official. "This water corridor is, you might say, their Achilles' heel."

"You might say it is a place where a whale could take a bite out of an elephant," remarked the son of Budd-Erling, with a smile.

XIII

Lanny said that he had an appointment, and called a taxi and was driven to his hotel. Spring hadn't come yet to these high regions, and the evening was cold but clear; the blackout was thwarted by a moon which was not under control of the city government. Lanny walked to the famous monument, which is in the form of a long rampart, with statues of the heroes of the Protestant Reformation standing upon it. He repeated his precautions to make certain that nobody was following him. He walked along the moat which is in front of the rampart and saw no one; but when he came to the Palace Eynard and turned the corner he heard footsteps behind him. He went on into a street, and turned another corner, the footsteps following. He slowed up, and heard the voice of Bernhardt Monck, whispering: "Follow me." He obeyed, and they turned three or four more corners, and came to a bit of park which Lanny had never seen before. Under the shadow of some trees the man halted.

The first time Lanny had met this anti-Nazi conspirator, six years ago in London, he had whispered: "*Wir sprechen besser Deutsch.*" This time he said: "Better we speak English"; and so they did. "I have to be especially careful," Monck began. "I hope to stay for some time, and may have important news from Germany. Can you arrange to come here now and then?"

"Very easily," was the reply. "I will proceed to re-establish my picture business here, and make one or two purchases."

"You got my letter. Which one?"

"At Juan—or I could not have got here so quickly."

"I do not know how long such letters will get past the censors; I can only try. This is the news I have now: Germany is going to seize Norway within the next week or ten days."

"You are sure of that?"

"Absolutely. I can't give any hint of how I got it, but it's from the top. The ships are assembled and being loaded; those which are going to the north may be already on the way. It is to be a surprise attack, and all the ports will be invaded. It is hoped the Norwegians will be asleep. Can you find any way to warn them?"

"I can go to London and try. The trouble is, the military men don't pay much attention to warnings from unknown sources. You can hardly imagine how many wild rumors are going the rounds in Britain and France. I myself have heard scores, and all upon absolutely the best authority."

"I know how it was in Spain. Do what you can, but of course without imperiling your own position. I will be here until I write again. I have made myself known as a student in the library."

"You will want money?"

"I can use some, not too much."

"I have brought the rest of your own money, one half in dollars and the rest in Swiss francs. If it is too much, I can take part of it back."

"I can use it now. You understand, I would like to tell you what I am doing, but it is against the rules."

"Most certainly. Tell me nothing but what you wish me to make public. What is the Nazis' idea in attacking Norway?"

"To protect their corridor to Narvik, and to have bases in the fjords for U-boat attacks on British commerce."

"They will be taking an extra war on their hands—and a stubborn one."

"They think otherwise. They count upon surprise, and the helplessness of civilians in the face of modern weapons in the hands of desperate and unscrupulous men."

"And what comes then?"

"A rush through Holland and Belgium; the old Schlieffen plan—but this time they will not make the mistakes which Kluck made."

"You believe they can break the Maginot Line?"

"I know they believe it, and I know they have been devising new weapons and rehearsing teams of men to perform precise and scientifically calculated duties. Unless the French are doing an extraordinary intelligence job, it will go badly with them."

"I doubt very much if they are doing anything of the sort. They are in a shocking state of morale."

"Are they going to make peace?"

"I don't think they are going to do anything definite; only quarrel among themselves until *Der Tag* arrives."

"And the British?"

"They will fight when they have to, and they will certainly not make peace. The government that tried it would be thrown out."

"And America?"

"Don't count upon my country for anything but trade. It will take a revolution in public sentiment to bring help from us."

"Even if the Nazis take Paris?"

"That's a long way off, my friend. At some point Americans would be frightened into giving help, but no one can guess what that point is."

"Tell them this," said the man of the underground. "If they do not give it, Europe will belong to the Nazis."

"I will do what I can," Lanny replied. "I'll take tomorrow to renew my acquaintance with Herr Fröder, a collector of old masters here. It is a small town, and word will spread quickly that I am looking for paintings, and thereafter I shall be welcome. I'll take the evening train to Paris and do what I can there, and then fly to London. You understand, I can no longer write letters from one country to another, on account of the censorship."

"I understand. It is like pushing against a steamroller; but we must do what we can."

XIV

Lanny unloaded one pocket after another into his friend's hands. They were afraid of attracting attention to themselves by standing too long, even in the shadow of the trees. Monck said: "Good luck to you." Then, as an afterthought: "What about our friend Laurel Creston?"

It was Lanny's turn to obey the "rules." He surely mustn't say that he had helped a rebel writer to escape from Germany, nor that she had been a guest at his mother's home. He never lied when he could help it, so he answered carefully: "The last I heard from her, she was about to leave for New York." Then he added: "What about your own family?"

"I have told them to move into Southwestern France, where they should be safe, at least for a while. They may be interned, of course; I have no way to hear from them."

"I wish I could help you, comrade; but you know how it is."

"I know exactly how it is. The cause comes first; the cause is everything. If we lose, there will be no place in Europe where you and I can hide, and in a very short time there will be no place in the world."

"I agree with you," said Lanny. He thought for a moment and then went on: "Will there be a chance of your finding out when the Wehrmacht plans to move against France?"

"There is a very good chance."

"All right. There is a French painter of war scenes, Meissonier. When you know definitely that the move is to be made, write me that you have one of his works. You can say that you have taken an option on it, for a week, or a month, or whatever the time is."

"It will not be a long time, I fear," said Monck. Then he gave his friend a handclasp and whispered; "So long, comrade!" and disappeared into the darkness,

28

The Sparks Fly Upward

I

ARRIVING at his Paris hotel, Lanny's first act was to arrange for a plane passage to London later in the day. Then he locked himself in his room, seated himself at his little typewriter, and wrote out the news which he held more precious than all the jewels in the world. He put it into a double envelope in the usual way and addressed it to the American ambassador, not mailing it in the hotel, but taking it outside to a postbox on the street. It would go by airmail, but might be three or four days in reaching F.D.'s eyes, and that might be too late.

Lanny could be sure that the President would pass this warning on to the Norwegian Embassy, but would they heed it? Would anybody in these days ever do anything before it was too late? The P.A. had come to have a deeply rooted distrust of all officials and bureaucrats. Each in his comfortable office was like a mole in his tunnel and had a mole's view of the world. How could it be otherwise, when office-holding was confined to persons who believed that the world would go on as it had been, and who were employed to keep it doing precisely that?

But what could Lanny do? There wasn't a single person in this city to whom he could impart his tremendous secret with hope that it would lead to action. He might go to Paul Reynaud, who had just replaced Daladier as Premier, and say: "I know this." The reply would be: "How do you know it?"—and what could he say then? No action could be taken without a Cabinet discussion; and what would this sharp little lawyer say to his colleagues? "I have a confidential agent whom I trust"? Straightway the rumor would go out; the Premier has a confidential agent, and who can it be? How long would it be before some secretary remarked: "Monsieur Budd, the American *connoisseur d'art*, was with him an hour or two previously"? And how long would it be before the German spies got hold of that hint?

What Lanny did was to go for a stroll until he came to a stationery shop, and there he purchased an extremely elegant sheet of paper with envelope to match. He wouldn't use his own typewriter, but strolled on to a place where they had these instruments to rent. He offered to hire one long enough to write a brief note, and was told that there would be no charge for the courtesy. He seated himself at a machine, and began:

"Sir: The following information comes directly from Germany, from a source which has never failed hitherto. The Germans intend to invade and seize all Norwegian ports within the next few days. They count upon deception and surprise. Some of the ships, for the northern ports, are already under way——"

Lanny was used to typewriters, and could lift his eyes occasionally as he wrote; he could even look behind him while the clicking went on, and thus he observed the proprietor of the establishment strolling casually up behind him. When he was near, the clicking stopped, and Lanny laid his forearm across the writing, looked around, and smiled at the stoutish, round-eyed gentleman his most amiable society smile. "*C'est un beau jour, monsieur.*"

"*Oui, oui,*" assented the other, the statement being beyond dispute. "*C'est une lettre d'amour,*" explained the writer, still graciously.

Such an appeal to French gallantry was beyond resistance. "*Pardon, monsieur,*" said the man, chuckling, and passed on.

Lanny removed his sleeve and the clicking continued: "The writer of this letter dares not sign his name, because his life might be forfeit if he did. Do not fail to warn your government, and advise them to search thoroughly all vessels of whatever character which have come from the south and from the Baltic within the past couple of weeks."

He signed this "A Friend," and addressed it to the Norwegian ambassador in Paris, a gentleman whom he had not had the honor to meet. He sealed it tightly, stamped it, and dropped it into a postbox; and that was all he could do in Paris.

II

At the Croydon airport Lanny telephoned to Rick at The Reaches. They had agreed upon their place of meeting, and all Lanny had to say was: "I want to see you." Rick had agreed not to tell even members of his family when such a call came. Lanny was motored to the city, and within a couple of hours was closeted with his friend in the room which the latter had taken in an obscure hotel.

Lanny wouldn't say: "I have just come from Switzerland, and there I learned such-and-so." What he said was: "I have this information and it is to be trusted. What can we do with it?"

The problem was complicated indeed. Rick couldn't take any action in his own name, for there were too many persons who knew that he was Lanny's friend, or had been. Nowadays Rick spoke rarely of his American friend, and then in a tone of sorrow; but even so people thought of them together, and for all they knew, some Gestapo agent, planted in London years ago, might be meeting Rick's friends at tea parties and collecting odds and ends of data about him. For six years he had been serving as a source of anti-Nazi information; and could he expect to go on with this forever? There can be such a thing as a perfect crime—but surely no series of them!

Someone had to be trusted; and after canvassing a score of different personalities, they decided that Sir Alfred Pomeroy-Nielson was the best bet. Rick's father was an incurable dilettante, and getting old and talkative; but he was a man of honor, and if he gave his son his word not to reveal a certain matter, he would keep it. His heart was deeply engaged in this war, and in the struggle over the issue of Norwegian neutrality which now filled the newspapers and the airways. Out of his large circle of acquaintances he would pick some member of the Cabinet or influential member of Parliament to whom he could take the information and who might go about ringing an alarm bell.

Rick wouldn't mention Lanny, or even that Lanny was in town. Since his father might guess that Lanny was the source of his information, it would be necessary to say that it came from a member of the German underground who had just arrived in England. Excusing himself, Lanny said: "I have been a member of the German underground for many years; and so have you! Therefore your father can say that *he* got it from a member of the underground, one that he has known for a long time—and he won't be telling any lies."

Rick's reply was: "If a man's conscience does not permit him to make up harmless stories, he is surely out of place as a secret agent in wartime."

III

Lanny rang up Ceddy at the Foreign Office. "I have come from Madrid and the Riviera, and have some impressions that might be of interest." The reply was: "We'll have dinner at the club."

So, in a private dining room of the Carlton Club, Lanny sat with Wickthorpe and Albany and a couple of their colleagues who had learned that this casual American had the knack of meeting the right people. Food was rationed, but not the more expensive sorts, so wartime made little difference to the important classes. Lanny talked about Spain and Italy and the Vatican, and the various eminent personalities who had traveled and stopped off at the Côte d'Azur. His own role was of modesty walking around in trousers. He would say: "I can tell you what Schneider said, and what de Wendel said, and Renault, and Duchemin; but don't ask me for an opinion, because I am just an art expert, and honestly, I am bewildered by the complexity of the world situation." He would stop in the middle of a discourse, and say: "Don't take this as my assertion; this is what Pétain said, and it is what his crowd is working for in Madrid. Naturally, you have to allow for the fact that they may not have spoken all their thoughts. This may be what they want me to report, and it's your job to guess what is really in their minds."

The person to whom Lanny Budd was talking was always the final authority, the one to be deferred to, the one to explain events and solve problems. In his life he had met few who did not enjoy that role and appreciate a deferential auditor. He would say: "May I repeat this to the Premier, or the Prime Minister, or the Führer?"—and there were few who were not flattered by the idea of having their words ascend to these exalted regions. After he had made himself agreeable for an hour or so, rarely asking any questions, the other person would become confidential, sometimes without meaning to.

Of these Foreign Office men, Ceddy had been the truest appeaser, the one who was willing to concede most to Adolf Hitler's inordinate demands. As an English gentleman, he had to be indignant at the Führer's manifold crimes in Poland; but Lanny knew from close watching, and from Irma's conversation, that his indignation was far outweighed by his fear of Red Russia. So Lanny mustn't be too patriotic for England, or for Poland, or for international law and order; he must be patriotic enough to satisfy the other men, but not enough to keep Ceddy from trusting him with confidences in the privacy of Wickthorpe Castle!

IV

Lanny didn't say anything about having been to Geneva. He couldn't afford to let these men know that he was in touch with the underground, or that he was a source of information about German military plans. There were bound to be German agents in London—not so many as in Paris, but one would be enough to ruin Lanny Budd forever, and possibly even cost him his life. When he reported what Hitler had told him to say, that was one thing, but it was quite another to report the most precious secrets of the Generalstab. Lanny might do it once, but not twice, and he had better wait until he was ready to give up his career.

Opinions, however, are different; any man can have opinions, even one who has just declared that he is not competent to have any. The conversation turned to the all-important question of where the enemy was going to strike, if at all. A fascinating problem, strategical and also psychological; the Nazis kept making threats, now here, now there, and each time you had to speculate: is that just another bluff, or do they mean it this time? Surely they wouldn't tell you what they had in mind! But then, that might be exactly what they would do, counting upon the fact that you would believe anything but that.

Just now the Nazis were pouring out threats against Norway, and saying what they would do if that country, small in population though not in area, should yield to the insolent threat of the British government to mine waters along the Norwegian coast. "The dirty egotism of England and France," had been the phrase of the *Völkischer Beobachter;* this being contrasted with the perfect altruism of National Socialism in all its international relations.

Said the guest: "I am surely no military authority, but it seems to me that Germany's best move right now would be to seize Norway."

"But Lanny!" exclaimed his lordship. "That would just be taking on another war!"

"They wouldn't count the Norwegians, because they are a peaceful people, not very heavily armed, and I suppose they could be surprised. The Nazis would figure that wherever they went to fight, you would have to follow them."

"Yes, but that would be our kind of war—a naval war."

"I'm not so sure about that. If they seized the Norwegian airports, it would be an air war, and they would have land-based aviation against your ships. If they got settled in those fjords, and got them mined, you'd have the devil's own time rooting them out. And think what submarine harbors they would make!"

"The Germans have their hands full in front of the Maginot Line," announced Gerald Albany. "They're not going off on any side adventures." Gerald's father was a clergyman, and spoke as God's deputy, without fear of contradiction. This attribute was not supposed to be hereditary, but it might be "catching," and Gerald had caught at least a mild form of it.

V

Lanny went out to Wickthorpe Castle by train, this being a safe and agreeable vantage point from which to observe the world plunging to its doom. He took up his residence in the ancient cottage, comfortable, even though he had to stoop slightly to get in. It had been made over with decorations in the modernist style, a bathroom attached, and a fireplace in which lumps of soft coal sizzled and bubbled, giving off blue and purple and golden flames in which you could imagine that you saw all sorts of faery shapes.

A maidservant came to wait on him now, the man having gone to war. She was no faery shape, but solid and substantial, with cheeks so rosy as to seem almost apoplectic. If he had offered to kiss her, no one would have objected, but he didn't; he was a serious gentleman who was usually to be found with his nose in a book, or else with his ear glued to a small radio set, listening to news, often in foreign languages. He was generous with his gratuities, and everybody gave him a good reputation. He rarely went to the castle unless his lordship invited him, for he was being careful not to have any gossip concerning her ladyship and himself. Her ladyship was kind to everybody, and so free with her riches that people said only good things about her. She was "expecting" again, and that was according to her Christian duty. The fact that she was a divorced woman and kept another man's child in the castle was something you had to call "American."

Frances came every day, after her lesson periods. They rode together, and danced to the music of a phonograph. Lanny read stories to her, and answered questions about the great world outside. The war, naturally, was cutting a deep groove in her consciousness; she wanted to know all about it and why it was, and this made difficulty for her father. He ventured the guess that neither mother nor stepfather would expect her to understand the subtleties which plagued their minds; she would have to be taught what every proper little English girl was taught at this time. He told her that Germany was a great nation which had fallen into the hands of evil men, and would have to be fought until those evil men had been driven out. He found her eager to listen to the story of Budd-Erling Aircraft, and to look at the pictures in a handsome pamphlet which her grandfather had prepared for his stockholders; her mother was one of the largest.

The refugee children had by now been fitted into the pattern of English country life. Scrubbed and deloused and supplied with underwear, they had learned the uses of cows and sheep, and also of manners; they went to school, and some of the more presentable had been invited, a few at a time, to have tea at the castle with Frances. They sat for the most part silent, and not knowing what to do with their hands; they stared at wonders which they knew only from the motion-picture screen. When they were alone they played noisy games, and Frances would have liked nothing better than to join them, but that, alas, was not to be thought of. She wasn't so rich as formerly, but still she was one of the richest little girls in the world, and it was almost as if she carried these riches on her person and might spill them out of her pockets.

VI

Ceddy came out for the week-end, and Lanny was invited to dinner. Afterwards they chatted, and the noble earl remarked: "By the way, you may have made a lucky hit. One of our intelligence groups has become convinced that the Germans are planning some move against Norway."

"You don't say!" exclaimed the guest.

"The idea seems to have gained currency in the House, and there may be interpellations."

"That is interesting, Ceddy." Lanny listened to his friend's renewed expressions of disbelief; meantime he thought, was that Sir Alfred's friend at work, and who would he be, and how far would he go? It ought not to require a great amount of warning to put the Norwegians on their guard. Lanny would have liked to send a telepathic message to commanders of air and sea and land forces in every harbor from Oslo to Narvik; but, alas, he had not been able to develop this technique in time.

He listened to the conversation of the week-end guests, which had to do entirely with the war and the world situation. He missed certain faces and voices, and gradually realized that there were shifts taking place in English social life. Politics and its controversies were breaking up lifelong friendships. People who were hot for the war didn't care to hear the opinions of those who were comparatively cool; and this made a tremendous difference to Irma, who, until recently, had been hostess to the majority, and now found herself hostess to a dwindling minority. Some of Ceddy's oldest friends pleaded previous engagements, and some told him frankly that his attitude was unworthy of an Englishman. Irma was worried, for she had visioned a splendid career for her handsome hardworking lord, and now, apparently, he had been led into a blind alley. She even asked the advice of her ex-husband about it, something which seemed to him slightly *gauche;* but then Irma had always seemed to him an insensitive person. He answered with most careful courtesy that he would have been glad to advise her, but these cruel events were every bit as bewildering to him as they were to her.

Controversy centered about the personality of the Prime Minister. Neville Chamberlain had voiced his indignation at German treachery, and declared his determination to punish international crimes; but there were many who didn't trust him, who refused to believe that his heart was in this war, or ever would be in any war. He was a trader, not a fighter; the thoughts of the rebels turned more and more to Winston Churchill, who really hated that ole 'Itler and meant to smack him down. Stormy scenes were occurring in the House, for some were convinced that the government was preparing, not for all-out war, but for some new and more infamous "Munich."

Here at Wickthorpe was the place to find out about it. By invitation of his host, Lanny repeated to a choice gathering the story of his visit to Madrid, and his talks with Marshal Pétain and those to whom the aged ambassador had introduced him. They had named Englishmen among the appeasers, and some of those named were here, and confirmed the idea that this was real statesmanship, this was what British diplomacy ought to be about in a crucial hour. Herr Hitler was difficult, and some of his aides were rowdies, nobody could deny; but at his worst he was better than the Bolshevists, and to destroy him and his partner, Mussolini, would be to deliver Europe up to Red revolution. Who but a blind man could fail to see that?

VII

The eminent ones went back to their posts of duty, and Lanny wrote out a report, and took a walk to a near-by town, where he could mail a letter to U. S. Ambassador Joseph Kennedy without attracting attention. A lovely country to walk in, with winding roads lined with hedges coming into bloom in early April. "O, to be in England!" the poet had sung—but you had better take your raincoat and hat on your strolls, for the sun kept no promises. The young men were gone from the landscape, and the middle-aged did the work; the very old men watched the sheep on the commons and the children brought in the cows from the meadows. There would always be an England, with lovely gardens, and quiet homes, and people reserved, never telling you their troubles unless they knew you well.

Lanny came back to his retreat. There was nothing more he could do, and he might as well be comfortable while he waited to see which way the world was going. He knew of books worth reading, and was fortunate enough to be able to buy them. The papers came regularly, and the magic radio was free for the turning of a couple of dials. One morning he went for a courtesy call on his ex-mother-in-law, and played a rubber of bridge with these people who found boredom the worst of all problems. There was Uncle Horace, now showing his age, and a niece who was visiting Fanny and served as an unpaid companion. They played a game, and while Horace was recording the score— they played for a penny a point and he hated to lose—Lanny suggested: "Let's try the BBC."

Nobody could object, in these times. He turned the dial, just in time to catch a bulletin: at five-fifteen that morning German troops had crossed the border of Denmark unresisted and were occupying the country. At the same time German warships and transports had entered the principal harbors of Norway and were taking possession of them. At Narvik a dozen destroyers had entered in a snowstorm, had torpedoed two Norwegian gunboats with the loss of all on board, had seized British vessels in the harbor and landed troops. At Trondheim, Bergen, Stavanger and Kristiansund it had been much the same. At Oslo the invaders had seized the harbor and also the airport, and were believed to be taking control of the city. The surprise had been complete, and the resistance gallant but probably ineffectual.

Words of sympathy followed, but these did not reduce the effect of the blow upon Lanny Budd's spirits. The rubber of bridge remained uncompleted and the debts unpaid; since Uncle Horace had been behind, there was no objection.

Such was the beginning of a period of heartache, almost of heartbreak, for the son of Budd-Erling. He had to sit, perfectly helpless, perfectly voiceless, and watch in the columns of newspapers and hear over the radio the murder of a nation and its culture: those quiet, inoffensive and decent people, about as near to a free democratic way of life as any in the world; a people whose ever-recurring task it was to conquer a harsh and inhospitable climate, to build homes on rocky shores and wrest a living from cold and stormy seas. Lanny had visited the country on his honeymoon with Irma; the yacht *Bessie Budd* had poked her prow into these fjords and her passengers had exclaimed

over the beauty of the towering mountains. That had been summertime, when the waters were blue, the clouds white, the shores green;
ladies and gentlemen of the luxury class had shuddered at the thought
of how it would be in winter, when almost perpetual daylight would
be turned to almost perpetual night. They had admired the sturdy
fisherfolk, and had gone ashore and ridden up to the *saeters*, the high
mountain-meadow farms.

These were a Northland people, according to the Nazis' own
formula as good as any in the world; surely as "Aryan" as Adi Schicklgruber the Austrian, or Hermann Göring the Bavarian or Josef Goebbels the dark and deformed Rhinelander. But it happened that geography was against them; the *Neue Ordnung* needed their harbors, and
so they were to feel the jackboot in their faces, they were to be turned
out of their homes and made into slaves of the conquering Nazi machine. They might have yielded, and been accepted as co-conquerors
and deputy-rulers; but they resisted, they stood by their faith in freedom and humanity—and so their story became one which made men
sick to watch.

VIII

The invasion began against six ports. German merchant ships came
in, supposedly in ballast, but really loaded with Nazi troops and weapons. They had sent their spies and secret agents ahead and had everything planned with true German *Gründlichkeit*. They had charts of
all the channels and minefields; they knew where the arsenals were, the
airports, the oil storage depots, the telephone exchanges, the radio stations. The troops, many of them, spoke Norwegian, for the reason that,
during the last war, the kindly Norwegians had accepted thousands
of refugee children, had taken them into their homes and treated them
as members of the family. Now they paid a return visit, in the role of
thieves and murderers.

Everything went precisely on schedule. The troops emerged from
the ships and seized the strategic places, while at the same time German
warships came into the fjords, destroying whatever vessels or fortifications attempted resistance. At Trondheim the warships surrounded
themselves with a fleet of small Norwegian vessels, so that the forts
hesitated to open fire. In the great Oslo fjord several German vessels
were sunk, but the troops came ashore, while the populace stared in
helpless incredulity. Since the Norwegian government refused to yield
to the invaders, fighting began and the small Norwegian army retreated
to the north and east.

These details Lanny gathered, hour by hour, day by day. It was hard to think about anything else, or to find anybody who wanted to talk about anything else. What would the British fleet do? Lanny was among people who could give him some idea. The fleet was already out in force, because mines were being laid in Norwegian waters. It would seek out the German fleet and begin action; but these waters were stormy, and fogs appeared suddenly, and who found what would be a matter of chance. The Germans would be willing to risk their fleet, and perhaps to sacrifice it, in order to seize Norway and hold it. Would the British fleet venture into the Skagerrak, and what would be its chances against German U-boats in those narrow waters?

Such were the questions debated by the family and guests at Wickthorpe during the following week-end. Somebody was always glued to the radio, and now and then would turn it higher so that others could hear. Never since World War I had there been so many incidents, piling one on top of another. For example, the fighting at Narvik —that far northern fjord into which the *Bessie Budd* had sailed, at the head of which you heard day and night the sound of iron ore roaring down a chute from railroad cars into ships. Here had come a German expedition, supply ships guarded by half a dozen of the latest and largest destroyers; five smaller British destroyers dashed in during a snowstorm, barely missing the black rocks of the shore, and sank the supply ships and one of the enemy destroyers and left two others in flames. One British destroyer was sunk and one had to be beached; a third, crippled, managed to get away with the other two.

A few days later came nine British destroyers with the battleship *Warspite*, and wiped out seven German destroyers then in the fjord. Those were feats in the old tradition of Drake and mighty Nelson; but alas, they wouldn't loosen the enemy's hold on the country they had seized. The Germans dug in, and fleets of airplanes brought them supplies; it would take a real war to remove them; and did Britain have the ships and the men and the guns to spare?

IX

Now and then Lanny went up to London. People there realized that the war had really begun now; you saw them carrying their gasmasks, something that had been forgotten during the winter. Lanny gave his time to luncheons, teas, and dinners in the town houses and clubs where he met Britons who knew what their country was doing and planning.

He let his role of art expert slip into the background and became the son of a great airplane manufacturer, which he discovered was a social distinction in England now; the man who bore it could sit before kings, he could speak like the Pope *ex cathedra*, he could utter that most offensive phrase, "I told you so!" and no one would take offense.

Margy came back from the Riviera, and Lanny spent a week-end with her. A curious phenomenon, how people were getting sorted out; there had been ardent appeasers at Bluegrass, but no more; for Margy's stepson, the new Lord Eversham-Watson, had a sister married to a Polish landowner, now a refugee, and her dreadful stories had turned the place into a rallying point for the Germanophobes. Margy herself, the dowager, hated all wars and war-makers, but she kept quiet and didn't count any more. Lanny, coming from a place where most men defended good old Neville and considered him a greatly wronged statesman, found himself in a place where everybody sang the praises of good old Winston, First Lord of the Admiralty and ninth lineal descendant of the Duke of Marlborough. Lanny took no sides, but listened attentively, and when he came back to London mailed another report in care of the American ambassador.

He wrote that the British would send an expedition, composed mainly of the troops which had been intended to aid the Finns. His guess was that they would try to take the port of Trondheim; later he revised this, and said that the port was too heavily mined; the expedition would land at fishing villages and try to take Trondheim from the land. "It is a race against time," he wrote; "the Germans have reopened the Skagerrak and are sending in tanks and heavy guns, and soon will be able to repeat in Norway what they did in Poland. Their claims that they have bombed and sunk British capital ships are probably false, but these falsehoods may be partly unintentional—Göring's airmen tend to see ships bigger than they are."

What happened after that must have brought quiet satisfaction to the president of Budd-Erling Aircraft Corporation, who had been foretelling it to the brass hats of Britain, France and his own country for several years. The Germans did not have much success against the British capital fleet, but they showed the helplessness of troops ashore, or trying to get ashore, in the face of land-based aviation. The Nazis had the Norwegian airports, and were flying their planes to these ports and supplying them by air transports. Their flyers dived upon the fishing villages and knocked their wooden docks to flinders; they bombed the landing vessels and the supplies on the shore; they machine-gunned the troops wherever they tried to hide. The Luftwaffe had had seven years in which to practice all this, and they had told Lanny Budd exactly what they meant to do.

Alfy came back from an encounter with them, having flown from a British carrier to raid an enemy supply dump. His plane had been shot full of holes by German flyers and he had barely managed to reach an airfield that was still in Norwegian hands. He had had to make his way to the coast by land, and had boarded a British transport which was bombed three times on its way back to Scotland. That sounded like a long adventure, but the whole thing had taken less than ten days. It had cost this slender young aviator some twenty pounds in weight, and his hands trembled like an aged person's. It wasn't fear, he said; it was grief and rage—to see these dreadful events and be powerless to prevent them, to know that his native land had been outwitted and out-guessed, and might be in jeopardy of her very existence, to say nothing of her imperial pride.

X

What made matters worse was the fact that these difficulties had been in great part concealed from the public. Day after day reports were given out that troops were going ashore, that they were advancing, that the Norwegians were holding the enemy, and so on. Even Lanny believed some of it, and the disillusionment was all the greater when at last people realized the truth—that the Nazi-Fascists were scoring another triumph at very small cost. The list of these was getting to be a tax on the memory: Abyssinia and Albania and Spain, Austria and Czechoslovakia and Poland, and now Denmark and Norway. The end of it was beyond any man's guessing, and certainly a long way off. Lanny sent a cablegram to his father, saying: "You may safely enlarge plant events make certain demand for product many years."

England began to boil, after the fashion of a democratic nation. Englishmen demand that their government shall succeed, and when they see it failing they accept no excuses. There were huge meetings of protest in Trafalgar Square, and those licentious, irresponsible newspapers which had so greatly displeased Adolf Hitler began to please him even less. A bundle of them came to the castle every morning and another in the evening, and really, it made you embarrassed to spread them out, or to let anybody see you reading them—they were so impolite to august personalities and to principles revered in these renovated ancestral halls.

Outwardly, everything at Wickthorpe was peaceful and safe. The sheep grazed on the lovely wide lawns and the deer browsed on the tender young buds of the shrubbery; little Frances rode her pony, and watched her father play at bowls with the palish and undersized curate. But politically speaking, and intellectually, and spiritually, the castle was under siege. It was named in all the Leftist press, along with Cliveden, as a center and source of the appeasement, the cowardice, the downright treason which had plagued Britain's public life and brought her to this shameful pass. Other persons might have a tendency to forget the list of humiliations, but a Liberal or Labor newspaper editor must keep it in large type on the wall in front of his desk, and never let an edition go to press without featuring it in news and editorials and cartoons.

The American guest, playing his role conscientiously, felt this pressure, and realized that it took a stout heart to withstand it. Did Cedric, fourteenth Earl of Wickthorpe, have that heart? In the gallery hung portraits of his ancestors, and assuredly they must have had it, to be able to walk around in the armor they wore. But Ceddy was a modern, who had lived a soft life; a game of rugger was the nearest he had ever come to a fight, and he had been brought up in the firm conviction that things were always going to be as they had always been. Now came these frightful shocks, one after another: battleships sunk by torpedoes, cruisers blasted by bombs, British soldiers forced to run like rabbits and hide in holes to escape streams of bullets from overhead. Even worse were the political shocks: the astonishing competence of the dictatorships, their speed and power, the paralyzing miasma which they poured out in the form of propaganda—brazen falsehood, cunning sophistication, which almost broke the heart of a lover of truth! How could anyone stand up against it, how believe in the possibility of righteousness, of its chances of survival in a world suddenly thrown back into barbarism?

XI

Lanny was especially interested in the reaction of the woman who had been his wife for six years, and whom he knew better than any other woman with the possible exception of his mother. Irma Barnes, Countess of Wickthorpe, had a stout heart, and was not plagued with a too-vivid imagination; but she, like his lordship, had had an easy life, and was accustomed to the idea that whatever she wanted would be handed to her on a silver platter. Now very certainly this wasn't happening, and appeared as if it might never happen again. Hosts of enemies rose up against her, screaming at her—in print, if not by voice. Indeed, she had been advised not to let herself be driven through any working-class district, for her picture had been widely published and she might be recognized, and have the unpleasant experience of having a rotten egg or a dead cat thrown into her limousine.

England wasn't just that green and pleasant land which had so attracted her that she wanted to own one of its picturesque old castles. England was a land of coal and iron, of heavy industry, and toiling masses who did not love their masters, but had their own ideas, their own press, their own leaders, wholly beyond the scope of Irma's mind. Now they were rising up against the betrayers of democracy, and it was a most unpleasant, even terrifying experience. Irma had not been entirely unprepared for it, of course; there had been Munich, and before that Spain, and she had played hostess to statesmen who had discussed these events in her presence, explaining them and providing her with arguments. What she had not been prepared for was the failure of these eminent persons; she had assumed that they knew England and the outside world, and would take the necessary measures to control events.

But they had not done this; on the contrary, they had let the world slip out of their grasp, they had let things happen the opposite to the way they wished. They hadn't made friends with Germany and got her into a war with Russia; they had let Germany divide Poland with Russia and then turn upon the West! The British Empire was being defied; actually, at this moment, Ceddy was reporting that they couldn't save Norway because that treacherous rotter, Mussolini, was mobilizing his fleet and threatening the Suez Canal, which was Britain's lifeline to India. So Britain's battleships and carriers had to go to Alexandria instead of to Trondheim! And suppose Mussolini should attack them with his fleet of submarines—it might mean the end of the British Empire in a single night!

So here was this titled pair, rich and fashionable, sitting on the apex of the social pyramid, and inside them they were two frightened and bewildered human souls who saw their world beginning to crumble and had no idea what to do to prop it up. Things got so bad that Ceddy didn't dare leave his office over the week-end, and Irma went to town so as to be near him and keep up his courage. Before she left she called her ex-husband over to the castle to ask him, would it do any good if she were to cable Robbie Budd, offering to sell some of her blue-chip stocks and put up the cash to pay for the immediate enlarging of the Budd-Erling plant!

XII

Lanny, too, was in need of encouragement, and he knew only one place where he could get it. The Reaches was only a short drive from Wickthorpe, and Lanny telephoned and made an appointment; he went for a walk on the road, and Nina and Rick picked him up. Petrol was hard to get, so they wouldn't have a holiday in the far-off Lake District, but content themselves with a picnic lunch in a sunny spot alongside one of the streams which run into the Thames. At least, it was sunny while they ate; later, when a shower came up, they carried everything to the car and continued their conversation inside.

They could find no cheerful subject; but old friendship and mutual trust are precious things in themselves, and Lanny and Rick were in their second quarter-century of shared experience. They had worried through one World War, and hoped never to see another; but here it was, and they had to live with it. Rick had come out of the first one with a crippled knee and the nuisance of a steel brace. Some seven or eight thousand nights he had unstrapped the brace, sitting on the side of his bed, and seven or eight thousand mornings he had strapped it on before getting up. Even so, he had managed to beget a family and to earn a living for it, and to make some contribution to his country's democratic thought. Now he was burning with the desire to be something more than a free-lance writer in this crisis; he would have liked a job on the BBC, but the fuzzyheads would never take him, because he was too Pink.

They talked about Alfy, who had gone back to his squadron. His superior officers had told him to go home and sleep; but how could a man sleep when his country was in such peril? They had put him to training some of the younger chaps, and that made it possible to think of him with a bit more hope. Poor Nina!—she had been through the same thing for more than a year with her husband, and here it was with her oldest son. She couldn't keep the tears from stealing into her eyes, and was embarrassed to wipe them away. Lanny asked about the younger children, whom he had not seen for a long time; he had had to drop out of the family's life, for it was too many people to trust with his secret.

Lanny imparted the news he had been collecting here and there, an important service to a journalist whose specialty was the predicting of world events. It had been a long time since he had predicted anything good; alas, he was a Cassandra going about in trousers, and he shared her sad fate, in that nobody believed him and nobody thanked him for being right while they were wrong. Now he was sure that the man with the black umbrella would soon be returned to his private business in Birmingham, and that the First Lord of the Admiralty would take the helm of the ship of state. Lanny told about the talks at Maxine Elliott's, and Rick said: "Why don't you go to see him now?"

The answer was: "I don't dare. I can't be known to associate with any real anti-Nazi."

"You could see him privately. I think that could be arranged without difficulty."

"There is nothing private in a time like this, Rick. You surely don't imagine that you've caught all the spies in England; and I am Cæsar's wife—I have to be above suspicion."

XIII

They discussed the war, and what was to be expected. They agreed that the British were in a hopeless plight in Norway, and that the expedition was probably being withdrawn at the present time. Rick told a curious story about that expedition; a friend of his had had a chance to observe what the British officers were taking with them, and besides the prescribed equipment, it had consisted mainly of salmon-fishing gear.

Lanny said: "I have reason to believe that Hitler means to move on France as soon as he is secure in Norway. I have the hope of getting some definite information about it; and if so, I'll get word to you."

There was material for much conversation here. What was the present state of the Maginot Line, and of its promised continuation to the north, in front of Holland and Belgium? This was one of the great military secrets, but Lanny could quote what Denis *fils* had told him, and this young *capitaine* ought to know, being stationed there. He reported that the extension was inadequate, for the reason that the heads of the government and of the army hadn't really expected war; Denis *fils* took part of the blame, because he and his family had done so much to encourage this attitude. "He repents, but that won't help France," explained Lanny.

The situation was drastically worse than in the last war. Then Belgium had been an ally, and from the moment of the war's outbreak their army had been one with the French. But this time the young King of the Belgians was an appeaser; he was more interested in his own country than in Poland, and he dreamed of keeping safe by letting the Nazis have a free hand in the East. The declaration of Belgian neutrality had been one of Hitler's great diplomatic successes, very little appreciated by the outside world. It left France with the northern part of her border exposed; the French armies could enter Belgium only after the German armies had done so, and would thus have no time to prepare positions.

In short, things were terrible, from whatever angle you approached them. Whether you looked at Scandinavia or Italy, Russia or Spain, the Mediterranean, the Atlantic, or even the far-off vast Pacific, you saw only black danger, and your heart was made sick by the spectacle of stupidity and incompetence, or of plain and simple treason to the cause of freedom and humanity. How could you explain it? How could it happen that all the brain power appeared to be on the side of the gangsters and the cynics, and all the dullness and futility on the side of the democracies?

"We have trusted the world too much," ventured the son of Budd-Erling. "It isn't nearly as intelligent or as honest as we imagined."

"We have trusted the capitalist system too much," responded the baronet's son, who refused to compromise in either his ideas or his language. "We thought it would know when its time had come, and would give up gracefully. We didn't dream that it would hire the worst knaves and murderers in all history to keep itself in power."

"It's partly that, of course, Rick——"

"It's wholly and completely that, and don't you swallow anybody's eyewash on the subject."

"The Germans really swallow their *Blut-und-Boden* eyewash, Rick."

"They swallow it because it's the only food they get, and it's fed to them at the point of a machine gun. Who put up the money to provide the machine guns, the pistols and the daggers and the uniforms and the flags and all the rest of the Nazi equipment? The iron and steel men, the big industrialists—you have told me so yourself, a hundred times."

"Yes, of course, Rick——"

"All right then; and they're reaping the biggest profits ever in all their lifetimes. They are the real masters of Germany today, and they can kick Schicklgruber out whenever they get ready."

"I'm not so sure of that. Some of them are worried, I can tell you."

"What price their worry? If gangsters turn against their employers —that surely wouldn't be the first time in history, and it wouldn't excuse the employers."

XIV

The showers had passed, and they got out and strolled for a while by the side of a gently flowing stream. It was the custom in this very old land for rights-of-way to be left free to the public, and there were delightful places to walk, with scenery ever changing. A land to be loved and cherished, and fought for if need be. Britons never shall be slaves! Rick quoted—and then his conscience began to trouble him, because he was enjoying a holiday while Britons were dying in Norway and in the seas about it and in the air above it. He wanted to get back home and write another article exposing those who didn't really want to beat the Fascists, because they were Fascists themselves at heart.

Nina drove them to the neighborhood of Wickthorpe, and put Lanny off by the roadside. When he entered his cottage, there was mail on his writing desk; a letter from Robbie—long delayed, because the British were holding up airmail for censorship in Bermuda, and they hadn't been able to get things properly organized. Ordinarily he would have pounced on such a letter, but this one waited, for there was another, in a plain envelope, with a Swiss stamp and a French censorship label. "Mr. Lanning Prescott Budd, Art Expert, Wickthorpe Castle, Bucks, England." He tore it open and read:

"Dear Sir: After considerable search I have located what I believe is a really desirable example of Meissonier. It is a large work, and rather expensive, but within the limit that you set. According to your instructions I have secured a ten-day option on it. I hope this letter finds you safe and well. Not being sure where you are I am sending a copy in care of your mother on the Cap d'Antibes, and one in care of your father in care of the Budd-Erling Aircraft Corporation in Connecticut.

Respectfully, Brun."

So there it was. Lanny lost not an hour, but packed a couple of bags and took the first train to London. On the way he thought over his plan of campaign. He had paper and envelopes, purchased in advance. Since it was after business hours, he couldn't stop in a typewriter shop as he had done in Paris; but the hotel porter would manage to find him a machine. In writing to strangers he dared not use his own, which he left in hotel rooms, where anyone might take a sample of its writing. He imagined the Gestapo being on his trail and having such a sample in its files. If one of his letters of warning fell into their hands, they could make a comparison under the microscope and establish his responsibility.

First he wrote his report to F.D.R.: "The German army will invade France by way of Belgium and Holland, starting about the 10th of May. This information comes from the same source as that previously sent, which proved correct. I have every reason to trust it." That was all; it wasn't his part to make appeals, or even suggestions. The President of the United States would know what use he wished to make of such information.

Then Lanny wrote three letters, much the same as he had written to the Norwegian ambassador in Paris; these to the Belgian, Dutch, and French ambassadors in London. Also a note to Rick, saying: "The date of the appointment is May 10th. Positive." Rick had agreed that when he got this word, he would put his father to work a second time. It hadn't done much good in the former case, but it might do more now, because the baronet could say: "Didn't I tell you about Norway?"

Lanny groped his way through the blackout, and dropped the letters into different postboxes on the street—all but the one for the Honorable Joseph P. Kennedy. For all Lanny could tell, there might be a diplomatic pouch leaving that night, and no chance must be missed. He stepped into a taxi and said: "American Embassy." By some paranormal sense which the taximen had developed in the past eight months, this one managed to draw up in front of the stately building. Lanny gave him the letter, saying: "Be so good as to hand this in, and say: 'Personal for Mr. Kennedy.'" With the request went a half-crown, and the driver replied: "Righto, guv'ner."

Lanny followed him part way to the door, near enough to see but not to be seen. Afterwards he let the man deliver him to a point near the hotel, but not at it. All this seemed to him to constitute the perfect crime, and he settled himself comfortably in bed to read the latest painful details from the fishing villages of Namsos and Andalsnes. "Too little and too late"—once more!

BOOK EIGHT

The Flinty and Steel Couch of War

29

Secret Dread and Inward Horror

I

LANNY had decided to stay in London and see if the movies and the theater could divert his mind. It was hard for him to read a book or to play the piano while waiting to see if his world was coming to an end. There wasn't a thing he could do about it; and what was the use of gathering facts and opinions which were going to be knocked into a chaos in exactly one week? His mind was haunted by visions of those crowded old towns of the Lowlands, with their fine churches and public buildings, and—more important to the Pinkish mind—their long rows of one- or two-story workers' homes built of brick or gray stone to last for centuries; each house with its white doorstep polished twice a day, and in the rear its tiny plot with tulips or other bright flowers now at their gaudiest. He saw with his mind's eye the Nazi steamroller passing over all these and reducing them to dust and rubble.

More dreadful yet, he saw the Nazi lie machine at work, forcing these free peoples to think and speak according to the Nazi formulas. The Jews would be robbed and driven into exile; the labor unions and the co-operatives would be destroyed and the newspapers suppressed, or made over in the Nazi mold; the children would be turned over to Nazi teachers and made into hateful little robots; the government would be put into the hands of those semi-lunatics in each country who espoused the Nazi cause, and who put on colored shirts with swastikas on them and went about heiling one another and denouncing the pluto-democratic-Jewish-Bolshevik institutions of their own land. Already you saw the whole thing in operation in Norway, where there was a creature by the name of Quisling who had the whole works and had been suddenly boosted into the seat of authority. There was something about his name which exercised a fascination upon the English mind, and it was becoming a symbol for everything horrid: a name, as the *Times* put it, "Suggestive of the questionable, the querulous, the quavering of quaking quagmires and quivering quicksands, of quibbles and quarrels, of queasiness, quackery, qualms and quilp."

The humiliating announcement came that the British were re-embarking at the Norwegian ports they had taken; and shortly afterwards Lanny Budd was a visitor in the House of Commons, listening to Chamberlain's defense of his course through the past four years. A lame defense indeed, and everyone sensed that his nerve was breaking. A member of his own party, attacking him as bitterly as any of his foes, called on him with the words of Oliver Cromwell to the Long Parliament: "You have sat too long here for any good you have been doing. Depart, I say. Let us have done with you. In the name of God, go!" The majority still supported the P.M. in his plea for "unity," but the margin was small and the end was near. Rick, at the picnic, had said: "The day he is out I am going to stand on my head!"

II

Lanny went about counting the days and hugging his direful secret. His credit as a P.A. was at stake, but he wouldn't hope for vindication; he would just wait, and leave it on the lap of Adolf Hitler. Lanny's mind went back to Berchtesgaden at the end of the previous August, when Adi had been agonizing and consulting the spirits, while a roomful of generals and adjutants downstairs champed and pranced like so many thoroughbreds lined up for a race. Would he have got some other medium this time—Professor Pröfenik of Berlin, or the little old lady of the Nymphenburgerstrasse in Munich? Was he getting a horoscope or a spirit communication and changing his mind this night? Or would he let the meteorologists and the militarists have their way?

The same burden of anxiety rested upon the minds of all Lanny's appeaser friends. The zero hour was approaching, and they hadn't done anything, at least not anything that counted. There was something going on, a negotiation so ultra-secret that Lanny was allowed only a hint of it; but there was a hitch, somebody had raised his demands, and, as usual, each side blamed the other, each suspected that the other had been playing for time, pretending good faith while having only guile. Europe was drifting to destruction, and there wasn't anywhere enough statesmanship, enough patience and wisdom to avert it.

On the evening after Chamberlain's speech, Lord Wickthorpe called from the apartment which he and Irma kept in town. "Could you come over, Lanny? It's something rather urgent." And when Lanny came: "Would it be possible for you to run over to Paris tomorrow?"

When Lanny answered in the affirmative, his friend inquired: "Do you know the Comtesse de Portes?"

Lanny had met her, but they had had only casual conversation. Now Ceddy said: "I will give you a letter. The French have got to act, if the situation is to be saved. We are helpless, because of the pressure which the opposition puts upon us."

"There's a war party in Paris, too, Ceddy."

"I know—but nothing compared to what we have here. If the Quai d'Orsay would make even the smallest public move toward peace, we could say that we were forced to join them. Even our madmen wouldn't want to fight Hitler alone."

So there was the P.A., in the very heart and center of the intrigue about which he had been hearing whispers for the past few weeks. It was too late from the point of view of a P.A., but he didn't say so; he listened patiently to the outline of an elaborate set of proposals for the reconstruction of Europe: a nominally independent Poland, under an administration satisfactory to the Nazis, and with the right of trade through a Corridor to be acknowledged as German; the independence of Norway and Denmark to be restored, but with German control of the waters leading to the Baltic; an agreement as to submarine and air-power ratios: in short, another Munich, but very much worse from the British point of view.

Said his lordship: "Our only hope is for Reynaud to accept it, and force his Cabinet to do the same. If the announcement is made public it will be like an Armistice Day in France; there will be such a wave of popular enthusiasm that the warmongers here will be cowed. It's either that, Lanny, or our own government will fall, and we can see no chance of anything but a Churchill Cabinet."

During this exposition, Irma sat by her husband's side, not putting in a word, but watching her ex-husband's face for signs of sympathy and hope. A curious situation for Lanny; it was his role to be gravely concerned, realizing that not merely the political career of Lord Wick-thorpe was at stake, and the prestige of the Barnes fortune, but the future of the present ruling class of Britain, and the safety of big money and big business everywhere. Fascism was law and order in Italy and Spain, Nazism was law and order in Germany, and the war on them would inevitably turn into a revolutionary struggle; which-ever side won, the holders of privilege would lose.

The son of Budd-Erling was supposed to understand this the more clearly, because in earlier years he had associated with the Leftists and had a chance to observe how treacherous and irresponsible they were.

Ceddy knew about Lanny's past, but it did not alarm him, because it conformed to a familiar pattern in the public life of Europe. One former Socialist, Ramsay MacDonald, had risen to become Prime Minister of Britain, and half a dozen such had become Premier of France in the course of the past generation.

III

Lanny wrote a report to Washington, and next morning flew to Paris, and in the afternoon presented his letter to Hélène de Portes, in her spacious and elegant apartment on the Place du Palais Bourbon just across the way from the meeting place of the Chambre des Députés. Here she lived quite openly with her Premier-lover, and the wits of Paris exercised themselves upon the situation, saying that the *fleur-de-lis*, the national flower of France, had become the *fleur-du-lit*, flower of the bed. Hélène had won out over her rival, Jeanne de Crussol, but wasn't happy in this triumph, because her lover had won by taking a course exactly opposite to what she desired. Hélène was an ardent *munichoise*, whereas Reynaud had an "anti-Munich" Cabinet, including Daladier, his hated rival, as Minister of National Defense, the most powerful post in time of war.

So that bed about which the jokes were made was far from being one of roses—or at any rate, the roses had plenty of thorns. The countess, a woman in her forties, domineering and shrill, wore her lover out with protests and arguments; she wore Lanny out in the course of a long conversation in which she discussed the members of the newly formed Cabinet and recited their crimes and failings. She was nervous and overwrought, a chain-smoker of cigarettes, and so blinded by hatred for her political opponents that she had apparently lost sight of any faults that might exist in Nazi Germany. That was the way of things in Paris; the clamor of the civil war drowned out the sound of the guns on the Maginot Line.

This busy political lady blamed the British, too; they did not appreciate the position of Paul Reynaud, who was practically a prisoner of the *bellicistes*, the war party. It was Wickthorpe and his friends who ought to be making the first move, because they still had a Cabinet and a Prime Minister. Instead, they were trying to put it off on their French friends, who were so much more exposed to the attacks of enemies both domestic and foreign. She asked Lanny to explain to her the circumstances which made it impossible for Chamberlain to act, but she didn't really want to listen—she broke in before he had said three sentences, and began scolding at Georges Mandel, the Jew, and other anti-Nazis in the Cabinet, and then at the pro-Nazis who were not in the Cabinet—Laval, Bonnet, Flandin—men who were intriguing against Paul, without having any appreciation of his difficulties. Poor little man, he was fairly worn out with the burdens heaped upon him, he was having to take sleeping powders, and public life was an accursed thing, incompatible with friendship, with love, with happiness, even with self-respect. Nothing but devotion to France and deep concern for her welfare had caused the Comtesse de Portes to have anything to do with politics, and now it was the dream of her life to return to the beautiful estate near Marseilles which her father had built.

But Monsieur Budd had come from London to see her, and she appreciated this, and hinted to him about one last effort that was being made, this time by way of Brussels. Hélène would appeal to Paul's wiser and better self; and meantime Lanny would interview Schneider and de Bruyne and de Wendel, and see what influences they could bring to bear and what chance there might be for an appeasement cabinet if Paul would consent to listen to reason. So Lanny went the rounds once more, and penetrated still more deeply into the ulcer that was eating out the heart of *la belle Marianne*. He went back to his hotel and dutifully wrote another report, saying:

"I fear this will be out-of-date before it reaches you. The appeasers are making a last appeal through the King of the Belgians, who is afraid of losing his throne if real war breaks out. All the monarchs of the small countries have the same fear, but they dare not stand together. Now King Leopold is awaiting Hitler's reply, and it is a question whether this will be delivered by Ribbentrop or by the Wehrmacht."

IV

Lanny telegraphed his mother that he was in Paris, and presently he received some mail forwarded from Bienvenu. There was no further word from Monck, but a note signed "Bruges," which meant Raoul Palma. On Lanny's last visit he had learned that the workers' school in Cannes had been closed; some of the pupils had gone into the army, while others, the Communists, had gone "underground." He hadn't known where Raoul and his wife were, and had been afraid to make inquiry. Now came a note, written in that code which Lanny had taught his friend: "I have come upon what purport to be some of the preliminary sketches by Doré for his illustrations of Dante's *Inferno*, and I thought you might be interested to examine them and pass upon their genuineness." That meant, apparently, that Raoul was in serious trouble of some sort, and needed Lanny's help. He gave an address in one of the factory districts which form a dark and dingy ring about *la ville lumière.*

Lanny was pleased to hear from this Spanish Socialist, who in times past had served in France as Rick had served in England, to make public important news. Lanny wrote, appointing a place of meeting on a street in Montmartre, where all sorts of people went, Bohemian artists and the well-to-do who patronized them. Lanny strolled on the other side of the street and saw his friend approach, with nobody following. Raoul knew all about taking precautions, and they joined each other, walking in obscure streets and lunching in an obscure café. The "Inferno," it appeared, was one of the concentration camps in the southwest of France, where a heartless government kept tens of thousands of refugees who had fled from Franco's hangmen and torturers. More than a year had passed since the collapse of the Spanish Republican government, but still the French politicians refused to turn any foreign "Reds" loose in France. They were not to be moved by the fact that these internees were the most determined foes of Nazism on the Continent, thousands of them soldiers with battle experience who craved nothing in the world but to go to the front and fight the Hitlerites. But no, they were "politically untrustworthy," and even Frenchmen who had fought for the liberties of Spain were denied posts of responsibility in the fight for the life of *la patrie.* Class was more than country!

Raoul had done his usual impetuous thing. Overlooking the fact that he was not a French citizen, he had tried to investigate the conditions under which these unfortunates were living. The result was that he had got himself arrested as a political suspect. During the period that Lanny had not heard from him he had been in jail in Toulouse, and only the tireless efforts of his wife, a Frenchwoman, had got him free. Neither of the pair had attempted to inform Lanny, because they knew they must never write anything which would do him harm if it fell into the wrong hands. Now here was Raoul, pale from confinement and bitter with resentment, not for one person but for a hundred thousand, asking Lanny what could be done to get the facts before the public. Another skirmish of the civil war in France!

Ordinarily, Lanny would have said: "I will take the story to Rick." But not now. He explained: "I have pretty good information, Raoul, that Hitler will attack through Belgium and Holland the day after tomorrow."

So, the Spanish refugees would have to be left inside their stockades for the present. Raoul wanted to know what he could do, and his friend said: "Go to *Le Populaire* and get them to publish a warning, a bugle call. *Aux armes, citoyens!* Tell them to cover the front page with it."

"But how can I tell them that I know it?"

"Say that you have a connection with the German Socialist movement. Make it positive and explicit, but nothing that could point to me. Do your best, for it is the most important thing you will ever have a chance to do. And try to keep out of jail, because you and Julie are the only persons in France who know my secret and can make use of my information."

"I don't know where I'll be," said Raoul. "The police have me marked, of course."

"Keep me informed wherever you go. But don't write anything except about paintings. Doré is good. Next time I hope it may be *Il Paradiso!*"

"A fine chance of that," was the reply, "if the Nazis enter Belgium the day after tomorrow!"

V

Lanny went back to his *deux cent familles*, and to the Comité des Forges, whose heads were striving desperately for an arrangement to have both sides spare the steel mills and coal mines. Lanny reported to Hélène de Portes, and became aware that he had made a hit with that ambitious lady. She entrusted him with the fact that there had occurred that day a violent quarrel between her Premier and the hated Minister of National Defense. Paul had wanted to replace the elderly General Gamelin, and put in someone who believed in attacking; but "Dala," timid and vacillating himself, insisted upon retaining the old gentleman who could be counted upon to stay behind his concrete. The situation was embarrassing for the Comtesse, for the thing she wanted was not what her lover wanted, but what the odious Edouard wanted, and she had been obliged to compel Paul to drop the unfortunate project. Such was the *fleur-du-lit de la belle France!*

The political lady went on to put her career in Monsieur Budd's hands—so she declared. She and her friends had under negotiation a matter of supreme importance, concerning which her beloved Paul had not yet been informed. The matter now hung in the balance, and they needed someone to travel to Brussels. Would Monsieur Budd possibly be willing to perform this great service? Lanny replied that he had no purpose and no thought at the present moment but to avert the calamity of war—real war, as opposed to "phony"—from the old continent which he had made his home.

Très bien! He was to be entrusted with a note of introduction to an important gentleman connected with the Belgian court, and he might even be invited to meet His Majesty. There was a certain set of proposals under consideration, and the answer might be too secret to be entrusted to paper—he might be asked to memorize it and bring it back in his head. The Comtesse apologized for putting such a burden upon him; she might have sent a Frenchman, but Frenchmen were known, and here had come an American, as it were *une merveille*, one who possessed the confidence of the British government, and his father was an airplane manufacturer, so that he might well be traveling on some such errand.

Lanny replied that he frequently attended to small matters for his father, and he had met through Baron Schneider an important steel man of Brussels, and might call upon him and enlist his co-operation in influencing the German industrialists. Madame la Comtesse was delighted, and wrote the note of introduction to His Majesty's man, and added: "I hope we are not imposing upon your kindness too greatly; also that you are not afraid of danger."

"Danger, madame?" said the messenger, missing no crumb of information that might fall from the table of a Premier's mistress. "You mean that hostilities may start so soon?"

"How can one tell, monsieur? One hears so many rumors, and meets so many persons who claim to know what is in the minds of statesmen and generals."

Lanny had given no hint of what he knew, or thought he knew. Now he smiled amiably and replied: "I can understand that your home must be a whispering gallery. As for danger, let me explain that I began visiting in Germany when I was a small boy. One of my oldest friends is General Emil Meissner, and when I was in Berchtesgaden last August I learned that he was commanding an army corps on the Belgian front; so you see, if I were captured it would be a social occasion, and I might be able to bring you even more important communications than the one I am scheduled to receive in Brussels."

"*Vraiment, monsieur!*" exclaimed the *grande dame*. "*Vous êtes un messager des dieux!*" Lanny kissed her hand, which was thin and wrinkled, with enameled purple nails, and knuckles stained yellow and smelling strongly of nicotine. Her dark eyes were set in deep hollows, and her skin was gray where it was not rouged. Lanny thought: "This woman is living on the last quiver of her nerves."

VI

This interview took place on the evening of the 9th of May, and his plane was to fly from Le Bourget field at ten the next morning, and put him down in Brussels in time for lunch with His Majesty's man. When he returned to the Crillon, *Der Tag* was less than two hours away—that is, if Monck's information was correct, and if Professor Pröfenik, or the little old lady on the Nymphenburgerstrasse with the much-worn deck of black cards, had not caused Adi Schicklgruber to change his mind. Rudi Hess was the one who would be collecting omens and bringing them to his master, and Lanny could picture the pair in the magnificent study of the New Chancellery, poring over the reports and worrying—the Führer rushing about and slapping his thighs and breaking out in scoldings at somebody who had given him advice contrary to the course which he wished to follow. It would still be Göring versus Ribbentrop, Hess versus Goebbels; they would come and present their arguments, each seeking some new extreme of flattery, some way to persuade *Die Nummer Eins* that the project they advocated was his, not theirs. One or the other would strike the right key, and the Führer of the Germans would have an inspiration, an intuition; he would know what his destiny called him to do, and he would give his thigh a still harder slap and shout: "*Ich hab's!*"

Lanny wondered, should he have gone to Berlin and tried to get the news at first hand, and perhaps to influence it? But what influence could he expect to have, a fellow-countryman and subject of the hated Rosenfeld, the pluto-democratic-Jewish-Bolshevik intriguer and enemy of the Herrenvolk; he, the son of a man who was making weapons for the British and the French, no longer for the Germans! No, there just couldn't be any more friendship, any more art-experting or piano-playing or philosophizing on the top of the Kehlstein; there couldn't be any more running back and forth, with messages from British statesmen and French cartel-masters. The son of Budd-Erling would have to sit, like any common man, getting his news about Germany via the radio or the newspaper page; and certainly he could no longer indulge in the luxury of imagining that he was changing events, even by the weight of an eyelash, the force of a midge's wing.

He wasn't going to sleep very much that night; he was going to sit up in bed, after the fashion of F.D.R., and search the London and Paris press for hints of what might be coming. He found several, for there had been alarms, one after another, for months. Now the Dutch army had canceled all leaves; and Lanny wondered, had his warnings had anything to do with that?

He turned the dials of his portable radio, keeping it low so as not to disturb his neighbors in the hotel. He imagined the Wehrmacht, most elaborate killing machine ever devised by mankind, massing its forces along the line, all the way from the North Sea to the Swiss border. They had been bringing up troops continuously over a period of years, and especially for the past eight months. There would be mass arrivals tonight, everything in darkness and silence. The attack, if it was coming, would be at dawn, which comes early at this season in the high altitudes of Europe. First would come bombing planes, and then an artillery barrage, the greatest in all history; for that, every gun would be in position, carefully camouflaged; the acres of hidden shells would be uncovered in the darkness and brought to the front. Every gun would be already laid on the target—that would be the work of spies who had obtained photographs, and of mathematicians who had calculated range and trajectory. Whole cities had been transplanted to the front lines, a thousand factories of death; and there they lay silent— except for the ticking of carefully synchronized watches.

Unless, of course, Adi Schicklgruber had changed his mind again, and decided to wait for another set of omens, or perhaps for a message from the mistress of the Premier of France, sent by way of the King of the Belgians. Lanny couldn't know; he could only await the ticking of his own watch, and ask himself, was there any word he could have spoken, any person he could have interviewed, any information he could have sent to the Great Father in the White House, that would have averted this continent-wide calamity? He wavered in his own mind, arguing perpetually with himself. Just what was he trying to do? To make another Munich? To postpone the decision, with Hitler getting ready twice as fast as any of his foes? War was such a ghastly thing, yet his reason told him that it had to be fought, and that it had better begin this very morning.

VII

The watcher dropped off to sleep with his bedside light still burning; and when he opened his eyes again he did not know how long he had slept. A glance at the window, and he realized that it was dawn. He reached for the radio and turned to one of the Paris stations. An excited voice was shouting, and it took Lanny a few moments to realize what he was hearing: bombings all over Holland, Belgium, and Northern France; German planes attacking one airfield after another, and rumors of parachute troops landing here and there. Suddenly the sirens of Paris began screaming, and at once the radio went dead.

Lanny realized that this must be it; this was the news for which the world had been waiting eight months and ten days. He slipped into his clothes and hurried down to the air-raid shelter, where guests and employees mingled in an irritated promiscuity. Apparently it was a false alarm; and when the "All clear" sounded he hurried back to his room. The radio had come to life, and he didn't want to do anything but stick by it, turning from one station to another, piecing together the details of the most frightful of man-made catastrophes. He forgot to order breakfast, and when the newspapers were brought he hardly glanced at them, for this put them out of date, it put everything else in the world out of date.

He listened as one who had traveled back and forth between France and Germany most of his life, and knew all these roads, these rivers, these bridges; when he heard the name of Venlo, or Arnhem, or Maastricht, it was not just a combination of syllables, it was a set of sights and memories—a town hall, a hotel, perhaps a meal eaten or a painting purchased. Even the shells and the bombs were personal, for he had seen the explosions before his eyes, felt them in his eardrums, and examined the ruin they had wrought in Madrid and Barcelona and Valencia and points between.

The Germans had repeated all the tricks they had used in Poland and Norway, and perfected in the interim. The first attack was upon the airfields of the three nations, in order to destroy their planes on the ground, or make it impossible for them to get into the air. Freight vessels had arrived in Rotterdam and Antwerp, supposedly loaded with merchandise, but really with troops which came out at the appointed hour to seize the arsenals and other strategic places. Paratroopers descended from the skies, and traveling salesmen and tourists emerged from the hotels to show them the way. The great Moerdijk bridge, which crosses the estuary of the Waal and the Rhine rivers, was seized before it could be destroyed; and so on for one place after another. Reports came in fragmentary form, but one who knew how to put them together discovered a pattern—it was like those wasps which prey upon grubs, and which have learned where each separate ganglion lies, and put their stingers in at the precise spot.

At eight o'clock in the morning Lanny took the liberty of calling the private telephone number which the Comtesse de Portes had entrusted to him. He listened for a while to her agonized exclamations and said polite words of sympathy; then he added: "I suppose, madame, there will be no use in my taking the proposed trip under the circumstances."

"No," she replied slowly, as if reluctantly. "I suppose not. What is going to happen, Monsieur Budd?"

"Sooner or later the enemy will be stopped, and there will develop a stalemate, the same as last time. Both sides will dig trenches and sit in them. They will have time to think, and then, perhaps, we can venture to have hopes again."

"You are a wise man," she exclaimed. "Come to see me again, and give me the benefit of your knowledge."

"Indeed, madame, you honor me," he replied. Assuredly no P.A. would say less to the first lady of a great nation—even if she was a left-handed lady!

VIII

A man cannot sit by the radio all day, even to listen to the end of the world. A civilized man has to bathe and dress and order orange juice, or coffee, and soft-boiled eggs and *petits pains*, "little breads," which strikes an American as an amusing phrase. There was mail to be read, and a cablegram from Robbie, a couple of days delayed, asking his son to see Schneider and de Bruyne and request them to use their influence to get a final decision as to whether the French government meant to put up its share for the building of a new Budd-Erling plant. The brass hats were still tied up in their red tape!

Lanny called up de Bruyne and made an appointment to lunch with him, and they talked over the dreadful news. Incidentally the younger man got an item of information which interested him greatly; the United States army and navy were turning back airplanes to Budd-Erling, and Johannes Robin was selling them to the French and British purchasing commissions in New York! A neat little device for helping your friends in trouble, and at the same time preserving the formalities of "neutrality"! The army and navy were getting the promise of much better planes than they turned in, so no ardent patriot could find fault with the arrangement; meantime the existing planes were being loaded onto French and British vessels in American ports, taking the chances of a race through submarine-infested waters. The arrangement was being kept secret, so much so that Robbie had written his son nothing about it; Denis had got the news from the French authorities. The new Minister of National Defense was Daladier, and Lanny and Denis would call on him in the course of the afternoon, and impress upon him the superiority of the Budd-Erling product and the importance of getting it quickly. Merchants of death!

Meantime the news was pouring in, and growing more and more frightful. The Germans were swarming all over Holland, and it was evident that the carefully prepared defenses of that little country were not counting for much. The main attack was centered at the southernmost tip, where Belgium and Holland and Germany meet; the defenses of two small countries had not been co-ordinated, since that might have been a violation of "neutrality." Now the Nazis didn't have to be neutral, so they rushed their tanks through Maastricht, and their spies and saboteurs and Dutch traitors held the bridges, or held the banks while the engineers built new bridges over the innumerable canals and streams of the Lowlands.

Everything was taken in a rush, because lives meant nothing to Adolf Hitler—not even German lives. Before he came to join his troops he made one of his grandiose speeches declaring: "The fight beginning today decides the fate of the German nation for the next thousand years." He had been getting the nation ready for more than seven years, and had been getting his own youth ready for almost a score. Now he had aroused in them the necessary spirit of "fanaticism"—his favorite word, which he rarely left out of a speech. It took them only five days to sweep over Holland and force its army to surrender and its Queen and government to flee. Just to teach the Dutch the proper fear of Nazi "fanaticism," the bombers came in broad daylight over defenseless Rotterdam and destroyed twenty-six thousand buildings, killing twenty thousand people.

Meantime the armies were on the way through Belgium. The Albert Canal was supposed to be the country's principal defense; it had concrete walls thirty feet high, and was supposed to make a perfect tank trap; but the Belgians had postponed blowing up the bridges, and the spies and paratroopers got there first. In the few cases where a bridge was blown, the Nazi engineers at once appeared with a sectional bridge to fit that spot. Fort Eben-Emael, supposed to be impregnable, was taken in a few hours by a combination of dive-bombers, smokescreens, flamethrowers, and grenadiers. Leopold, King of the Belgians, who had refused Allied help in advance, now called for it loudly, and became angry when it did not arrive in sufficient force. He had lived surrounded by "Rexists," the Fascists of his country, and now he first got the Allied armies into his country, and then surrendered his own armies and left his allies cut off.

IX

Lanny carried out his promise and went to call on Madame de Portes. He found her in a state bordering on hysterics, for she took this Blitzkrieg as a personal affront, a betrayal of her hopes, an exposure of herself as an incompetent political guide. She wanted Lanny to tell her what to do, and of course he had to tell her what he knew she wanted to be told—that some way must be found to stop this cruel slaughter, so ruinous to both France and Germany, and beneficial only to Bolshevists.

There wasn't much for a P.A. to do at the moment; events were happening so fast that nobody could keep up with them, to say nothing of keeping ahead. F.D.R. would get his news in the same way as everybody else, from radio and newspaper correspondents who were posted all over Europe and who told everything the censors would permit. It is in the nature of both armies and governments to try to suppress bad news; but all that anyone needed these days was a map of the countries involved and the names of the places where there was fighting. That frightful new weapon, the German Panzer division, could not be stopped by anything the Allies had. The tanks rolled, and the motorized artillery, and the armored trucks full of men with machine guns and mortars; overhead came the dive-bombers, screaming down from the clouds, blowing up enemy tanks and machine-gunning enemy troops. Nothing could stand up against this combination, and apparently they had no fear of being outflanked—they just raced on and on, and the infantry behind them had nothing to do but hold the places which parachute and air-transport troops had seized.

The Germans had five thousand tanks; and, by an odd quirk of fate, the best of them, with the deadliest fire-power, had come from Czechoslovakia—that magnificent Skoda plant which Baron Schneider had owned and which the Nazis had so rudely wrested from him. What a blow to the men of Munich, what a mockery of their dreams! They might have had those tanks on their own side; they might have had the excellent Czech army, and the Polish army, and, with a little wisdom and good faith, the Russian army; but instead, the tanks came crashing through the Ardennes forest and broke the line which the French had extended there. Only five days after the start of the offensive they crossed the river Meuse and took Sedan; Lanny remembered the steep wooded sides of that valley, thickly studded with pillboxes, and he wondered, where was the French army and what was it doing? In the drawing-rooms of Paris, ladies and gentlemen looked at each other, dazed by this news, and saying: "Our real forces have not gone into action yet." They tried to comfort themselves: "Gamelin is holding back; he is waiting to strike them on the flank; he is leading them into a trap from which they will not escape."

But the insiders, those who were close to the government, were not fooling themselves; they knew by the end of the first week that the Nazis had created a weapon that neither the French nor the British could stand up against. The breakthrough on the Meuse was widened to more than a hundred miles, and there were tank battles on the plains beyond the river. The only question was, which way would the Germans head—straight west toward Paris, or north to outflank the British army, or south to take the Maginot Line from the rear, a possibility which had not been considered when that one-hundred-thousand-million-franc monstrosity was constructed. The Germans did not delay to let them know; in one day they drove to the river Somme, and turned north up that valley, all the way to the Channel, penetrating like a scythe and ready like a scythe to cut down everything within the sweep of its blade.

X

Strolling past the Café de la Rotonde, Lanny was hailed by a familiar voice and saw a familiar shock of red hair, belonging to one of the newspaper fellows whom he had known in the good old days of the League Assemblies in Geneva. Ordinarily he dodged publicity perils, but now he wanted to listen to somebody, anybody. Here, it turned out, was a man who had been up at the Sedan front, and now was having a drink to restore himself after a futile bout with the French censors. This was a story for which the whole world sat waiting, a story of the French army in a sort of general abdication of its functions, the soldiers stopping to fight here and there at the word of some officer whom they knew and trusted, but mostly marching cross-country away from the battlefields and in the general direction of home; now and then tumbling into a ditch when strafing planes came roaring down upon them, but otherwise having slight interest in the war.

"Nothing like it has ever happened in the world," said "Knick," and spread out an afternoon paper, in which the public of Paris was told under startling headlines that the heroic *grande armée de la république* was now ready and that the great counterattack was to be expected at any moment, the hammer blow that was going to shatter the German scythe, and cut off those Panzer divisions which thought they had cut off the British and French. "Listen to this sapient expert," said the correspondent, and read how the Germans had overextended themselves as no army had ever dared to do in history; the distance from their base to the Channel was some three hundred kilometers, and every meter of it was exposed to attacks from both sides, by powerful and perfectly equipped French and British forces. "They have committed suicide," declared this expert.

"What he says would be perfectly correct," declared Knick, "if only the French wanted to fight; but they don't."

"How do you explain it?" inquired the P.A.

"There's only one explanation possible—that is, treason at the top. The heads of the French army are Nazis at heart, and don't want to fight their best friends."

"That sounds like motion-picture stuff, Knick," said Lanny.

"Call it what you please," replied the other. "It's what a lot of us Americans have decided is the truth. How can you have lived all these years in France and not realized how the German and Italian and Spanish agents have been working here, and the billions of francs they have been pouring out? Now they are cashing in."

"Well, you know," explained Lanny, "I'm an art expert, and I've been hunting old masters and not paying much attention to political talk. But I agree with you that the facts ought to be told somehow."

"We're going to find a way to outwit the damned censors, and it won't be long, believe you me!" exclaimed the red-headed and hotheaded correspondent.

XI

Lanny went out to spend a week-end at the Château de Bruyne. In an upstairs room lay *le capitaine, Denis fils,* with a bullet hole through his right shoulder blade and another through his left arm. He had got these near Maubeuge, where his regiment had been rushed forward to the aid of Belgium. The Blitzkrieg had rolled over it, and Denis had crawled into some thick brush and lain there till dark. Then he had found a couple of his men and with their help had got out by a side path and been taken to the rear in a French car. When his wounds had been dressed and he had had a night's sleep, he had made his own way home. Obviously, they wouldn't want anybody in a hospital who was able to walk, and to stay near the front would not help to win the war but merely invite capture by the onrushing hordes.

His devoted wife was taking care of him, and his father let him alone, for they had had a violent disagreement concerning the war and its causes. Eight and a half months at the front had sufficed to make the son into a patriot, convinced that his country had been tricked into inaction, and that the Nazis meant to conquer it completely, take away its industries, and set it to growing wheat and wine and fruit for German tables. He was lying helpless, unable to lift a newspaper or turn a radio dial, but chafing like a caged animal, eager to get back into the fight. He could hardly bring himself to believe the news he heard, and the tears ran down his cheeks as Lanny assured him that the worst was true, the Germans had taken Abbeville at the mouth of the Somme, and cut off the British army and a large section of the French, including Denis's own division. Now the British were making a desperate stand in Calais, but how they could escape was impossible to imagine.

Lanny sat with his hand resting on the younger man's knee and let his tears flow. This was Marie's son, and Lanny had known him since he was a lad in short trousers, and had shared his confidences, and of late years managed to avoid argument, no matter how far apart they drifted. Now he listened to Denis's story, and answered his questions. Yes, it was terrible, incredible; Lanny had been staggered, like everybody else. The German armor had been stronger and their airplanes far more numerous. Denis cried out that it wasn't only that, it was the French spirit that had failed; not the common soldier, who was still the *brave garçon* he had always been, but the men at the top, *les sales politiciens*, quarreling among themselves——

"France is a free country," put in the older man. "There must be disagreement in a republic."

"Yes, but we have abused our freedom. In the face of such a foe, it was our necessity to come to an understanding, and to protect our heritage. We could have had just as good tanks, just as good planes as the Germans."

"You know I did what little I could on that score, Denis."

"Where were our planes while we were fighting? I pledge you my word I never saw one, not one the whole time. But the Germans were over us all day, like a swarm of bees, diving down with screaming noises, that were supposed to frighten us worse than the bullets—and they did, with some. *Mon dieu, c'était affreux!*"

XII

Such was the conversation upstairs; and downstairs Lanny entered the drawing-room and found his elderly host in conference with a visitor whose face was known to everyone in France, and indeed wherever people read newspapers. It was a wide face with prominent cheekbones, heavy-lidded dark eyes, and large lips partly concealed by a thick black mustache. The man's complexion was olive green, and his heavy hair drooped and needed cutting; when he became excited the muscles swelled in his bull's neck, he shook his head violently, and a lock of hair fell over into his eyes. He was rarely without a cigarette, and kept it between his lips so long that you worried about the possibility of his mustache catching fire.

He had one of those unusual names which spell backward the same as forward, and he had taken that as a lucky omen, the promise of a great career. He had been born in a small village in Auvergne, where his father had been butcher, tavernkeeper, and postmaster. Little Pierre had had to drive twelve miles every day to get the mail, and on the way he had read newspapers and learned about the world. He had become a lawyer, and espoused the cause of the poor and lowly; he was one of those Frenchmen who learn politics in the Socialist movement, and then climb out of it to fame and fortune. The Auvergnats play in French humor the same part as the Scots in England; they are supposed to love and cherish money, and Pierre had set out to make immense amounts of it, and now was said to be worth a hundred million francs. It was the French version of the theme, "Home-town boy makes good," for he had come back to his village of Chateldon and bought the medieval castle on the hill, also the medicinal springs, and was making a fortune out of exploiting the water.

He rose politely when Lanny came in; and Denis said: "This is my old friend, Lanny Budd. Monsieur Laval."

"I have had the pleasure of meeting Monsieur Budd," replied the ex-Premier.

"More than once," said Lanny. "The last time I saw you was on the beach at Cannes." He knew that under that proper black vest was a mat of hair like a bear's.

"Lanny is one of us," added the elderly host. "You may speak freely in his presence." He addressed the visitor as "*mon cher Maître,*" which meant that he thought of him as a lawyer, in which capacity he had served Denis for many years. Laval in return used the phase *"mon vieux,"* which is about equivalent to "old fellow," and meant that when a man has been three times Premier of France and is now a Senateur, he is on familiar terms with even the richest and haughtiest.

They resumed their seats, and Laval gave a tug at his stiff collar, as if his tie was too tight. He invariably wore a white string tie of wash material, a practice which his foes called a measure of economy, but which Lanny guessed was a political device, on the theory that in a democratic land a statesman should have some harmless eccentricity to amuse his constituents.

Said Denis: "Monsieur Laval has come to discuss with me the measures which will have to be taken to save *la patrie*."

Lanny understood that this was intended to get the conversation started in its former confidential vein. He assisted by remarking: "I hope it is something which can be done without delay, so that we may spare Paris the calamity which we have witnessed in Rotterdam."

"Vous avez raison, Monsieur Budd!" exclaimed Laval, and realized that this was a man of sense. "I have, as you may know, felt it necessary to retire from public life for a time, and let a band of Leftist adventurers have their way with France. I had done all I could to check them."

"I understand that you breed beautiful race horses on your estate in Normandy," remarked Lanny, with his most winning smile.

"Vraiment, Monsieur Budd! You should come and visit me some day and see them."

"First we have to make peace, Monsieur Laval. I hope that you are using your immense political influence to that end."

XIII

After that there was no reason for a statesman to hesitate. He explained that it had been the dream of his life to bring about a Mediterranean Federation, to include France, Italy and Spain; in such a group France, with her greater wealth, population and culture, would inevitably have become the leader. But this aim had been thwarted, and now it was necessary to recognize the fact that Germany had won the leadership, and was going to establish the new European order. To resist further would be suicide; it was obvious that the greater the expense to which Germany was put, the greater the reparations which France would be expected to pay.

"It should be obvious to any thinking man that once we have made friends with Germany, she no longer has any interest in hurting us; Russia is her true foe, and ours, and only camouflaged sedition could keep us from recognizing that. Now we shall have to submit to humiliation for a time, but once we convince the Germans of our good faith we can become full partners in the New Order. All that Hitler is trying to do is to put the right men in control of France."

Who these right men were could be a matter of no uncertainty to Pierre Laval. Unquestionably the man to become President of the new government was Marshal Pétain, who had abandoned his Spanish mission and was awaiting the new call to serve his country. As for Premier, Laval would not have been himself if he had been shy about submitting his claims. He was the intimate friend of Otto Abetz, and trusted by all the Germans; they knew that he had been the determined advocate of peace between the two nations, ever since the days before Hitler, when he, as Premier, had taken Briand, his Foreign Minister, to visit Hindenburg in Berlin. Now he named a proposed Cabinet, composed of the old-time pacifists, renegade Socialists like himself, and German agents. Bonnet, he declared, had raised a fund to promote this cause, though he did not meet Laval publicly, for reasons of politics.

Lanny listened, and found it according to the reports which he had already sent in. He ventured to suggest one or two names, and Laval revealed that he was in touch with these persons. Owner of a great chain of newspapers, this *fripon mongole*, as his enemies called him, knew everybody in France who could be bought or influenced to work against the cause of democratic Socialism which had given him his education and his career. Lanny observed with repugnance difficult to conceal the rancid hatred which Laval manifested for those men in public life who had remained true to their youthful ideals. He who was suspected of having Mongolian blood—and with good reason, since the hordes of Attila had penetrated into central France—did not hesitate to spit upon Mandel and Blum because they were Jews, and to accuse Daladier of corruption—this man who had made his millions by protecting every kind of stockmarket racketeer, and by showing the great rich masters of the Comité des Forges how to conceal their profits and their frauds.

Lanny knew all this because Denis had described it to him in past years. This *"cher Maître"* knew nothing of the law except such devices, and his ignorance of all cultural subjects was so great that he had to make a joke of it. Maître Torrès had asked him which of two painters he preferred, and he had answered that he had no time to attend vaudeville. He laughed uproariously over this. A coarse, hard countryman, who knew the ways of this world, and had no friend but his own pocketbook, he had admired, first the Fascists, then the Nazis, because they were fellows of that sort, and he wanted such to take charge of France and make it over in their own image. Since the French voting public—heirs and victims of a revolutionary tradition—wouldn't do it themselves, let Hitler and Mussolini and Franco step in and do it for them.

"Put me in charge," said Pierre Laval, "and I'll stay in. Believe me, *mon vieux*, the job won't have to be done a second time!"

XIV

Lanny returned to the Crillon and wrote a report concerning the program for a collaborationist France. He mailed it to the Embassy, and breathed a silent prayer that the American diplomatic pouches were not being tampered with en route. If any government knew their contents, the Nazi-Fascist agents would soon share the secret, and it would be all up with Lanny's career, and perhaps with Lanny.

Two weeks and two days after the start of the Blitzkrieg, Lanny heard over the radio that Calais had been taken, and heard the Germans claim that they had a million French and British troops pinned against the Channel coast. In the evening he went to Baron Schneider's home, and met some of the bewildered industrialists who were still trying to figure how to save their properties. What a tragic blunder that they had failed to appease Hitler, by giving him colonies, and perhaps even Alsace-Lorraine!

One or two who still had the idea of fighting wanted to know how many planes were coming from America, and Lanny had the sad duty of telling them that there weren't many to come. Fighter planes couldn't be flown across, but had to be crated and stowed in ships, which took both time and space. They were being sent now to Casablanca, and French mechanics, unfamiliar with the plane, were slow with the work of assembly. The men of great affairs shook their heads sadly and wished they had taken the advice of the Budds, *père et fils*, a year or two years ago. The sirens sounded while they were talking, and they turned pale; they were not fighting men, but dealt with one another on the basis of engraved or signed pieces of paper, and on any other basis they could not imagine how to live.

When Lanny returned to his hotel, quite late, he found a note from Madame de Portes, asking him to call her. She was a difficult person to see, for she spent most of her time sitting on the desk of the Premier of France, giving orders to admirals and generals and Cabinet members, and threatening them if they did not obey. Her Paul had been ill and was only partly recuperated; he spent his time in an inner room, receiving one person after another, and trying to get up the courage to counter some of the decisions his *amie* had made. Their disagreements were public, and were surely not good for the morale of Marianne.

Lanny called the apartment and she was not there. He called the Quai d'Orsay, where the Premier had his office, and then he heard her voice. She asked if he could come to her apartment at a half hour after midnight; there was to be an important conference—*très, très,* she said, and they might need his help. He replied that he would be at her service.

It was a brisk walk across the Place de la Concorde. Lanny remembered this as it had been after World War I, with rows of captured German cannon of many sizes. He crossed the great bridge where, six years ago, he had watched a Fascist mob trying to get to the Palais Bourbon, where the Chamber of Deputies was in session. Some people had been shot, and "Dala," then in his first premiership, had got the blame; it had broken his nerve, and he had never been the same man since.

Now it was little Paul's turn, and his nerve, too, was failing; the blood had gone out of his face, and he looked ghastly. A strange face it was, with eyebrows not curved but bent in a sharp angle, and a wide mouth like a clown's mask; his enemies called him "the Mickey Mouse of France." He did not know which way to turn, or whom to trust; he could not appoint any real *belliciste* to any position of importance, because Hélène would fly into hysterics and make it impossible for him to sleep.

Madame had not arrived, so Lanny sat in the overdecorated drawing-room with silk-upholstered furniture. Presently the door bell rang, and he heard a familiar quavering voice, and realized who was the important person he was to meet. He arose and went to the door, and saw two military aides taking the elaborate bandbox hat, with three rows of golden oak leaves around it; also the heavy overcoat which the caller wore even at the end of May. They led him into the room—poor old gentleman of eighty-four, it was at least three hours after his bedtime, but he was toddling about trying to save his beloved native land. The front of his gray uniform bore many decorations, and he had enjoyed about every honor a French soldier could win—Generalissimo, Inspector-General of the Armies, Chef de la Defense du Territoire,

Inspector-General of Aviation, Vice-President of the Supreme War Council, Minister of War, Permanent Member of the Inner War Council, and, since the last ten days, Vice-Premier of France.

Lanny rose respectfully, and stood until the venerable caller had been seated; then he approached, and, taking no chances with senility, said: "You may remember me, Monsieur le Maréchal; I am Lanny Budd, who had the honor of calling upon you recently in Madrid. I am the son of Robert Budd, of Budd-Erling Aircraft."

"*Ah, oui, oui!*" replied the quavering voice. "I remember you very well. You were sent to me by—by——"

"Denis de Bruyne," put in Lanny, without delay.

"*Ah, vraiment*, I remember you well. Your father should send us more aircraft, Monsieur Budd; they would be useful at this moment."

"I am sure that my father is doing everything in his power, Monsieur le Maréchal."

There was nothing wrong with Lanny's memory, and he had in mind the positive assurance which the elderly officer had given him in Madrid that the part which airplanes would play in this war had been greatly exaggerated. Furthermore, this eminent authority had declared that he would ask for nothing better than to see the Germans come out from their so-called Siegfried Line and attack the Maginot. "I should pray to be in command of the French armies at that time, Monsieur Budd!" Now word had just come that the King of the Belgians was on the point of surrendering his army and his country; and Lanny ventured the guess that this had something to do with his being called to renew his dealings with the venerable Henri Philippe Benoni Omer Joseph Pétain.

XV

Madame la Comtesse arrived, apologizing volubly for keeping the hero of Verdun waiting, even for a minute. After her hand had been kissed, her first action was to light a cigarette. A servant placed a tabouret by her chair, with an ashtray upon it; and thereafter during the conference she was not once without a lighted cigarette in her fingers. She was almost beside herself with nervousness, and would jump up and pace the room, gesticulating in the excited French manner. Now and then she would move to the tabouret and dump off a load of ash, without for an instant ceasing her rattle of conversation.

Lanny had guessed correctly; the calamity in Belgium made a decision necessary in France. To him the King's action seemed a cowardly betrayal, and Hélène revealed that her Paul was going to say that over the radio in the morning. She herself exclaimed: "What else could the poor man do?"—and so Lanny could be sure there had been another battle between them, and might be one all this night, or rather, early this morning.

"Our situation has become desperate. We may have bombs falling on this building before daylight!" Such were the words of the Premier's guiding spirit. "You know as well as I do, Monsieur le Maréchal, that Hitler does not wish to destroy Paris, and that only our insensate folly can cause it to happen."

"You are entirely right, madame," replied the idol of France. His hands trembled as he gestured, and his pointed white mustache revealed that his lips were trembling also. Lanny had taken a chair close to him, and could look into his bright blue eyes. "I have received every possible assurance of friendship from Baron von Stohrer in Madrid, and only this morning I received a message from him through Señor Beigbeider." The former of these was the Nazi ambassador to Spain, and the latter was the Spanish ambassador to France, for all practical purposes a Nazi agent in Paris. Franco had been a pupil of the French Marshal in the École Militaire of France, and both of them were Catholics, both Royalists, both believers in a Fascist alliance and in a Europe populated by devout, industrious, and obedient peasants.

The Marshal went on to repeat the ideas with which his mind had been stuffed during several months in Madrid. The Führer wanted what you might call a polite war, and a purely technical victory over France. He had no real quarrel with the country, only those vile Leftist elements whom the Marshal hated as much as did the Führer. *Eh bien, alors*, why should not friends combine against their true enemies? Let the French make an honorable retreat and then a nominal capitulation, and the New Order could be made safe for all Europe. The old gentleman talked Nazi talk, and Cagoulard talk, both of them comparatively new; later on, he was talking an older kind, which he had learned when he was a toddling child instead of a toddling dotard. That was Catholic talk; said he: "Liberty is immorality." And presently: "France is being punished for her loss of faith." Then, to this raging political woman: "Calm yourself, madame, and remember that what happens in this world is of minor concern to us or to anyone; our destiny lies in eternity, and what is important is the salvation of our own souls and our country's."

XVI

To speak of the Premier's mistress and the Vice-Premier of France might sound like a cruel pun, but it was one which had been created by history and the language makers. This pair assuredly had no humor concerning themselves, or the effort they were making to keep their native land in its ancient patterns. Better to turn it over to its hereditary foe, who would discipline it well, than permit it to fall into the hands of atheistic, libertarian, and collectivist revolutionaries. *Semper eadem*, always the same, was the motto of their Holy Mother Church, and within the last century her Popes have solemnly repudiated all that charter of liberties upon which the democratic world is being built—freedom of speech, press and worship.

What this reactionary pair wanted of Lanny Budd was that he should return to the powerful friend who had sent him here, and say: "France is done for, France must save herself by quitting the war; but she does not wish to humiliate her great ally by leaving her alone; indeed, it would not help France to withdraw alone, for she would only become a launching platform for an attack upon Britain. The wise course is for the two countries standing together to make the best terms they can, which Hitler has promised us will be lenient."

Said Marshal Pétain: "I have been assured by several authorities that the Führer is prepared to guarantee without qualification the integrity of Britain and the British Empire."

"He has told me that himself," agreed Lanny.

"Then you will do this for us?" inquired the Comtesse, eagerly.

"I will go, madame, and will do my best; but do not ask me to promise to succeed. You must bear in mind that Winston Churchill is now Prime Minister and he is an extremely arrogant man. I have had opportunities to talk with him and I know."

"He is a dreadful man, an unscrupulous man!" exclaimed Hélène. "He must be put out of office before the world can have peace."

"I doubt very much, madame, if Lord Wickthorpe has any power to put him out of office, unless it were by killing him. All that I can do is to take your message and explain the circumstances as I have found them in France. Of course, as the military situation worsens, the advisability of your course will become more clear. If the armies in Flanders should be forced to surrender, then I doubt if Churchill would have the power to resist, even if he wished to."

"What you say is true," admitted the woman. "But it is also true that the longer we wait, the more severe the terms will grow, and the greater the reparations we shall have to pay. If we had had enough political sense we should have made terms before this dreadful fighting started."

"Quite so, madame; but political sense is, alas, not always to be had upon demand. I will plead your cause in London to the best of my ability, and if I have any effect, Monsieur Reynaud will learn of it through the regular diplomatic channels. In order that there may be no misunderstanding, please tell me explicitly, am I to say that this course is one which the Premier himself desires and recommends?"

Lanny expected to see the woman show signs of hesitation at this point; but she was an old intriguer, and had anticipated the question. "You are to say that this is the course to which Monsieur Reynaud is being forced by the tragic events of the hour. It will quite probably be his decision by the time you arrive in England. Strictly between us, it is my intention to bring him to that point of view."

"I understand, madame; and France is fortunate in having someone in her service who is capable of looking ahead and making decisions. Have you any way in mind for me to reach London?"

"I have arranged for a military plane to fly you there, leaving Le Bourget at eight this morning."

This wasn't so agreeable to Lanny, because it was getting him established as an official person; but he didn't see quite how to get out of it. "Madame," he said, "I am not a coward, but I assume that you want your messenger to arrive. The German planes are active now, I have been told."

"Your pilot will have orders to fly west, and to approach England by way of Cherbourg. That, I am assured, will be quite safe."

"Thank you, madame." He kissed the tobacco-stained hand—for the last time, though he did not know it. He was tickled on both cheeks by the aged Marshal's white mustachios—something which was more than the proprieties required, and was meant as a paternal demonstration, in honor of a faithful son who was going into danger. He took it as an honor, and said: "*Merci, mon cher Maréchal.*" He, too, enlisting!

XVII

He went back to his hotel and wrote a report on the hopes and plans of the French Fascists. He put it into the mail, and then slept for a while, until the hotel desk awakened him. He was up, and bathed and dressed, radioed and breakfasted—if one can put it that way—by a little after seven, when Madame's own car came to take him to the airfield. The driver was a young man from the South, Madame's own estate, and Lanny sat by him on purpose and encouraged him to talk—which is seldom difficult with the people of the Midi. He expressed his opinion of the *Fridolins,* and didn't seem to love them, or to be particularly anxious to surrender France to them. He wanted his passenger's idea of the prospects, and Lanny had to evade, saying that nobody knew anything except what came over the air, and you had to choose your station carefully.

This enquiring American had for some time been convinced that now and then, under circumstances as yet beyond guessing, it happened that the human mind was able to pierce the veil of the future and get a glimpse of events which were on the way. But he possessed no trace of that strange faculty himself, and he rode in this car and listened to this dark-skinned Marseillais, and had no slightest intimation of the fact that exactly one month from this date the man was destined to crash the car into a tree and kill Madame de Portes and seriously injure her lover. This was after the French government had fled to Bordeaux, and after Laval had succeeded in ousting "the Mickey Mouse of France." She was taking her Paul to that estate which she loved, but was not destined to see. Hélène Rebuffel, daughter of a wealthy contractor, had had ambitions, and had risen as high as it was possible for a woman to rise in the France of her day, where women did not vote or hold office, but intrigued in the *salons* and the *lits.* Her death was considered a cruel stroke by her friends; but perhaps fate was wiser than any of these, and was sparing her sights and experiences which might have been beyond her power to endure.

30

Those in Peril on the Sea

I

FROM Paris to Cherbourg and from there to Southampton and into the interior of England is a journey which would have taken Lanny's forefathers at least a week; but now, by the eagle's route, he made it in less than an hour. They put a flying suit on him, and a parachute, and gave him an oxygen mask to be used in case of need. Speed was safety, and the pilot poured it on; they climbed and climbed, and there was a crackling in Lanny's ears. He looked down upon the tiny checkerboard fields of France, most of them bright green at this season; he looked at the Channel, gray, with faint irregular lines like haircloth. Then it was England, with stretches of open downs, and woodlands, and fields with the pattern of a crazy quilt.

The roar of the engine drowned out all other sounds. Lanny could have talked with the pilot by putting on a headset; but he observed the young officer scanning the sky, above, below, and at all points of the compass, stopping only now and then for a glance at his instrument panel. Lanny decided that this was a worthy work, not to be interrupted. He wondered, what would this handsome lieutenant of aviation be thinking about carrying a civilian passenger while his country's armies were in rout? Lanny knew from young Denis what the French soldiers in the field were thinking about this fighter plane not being over their heads, and the idea confirmed him in the decision to keep still.

He had chosen an airport toward the west as his goal, both because it was safer than Croydon, and because he would be less apt to meet anyone who knew him. The pilot had a couple of strip maps in his pocket, and now and then he glanced at them; when he made out the airport ahead he nodded to Lanny and pointed. Their coming had of course been announced, but there would be no radio beam; the plane circled once, so that its identity might be established, and a man ran out into the field onto the runway, waving a flag. Then the plane began to slide down, and soon came lightly to rest on the field. Military police hurried up, and the arrivals established their identity; Lanny displayed his passport, properly visaed, and then he shook hands with his pilot. "*Merci bien, mon lieutenant.*" The pilot bowed from the waist, he bowed to the Englishmen, and then turned his plane about and was off for home.

Lanny asked to be taken to the railroad station. He did not say where he was bound or what was his errand, and nobody asked him. From the station he called Ceddy's private number in London, and left word that he would be waiting at the Castle, a short ride distant. He was sure that Ceddy would come there, and guessed that he'd prefer to have the meeting unobserved.

Lanny found a garage man who would drive him to the Castle for no excessive fee—"business as usual"; but on that short drive he learned that there were many changes taking place in England. For one thing, all the road signs had been taken down or hidden; the order had come over the radio and it had been done in one night. Roads were being blockaded, except for narrow, one-way passages which could be quickly closed. Every field that was big enough for a plane to land on was having deep trenches dug across it, and dead trees and derelict automobiles dragged out as obstacles. England had waked up all of a sudden, and every evening on the village commons you would see the middle-aged men and the half-grown boys drilling—with broomsticks if they had nothing better. So the driver informed this American stranger, and added: "The bloody Hun won't have as easy a time on this island as he expects."

II

At the Castle Lanny received a message; his lordship and her ladyship were taking the first train. They came in just at lunchtime, but they didn't want to eat—they wanted to get Lanny off in Ceddy's study and hear his report. But very soon it turned out that they didn't want to hear much, because it was all useless, all out of date, there was nothing that could be done along those lines. Lanny thought that never in his life had he met two such completely bewildered and disorientated persons. Quite literally, their world had come to an end, and they knew it but couldn't make it real to themselves; they would say that there was a new England, but in the next sentence they would be talking about the old England and what they were going to do with it; they would stop in the middle of the sentence, realizing that what they were saying must sound like nonsense to the hearer.

The Nazis had won the war. There could be no question about that; the French armies were trapped or routed, the British army would have to surrender, and there simply was nothing left to fight with— no troops, no guns, no equipment, absolutely nothing. It was madness to try to go on—and yet, there was that madman, Winston, refusing to listen to reason, the bull-headed, roaring maniac, shouting people down, ordering impossibilities, turning Number 10 Downing Street into a lunatic asylum. And the worst of it was he had got the people behind him; they were determined to fight, even though they had no weapons, even though it could mean nothing but the destruction of their homes and the death of everybody in them.

"They just hate the Germans, Lanny," declared the Earl of Wickthorpe. "They hate them with a blind, insensate hatred there's no controlling. What the Nazis have done in Poland and Norway and Holland has been too shocking to everybody."

"I know," admitted the American. "It's too bad they couldn't have been more tactful."

"The French don't seem to feel so bitter as we do—at least, so I gather from various sources."

"Some do, but not so many as here. The French have been beaten in war now and then, and they find it easier to imagine giving up and starting all over."

Bit by bit, Lanny made his report. He told what the steel men had said, and the great industrialists, and the statesmen; what Laval was planning, and what Pétain and Madame de Portes had commissioned him to propose. "We should have done it six months ago if we were going to do it," said the Foreign Office man. "Now it's hopeless, and no good even to talk about it. The P.M.'s head is set, and if he hears even so much as a whisper of reconcilement, or even of discussing terms, out you go on your ear."

Lanny permitted himself a comment. "I was certainly surprised when I heard that Chamberlain had taken a post in the War Cabinet."

"It's like a hurricane, Lanny; nobody can stand against it. It's the cant of the hour that Britain is a democracy, and that the people rule; well, the people have made up their minds that Hitler is anti-democratic, and so they are determined to fight him. What you and I can do about it seems to be very little."

"I suppose I'll have to go back to buying old masters," remarked the American, sadly.

III

They had to go on living, so they went in and ate lunch, and meanwhile, since gossip is always in order, Lanny described his visits to the Premier's mistress, and the final interview with the Vice-Premier. Both Ceddy and Irma did him the honor to say that he had executed his commission with admirable skill; both thanked him, and agreed that the failure of the mission was in no way his fault. All three had done their best, and their defeat was owing to forces beyond their power. "Our time will come later," declared Irma.

"God grant that we don't find London in ruins before that!" exclaimed her husband.

The pair were going back to their duties at once, and Lanny was planning to resume his quiet life with Frances. He said to Irma: "She will ask me questions about events, and you must tell me what you want me to say. I suppose she'll have to be patriotic, like all the other children."

"Of course, Lanny; much as I hate it, I can't expect her to stand out against her whole environment."

They were on their way to visit the child—they made it a practice to see her together now and then, so that she might have no sense of anything abnormal between them, any avoidance of one another's company. Everything must always be as if nothing had ever happened; the words were Irma's, and no sense of humor troubled her as she said them.

She lowered her voice, and continued: "There is something else I want to speak to you about, and that is Ceddy. He is in a most embarrassing position, with the sudden changes that have taken place at the Office."

"I have imagined it," responded the ex-husband, sympathetically.

"You know it is the British tradition that foreign policy is continuous, and the permanent officials stay on. Ceddy isn't supposed to influence policy, but you know that really he does."

"Of course, Irma."

"He might resign; but I think that would break his heart. You can have no idea how proud he is of his career and how much it means to him. He didn't want to be just a member of the House of Lords, an idler, like so many; he wanted to do something worth while, to make good on his own. He has been willing to take orders like anybody else, and to win his promotions."

"I understand perfectly, Irma. I have always admired him for it."

"Now, he's a cog in a machine; and he can't go about quarreling with his colleagues—he has to consider that the decision has been taken, and he has to play the game, to the best of his ability. I shall have to adjust myself. I am an Englishwoman now."

"I think it is a wise decision, Irma; and you may be sure that I won't do or say anything to embarrass you."

"Lanny, you're a brick!" was his ex-wife's verdict. "Don't ever fail to realize that you have taught me a lot."

The ex-husband went off saying to himself: "Good grief! Wickthorpe Castle has gone anti-Nazi! The first thing I know, Nancy Astor will be carrying a gun!"

IV

Lanny listened to the radio. Nine Panzer divisions, each with four hundred tanks and self-propelled guns, had driven through to the Channel, completely cutting off a million French and British troops from connection with the rest of France. The vast might of the Wehrmacht was closing in from the east and south, and crowding the victims into a small pocket against the coast at Dunkirk. The British rearguards were holding desperately, forcing a house-to-house battle at Calais and other places; but they were being steadily driven back, and surrender of the whole force seemed inevitable. A call was going out for the British to organize for home defense; every able-bodied man and boy must prepare to fight with whatever weapons he could lay hands on.

It was the most terrible moment in British history since the days of the Spanish Armada. Lanny had to have comfort, and knew only one place to get it; he went for a walk and telephoned to Rick, making an appointment to meet him by the roadside, as before. They came, Nina driving; and Lanny's first word was: "How is Alfy?"

"He's somewhere in the show," said Rick. "They don't keep us informed."

"No news is good news," ventured the American, thinking of Nina.

"Good news is a scarce commodity this day," countered the Englishman.

They had no special place to go and no petrol to waste, so they stopped in a quiet spot by the roadside, and Lanny listened while Rick confirmed Ceddy's story of this small island's plight. Everything had been sent across to help the French: trained men, guns, ammunition, every sort of equipment; a couple of thousand field guns, nearly a thousand tanks, fifty thousand vehicles! Britain was left naked to her enemy, and the enemy was bound to know it. "We won't even have a chance to destroy anything, Lanny; the Nazis will use it against us."

"Won't you be able to rescue some of the men?"

"We'll be doing all we can, I've no doubt; but think of the situation! The port of Dunkirk will be wrecked by bombs, and there'll be nothing but the open beaches, where the men will be under constant shellfire and strafing from the air. You know what the Channel weather is; and there'll be submarines and motor torpedo boats—we'll probably lose half the ships we send. And even if we get the men, what will they fight with? I doubt if we have more than a full division of properly equipped troops on this island; I'm told we haven't a hundred field guns. You understand all this is confidential."

"Oh, surely!"

"Will they send us anything from America, do you suppose?"

"I can't answer, Rick. I haven't been in touch with America. The events of the last few days are bound to have made a deep impression. Our people will wake up sooner or later."

"It's got to be sooner, Lanny. Time is of the essence. What do you think Hitler will do—take Paris, or try to cross the Channel at once?"

"I wish I had some way to find out. All I know is Paris, and I'm afraid that won't hold him up very long."

He told the story of his visit and what he had found. He didn't mention having been commissioned by Wickthorpe—Rick and Nina could guess about that if they chose. The important thing was the decay in French morale, the fact that what was supposed to be a War Cabinet had a large element of appeasement in it, and that a fighting Premier was being kept awake at night by the scoldings of a mistress who wanted peace at any price and who hated her foes at home more than those abroad.

Rick said: "That's one thing we'll be free of from now on. Our rats have been driven into their holes, and there won't be any more appeasement talk in Parliament or the press. It's a fact about the Englishman—it takes adversity to bring out his strong qualities."

Lanny thought, how true about Rick himself! He was the most pessimistic of men on the subject of his own country; for years now, ever since the coming of Fascism, his conversation had been full of black despair, and he had rarely had any good thing to say about any man in public life. But now he was an Englishman, one among millions who would fight for their freedom and for the cause of freedom throughout the world. "Believe me, Lanny," he declared, "we'll not give up like the Belgians. We'll fight with whatever we have. We'll fight the first German who lands on this island, and we'll fight the last one. The men and the boys and even the women will help."

Rick went on to say that he had joined the Home Guard. Lanny exclaimed: "But you can't march!"

"I can hide in a ditch or a foxhole. I've an old double-barreled shotgun, and some buckshot, and I can get a couple of Nazis before they get me."

V

Lanny went back to the Castle, considerably cheered. After all, the Channel was twenty-two miles wide at its narrowest point, and the Royal Navy had not merely big battleships but a vast fleet of small craft which could do execution upon enemy transports or barges or whatever they would be using. The important thing was that England was awake; everybody knew what had happened in Norway and Denmark, in Holland and Belgium; there were no more tricks that could be sprung. The beaches were being wired and mined, the roads were being blocked; the strategic points were watched day and night, and if paratroopers came down there would be wardens to detect them and a system of warning and rushing defenders to the spot. The lion had his back to the wall now, and his aspect was encouraging—to his friends.

Lanny sat glued to the radio in his cottage, listening to alarms and programs for action at home; but not a word about any efforts at rescuing the trapped forces across the Channel. Whatever was being done, the enemy was not to be told. Not long after dinner there came a telephone call for Lanny, and a familiar voice said: "No names, please. Would you like to see a bit of the war? We have a neighbor whose sons are in the show, and he's lending their motorboat—a pretty fair one. There's a chance for civilians to help."

It seemed manifest that a P.A.'s duty was to say: "Sorry, old chap, but I'm under orders, and not permitted to do anything else." But he had got wrought up by the things he was hearing and reading, and this message produced a sort of brainstorm. He said: "Wait a moment. How long will it take?"

"Three or four days is a reasonable guess. It's only fair to mention that it's dangerous. We're likely to be under fire a good part of the time."

"I've been under fire before. The question is, some other things I have to do."

"It's a temptation, I know, and perhaps I shouldn't bother you."

"Wait a moment. It may fit in with something I've had in mind. When do you plan to start?"

"At daylight tomorrow. I have to know soon, so as to get somebody else if you think you shouldn't. Be sure I won't misunderstand if you say No."

"Give me a minute or two to think it over."

Rick waited. After a while he asked: "Would you like me to call you again, say in a quarter of an hour?"

"No, I think I can fit it in with my job. Where shall I meet you?"

"You'd have to come over here tonight, or else let me pick you up at one of the docks in London. Perhaps the latter would be less conspicuous."

"That's right."

"Well, do you remember the place where the ship was docked when you took your mother to a fancy-dress ball—the one that was called 'A Voyage to the Island of Cythera'?"

"I remember it well."

"That was Charing Cross Pier, and it'll be easy for both of us to find. I can't tell you the hour, because there are locks on the river, and there'll be many boats coming and may be bottlenecks. My guess is, I ought to be there by ten o'clock. You'll just have to sit and watch for me, and I'll come and watch for you. Get yourself some oilskins, and a hat. I'd say wear old clothes, only you haven't any. Wear whatever you value least. The weather may be anything; we take our chances."

"O.K., and thanks."

"I'll bring food and water, but if you pick up some small stuff, like chocolate or raisins, it'll be welcome. A bottle or two of whisky will help the men—they'll be pretty well done up, you know."

"And how about petrol?"

"That'll be furnished on the way."

"It's a date. I'll take the late train from here and spend the night at the hotel. You can call me there if there's any change."

"Cheerio!—and pleasant dreams for your last night on earth!"

Lanny recognized that as typically English. Always take the gloomiest possible view of everything, and keep smiling while you say it!

VI

Lanny put on the suit of clothes which he valued least, and packed his newest and best in a suitcase, a complete outfit: underclothing and socks, shirt and tie and handkerchief, a safety razor, shaving cream, a practically new pair of shoes. He was motored to the station, and took the night train to that strange immense city where theaters and cinemas, restaurants and night clubs were going full blast behind double blackout doors, while the streets outside were dark and silent as if the city were dead. It took him an hour to find a taxicab, but it would have taken still longer to grope his way to the Savoy. Settled in his room he wrote a report on the change of spirit of the British people, and on their dire need. No doubt F.D. would get all that through the regular diplomatic channels, but it was important enough to repeat. His last words were: "I am on my way to see if I can find out who is next on the list. It may be some time before I am able to report."

He slept, as men in war must learn to do when they can. In the morning he went shopping, and found some chocolate, perhaps the last in London, and a few other concentrated foods, some whisky and cigarettes, and a suit of yellow oilskins, including a hat with a strap under the chin. Also he purchased a strip of oilcloth more than a yard square, and took that back to the hotel and wrapped his immaculate outfit and tied it up safely. He left the suitcase in care of the hotel, and had his two large bundles carried out to the taxi by an elderly man who had become a bellboy in the last few weeks. "Goin' on a sea trip, sir?" this functionary inquired, and smiled knowingly. Apparently all London knew what was "up."

"Charing Cross Pier," said the traveler to the taxi driver, and when he arrived, lugged his bundles out to the pier's end. He remembered it from something like eleven years ago, when a ship tied here had been the scene of one of the most fantastic entertainments in fashionable history. It was just before the great panic hit Wall Street and the great depression spread over the world; incidentally it was just before Lanny's marriage to the daughter of J. Paramount Barnes. What a lot of things had happened to him and to the world in those few years!

Now he sat on the end of a short pier and looked across one of the most written-about rivers of the world. There was a haze, and the water looked gray and dingy. On the far side was a solid line of stone piers and embankments, and behind them brick and stone houses— nothing but city as far as the eye could reach, and for miles farther. There were bridges, under which the traffic slipped, and Lanny noticed a peculiar phenomenon—nearly all the traffic was one way. Everything from tiny speedboats to river tugs with as many as fifteen or twenty cabin launches in tow, all gliding silently in the general direction of the morning sun. It was as if they had been seized by what the learned scientists call a phototropism, an impulse to move toward the light. Moths have it, certain flowers have it, and sea-urchin larvae when you drop chemicals into the water, with them. What chemical had been dropped into the River Thames which had caused all the pleasure boats and the work boats to be seized with a common impulse to come chugging out of their houses and their basins and sliding down-current into the pale broad streak of sunlight on the dirty river?

VII

Lanny didn't know exactly what he was watching for, and he kept his eye on every boat which came in sight near the right bank. He hoped that Rick's might be large and safe, with a cabin for comfort; but no such luck—she was just an open launch with an engine in the cockpit under a hood, a steering wheel in front, and a row of seats on each side in which your guests sat while you went put-put-putting on the narrow stream to a tea party or a cricket match. *Gar* was her name, and she was about fifteen feet overall, Lanny judged. He knew it was no boat to cross the Strait of Dover in; but they would have a lot of company, and if they shipped more water than they could bail out with buckets, there would be some of the bigger fellows to pick them up.

The matter of importance was that here was Rick, sitting at the engine, with one leg stretched out straight as it had to be. It was an effort for him to get up, so he didn't, but just waved his hat. At the steering wheel was another man, and the pair of them brought the small craft comfortably against the stone platform at the foot of this ancient wooden pier. "Hello," said Rick, in his casual way. "This is Tom; he's going back for another boat. You're supposed to steer. Do you think you're up to it?"

"I'll learn by doing," replied Lanny, with a grin. He had never owned a motorboat, but he had done his share of sailing, and the steering wheel wasn't so different from that of a car. "I notice the traffic is all one way, so there won't be much chance for collisions."

"Tom," who was somebody's middle-aged handyman, took Lanny's dunnage and stowed it in a dry compartment up forward. Then he got out, and touched his cap, saying: "Good luck, Mr. Rick," and, to Lanny: "Good luck, sir." The engine began its vigorous persistent noise for which there is no name, and by following Rick's instructions Lanny managed to back and turn, and soon they were out in the current, reinforced by an outgoing tide.

On they went, under one bridge after another, past the endless docks and shipping of what had been for a century or two the greatest port of the world. To Lanny these sights brought back one of the unforgettable moments of his life, when he had got married to Irma by the captain of a freighter out in the North Sea, and they had waited at Thames Mouth for the tide, and then a long procession of dingy vessels had come up the river, dropping off, one here and one there, into the great basins where most of the docks were, and the warehouses and railroad terminals. Now everything was bound the other way; apparently all the small craft of the river and a good part of the medium-sized were putting out to sea.

VIII

There was plenty of time for talk. "I suppose you know we're bound for Dunkirk," said Rick; and Lanny answered: "I guessed it. I don't mind the trip, but I'm worried because we can bring back such a small number of men."

"We'll not be bringing them back, Lanny; we're to deliver them to the larger craft. We little fellows with shallow draft will be able to pick them out of the surf if it's not too high."

He explained the situation as it had been made known to the insiders. The harbor had been wrecked and mines had been dropped in the Channel by enemy aircraft. The great pier was being bombed, and might be burning by the time they arrived. The men would be on the beaches, and would wade out into the water as far as they could. "We may be under fire the whole time, and it'll be pretty rugged. I'm not sure I ought to have asked you."

"It's my fight as much as yours," replied the American.

For once, Rick could say that his government had acted promptly and efficiently. Two weeks ago the Admiralty had foreseen the possibility of trouble, and on the day before Holland gave up, the BBC had broadcast an order for all owners of motor craft of between thirty and a hundred feet length to register the same with the Small Vessels Pool. "That doesn't include us; we're just minnows—but I'm told they'll let us go. I saw a couple of chaps setting out down river in canoes with outboard motors. Maybe they'll put them aboard one of the larger vessels; they'll be using washtubs over there, no doubt."

What all Britain was praying for was a spell of decent weather. So far, the damned Führer had got all the breaks: continuous dry weather for his raid on Poland, and again for Holland and Belgium. Now, if only the winds would hold up for a few days, they might be able to save a good part of the British army. "But you know what the North Sea is; a storm can blow up in an hour and swamp all these little craft, and force the big ones away from shore. It can happen at the end of May as well as any other time of the year. God grant us a week's respite!"

Rick wasn't much on piety, as a rule, but this was one of the solemn occasions when an Englishman reverted to the faith of his childhood. "O, hear us when we cry to Thee for those in peril on the sea!"

IX

Past the tidelands and marshes of the lower Thames, they came in early afternoon to Sheerness, at the river's mouth. All boats seemed to be concentrating at the pier, so they joined the immense flock—literally more than either of them had ever seen in one place, and certainly more kinds than they had known existed in the ports of Britain. There were coasters and fisherboats, drifters and tugs, speedboats and yachts, minesweepers, trawlers, and the fast new vessels called "sloops"; there were whalers, pilot cutters, target-towing boats; there was a ferry vessel which had taken railroad cars across the Thames, and which was now going to sea for the first time in its long career; there were fireboats and lifeboats—some old ones from ships which had been sunk years ago; there were ancient paddle steamers, the *Brighton Belle* and the *Brighton Queen*, converted to minesweepers; there were mud-scows with fancy names such as *Galleon's Reach* and *Queen's Channel*. The inhabitants of this little island had been a sea people since the earliest days recorded, and had built every sort of craft for every purpose; now, seized by the tropism called patriotism, they had come put-putting out from their coves and inlets, ready to do what had never needed to be done in all those previous centuries.

Some just went on their own, without any word or assistance. But Eric Vivian Pomeroy-Nielson, former army flyer, was a man of discipline; he reported to a naval patrol, and was ordered to a place at the pier where boats were being checked and supplies handed out freely: parcels of food, first-aid kits, fresh water, fuel for the engines. Only one question: "Will you go to Dunkirk?" Each man must be fitted with a steel helmet and a gas mask—this set two amateur sailors to thinking about the seriousness of their venture. They might have had a Bren gun on their foredeck if the *Gar* had had space for it.

They were told to proceed to Ramsgate, some thirty miles farther to the eastward, around the point which sticks out into the North Sea. It was pretty much like Derby Day on a highway, Rick said; a regular procession. Some boats were faster, and crept by them; others, such as fishing boats and barges, were slower. Well-bred yachtsmen kept their eyes ahead, and refrained from speaking to persons to whom they had not been introduced. It was a picture gallery of Englishmen, of every age and station: fishermen and sailors, boatbuilders and dockers, in America called longshoremen, and engineers, called machinists; yachtsmen and employees of yacht clubs, naval and professional people—anybody who had ever handled a boat or had listed himself with the "Small Vessels Pool." The vessels they had brought, or had been assigned to, were as varied as their crews: some sleek and shining with chromium and brass and white paint, others rusty and weatherbeaten, with old tire casings hanging at their sides to serve as fenders.

This Kentish shore was familiar to Lanny—seaside towns running into one another and forming a continuous line of villas and hotels. At one little inn he had sat under an arbor and eaten with Irma a pre-wedding luncheon of cold mutton and beer. The town of Ramsgate was where he and his bride-to-be had met the yacht *Bessie Budd*, and been taken out to sea in order to circumvent the Archbishop of Canterbury, who wanted sixty pounds for a special marriage license! Very gay it had all seemed at the time, but now a little sad to look back on. "Too bad we couldn't have hit it off!" Lanny remarked.

But his friend had no sympathy with that kind of sentimentality. "Irma's got what she wants, and you didn't have it. So that's that."

X

There was a breeze springing up, and when they came round into the Strait of Dover there was a bit of a sea—at least so it seemed from the disadvantage point of a tiny craft. She began to pitch, and the spray shot over them, and they dug out their sea suits and put them on. Rick began to look rather pale, and Lanny, usually a "good sailor," inquired: "Are you going to be sick?" The answer was: "I don't know, but I'll stick it, whatever happens." They didn't have far to go before they slid into the still water of Ramsgate basin, perhaps a quarter of a mile each way, and with hundreds of boats in it.

From that time on they were under naval orders; in fact, they had a regular Admiral—and assuredly no Admiral of the King's Navee had ever commanded a more fantastic armada. The high personage—his name was Taylor—dashed about in a motor launch some thirty feet long, with twin engines and mounting two Bren guns; for a crew he had one sub-lieutenant, one stoker, and one gunner; but his flag gave him authority, and all his "small vessels" did what he told them. They were to wait until just before dawn and go in convoy; meantime their supplies would be checked again—they must have petrol for several days' work at the beaches, and they must have enough food and plenty of fresh water. The navy was in a generous mood; they got real butter and live eggs, which had already become a rarity in London. They were advised to tie up and sleep for a while, and to keep their "tin hats" handy. A patrol ship passed out buckets of hot tea, priceless to Englishmen.

There wasn't much order to the procession which set out in the early morning hours. No two vessels had the same speed, and the fast ones were not required to wait for the slow; they were soon spread out over the forty miles between Ramsgate and Dunkirk. Nobody had difficulty in finding the way, even in darkness, because there was a red glare in the sky, and when you got nearer you could see flames and pillars of thick black smoke. When dawn came, the convoy was scattered all over the sea in front and behind; they had been joined by redsailed French fishing boats from as far as Caen and Le Havre, boats with pious names such as *Ave Maria* and *Gratia Plena, Stella Maris* and *Ciel de France;* also escaped Dutch and Belgian vessels, stout and stubby, called *schouts*. Here and there through the stream of vessels dashed patrol torpedo boats and destroyers on watch for submarines and enemy vessels; Lanny soon found that the wash from a destroyer was as dangerous to his puny *Gar* as anything German; he had to head quickly into the swells, and prepare to be pitched and tossed and covered with spray.

There was a condition in the Strait known as a "chop," and open motorboats had no business being out there; poor Rick lost first his breakfast, and then everything else he had. It was hard for him to get up to the side of the boat, so he had to use a can, and just lie there by his engine, turning first pale, then yellow, then green. But there didn't come a single groan from him, and he didn't want Lanny to talk about it—just "carry on." He didn't have much to do, for the engine was a good one, and its pace, once set, continued for four or five hours. Rick knew about internal combustion engines because he had been a flyer, and Lanny because he had been driving a motorcar most of his life and had had to stop by the roadside many a time to tinker.

With daylight came the enemy planes, bombing the larger vessels and machine-gunning the little ones as they roared on; the bullets made a line like a plowshare rushing at you, a scary sight. Anti-aircraft fire opened up from every vessel which had a gun, and presently came the British planes; there were dogfights in the sky, and now and then one of the planes would plunge into the sea, or race away streaming black smoke behind it. Rick knew the different types, and would say "Messerschmitt" or "Spitfire." He had always insisted: "Our planes are better, our men are better; the only question is, have we enough?" This time, apparently, the R.A.F. was going all out, and made it hot for the "Jerries" from dawn to dark. A great show to watch, but rather hard on the nerves; they put on their helmets, and made themselves as small as possible while shell fragments spattered the sea about them.

X

Ahead lay Dunkirk, once a peaceful fishing port and summer resort for the French and those who liked French food and conversation. There were two parallel jetties running out to the sea, with a lighthouse at the end of one. Also there was a long mole, and inside it many small basins and docks. The port was still held by the British rearguards, being constantly bombed and shelled by the enemy. Huge fires were burning, including oil depots and ammunition dumps; a black pall of smoke hung over everything, and an incessant clatter of explosives large and small was never out of any man's ears, day or night. Not all these explosions were a danger to the crew of the launch *Gar*, but they were all a danger to somebody, and an imaginative person like Lanny Budd couldn't get away from that thought.

Some of the larger vessels, bound into the port, had to take a roundabout course which had been marked with buoys, for the enemy had dropped mines in the regular channel, and kept dropping them into each new channel that was discovered and marked. Such is war: move and counter-move, one set of brains matched against another set, and the victory going to the better. Or was it necessarily the better? The idealist in Lanny Budd kept asking, and trying to figure out some way whereby the two sets of brains might manage to combine against their common enemy, the blind forces of nature. Even amid the hell of Dunkirk, Lanny kept thinking about that! When he voiced it, Rick said: "I'll not combine with any Nazi brain!"

Little boats were not going into the harbor; little boats could approach the beaches, where the water was shallow, and men could wade out, in some places a quarter of a mile before they were up to their necks. The orders to the *Gar* had been brief: "Go wherever there are men on the shore, and bring them out to the nearest larger boat." They moved slowly past the mole, and on to the eastward, where there stretched a beautiful wide beach on which children had built sand castles and men and women had browned themselves in scanty bathing suits. Now the entire beach was crowded with khaki-clad men—more men, Lanny thought, than he had ever seen in one place in all his life; but then he remembered the Parteitag in Nuremberg, where more than a million Nazis had been assembled on the great airfield in one of those demonstrations which the genius of the Führer and his Doktor Goebbels had devised. Now those same men of Nuremberg were here, shelling and attacking day and night; overhead they were coming down in screaming dives, machine-gunning their enemies, who stood and took it because there was no place to go and nothing else to do.

As far as the eye could see, the beach was dark with men, and they formed thick lines coming out into the water—wavy, irregular lines, marking the presence of sand bars and shoals. All night they had hidden in the dunes, but now they saw the ships, and not all the power of the Luftwaffe could keep them out of the water. They had been marching and fighting for almost three weeks, and many were wounded and bloody; all showed pitiful signs of exhaustion—haggard faces, red-rimmed eyelids, trembling lips. Some stumbled, and had to be lifted and held up by their comrades.

Lanny and Rick found their job quickly enough. A good-sized tug had come in ahead of them, towing behind it a bunch of wherries and dinghies, perhaps a score. The tug had crept in as close as it dared and then cast anchor; the master called to Lanny: "Sir, you can save a lot of time for us if you'll take this tow in." The *Gar* backed up and the towline was made fast to her stern; oarsmen from the tug got into the boats, one for each; the engine set the water to boiling, and slowly the bunch of boats crept in toward the beach. The men on the sand bars started coming closer, many up to their necks; and when the boats were cast loose, the oarsmen started dragging the men in. There was no panic, no confusion; a subaltern took charge and gave the orders; they brought the wounded and got them in first. Whatever number the oarsmen specified, that number was put in, and the boat was turned and rowed out to the tug. When the tug was loaded, it took the load out to one of the steamers and then came back for more.

XII

Such was the pattern, and it went on all day without let-up. Swarms of enemy bombers appeared overhead, and bombs fell in showers, and now and then a vessel was hit and sometimes set on fire, sometimes sunk; small boats came to the rescue and the survivors were transferred to other vessels. Farther down the shore, at a small place called Nieuport, enemy batteries were hidden, firing 5.9 shells at the crowds on the beaches and at the mole; but nobody paid much attention to this, they just went on with their jobs. When British fighter planes came to the rescue, the men looked up for a moment; when a bomber came rushing down under full power and hit the sea and exploded—that was just one more bang to be added to the fireworks. "Good work!" Rick would say, with a grin. The wind had mercifully gone down, and he nibbled a bit of biscuit in between filling the grease cups of his engine. "Don't be downhearted!" he would call to the men, and they would turn their thumbs up and answer: "Give us another go at them!"

The name of the tug to which they had attached themselves was the *Gentle Annie*, and she had come all the way from Battersea. Because Rick wasn't much good for lifting men out of the sea, she loaned him a husky docker with an accent which Lanny would have liked to record on a phonograph. He was unceremonious in his handling of Tommies; he would stand on the gunwale and hook his right hand firmly in the back of a man's collar and just heave until the man was on the gunwale; after that he could fall in if he was too tired to lift his legs. As a rule the arrival's first call would be for water, for the German bombers had destroyed the city's water supply, and the men had long ago emptied their canteens. Lanny would give him a cup with a tot of whisky in it and his gratitude would be touching. Then he would get a sheet of hardtack to munch, and maybe a piece of chocolate, and would settle down in the bottom of the launch and sometimes fall asleep before he had finished eating.

Toward evening a hospital ship, white-painted and with conspicuous red crosses, was dive-bombed and got a great hole in her side; many of the wounded had life jackets put on them and were dropped into the sea. The Admiral's launch came along and ordered both the *Gar* and the *Gentle Annie* to the rescue, and that was a job that took several hours. Lifting wounded men out of the water couldn't be done quite so unceremoniously; and presently it was dark, and there couldn't be any lights, not even a cigarette, because that would bring the bombers again. You had to creep here and there at a speed of a mile or two per hour, calling, and trying to hear the responses of men and women in the water. Lanny had to be prepared to give a whirl to the wheel if he saw any phosphorescence which might mean the presence of a swimmer; Rick had to be on the *qui vive* to stop or to reverse the engine, for the sea was blowing up again, and if you heard a cry it might be a man's last. They had two husky chaps with them to do the lifting; and because the victims were half dead with cold they had to make frequent trips to the tug.

The time came when they themselves were utterly exhausted, drenched with spray and half frozen by the north wind, and Rick seasick again. They had to turn the launch over to others and seek shelter in the *Gentle Annie's* bosom. Rick was lifted on board—he really had no right to be doing this work, with his game leg, and everybody treated him with special care, even while hiding the fact to save his pride. Because he couldn't bend one knee it was slow work getting up or down a companionway; as a rule he did it with one leg and two arms to let himself down a step at a time; but now, for the first time since Lanny knew him, he had to admit that he was at the end of his strength and let himself be carried, pick-a-back.

Have you ever been inside the boiler room of a tug—one of those soft-coal-burning tramps that fills the air with thick black smoke which in the course of nearly a century has made the London docks and the London dockers as grimy as itself? Ordinarily you wouldn't think of one of these tugs as especially lovable, but when your very bones are frozen and your teeth are chattering and you are dazed with exhaustion, you are taken into a room where the heat clasps you like a mother's arms and penetrates to the very center of your being; nor does it fail, but is renewed every few minutes by the opening of an iron door and an outpouring from a golden-hot furnace. You sink to the floor and don't care how black it is, because it is warm. You strip off your wet clothes and lay them over the boiler and in five minutes they are dry again.

And meantime, the tea! Such tea as British seamen get, made in a big cooker and full of tannin, of which the hygienist does not approve; but it is hot and sweet, and warms your insides and makes a new man of you—especially if you get a ham or cheese sandwich at the same time. You swallow it down quickly, because you feel that your eyes are closing and you know that you can't hold on much longer. Presently you keel over and are fast asleep; if other men stumble over you you don't know it, and they have to shake you hard and tell you that it's daylight, and the launch is back, and newly supplied with water and food and fuel.

XIII

Such was the life of two men of gentle rearing for a matter of five or six days and nights. They lost track of the time, and thought about nothing but the streams of men who kept magically appearing out of the streets of Dunkirk and wading into the sea. The pair soon lost the maternal care of the *Gentle Annie*, for a bomb hit her and she went down and they helped to rescue her gentle crew. Her tall, rusty smoke-stack remained sticking out of the sea, along with scores of others—nobody ever counted them, so far as Rick or Lanny knew. There were officially said to be eight hundred and eighty-five vessels taking part in the rescue, but that didn't include the many which went in on their own and didn't come back to report. The British and French navies admitted the loss of thirteen destroyers and twenty-four minor war vessels. The crew of tiny *Gar* saw many of them go down, and went on with their job of taking men off the beaches.

They attached themselves to that *Brighton Belle* which was officially classified as a "paddle minesweeper." She was older than Lanny himself; painted white with gold trimmings, she had been carrying "trippers" at the time of the Boer War. Now a dingy war gray, she was loaded with more humans than ever before in her long history. She struck a mine, and all the load had to be transferred to her sister ship, the *Brighton Queen*—and then she went down in her turn. But more ships kept coming, and the R.A.F. kept clearing the skies—they were getting four Jerries to one, the navy men reported, and Rick announced, proudly: "I've a son up there." To Lanny he said, no less proudly: "I told you so! We're better!"

Men, men, men! Endless streams of them, the whole British army, it seemed, and a good chunk of the French, and some black Senegalese. From first to last, Lanny didn't see a single man, rescued or rescuers, flinch from a duty; he heard tales of Frenchmen rushing the boats, but the ones he helped invariably shook hands with him and said "Merci, monsieu'." When they discovered that he knew their language, they told him something of their adventures; and Rick, a professional in spite of weariness and seasickness, would say: "Somebody will get a great story out of this!" Lanny met Americans who had been driving ambulances, and what the British called "tea cars" for the Y.M.C.A. He met a British officer who had galloped onto the beach on a stolen French carthorse, and another who had ridden a lady's bicycle and didn't say how he had got it. The Tommies had many such tales to tell and were glad of a chance to laugh. They had much fun with French peasant boys who had never seen the sea, and were as much afraid of a small boat as of a German tank.

The docks of the city were blasted and the warehouses burning, and the waterfront became too hot for men or ships; so more and more men appeared on the beaches, and on the jetties which protected the roadstead. The largest of these was made by driving piles into the sand, two parallel rows close together. Nobody had ever contemplated using them as a pier; but some bright fellow had the idea of the mess tables of the vessels, and they were brought out and laid upside down on the pilings, making a gangway of a sort. Over that precarious footing something like a half million British and French boots passed in the course of several days and nights. The ships drew up alongside and the men stepped aboard, and that was a lot faster than wading into the surf. The Germans bombed that jetty incessantly, but they never once hit it; the Spitfires came in droves and sent many of the bombers plunging into the sea. The destroyers and the ack-ack guns on the beach kept up an incessant pounding at them. Also the cruisers, which had enormous eight-barreled anti-aircraft guns, known as "Chicago pianos." There was such a racket that you had to shout to be heard.

Rick contributed another bright idea to this haphazard procedure. The wide beach was sprinkled with vehicles of every sort, ambulances, tanks, lorries which had been driven here and could go no further. Why not drive them into the sea, as far as they would go—two of them side by side and then another pair, and another, until you had a pier of a sort. With planks laid on top, men would walk to the end and boats of medium size could come and get them handily. Rick shouted the suggestion to a young lieutenant, who put men to work; and in an hour or so it was done, and things went much faster at that spot. The enemy had a new target, but his shooting wasn't any too good, and presently a new flock of destroyers would sweep in and put his guns out of action.

XIV

The battle behind the town, and in an arc all around it, went on without a moment's cessation, day or night, for an entire week. The enemy was in Nieuport to the east and Calais to the west and in the suburbs of Dunkirk all the way around, trying desperately to break through to the beaches, and being as desperately fought by the British and French rearguards. Buildings were shot to pieces, great fires were started, and a black pall hung over the whole scene. The men who dragged themselves out of that battle were pitiful to see, many without shoes and their clothing in shreds. The ambulance men and litter bearers stayed on the job, and carried the wounded to the boats, which never stopped coming. One of the regular Channel steamers made eight round trips to Ramsgate, with some two thousand men at each trip.

Until at last there were no more except the rearguards, and the navy was going to care for them. "Gentlemen, your work is done," said the Admiral, darting here and there on his tiny flagship. "You can go home whenever you please. Be sure you have enough petrol, and if you want a tow, come to one of the assembling stations."

Poor old Rick! He was surely glad to hear those words—so glad that he didn't try to hide it. His face was drawn and every step was pain; the ordeal must have cost him twenty pounds of his not too abundant weight. They had taken the last man off a shoal where once there had been thousands standing; and now they looked about them at the never-to-be-forgotten scene. Hundreds of vehicles had been wrecked and burned on the beach, which was so littered with debris that you couldn't see the sand. The funnels and masts of vessels of all kinds and sizes were sticking up out of the water, and every sort of debris was afloat, including a number of cork boats which seemed to have nothing wrong with them. Several horses galloped here and there on the beach, trying to get away from the racket; and strangest thing of all, the surface of the water was white with dead fish—millions of them killed by the bombs, and a few with life enough left for a feeble wriggle. Rick said: "If our lads had been Japs, they wouldn't have gone hungry. Just take out your pocket knife and cut off a thin slice, and you have the choicest table delicacy."

Lanny's reply was: "That reminds me!" and he started to open a can of bully beef. They hadn't had a real meal for a week; just picking up something when they thought of it, and nibbling while they worked, or waited for their small boat to be emptied.

"I think we've a right to be towed in," Lanny continued. "It looks to me as if the weather had about exhausted its patience."

"Righto!" was the Englishman's reply. "I won't mind having a good snooze in a boiler room."

His friend began, very seriously: "I must tell you something I've had on my mind from the beginning. I want you to put me ashore, and work out some way to get to the assembling station by yourself, or pick up someone who can help you to it."

"What are you thinking of, Lanny?"

"You're not to say a word about it, understand. I want to join the German army."

"Good God, man! Are you out of your mind?"

"I've thought it out carefully. I want to join Hitler, and find out if and when he means to invade Britain. It'll be the most important job I've ever tackled."

"But they'll shoot you for a spy, Lanny!"

"I don't think so. I'm an American civilian, and the Führer's personal friend. He gave me a commission—certain things I was to say to people in London and Paris, and I've said them, and it will seem to him the most natural thing in the world that I should come back and tell him what they answered."

"But the army, Lanny—the Germans you will run into in this town!"

"I don't think there's much to worry about. I know their language, and how to talk to them. I have reason to believe that Emil Meissner is commanding a division somewhere on this front, and if I say I'm a friend of his, nobody's going to shoot me until they ask him."

"Well I'm blowed!" said the baronet's son. Remembering his lifelong habit of not interfering in other men's affairs, he added: "You know what you want to do."

"The main thing is that you should keep the secret—otherwise I might have a hard time getting back into England. You can put me off at our pier; and if you wait there for a bit, someone will be coming along and help you to an assembling station."

"I'll manage that part of it all right," was the reply; but Lanny knew that his friend was so tired he could hardly drag his game leg.

XV

"Our pier" meant the contraption which Rick had invented, and which was now standing deserted in the fast-falling twilight. Its landing stage, at the end, consisted of a number of planks laid across two heavy trucks, or lorries as they are known to the English. (Some tens of thousands of them had been left behind for the Germans to use.) Lanny steered the *Gar* to the spot and made her fast. He got out his precious bundle, which had been stowed in a closed compartment and appeared to have escaped the spray. "I have an outfit," he explained, "so that I'll look like a tourist and not like a shipwrecked mariner."

"You'll be wanting food?" inquired Rick.

"Other people will feed me, if I look right. But I must have water, to wash off and shave. I have changed most of my money into francs, and I'll leave the small change with you."

"But your passport is wrong, Lanny! It won't show your entrance into France."

"I hired a launch to bring me, and when we got to Dunkirk we found everything disorganized, so I just came ashore. I've a right to have been in England; that's where Hitler asked me to go."

"Well, good luck, old fellow. If anybody asks about you, I'll say you got on another boat."

"Everything's pretty well shuffled, and nobody will worry about any one man. How many do you suppose have been saved?"

"God knows! I'd guess half a million." When the figures were announced, the world learnt that this civilian effort had saved a total of 122,000 Frenchmen, and just twice as many Britons.

Lanny set his bundle onto the landing stage, also a gallon tin of water. He exchanged a handclasp with his friend—it might be a long time before they met again—and then he climbed up. "So long, Rick!" He tucked his bundle under one arm and took his precious tin in the other hand and started walking cautiously along the irregular planking. Half-way to the shore he saw two figures approaching, a Tommy helping his wounded buddy. They stopped when they were near, and Lanny, disguising his American accent, remarked: "There's a boat out there that will tyke you, if you can steer her."

"I can myke a stab at it, pal."

"I'm tykin' in some medical supplies. There'll be another boat a bit lyter, so don't wyte for me."

"Back to Blighty for mine!" remarked the Tommy.

31

Even in the Cannon's Mouth

I

As BACKGROUND to the beach and its scenes there had stood in Lanny's eyes for five or six days an immensely long building which he took to be the casino or pavilion of Dunkirk, or perhaps of Maloles-Bains, as part of the beach was called; in an idle moment he had counted sixty windows in one continuous front. He had imagined what had gone on there in happier times—the dining, dancing, and gambling which made up the life of the *beau monde* of the Continent. Now the building was dead, its windows dark, and every pane of glass shattered by shell and bomb blasts. Had all the people fled—and where to, with the sea on one side and a semicircle of flame and steel on the other? Were they hiding in the cellars, taking their chances of the collapse of the building and the spreading of fire?

Lanny found the esplanade as badly littered as the beach. He did not dare to use his pocket flashlight, but stumbled along in fast-gathering darkness, and when he was past the pavilion, turned up a side street. Not a light anywhere in sight, but from the shape of the buildings he judged it to be a street of apartment houses and pensions. Some were partly wrecked, others intact; he stopped at one of the latter and rang the bell, then stood for a while. When no answer came, he tried the door, and finding it unlocked, stepped in and closed it behind him. He ventured to turn on his pencil of light and flash it about. He was in a somewhat pretentious establishment, with spacious entrance hall and drawing-room beyond; there were heavy portieres and elaborate carvings on the woodwork.

This would suit the P.A.'s purpose well enough, and he wasn't concerned to find the proprietor. He went up the wide stairway quietly, something made easy by heavy carpets. At the *premier étage* he flashed his torch again and went to the nearest door, tried it, and when it opened, went in and flashed again; there was a sitting-room in perfect order, except that the glass of the windows was scattered over the carpeted floor and the cold night wind was blowing in. Lanny judged that there would be a bedroom and bath attached, and so there was. No person in sight, and he wanted none. There was a key in the door, and he locked himself in.

He was so tired that he could hardly keep away from the bed; but he had fixed in his mind for the past week exactly what he meant to do, and he did it half automatically. He undressed in the bathroom, taking the precaution to keep his wet shoes on because of the glass. No water came from the spigots, but he poured part of his gallon into the basin, wet a towel and rubbed himself clean all over; it can be done with very little water, if you work hard. He unrolled his precious bundle and put on his clean underclothes, his dry socks and new shoes. Then he poured out more water and shaved himself carefully, using the precious torch for the finishing touches.

He put on his clean shirt, and tied his tie in the dark and inspected it in the light. He combed his wavy brown hair, and was surprised to note that some of it looked gray at the roots. Had Dunkirk done that? He put on his trousers, and made sure they had not got too badly wrinkled in their sea journey. He put on his coat and his gray Homburg hat, and there he was, a perfect gentleman, ready for the best society. The bedroom closet had a pierglass mirror, and he flashed his torch and inspected himself. A gentleman has to be exactly right, or he might as well not be at all.

He took his ruined clothes and hung them in the closet, which was full of elegant ladies' costumes. He folded the sheet of oilcloth and tossed it onto the closet shelf. He took a good drink of water, and then tossed the empty can out of the window. No doubt it made a racket, but it was inaudible amid the sounds of war, which appeared to be coming nearer every minute. In the inside pocket of Lanny's new gray suit he put his billfold, his passport book, and a few letters from American millionaires—one of them Edsel Ford—having to do with the procuring of old masters. With these he was prepared to face the Wehrmacht.

He groped his way downstairs again. He didn't want to face the Wehrmacht in the dark, nor while it was fighting. What he wanted was to sleep, and he wanted that the worst way in the world. He had seen so many shells and bombs exploding that he had become rather indifferent; he would take his chances and hope that none had his name on it. He went into the drawing-room with the overstuffed furniture, but no glass in the windows. Things were exploding outside, and by their light he observed a couch with plenty of cushions. He went to one of the portieres, stood on a chair and slipped the rod out of its holder, then slipped the rings off the rod and carried the portiere to the couch. He lay down on his back, so as not to wrinkle his clothing too much. He pulled the portiere over him, and in half a minute was lost to the world and all its evil doings.

II

When he opened his eyes again it was broad daylight, and the sun was streaming in at the smashed windows. Lanny's first sensation was of bewilderment; there was something wrong with the world—it had become silent! No more ear-splitting explosions, no monstrous banging of Chicago pianos, not even the whirring of machine-gun fire. A moment's thought, and he realized that this was the condition he desired;

the British rearguard has been taken away by the navy, and the Germans, no doubt, would be coming in on their heels. It was the moment to move into action.

He got up and inspected himself in a mirror. There were wrinkles in his clothes, but not too serious; he passed a small pocket comb through his hair, then put on his hat. He didn't want any conversation with people in this place, so he stepped quickly to the front door and went out, closing it behind him. Alongside the door was a brass plate reading "Pension Albertine." He kissed it good-by in his thoughts, and set out along the debris-littered street. Not far ahead was the sight he expected—half a dozen green-clad Nazi soldiers, advancing slowly, guns in hand and ready for action.

It is like dealing with dogs—the first essential is not to show fear. Lanny continued his strolling pace, and when the men were near he extended his right hand and arm. "*Heil Hitler!*" To return the salute was obligatory, and it made them friends for the moment. Lanny did not wait to be questioned, but said: "*Bitte, wo ist die Kommanditur?*"

"*Weiss nicht, Herr.*" Common soldiers in the midst of battle do not possess such information; they know only their immediate tasks. Lanny asked where he could find their superior officer, and they reported he was back there somewhere. Lanny strolled on.

He repeated this performance with two more groups. A *Feldwebel* directed him to a *Leutnant*, and to this latter he explained: "*Ich bin ein amerikanischer Kunstsachverständiger, Freund der Regierung.*" He wouldn't claim too much in dealing with a subordinate. "I have some information, and request that you will kindly have someone escort me to your nearest command post."

A despatch bearer chanced to arrive, on a motorcycle with a side car, and Lanny was invited to become a passenger. As he took his seat, he recalled that the Gefreiter, Adolf Hitler, had driven just such a machine as this, and had seen the fighting here at Dunkirk in the last war. Lanny rode through the advancing German army, tanks and trucks and battle-worn men, grimy, stubble-bearded, a few of them bloodstained. They had been fighting for nearly a month, and walked without heeding anything about them, almost as if they were asleep. Alongside the roads was all the wreckage of war, exactly as on the beaches. The British had held this ground for the past week; their dead men had been buried, but not their dead horses. Lanny decided that it was pleasanter to do one's fighting on the sea, where corpses disappeared, at least for a while.

III

They stopped at a group of tents, with telephone wires running to them and staff cars parked near by. Obviously, this was what the visitor had asked for; and presently he found himself seated on a camp chair, in front of a shaven-headed and bespectacled young staff officer. Lanny introduced himself, and added: "I am an old friend of General Emil Meissner, and have been told that he is somewhere on this front. I have some information which I know would be of importance to him, and I would appreciate it if you would communicate with him and let him know that I am here."

"That would be somewhat difficult, Herr Budd," was the reply. "General Meissner's command is on this front, but I don't know his position, and I should have to explain matters to the Korps Hauptquartier. May I ask if your information is of a military nature?"

"Not military, but political, Herr Hauptmann. I ask for General Meissner because he knows me intimately, and will credit a story which a stranger like yourself might find difficulty in accepting."

"I can see that you are a gentleman, Herr Budd," said the officer; "also that you are familiar with our country and our language. Can you not trust me so far as to tell me a little about yourself? We are in the midst of a hard campaign, and our means of communication are overtaxed, also our time."

So Lanny explained the circumstance that he had been a friend of General Meissner's brother, the Komponist Kurt Meissner, since boyhood, and had assisted Kurt in his work for the Reichswehr in Paris both after the last war and before the present one. Also he was a friend of Heinrich Jung, of the Hitlerjugend. "Judging from your age, Herr Hauptmann, you may have belonged to that organization, and may know Heinrich. He was a friend of the Führer's and visited him when he was a prisoner in the fortress of Landsberg; so it happened that I was taken very early to hear the Führer speak and later to call on him in Berlin."

"Oh!—so you know the Führer personally?"

"I have been his guest a number of times. I was at the Berghof for a week or two just before the Polish campaign began. If you know any member of the Führer's staff or his household, they will confirm my statements. I am a friend also of Herr Reichsminister Hess and was his guest at the last Parteitag—that was the year before last, as you know.

Any of the persons I have named will tell you that the Führer always receives me when I call."

"Then your information is really for the Führer—is that what I am to understand?"

"*Ganz richtig, Herr Hauptmann.* The Führer requested me to interview certain persons in Paris and London, and to give them certain messages; this I have done, and have returned at considerable risk, as you can guess. I assure you that the matter is of importance, and if you will convey the name of Lanny Budd to the Führer or to anyone on his staff, you will find that you have not wasted your time."

"Your story is most interesting, Herr Budd. Would you mind letting me see your passport and other papers?"

Lanny emptied his pocket promptly. "You will understand that, coming from England, I carry no German credentials. I wish you to know that I am not a paid agent, but a friend of National Socialism. What I am doing has been at the Führer's request, and as a personal favor."

The captain studied the passport with its unmistakable photograph of a handsome gentleman with a fashionable small mustache. "Am I at liberty to look at these letters, Herr Budd?"

"*Freilich, Herr Hauptmann.* They have to do with my profession of art expert, and will not tell you very much. I have disposed of a number of valuable paintings for Reichsmarschall Göring, and have purchased some which the Führer has at the Berghof. If you are familiar with his home, or with Karinhall, Marshal Göring's estate, and will ask me questions about them, I will quickly be able to satisfy you that I have been there."

"*Leider, mein Herr,* I have never moved in those exalted circles. But your story impresses me, and I will ask my chief's permission to send the necessary message to the Oberfeldkommando."

IV

Lanny's story was accepted provisionally, and they invited him to lunch with the staff. Folding tables were put together in the open, and a palatable hot meal was served to a dozen officers, from the divisional commander down to humble lieutenants. This was the Wehrmacht, the regular army, all absolutely correct, formal, severe; they used the military salute, not the Nazi *Heil.* Were they play-acting, in front of a foreigner? Lanny couldn't be sure, but he observed that from the highest to the lowest they revealed none of the exultation which must have been in their hearts. No, no, this was just routine, this had been rehearsed for years, every detail had been planned, and everybody behaved as if these were field maneuvers and not the conquest of Western Europe. They talked freely about the progress of the offensive, and Lanny could understand the reason. If he, the foreigner, was what he claimed, he had a right to know, and if he wasn't what he claimed, he would be shot, so it wouldn't matter.

The substance of what he heard was: "*Heute geht es weiter nach Paris.*" Not: "Today we begin a great offensive," or anything involving doubt or difficulty, but "Today we are setting out for Paris." The clean-up of Flanders had been completed, and fresh armies were striking straight westward on a front of a hundred and fifty kilometers. The Führer had that day issued a proclamation which had been read to the troops, and Lanny was permitted to read it in mimeographed form. The Führer thanked his soldiers for winning "the greatest battle in the world's history," and he went on: "Today another great battle begins. . . . This fight for freedom and the existence of our people will be continued until the enemy rulers in London and Paris are annihilated." He went on to order the church bells to be rung for three days and flags to be flown for eight days all over Germany.

The attack had started at dawn that morning, with the customary immense barrage of artillery. Now the guns sounded distant, and when Lanny commented upon the fact the officers smiled and told him that that represented the day's advances; this divisional headquarters would strike its tents in the latter part of the afternoon and follow. "The longer we wait, the farther we can go," said Leutnant Bedow from East Prussia, sandy-haired, with a tiny little spike mustaches and pince-nez. He brought the visitor a copy of that morning's *Kölnische Zeitung*, a priceless possession, since Lanny had been out of touch with the world for a week. A Nazi paper, like all the others, but the communiqués of the High Command would probably be correct.

He took a folding chair out into the pleasant June sunshine and read the High Command's summary of the battle of Flanders, just completed by the taking of Dunkirk. It was "the greatest battle of destruction of all time." With total casualties of about sixty thousand the Germans had taken one million, two hundred thousand prisoners, including Belgians and Dutch. A considerable navy had been destroyed, including five cruisers sunk and ten damaged. Lanny hadn't seen any cruiser sunk and he decided right there that the Nazis had taken charge of the Wehrmacht's publicity department.

There was all the customary hate-stuff, including exultation over the first bombing of Paris which had taken place a couple of days previously. Italy was on the point of entering the war, mobs in Milan and Rome were clamoring for it, and Göring and Hess had gone there to arrange co-operation. Also, according to the Nazis, the British were planning to torpedo the American liners which were taking Americans home, and then blame the act on the Germans. Since it was obvious that the Germans couldn't know this if it were true, Lanny wondered if they were preparing to torpedo the liners themselves and blame it on the British. They had already done that in the case of the *Athenia*, at the very outbreak of the war, when twenty-five Americans had lost their lives.

V

By mid-afternoon Lanny had arrived at page eight of the *Zeitung*; the advertisements were revealing of what the Germans wanted and what they were supposed to be thinking. But he didn't finish; for here came the Hauptmann, beaming with amiability, pleased to inform Herr Budd that his story had been verified. A great honor, indeed, to shake the hand of an intimate friend of the Führer; also, Lanny could guess, for the Hauptmann to have his judgment confirmed against the judgment of some other members of the staff who had refused to believe that the Führer ever had or would have an American friend. Anyhow, it was settled. *"Ein grosses Vergnügen, Herr Budd. Sie fahren sofort nach des Führers Feldquartier."*

Funny thing, to have no luggage to pack, and not a thing to do but return the newspaper to the Leutnant, and shake hands with half a dozen officers who took time to think about him. Bowing and heel-clicking, he stepped into an open staff car; a military chauffeur and a guard with a submachine gun in front, and Lanny in the back seat in solemn state. *"Gute Fahrt, Herr Budd.* We will see you in Paris in one week, or two at the most." So sure they were, having planned every detail!

The course lay southward and to the east, since a one-and-only Führer would never be permitted too close to the battle line. Lanny knew this border country, and if he had any doubts where he was, there were road signs at every crossing; the Belgians and French had had no chance to destroy them, and the Germans found them useful. On every side was the wreckage of war; not much destruction of houses, for the battle had passed too swiftly; but the ditches and roadsides were piled with wrecked vehicles of every sort. The French had been using horse artillery, and had been bombed on the roads; dead horses lay beside the guns, and lime had been poured over them, but this had little effect upon the awful stench. Repair crews swarmed over the damaged vehicles, setting them right side up and working on them day and night. German planes hovered in the sky; but nowhere on this trip did Lanny catch sight of a French or British plane, or of any air fighting.

All the roads leading west were filled with traffic bound for the front; a seemingly endless procession of guns, half-tracks, field kitchens and supply trucks. Great six-inch guns hauled by caterpillar tractors going forty miles an hour, and followed by trucks loaded with shells, and crews to serve them, and men with machine guns and light mortars to defend them—all rushing into France, appearing suddenly where nobody expected them, and firing under the direction of spotting planes! Lanny doubted very much if the French had provided anything like that, and the French were all alone now! He had read in the *Kölnische Zeitung* that General Weygand had been put in command of the *grande armée*, and the line they had set up along the Somme was called the Weygand line. Lanny recalled this dapper, wizened old gentleman whom he had met socially; he was one of the most ardent appeasers, and only three years ago the Cagoulards had chosen him as one of a committee of five who were to govern their counter-revolutionary France.

Lanny's route lay crosswise to that massive stream, and if he had been an ordinary civilian he would have had a difficult time. But the chauffeur would go forward and show a document with which he had been provided, and its effect would be magical; other traffic on the cross road would be got out of the way, and the rolling army would be flagged to a halt, just long enough for the staff car to shoot across. Lanny knew better than to ask any questions, but he could safely reckon his southerly direction as a conclusive proof that the Führer was going to take Paris before he tried London. That would have been an interesting item of information to persons in both cities, but they would probably know it before Lanny could get it to them.

VI

The Führer's field headquarters were in a special train which had been built and equipped for this purpose. It had been halted on a spur track in a pleasant spot in thick woodlands, where the Führer would be safe from attack by airplanes, and where, incidentally, he could enjoy his favorite pleasure of pacing up and down in solitude and contemplating his destiny. Wherever a halt was made, guards were at once thrown round the place; the staff car, coming in by an inconspicuous dirt road, was halted, and its pass examined. There was a field telephone to the train, and inquiry was made; Lanny was asked to produce his passport, and his features were compared with the photograph therein. "*Alles in Ordnung,*" and they were to proceed.

A very elegant train of about a dozen cars, painted in camouflage, with an observation car at the rear; and after more investigations, Lanny was invited to enter. He did not forget *Trinkgeld* for the chauffeur and the guard. *Französisches Papier,*" he remarked, with a smile; "*aber, in Paris wird es gut sein.*" They appreciated the prophecy.

More than nine months ago the Führer of the Germans had told his tame Reichstag that he was putting on his old army coat and would not take it off until the victory was won. This coat was a short double-breasted jacket, gray in color, and with no decorations whatever—so different from *Der Dicke* and others of his entourage. A simple man of the people was *Der schöne Adolf,* and his thoughts were only of his beloved *Volk,* and the happiness he was going to bring them when he had made them safe from their foes; a frank and friendly man, not stiff and solemn like those who were unsure of their position and had to manifest it to the world. When he felt an emotion, he was not afraid to express it; and now of all times, when he saw all his prophecies coming true, his harvest being reaped, his glory spreading like a sunrise from the east.

VII

When his visitor entered the car he came forward with hands out-stretched. "*Herr Budd! Wie herrlich!* Where do you come from?" Lanny thought that he had never seen him looking so well, or so radiant.

"You drew me like a magnet, *mein Führer.* I could not stay away. I came to tell you how pleased I am in your success."

"It is only what I promised you. You know that."

"Indeed I know it. There has never been anything like it in the world."

"*Aber*—how did you get here?"

"I came to Dunkirk. I had what I thought was important news for you, and I thought your armies would have got there."

"What is the news?" Impossible to wait a moment for information about enemy lands.

"*Leider*—it is all out of date. You see, it was a week ago. The British were still in Dunkirk, and I had to wait for your fellows to drive them out."

"What did you do?"

"I holed up in a pension and took my chances. Believe me, I can testify to the accuracy of your artillery!"

"*Jawohl!* But tell me—what is it you have to report?"

"I had a conference with Pétain, and with the Premier's mistress. You have heard of her, no doubt—Madame de Portes?"

"Indeed, yes. It is an excellent thing for us that our enemies are governed by women. What did they have to say?"

"They wanted peace. It was their idea to offer token resistance, and that you would then be gentle in your terms."

The Führer burst into a laugh and slapped his thigh. "Token resistance? *Ausgezeichnet!* So that is why my armies have been moving so fast!"

"The French leaders are in a state of utter bewilderment, Exzellenz. They are frantic to save their beautiful *ville lumière*."

"Tell them they do not have to worry. I am bombing only their airports and munition centers. I have my own purposes with Paris; it is to be our playground, our recreational center. I will send my able-bodied lads there, and presently there will be a new race of Frenchmen, understanding what discipline and order are. They will come to like it."

"Quite so, *mein Führer*. They are hoping that you will do what you have done in Norway—set up a government of your own sympathizers. They have come pretty much to an agreement that Pétain is the man."

"Ah, so that old *Trottel* is finding a soft berth for himself! *Jawohl*, it may be the thing to do. Abetz is keen for it; he insists that he can make use of them all. I shall make him my governor of Paris."

"A sweet revenge for Otto, indeed."

"Sweet for us all. Shall I tell you what I am going to do the first thing?"

"If it is not a secret. I have learned that secrets leak, and I prefer not to carry the responsibility."

"It will all be over in a week or two. You remember that dining car in which we were compelled to sign the last armistice?"

"I remember it very well; they have taken it to Paris and set it up in the Invalides."

"Also they have set up a monument to Marshal Foch on the spot in the forest of Compiègne where the car stood when the armistice was signed. Well, I am going to have the car taken back to that same spot, and there the French will come and sign *my* armistice; after which I will take the car to Germany and build an Invalides of my own for it. Will not that be a fair riposte?"

"An eye for an eye, Exzellenz!"

VIII

All his life Adi Schicklgruber had liked to talk; they had threatened to put him out of the home for the shelterless in Vienna because he wouldn't stop talking, and many a time he had had beer mugs thrown at his head in Munich for the same reason. All he required was one auditor, preferably sympathetic; and Lanny Budd had come resolved to be the most sympathetic in the whole Third Reich. Really, it was incredible what this man had done; this one man, by his vision, his persistence, his driving *daimon*. There had been nothing like it in the world for more than a thousand years. Lanny reminded him of the talk they had had on the top of the Kehlstein, where Adi had his ultra-secret retreat; he had there confided to the American guest his admiration for an Arab shepherd named Mohammed, who had founded a new religion and had enforced it by the sword. That was the way to make it stick, and not the futile way of martyrdom which Jesus had tried. The religion of Mohammed was still practiced, exactly as he had laid it down thirteen hundred years ago, whereas the abortion called Christianity bore no resemblance to what the Jewish carpenter had wanted. That was all to the good, for it was a lot of fool stuff, the product of a degenerate race.

Now Adolf Hitler had laid down *his* religion, and as Führer of the Germans he was enforcing it by means of dive-bombers and tanks. He had forged a new weapon called the Panzer division, and by its means he was going to establish order in Europe for the next thousand years. He had dreamed it in the trenches of the last war; he had labored at it through humiliation and defeat; he had shouted it to several thousand audiences, constantly growing bigger, until now they included the entire civilized world. There had literally never been anything like it in all history, for the reason that modern technology made possible achievements, oratorical, political, military, which had never before been imagined. Adolf Hitler was the man who had had the wit to seize these weapons and put them to use, and now nobody could get them away from him. By them he was going to become master of the world.

So he told his audience of one, and his audience agreed with every word. Lanny had decided that this was the time to pile the flattery on; when he saw the glow on Adi's cheeks and in his eyes, he decided that nothing would be too fulsome. He told Adolf Hitler that he was, beyond any question, the greatest leader who had ever lived, the chosen commander of the race which was destined to make over European civilization and cure it of its manifold diseases. He told how this realization had come to him, the first time he had heard Adi speak in the Bürgerbräukeller in Munich in the year 1923; how thereafter he had sung his praises wherever he went, and had sought the honor of his acquaintance through Heinrich Jung. Adi had converted him from a Socialist to a National Socialist, a different and truly practical thing.

That was the sort of thing Adi liked to listen to. Perhaps he had got a little tired of hearing it from his own court circle, and it came with a fresh flavor from an American who had become a world citizen. He was not the least bit shocked to hear that God had sent him to direct his armies through Holland, Belgium, and France—all in four weeks. He listened with pleasure while Lanny translated what an English poet had written about an angel who, by divine command, with rising tempests shakes a guilty land:

> Calm and serene he drives the furious blast,
> And, pleased the Almighty's orders to perform,
> Rides in the whirlwind and directs the storm.

IX

The Führer was a dreamer and an ecstatic, but he was also a practical man, with an immense job on his hands. He was not leaving the direction of his armies to his generals; on the contrary, he was watching every step, and making the major decisions. Messengers came with despatches. The mechanized forces under General von Reichenau had broken across the Somme at Amiens. Guderian and Kleist were heading for Soissons. Hitler read these reports to his guest and compared the swift advances to the long siege of fighting over these same places in World War I.

Then he said: "Now to business, Herr Budd." He wanted to know everything Lanny could tell him about the present attitude of high personalities in the French government, the women as well as the men.

Lanny talked freely, because that was the way he got Hitler to talk, and it still worked. He expressed his opinion that the French would soon evacuate Paris and seek refuge in Bordeaux; but he didn't believe they would fight long from there. The dissension in the Cabinet was too great; there were too many politicians who saw their future in co-operating with Hitler rather than in opposing him. "I have worked hard to persuade them," declared the American. "I hope I have not been wrong in giving them the assurance that you will know how to make use of them."

"*Absolut!*" exclaimed the Führer. "What do I want to fight the French for? What do I want to fight any European people for?—once they have got rid of their Jews and their democratic dogs that keep snarling at my heels. I am a man of peace, a builder, and everything I do is to that end. Under my *Neue Ordnung*, all the peoples will be free, all will have their own National-Socialist culture, and only the demagogues and misleaders will be exterminated."

There was only one fly in this sweet Nazi ointment, and that was "*diese verdammten Engländer.*" The poem which Lanny had quoted had been written about the Duke of Marlborough, the forefather of Winston Churchill—and this was the man whom Adi hated above any other now living, not excepting the Jew Rosenfeld in the White House. Churchill had made a report on Dunkirk to the House of Commons on the previous day, and the BBC had been broadcasting the text ever since. Hitler had had a recording made, and a translation for his own use. He told Lanny about it with a mixture of ridicule and rage: a lot of *dummes Zeug* about "fighting on beaches, landing grounds, in fields, in streets and on the hills." Said the Führer: "What will they fight with? Don't they know they have left all their equipment behind in Flanders? And don't they know that I know it?"

Lanny explained to the best of his ability how a staunch Tory could fail to appreciate the advantages of National-Socialist *Zucht und Ordnung*. The British had been sailors, mostly in small ships, and each captain was a law unto himself, and that was the basis of their individualism. Also, the fact that there was a wide and rough Channel between them and Europe gave them a feeling of security and tempted them to insolence.

"But it is madness!" exclaimed the Führer. "What protection will the Channel give them against the fate of Rotterdam?"

"They know that the bombing plane has been created, Exzellenz, but they hate to face the implications of it. They are a stubborn people."

"I will wipe out London, I will wipe out Birmingham and Sheffield and all their manufacturing cities. They challenge me, and make it impossible for me to spare them. I am getting barges ready, and transports, and will put an army on their coasts as soon as I finish with France."

That was what Lanny had come here to learn; but he wanted to be sure it wasn't just angry rhetoric. Said he: "If you say that you will do it, *mein Führer*, I know that you will. But it is bound to be a costly operation."

"Everybody was sure it would be costly to breach the Maginot Line; but we breached it at almost no cost, and so we have plenty of expendables for the taking of Britain. I will show my generals how to save many lives—by putting down paratroopers who will paralyze all the brain centers of the island before the invasion starts."

"I made up my mind," said the worshipful Lanny, "that I will never question your promises again. Every time you have told me you would do something, it has been done."

"*Also, Herr Budd!* I have told my enemies, too, but I am safe because they think I must be going to do something else."

"An odd but most effective kind of secrecy!" smiled the visitor. "If I find myself back in England, shall I tell them what you have said?"

"By all means! They will straightway begin making preparations to resist me in Sweden or the Balkans."

"They are making preparations in England now, I can assure you; I have seen some of them. I am not a military man and my opinion on such matters would be worth nothing; but I can tell you that there are many friends of your cause on that island, people who are not moved by fear, but by a genuine understanding of your program. They are doing their best to avoid further waste and destruction, and they beg you for time, so that the British people can realize the meaning of your tremendous victory in France, and the hopelessness of trying to stand against you.

"*Jawohl!*" exclaimed Adi, with a gesture of impatience. "If there are so many of them, let them make themselves heard. Let me have their proposals!"

"You are having them at this moment, Exzellenz. I am here at the urgent request of Lord and Lady Wickthorpe and their friends in the Foreign Office. They wish you to understand that they are working tirelessly, and making great headway. They have asked through their representatives in Madrid and in Stockholm to know your terms——"

"*Zum Teufel!* I have stated my terms again and again. I want no part of the British Empire—unless you count German East Africa and the Cameroons. The Belgian Congo will suffice, with these; but of course Il Duce must have a free hand in dealing with Spain, Yugoslavia and Greece. And of course I have a free hand in dealing with Eastern Europe. That I have won and no one can dream of taking it away from me."

"Understand, Exzellenz, I am not speaking for myself—I am just an errand boy for my friends on both sides. The British want time——"

"*Ja, ja, das weiss ich gut!* They want time to recover from what I did to them in Flanders! Tell them they may have exactly this much time—what it takes me to resupply my armies and move them to the Channel ports. That much, and not one hour more, Herr Budd!"

X

Lanny had got what he wanted, and it wasn't his job to argue or plead. He said: "I was thinking of offering to bring Madame to you again, and see what the spirits had to say. But you have taken matters out of their hands and are making the future for yourself."

"The spirits had their turn, and did very well." Adi dropped the subject, and Lanny guessed that he would not wish to recall Miss Elvirita Jones. This was no time for women; this was war, the business of men.

"Tell me what your plans are, Herr Budd." This was a command, and Lanny replied promptly: "I should like to be in Paris to see the inauguration of your *Neue Ordnung*, and what it will mean to that city of elegance and fashion. I might be able to bring you some useful reports."

"Assuredly; it would be appreciated, as always."

"Prior to that, I don't want to be in your way. I will find myself some agreeable resort, where I can read the newspapers and follow the course of the campaign."

"It might interest you to know that Kurt Meissner is at Godesberg."

"*Oh, wie schön!* I haven't seen him since he left Paris. He is at the Dreesen?"

"Yes. He has promised to write me a march, for my bands to play when we have our parade under the Arc de Triomphe."

"He will have to hurry," smiled Lanny. "That is where I will go. Kurt and I are old friends, and he knows that I never interfere with his inspirations. When he wishes to be alone he tells me so, and I find a book to read."

So matters were left. The Führer apologized because he could not invite Lanny to travel to Paris with him; he had no guest car, and, besides, his generals were very exacting. Even now, they would be fretting because he was not with them, poring over their large-scale maps of the valleys of the Somme and the Vesle. "*Auf Wiedersehen, Herr Budd!*"

32

They That Worship the Beast

I

GODESBERG is a small health resort on the Rhine, not far above Cologne. Its Hotel Dreesen was owned by an old pal of Adi's, who boasted that the Führer had been its guest no fewer than sixty-seven times—at least that was the number when Lanny had last heard it. The most conspicuous occasion had been the second visit of Prime Minister Chamberlain in the course of the Munich settlement. The man with the black umbrella had stayed on the other side of the river and come across on the ferry to argue and plead. It had been only twenty months ago, but already it seemed twenty years.

"Mountain of the Gods" is the meaning of the name in old German, and all this Rhine country is haunted ground to the worshipers of blood and soil. So it was a natural place for a great Komponist to choose, in the path of the triumphant armies—he had seen them going by, had sat by the roadside for hours, filling his soul with German glory; sometimes he had marched with them, to see how it felt. The hotel, which was not crowded, had given him a remote room with a piano in it, where he could pound to his heart's content; he would go out and walk in the forests near by and see himself as another Wagner, with whom the little birds and the big dragons, the dwarfs and giants and Rhinemaidens came to commune.

No man can be inspired all day and all night, and so Kurt was pleased as well as surprised to see his boyhood chum. His long somber face lighted with real cordiality. When he heard the story of how Lanny had come to join the Wehrmacht, he exclaimed: "*Ach, so!* You are as crazy as you were the first day I met you!" He lost little time before taking Lanny upstairs to hear his new composition, which thundered monstrously. Lanny listened, and thought: "Good Lord, is this what he has come to?" Tum-tum, tum-ty-tum—he had heard one thousand and one German military marches, including the *Badenweiler*, Adi's favorite to date. It seemed to Lanny that there were only a certain number of possible combinations of notes in this rhythm, and certainly Kurt had not found a new one. Compared with this, Sousa was really stirring, and Elgar's *Pomp and Circumstance* magnificent.

But of course he had to lie like the devil; he had to say that the work was just what the occasion called for, and would be associated in the minds of all Germans with their greatest series of victories, and the establishment of a new order, for Europe if not for the world. Wagner had written a Kaisermarsch, and Meissner a Führermarsch. Kurt glowed with pleasure—for Lanny had come straight from the Führer, and brought some of the magic with him; it was possible to believe that what he said was what the Führer would say, and France and America in course of time. "Lanny, it is a sublime hour we are living in, and our art works must strive to be worthy of it." Lanny assented; and in his traitor heart he wondered: was there, perchance, in some one of the Nazi concentration camps, a comrade who was jotting down on a scrap of paper the notes of a death march which would some day sweep the world, and might be played at the funeral of Adolf Hitler's *Drittes Reich?*

These two roamed the forests and climbed the mountains and looked at old Rhine castles, just as they had looked at even older Roman castles and aqueducts and what-not on the French Riviera more than twenty-six years ago. Now, as then, Kurt talked his hifalutin German metaphysics, magnificent long words of Latin and Greek derivation which were impressive so long as you did not seek to apply them to anything in the everyday world. Then, as now, Lanny listened reverently and expressed his agreement; but in his traitor soul he was using one of Hitler's rowdy phrases: "*Das kümmert mich einen Dreck!*"

Sitting on the ruins of the old Godesberg castle, lost in damp clouds, the art expert said: "Kurt, I wonder if it is considered unethical to travel during the height of this campaign."

"It depends on where you want to go."

"I have had word about a collection of paintings in Basel, and sooner or later I must take a look at them. This might be a good time, before the march to Paris is completed. But the road lies across the pathway of the armies."

"We have switchmen who attend to matters like that," said Kurt, in the patronizing tone he had always taken to an American two years younger than himself. "If the trains are running, I'm sure there's no reason why you shouldn't be on one of them."

"Well then, I'll make inquiry. You are presenting the Führer with a splendid march, and it occurs to me that if I found some painting he would like, it might be a gracious way of expressing my congratulations."

"*Famos!*" exclaimed the Nazi Beethoven.

II

So Lanny enjoyed a daylight rail trip up the storied Rhine. In the wealthy and pious Swiss city with the ancient cathedral he got himself a hotel room and a typewriter, and wrote:

"The Germans expect to take Paris within one week from date. Pétain will be the head of the new French government and Otto Abetz will be Governor of Paris. The present program is to attack England by means of bombers, parachutists, barges and transports, as soon as the armies can be moved to the Channel ports and resupplied. In the meantime appeasement negotiations are going on with British agents in Madrid and Stockholm. German demands are for the Cameroons, German East Africa, and the Belgian Congo, a free hand for themselves in Eastern Europe, and for Mussolini in dealing with Spain, Yugoslavia and Greece. This comes from the highest authority and is to be accepted."

This he double-sealed in the usual way, and addressed it, not to the American ambassador as such, but to Leland Harrison, Esq., 4 Weststrasse, Bern. Lanny knew that Basel would be swarming with German agents, and that anyone coming from that country would be closely watched; so he took a long walk and turned many corners before at last he dropped the letter into an inconspicuous box. After that he went straightway to look up art dealers, and made himself as prominent as possible, inspecting what they had to offer, and inquiring as to what there was to be seen in private collections, and whether any of them could be purchased for American collectors. He spoke German, and looked at German paintings, and made quite sure that the Germans would know he was there.

He had the good fortune to come upon a Defregger, one fairly small, which could be taken out of its frame and carried under a gentleman's arm in wartime. This Austrian painter was the Führer's favorite; he would delight to look upon the weatherbeaten countenance of an old *Bauer* of the Innthal, where the greatest man in the world had been born. Adi would find in those wrinkled features the honesty, fidelity and credulity which were the virtues he wanted in his peasants, and meant to teach to all the peasants of the earth, not excluding North America. He would hang the work in his private car, and take it back to Berchtesgaden and put it in one of his guest bedrooms. The price was only fifteen hundred Swiss francs, which Lanny arranged to pay through his bank in Cannes. When he took possession of the work he did not fail to say what he was going to do with it. He knew that the story would go all over town, and certainly ought to satisfy the agents of the Gestapo!

III

Back to the Mountain of the Gods. Kurt admired the painting, and listened while Lanny explained the peculiarities of the painter's technique, and its derivations. They played four-hand piano compositions which Lanny had purchased; and in between times they listened to the radio and marveled at the achievements of the Führer's armies. Nothing like it in the world! They had broken through along the coast, and by the 10th of June were at Dieppe, and from there in a great bulge through Compiègne and Soissons. In two days more they were at Le Havre, and all the way along the Seine, as close to Paris as the mouth of the Oise. They had begun a giant new offensive farther west, and had broken through to the west of Paris and reached the Marne. They had taken Château-Thierry—name full of significance to Americans as well as French.

It was incredible. Kurt was like a man walking on air, or flying on one of the steeds of his Valkyries. He hummed new music, and started to write a march that would be better than his first. Lanny had to act the part; and it is a fact to which the psychologist William James has called attention, that if you enact certain emotions, you presently begin to feel them; the reflexes work both ways, and an anti-Nazi spy cannot help becoming a Nazi, at least for the nonce. After all, it is impossible not to pay tribute to a professional job well done—even if the job is the wholesale slaughter of your fellow-men. If you go to a football game, and the home team is being overwhelmed beyond hope, you might as well get your money's worth by admiring the way the victors are doing the job, the new formations they have devised, and the amazing accuracy of their forward passes.

Mussolini summoned his Fascist mob to the plaza in front of the

Palazzo Venezia. The band struck up and he made his dramatic appearance on the balcony, thrust out his pouter-pigeon chest, and roared one of those pompous pronouncements which had caused Rick to call him the world's most odious man. "Fighters of land, sea and air, Blackshirts of the revolution and of the legions, men and women of Italy, and of the empire, and of the Kingdom of Albania, listen! The hour destined by fate is sounding for us. The hour of irrevocable decision has come. A declaration of war has already been handed to the ambassadors of Great Britain and France. We take the field against the plutocratic and reactionary democracies which always have blocked the march and frequently plotted against the existence of the Italian people. . . ."

And so on, through a long tirade, which the Nazi press featured on their front pages. Lanny was concerned, because one of the Duce's demands was for Nice, and that might include Cannes and the Cap d'Antibes, Bienvenu and Beauty Budd. But Kurt said: "Do not worry. The jackal only takes what the lion allows him." Such was a Nazi agent's opinion of his ally. He went on to predict that Mussolini would do no invading or fighting in France; he was afraid of the French army, even crippled as it was, and still more afraid of the British Mediterranean fleet. It was understood that he was to be in on the armistice, and to have French North Africa if he could take it.

Very convenient, to be close to the seat of authority, and to know what was coming next! They talked about Paris, and the future which the *Neue Ordnung* was preparing for it. Since the Führer had honored Lanny with his confidence, there could be no reason why Kurt should not speak frankly. *La ville lumière* had been his stamping ground for years, and he knew everybody and everybody's wife and everybody's *amie*. Lanny knew many of them, and it was useful to review the parts these persons had played in the débacle. Like putting together a jigsaw puzzle, of which each furnished parts. Kurt said he was planning to take up his residence in Paris, and do what he could to assist Abetz in making real friendship between the two nations. "What do you plan, Lanny?"

The American replied: "I can't think of any better work than that. I'll be somewhere around, to run errands for you when you call."

"*Herrlich!*" exclaimed Kurt. "Perhaps we can devise a way for you to get to England now and then. We must set to work immediately to try to keep that war from going to extremes. Your connection with Irma and Ceddy may be most fortunate for us."

IV

A telephone call for the Komponist. The Führer had promised that he should hear his march played when the Germans entered Paris; and the Führer never forgot a promise. A limousine would call for him the next morning. "Would you like to come along?" asked Kurt; and Lanny replied: "What would I like better?"

So he was driven once more through the fields of battle, and breathed once more the air polluted with the effluvia of dead horses and cattle. You got an overwhelming impression of destruction, because, in this new Panzer war, most of the fighting was along the roads, and the ditches were filled with wrecks of every sort. The dead humans had been buried where they lay, but the living still sat among the ruins. They had piled their belongings into carts or baby carriages, fleeing from bombs and shells; they had cumbered the highways, and had been one of the reasons why the French had been unable to move their armies. The Germans had cleared the roads ruthlessly; and now, after weeks of wandering, many of the people had given up in despair, and settled down to die of starvation where they lay. It was nobody's business to feed them.

When the car traveled westward things were better, for there had been less fighting. The poilus had given up and taken the road home; if some Germans came along in an armored car and told them they were prisoners, *eh, bien,* they shrugged their shoulders and gave up. Altogether, Kurt reported, the Germans had taken close to a couple of million prisoners, with German casualties of all kinds less than a hundred thousand. Six nations conquered in nine weeks! There had been nothing like it in history.

Lanny said: "It was your work, Kurt; I mean, yours personally. You cut the motor nerves between the French head and the French body." That is the way to make friends and influence people!

The highway passed within a couple of miles of Les Forêts, familiar to them both. Lanny suggested: "Let's stop and see if Emily is here." They did so, and found the place turned into the headquarters of a Reichswehr corps. Emily had fled to the Riviera, as Lanny had advised some time ago, and heel-clicking officers were in possession of her splendid château, which Lanny had visited from childhood, and in which Kurt had first met the élite of French society. It was a lot better than having the furniture smashed, as in the previous war, and several thousand dead men in the great beech forest. Lanny said: "It will be a pleasure to tell her."

"You can say," replied the Komponist, "that if any damage is done, it will be paid for fully."

When the car neared Paris, Lanny said: "I want to retain my ability to help you and the Führer, and for that reason I ought not be seen riding in a German staff car. It might give the idea that I am in the pay of your government, and that would hurt my standing with some of the French."

"No doubt you are right, Lanny. What will you do?"

"I'll get out when we come to a Metro station. I'm not sure if it's running, but if not I can walk."

Kurt was going to the Crillon—an odd reversal; for thirty or forty years this had been Robbie Budd's hotel, and Lanny's when he wanted to be fashionable; Kurt had come as Lanny's guest, or had hovered around in the shadow while Lanny went inside to meet American officialdom. Now the wheel of fortune had turned; the Germans had taken over the hotel, and it would be Kurt's address, and Lanny would find himself a less elegant abode. Kurt would ride in state, and Lanny would walk, or ride a bicycle, if he could find one. That was to be the new custom of Paris, he guessed, a custom good for the health, except, perhaps, when it rained. The son of Budd-Erling stepped from a well-padded limousine, with his newly purchased suitcase in one hand and his carefully wrapped Defregger in the other, and mounted shanks' mare along the Grand Boulevard.

V

You could just about have your choice of accommodations in the city. Many hotels were closed, others empty of both guests and staff. More than half the population of Paris had fled to the south—they had been told that the Germans would plunder everything, shoot the men and rape the women. The result had been a frightful calamity; the roads had been blocked, and the Germans had bombed and machine-gunned them indiscriminately, killing tens of thousands of women and children. They still lay where they had fallen, and hundreds of thousands of refugees were sitting by the roadside, exhausted and despairing, with no place to go and no power to go there. This and other news you could get from radio stations in the south, if you could get access to a set; there was, as yet, no one to prevent your using it.

Lanny settled himself comfortably in the hotel where his mother had stayed at the time of the Peace Conference, and where she had hidden Kurt and helped him to escape into Spain. That had been a long time ago, and nobody remembered this elegant American gentleman who strolled in and engaged a suite. There was still food, if you had the price. To Lanny's surprise he found that it was possible to get Bienvenu on the phone. He had a good chat with his mother; he didn't say where he had been, but said Kurt was here, and thought she had nothing to worry about. Beauty answered that she was not the worrying kind. They were all well, and Parsifal still loved everybody, French, German, Italian. She had had a letter from Laurel Creston, safe in New York. There were letters for Lanny, but he didn't believe that mail would reach him now. "What are you going to do?" she asked, and he said: "There will always be old masters!"

He hunted up some of his friends. Denis de Bruyne was not running away; he was staying and looking after his investments. His elder son had fled to the south, with the mad idea that the war should be continued from there. Charlot had not been heard from; presumably he was a prisoner, as there had been no heavy fighting in or near the Swiss border. Lanny said: "I was in Basel a few days ago. Many thousands of French troops were crossing the border and giving themselves up for internment."

He accepted an invitation to spend the week-end at the chateau. Denis still had his car and chauffeur, everything which a member of the *deux cent familles* claimed as his right and meant to keep, regardless of victory or defeat. He would bring Lanny up to date as to what had gone on behind the scenes; and from the radio they could learn what was going on now, or at least a part of it. Churchill had flown to Tours, whither the French government had fled; he was seeking to persuade Reynaud to continue the fight. The French Premier had made a public appeal to President Roosevelt, to send "clouds of planes" to the rescue of France. The President had answered with a promise of every sort of material, but ended with the warning that he could not promise military aid, since only Congress had the power to declare war.

"*Les imbéciles!*" exclaimed Denis, meaning the whole lot of them who wanted to wage war on Hitler. Why should anybody quarrel with that splendid system he had set up, and which had proved itself so marvelously in the past weeks. Denis had received the assurance that the Germans were going to behave with the utmost correctness in Paris, and certainly their advance guards had done so. Very soon there would be nobody to challenge the New Order, and France would settle down to life without labor unions, riots, strikes, and all the other appurtenances of democracy.

VI

This was Sunday, the 16th of June, and the German army was making its formal entry into Paris, with a grand parade down the Champs Élysées and under the Arc de Triomphe. The bands would be playing Kurt's new *Führermarsch*, but Lanny didn't go, for already he knew it by heart, and he knew every foot of that great double avenue, lined with trees on each side; he knew the gray-green soldiers, who held their guns with their left hands and swung their right arms, and threw out their legs straight before them and brought their heels down hard upon the pavement—the goosestep, it was called by their enemies. Their big tanks and mounted guns and half-tracks would roll, and their planes would roar overhead. The bands would blare, and all German hearts would swell with glory, seeing immense swastika flags floating over the Arc de Triomphe, the Chambre des Députés, the Eiffel Tower, and the golden dome of the Invalides. Not to mention the Hotel Crillon, hitherto a sort of clubhouse for Americans who had money!

Lanny preferred to spend this lovely day in the garden where he had had so many happy hours with Marie de Bruyne. Apricot trees carefully trained against the south wall were loaded with half-grown fruit; roses were in bloom, and bees were busy, and Marie's grandchildren knew nothing about old sorrows—it was the blessed renewal of nature. When Lanny tired of play, he could go in to the radio and hear about Winston Churchill's proposal of a complete union of the British and the French peoples and governments. It had come rather late, and to an elderly French capitalist it seemed the apex of lunacy. "If we have to merge with some nation, why not the German? They are already here, and we don't have to fight a bloody war and have our cities and homes destroyed in order to consummate the union."

VII

Lanny went back to Paris, that strange, half-deserted city, with a curfew at nine o'clock and a blackout from sundown. The greater part of the shops were covered with iron shutters, and there was practically no traffic except military in the streets. Imagine, if you could, being able to cross the Place de l'Opéra at your leisure, and with no danger to your bones! The shouting traffic police were gone, the Café de la Paix was closed tight, and the front of the great opera house was covered with sandbags. Only two newspapers now on the kiosks, both humbly subservient—one, *Le Matin,* and the other, oddly enough, *La Victoire!* It wouldn't be many days before the Nazis would revive others—the old names but new policies. Already they had taken over the radio stations, and had set up loudspeakers in the public squares, to tell the French what they were going to think for the next thousand years.

The government had been bombed out of Tours, and was now being bombed in Bordeaux. Lanny could imagine the scenes there: the frantic debates, the Cabinet shifts, the futile balloting—and Hélène de Portes sitting on the Premier's desk, shrieking at politicians and officials who dared to differ with her. Lanny put his wits to work on the problem of how to get to Bordeaux; it appeared to be his job to find out what the decision would be—surrender, or continuing the fight from Africa. Before he could hit upon a plan, he stopped in a crowd to listen to a loudspeaker on a street corner, and heard the quavering voice of Marshal Pétain, telling his beloved children that the welfare of *la patrie* required him to ask an armistice of the Germans.

There could be no doubt that it was his voice, and the P.A. found no difficulty in believing it; but to the people about him it came like a thunderbolt, staggering, paralyzing. They had assumed that the *grande armée* was falling back, as armies did, in order to fight from a better position. They had understood that Paris must be abandoned, so as to save it from destruction. But to surrender, to turn all France over to the boches, to desert Britain and give up the promised aid from America?—*c'était la honte, la trahison!* Some stood with tears running down their cheeks.

Lanny thought, it was as he had said to Kurt, the French body had been separated from the head, and the body was paralyzed. He put what he had learned from Kurt and from Denis into a report and mailed it to the Embassy, which was still functioning. The head Nazis hated Bill Bullitt like poison, but he had stayed on, and they treated him with careful formality. They wanted no trouble with America at this stage.

They were formal with Paris, too, for they wanted no trouble there. The armistice was almost as unbelievable to them as to the French. The troops had strict orders to be polite to everyone; when they were off duty they wandered about staring at the sights, exactly like tourists. Oddly enough, they all appeared to be camera fiends, and wanted pictures of the Eiffel Tower and Notre Dame and the Arc de Triomphe to send home. Standing before the eternal flame which guards the Unknown Soldier's tomb, they bared their shaven blond heads. If they were officers, they saluted, and it was all *absolut korrect*. When the shopkeepers discovered how it was going to be, the iron shutters came down, and the *"Fridolins"* poured into the shops, and soon there was a flood of silk stockings and kid gloves and perfumes going back to the pregnant *Mädchen* of Naziland. "Pregnant *Mädchen*" might sound like a joke, and so it was—a Nazi joke.

VIII

Long trains poured in from Berlin, bringing staffs, editorial, radio, administrative staffs. They were going to take charge not merely of Paris but of all Northern France, the part where the great factories and mines were. They had been in training for their jobs for years, and all spoke French of a sort. The Crillon became a beehive—bees who clicked their heels and saluted, this way and that way, wherever they flew. Lanny went among them, because it was his job; he watched for signs whether the Wehrmacht was going after England at once, or whether it would wait and give the Quislings a chance. Hitler had told him, but Lanny was one of those foolish people who didn't know whether to believe Hitler or not. Perhaps he would tell the truth fifty times, and then on the supreme occasion he would lie.

Kurt invited his old friend to the Crillon to lunch, and the invitation was accepted. A strange thing, to sit in that spacious elegant dining room full of every sort of Nazi uniform, and look back twenty-one years to the time when it had been full of American uniforms, and a few French and British; also with the sack coats of American professors, some of whom were now dead, and others who were college presidents, or diplomats, or members of the "brain trust." At this very table, or at any rate a table in this same position, Lincoln Steffens and Bill Bullitt had sat after their mission to Russia, and Stef had teased the conservative professors, asking them questions in his Socratic way, and assuring them that the Communist revolution was not the flash in the pan as they chose to believe, but a new stage in social evolution. "I have seen the future, and it works!"

Now at this table sat Kurt and his agreeable blonde secretary; also Graf Herzenberg and his *schöne Lili*, and red-headed Otto Abetz, handsome, genial, full of conversation. Victory is such a delightful thing; it expands the ego, and produces amazing sensations. This once humble student, who had thought he had reached the heights when he was able to lecture fashionable ladies in the Cinéma Bonaparte, was now the master of all Paris; he *was* all Paris, for practical purposes. He had been chased out in disgrace, and now the chasers were the chased, and if any of them hadn't got away, he was going to find them and lock them up.

These Nazi great ones were taking their duties with the utmost seriousness, and wanted all the help Lanny could give them. Who was there among the French who had not fled, and could be trusted to co-operate? Lanny mentioned Denis de Bruyne and others who should be consulted, and perhaps used in some official capacity. In return for such advice, he was privileged to hear an outline of Nazi intentions regarding Spain, Italy, France, and French North Africa. All most interesting, and he returned to his hotel room and wrote a report and mailed it to Mr. W. C. Bullitt, just around the corner. He would have liked nothing better than to drop in and have a chat about times old and new, but he didn't dare to, for fear that Bill might connect him in his mind with those mysterious reports which came frequently for periods and then stopped for still longer periods. Somebody was going to the Big Boss over the ambassador's head, and who the devil could it be, and what the devil would he be saying, perhaps about the ambassador!

IX

The Führer's train chugged to Munich, so that he could consult with Mussolini about the armistice terms for France. The train chugged back, and the Führer proceeded to put through that elaborate insult which he had outlined to his American visitor. Rumors of it had leaked out, but not through Lanny. Perhaps it was because the sacred armistice car was rolled out of the Invalides, and put upon two heavy trailers; it disappeared into the night, and the natural inference was that it might be on the way to the place where it had acquired its special status, making it different from all other dining cars on the railroads of France.

The ceremony took place on the 21st of June. Lanny didn't attend because, for one thing, he was sick of Nazi glory, and for another, he didn't want to make himself conspicuous. He could imagine the scene well enough, and a few hours later could see it in the newspapers which the Nazis had set up, and which from now on would be full of Nazi glory. The Führer had a court favorite by the name of Hoffmann who had become the official photographer; small, alert, with bright blue eyes and a sharp nose like a dog's, he haunted *die grosse Welt* with a tiny Leica camera, snapping shots of everybody and everything. So posterity would be assured of being able to see the Führer eating his vegetable plate with a poached egg on top, the Führer playing with his seven German shepherd dogs, the Führer smiling at or scolding premiers and kings.

The sacred car was moved to the spot in the forest which had been marked with a great flat stone inscribed *Le Maréchal Foch*. A park had been built around it, with a statue of the victorious commander. Now a German guard of honor marched and stood at salute; then came Hitler, in his simple gray uniform, and no decoration but his iron cross. Admiral Raeder marched on his right and Marshal Göring on his left, both carrying their batons of office. General Brauchitsch marched on Raeder's right, and behind them came Hess and Ribbentrop, both in uniform and with their decorations. In front of the armistice car was a huge granite block with an inscription, and no doubt Hitler had read its insulting words many times; but it was part of the ceremony that he should stop and read them in the granite original: "*Here on the eleventh of November 1918 succumbed the criminal pride of the German Empire . . . vanquished by the free peoples which it tried to enslave.*"

All the hatred in the fiercest heart in Europe showed in the Führer's face as he walked from that granite block to the steps of the car. He entered, followed by his friends, and sat waiting. The French delegates arrived promptly on time, and there were salutes by the military men outside, but no handshakes. When the French entered the car, Hitler and the others rose and gave the Nazi salute, but did not speak. They sat, and General Keitel read the preamble to the armistice terms, in which Adi exploited the theme upon which he had been pounding for twenty-one years, the "dishonor and humiliation," the "broken promises and perjury" of the Versailles *Diktat*. The terms proper were long, some thirty pages, and Hitler knew them and did not choose to hear them again. When the preamble was finished, he and his party rose, saluted, and stalked out, leaving General Keitel to complete the reading.

For a day the discussions over the terms went on, the French delegates and their government leaders telephoning back and forth. Hitler had set a time limit, and just before it expired the French gave way. There was a second meeting in the armistice car, and the document was signed. When the Führer came out from that ceremony he could no longer contain himself, but executed a series of capers, a sort of little jig, in front of the cameras of the world. The French would pay— and oh, how they would pay! Four hundred million francs per day for the keep of the German army of occupation—as long as they chose to invite themselves!

X

So came the New Order to Paris; and now the conqueror paid a visit to that frivolous city about which he had heard so much. He drove down the Champs-Élysées and surveyed the Place de la Concorde, per- haps the most splendid in the world; he stopped at the Arc de Triomphe and gave the Nazi salute to the Unknown Soldier of France. After this tour he came into the Crillon, where Kurt and Lanny paid him a call. Kurt brought two manuscript copies of the *Führermarsch*, one rever- ently inscribed to the greatest man in the world; upon the other the greatest man wrote: "*Dem Meister Musikanten des Nationalsocialis- mus.*" Kurt would cherish this all his life, and then bequeath it to the Staats Bibliothek in Berlin.

The American unveiled his little Defregger: an accidental discovery, he explained, not that painter's greatest work, but a rather charming genre piece. Hitler agreed, and thanked him cordially. He said he didn't know if he ought to accept so valuable a gift when he was not permitted to make any sort of return. Lanny replied: "*Mein Führer,* you have made a return to the human race." The way to get along with dictators!

The greatest man was going to pay a visit to the tomb of Napoleon in Les Invalides, and graciously invited his two friends to accompany him. They accepted; but after Lanny had time to think, he said to Kurt: "There will be photographers there, and it won't be a good thing for either of us to be in the newspapers." Kurt agreed, and spoke to Hitler, who laughed and said: "You can join the photographers in- stead of the photographed." That eager little blue-eyed beaver, Hoff- mann, was in the room, and Adi said: "Lend each of them a camera, and see that they have passes."

So Kurt and Lanny strolled across the Place to the group of build- ings constructed by the Sun King for his invalid soldiers. It includes the royal church, a golden-domed building to whose crypt the bones of the dead Emperor had been brought, exactly a century ago. On the way they talked about him, and the curious resemblances between his career and that of the man who was about to honor him. Napoleon had been known as "the little corporal," and Adolf had been almost a corporal and was almost little. Both had been foreigners, from the point of view of the country they had led to glory: Napoleon a Corsican and Adolf an Austrian. The difference between them was that Napoleon had failed, whereas Adolf was going to succeed; so declared Kurt, and Lanny hastened to assent. The dictator of France had written a code of laws, a part of which still survived; the Austrian was going to write a code for Europe which he himself predicted would last for a thousand years.

XI

The walls of the Église Royale, like most of the other public buildings of Paris, were now protected by sandbags. The building was closed to the public for this occasion, but accredited photographers, including some from America, were admitted by one entrance; they were to stand on one side of the circular gallery which runs around the crypt, while the Führer and his staff would stand on the opposite side. The lighting comes from above, and thus from the point of view of photography the situation would be ideal. Lanny and Kurt stood apart, attracting no attention; when the new master of Europe entered with his entourage and the cameras began to click, they took their shots also.

The sarcophagus is of red porphyry, and of great size; its cover is shaped like the top of an Ionic column, a sweeping curve turning at each end into a circle. The great dome of the building is upheld by twelve massive figures, each representing one of Napoleon's victories; as some of these had been won over Austrians and Germans, Hitler was not interested. He stood looking down at the tomb, a conspicuous figure in the gray linen duster which he always wore when motoring, and which he frequently did not trouble to remove. Perhaps it reminded him of the old raincoat he had worn all through the early days of his campaigning; it had become a sort of trademark, a proletarian symbol, and he had carried a riding whip, perhaps as a forecast of the authority he was going to win.

That was all there was to the ceremony; Hitler just stood and gazed at Napoleon's tomb. But it was a long ceremony, even so; he did not move, and no one of the score of his staff members moved. The photographers, having duly shot the scene, waited on chance that he might do something else—make a speech to Napoleon, or give him the Nazi salute. But he didn't speak or move; he just stood and stood and stood. Lanny wondered, was it a pose, a dramatic performance for the French public and for the world? He guessed it was more than that; for Adi had told him that he considered the Emperor one of the greatest of minds; and Adi was a man of fervors and transports. He would enter into spiritual communion with the soul of the great conqueror; he would say:

"Thank you, master, for all that you have taught me. You will see that I have learned your lessons. I will succeed where you failed. I will impose order upon Europe. I will give them a new code, adapted to modern conditions. I will establish a regime which will endure for a full millennium, and perhaps as long as the Continent exists. Be at peace, great soul, for your work was not in vain."

And the others—what would be their thoughts during this long sojourn in the silences? The photographers would be thinking: "What the heck?" The staff members would be thinking: "*Um Gottes Willen, wann essen wir?*"—when do we eat! Kurt would be thinking: "He has recognized me as the *Musikant* of his New Order, and my name and work will go down into history with his."

And the presidential agent? When he got through thinking about the others, he found himself saying: "Oh, God, when will the world be done with dictators? When will the people arise and take charge of their own destinies? When will they stop following leaders who build their monuments out of millions of human skulls?"

The son of Budd-Erling was perhaps the least happy man in that famous old church at the moment. He had little admiration for Napoleon Bonaparte, and still less for his Austrian imitator. If wishes had been magic, Adi Schicklgruber, gray uniform, linen duster, and all, would have vanished into nothingness and never been seen or heard of again. Indeed, Lanny had sometimes wondered whether he ought not to use his privileged position to take a gun and shoot the one-time Gefreiter. But he realized that it wouldn't help; the odious Nazi system would have a martyr, and Göring or Hess would carry on—and be no improvement.

France was down, Britain was sinking, and the one chance for freedom and human decency lay in the homeland of Lanny's forefathers across the seas. He thought: "It is my duty to go back and make F.D. realize the frightfulness of this crisis." But no, the great President of the United States understood; his speeches showed it, and he would do his best. He would act with every ounce of the strength that was in him. And sooner or later the freedom-loving people of America would understand, also. Theirs it would be to decide what was going to dominate the next thousand years, Hitler's New Order or American democracy. Through Lanny Budd's mind, tortured for so long by the roaring of Nazi blood songs and military marches, came the chorus of one of his own country's so different hymns:

America! America! God shed His grace on thee,
And crown thy good with brotherhood from sea to shining sea!

BOOKS BY UPTON SINCLAIR

PRESIDENTIAL AGENT
WIDE IS THE GATE
DRAGON'S TEETH
BETWEEN TWO WORLDS
WORLD'S END
EXPECT NO PEACE
YOUR MILLION DOLLARS
LITTLE STEEL
OUR LADY
THE FLIVVER KING
NO PASARAN!
THE GNOMOBILE
CO-OP: A NOVEL OF LIVING TOGETHER
WHAT GOD MEANS TO ME: AN ATTEMPT
    AT A WORKING RELIGION
I, CANDIDATE FOR GOVERNOR AND HOW I
    GOT LICKED
THE EPIC PLAN FOR CALIFORNIA
I, GOVERNOR OF CALIFORNIA
THE WAY OUT: WHAT LIES AHEAD FOR
    AMERICA
UPTON SINCLAIR PRESENTS WILLIAM FOX
AMERICAN OUTPOST: AUTOBIOGRAPHY
THE WET PARADE
ROMAN HOLIDAY
MENTAL RADIO
MOUNTAIN CITY
BOSTON
MONEY WRITES!
OIL!

THE SPOKESMAN'S SECRETARY
LETTERS TO JUDD
MAMMONART
THE GOSLINGS—A STUDY OF THE AMERICAN
    SCHOOLS
THE GOOSE-STEP—A STUDY OF AMERICAN
    EDUCATION
THE BOOK OF LIFE
THEY CALL ME CARPENTER
100%—THE STORY OF A PATRIOT
THE BRASS CHECK
JIMMIE HIGGINS
KING COAL, A NOVEL OF THE COLORADO
    COAL STRIKE
THE PROFITS OF RELIGION
THE CRY FOR JUSTICE
DAMAGED GOODS
SYLVIA'S MARRIAGE
SYLVIA
LOVE'S PILGRIMAGE
THE FASTING CURE
SAMUEL, THE SEEKER
THE MONEYCHANGERS
THE METROPOLIS
THE MILLENNIUM
THE OVERMAN
THE JUNGLE
MANASSAS, A NOVEL OF THE CIVIL WAR
THE JOURNAL OF ARTHUR STIRLING

Plays

PRINCE HAGEN
THE NATUREWOMAN
THE SECOND STORY MAN
THE MACHINE
THE POT-BOILER
HELL

SINGING JAILBIRDS
BILL PORTER
OIL! (DRAMATIZATION)
DEPRESSION ISLAND
MARIE ANTOINETTE